# DECENT WORK IN THE DIGITAL AGE

This book explores the legal and practical implications of the digital age for employment and industrial relations. To that end, the book analyses the problems arising from the digitalisation of work and the negative effects on working conditions in fields such as platform work, robotisation, discrimination, data protection and freedom of speech. It also looks at how to ensure decent working conditions for workers affected by digitalisation, by investigating the minimum standards that should be ensured to mitigate negative effects – and how these could be best guaranteed by legislation and collective bargaining.

The book presents a theoretical framework on the impact of automatisation, robotics, and digitalisation on the very basic principles of individual and collective labour law. The chapters provide an in-depth analysis of new patterns of work prompted by digitalisation, including: classification of platform workers; recognition of employment and social security rights; competition law aspects of platform work; remote (tele)work arrangements; algorithmic decision-making and remote surveillance; data protection and privacy; and social media in working environments.

The book is an important reference for academics and researchers, social partners, and policy makers with an interest in labour law and industrial relations.

# Decent Work in the Digital Age

*European and Comparative Perspectives*

Edited by
Tamás Gyulavári
and
Emanuele Menegatti

• HART •
OXFORD • LONDON • NEW YORK • NEW DELHI • SYDNEY

HART PUBLISHING

Bloomsbury Publishing Plc

Kemp House, Chawley Park, Cumnor Hill, Oxford, OX2 9PH, UK

1385 Broadway, New York, NY 10018, USA

29 Earlsfort Terrace, Dublin 2, Ireland



First published in Great Britain 2022



A catalogue record for this book is available from the British Library.

A catalogue record for this book is available from the Library of Congress.

Library of Congress Control Number: 2022940532

ISBN: HB: 978-1-50995-823-8
ePDF: 978-1-50995-825-2
ePub: 978-1-50995-824-5

Typeset by Compuscript Ltd, Shannon

The manuscripts for this volume were produced under the programme 'The Elevation of the Standards of Legal Education' of the Hungarian Ministry of Justice.

# FOREWORD

This is an exciting collection of essays on a challenging topic. Digitalisation of working lives has accelerated and, as labour lawyers, we now find ourselves reflecting on the consequences. As the editors of this remarkable volume observe, emerging technologies and their diverse consequences for work are prompting the re-evaluation of what seemed to be previously successful regulatory strategies and their merits in a rapidly innovating sphere of the labour market.

The editors present these concerns in a European and comparative frame, which is likely to have global relevance. It is hard to find many countries that have not been affected by various different kinds of platform work and digital outsourcing.[1] What the European Union provides is a framework for transnational debate and an experimental regulatory forum from which other states and policy actors can learn, perhaps as much from any missteps as successes.

This volume begins by posing fundamental questions about how we view regulation of work in a digital age. Manfred Weiss asks questions regarding the 'basic principles of labour law' and the extent to which these can be applied in a new contextual matrix of digitalisation. He presents the potential tensions, given the emergence of new forms of precarious non-standard work, and the challenges to be overcome to avoid a 'recommodification' of labour. These are ably set out in this book in part I which explores the actual impact of forms of automatisation and digitisation on work relations, while part II considers particular emergent features of platform work and part III examines issues raised by the phenomenon of algorithmic control. Part IV addresses the data protection and privacy concerns associated with digitisation of work. In a short Foreword, it is difficult to do justice to the rigour and complexity of the arguments presented by all the contributions presented in each part. Suffice to say that, throughout the volume, they pose various difficult questions, which are worth highlighting here.

For example, at what level of generality can regulation be made, so as to capture not only recent innovations but future technological innovations, which at present can be only scarcely envisaged? After all, we are embarking on a creative enterprise to craft appropriate solutions to new problems that will not merely pause at this point,

[1] M Graham and M Anwar, 'The Global Gig Economy: Towards a planetary labour market?' (2019) 24(4) *First Monday* 21; M Graham, V Lehdonvirta, A Wood, H Barnard, I Hjorth and PD Simon, *The Risks and Rewards of Online Gig Work at the Global Margins* (2017), available at: ora.ox.ac.uk/objects/uuid:8c791d5a-e3a5-4a59-9b93-fbabea881554; and the ILO World Employment and Social Outlook Report, *The Role of Digital Labour Platforms in Transforming the World of Work* (Geneva, ILO, 2021), available at: www.ilo.org/global/research/global-reports/weso/2021/WCMS_771749/lang--en/index.htm.

but which are likely to further morph and develop.[2] Is rapid adoption and review of specific legal instruments, such as new laws aimed at particular forms of platform work or algorithmic management, preferable to norms set at a broader level of generality that might encompass ongoing accelerated change? And could the latter even be achievable?

Can we future-proof labour law when, as EP Thompson observed, mechanical change once transformed notions of working time, as does now the use of social media and the internet today.[3] With acceleration in changed working demands, regarding tasks and hours, and perhaps training and know-how, including new issues of confidentiality and fidelity, how does law recognise such transformations?

Further issues also arise. Digitalisation offers, ironically, a return to home-based working or even working almost anywhere,[4] as we have seen in the context of skilled online labour provided during the coronavirus pandemic.[5] As such, when we seek to promote 'Decent Work in the Digital Age', it may become necessary to look beyond the safety and health not only of 'the workplace' as constructed and managed by an employer, but also to broader environmental concerns which affect where and how we work. This, in turn, raises broader questions regarding the substantive values that inform labour law.

In the construction of future ongoing regulation of digitalisation, how do we maintain a principled approach, or as Ruth Dukes would have it, a 'Labour Constitution' reflecting values other than merely 'the law of the labour market'?[6] Can this be achieved, given the pressure not to obstruct technological progress and the economic growth to which digitalisation of work is often tied? It may be notable that Sustainable Development Goal 8 proclaimed in the 2030 Agenda[7] is concerned not only with the promotion of 'decent work' but 'economic growth', including 'full and productive employment'. That tension is again apparent in principle 5 of the European Pillar of Social Rights in relation to 'secure and adaptable employment', which does not only engage with 'working conditions' (in paragraph 1) but with 'the necessary flexibility for employers to adapt swiftly to changes in the economic context' (in paragraph 2).[8]

Given the conflict likely to ensue between different interests over the normative objectives and their manifestation in legal forms, who is to make such decisions? What scope is to be given to managerial prerogative (enabling discretion based on perception

[2] eg, see V De Stefano, A Aloisi and N Countouris, 'The Metaverse is a Labour Issue', February 2022, available at: socialeurope.eu/the-metaverse-is-a-labour-issue.

[3] EP Thompson, 'Time, Work-Discipline and Industrial Capitalism' (1967) 38 *Past & Present* 56.

[4] P Tomassetti, 'Labor Law and Environmental Sustainability' (2018) 40 *Comparative Labor Law & Policy Journal* 61, 63.

[5] For early reviews of these worldwide developments, see (2020) 13(1S) *Italian Labour Law E-Journal*: Special Issue: Covid-19 and Labour Law. A Global Review, available at: illej.unibo.it/issue/view/868. For an admission of this shift from employers, see ILO, *An employers' guide on working from home in response to the outbreak of COVID-19* (2020) available at: www.ilo.org/wcmsp5/groups/public/---ed_dialogue/---act_emp/documents/publication/wcms_745024.pdf.

[6] R Dukes, *The Labour Constitution: The Enduring Idea of Labour Law* (Oxford, Oxford University Press, 2014).

[7] UN General Assembly Resolution Transforming our world: the 2030 Agenda for Sustainable Development, 25 September 2015, A/Res/70/1, available at: sustainabledevelopment.un.org/post2015/transformingourworld/publication.

[8] Interinstitutional Proclamation on the European Pillar of Social Rights 2017/C 428/09, 13 December 2017 OJ C 428/10.

of commercial needs) versus collective bargaining exercised through worker representatives (enabling workers' interests to enter the frame)? In this context, the exploration by Edoardo Ales in this volume of 'the impact of automation and robotics on collective labour relations' is most welcome, as is the careful reflection by Jeremias Adams-Prassl on both individual and collective aspects of 'management by algorithm', and the exploration by Tamás Gyulavári of collective labour rights amongst a wider 'floor of rights'.

The resolution of such tensions may fall to be decided at first instance by the state legislature and the courts in any given nation state. Yet, one might wonder also what scope would there be for regulating the terms of regional and global competition between nations? For this reason, the insights of Iacopo Senatori on 'EU law and digitalisation of employment relations' are also most welcome. Here we can look to the simultaneous issue by the European Commission of a proposal for a Platform Worker Directive,[9] alongside proposed Commission Guidelines on the application of EU competition law to collective agreements regarding the working conditions of solo self-employed persons.[10] Yet, we may also wish to consider higher level coordinated regulation through the International Labour Organization or a broader species of multifaceted 'global law', as Frank Hendrickx suggests in this collection.

Last, but certainly not least, this impressive collection of essays directs us towards considering regulation of working life in the digital age, not only with reference to the traditional field of labour law, but in other spheres of law which can secure 'decent work'. It has been acknowledged for some considerable time that the wellbeing of workers is shaped by other legal disciplines, such as company law.[11] In part IV of this volume, the contributors offer analysis of data protection law and of course human rights law relating to privacy, all of which are highly relevant to work in a digital age. Also, earlier in the book we find other helpful intersections, when the significance of competition law is interrogated by Tihamér Tóth and the importance of social welfare law is highlighted by Marius Olivier.

This may not be a book that pretends to offer neat or straightforward solutions to the taxing problems posed by the digital present and future of work. However, it will provide a vital reference point for those exploring regulatory possibilities and considering their implications. The editors are to be congratulated, as are all the contributors.

Tonia Novitz
*Professor of Labour Law, University of Bristol*
*28 February 2022*

[9] COM(2021) 762 final.
[10] C(2021) 8838 final.
[11] See, eg, on the interplay between the two, C Villiers, 'Corporate Governance, Employee Voice and the Interests of Employees' (2021) 50 *Industrial Law Journal* 159. See more generally, on the interplay between disciplinary areas of law, A Bogg and T Novitz (eds), *Voices at Work: Continuity and Change in the Common Law World* (Oxford, Oxford University Press, 2014) 30–31.

# CONTENTS

# LIST OF CONTRIBUTORS

**Tamás Gyulavári** is a Professor of Labour Law and Chair of the Labour Law Department at Pázmány Péter Catholic University in Budapest, Hungary. He studied and did research at the Universities of Budapest, Warwick, Groningen and Aix-Marseilles and was also a visiting fellow at the European University Institute in Florence in 2013 He has lectured at several universities, including Porto, Bologna, Vienna, Quito, Jakarta and Chicago. He is the founding editor of the *Hungarian Labour Law E-Journal*. He is the member of the European Labour Law Network and the Academic Network of Experts on Disability.

**Emanuele Menegatti** is Professor of Labour Law and President of the Forlì Campus, University of Bologna. He has been a visiting professor at many universities, including the University of Illinois, Monash University (Melbourne), Curtin University (Perth), Pázmány Péter Catholic University (Budapest, Hungary). He is the editor-in-chief of the *Italian Labour Law E-Journal*. His main fields of specialisation are Comparative and EU Labour Law. His main current research interests include the balance between social rights and economic freedoms in European Union law, minimum wage regulation, new forms of work in the gig-economy. He is the author of two books and a broad number of scientific publications on high-ranking Italian and international journals.

**Jeremias Adams-Prassl** is Professor of Law at Magdalen College, and Deputy Director of the Institute of European and Comparative Law in the University of Oxford. He studied law at Oxford, Paris, and Harvard Law School. His work has been recognised by prizes for teaching, research and public impact, including the *Modern Law Review* Wedderburn Prize, a British Academy Rising Star Engagement Award, and the 2019 St Petersburg Prize. Since the start of 2021, he has led a five-year research project on Algorithms at Work, funded by the European Research Council and a 2020 Leverhulme Prize.

**Edoardo Ales** is Full Professor of Labour Law and Industrial Relations at the Departme of Law of the University of Naples 'Parthenope' (Italy). He also teaches Social a Labour Market Regulation at the LUISS – G Carli in Rome (Italy). He is invited pro sor of International and Comparative Labour Law at the Pontifical Lateran Unive (Vatican State). He is member of the Board of the Italian Labour Law and Social Se Association (AIDLaSS). He is Member of the Board of Directors of *Giornale del D del Lavoro e delle Relazioni Industriali*, *Rivista del Diritto della Sicurezza Sociale*, *Labour Law e-Journal*, *Diritti Lavori Mercati* and DLM.int. He is a Membe Scientific Committee of the Marco Biagi Foundation of the University of Mo Reggio Emilia (Italy). He is the National Expert for Italy in the ICF-ECE ar Networks supporting the EU Commission in the field of labour law and free of workers.

**Antonio Aloisi** is a Marie Skłodowska-Curie fellow and assistant professor of European and Comparative Labour Law at IE Law School, Madrid, Spain. Before joining IE University, he was a Max Weber postdoctoral fellow at the European University Institute (EUI), Florence, Italy. He holds a PhD in Business and Social Law from Bocconi University, Milan, Italy (2018). His research focuses on the impact of digital innovation on labour regulation and social institutions in the European Union and beyond. The aim of his Boss Ex Machina project, which has received funding from the EU Horizon 2020 programme, is to map practices of algorithmic decision-making and assess the adequacy of existing legal frameworks when it comes to enabling sustainable data-driven workplaces. Antonio was a visiting researcher at the Saint Louis University, USA, and worked for the Italian Ministry of Education. He has been involved in various projects on platform work, non-standard employment and collective rights, commissioned by international organisations and research centres. He has co-authored *Your Boss is an Algorithm: Artificial Intelligence, Platform Work and Labour* (Hart Publishing, with Valerio De Stefano) and authored several articles, book chapters and op-eds.

**Martin Gruber-Risak** is Associate Professor in the Department of Labour Law and Law of Social Security at the University of Vienna (Austria). He was an associate with the international law firm CMS Reich-Rohrwig Hainz, Professor of Labour Law and Civil Law at the University of Passau (Germany) and a Marie Curie-Fellow at the University of Otago (New Zealand). Professor Gruber-Risak is the national expert for Austria of the European Centre of Expertise (ECE) in the field of labour law, employment and labour market policies that advises the European Commission. His main research interests lie in the effects of the digitalisation on the world of work and the labour law.

**Frank Hendrickx** is full Professor of Labour Law at the Law Faculty of KU Leuven
Belgium). He has been a visiting scholar at the Wharton School of the University
Pennsylvania (2008) and has held a part-time Chair in European Labour Law at
rg University (The Netherlands) between 2001 and 2018. He is General Editor
*International Encyclopaedia of Laws*, Editor of the *International Encyclopaedia*
*Law and Industrial Relations*, Editor of the *Bulletin of Comparative Labour*
nd Editor-in-chief of the *European Labour Law Journal*. He was President of
Association for Labour and Social Security Law from 2016 to 2018 and is a
of the Belgian Association for Labour Relations.

orks as Associate Professor in the Labour Law Department of Pázmány
ersity (Budapest). His main research fields are posted workers in EU
y work, other multiparty employment relationships and working
lved in a number of international research projects, including
found. Between 2018 and 2021 he supported the labour law
Court of Hungary as Advocate General.

professor at the University of Public Service (Budapest).
Pázmány Péter Catholic University Faculty of Law and
Hungary. He received his LL.M degree in public law
006, and his PhD degree in law at Pázmány Péter
author of more than 400 publications, and numer-
; in English: *Freedom of Speech – the Unreachable*

*Mirage* (Wolters Kluwer, 2013); *The Troubled Relationship between Religions and the State. Freedom of Expression and Freedom of Religion* (Whitelocke, 2017); and *New Media and Freedom of Expression* (Hart Publishing, 2019).

**Sylvaine Laulom** is Advocate General in the Social Chamber of Cour de Cassation in France. Before she came into office at the Court in 2019, she held a position as Professor of Private Law at Université Lumière Lyon II. There, she was the Director of the cross-disciplinary Institut d'Études du Travail de Lyon (IETL) and was part of the research team of the multidisciplinary Centre de Recherches Critiques sur le Droit (CERCRID). Laulom was awarded her PhD in 1996 at the European University Institute in Florence. Her research interests are mainly national and comparative labour law, and the social policy area of EU law. She has published several books and articles on these issues and she directed and/or was involved in several researches in particular on collective bargaining in times of crisis, on discrimination, transnational collective bargaining, etc.

**David Mangan** is Assistant Professor at the School of Law and Criminology, Maynooth University, Ireland. His research in labour, common law obligations and information technology has been published internationally. He is a barrister and solicitor in Canada. David has worked in Canada, France, Ireland and the United Kingdom.

**Marius Olivier** is an experienced Social Security and Social Protection Consultant, Legal Expert, Scholar and Researcher. He holds ad hoc professorial appointments with Nelson Mandela University and Northwest University (South Africa) and the University of Western Australia (Australia). He has published widely and has rendered comprehensive legal, advisory and policy services to international and regional organisations, several governments, social security institutions, and development agencies and donor institutions involved in social protection.

**Iacopo Senatori** is Assistant Professor of Labour Law at the University of Modena and Reggio Emilia. He received a PhD in labour law and industrial relations at the University of Bologna. He is a Member of the Academic Advisory Board of the Marco Biagi Foundation, University of Modena and Reggio Emilia; Coordinator of the Labour Law Area in the PhD Programme of Labour, Development and Innovation at the University of Modena and Reggio Emilia; Managing Editor of the *Italian Labour Law E-Journal*. His research interests include EU labour law, freedom of association and collective bargaining, workers' wellbeing, law and tech and the regulation of new forms of work. He is the author of one book and several articles and essays written in Italian and English, published in high-ranking national and international journals. He has been the principal investigator in several international research projects co-funded by the European Commission.

**Carla Spinelli** is Associate Professor at the Department of Law, University Aldo Moro of Bari. She was visiting professor at Lyon 2 University and has participated in several Erasmus teaching staff exchanges in Belgium and Spain. She is member of the scientific committee of two Italian labour law journals (*Diritti Lavori Mercati* and *Rivista Giuridica del Lavoro*). She participates in a number of research projects on labour law and European labour law. She has been a speaker at many scientific conferences, both national and international. She published two books in 2012 and 2018 and co-edited the book *El empleo publico. Puntos criticos en los ordenamientos italiano y español* (Thomson Reuters-ARANZADI, 2018) and *Los derechos fundamentales en el empleo publico* (Editorial Comares, 2021). She is the author of many articles and essays published in Italian and in English in national and international collective volumes and journals. Her main research interests are currently focused on the digital economy and new forms of work; anti-discrimination law and reasonable accommodation for people with disabilities; work–life balance; and labour law in the public sector.

**Tihamér Tóth** is a Professor of Competition Law and Associate Dean of the Faculty of Law and Social Sciences at Pázmány Péter Catholic University in Budapest, Hungary. He taught courses in English at the University of Notre Dame, Loyola University of Chicago, the Catholic University of Leuven and the Catholic University of Lyon. He has recently been granted a Jean Monnet chair position. He is a member of the scientific committee of the LIDC, member of the board of the Hungarian Competition Law Association, editor of Hungarian law journals *Competition Mirror* and *State Aid Law*. He also works as an attorney, co-heading the competition team of Dentons Réczcicza LLP.

**Manfred Weiss** has been a full Professor of Labour Law and Civil Law (first at the University of Hamburg and since 1977 at the Goethe University in Frankfurt); Professor emeritus since 2008; 2000–03 President of ILERA; 1998–2002 Deputy President of the German Lawyers' Association (DJT); for many years, Consultant to the International Labour Organisation since 1980 and to the Commission of the EU. He received honorary doctorates in Budapest (2005), Bordeaux (2011), Northwest University (NWU) in South Africa (2015); Award of the Labour Law Research Network (LLRN) for outstanding contribution to labour law (2015).

**Leonardo Battista** and **Gábor Kártyás** worked as assistant editors on this book.

# 1

# Labour, Law and Digitalisation

TAMÁS GYULAVÁRI AND EMANUELE MENEGATTI

## I. Introduction

Digital transformation of work has recently become the hot topic of labour law research, probably for more than one simple reason. New digital technologies have rapidly spread all over the world in the field of work (as well), and their future seems to be even brighter. We must reasonably expect that its role in economic, as well as work relations will increase both in the short and long term. At the same time, digital technologies and related socio-economic legal changes have serious implications for labour markets and work relations. Above all, digitalisation has given a new impetus to the expansion of non-standard forms of work and a rearrangement of standard employment.

Most importantly, technological changes have profound results in the working conditions of an increasing group of workers. Indeed, these forms of work are new in many senses, but warm up the traditional debate on which securities should be guaranteed for which workers. This leads us to the usual questions about personal scope, but also carries on to the details of standard employees' rights. Consequently, labour law faces the challenge of whether new problems may be solved with the old, classic labour law framework; although, this theoretical, but also practical debate does not really stop at the borders of labour law. Beyond labour law, several other fields of law and policy are relevant in this regard, such as competition, freedom of speech, data protection and privacy. Therefore, the effects of digitalisation must be seen in an interdisciplinary scenario.

In this introductory chapter, the editors investigate the general issues discussed in the book. In section II, we map the meanings of digitalisation at work, that is to say the fields and forms of digitalisation which have an impact on workers and employers alike. In section III, we focus on the positive and negative effects of digitalisation on workers. Section IV raises the underlying question of whether labour law is capable of addressing the negative outcomes of digitalisation for affected workers by means of the traditional legal institutions of labour law. Section V looks into the future of labour law and strives for some projections on how labour law could and should react to the challenges deriving from expanded digitalisation of work in the short and longer term. Finally, section VI presents the aims, structure and authors of the book.

Several books have been published recently on various aspects of the counteraction between digitalisation and labour law.[1] This book aims at addressing the same issues with a more comprehensive and multidisciplinary approach, considering all the forms of digitalisation and regulatory matters involved. It has the central theoretical objective to outline the main obstacles and possible ways of providing decent working conditions in the new digital age. Therefore, the book focuses on digitalisation forms which directly involve work relations only. An investigation into those digital platforms dealing with services such as *Airbnb* or *Ebay*, where the labour factor is not preponderant (a physical capital or a good is instead), falls outside the scope of our work.[2] Furthermore, electronically made legal statements (eg, employment contract conclusion by email), how they are made and accepted as lawful by labour law, is not part of our scrutiny.

In this context, this introduction attempts to summarise the most relevant legal and policy matters, which are discussed in detail by the contributions in this volume.

## II. Four Pillars of Digital Transformation of Work

Digitalisation manifests itself in many ways and forms in the world of work. In this book, we focus on the legal aspects of digital transformation of labour markets and work relations. Although it is labour law, which has the exclusive mission to regulate employment rights, other related legal branches are also included in our work, such as competition, social security, occupational health and safety, equal treatment, data protection and freedom of speech. Against this theoretical background, we identify the following four pillars which have been driving the digital transformation of work relations:

a. Digital platforms running digital marketplaces for non-standard work.
b. ICT entailing new forms of remote and more flexible work.
c. Production processes managed by algorithm.
d. Digital surveillance vis-à-vis employees' privacy.

In our view, these four forms (above all others) pose fundamental challenges for labour law.

These challenges take place within the (almost) new form of non-standard work, such as the various forms of platform work. They also relate to the 'evolution' of traditional employment prompted by digitalisation. Even though platform workers and more traditional employees present different issues, they do share several questions raised by algorithm decision-making and the intensity of control and monitoring permitted by

[1] MT Carinci and F Dorssemont (eds), *Platform work in Europe* (Cambridge, Intersentia, 2021); E Ales et al (eds), *Working in Digital and Smart Organizations: Legal, Economic and Organizational Perspectives on the Digitalization of Labour Relations* (London, Palgrave Macmillan, 2018); A Perulli and T Treu (eds), *The Future of Work: Labour Law and Labour Market Regulation in the Digital Era* (Alphen aan den Rijn, Kluwer Law International, 2020); J Carby-Hall and L Mella Méndez, *Labour Law and the Gig Economy* (London, Routledge, 2020); JM Miranda Boto and E Brameshuber (eds), *Collective Bargaining and the Gig Economy: A Traditional Tool for New Business Models* (Oxford, Hart Publishing, 2022).

[2] For a taxonomy of digital platforms and platform work, see C Codagnone, F Abadie and F Biagi, *The Future of Work in the 'Sharing Economy'. Market Efficiency and Equitable Opportunities or Unfair Precarisation* (Luxembourg, Publications Office of the European Union, 2016).

digital technology. For example, management by algorithm is at the core of the business model created by gig-work platforms, even if on-demand-work via app often involves traditional work on the spot.[3] Moreover, digitalisation in support of traditional business operations has permitted algorithms to dictate the organisation and conditions of work performances.

Not all the models of work permeated to some extent by digitalisation have to do with algorithms. That is the case in remote work arrangements, where the work is performed outside the business premises and in some cases outside the employer's usual control, as to the working-time and the way work is performed. The relevance of digital technologies is for employee–employer communication and, very often, for the performance of work. In many cases, as much as for computer-based work performed in the traditional way (inside the company's premises), the legal problems concern surveillance over employees, privacy and freedom of speech. They are generated by the use of GPS, web camera, email communication and internet through social media. Remarkably, these digital tools are able to intrude into work performance as well as rest periods and leisure time.

As just shown, the legal and practical issues entailed by digitalisation are colourful and different in relation to the different forms of work and work organisation prompted by the highlighted four drivers of work transformation. Not surprisingly, labour law answers are inevitably heterogeneous too.

## III. The Profound Impact of Digitalisation on Work Relations

The transformation of employment patterns prompted by the digital revolution has been having a profound impact on work. We must emphasise that there is a positive and a negative side to such effects. Therefore, it is important when looking at the possible legal solutions for addressing the issues that we bear in mind both sides, in order not to waste the good opportunities brought by digitalisation.

As for the positive impact, gig-work and remote work arrangements must be mentioned. They are both characterised by increased autonomy for workers, including working time flexibility. Moreover, the new digital marketplaces created by platforms increase job opportunities for disadvantaged labour market segments (ie, migrants, young unexperienced, women)[4] and the overall employment rate.[5] It may represent

[3] See ch 5 in this volume by Martin Gruber-Risak on the differentiation between on-demand work via apps and crowdsourcing.

[4] Eurofound, *Employment and working conditions of selected types of platform work* (Luxembourg, Publications Office of the European Union, 2018, 60). www.eurofound.europa.eu/sites/default/files/ef_publication/field_ef_document/ef18001en.pdf.

[5] S Engblom, 'Atypical Work in the Digital Age – Outline of a Trade Union Strategy for the Gig Economy' (2017), 220, available at: www.academia.edu/32900838/Atypical_Work_in_the_Digital_Age_Outline_of_a_Trade_Union_Strategy_for_the_Gig_Economy; European Commission, 'Communication from the Commission to the European Parliament, the Council, the European Economic and Social Committee and the Committee of the Regions. A European agenda for the collaborative economy' (SWD(2016) 184 final) 2, available at: www.europarl.europa.eu/RegData/docs_autres_institutions/commission_europeenne/com/2016/0356/COM_COM%282016%290356_EN.pdf.

a supplementary source of income for those already engaged in another main work activity or for pensioners and students.[6] As for employers, thanks to crowdworking, companies have access to an unlimited pool of workers with lower administrative and other costs.

Management by algorithm and, more generally, organisations taking advantage of artificial intelligence (AI) brings fast, cheap, innovative solutions in a flexible way.[7] It increases work productivity and improves the quality of products and services. It can also improve working conditions by securing healthy and safe working conditions, and a better allocation of tasks between human and machine.[8]

One cannot deny that the negative consequences are far more numerous. At the same time, these practical and theoretical problems are significantly different regarding the four pillars of digital transformation of work. Platform work is by far the most problematic with an extensive blacklist,[9] stemming from a general lack of employment[10] and social protection,[11] when platform workers are not considered as employees;[12] consequent low pay,[13] mostly not covered by the minimum wage,[14] unpredictable working time, long working hours, often at night, at weekends and on bank holidays;[15] missing protection against dismissal, disciplinary measures and unfair performance appraisal;[16] child labour[17] and forced labour[18] especially in crowdsourcing; lack of collective bargaining and collective rights; no employers' liability for employees' damages; dependence on algorithmic decision-making.

[6] M Risak and J Warter, 'Legal strategies towards fair conditions in the virtual sweatshop', Paper presented at the fourth Regulating for Decent Work Conference (ILO, Geneva, 8–10 July 2015), available at: www.rdw2015.org/download, 4.

[7] JM Leimeister, S Zogaj and D Durward, 'New Forms of Employment and IT – Crowdsourcing', 4th Conference of the Regulating for Decent Work Network, 2015, 8, available at: www.papers.ssrn.com/sol3/papers.cfm?abstract_id=2736953.

[8] *European Social Partners Framework Agreement on Digitalisation*, June 2020, 11, available at: www.etuc.org/system/files/document/file2020-06/Final%2022%2006%2020_Agreement%20on%20Digitalisation%20 2020.pdf.

[9] See ch 7 in this volume by Tamás Gyulavári for details on the floor of rights for platform workers.

[10] J Prassl and M Risak, 'Uber, Taskrabbit, & Co: Platforms as Employers? Rethinking the Legal Analysis of Crowdwork' (2016) 37 *Comparative Labor Law & Policy Journal* 619, 626; Risak and Warter (n 6).

[11] ILO, *Digital labour platforms and the future of work. Towards decent work in the online world* (Geneva, ILO, 2018) available at: www.ilo.org/wcmsp5/groups/public/---dgreports/---dcomm/---publ/documents/publication/wcms_645337.pdf, xviii.

[12] See ch 6 by Emanuele Menegatti and ch 5 by Martin Gruber-Risak in this volume on the classification of platform work.

[13] A Felstiner, 'Working the Crowd: Employment and Labor Law in the Crowdsourcing Industry' (2011) 32 *Berkeley Journal of Employment and Labor Law* 143, 156.

[14] For instance: GMB, *Uber Driver Not Paid the Minimum Wage* (7 September 2015), available at: www.gmb.org.uk/newsroom/uber-driver-not-paid-minimum-wage.

[15] ILO, Digital labour platforms and the future of work (n 11) xvii.

[16] R Florisson and I Mandl, *Digital age Platform work: Types and implications for work and employment – Literature review* (Luxembourg, Eurofound, Publications Office of the European Union) 4; V De Stefano, 'The Rise of the "Just-in-Time Workforce": On-Demand Work, Crowdwork, and Labor Protection in the "Gig-Economy"' (2016) 37 *Comparative Labor Law & Policy Journal* 471, 478.

[17] A Todolí-Signes, 'The End of the Subordinate Worker? Collaborative Economy, On-demand Economy, Gig Economy, and the Crowdworkers' Need for Protection' (2017) 33 *International Journal of Comparative Labour Law and Industrial Relations* 241, available at: www.ssrn.com/abstract=2899383.

[18] V De Stefano and A Aloisi, 'Fundamental Labour Rights, Platform Work and Human-Rights Protection of Non-Standard Workers' (2018) Bocconi Legal Studies Research Paper 1, available at: www.papers.ssrn.com/sol3/papers.cfm?abstract_id=3125866, 7.

In this latter regard, the recourse to AI, including algorithmic decision-making, can jeopardise human involvement and capabilities,[19] and it is a potential source of non-transparent discriminatory decisions. It might also result in the intensification of workloads, posing a potential threat to human physical and psychological integrity, especially if it does not follow the human-in-control principle.[20] From the labour market perspective, digital transformation involves risks for employers and workers, since some jobs will disappear and change.

Telework and other forms of remote work are dominantly performed in an employment relationship, so most of the above-mentioned problems are resolved by labour law. However, the flexibility it entails may create risks not yet properly addressed by labour laws,[21] stemming from the blurring of the division between work and private life, both during and beyond working time. The right to rest and, in particular, to disconnect from work could be difficult to enforce. Similarly, the privacy of the worker is considerably curtailed by digitalised life and work. Personal monitoring, facilitated by digital technologies can compromise the dignity of workers.[22] The surveillance could even extend to off-duty activities, in social networks.[23] This risk affects standard employees as well, whose work is performed by digital devices/tools. Remote workers can also find particular risks, not included in standard work: isolation; possible reduction of career opportunities; and the lack of a fair cost sharing between employer and employee regarding expenditure inevitably deriving from working from home.

Therefore, the digital scenario of work relations is rather varied, just like the potential answers from labour law. It calls into question the capacity of existing legislation to ensure the protection of workers' rights. Statutory law and international institutions may respond to these comprehensive changes in work with a complex set of amendments. Moreover, case law also has a unique role in some parts, particularly in the protection of privacy and freedom of speech, where an adequate balance should be found based on the general rules in statutory law. Therefore, in the next section we look into the regulatory challenges labour law is facing at this moment.

## IV. Regulatory Challenges: New Problems versus Traditional Labour Law Institutions

During the twentieth century labour law has elaborated a comprehensive and high-quality framework of protection for workers, thus, it has a long-standing, traditional institutional architecture and logic. The entire body of this protection has been built

[19] European Social Partners Framework Agreement on Digitalisation (n 8). See details in ch 3 by Edoardo Ales in this volume.

[20] See details in ch 12 by Jeremias Adams-Prassl in this volume.

[21] See ch 11 by Carla Spinelli in this volume for details on agile work/telework.

[22] *European Social Partners Framework Agreement on Digitalisation* (n 8). See details in ch 14 by Sylvaine Laulom in this volume.

[23] See details in ch 16 by David Mangan in this volume.

on the abstract model of the 'employee' in the standard employment relationship. The scope of labour law was targeted on workers belonging to the industrial economy and their need of protection resulting from a position of legal subordination and weak bargaining power.[24] The employment relationship was a real success in this regard for almost the entire twentieth century. However, in the last decades the switch to the post-industrial economy, accompanied by de-verticalisation of companies in the framework of enhanced global competition, favoured the headway of non-standard (precarious) employment.[25] It brought about shrinking coverage of the employee status, and the weakening of associated protections.[26]

Nonetheless, many workers not matching the traditional 'employee' paradigm present a similar or even higher need for protection than traditional employees, because of their economical, functional and operational dependence on a client's business.[27] 'Dependent' self-employment and bogus self-employment have in many cases become a survival strategy for those who are not able to get a 'regular' job through an employment contract, typically those belonging to the weakest segments of the labour market (migrants, young workers, disabled, etc). This has led many to question the adequacy of the binary dichotomy between employee and self-employed and the attached logic of all-or-nothing in terms of employment protection and social security rights. The changes brought by digitalisation have emphasised this issue even more.[28] Platform work, especially, has become the typical area of debate on the personal scope of existing employment protection.

However, not only is the personal scope of labour law challenged, but the traditional pillars of labour law protection are also under pressure. Labour law has traditionally been founded on the following basic principles and values: social protection in line with human dignity; a collective voice; and a democratic workplace. Digital transformation has several implications for these basic labour law principles, such as the need to support lifelong learning by an appropriate legal framework; to reshape the personal scope of employment and social protection; to adapt working time rules to 'autonomised' employees; to assure an adequate work–life balance; to protect health and safety and privacy from unprecedented challenges relating to workers' psychological sphere; and to prevent new subtle forms of discrimination created by apparently objective decisions made by algorithm. Last but not least, all workers should be granted access

[24] See G Davidov, *A Purposive Approach to Labour Law* (Oxford, Oxford University Press, 2016) 14.

[25] ILO, 'Meeting the challenge of precarious work: A worker's agenda' (2013) 1 *International Journal of Labour Research*, available at: www.ilo.org/wcmsp5/groups/public/---ed_dialogue/---actrav/documents/publication/wcms_216282.pdf, 30, 42.

[26] N Countouris, 'The Employment Relationship: A Comparative Analysis of National Judicial Approaches' in G Casale (ed), *The Employment Relationship: A Comparative Overview* (Oxford, Hart Publishing, 2011) 35.

[27] H Collins, 'Market Power, Bureaucratic Power and the Contract of Employment' (1986) 15 *Industrial Relations Journal* 1 defines this dependence as 'bureaucratic': independent contractors' activities are integrated into the client's 'bureaucratic structure', which gives the latter a 'bureaucratic control' – something de facto similar to direction and supervision – over the former.

[28] A Supiot, 'Les nouveaux visages de la subordination' (2000) 2 *Droit Social* 131; M Freedland, 'Application of Labour and Employment Law Beyond the Contract of Employment' (2007) 146 *International Labour Review* 3; M Freedland, *The Personal Employment Contract* (Oxford, Oxford University Press, 2003).

to collective representation, which can be very difficult when the workplace becomes virtual. As Manfred Weiss summarises:

> [I]t has to be kept in mind that labour law since its foundation has seen many changes and met many challenges. The so-called fourth industrial revolution is only another step, even a dramatic one … The main task will be that the digital Era will not lead to a re-commodification of labour and that the respect of human dignity with all its implications can be guaranteed.[29]

Along these lines, recent research has often simplified this question to the single legal issue, whether the employee status shall be ensured for platform workers. So, the debate is of a general nature: shall we apply the rules of the employment relationship automatically to platform workers? Judicial interpretation is playing the primary role in expanding the personal scope of the employment relationship.[30] In international labour law, the European Court of Justice (ECJ) has also been slowly and gradually moving towards a wider interpretation of the concept of worker.[31] This solution has many evident advantages, since all existing employment standards may be easily and automatically applied to more workers, in particular non-standard, including platform workers.

But the legislative expansion is remarkably hardened by the distinctive features of many of these new work forms, so the employee status may extend to only a fragment of them. Therefore, employee status may not provide a solution for all affected workers.[32] Moreover, some rules of national labour law cannot be automatically applied due to the special nature of platform work. There are specific rules of labour law, where the application of old rules may prove difficult to apply: working time; competition law obstacles of collective bargaining; and algorithmic management and decision-making.

As an alternative solution, it has also been argued that a specific (other) legal status should be elaborated (applied) by creating new, intermediary statuses, like economically dependent workers.[33] It is of course an ongoing discussion which tries to identify all the pros and cons regarding this option. The theoretical criticism of such a solution concerns the weakening of the employment relationship as a whole and of the entire structure of labour law.[34] From a practical point of view, gradual implementation of the floor of rights may be a part of the solution for those not fitting into the employee status. In this respect, it seems to be inevitable to move towards universalisation of

[29] See ch 2 by Manfred Weiss in this volume on labour law principles and their potential to adapt to the new economic and social reality.

[30] See ch 6 in this volume by Emanuele Menegatti on judicial developments regarding the personal scope of labour law in relation to platform work.

[31] N Kountouris, 'The Concept of "Worker" in European Labour Law: Fragmentation, Autonomy and Scope' (2017) 47 *Industrial Law Journal* 202; M Risak and T Dullinger, 'The Concept of "Worker" in EU Law: Status Quo and Potential for Change' (2018) ETUI Research Paper – Report 140; S Giubboni, 'Being a Worker in EU Law' (2018) 9 *European Labour Law Journal* 223; E Menegatti, 'Taking EU labour law beyond the employment contract: The role played by the European Court of Justice' (2020) 11 *European Labour Law Journal* 26.

[32] See the arguments in detail in ch 5 by Martin Gruber-Risak in this volume.

[33] See, for instance, SD Harris and AB Krueger, 'A Proposal for Modernizing Labor Laws for Twenty-First-Century Work: The "Independent Worker"' Hamilton Project Discussion Paper 2015-10 (December), available at: www.hamiltonproject.org/assets/files/modernizing_labor_laws_for_twenty_first_century_work_krueger_harris.pdf.

[34] N Countouris, *The Changing Law of the Employment Relationship: Comparative Analyses in the European Context* (Aldershot, Ashgate Publishing, 2007) 8.

employment protection by a floor of rights for all workers, including those working at digital platforms.[35]

Nevertheless, the full range of employment protections are guaranteed for other kinds of work relations impacted by digitalisation. We refer to standard employment relationships where AI is in charge of managing work organisation. We refer also to employees engaged in remote work arrangements. In these cases, the protection of the entire body of labour law is not in question, however, traditional employment rules are under 'digital pressure'. Digital technologies (GPS, algorithm, web camera, social media etc) suddenly blew up and made more visible many existing malpractices. The possibility for the employer to monitor an employee's social media activities offers many data about the latter, not normally accessible from traditional workplace interactions.[36] Labour law is prepared for this kind of problem with national and international standards; however, the scale, intensity and nature of violations are noticeably different from before.

Overall, digital transformation of work is an excellent example, when old legal institutions have to answer new challenges. This is a bit of exaggeration of course, because not all the applicable labour law provisions are old (eg, data protection), and even the challenges are not absolutely new, but different. It is also true that the speed of the digital transformation forces the legislator and the judiciary to pursue the changes. Anyway, the good news is that the basic labour law institutions are not questioned as a whole in the course of the digitalisation debate. Protection of human dignity, social protection, collective rights and a democratic workplace are still valid and meaningful values, which must be provided either for new persons, or in a novel way.

We can conclude that the entire system of labour law is capable of adapting to the new changes, but this process is slow and full of legal obstacles (eg, antitrust rules versus collective bargaining). And we find this evaluation equally valid for national and international employment labour standards. The present and potential methods of this adaptation will be discussed in the next section.

## V. What Future for Labour Law in the Digital Era?

We must emphasise that our focus here is not the future of labour law in general, but exclusively the impact that digital transformation and its relevant drivers will have on labour regulation. We propose two investigations in this regard. The first one is about the state of the art, considering what amendments and laws have already responded to the digital transformation of work in recent years. The second question relates to our prediction for the immediate future and medium term. In light of the ongoing changes, shall we expect new directions in labour regulation, and if so, what are these?

For both questions on present and future developments, we scrutinise three aspects: (a) why is labour law moving and shall move forward; (b) in which directions is it exactly going; and (c) how fast are the changes? We will structure this section along these three

[35] See ch 7 by Tamás Gyulavári in this volume on a possible floor of rights for platform workers.
[36] See the details in ch 16 by David Mangan in this volume.

aspects, starting with the reasons for changes, continuing with the clustering of legal developments, and closing with the evaluation of the speed of digital transformation of labour law.

We must also remark that there are several, considerably different levels (sources) of changes, like national law, international standards and case law at both levels. National employment legislation seems to be the ideal level for a fast and decisive answer. Digital transformation is moving fast in the developed countries, where the most crucial problems are already well represented in the labour market. These countries have already elaborated a high level of employment protection and institutional framework. Equally, they have the will, which derives from a certain responsiveness to social pressure, and the methods to adjust to rapidly moving economic and social changes. Unsurprisingly, the authors of this book take most of the examples of developments from the legislations of European and North American countries, as well as from the European Union (EU) law.

International standardisation should also play an important role, as some of the new forms of digital transformation have a global nature. Thus, a global response is both appropriate and for some of the phenomenon inevitable (eg, crowdsourcing). International and supranational standards may have two separate functions: universalisation and innovative functions.

Regarding the first, universalisation function, employment standards elaborated in some national labour laws may in this way be incorporated and then become international obligations. EU law is an excellent example of this,[37] where digital transformation is happening at a large scale in the rich centrum countries of the EU (in particular platform work), so they react the fastest in their labour laws. These national legal solutions are already on the way to becoming EU level standards, in some form of compromise among Member States. This is happening, for example, with the recent Proposal for a directive on improving working conditions in platform work,[38] or it has happened with the European Social Partners autonomous framework agreement on digitalisation.[39]

The second, innovative function of international labour law may mean that international legal standards and court decisions (eg, ECJ) invent some new solutions not known before in national laws and give impetus to those national legislations which are slower to adapt to social needs. Evidently, the wider scope of international standards, and the mediation always underlying these standards, quite often leads to softer standards at the end compared with those enacted by developed countries' national labour laws.

## A. Reasons for Adjustment

So, our first question is: why is labour law on the move, in other words, why do we experience an intellectual and legislative upheaval around the digitalisation of labour market

[37] See ch 4 by Iacopo Senatori in this volume for developments in EU law.

[38] European Commission, 'Proposal for a Directive of the European Parliament and of the Council on improving working conditions in platform work' COM(2021) 762 final.

[39] *European Social Partners Framework Agreement on Digitalisation* (n 8).

and work relations? The short answer is that digitalisation is experienced intensely in many countries and perceived as a problem to solve. Platform work is certainly now only affecting some developed countries, but the problems deriving from the other pillars of digital transformation (telework, social media, privacy, data) are widely present all over the world. Although many of these forms (eg, platform work) are still at a low scale, there is a rapid and constant increase. Just think of the smartphone revolution in developing countries, which helps to overcome the barriers of expensive laptops. The number of smartphone users in India reached 748 million in 2020, and worldwide it is forecast to exceed 1.5 billion users in 2040.[40]

The present overrepresentation of developed countries in digitalisation of work derives from the high availability and use of digital technologies at work and the related limitation of digitalisation to the services sector. The sectoral limitation may rapidly change, as platform work, digital surveillance and telework has a lot to offer for companies and consumers alike in terms of cost, availability, quality control, etc. We would not be surprised, for instance, if more and more Indian agricultural workers are hired through apps in the near future. The involvement of other sectors, such as agricultural production, may cause a real boom in digital aspects of work. What we see now is only the beginning of the digitalisation story.

The widespread use of digital technologies in the framework of work relations has increased the impact and speed of the highlighted four drivers of digital transformation of work: digital platforms; the increasing use of flexible remote work; management by algorithm; and digital surveillance. This has increased the attention paid to the misalignment between employment and social protections, their scope of application, and the reality of production models and business organisation.

At the very beginning, labour courts have been at the forefront, when they had to adjudicate disputes deciding over the application of labour law or single employment protection, by making use of not always suitable labour law tools. At the same time, grassroots movements have emerged among the new workers of the gig economy in the attempt to raise a collective voice. Workers reacted almost immediately, even before labour law scholars understood the disruptive effects on the common understating of employment categories that the digital revolution was causing. Almost immediately trade unions and politics have stepped into the debate at all levels – national, international and supranational.

## B. Regulatory Tendencies

The second question is what answers labour law has given to the digital challenge, and what policies we can foresee. So far, we may identify five distinctive tracks of improvement of employment rights in the digitalised world of work:

1. Full application of employment standards.
2. Application of certain employee rights to non-employees.

[40] www.statista.com/statistics/467163/forecast-of-smartphone-users-in-india/.

3. Introduction of a third-worker status.
4. Improvement of specific employees' rights taking into consideration the issues entailed by the new digitalisation context.
5. Adaptation of employment rights to changing models of work organisation.

As for the first track, extension of the employment relationship (employee status) to a wider range of workers, including platform workers, is happening through the case law of ever more national high courts. A few national legislations have already introduced a broader concept of employee in order to cover platform workers alongside economically dependent workers. This has happened so far mainly by legal presumption of employment. Examples are the California Assembly Bill No 5 (AB5) and the Spanish riders law.[41]

The second track is the provision of certain employee rights. In some national laws (eg, in France, Poland), the universal application of a few employment rights has been strengthened, since specific rights (trade union membership, collective bargaining, minimum wage) are provided for non-employee workers as well.[42] EU law is moving in a similar way, in the first instance, with the ECJ's elaboration on a wide concept of worker – broader than the national concepts of employee – with a view to enlarge the scope of application of some EU directives[43] and some other fundamental rights such as pay equality,[44] or the right to collective bargaining as an exception to antitrust law.[45] In this way the EU broad concept of worker has become obligatory regarding the implementation of some EU laws, but it may have an effect on the national interpretation of the employee status in general. Furthermore, the latest EU legislation addressing the issues of non-standard workers, such as the Directive on transparent and predictable working conditions, make use of the ECJ's elaboration on the concept of worker to determine the scope of application, though in a rather ambiguous way.[46]

[41] Real Decreto-ley 9/2021. As for the implications of these bills see ch 6 by Emanuele Menegatti in this volume.

[42] I Daugareilh, D Degryse and P Pochet (eds), 'The platform economy and social law: Key issues in comparative perspective' (2019) ETUI Working Paper 10 (Brussels, ETUI, 2019), available at: www.etui.org/sites/default/files/WP-2019.10-EN-v3-WEB.pdf, 55; L Pisarczyk, 'Collective Bargaining in the Shadow of Legislation: Labour Law Sources in Poland' in T Gyulavári and E Menegatti (eds), *The Sources of Labour Law* (Alphen aan den Rijn, Kluwer Law International, 2020) 281, 285.

[43] Kountouris, 'The Concept of "Worker" in European Labour Law' (n 31).

[44] Case C-256/01 *Debra Allonby v Accrington & Rossendale College, Education Lecturing Services, trading as Protocol Professional and Secretary of State for Education and Employment* ECLI: EU: C:2004:18 [2004].

[45] Case C-413/13 *FNV Kunsten Informatie en Media v Staat der Nederlanden* ECLI:EU:C:2014:2411 [2014]. See ch 10 by Tihamér Tóth in this volume for details of this case law and the related competition law rules and case law.

[46] Directive (EU) 2019/1152 of the European Parliament and of the Council on transparent and predictable working conditions in the European Union (Transparent and Predictable Working Conditions Directive) [2020] OJ L186/105, Article 1.2, refers the rights provided by the Directive to 'every worker in the Union who has an employment contract or employment relationship as defined by the law, collective agreements or practice in force in each Member State with consideration to the case-law of the Court of Justice'. Linking the access to the rights offered by EU directives to those who are 'employees' under national law and referring, at the same time, to the criteria established by the ECJ for determining the status of a worker is quite contradictory. That because, as reported above in the text, the concept of 'worker' elaborated by the ECJ is broader than most of the national concepts of employee. See B Bednarowicz, 'Delivering on the European Pillar of Social Rights: The New Directive on Transparent and Predictable Working Conditions in the European Union' (2019) 48 *Industrial Law Journal* 604, 609.

As for the third track, some jurisdictions have in place a third labour law category, able to extend the scope of some rights to those falling under this employment status. The UK and Spanish legislations are clear examples of this approach. In the UK, the 'worker' category includes those who have a contract or other arrangement to perform work or services personally, a limited right to send a substitute to do their work, and not doing the work as part of their own limited company in an arrangement where the 'employer' is actually a customer or client. Workers who are not employees share some employment rights such as the minimum wage, a statutory minimum level of paid holiday, a statutory minimum length of rest breaks, some working time limitations, protection against unlawful discrimination and for 'whistleblowing'.

Spanish law recognises the category of Economically Dependent Worker (TRADE), that is to say those who are not under a principal's directives bear the entrepreneurial risk and have the ownership of the tools and instrumentalities of production. At the same time, they depend on a principal for at least 75 per cent of their income, for whom they perform an economic or professional activity on a continuing basis. These workers are entitled by the legislation to several employment rights like annual leave, some working time limitations, leave for family or health reasons, unemployment benefits. In both countries, several court decisions recognised the intermediate category status of some platform workers.[47]

This may be followed in countries where the third category (economically dependent worker) exists, or another specific status is created for some groups of non-employees. This option has some flaws, because it comes up with a narrow scope and weaker rights than that of employees, and it also adds a new front line to the litigation on the personal scope of three groups (employee, worker, self-employed) instead of the binary divide.

The fourth track concerns the improvement of some employee rights which are already regulated in labour law. In EU law, the General Data Protection Regulation (GDPR) is a crucial development because it introduced a higher-level regulation for data protection.[48] This may serve as an example for other regional and universal organisations to elaborate a comprehensive regulation of data protection.[49] Regarding the right to freedom of speech and privacy, existing statutory law has been improved primarily by national courts, which judicial tests may contribute to the strengthening of employee protection in the digital setting.[50]

[47] See, for instance, *Aslam and Farrar v Uber BV, Uber London Ltd and Uber Brittania Ltd*, first decided by the Central London Employment Tribunal (www.judiciary.uk/judgments/mr-y-aslam-mr-j-farrar-and-others-v-uber/); decision confirmed by the Employment Appeal Tribunal (www.assets.publishing.service.gov.uk/media/5a046b06e5274a0ee5a1f171/Uber_B.V._and_Others_v_Mr_Y_Aslam_and_Others_UKEAT_0056_17_DA.pdf); and finally by the Court of Appeal (www.judiciary.uk/wp-content/uploads/2018/12/uber-bv-ors-v-aslam-ors-judgment-19.12.18.pdf). In Spain, the TRADE status has been recognised by the Madrid Labour Court *Beatriz Victoria Prada Rodriguez v Glovo* (www.jurisprudencia.vlex.es/vid/740259545).

[48] Regulation (EU) 2016/679 of the European Parliament and of the Council of 27 April 2016 on the protection of natural persons with regard to the processing of personal data and on the free movement of such data, and repealing Directive 95/46/EC (General Data Protection Regulation) [2016] OJ L119/1.

[49] See details in ch 15 by Frank Hendrickx in this volume.

[50] See the chapters by David Mangan (ch 16) and András Koltay (ch 17) in this volume.

The fifth track involves the adaptation of existing rules to the new issues stemming from the digital revolution. The reference is to the surveillance over workers, including private lives, which may now take place via monitoring of social network activities. These aspects have not significantly been addressed at this point either by legislation or by case law. Nonetheless, some interesting – still embryonic – developments, both at international and national level, are on the way.[51] Another important example is that of the adjustment of working time for new remote work arrangements, and in general for all those work arrangements facilitated by digital technologies entailing more employees with discretion over when they work.[52] Coordination about the maximum extension of work performances should be provided by legislation, such as happens for example with agile work in Italy. A right to disconnect is important in order to prevent workers from checking and answering emails 24/7. This leads to the health and safety angle. Possible intensification of workloads favoured by mobile devices and flexibility may dramatically increase issues relating to psychological stress and burn-out. The same may happen because of the possibility permitted by algorithm management and digital tools to impose higher performance targets.

Solutions are on the way too. Work-related stress is at the forefront of EU policies targeted at health and safety protection. The issue has already been dealt with by the Framework Agreement on Work-related Stress signed by the European Social Partners in 2004, providing rules for identifying, preventing and managing the related problems. Concerns about health and safety for teleworkers have been increasingly addressed at national level, especially in the wake of the Covid-19 pandemic and the massive resort to remote work prompted by lockdowns. An important role here is played by collective bargaining in place of, or in addition to, legislation.[53]

## C. Pace of Change

It is often the case that labour law academics are unsatisfied with the speed with which legislation reacts to the transformation of labour markets. Thus, it is a suitable question to raise: how fast are we moving towards an amended labour law framework? Can we reasonably expect an improvement regarding the reaction time of legislations at national and international level? Let us start with a time line of labour law developments concerning digital transformation, and particularly platform work. In the early

[51] The European Court of Human Rights jurisprudence dealing with the workers' right to privacy vis-à-vis the surveillance permitted by technology is perhaps the most interesting. For example, in *Bărbulescu v Romania* A no 61496/08 ECLI:CE:ECHR:2016:0112JUD006149608 [2017] has concluded that Article 8 ECHR, dealing with the right to respect for private and family life, is capable of adapting to the technological challenges, precisely to the employer's over employee's social network activities. See ch 16 by David Mangan in this volume for a comprehensive analysis on the development of the ECtHR, ECJ and some national jurisprudence on the topic.

[52] On the ambiguous nature of 'work time autonomy', see ch 8 by Gábor Kártyás in this volume on working time.

[53] That is, eg, the case of the French Intersectoral Agreement of 26 November 2020, the Dutch Flexible Work Act of 2015, Italian Law no 81/2017 on Agile Work Arrangements. See on this ch 11 by Carla Spinelli in this volume.

days – 2006 – platform work was labelled (crowdsourcing), which can be considered as the start of real debate. The first decade following this brought about the increasing discussion of labour lawyers at academic level.[54]

It was only within the last five years or so that legal changes have shown up at two levels. On the one hand, several high-level courts have passed decisions (mostly in the EU and the US) on the classification of platform work.[55] At the same time, courts have also been quite active in data protection, privacy and freedom of speech cases over a longer period of time, but this line of interpretation has definitely turned towards digitalisation issues in recent years (eg, social media use). At the international level, the European Court of Justice (ECJ) and the European Court of Human Rights (ECtHR) have also responded to these changes in many decisions. At the same time, the past few years has resulted in new laws both at national and supranational level. We have already mentioned the Transparency Directive, the GDPR and the Proposal for a Platform Work Directive, US Bill No 5, and the Spanish riders law, alongside other important changes in national laws. We can also mention that collective agreements in the platform economy are similarly new, starting in 2019.

In the near future, it is certain that we will see an increasing focus on various forms of digital transformation in legislation and case law. More and more countries will be affected on a large scale by various forms of digitalisation of work; thus, national answers may be expected in a wider range of national laws. This will also hopefully reflect in an attempt at standardisation of the national solutions at supranational and international level.

# VI. Aims, Structure and Authors

## A. Aim of the Book

The aim of the book is to undertake a comparative research on the broader topic of 'labour, law and digitalisation', mainly, but not only, from a labour law perspective. The main theme is on how to guarantee decent working conditions for those workers, whose everyday work is largely affected by digital technologies. Decent work means to

> promote opportunities for women and men to obtain decent and productive work, in conditions of freedom, equity, security and human dignity … Decent work is the converging focus of … four strategic objectives: the promotion of rights at work; employment; social protection; and social dialogue.[56]

[54] See among the first contributions published on the topic: De Stefano (n 16); Prassl and Risak (n 10); G Davidov, 'The Status of Uber Drivers: A Purposive Approach' (2017) 6 *Spanish Labour Law and Employment Relations Journal* 6, available at: www.doi.org/10.20318/sllerj.2017.3921.

[55] See the extensive case law review of C Hießl, 'Case Law on the Classification of Platform Workers: Cross-European Comparative Analysis and Tentative Conclusions' (2022) *Comparative Labor Law & Policy Journal* (forthcoming), available at SSRN: www.ssrn.com/abstract=3839603 or www.dx.doi.org/10.2139/ssrn.3839603.

[56] ILO, *Decent Work. Report of the Directorate General, International Labour Conference*, 87th Session 1999, available at: www.ilo.org/public/libdoc/ilo/P/09605/09605(1999-87).pdf, 3.

In achieving this, the book focuses on the legal implications of recent, and also foreseeable future technological changes in employment, labour market and industrial relations, also giving space to considerations relating to consumer profiling, social network regulation, privacy, data protection, etc.

As for the geographical coverage of the book, it is not confined or even focused on developments at national level, but rather has a global character in accordance with the similarities across the countries of the new forms of work and of the challenges brought to labour regulation. The book includes examples from all over the world, with special emphasis on Europe and the United States. Nevertheless, EU law is a forerunner in many fields, such as overcoming the competition law obstacles of collective negotiations, general data protection regulation, the organisation of working time, or debating employee status. Therefore, EU law will be mentioned in detail in several chapters, as the source of good practices, but also of ongoing legal debates.

Our endeavour is to analyse the legal and practical problems deriving from digitalisation tendencies in work relations, and also to outline the ways in which decent work standards could be ensured in order to better working conditions for those workers affected by the digitalisation of their work. The main theme will be the regulation of decent working conditions in the light of the digitalisation of work. In this context, the following conceptual line of research will be followed:

- What problems arise from the digitalisation of work for the various groups affected?
- The negative effects these problems and malpractices have on working conditions.
- What minimum standards could and should be ensured in order to mitigate these negative effects?
- How these minimum working standards could best be guaranteed and legislated.

These are the common issues in the different fields – from telework and classification of platform workers, to data protection and privacy, or freedom of speech in the digital era. All the analysed fields are arranged around the main theme of ensuring decent working conditions for workers affected by digitalisation.

## B. Structure of the Book

The volume is divided into four parts. Part I of the book elaborates on the impact of automatisation and digitalisation on work relations. In this respect, particular consideration will be given in three chapters to the general trends and basic issues on the challenges coming from the fourth industrialisation. At the outset, Manfred Weiss outlines the goals and basic principles of labour law and how these can be adjusted to the new digital economic panorama. After this general approach, Edoardo Ales continues with the impact of automatisation and robotic production on collective labour relations. Collective rights are the distinctive features and indeed cornerstones of labour law protection even in these forms, but with many new challenges, which will be examined in detail. Part I closes with a chapter by Iacopo Senatori dedicated to developments in EU law. This chapter will provide a systematic reconstruction of the role that EU law can play in aligning employment protections to the challenges of digitalisation, pointing out the strengths and weaknesses of the present regulatory framework and assessing the policy proposals put forward by the European institutions.

Part II of the book considers the new work arrangements prompted by the digital revolution: platform work and telework. In the first chapter, Martin Gruber-Risak summarises the scholarly perspective on platform workers with special attention on the most popular question of classifying platform workers. In this regard, the different approaches will be evaluated from the perspective of providing platform workers with good working conditions. Based on this, in the second chapter, Emanuele Menegatti provides a comparative analysis on the classification of platform workers through the lens of judiciaries as a rapidly changing and improving scenery. In the third chapter, Tamás Gyulavári enlists the necessary employment standards inevitable to improving platform workers' working conditions, including the possible ways of ensuring these rights or part of them.

In the fourth chapter in part II Gábor Kártyás highlights that the basic institutions of working time have their roots in the protection of health of the worker, and thus shall be respected regardless how technology evolves. For that aim, primarily union law will be examined. The fifth chapter moves on to the details of selected specific rights, as Marius Olivier investigates the present obstacles and possible ways to improve the welfare of platform workers through an amended system of social security rights. Collective rights are again on the table in the sixth chapter, however, from a remarkably different angle. Tihamér Tóth delicately approaches the difficulties in collective bargaining from a competition lawyer's perspective. Telework is the topic of the final chapter as Carla Spinelli investigates telework and ICT-based mobile work arrangements, that have emerged in response to societal developments, including digitalisation, increasing labour market flexibility, participation of women, and global competition.

Part III is dedicated to the potential regulation of algorithms. First, Jeremias Adams-Prassl explains individual and collective aspects of labour law challenges of management by algorithm. The chapter attempts to answer the crucial question hovering in the background: in regulating the deployment of algorithmic management systems, how can we ensure that the peculiarities of the employment relationship are sufficiently taken into account? In the second chapter, Antonio Aloisi goes into the details of labour regulation and the technological transformation of managerial prerogatives. This chapter aims at disentangling the main trajectories of the digital transformation of work. It grapples with the conventional wisdom on the alleged 'end of work' and discusses the impact of new technologies on the quality of jobs. The final chapter focuses on algorithmic discrimination. Sylvaine Laulom argues that not only can algorithms be discriminatory, but they can also exacerbate it.

Part IV is about the digital dimension of data protection and privacy at work. The chapter by Frank Henrickx starts this part with a comprehensive analysis of international and supranational regulation of data protection and privacy. This chapter gives an overview of the global regulatory frameworks and critical insights into trends and principles. In the next chapter, David Mangan presents a comparative analysis of the legal constraints to remote surveillance by employers. The chapter compares treatment of remote surveillance between Europe and North America through the differing engagement with privacy. And the final chapter of the book is about the social media and freedom of expression in labour relations. András Koltay gives an overview of the most important issues relating to the use of social media at the workplace or generally in a working environment.

## C. Authors

The authors represent various, but dominantly European legal systems. However, their research focus includes global and national legal developments in various continents, so their interest is not limited to the European legal systems or EU law. As a consequence of the global nature of the research theme, the authors do not write about their own national laws, but the chapters are founded on a comparative method. The authors have remarkable academic backgrounds and expertise in the field of labour law, digitalisation and the topic of the chapters. We must also emphasise that remarkable effort has been put into ensuring gender equality in the selection process; however, the equal participation of male and female scholars was largely impeded by the availability of experts in this narrow field. Overall, the editors strived for ensuring a high quality of expertise and research throughout the editing process. In this regard, we must acknowledge the precious work of all authors and the editing team at Hart Publishing.

# PART I

# The Impact of Automatisation and Digitalisation on Work Relations

# 2

# Digitalisation and Basic Principles of Labour Law

MANFRED WEISS

## I. Introduction

Labour law is a product of industrialisation. It has been developed in view of a social and economic reality which is no longer the reality of today. The point of reference for the development of labour law was the Fordist model.[1] The workplace was embedded in a factory of manufacturing industry, a more or less large unit, where employees – mainly blue-collar and only to a small extent white-collar – did not work in splendid isolation but as a collective entity. The employment contract was no longer conceived as a merely individual relationship between employee and employer but as an element of the collective relationship between the employer and the workforce. The workforce was relatively homogeneous as were the employees' interests. Prototype of this workforce was the male employee in an undetermined full-time employment relationship. This male employee regularly was functioning as 'breadwinner', responsible for the family's budget. Continuity and stability were features of employment. The enterprise was characterised by a clear structure of hierarchies. It was easy to define subordination and the employer's power to command and control as criteria for the employment relationship and at the same time as a reference point for labour law. The homogeneous interests of the workforce as well as the experience of being part of the collective were ideal preconditions for unionisation. Thereby protection by collective bargaining could be organised without serious problems. Labour law was focusing on the domestic labour market. Globalisation was not a real issue.

In today's post-industrial era practically everything of this scenario has disappeared. The factory as a location where employees cooperate with each other is eroding to an increasing extent. Outsourcing, networking, sub-contracting and similar dislocating strategies are on the agenda. The enterprise is often turned into a merely virtual entity. Vertical structures are replaced by flat hierarchies. Manufacturing is becoming an ever

[1] See especially, D Watson, 'Fordism: A Review' (2019) 2 *Labor History* 144.

smaller part of the economy, the service sector is increasing. Due to technological changes work organisation has changed dramatically. The workforce is no longer homogeneous, it is fragmented and segmented into core groups and marginal groups, less traditional employment and more and more new forms of work. The number of part-time jobs, of fixed-term contracts as well as of temporary agency workers is significantly increasing. There are growing numbers of economically dependent self-employed. The labour market is no longer male dominated, feminisation of the labour market has become an important feature. The male 'breadwinner' model belongs to the past. Balance of work and family obligations, thereby, has become a serious problem. Globalisation puts pressure on the national economies. Relocation of production to other countries is on the agenda. New communication technologies allow for dividing the process of production and providing services between different countries all over the globe.[2]

These very sketchy and admittedly superficial and simplistic observations may be sufficient to illustrate that technological and organisational innovations as well as globalisation have significantly changed the reality for which labour law was originally founded. However, all these changes meant perhaps a less dramatic reorientation of the world of work than the one which is introduced by way of digitalisation.

This leads to the question whether and how in the era of digitalisation the world of work can be brought into line with the basic principles of labour law which were developed in view of a very different reality. To demonstrate how much of a challenge this is, it will be necessary to first identify the basic goals and principles of labour law (section II), then to highlight the main implications of digitalisation for the world of work (section III) and finally to illustrate the chances and difficulties in reorganising the instruments of labour law in order to be in line with the basic principles (section IV). A short overall assessment will conclude the chapter (section V).

## II. The Basic Principles of Labour Law

### A. The Peculiarity of the Labour Market as a Starting Point

For a long time, the labour market was understood as being a market like any other. According to this approach the same market rules had to apply as in any other markets where products and services are the objects of trade.[3] It was only in the nineteenth century that this view started to be contested. It first came under attack by Karl Marx who pointed to the fact that the object of the labour market is not labour but the worker, a person with flesh and blood, who sells the labour power. But according to him the labour power is not an independent entity, since it cannot be separated from the worker as a human being. Therefore, the labour market cannot be the same as any other market

[2] For this changed reality, see M Weiss, 'Re-Inventing Labour Law ?' in G Davidov and B Langille (eds), *The Idea of Labour Law* (Oxford, Oxford University Press, 2011) 43, 45.

[3] A Smith, *The Wealth of Nations, Books I–III, Chapter VIII Of the Wages of Labour* (London, Penguin, 1999) 134, 167–69.

and needs specific rules.[4] This view in the meantime has become common knowledge. It is expressed in the International Labour Organization's (ILO) Philadelphia Declaration of 1944: 'labour is not a commodity'. This formula somehow has become the trademark for labour law and has been reconfirmed in many national and international documents.

## B. Implications for Labour Law

### *i. Social Protection in Line with Human Dignity*

The insight that labour is not a commodity first of all means that the labour market cannot be totally left to the rule of offer and demand. Contractual freedom has to be limited in a way which respects human dignity. The underpinning idea of the formula that labour is not a commodity, as O'Higgins in his seminal article of 1997 has convincingly demonstrated,[5] is the need to protect the human dignity of the worker. Human dignity as the overarching goal of labour law is explicitly mentioned in quite a few international legal documents.[6] For example, the key concept of the ILO's decent work agenda is human dignity. And it is particularly prominent in the texts of the European Union (EU). It is not only the predominant right of the Charter of Fundamental Rights of the European Union (CFREU) as a whole but particularly mentioned in the chapter on 'Solidarity' which contains the fundamental social rights. According to Article 31 paragraph 1: 'every worker has the right to working conditions which respect his or her … dignity'. This reference to human dignity is by the way decisive for the interpretation of all fundamental social rights contained in this chapter of the Charter.

Labour law never has denied the legitimate role of the employer. It has recognised the power to recruit, to direct and control the employees and to terminate the contract. This is the implication of the freedom to conduct a business, as it is for example guaranteed by Article 16 CFREU. However, the recognition of the legitimate role of the employer is linked with the recognition of the asymmetric power relationship between employer and employee. Therefore, in order to overcome this asymmetric structure one of the basic principles of labour law is to limit these so-called management prerogatives by rules protecting the employees in a way that their human dignity is respected. These rules, which are no longer the object of contractual freedom but are to be strictly respected by the parties of the employment contract, may be embedded in statutory law or in collective agreements.

The result of this balancing differs from jurisdiction to jurisdiction, depending on the circumstances and the overall legal framework of the respective country or region. Whereas for example in European countries the limitation of the employer's power to dismiss employees plays a big role,[7] this is different in countries where employment

[4] K Marx, 'Das Kapital Bd I' in K Marx and F Engels (eds), *Werke Bd 23* (Berlin, Dietz 1968) 557, 559.

[5] P O'Higgins, '"Labour is not a Commodity" – An Irish Contribution to International Labour Law' (1997) 26 *Industrial Law Journal* 225.

[6] For a profound analysis of the concept of Human dignity, see A Barak, *Human Dignity* (Cambridge, Cambridge University Press, 2015).

[7] According to Article 30 of the Charter of Fundamental Rights of the European Union (CFREU) 'every worker has the right to protection against unjustified dismissal'.

at will prevails. This shows that the level of limitation of the freedom of contract may be different from jurisdiction to jurisdiction, the principle, however, is clear: protective rules which are not at the disposal of the contracting parties have to make sure that working conditions are in line with human dignity. The ILO's 1998 Declaration on Fundamental Principles and Rights at Work has established a minimalistic approach to workers' core rights: freedom of association and the effective recognition of the right to collective bargaining; the elimination of forced or compulsory labour; the abolition of child labour; and the elimination of discrimination in its broadest sense. This list has been amended by adding health and safety. But, of course, protection has to include many more items as for example protection of employees' privacy, fair remuneration and limitation of working time, to mention just a few important topics. And it has to be kept in mind that the founding fathers of labour law, for example Hugo Sinzheimer, insisted that labour law cannot be perceived as merely law for the employment relationship but has to include social protection in its broadest sense, covering all the needs and risks which have to be met in an employee's life.[8]

Therefore, conditions in line with human dignity not only refer to the situation within an employment relationship. They also include social security as well as the conditions for access to such a relationship. Labour law, therefore, has to promote the worker's capacity to make use of job opportunities, to achieve employability. Only if this precondition is fulfilled, will individuals have a fair chance to participate in the labour market.

### *ii. Collective Voice*

The asymmetric power between employers and employees has an important implication: the need to promote the collectivisation of employees.[9] The possibility to act collectively, to get organised in labour unions and to conclude collective agreements with the employer's side, is of utmost importance. As long as workers merely act as individuals competing with each other in the labour market, exposed to the mechanism of supply and demand, the danger of a race to the bottom is always present. In cases where the supply is higher than the demand for labour, impoverishment might be the result of individual competition between workers. Therefore, the restriction of competition between individual workers should not be forbidden but allowed and encouraged. Only if workers are able to join forces, can they prevent the race to the bottom by negotiating and if necessary fighting via collective action for minimum standards or better standards than those fixed by statutory law. This is the reason why freedom of association including the right to collective bargaining is listed in the above-mentioned ILO Declaration of 1998. It is a characteristic feature of labour law that the norm-setting activity is shared by legislation and collective bargaining, again with big variations from jurisdiction to jurisdiction.

[8] H Sinzheimer, 'Das Wesen des Arbeitsrechts' (1927) in H Sinzheimer (ed), *Arbeitsrecht und Rechtssoziologie*, vol 1 (Frankfurt am Main, Bund-Verlag GmbH, 1976) 108, 110.

[9] See, in particular, O Kahn-Freund, *Arbeit und Recht* (Frankfurt am Main, Bund-Verlag GmbH, 1979) 7.

### *iii. Democratic Workplace*

An important implication of respect for human dignity is the fact that workers are not supposed to be mere objects of management's decisions but must have an opportunity to influence this decision-making. The founding fathers of labour law were already pleading for a democratic workplace as a precondition for labour law in line with human dignity. This insight of the founding fathers of labour law is as valid today as it was in the formative era of labour law. In the context of the EU the actuality of this concept is particularly shown by Article 27 of the Charter of Fundamental Rights where 'information and consultation' for 'workers or workers representatives' 'in good time' and 'at the appropriate levels' is guaranteed as a fundamental right.

Institutionalised patterns of workers' participation exist in many countries, however, there are big differences from country to country. These differences refer to the degree of participation, ranging from information and consultation via veto rights up to co-determination where management and workers' representatives are on the same footing in decision-making for a whole range of topics. They also refer to the level of participation, ranging from the shop-floor level up to the headquarters of companies or groups of companies. The composition of bodies of workers' participation is different from country to country. Some countries even recognise employee representation on company boards where again the differences are tremendous.[10] All systems of worker participation are embedded in the cultural tradition and overall institutional framework of the respective country.

## C. The Concept of Basic Principles

As has become visible from the foregoing my understanding of basic principles is by no means identical to the notion of fundamental principles in the ILO Declaration of 1998. It goes far beyond and is rather a description of the very idea of labour law. It is not dependent on the incidental consensus already reached in the international arena of norm setting, but derived from the overarching insights that labour is not a commodity, and that human dignity is to be respected. It, therefore, is much more comprehensive than the ILO Declaration.

As has been shown above it boils down to three areas of regulation: (a) social protection in line with human dignity, not only covering rules on the employment relationship as such, but including rules on employability and even social security; (b) collective voice; and (c) a democratic workplace based on workers' participation in management's decision-making.

Whether and in what way this concept of basic principles of labour law as presented here is challenged by digitalisation is to be discussed in the following paragraphs.

[10] For an overview of the different patterns, see M Biagi and M Tiraboschi, 'Forms of Employee Representational Participation' in R Blanpain (ed), *Comparative Labour Law and Industrial Relations in Industrialized Market Economies*, 9th edn (Alphen aan den Rijn, Wolters Kluwer, 2007) 503.

# III. The Digital Workplace

## A. The Different Types of Digital Work

Digitalisation of working patterns has many faces, it is not to be conceived as a uniform or homogeneous phenomenon. Different technologies from communication technologies up to artificial intelligence (AI) are involved and different working patterns result from these technological innovations. Many details are still rather unclear. But undoubtedly this development means a dramatic transformation of the world of work. Each of the different working patterns leads to different challenges for labour law. Three types are most relevant in this context.

For several decades, communication technologies have already made it possible that work does not have to be performed in the premises of the employer but can be executed anywhere. Commonly the labels used for this type of work are 'telework' or 'mobile work'.[11]

Another trend in this digital evolution is labelled 'Industry 4.0' which stands for the fourth industrial revolution.[12] The label is somewhat misleading because this type of work not only refers to manufacturing, but in the same way to services. Collaborative robots become intelligent, which means able to adapt, communicate and interact. Smart robots communicate with each other and with humans on interlinking tasks. These cyper-physical systems (AI)[13] are quickly widening, including various functions in production, logistics or management, ranging from recruiting employees, assigning tasks, controlling the performance of work up to sanctioning unsatisfactory performance.[14] Or as Jeremias Adams-Prassl predicts: 'In the long run, no sector of the economy will remain beyond algorithms' reach'.[15]

The third important trend is the increasing platform economy where, of course, AI also plays a dominant role.[16] Here basically two types are to be distinguished: 'internal platforms' to which only the workforce of a specific company has access; and 'external platforms' with open access for anyone meeting specific criteria. Among the

[11] For the problems arising in the context of telework, see the contributions in R Blanpain (ed), *European Framework Agreements and Telework: Law and Practice, A European and Comparative Study, Bulletin of Comparative labour Relations* (Alphen aan den Rijn, Wolters Kluwer, 2007); L Mella Méndez) and A Villalba Sánchez (eds), *Trabajo a Distancia y Teletrabajo, Estudios Sobre su Régimen Jurídico en el Derecho Español y Comparado* (Pamplona, Editorial Aranzadi, 2015).

[12] F Almada-Lobo, 'The Industry 4.0 revolution and the future of manufacturing execution systems (MES)' (2016) 3 *Journal of Innovation Management* 16.

[13] For an assessment of different forms of AI in the workplace, see PV Moore, 'The Mirror for (Artificial) Intelligence. In whose Reflection?' (2019) 41 *Comparative Labor Law & Policy Journal* 47; See also Commission, 'Proposal for a Regulation of the European Parliament and of the Council laying down harmonised rules on artificial intelligence (Artificial Intelligence Act) and amending certain union legislative acts' COM (2021) 206 final.

[14] For the enormous potential of algorithmic management, see J Adams-Prassl, 'What if your Boss was an Algorithm? Economic Incentives, Legal Challenges and the Rise of Artificial Intelligence at Work' (2019) 41 *Comparative Labor Law & Policy Journal* 123.

[15] ibid, 128.

[16] For the different types of work in the platform economy, see V De Stefano, 'Introduction: Crowdsourcing, the Gig-Economy and the Law' (2016) 37 *Comparative Labor Law & Policy Journal* 461.

'external platforms' again two types are to be distinguished: 'work-on-demand via app' where the work is performed in a traditional way (transport, cleaning etc); and 'online crowdwork' where work is performed by a crowdworker online. Again, there has to be a distinction between platforms where relatively simple tasks are performed by unskilled or low-skilled persons, and complex platforms where highly skilled persons are confronted with complex tasks.

## B. The Implications for the Labour Market

There is no doubt that, at least to a certain extent, human beings will be substituted by AI, by robots etc, thereby losing their jobs. The challenge will be to keep the number of these people as small as possible and to upskill those who are substituted in order to reintegrate them into the labour market.

# IV. Implications for Basic Principles of Labour Law

## A. Implications for Social Protection (Examples)

### *i. Reconceptualisation of Employability*

Previously it might have been sufficient to get trained for a job at the beginning of a career, thereby getting the skills needed throughout professional life. This is no longer the case. Digitalisation not only makes many traditional skills obsolete, but due to the exponential speed of technical innovations leads to an ongoing rapid change in required skills. Therefore, continuous upskilling has become more urgent than ever before.[17] Its content and organisation have to be fundamentally reconceptualised. Law has to provide the framework for such opportunities for lifelong learning to a greater extent than ever before. It is not only government, but the actors in collective bargaining that are confronted with this task. Joint efforts from all these actors are needed.[18]

Many questions have to be resolved in this context: whether there should be an individual right for all employees to participate in such training; what incentives for employees and employers should be envisaged; how the costs should be shared between employees, employers and the state; how the responsibilities are to be shared between legislation and collective bargaining; and last but not least, what should be the content of lifelong learning in view of the fact that due to the fast-changing technological developments no one knows what skills will be required in the future. These are difficult questions, but they have to be answered. As the report of the ILO Global Commission

[17] This is particularly stressed by the inter-professional *European Social Partners Framework Agreement on Digitalisation* of June 2020 which as its first priority emphasises 'Digital Skills and Securing Employment'.

[18] See also, in this context, the EU Commission's European skills agenda for sustainable competitiveness, social fairness and resilience, COM 2020/274 final of 1 July 2020.

on the Future of Work[19] as well as the Centenary Declaration of the ILO[20] tell us: lifelong learning for all is the precondition for coping successfully with the challenges of digitalisation.

The Global Commission's report contains many helpful recommendations. In particular, the idea of an entitlement to training during working hours is to be supported. One might go even further and recommend an individual right for training during working hours, of course without loss of remuneration.

And as far as financing of continuous training is concerned, the establishment of an 'employment insurance', as suggested by the report, deserves strong support. Thereby, the costs for such a training scheme may be covered to a great extent by contributions from employers and employees together. The question, of course, remains whether and how far such a training scheme – which is not only in the interest of workers and employers but for the society as a whole – is to be subsidised by the system of taxation.

The biggest problem, however, is the content of continued training. So far training has been focusing on skills required for the different well-known professions. In the future it will no longer be possible to focus on such well-established skills. The new skills which are needed are unknown to a great extent. And they will quickly be replaced by others. Therefore, the report of the Global Commission is correct by insisting that in future the focus has to be much more on 'learning how to learn' in order to become able to adapt to new situations. This, of course, requires highly qualified teachers: an enormous challenge for all who are responsible for the educational system.

In short and to make the point: the deskilling of workers by digitalisation needs a tremendous effort of upskilling in order to improve the chances of workers to either keep or regain their jobs. Labour law has to significantly reconceptualise the framework for such a strategy. However, all relevant problems in this context still are unresolved.

### *ii. Reconceptualisation of the Scope of Labour Law Protection*

The reference point for labour law so far has been the traditional employment relationship. Thereby, the coverage of labour law protection has been limited to employees. Due to technical and organisational changes in the world of work, and especially due to digitalisation, the demarcation line between employment and self-employment is very difficult to draw.[21] This is not a new phenomenon. But it has become particularly problematic in the context of the platform economy where many are self-employed (so called solo self-employed). Many of those who are engaged in crowdwork are certainly not employees but rather self-employed.

Of course, many who are labelled as being self-employed are in reality employees (so called 'bogus self-employed'). Even if the degree of autonomy in performing digital work makes it more and more difficult to categorise the persons involved in such work,

[19] ILO, Global Commission on the Future of Work, *Work for a brighter future* (ILO, Geneva, 2019).

[20] International Labour Conference, ILO Centenary Declaration for the Future of Work, adopted by the conference on its 108th session on 21 June 2019.

[21] See, for a comprehensive discussion of this problem, G Davidov and B Langille (eds), *Boundaries and Frontiers of Labour Law* (Oxford, Hart Publishing, 2006).

often a closer look reveals that the autonomy is ambiguous because new mechanisms of more efficient algorithmic control are in place. Then those who are wrongly labelled as self-employed turn out to be employees. They are not the main problem. The focus rather should be on those who undoubtedly are self-employed and work alone without employees but are economically in a similar position as employees. They are not reached yet by labour law protection. They are not included in minimum wage schemes, in health and safety arrangements or in guarantees of decent working time, to give just some examples. This is an unsatisfactory situation.

Theoretically there are different possibilities to provide them with the necessary protection: the broadening of the notion of employee; the creation of a specific intermediate category; or the extension of the scope of labour law to economically dependent self-employed (solo self-employed).

The broadening of the notion of employee is the pattern which can presently be seen in the many lawsuits all over the world determining the question whether, for example, Uber drivers are employees or self-employed. In many countries the notion of employee has been extended significantly, be it by case law or even by legislation. However, this strategy has limits. If the notion is extended too far, it becomes meaningless. And it will never be possible to include all economically dependent self-employed.

The introduction of an intermediary category between employment and self-employment might be a solution.[22] However, as the examples in quite a few countries show this strategy has only provoked uncertainties and led to many controversies. It increases the complexity, thereby rather leading to more problems than fewer. The same problems arise if special legal relationships beyond the classic employment relationship are created where only some specific labour law protection applies.

A more radical possibility would be the inclusion of the self-employed up to a certain wage level under the protective roof of labour law and social security law. As far as the inclusion in the social security system is concerned, some countries – for example Austria – have followed this path already and it seems to work quite well.[23] Whether, however, such a strategy might also work for labour law in a narrow sense, may be doubted. It cannot be denied that many protective patterns are linked to the relationship between employer and employee in the employment relationship. The rules on protection against unfair dismissal might be a good example to illustrate what I mean. Therefore, a mere extension of labour law to the self-employed may not be the right strategy.

In view of all these difficulties a change of paradigm might be more helpful. Instead of putting workers in different categories, it might be preferable to discuss the floor of rights all working people need, no matter their status. This is in line with the idea of a universal labour guarantee as suggested by the ILO Commission on the Future of Work (and unfortunately no longer contained in the ILO Centenary Declaration of June 2019).

[22] Germany has such a pattern. For details see B Waas, 'Crowdwork in Germany' in B Waas, WB Liebman, A Lyubarski and K Katsuka (eds), *Crowdwork: A Comparative Law Perspective* (Frankfurt am Main, Bund-Verlag, 2017) 142, 160–62.

[23] For such a solution, see also the EU Council Recommendation of 8 November 2019 on access to social protection for workers and the self-employed [2019] OJ C387/1.

It focuses on protection of workers regardless of their contractual arrangement and of their employment status. The focus should be on the shape of the protective umbrella, not on the boxes that workers are put in. This, however, indicates another problem: who is responsible for providing the protection? The solution might be relatively easy in the case of platform work. But it is certainly difficult for other self-employed workers. Most probably, the state administration has to play an essential role in this context.

### *iii. Impact on Protection of Privacy and Against Discrimination*

Protection of employees' privacy and of employees' personal data as well as protection against discrimination for a long time have been essential elements of working conditions implied by the respect for human dignity as explained above. This, of course, remains a requirement in the era of digitalisation. However, to provide this protection has become much more difficult in the era of algorithmic management.

Digital tools provide for a totally new quality of supervising and controlling employees' performance. Algorithmic management allows for far-reaching substitution of decision-making by humans. Much more than ever before digital tools allow for an excessive amount of data collection and methods of data processing. Decisions based on algorithms are processed by mathematical rules and, therefore, supposed to be objective, even if, of course, they may simply transport and reinforce the bias of the humans who organise the inputs. This makes it much more difficult for job applicants or employees to discover discrimination, in particular if data are given priority which only indirectly advantage or disadvantage certain groups (socio-economic status etc).

Computer science is aware of these problems of traceability and fairness of decision-making. There is a specific branch named 'Ethical algorithm' trying to reduce the danger of biased decision-making by algorithm by correcting biased inputs towards fairness.[24] But, of course, this only can be done to a limited extent.

As far as protection of personal data – so-called informational privacy – is concerned, the General Data Protection Regulation (GDPR) of the EU is a good example for an important step in the right direction.[25] It only allows collection and processing of personal data for specific purposes implied by the very nature of the employment relationship. Additional personal data may only be collected and processed if the employee agrees. This consent, however, has to be voluntary. Whether it is voluntary has to be evaluated in view of the dependency of the employee in an employment relationship and in view of all the circumstances in which the consent is given. The consent always has to be in written form. The aim of the rather complicated regulation is clear: only exceptionally will the consent be evaluated as being voluntary. In addition, there is an obligation for the employer to inform the employee about all personal data to be

[24] For a good overview of this debate, see BD Mittelstadt, P Allo, M Taddeo, S Wachter and L Floridi, 'The ethics of algorithms: Mapping the debate' (2016) 3 *Big Data & Society* 1; and recently M Kearns and A Roth, *The Ethical Algorithm* (Oxford, Oxford University Press, 2019).

[25] Regulation (EU) 2016/679 of the European Parliament and of the Council of 27 April 2016 on the protection of natural persons with regard to the processing of personal data and on the free movement of such data, and repealing Directive 95/46/EC (General Data Protection Regulation) [2016] OJ L119/1 (GDPR).

processed on him or her. Whether this requirement of consent is sufficient in view of the fact that automatic collection and processing of personal data remains invisible for the employee, may well be doubted. However, an efficient alternative is not yet in sight.

It always should be kept in mind that algorithmic management is a human construct. In this context a rule in the GDPR protecting employees from the effects of automatic decision-making is of utmost importance. It prohibits decisions 'based solely … on automated processing … which produce legal effects' for the individual 'or similarly affects him or her'.[26] In other words, there always has to be a human being as a visible, and at the end, responsible decision-maker.[27] Even if this requirement is to be welcomed, this does not prohibit the human being relying on the outcome of the algorithm. And it should not be ignored that in the GDPR this requirement is not without exceptions.[28]

Since the supervisory and potentially discriminatory effects of algorithmic management are not transparent for individual workers, resistance against the use of such systems might easily develop. Acceptability perhaps can only be achieved if those systems are introduced and performed in cooperation with workers' representatives as will be discussed below.[29]

### *iv. Reconceptualisation of Working Time*

In the context of digitalisation workers will have to focus more on goals to be achieved in a certain time frame. Presence at the workplace will be less important. How and when within the given time frame work is to be performed, is more or less left to the discretion of the worker. This 'autonomy' leads to the question whether traditional working time regulations are still appropriate to cope with this situation. Working time regulation has so far focused mainly on daily and weekly maximum working time, on breaks and rest periods between the days, and providing holidays and vacations. Step-by-step flexibility has been built in. Daily and weekly maximum working time could be exceeded to a certain extent if compensated by a reduction in working time within a certain period. However, in spite of the flexibility element working time regulation still remains rather rigid.

In the digital world, in particular in the context of telework and all forms of mobile work including work in the home office, which has become widespread in the pandemic, there is the danger that working time never ends. Workers may be expected to remain online, to answer emails and phone calls after normal working time as well as on days off and on vacations. And even if the workers are not asked by the employer to do so, they might do it voluntarily. This has far-reaching implications for the health and safety

[26] Article 22, GDPR.

[27] Very enlightening in this context is Part 3 of the already quoted European Social Partners Framework Agreement on Digitalisation, 'Artificial Intelligence (AI) and Guaranteeing the Human Control Principle'.

[28] For an enlightening discussion of the problem, see A Aloisi and E Gramano, 'Artificial Intelligence is Watching You at Work: Digital Surveillance, Employee Monitoring, and Regulatory Issues in the EU Context' (2019) 41 *Comparative Labor Law & Policy Journal* 95, 106–08.

[29] In this sense see Part 4 of the *European Social Partners Framework Agreement on Digitalisation*, 'Respect of Human Dignity and Surveillance' where 'Enabling workers' representatives to address issues related to data, consent, privacy protection and surveillance' is a core request.

of the workers as well as for their private life. Relaxation and rest, as it is meant by traditional working time regulation, is no longer possible under these conditions. Self-exploitation is an ever-increasing danger. The eight hours day – the big achievement of the labour movement in the early twentieth century – is in danger of being abolished.

The question is whether regulations are possible at all. Even if it might be very difficult to prevent self-exploitation, it still might be regulated that the worker is not obliged to work beyond a certain time. The keenly discussed right to non-availability or right to disconnect may be a step in the right direction.[30] Of course this right has to be combined with the employer's obligation to disconnect. Technically it might be executed by blocking the use of servers for certain times as is already done in some companies. However, this only can be a first step. And it cannot be implemented everywhere (eg, not in hospitals where access to servers is needed around the clock). Things are even more complicated when workers are involved in production or service processes with workers in other time zones. Then such disconnection might be counterproductive.

Maybe the solution is not to be found in giving up daily and weekly maximum times or rest periods, but within these limits to allow more flexibility and – most importantly – to provide reliable tools for documentation of when and how long work is performed. In short and to make the point: the traditional working time regulation is no longer feasible, but an appropriate alternative is not yet in sight.

### *v. Reconceptualisation of Health and Safety*

Digitalisation will make it necessary to totally rethink the concept of health and safety. The traditional focus on physical dangers has to be radically enlarged in relation to psycho-social problems. It is already common knowledge that the danger of psycho-social disorders has significantly increased in the information society. This will further increase if to a greater extent work is characterised by technology driven forms of work. On the one hand de-localisation, flexibility of working time patterns, the focus on work results to be produced in a certain period and no longer on presence at the workplace, as well as the loss of clear-cut hierarchies, promotes workers' autonomy which is considered to promote creativity and innovation. But in reality, this new autonomy is very ambiguous, it implies – as already mentioned – the danger of self-exploitation. This implies a need for new patterns of stress prevention and new strategies on how to cope with the consequences of stress. The cross-sectoral Framework Agreement on Work-related Stress concluded in 2004 by the European Social Partners in the context of the Social Dialogue is a step in the right direction.

As already indicated, due to the pandemic the digital home office has become a widespread arrangement, which will remain or even further increase in the future. This leads to new challenges for health and safety. In particular, the problem arises whether the equipment is in line with ergonomic requirements. In this context the question arises as to how it may be guaranteed that these requirements are enforced and controlled in the

[30] For potential measures in this context, see Part 2 of the European Social Partners' Framework Agreement on Digitalisation, 'Modalities of Connecting and Disconnecting'; see also, European Parliament, 'Resolution of 21 January 2021 with recommendations to the Commission on the right to disconnect' 2019/2181(INL).

worker's private home, whether and how far there is access by the employer, by labour inspectors and/or by other supervising authorities. An unresolved area so far.[31]

### *vi. Reconceptualisation of Work–Life Balance*

So far labour law has tried to develop patterns which make it possible to find a better balance between work and private life, family obligations etc. Part-time work, parental leave or leave for care of sick or elderly family members are well-known examples of such a policy. However, these strategies were all developed under the assumption that work and private life are two different entities. This distinction may increasingly fall apart due to digitalisation of work. De-localised work and work without clear time limits is more and more intruding into private life, thereby eliminating to a greater extent the demarcation line between the two spheres of human life. This will not only have a significant impact on family life, but for society as a whole. It is an open question whether, in how far and by what kind of regulation the private part of life can be rescued.

This development has been intensified and accelerated during the Covid-19 pandemic where – as already indicated – the home office has become an important option to prevent infection and to fight the virus. This is a sort of revival of the traditional home work which was to a great extent overcome by industrialisation. In that period this was understood as a step towards emancipation. Now it is often celebrated as an ideal model for work–life balance. This perception, however, may be too quick and rather one-sided. Of course, the home office allows for much flexibility and autonomy which is definitely a very positive effect. But the negative side-effects in the context of work–life balance should not be underestimated. Much research in particular on the psychological effects for the worker and for his or her family is needed as a precondition for regulatory strategies guaranteeing a sound coexistence of professional and private life.

## B. Collective Voice

The traditional Fordist model was characterised by a relatively homogeneous workforce in a hierarchically structured factory or office. As already indicated above, this model already fell apart with the segmentation and fragmentation of the workforce, divided into core groups and non-standard groups with significantly diverse interests. This trend has dramatically increased with the digitalisation of work. The example of the platform workers shows that there is no longer a link between the acting individuals, they – at least in principle – do not know each other and work in isolation. But the need for collectivisation is as urgent as ever. However, the conditions for collectivisation and the consciousness of being part of a collective are rapidly declining, particularly due to working patterns in the era of digitalisation.

[31] For all the problems arising in this context, see the voluntary framework agreement on teleworking concluded by the European Social Partners in the context of the Social Dialogue on 16 July 2002, last amended on 4 October 2017.

The big question is whether and how individualisation can be overcome by patterns of collectivisation, whether such collectivisation can be embedded in existing structures of industrial relations, in particular collective bargaining, or whether new specific structures are to be developed, as for example trade unions or alternative associations exclusively for platform workers.

From a merely legal point of view, the problem might be that these workers – as explained – are by no means only employees in a traditional sense but are, to a significant extent, genuinely self-employed. According to the Court of Justice of the European Union (CJEU) they cannot be included in collective agreements because of the competition rules contained in the Treaty on the Functioning of the European Union (TFEU).[32] This archaic and narrow-minded view of competition law which is based on a reality of the past, of course, needs to be overcome. At least the EU Commission has understood the problem, as on 30 June 2020 it launched a process of consulting all stakeholders to address the issue of collective bargaining for the self-employed. There is hope.

Instead of discussing this any further, I would rather like to focus on the practical problems. However, it at least should be kept in mind that according to ILO Convention 87 on freedom of association, self-employed workers are also fully covered. And at least it is a good sign that in quite a few countries the statutes of trade unions by now allow the self-employed to become members which has already led to landmark collective agreements in the platform economy.[33] And more and more trade unions are offering services and support to the economically dependent self-employed.[34]

It is still controversial whether it might be better to integrate platform workers into existing trade unions or to develop genuine alternative associations to promote their interests. There are attempts in both directions.[35] The question is whether alternative associations will be powerful enough to form an efficient counterweight against the platforms which in many cases are powerful oligopolies. This might of course be different for high-skilled platform workers who cannot easily be substituted, than for low-skilled platform workers whose substitution is not a problem. And it might also depend on the possibility of how traditional forms of industrial action could be substituted or even strengthened by using digital tools.[36]

Whether collectivisation might succeed will also depend on the question whether and how far digital tools can be used to organise and put pressure on the employers' side. This might be difficult in view of the increased asymmetry of bargaining power, and in particular in view of the powerful multinational platforms.

[32] Case C-413/13 *FNV Kunsten Informatie en Media v Staat der Nederlanden* ECLI:EU:C:2014:2411 [2014].

[33] See the comprehensive overview in A Aloisi, 'Negotiating the digital transformation of work: non-standards workers' voice, collective rights and mobilization practices in the platform economy' (2019) European University Institute (EUI), Max Weber Program Working Paper (MWP) 1, 11–20.

[34] C Jolly, 'Collective Action and Bargaining in the Digital ERA' in M Neufeind, J O'Reilly and F Ranft (eds), *Work in the Digital Age: Challenges of the Fourth Industrial Revolution* (Lanham, MD, Rowman & Littlefield International, 2018) 209, 215.

[35] Aloisi (n 33).

[36] ibid, 218.

## C. Democratic Workplace

The more the world of work is changing, the more important becomes the workers' involvement in management decision-making. Such involvement increases the legitimacy and thereby the acceptability of management decisions. It is a necessary element of workplace democracy which – as shown above – is a traditional goal of labour law.

Technological innovation cycles by the digitalisation of work are becoming faster and faster. The legislator will not be able to keep up with the changes and adapt the rules to the respective needs. The legislator can only provide a relatively vague framework. Solutions balancing the needs of the platforms and of the workers need to be developed on a decentralised level in the companies. These solutions cannot be left unilaterally to the employer, but must be developed in cooperation with representative bodies of the workforce. In other words: the working conditions fitting with the specific conditions of each company should be shaped and monitored together with the employees' representatives, be it by way of information and consultation or even by co-determination. 'Cooperative turn' has become the catchword for this approach.

The difficulties for workers' participation have grown due to digitalisation. The preconditions for efficient functioning of workers' participation in management decision-making can no longer be taken for granted. These are, in particular, an identifiable workplace where employees are working together in the premises of the employer; a hierarchical structure between management and employees with more or less homogeneous interests; a relatively clear method and easily recognised criteria on how to identify who is an employee; and – last but not least – an identifiable employer, namely a company to which the employees belong. All these preconditions have become increasingly problematic. And this leads to the question whether and how workers' participation can survive in the future and how it has to be restructured.

The need to be present in the premises of the employer is fading. As already indicated above, digitalisation to an increasing extent allows that work can be performed from anywhere.

Vertical structures are increasingly being replaced by so-called flat hierarchies. Instead of subordination, autonomy is becoming the new catchword. But control prevails. Thereby the still existing conflict of interests between management and employees, of course, is not disappearing, it is only becoming less visible.

There is not only an increase in fragmentation and segmentation of the workforce leading to very heterogeneous interests, but the erosion of company structures which makes it difficult to define who is the employer. For quite a while, companies have achieved a 'new mobility' as regards company patterns and cooperative structures. It makes sense to talk of a 'volatility' of legal structures, as virtual corporate networks emerge, areas are outsourced, companies are run without formal group structures, and transnational cooperation is becoming an increasingly common feature. Dislocating strategies are on the agenda. It is often now difficult to identify the employer. The 'fissured workplace' has become a sort of catchword term for this extremely complex development. Digitalisation and globalisation are further and mutually pushing this trend.[37]

[37] For this development, see T Klebe and M Weiss, 'Workers' Participation 4.0 – Digital and Global?' (2019) 40 *Comparative Labor Law & and Policy Journal* 263, 270.

To sum up these observations: the more urgent the need for workers' participation, the more difficult it might be to maintain or establish such systems in the new world of work. There are quite a few obstacles which have to be overcome in order to maintain or establish functioning workers' representation in modern company structures, in particular in the platform economy.

In addition to collectivisation and establishing collective consciousness, thereby also overcoming the separation between employees and economically dependent self-employed – as discussed above – it will be necessary to clarify who is the counterpart on the management side. This is getting more and more difficult the more company structures are scattered. And it is particularly difficult in the context of the platform economy. Who – to take just this example – in the case of crowdwork is treated as employer, the platform operator, or in the case of crowdwork the crowdsourcer or both of them? The categorisation cannot be left to the platforms themselves. Objective criteria and a functional approach are necessary to identify the employer.[38] The problem is particularly complex in a crowdwork structure, where it is not the platform operator but the crowdsourcer as client of the platform who is receiving the crowdworkers' achievements. In this tripartite structure, the employer's role might be split between platform and crowdsourcer, or fulfilled by one of the two actors.

Of course, the problem of tripartite structures is not new. It is well known in the context of temporary agency work. However, it has become much more dramatic in view of the platform economy. Therefore, efforts need to be made to develop appropriate solutions to identify who, in such a constellation, is the employer and in what way.

The final challenge is the fact that the workforce, again particularly in the context of crowdworking, is transnational. This leads to the question whether schemes of workers' participation can be established covering all workers, no matter to which jurisdiction they belong. All those workers might be included in voting for workers' representatives. And the workers' representatives might possibly speak for all of them. This would need worldwide transnational regulation which is not easy to develop. This problem, of course, is not new: it has been a challenge for workers' participation along with the existence of transnational companies, but it has been intensified by digitalisation. The EU has responded with several directives, most importantly the Directive on European Works Councils.[39] But on a global scale still is nothing.

It also has to be kept in mind that the procedure of decision-making has changed due to digitalisation. As indicated above, management by algorithm plays an important role today and will in the future perhaps even more. As also shown above, one of the big problems in this context is the lack of transparency in algorithmic decision-making. One of the tasks of workers' participation should be to make this mode of decision-making transparent in order to be able to evaluate whether it is in line with the

[38] J Prassl and M Risak, Uber, 'Taskrabbit, & Co: Platforms as Employers? Rethinking the Legal Analysis of Crowdwork' (2016) 37 *Comparative Labor Law & Policy Journal* 619.

[39] Directive 94/45/EC of 22 September 1994 on the establishment of a European Works Council or a procedure in Community scale undertakings and Community-scale groups of undertakings for the purposes of informing and consulting employees, [1994] OJ L254/641, replaced by Directive 2009/38/EC of 6 May 2009 on the same topic, [2009] OJ L122/28.

protective needs of employees. This might be beyond the capacity of workers' representatives. Therefore, if the goal to increase transparency does not remain a mere illusion, it might be necessary to provide easy and cost-free access to independent experts for workers' representatives.

In short, and to make the point: whether and in what way functioning and effective workers' participation in management decision-making can be established in the digital era, is to a great extent an open question.

## V. Conclusion

This introductory chapter is not supposed to provide solutions for problems arising at the digital workplace. Rather it is meant to just give an idea of the manifold challenges implied by this technological development for the basic principles of labour law. It has to be kept in mind that labour law since its foundation has seen many changes and met many challenges. The so-called fourth industrial revolution is just another step, even a dramatic one. It bears dangers as well as chances. On the one side there are fears of job loss and of deskilling. But on the other – as any technological progress – it also provides many chances to improve the situation of workers.

The main task will be to ensure that the digital era will not lead to a re-commodification of labour, and that the respect for human dignity with all its implications can be guaranteed. The sketchy overview in this introductory chapter is mainly meant to demonstrate the difficulty of this task and to show the challenges for labour law regulation. There are no definite answers, but merely a set of unresolved questions. Possible solutions are to be discussed in specific chapters in this volume.

It has to be stressed that many challenges for labour law are by no means new (eg, the implications of fragmentation and segmentation of the workforce, the challenges for workers' privacy, the problems of discrimination, the erosion and trans-nationalisation of companies). They have only become more dramatic and more difficult to be met. Therefore, digitalisation should not be treated as an isolated phenomenon but in the context of the ongoing changes of the reality of work to which labour law has, and has had to adapt, in order to keep its regulatory power. Digitalisation is only a further step in this continuum.

# 3

# The Impact of Automation and Robotics on Collective Labour Relations: Meeting an Unprecedented Challenge

EDOARDO ALES

## I. Introduction

The relationship between automation, robotics and labour has been investigated thoroughly by all the branches of scholarship that deal with labour. The literature is immense. It touches the different angles of the subject, mainly focusing on the impact of technology on work and how to mitigate its negative consequences on workers. Some studies, however, highlight the beneficial effects of technology in eliminating monotonous, dangerous and heavy jobs or tasks, as they can be performed, even more efficiently, by machines or robots controlled by artificial intelligence (AI).[1]

Nevertheless, room for reflection on some particularly sensitive issues still remains. These are, in my perception, the competition between technologies and humans, and the way in which entrepreneurs' decision-making processes to introduce or enhance technologies can be influenced by workers. Both points affect the collective dimensions of labour relationships, which is the topic of this chapter.[2]

As is well known, collective labour (or industrial) relations primarily aim at regulating working conditions homogeneously, in order to avoid the race to the bottom that is likely to characterise the individual negotiation between an employer and her employees. The wider the application of collective regulation to employers, the lower the risk of individuals and groups already covered by more favourable (and expensive) agreements being dumped. Falling within the scope of a collective agreement means that workers enjoy the same interests settlement (ie, rights), thus excluding competition, at least within the same professional group. Therefore, one can argue that the essential feature and added value of an effective collective labour relations system is the recognition of fair and just working conditions that cannot be worsened at employers' will.

[1] See CB Frey, *The Technology Trap: Capital, Labor, and Power in the Age of Automation* (Princeton, NJ, Princeton University Press, 2019).

[2] More in general, see B Keller, 'Interest representation and industrial relations in the age of digitalization – an outline' (2020) 27 *Industrielle Beziehungen* 255.

When it comes to AI, robots and machines, the issue of fair and just working conditions, as set by collective agreements or by law, seems to be irrelevant. Apparently, they have no need or interest in remuneration, rest, or health and safety whatsoever, which makes them undefeatable competitors for humans and perfect cost-saving, trouble-avoiding tools for entrepreneurs. However, there is a wide literature pleading for the recognition of some protection for non-human labour, starting, of course, from that performed by animals,[3] which suggests scrutinising the argument with reference also to other non-human entities like, above all, AI controlling machines and robots.

What is at stake here is the very notion of worker to which protection of any kind is attached. This has nothing to do with the qualification of the work relationship as subordinated or autonomous, as it happens with platform workers.[4] The point is to protect any persons *who or that* work for somebody else. In fact, my proposal is to rethink the personalistic principle, which underpins labour law, by ceasing to look at the person only as a human being. Animals, as well as AI controlled machines or robots, work – not just in the sense that they are functioning. From such a stipulative perspective, a person is anyone or anything who or that works. As a consequence, a worker is a human as well as a non-human person, who or that, just for this reason (being a person), deserves to be protected.

A reasoning of this kind is in line with the idea that work is not a commodity since anyone or anything who or that works has her or its personal dignity to be safeguarded. Such a perspective also allows making the distinction between workers' rights and human rights clearer and more convincing: the proposed notion of worker is more comprehensive than that of human being, including animals, AI, machines and robots working for or instead of humans. Therefore, the notion of workers' rights is wider than that of human rights.

From that approach, which rejects the anthropocentric vision of labour and of person, not only can non-human work profit but also human. In fact, by recognising dignity for non-human workers, they will fall within the scope of labour law as humans do, nullifying the competitive advantage inhuman treatments provided to human entrepreneurs/shareholders who are allowed at present to abuse them as non-human. The proposal to extend the notion of worker to non-humans is inspired by the altruistic and, at the same time, utilitarian aim of avoiding the exploitation of workers, being human or non-human, on the ground of the well-established idea of interspecies justice.[5]

[3] See CE Blattner, K Coulter and W Kylicka (eds), *Animal Labour: A New Frontier of Interspecies Justice?* (Oxford, Oxford University Press, 2020).

[4] See, among others, E Ales et al (eds), *Working in Digital and Smart Organizations: Legal, Economic and Organizational Perspectives on the Digitalization of Labour Relations* (London, Palgrave Macmillan, 2018); J Prassl, *Humans as a Service: The Promise and Perils of Work in the Gig Economy* (Oxford, Oxford University Press, 2018); J Prassl and M Risak, 'Uber, Taskrabbit, & Co: Platforms as Employers? Rethinking the Legal Analysis of Crowdwork' (2016) 37 *Comparative Labor Law & Policy Journal* 619; V De Stefano, 'The Rise of the "Just-in-Time Workforce": On-Demand Work, Crowdwork, and Labor Protection in the "Gig-Economy"' (2016) 37 *Comparative Labor Law & Policy Journal* 471; M Delfino, 'Work in the age of collaborative platforms between innovation and tradition' (2018) 9 *European Labour Law Journal* 346; E Gramano, 'Digitalisation and work: challenges from the platform-economy' (2020) 15 *Contemporary Social Science* 476.

[5] See CE Blattner, K Coulter and W Kymlicka, 'Introduction: Animal Labour and the Quest for Interspecies Justice' in CE Blattner, K Coulter and W Kylicka (eds), *Animal Labour: A New Frontier of Interspecies Justice?* (Oxford, Oxford University Press, 2021).

The adoption of such a model will also allow getting rid of speciesism[6] as a regulatory principle of social protection, to be recognised, on the contrary, to workers of all species.

I am well aware of the fact that there are at least two aspects of this proposal that have to be clarified.

The first relates to the kind of protection non-human workers should enjoy.

Here, a distinction has still to be made between non-human animals, on the one hand and AI, machines and robots, on the other. Non-human animals may also enjoy fair remuneration to be understood as an appropriate level of welfare, in terms of food, accommodation and care. Fair and just working conditions shall be added in terms of limited working time and health and safety, thus excluding their exploitation to death. Machines, which cannot enjoy those benefits shall, however, be protected against abuses and misuse that may lead them to breaking point. AI and robots, all the more robots controlled by sophisticated AI, which may replicate some human behaviour should, at least, enjoy just and fair working conditions with an eye to remuneration and care, as predicted by science fiction as not far from reality.[7]

The further aspect to be clarified refers to the way in which protection should be granted.

A first route is *legislative* which, without any modifications of the status quo in terms of 'constitutional' recognition of non-human workers' rights, might be activated on the premise of the right to work (for humans), the protection of work in all its forms and applications as well as the prohibition of slavery and forced labour (both for humans and non-humans). All these are recognised by several international, supranational and national instruments. They are realised mainly in terms of freedom to choose an occupation and the right to engage in work, placement services, fair and just working conditions, protection against dismissal, support for stable and decent work. In order to substantiate my proposal, a further perspective should be added: the protection of non-human work to avoid its exploitation and the replacement of human work or its degradation (see below).

A second route is the *judiciary*, which can be viable if an applicant provided with the necessary *locus standi* files a case in favour of a non-human worker as defined above. However, even if someone is available it would not be easy to claim the violation or the denial of a (non-existing) right to protection unless one adopts a relational notion of such a right. Under a relational notion of right, I understand a right that can be recognised to a non-human, incapable of interest or will in a human perspective,[8] on the ground of the benefit such a recognition may bring both to the non-human and to the human in the altruistic/utilitarian view already envisaged above. However, as judge-made – at least in civil law jurisdictions – any protections recognised for a non-human worker will not per se be enjoyed by the rest, nor can the extension of the notion of worker to non-human for such protections be taken for granted *erga omnes*.

[6] See O Horta, 'What is Speciesism?' (2010) 23 *Journal of Agricultural & Environmental Ethics* 243.

[7] On this point, see R Alexy: www.DatasMenschenrechte.pdf (uni-kiel.de) as commented and elaborated on by A Punzi, 'Alexy and the "Rights" of the Machines' (2020) 2 *Rivista di filosofia del diritto* 333.

[8] See CE Blattner, 'Animal Labour: Toward a Prohibition of Forced Labour and a Right to Freely Choose One's Work' in CE Blattner, K Coulter and W Kylicka (eds), *Animal Labour: A New Frontier of Interspecies Justice?* (Oxford, Oxford University Press, 2020) 91.

A third route is *collective bargaining*, which can be regarded as the most effective solution in the view of realising the relational notion of rights to the benefit of both human and non-human workers. In fact, nobody is clearer than the European Social Partners in perceiving the sensitivity of the human/non-human competition, the risk of a race to the bottom and degradation of work. In the meantime, only unionised labour might have the strength to compel business to understand that the degradation or the end of human work is socially unacceptable, endangering the very survival of the human species.[9]

Until AI acquires the capacity to exercise freedom of association,[10] it will be indispensable that someone (human) takes on its agency, in order to look after its interests which, in turn, shall be conceptualised in a relational perspective, as proposed for rights. The relational notion of interest(s) assumes that non-human workers (AI, robots and machines: it does not apply to animals)[11] are still unable to elaborate and express interests of their own. As a consequence, the same construction of interests shall primarily rely on the capacity and the willingness of the human agent to bring out claims which consider needs shared by human and non-human workers as persons. To this aim, what is required, in my view, is a universal workers' representation beyond the human, based on the altruistic/utilitarian approach, according to which protection of non-human work is strictly connected to the fight against unfair competition to the detriment of human workers. On the other hand, the idea that by making robots and AI work as hard as possible and by taxing their work one could be able to release human beings from work or at least make them work less, implies an earmarking of the relevant resources in favour of the social security systems supporting those thrown out of the labour market, which may remain wishful thinking.

Against that systematic background, this chapter aims at analysing the structural and functional impact of automation and robotics (A&R) on Collective Labour Relations (CLR), in terms of their quali-quantitative potentially negative effects (section II), and of the different attitudes towards them human workers' representatives may have, depending on whether they participate or not in entrepreneurs' choice to introduce A&R as innovations in already existing undertakings or within startups (section III).

## II. The Structural Impact of Automation and Robotics on Collective Labour Relations: Quali-Quantitative Potentially Negative Effects and their Remedies

It is common understanding that A&R, as any technological changes, impact on labour relations, individual and collective. Such an impact (positive and negative), in my view, can be seen as *quali-quantitative* in the sense that it may affect both the quality and the quantity of human work.

[9] As envisaged by K Čapek, *RUR Rossum's Universal Robots*, 1920, various editions.

[10] As envisaged by Čapek (n 9).

[11] See K Coulter, 'Toward Humane Jobs and Work-Lives for Animals, in CE Blattner, K Coulter and W Kylicka (eds), *Animal Labour: A New Frontier of Interspecies Justice?* (Oxford, Oxford University Press, 2020) 29.

From the qualitative point of view, there is some agreement on the fact that A&R may have a simultaneous negative and positive effect on human workers' skills in terms of deskilling and reskilling or upskilling. Disputed is, on the contrary, which effect will prevail. This has much to do with the reflection on the very nature of new technologies, whether they are labour replacing or labour enabling.[12] Whatever the case, my point is rather that the introduction of A&R, if it does not produce technological unemployment, leads at least to a polarisation of the workforce that is likely to have a troublesome impact on CLR (section II.A). This will happen, in particular, as for the very notion of collectivity (section II.A.i) and in terms of individualisation of the work relationship of high-skilled cognitive workers (section II.A.ii).

From the quantitative point of view, A&R, as labour-replacing technologies, on the one hand reduce the number of human workers and, as a consequence, the potential union membership (section II.B). On the other, they increase the presence of non-human workers, both in the management (algorithm) and in the workforce (robots), on the assumption of, and resulting in a dehumanisation of the employment relationship (section II.C), which in turn is likely to reduce or to nullify the room for negotiation between management and labour in the workplace (section II.C.i) and to deprive workers of their needs, interests and rights through a kind of eugenic process (section II.C.ii).

## A. Deskilling and Reskilling or Upskilling: The Polarisation of Workforce and its Consequences for CLR

As mentioned above, from a qualitative point of view, A&R are likely to impact on labour relations both in a negative and in a positive way. On the one hand, as advocated by Harry Bravemann in his seminal contribution,[13] A&R may increase the fragmentation of tasks with the consequence of deskilling human work, to be understood also as less (or no) control over the labour process, now dominated by AI. Such a degradation of work[14] still represents a major concern for the European Social Partners as witnessed by the reference they have made to 'guaranteeing the *human in control principle*' as one of the main issues attached to the digitalisation of work.[15]

On the other hand, as advocated by the same European Social Partners, they

> have a shared interest in facilitating access to quality and effective training and skills development while respecting the diversity and flexibility of training systems, which vary according to diverse industrial relations practices. This entails employers' commitment to use digital technology positively, seeking to improve innovation and productivity, for the long-term health of enterprises, and for the employment security of the workforce and for better working conditions.

[12] Frey (n 1) 12 ff.

[13] H Bravemann, *Labour and Monopoly Capital: The Degradation of Work in the Twentieth Century* (New York, Monthly Review Press, 1974).

[14] ibid.

[15] Quotations from the European Framework Agreement on Digitalisation' signed by the European Social Partners on 22 June 2020. On the EFA, see L Battista, 'The European Framework Agreement on Digitalisation: A tough coexistence within the EU mosaic of actions' (2021) 14 *Italian Labour Law e-Journal* 105; I Senatori, 'The European Framework Agreement on Digitalisation: A Whiter Shade of Pale?' (2020) 13 *Italian Labour Law e-Journal* 159.

Hence the need to highlight that the positive qualitative effects of A&R, although easy to envisage, cannot be taken for granted, considering the common understanding of the adverse reaction they may produce on skills, if they do not 'respect human dignity'.

By mentioning human dignity only, the European Social Partners have adopted an anthropocentric approach to labour protection, based on 'employers' commitment to use digital technology positively'. On the contrary, if they had also referred to non-human dignity, they would have opened the way for the *relational notion of interests and rights*, as proposed above, and for consideration of the *altruistic/utilitarian approach* as the leading principle of CLR; a call that would have strengthened the position of unions as agents of both human and non-human workers.

Whatever the stand one takes on the effects of A&R, the risk of the polarisation of the workforce on skills is real. By *polarisation* I understand the professional divide between deskilled and reskilled or upskilled workers, which is likely to produce negative effects on the capacity of unions to represent and show solidarity between groups at the very top and at the very bottom of the corporate ladder. Not by chance, the European Social Partners' goal (or wish) is reskilling or upskilling of the entire workforce.

But what if such expectations are not met? In my view, there are two dangers. On the one hand, it will be difficult if not impossible to maintain the traditional feature of (branch) collective bargaining and agreements for providing common working conditions for such heterogeneous groups, withdrawing the very notion of collectivity (section II.A.i). On the other, workers with highly developed cognitive skills will be prompted to claim or accept individually negotiated working conditions (section II.A.ii), breaking the unity of that collectivity as well.[16]

### *i. New Collectivities*

Against such a background, it is questionable that the crisis of the traditional notion of collectivity, based on evenly distributed cognitive skills, might be avoided, at least in those sectors in which A&R prevail. The polarisation of the workforce in terms of uneven distribution of cognitive skills has to be added to the many challenges branch collective bargaining has been facing, not always successfully, over the last decades.

In terms of representation and negotiation strategies, unions may choose either to resign themselves to the situation and adopt a *two-track approach*, differentiating and specialising their action according to the cognitive skills divide that characterises such polarised collectivities, or to resist and look for a new common denominator, overcoming that divide, on which a new collectivity can be established.

In my view, that denominator is to be sought within the above-mentioned relational perspective, which allows holding together interests and rights, as well as the needs not only of human and non-human, but of cognitive and non-cognitive workers. In this case, the *altruistic/utilitarian approach* applies in terms of the still inescapable necessity

[16] Individualisation and new collectivities have nothing to do with the dichotomisation of freedom of association between individualism and collectivism, as convincingly criticised by A Bogg, '"Individualism" and "Collectivism" in Collective Labour Law' (2017) 46 *Industrial Law Journal* 72.

of non-cognitive work in order to allow cognitive work to deliver, above all when cognitive workers are non-human (AI).

Designing representation and negotiation strategies within the framework of the relational perspective would empower unions to emphasise the *complementarity* of cognitive and non-cognitive as well as that of human and non-human work. Admittedly, it will not be easy for unions to convince employers and their organisations to adopt such an approach. Indeed, the renewal of traditional collectivity based on complementarity will result in the claim of reducing the working conditions gap created by the cognitive divide. Something that will be excluded in cases where polarisation ends up in separate collectivities.

For these purposes, the well-targeted use of participatory tools and the right to collective action, as recognised by the legislator and/or by the industrial relations system would be crucial. I will come to this below.

### *ii. The Individualisation of the Work Relationship of Workers with Highly Developed Cognitive Skills*

In my view, there is a further reason why unions should not give in to polarisation. In fact, such a process is likely to indulge or even enhance the propensity of high-skilled cognitive workers (and their employers) for the agreement on tailor-made working conditions, outside any collective framework. Actually, the very creation of a separate collectivity of those workers will act as a stepping-stone towards the individualisation of their employment relationships. Indeed, this is the kind of collectivity that, due to the remarkable individual negotiating power of its potential members, hardly finds reasons to exist.

Insisting on *complementarity and inclusivity* as rationales of renewed collectivities, which may be established at branch as well as at company level, union representation and negotiation strategies may play a key role in countervailing the degradation and even the extinction of human work in highly automatised and robotised sectors. On the contrary, focusing exclusively on human workers and human dignity, neglecting the non-human 'side of the moon', and relying on the 'employers' commitment to use digital technology positively', will not fit that purpose, leaving non-human, and as a consequence, human work to the mercy of shortsighted entrepreneurs. On the contrary, forward-looking entrepreneurs are needed, willing and ready to share the responsibility to countervail the degradation and extinction of human work.

Of course, the Social Partners' responsibility may be stimulated by the existence or the introduction of public policies and legislative frameworks committed to the same goals.

## B. The Replacement of Human Labour and the Reduction of Union Members

From a quantitative point of view, the most striking effect of A&R on CLR is the reduction of human workers in absolute numbers, which leads to a drop of potential union membership. However, in relative numbers one may argue that, on the one hand, the degradation is likely to concentrate human work into the lowest ranks of the labour market where the need for representation in order to obtain better working conditions is felt to be the most urgent. On the other, as highlighted above, A&R may lead to an increase in the relative number of high-skilled cognitive workers provided with a remarkable individual negotiating power. Therefore, in terms of representation strategies, the least unions could do is to widen their membership among low-skilled workers, trying to remind the high-skilled ones of the complementarity on which their wellbeing is based.

More generally, a large number of unionised low-skilled human workers will constitute a critical mass that, in the framework of renewed inclusive collectivity, may also serve the interests of a few high-skilled cognitive human and non-human workers. However, this means that unions should not adopt a craft model but rather invest in a federative representation at branch or (large) company level.

## C. The Dehumanisation of Work Relationships and its Effects on CLR

Even if, according to the personalistic principle as revisited above, non-humans should be regarded as workers as far as their protection is concerned, they are, tautologically, non-human from a relational point of view. This means that AI, robots and machines may (learn to) calculate decisions but cannot negotiate them driven by individual or collective needs and interests as human do. In the view of many this is something positive, since it can be looked at as an unbiased decision-making process, guaranteeing fairness and avoiding discrimination. In my view, and also in the opinion of some national courts,[17] algorithms may be as biased as humans, since at the very top of their creation, one finds human (economic) interests to be served, hidden behind a scientific and thus by definition (!?) a fair, dehumanised decision-making process.

The adoption of such dehumanised, apparently unbiased, unquestionable, and for most of the time unintelligible, decision-making processes, is likely to withdraw any room for negotiation between (AI) management and labour, thus, absolutising the unilateral exercise of managerial prerogatives, above all at plant level (section II.C.i). On the other hand, the increasing presence of non-human work may have the consequence of making negotiations pointless, on the grounds that non-human workers have no needs and interests (section II.C.ii).

### *i. The Algorithm as Manager: No Negotiation Allowed*

The fact that, in a growing number of cases, managerial prerogatives are exercised by algorithms,[18] which are not allowed to or are incapable of negotiating, constitutes in my

[17] See I Purificato, 'Behind the Scenes of Deliveroo's Algorithm: in the Blindness of "Frank" its Discriminatory Potential' (2021) 14 *Italian Labour Law e-Journal* 169. More in general, M Kullmann, 'Platform Work, Algorithmic Decision-Making, and EU Gender Equality Law' (2018) 34 *International Journal of Comparative Labour Law and Industrial Relations* 1; V De Stefano, '"Negotiating the Algorithm": Automation, Artificial Intelligence, and Labor Protection' (2019) 41 *Comparative Labor Law & Policy Journal* 15, 28.

[18] See J Adams-Prassl, 'What If Your Boss Was an Algorithm? Economic Incentives, Legal Challenges, and the Rise of Artificial Intelligence at Work' (2019) 41 *Comparative Labor Law & Policy Journal* 123.

view a violation of the right to collective bargaining as recognised by international and EU legislative instruments. As for the former, the reference is to International Labour Organization (ILO) Convention 98 of 1949 on the Right to Organise and Collective Bargaining, and to Convention 154 of 1981 on Collective Bargaining, as well as to Article 6 of the Revised European Social Charter. As to the latter, to Article 28 of the Charter of Fundamental Rights of the European Union (CFREU).

As far as international labour law is concerned, one has to be aware of the fact that the mere promotion of collective bargaining is at stake. In fact, according to Article 4 of Convention 48:

> Measures appropriate to national conditions shall be taken, where necessary, to encourage and promote the full development and utilisation of machinery for voluntary negotiation between employers or employers' organisations and workers' organisations, with a view to the regulation of terms and conditions of employment by means of collective agreements.

Something more precise is provided by Convention 154, when it specifies the aims of 'measures adapted to national conditions … taken to promote collective bargaining',[19] in terms of 'collective bargaining [that] should be made possible for all employers and all groups of workers in the branches of activity covered by this Convention'[20] and 'should be progressively extended to all matters covered by … this Convention'.[21] Indeed, also the statement that 'the establishment of rules of procedure agreed between employers' and workers' organisations should be encouraged',[22] may be seen as a tangible sign of the commitment required of the Members of the ILO. On the other hand, 'measures taken by public authorities to encourage and promote the development of collective bargaining shall be the subject of prior consultation and, whenever possible, agreement between public authorities and employers' and workers' organisations'.[23]

The same *promotional approach* is adopted by the Revised European Social Charter. According to Article 6,

> with a view to ensuring the effective exercise of the right to bargain collectively, the Parties undertake: 1 to promote joint consultation between workers and employers; 2 to promote, where necessary and appropriate, machinery for voluntary negotiations between employers or employers' organisations and workers' organisations, with a view to the regulation of terms and conditions of employment by means of collective agreements.

Even if confined within a promotional approach, the systematic relevance of ILO and Revised European Social Charter provisions shall not be underestimated, above all when it comes to the impact of A&R on CLR. In fact, one can argue that the commitment to promote collective bargaining cannot be compatible with its denial, as happens when algorithms exercise managerial prerogatives. Therefore, the promotion of collective bargaining shall result, at least, in the possibility for workers and their representatives to have a counterpart capable of negotiating with them on working

[19] Article 5(1).
[20] Article 5(1)(a).
[21] Article 5(1)(b).
[22] Article 5(1)(c).
[23] Article 7.

conditions. The alternative would be to deny such a role to algorithms and to consider them mere organisational tools, which should be bypassed by unions referring directly to the human entrepreneur.

Moreover, the fact that according to Article 6(4) of the Revised European Social Charter, the Parties 'recognize the right of workers and employers to collective action in cases of conflicts of interest, including the right to strike, subject to obligations that might arise out of collective agreements previously entered into', confirms that counterparts shall be *stakeholders* and not organisational tools.

As far as EU law is concerned, the CFREU adopts, rather, a mandatory approach to the right to collective bargaining (and action). Article 28 recognises for 'workers and employers, or their respective organisations', the right to negotiate and conclude collective agreements at the appropriate levels and, in cases of conflicts of interest, the right to take collective action to defend their interests, including to strike. As is well known, both rights are recognised 'in accordance with Community law and national laws and practices', a statement that has produced serious difficulties with the view of affirming the existence of fundamental rights to collective bargaining and action at EU level. On the contrary, in the realm of algorithmic management, such a statement, above all for the right to collective bargaining, could be an advantage, allowing legislators who have obliged themselves to promote that right to intervene in order to assure that managerial prerogatives would be exercised by human agents to guarantee any prospective negotiations.

### *ii. Workers without Needs: The Deprivation of Interests and Rights through Eugenics*

If one does not accept the relational notion of rights and interests as proposed above, there is a further point on dehumanisation of work that has to be made from the CLR perspective, this time from the workers' side. Until AI is given human feelings, it will have no needs. This means that it will have no interests and no aspirations to settle needs in terms of rights, among others, as far as labour is concerned. As a consequence, if deprived of the human agency advocated above, AI will have no claims against its 'employers' and no need of collective bargaining.

If one accepts the comprehensive definition of person and worker as stated earlier, one has to admit that a kind of eugenics is at stake when it comes to the design of non-human (non-animal) workers. Indeed, they are deprived of needs, interests and rights in order to be more efficient and productive. In the comprehensive perspective of the personalistic principle I have suggested, this would clearly be a violation of the 'right to the integrity of the person' as affirmed by Article 3 CFREU which, in the field of medicine and biology (extendable to biotechnology), prohibits 'eugenic practices, in particular those aiming at the selection of persons'. Such a manipulation, as acceptable as it can be, may result in one of the 'genetic features' Article 21 CFREU looks at as a prohibited ground of discrimination. Discrimination that happens, for instance, when (non-human) workers are deprived of the right to collective bargaining because of their failure to conceive interests.

To the objection that non-human workers cannot have needs and interests, I have already responded by advocating the relational notion of interests.

# III. The Functional Impact of Automation and Robotics on Collective Labour Relations between Innovations and Startups

From a structural point of view, A&R prompt a profound rethinking of some basic conceptual categories of labour law, such as the personalistic principle and the interests/rights theory. On the other hand, A&R also produce a significant impact on the functioning of CLR, in terms of role and attitude towards them of workers' representation. However, one may argue that such an impact varies depending on whether A&R are introduced as *innovations* (section III.A) within an already existing organisation, or they are original features of a *startup* (section III.B).

In the first case, it is plausible that workers' representation at undertaking or establishment level already exists or that branch unions are strong enough to be involved in entrepreneurs' decision-making processes. In the second, the physical or legal person(s) starting up a new activity may aim at creating a 'collective-dimensions-free business model',[24] in particular a non-unionised one. As mentioned above, the prevalence of high-skilled cognitive workers is likely to facilitate such a perspective.

## A. Innovations

Starting from A&R as innovations within an already existing organisation, once again one may adopt a binary analytical model of the role workers' representatives can play. In fact, on the one hand there is the case of their inclusion in the entrepreneurial decision-making processes (section III.A.i); on the other, that of A&R as unilaterally imposed innovations (section III.A.ii).

### *i. Workers' Representatives' Inclusion in the Entrepreneurial Decision-Making Processes*

In turn, as is well known, workers' representatives' inclusion in the entrepreneurial decision-making processes may result from legislatively regulated participation, codetermination included (section III.A.i.a) or from the exercise of freedom of association and the right to organise (section III.A.i.b).

#### a. The Legislatively Regulated Participation and Codetermination

The existence of a legislative framework regulating participation, codetermination included, proves the relevance of workers representatives' involvement in the entrepreneurial decision-making process for the legal order providing for it. A&R, as (relatively)

[24] On the notion of the collective dimensions of labour relations, see E Ales, 'The Collective Dimensions of the Employment Relationship: Ways Beyond Traditional Views' in T Addabbo et al (eds), *The Collective Dimensions of Employment Relations: Interdisciplinary Perspectives on Workers' Voices and Changing Workplace Patterns* (London, Palgrave Macmillan, 2021) 63.

new issues fall within the scope of application of that framework as any other technological changes modifying the organisation of the relevant company, affecting skills or employment levels. As a consequence, works councils, named as they may be within that legal order, are entitled to prerogatives that range from information and consultation to codetermination, with or without real veto power on entrepreneurial calls.[25] Whatever the depth of their involvement, the crucial point in my view is whether it occurs in the decision-making process or happens when the negative consequences of that process show up.

The relevance of entrepreneurial social accountability in terms of alternative solutions to be agreed upon with workers' representatives or compensation to be paid to the workers affected by those calls should not be underestimated. However, it is rather clear that considering the radical and irreversible nature of A&R, workers' representatives' involvement should be concentrated on the decision-making process that could result in their introduction as innovations. In that phase, a joint assessment of the negative consequences that may follow those calls is also decisive from the perspective of avoiding the end of human work, which cannot be tackled by the usual tools adopted to alleviate the impact of any technological changes once they have occurred.

Therefore, A&R are likely to require upgrades even of well-established participation and codetermination systems if they do not already allow workers' representatives an effective voice in the entrepreneurial decision-making process. This may be obtained in the most effective way by providing workers' representation on managing and surveillance boards rather than by enhancing involvement at establishment level, where those calls are just going to be implemented.

However, even if workers' representatives' participation takes place in the decision-making process, at least three problematic aspects have to be highlighted. I will enumerate them in my personal order of relevance: (i) the independence of workers' representatives from the employer; (ii) adequate expertise, in our case, in A&R, algorithms included; and (iii) the effective influence on the decision-making process.

(i) Independence, in my view, implies the capacity of workers' representatives to realise when the interests of business and labour coincide and when, on the contrary, they diverge. Such an awareness, which is worth much more than any ideological opposition, is not easy to acquire if workers' representation within the undertaking is not backed up by an external partner seeing the bigger picture the former may fail to see (corporate friendly approach). Unions at branch level are the most suitable and best qualified for this purpose. A solution could be to have one or more workers' representative appointed by branch unions in order to establish a structural and functional linkage.[26]

[25] On the works council model, see M Weiss, 'Challenges for Workers' Participation' in T Addabbo et al (eds), *The Collective Dimensions of Employment Relations: Interdisciplinary Perspectives on Workers' Voices and Changing Workplace Patterns* (London, Palgrave Macmillan, 2021) 15. See also, T Klebe and M Weiss, 'Workers' Participation 4.0 – Digital and Global?' (2019) 40 *Comparative Labor Law & Policy Journal* 263.

[26] See E Ales, 'Who is afraid of unions representation? Some considerations on the *SAP SE* case in the light of EU Labour Law' (2021) 14 *Italian Labour Law e-Journal* 71.

(ii) The same reasoning may apply to the adequate expertise workers' representatives shall possess in order to play an active role in the decision-making process. In case A&R are introduced as innovations, one cannot take for granted that workers' representatives within the undertaking are acquainted with their impact on human labour and with their functioning. Unions at branch level or the inter-branch confederation they may be affiliated to should be able to offer any support needed by monitoring the bigger picture (looking for best and worst practices) and by activating think-tanks, research departments as well as societal debates on those issues.

(iii) Made aware of the bigger picture and provided with the adequate expertise, workers' representatives within the undertaking are able to contribute effectively to the decision-making process. The point is how the system in place is going to handle (hopefully infrequent) cases in which no consensus is achieved, and opinions differ between entrepreneurs and workers' representatives. The appointment by agreement of an independent chairperson may help in such cases. However, one may wonder whether the linkage of workers' representatives with branch unions might be used in the view of taking workers' interests up through collective action even if a decision has been made by majority within the competent body. In my view, since interests are at stake and no collective agreement has been concluded that option can be acceptable (see below).

### b. The Freedom of Association and Right to Organisation Model

Workers' representation within the undertaking stemming from freedom of association and the right to organise (hereinafter also union representation) can be looked at by the legal order as exclusive or complementary to legislatively regulated participation and codetermination. In many cases, legislation provides rules and requirements for its establishment in order to strike a reasonable balance between business and labour interests and to avoid recognition conflicts. In CLR systems that allow company level collective agreements, union representation is entitled to bargain them, usually backed up by the relevant branch union(s), frequently within a double-level (branch and company) collective bargaining model.

Being traditionally focused on the setting of wages, working time and skills scales, branch collective bargaining, at least as far as its *normative function* is concerned, does not seem to fit the purpose of union representation's involvement in the organisational decision-making process of the undertaking in its individuality.[27] The very idea of making freedom to conduct a business a collective bargaining issue is not attractive at all for entrepreneurs, because it also implies the risk of facing collective action while organising their activities. One could argue that work organisation as such, A&R included, is not a very popular subject for collective bargaining.[28] On the contrary, it can be for participation and codetermination.

[27] However, on the duty to bargain A&R in the US Labour Law System, see DJ Zidich, 'Robotics in the Workplace: The Employer's Duty to Bargain over its Implementation and Effect on the Worker' (1984) 24 *Santa Clara Law Review* 917.

[28] For a different view, see De Stefano, '"Negotiating the Algorithm"' (n 17) 45.

In such a perspective, as the Italian experience shows,[29] the *obligatory part* of branch collective agreements may provide a participation machinery which also encompasses joint decision-making on A&R, including the creation and implementation of algorithms. This may happen through the establishment of bilateral bodies at territorial level or by committing union representation and management within the undertaking. A ban on collective action may be agreed upon, and conciliation, mediation or arbitration mechanisms put in place.

Needless to say, any participation machineries established by collective agreement have increased chance for success, stemming from a joint decision of the parties involved, who are also accountable for the monitoring and their well functioning.

### *ii. Unilaterally Decided Innovations*

The freedom to conduct a business might justify the introduction of A&R as unilaterally decided innovations, without any involvement of workers' representatives in the organisational decision-making process. However, at least within the EU, this cannot happen without information and consultation being guaranteed at the appropriate levels as well as in good time, 'in the cases and under the conditions provided for by Community law and national laws and practices'.[30] From such a perspective, the full and correct implementation of Directive 2002/14/EC by Member States is crucial, as highlighted by the Court of Justice of the European Union in its case law.[31]

Although to be provided at the appropriate levels and in good time, information and consultation, per se, do not guarantee the participation of workers' representatives within the relevant phase of the decision-making process and may prove to be unfit for the purpose of countervailing deskilling and/or the very end of human labour. In the absence of participation, the only possibility left to human workers is collective action taken to defend their interests, jeopardised by such unilaterally decided innovation. This is, in my view, a very important point, since in many legal orders collective action is necessarily linked to the conclusion or the renewal of a collective agreement, which is not the case when unilaterally decided innovations are at stake. Moreover, in many legal orders the call to strike is a prerogative of already established unions, a notion from which spontaneous workers' coalitions are excluded.

Given this, in my view, the right to exercise collective action, strike included,[32] should be recognised, as a last (and only) resort, to workers in undertakings that are going to adopt unilaterally decided innovations affecting the skills or the very existence of human labour. In the same vein, any kind of solidarity actions in such circumstances should be deemed to be lawful on the ground of the relational approach to interests and rights as illustrated above.

[29] See E Ales, 'La tutela della salute sul lavoro nel prisma del metodo partecipativo' in L Zoppoli (ed), *Tutela della salute pubblica e rapporti di lavoro* (2021) 11 *Quaderni della Rivista Diritti Lavori Mercati* 231.

[30] Article 27, CFREU.

[31] Case C-176/12 *Association de médiation sociale v Union locale des syndicats CGT and Others* ECLI:EU:C:2014:2 [2014].

[32] Article 28, CFREU.

### iii. Proactive or Reactive Attitudes Towards A&R

It is common sense to observe that workers' representatives' effective participation in the organisational decision-making process increases the chances of their positive and even proactive attitude, among the others, towards A&R. Participation, as argued above, seems to be the right call in the view of striking a balance between entrepreneurs' and workers' interests, even if it could cause delays and require compromises to be reached in order to adequately protect human and non-human work.

It is also common sense to observe that the more widespread the adoption of participation as a functional tool of CLR, the higher its effectiveness in avoiding technological dumping by undertakings introducing unilaterally decided innovations. The global implications of unregulated A&R are apparent, as it happens with any other diversities in entrepreneurial decision-making processes affecting working conditions in the broader sense.

A recent and relevant example of efforts made to cope with such negative implications is the comprehensive plan to ensure that international labour standards are being enforced at the General Motors' facility in Silao, Mexico, announced on 8 July 2021, by the United States and Mexico. 'The plan represents the first step of remediation under the United States–Mexico–Canada Agreement. Through this type of enforcement, American workers are protected from unfair trade practices and are able to compete and succeed in the manufacturing sector'. In the words of US Secretary of Labor Marty Walsh: 'If we are to succeed in protecting workers' rights at home, we must ensure that those rights will not be undermined by exploitative labor practices and violations of collective bargaining rights around the world'.

Although extremely cautious, noteworthy in a similar perspective is the establishment of the European Labour Authority by Regulation 2019/1149, a body provided with some promising prerogatives in coordinating, supporting and suggesting concerted and joined labour inspections in the Member States, in order to facilitate cooperation among them and to support the effective compliance with their cooperation obligations in the field of workers mobility.

Widespread workers' representatives' participation in the entrepreneurial decision-making process may also constitute a way to make public authorities' intervention superfluous and to stimulate a proactive attitude of labour towards innovations by striking a shared and sustainable balance between human and non-human work. This implies keeping the decision-making process as human as possible, ie, steered (or biased, if you like) by the interests of the parties, inconceivable to AI.

The alternative, in the case of unilaterally decided innovations, is workers' reactive attitude, which is likely to result in conflict and collective action against decisions that have already been made. As highlighted above, the same lawfulness of such actions is questioned, in many legal orders. If the latter intend to support workers' reaction, national legislators and the courts will need to adopt a more generous approach towards non-contractual strikes and secondary action. However, this may not be enough since strikers could have already been made redundant by A&R, thus nullifying the effects of any primary collective actions. Secondary action too, in cases of free-rider companies not member of employers' organisations, will be futile.

## B. Startups

The issue is even more complicated if, as already mentioned above, the physical or legal person starting up a new activity, being it on platform or traditional, aims at creating a 'collective-dimensions-free business model', in particular a non-unionised one. In the era of A&R, this may happen without a manifest violation of freedom of association and the right to organise, by establishing a work environment with a high rate of non-human labour, in which the few humans are not physically interconnected since they interact remotely with and through a platform.[33] Individualised work relationships will be the rule, not the intended or unintended consequence of any innovations.

Such undertakings lack the very basis of the collective dimensions, making difficult, if not impossible, the spontaneous establishment of union representation. The same applies to collectively bargained participation since undertakings like these will not be affiliated within any employers' organisations. The one and only chance is to rely on the establishment of workers' and union representation bodies within the undertaking as provided by the law. However, as is well known, with a few exceptions, this is conceived as a right workers may exercise subject to certain conditions, for example a minimum threshold of employees within the establishment or the undertaking. Even if those conditions are fulfilled, it will be up to them to trigger the establishment mechanism, through election or designation. Rhetorically, one may wonder whether the work environment as described above will be the most stimulating or welcoming for workers' and union representation.

Moreover, if the workforce is mainly non-human there could be a problem of meeting the required dimensional threshold, still to be calculated with reference to humans, although the overall number of (human and non-human) workers exceeds it by far. From the relational perspective proposed above, non-human workers shall matter too. On the other hand, a group of human workers managed by (or through) a non-negotiating algorithm may find that establishment of a representation is a pointless exercise.

By consequence, in my view, the proliferation of highly automatised and robotised startups emphasises two issues, indeed of general significance: the guarantee of an adequate number of human workers within the undertaking (section III.B.i); and the necessity to have some form of workers' representation at the same level (section III.B.ii).

### *i. Automatised and Robotised Startups and the Difficulty to Establish CLR: Towards Human Quotas?*

In the absence of any collective dimensions regulating the use of A&R also from a quantitative point of view (see, for instance, the limitation to fixed-term contracts provided by collective or works council agreements), this can be achieved only by the law.

[33] See E Ales, 'Adapting Labour Law to "Digital" Work: Between Scholarly Interpretation, Case Law and Legislative Intervention' in A Perulli and T Treu (eds), *The Future of Work: Labour Law and Labour Market Regulation in the Digital Era* (Alphen aan den Rijn, Kluwer Law International, 2020) 225, 232.

If, in my view, quotas are not necessarily the fairest and most efficient solution where competition between groups of humans (based on sex, ethnic origin, age, disability etc), when humans are obliged by other humans to compete hopelessly with AI, robots and machines, quotas would seem to be the only way to save human work from succumbing.

To the question whether human quotas imposed by law are compatible with the freedom to conduct a business, one can answer by invoking the right (of humans) to work and, to a certain extent, to life, as long as work represents the only means of subsistence for the majority of them. From such a perspective, quotas should be provided for different levels of skills, as this will still be a feature of human work, despite the trend to polarisation mentioned above. However, in the light of the aforesaid, quotas will be crucial in managerial positions, which should be mainly, if not exclusively, held by humans.

Human quotas, in my view, should be provided not only within startups but within already existing undertakings, if required by the absence of agreement between the parties on a sustainable use of A&R.

### *ii. From Workers' Right to Employers' Duty to Activate Participation Systems*

In the presence of a 'collective-dimensions-free business model' the recognition of workers' right to establish union representations or works councils within the undertaking does not fit the purpose of guaranteeing their effective participation in the decision-making process at any stage. In my view, the solution should be to impose, by law, a duty to the entrepreneur to establish any kind of works council, as happens in France with the Comité Social et Économique in undertakings employing more than 11 workers.[34] The mandatory establishment of a works council will avoid any violation of freedom of association, as will be the case if union representation is at stake.

In fact, the same mandatory presence of workers' representatives within management and surveillance boards should be seen rather as a structural requirement for their legitimate establishment and functioning than as the free exercise of a right.

On the other hand, the effective functioning of a workers' representatives' participation system may mean that human quotas are no longer required.

## IV. Conclusion

From the aforementioned, one can conclude that A&R are going to produce an unprecedented impact on labour relations in general and on CLR in particular. At stake, in the short term, is the very existence of CLR; in the medium term, human work which, in turn, is still the basis for human living. In order to meet such an unprecedented

[34] Introduced on 29 December 2017 by Décret n 2017-1819, which added Article 2312-1–2312-61 to the Code du Travail. The Comité Social et Économique replaces the Comité d'Entreprise, the Comité d'Hygiène, de Sécurité et des Conditions de Travail and the Délégués du Personnel.

challenge, an unprecedented joint effort between legislators and social partners would be needed. Scholars convinced of the importance of the collective dimensions of labour relations, in terms of cooperation between union and non-union representation in the view of workers' participation within the entrepreneurial decision-making process, may contribute to it. Indeed, the establishment or the enhancement of effective participation systems is likely to stimulate a positive and even proactive attitude of workers towards A&R, facilitating their introduction in a balanced version that should be particularly aware of the existential nature of interests involved, which cannot be sacrificed in the name of the freedom to conduct a business.

# 4

# EU Law and Digitalisation of Employment Relations

IACOPO SENATORI

## I. Digital Transformation of the World of Work: Naturally a Matter for the EU?

The relationship between the technological transformation and employment relations involves many topics on which European Union (EU) law may claim a regulatory competence.[1] One may look at the recent European Commission's Proposal for a Directive on platform work (Platform Proposal),[2] where the justification for the intervention of EU law on grounds of subsidiarity is found in the transnational character of the platform business.[3] More generally, the changed employment and organisational patterns that come as a result of the use of 'enabling' technologies in workplaces cross-cut the scope of several established instruments of primary and secondary EU labour law, including fundamental rights and economic freedoms, and call into question the effectiveness and the adequacy of the current EU *acquis*. It comes as no surprise, then, that several contributions in this book include detailed references to the influence of EU law on the corresponding subjects.

This chapter aims at complementing the discussion, by adding a specific focus on what role EU law may play in shaping the responses of labour law to the digital challenge, and particularly whether it can bring about the right balance between the quality of employment and the profitability of businesses. In this respect, it is worth noting that the impact of technological transformation is not just about devising new policies and new regulatory instruments. It also implies the need to review

[1] N Potocka-Sionek and A Aloisi, '"Festina Lente": The ILO and EU Agendas on the Digital Transformation of Work' (2021) 37 *International Journal of Comparative Labour Law and Industrial Relations* 35.

[2] European Commission, 'Proposal for a Directive of the European Parliament and of the Council on improving working conditions in platform work' COM(2021) 762 final.

[3] As the Commission has noted, '59% of all people working through platforms in the EU engage with clients in another country', and a single market for digital labour platforms is quickly developing: European Commission, ibid, 8.

the current legal framework to ascertain whether existing instruments and categories can be adjusted by means of interpretation to fit the new technological environment.[4]

## A. The State of the Art in EU Law and Policy

The EU body of regulation presents a certain degree of ambivalence when it comes to protecting the rights of 'digital workers' (a category which is used in this chapter for the sake of simplification, while remaining well aware of the vast diversity of situations that it entails). On the one hand there are instruments – like, for example, non-discrimination law and information and consultation rights[5] – that embody a strong potential to cover the needs arising from the new organisational and contractual arrangements and, as a result, may gain a central systemic role.[6] On the other hand, there are rules based on concepts and techniques that seem seriously misaligned with the changes prompted by digitalisation, as is the case of the Working Time Directive. Another example of the same kind is antitrust law, which for a long time has threatened to deprive increasing sectors of the workforce of fundamental rights like collective bargaining, at least until the latest developments that will be addressed below. It seems therefore a legitimate question to ask whether the unescapable influence of EU law on the technological transformation will represent for the quality of working conditions a booster or a brake.

The same ambivalence that characterises 'hard' EU law can be found in the field of EU policymaking. Some commentators have criticised a number of recent actions, such as the 'Digital Services Act'[7] and the 'Artificial Intelligence Act',[8] for their market-biased character, that purportedly overlooks the specific needs linked to the application of the digital technologies in the employment context and, as a result, fails to provide sufficient guarantees for workers' rights.[9] Nonetheless, a certain degree of 'labour sensitivity' can be recognised in a set of EU initiatives undertaken under the framework of the European Pillar of Social Rights.

[4] According to J Adams-Prassl, 'What If Your Boss Was an Algorithm? Economic Incentives, Legal Challenges, and the Rise of Artificial Intelligence at Work' (2019) 41 *Comparative Labor Law & Policy Journal* 123, 124, for instance, certain elements of the technological transformation, such as the rise of platform-based forms of work, can be adequately tackled by 'the consistent application and enforcement of existing regulatory models', whereas other elements, like those brought about by artificial intelligence and automation, 'require a fundamental rethink of key elements of the traditional apparatus of employment law and labor market regulation'.

[5] Employee involvement is the main instrument envisioned by EU law for the collective control of organisational decisions that may affect the interests of workers, as it is certainly the case for any kind of 'digital restructuring' of the undertaking.

[6] This does not mean that a maintenance of such instruments is not needed. For instance, the machinery of non-discrimination law faces the challenge of algorithmic management techniques that may hide biased decisions and obscure the employer's accountability on such decisions: see below at section II.B.

[7] European Commission, 'Proposal for a Regulation of the European Parliament and of the Council on a Single Market For Digital Services (Digital Services Act) and amending Directive 2000/31/EC' COM(2020) 825 final.

[8] European Commission, 'Proposal for a Regulation of the European Parliament and of the Council Laying Down Harmonised Rules on Artificial Intelligence (Artificial Intelligence Act) and Amending Certain Union Legislative Acts' COM(2021) 206 final (Artificial Intelligence Communication).

[9] A Ponce Del Castillo, 'The Digital Services Act package: Reflections on the EU Commission's policy options' (2020) 12 *ETUI Policy Brief*; A Ponce Del Castillo, 'The AI Regulation: entering the AI regulatory winter? Why an ad hoc directive on AI in employment is required' (2021) 7 *ETUI Policy Brief*.

The landmark Commission's Communication titled 'A Strong Social Europe for Just Transitions', released on 14 January 2020,[10] set out an action plan for the implementation of the Pillar, expressing the intention to put people 'at the heart' of the digital economy. The driving principle was to grasp the employment opportunities generated by technological transformation while preserving the quality of jobs. The envisaged measures covered a wide array of topics that entail significant labour law implications: vocational training (a crucial means to adapt workers' skills to the changing patterns of the labour market triggered by the new technologies); gender equality (hindered by the unbalanced representation of women in 'digital professions'); working conditions of platform workers; and changes in the workplace that entail new risks of discrimination, exclusion and impairment of workers' physical and mental health.

With the subsequent Communication entitled 'The European Pillar of Social Rights Action Plan'[11] the Commission brought its strategy one step forward, sketching out a more specific body of initiatives and targets which necessarily take into account the abrupt change of scenario prompted by the Covid-19 pandemic. The document called for integration between the 'digital transition' policies and the instruments specifically adopted by the Union to support the post-pandemic recovery, notably the plan 'Next Generation EU'.[12] The actions envisaged under the Plan addressed the enhancement of digital skills, reinforcement of social dialogue in promoting workplace innovation and digital restructuring, improvement of working conditions, and the protection of new digital rights at the workplace.

To tackle the skill shortage issue, the Plan committed to increase the adult participation in training, setting a target of 80 per cent of people aged between 16 and 74 equipped with basic digital skills, considering this target as 'a precondition for inclusion and participation in the labour market and society in a digitally transformed Europe'.[13] With regard to the role of social dialogue, the Plan aimed at introducing specific modalities to improve the implementation and enforcement of the *acquis communautaire* in the field of information, consultation and participation rights.

As for the new forms of digital work, the Commission confirmed the intention to introduce a legislative proposal on the working conditions of platform workers and an initiative 'to ensure that EU competition law does not stand in the way of collective agreements for (some) self-employed', including – again – platform workers.[14] Finally, the Commission addressed the rise of telework triggered by the pandemic and the problems linked to the adoption of algorithmic management in workplace practices. On the first point, it undertook to follow up the European Parliament Resolution with recommendations to the Commission on the right to disconnect[15] and to present in 2022 a report

[10] European Commission, 'A Strong Social Europe For Just Transitions' (Communication) COM(2020) 14 final (Just Transitions Communication).

[11] European Commission, 'The European Pillar of Social Rights Action Plan' (Communication) COM(2021) 102 final.

[12] European Commission, 'Europe's moment: Repair and Prepare for the Next Generation' (Communication) COM(2020) 456 final.

[13] European Commission, 'The European Pillar of Social Rights Action Plan' (n 11) 6.

[14] European Commission, Artificial Intelligence Communication (n 8) 14.

[15] European Parliament, 'Resolution of 21 January 2021 with recommendations to the Commission on the right to disconnect' 2019/2181(INL) (Resolution on the right to disconnect).

on the implementation of the Working Time Directive,[16] presumably aimed at testing the enduring fitness of the current provisions in the face of the risks that the modern remote work arrangements pose for the stability of the boundaries between work and personal life. On the second point, the Plan anticipated the introduction of a proposal for an EU Regulation on Artificial Intelligence, 'for the uptake of trustworthy AI use in the EU economy, including in the workplace for all forms of work'.[17]

## B. Chapter Outline

Against such a background, the following sections of this chapter will go through the existing regulatory framework and the announced reform initiatives, trying to reconstruct the general trends and point out the critical elements.

Two general propositions will serve as a methodological guidance to the arguments discussed below:

1. Technological transformation is a multidimensional phenomenon, whose constitutive elements (as well as the interests attached to them) are so closely intertwined that the consequences of any specific regulatory intervention almost necessarily will exceed its original scope and purpose. The European Social Partners took the same position in their 'Framework Agreement on Digitalisation',[18] signed in June 2020. They maintained that 'the digital transformation of the economy is a multifaceted topic with large implications for labour markets, the world of work and society at large', in which 'multiple topics play a role or should be taken into account', whereas 'most of these topics are interlinked and should not be dealt with in isolation'. This suggests that a holistic approach, attempting to keep track of the interdependencies between different regulatory instruments and the interests they aim at protecting, is the best analytical tool to address the relationship between technology and (labour) law.
2. The policy discourse on technology, work and the law at the EU level revolves around the dichotomy between risks and opportunities. This is a recurring motif in the documents mentioned above,[19] which echoes the rejection of the deterministic interpretations of the digital transformation. In other words, technology is a neutral phenomenon, whose values and effects, as well as the allocation of the benefits and costs related to its adoption in any economic or social context,

[16] Directive 2003/88/EC of the European Parliament and of the Council of 4 November 2003 concerning certain aspects of the organization of working time (Working Time Directive) [2003] OJ L299/9.

[17] European Commission, 'The European Pillar of Social Rights Action Plan' (n 11) 14. The Proposal was published on 21 April 2021: see European Commission, Artificial Intelligence Communication (n 8) and below at section IV.B for comments.

[18] See ch 3 by Edoardo Ales in this volume. For further references see I Senatori, 'The European Framework Agreement on Digitalisation. A Whiter Shade of Pale?' (2020) 13 *Italian Labour Law e-Journal* 159; L Battista, 'The European Framework Agreement on Digitalisation: a tough coexistence within the EU mosaic of actions' (2021) 14 *Italian Labour Law e-Journal* 105; D Mangan, 'Agreement to Discuss: The Social Partners Address the Digitalisation of Work' (2021) 50 *Industrial Law Journal* 689.

[19] The dichotomy is also recalled in the Commission's Just Transitions Communication (n 10) 3: 'Together, we will upgrade Europe's social market economy to fit the opportunities and challenges of today and tomorrow and ensure just transitions for all'.

depend on the decisions made by rule makers with regard to the various (and often competing) interests involved.[20]

As for the structure of the chapter, section II will address the scope of EU labour law, ie, the extent to which the available instruments are applicable to workers whose contractual schemes are framed into the business models enabled by the digital technologies (like platforms). Such schemes often result in an uncertain employment status, which in turn hampers the effectiveness of labour law protections. Thus, the analysis will also review the measures undertaken by EU policymakers to tackle the under-protection of such workers. Section III will focus on the way in which working conditions are affected by technological innovations. It will assess the fitness of the current regulatory framework to respond to such challenges, referring as examples to the legislation on working time and information and consultation. Section IV will look into the policy context, with a focus on the undergoing proposals for the introduction of new statutory provisions. Section V will conclude.

## II. The Scope of EU Law and the Employment Status of Platform Workers

As Martin Gruber-Risak and Tamás Gyulavári explain in their chapters, the business models put in place by digital platforms permit the covert exercise of managerial prerogatives and the avoidance of the accountabilities linked to the formal status of employer: for instance, by substituting traditional command and control schemes with more subtle reputational mechanisms that can similarly influence the execution of the work performance.

In theoretical terms, there is no clear position on whether such a condition of under-protection should be addressed by an 'universalistic' extension of the scope of labour law (which could be obtained either by broadening the concept of employee[21] or by manipulating it to match more closely the phenomenology of platform work)[22] or with a selective approach, based on a case-by-case assessment of the actual needs of each category of workers and of the rights required to fulfil those needs.[23]

[20] I have tried to develop this argument in I Senatori, 'Regulating the Employment Relationship in the Organization 4.0: Between Social Justice and Economic Efficiency' in A Perulli and T Treu (eds), *The Future of Work: Labour Law and Labour Market Regulation in the Digital Era* (Alphen aan den Rijn, Kluwer Law International, 2020) 191.

[21] G Davidov, 'Setting Labour Law's Coverage: Between Universalism and Selectivity' in A Perulli (ed), *Lavoro autonomo e capitalismo delle piattaforme* (Milan, Wolters Kluwer-Cedam, 2018) 49; A Aloisi, '"Time Is Running Out". The Yodel Order and Its Implications for Platform Work in the EU' (2020) 13 *Italian Labour Law e-Journal* 67, 81, who maintains that 'To avoid conflicts concerning the specific connotations of the categories, a broader construction of the subjective scope of protection could be developed, without dissolving the very notion of employment'.

[22] N Countouris and V De Stefano, *New Trade Union Strategies for New Forms of Employment* (Brussels, ETUC, 2019).

[23] This position includes the advocates of 'intermediate categories': see A Perulli, 'Platform Capitalism and Labour Law' in A Perulli and T Treu (eds), *The Future of Work: Labour Law and Labour Market Regulation in the Digital Era* (Alphen aan den Rijn, Kluwer Law International, 2020) 111.

The authors mentioned above convincingly argue that the phenomenology of platform work is too diverse to assume a one-size-fits-all solution, and claim that the plain application of labour law resulting from the attribution of employee status to all the platform workers would really benefit only a share of them.

EU labour law mirrors very closely the terms of this theoretical debate. On the one side, it features such instruments as the Directive on Transparent and Predictable Working Conditions in the European Union,[24] which applies only to 'employees' under the meaning elaborated by national jurisdictions and the Court of Justice of the European Union (CJEU), and whose extension to platform workers is therefore problematic.[25] On the other side, there are instruments whose coverage exceeds the boundaries of employment status, which can be applied at certain conditions to platform workers irrespective of the classification of their employment relationship. An example of this kind is the legislation on non-discrimination. With the publication of the European Commission's 'Guidelines on the application of EU competition law to collective agreements regarding the working conditions of solo self-employed persons',[26] this group of instruments now also includes the right to collective bargaining.

The picture must also take account of the Platform Proposal (referred to in section I), which, as it will be explained below, introduces a 'mixed' regulatory approach to the issue. Its main elements and expected impact will be addressed into detail in section IV of this chapter, together with other relevant reform initiatives. However, since its contents are partly coordinated with the instruments analysed in the following sub-sections, it will also be mentioned, when necessary, in this part.

## A. The Transparent and Predictable Working Conditions Directive

The Directive on Transparent and Predictable Working Conditions contains provisions that are specifically designed to guarantee minimum protections to non-standard workers who operate under unpredictable work patterns. For instance, it places an obligation on the employer to inform such workers on specific elements of the employment contract like the number of guaranteed paid hours, the reference hours and days within which the worker may be required to work, the minimum notice period to which the worker is entitled before the start of a work assignment and, where applicable, the deadline for cancellation.[27] Furthermore, it provides that in case the above requirements are not met, a worker shall have the right to refuse a work assignment without adverse consequences.[28]

[24] Directive (EU) 2019/1152 of the European Parliament and of the Council of 20 June 2019 on transparent and predictable working conditions in the European Union (Transparent and Predictable Working Conditions Directive) [2019] OJ L186/105.

[25] E Menegatti, 'The Evolving Concept of "Worker" in EU Law' (2019) 12 *Italian Labour Law e-Journal* 71; N Kountouris, 'The Concept of "Worker" in European Labour Law: Fragmentation, Autonomy and Scope' (2018) 47 *Industrial Law Journal* 192.

[26] European Commission, 'Guidelines on the application of EU competition law to collective agreements regarding the working conditions of solo self-employed persons' (Communication Annex) C(2021) 8838 final.

[27] Transparent and Predictable Working Conditions Directive (n 24) Article 4(2)m.

[28] ibid, Article 10(2).

Finally, the Directive grants a specific protection to on-demand workers (a category perfectly fitted to most platform workers) with the aim of preventing the abuse of this form of work. It obliges Member States to provide for limitations on the use or the duration of such arrangements, or alternatively for a rebuttable presumption of the existence of an employment contract with a minimum amount of paid hours, based on the average hours worked during a given period.

The critical point about the personal scope of this piece of legislation consists of the adoption of a mixed definition of the employment relationship. The definition refers on the one hand to the laws, collective agreements or practices in force in each Member State, whereas on the other hand it requires to pay consideration to the case law of the Court of Justice. The adoption of such a 'hybrid' definition has been criticised by commentators on the ground of the difficulties that may emerge in the application of the provision when domestic and European notions are irreconcilable.[29] A circumstance that, as it has been noted, may bring to the exclusion of platform workers, as a result of the prevalence of the more restrictive definitions usually adopted in domestic jurisdictions. This is however a merely hypothetical 'worst scenario' perspective, as the principle of the primacy of EU law should lead to the prevalence of the interpretation elaborated by the Court of Justice, in which most platform workers should be easily accommodated.[30]

The complementarity between the Directive on Transparent and Predictable Working Conditions and the Platform Proposal may result in the increased protection of platform workers on two levels.

In fact, the Platform Proposal adds to the list of rights and protections enshrined in the Directive on Transparent and Predictable Working Conditions, mainly concerning the transparency of working time arrangements, a focus on another recurring issue of platform work, ie, the transparency of the automated monitoring and decision-making systems which usually govern the work performance. Article 6 (Chapter III entitled 'Algorithmic Management') requires, without prejudice to the obligations and rights set out by the Directive on Transparent and Predictable Working Conditions, that platforms inform workers of the existence of automated monitoring and decision-making systems in use, the categories of actions monitored, the decisions taken or supported by the automated systems, and the main parameters and grounds for those decisions.

Thus, for the workers who pass the employee test under both instruments, the interest to the transparency of organisational arrangements will be protected in both the crucial areas of working time and algorithmic management. For the workers who do not qualify as employees, and are therefore excluded from the scope of the Directive on Transparent and Predictable Working Conditions,[31] the Proposal provides for at

[29] B Bednarowicz, 'Delivering on the European Pillar of Social Rights: The New Directive on Transparent and Predictable Working Conditions in the European Union' (2019) 48 *Industrial Law Journal* 604.

[30] Potocka-Sionek and Aloisi (n 1); L Ratti, 'A Long Road Towards the Regulation of Platform Work in the EU' in JM Miranda Boto and E Brameshuber (eds), *Collective Bargaining and the Gig Economy: A Traditional Tool for New Business Models* (Oxford, Hart Publishing, 2022) 39.

[31] As expressly confirmed by Recital 10 of the Platform Proposal.

least a minimum floor of rights. In fact, according to Article 10, the obligations set out in Article 6 apply also to 'persons performing platform work'. The latter is the umbrella-category defined in Article 2.1 of the Platform Proposal, which embraces 'any person performing platform work, irrespective of the contractual designation of the relationship between that individual and the digital labour platform by the parties involved'.[32]

## B. Non-Discrimination Law

Among the sectors of European labour law whose scope of application is not restricted in principle to the realm of the employment contract, and that therefore can be used to reinforce the universalistic approach to labour protections and embrace platform workers, a remarkable example is non-discrimination law.[33]

Article 21 of the Charter of Fundamental Rights of the European Union (CFREU) and Directive 2000/78/EC, establishing a general framework for equal treatment in employment and occupation (Equal Treatment Directive),[34] prohibit discrimination based on a wide series of grounds like religion, belief, disability, age and sexual orientation.[35] Directive 2000/78/EC is part of the 'second-generation' EU equality legislation, which was aimed at expanding the scope and systemic role of anti-discrimination law in the Union.[36] Article 21 CFREU has reinforced this strategy, not only by elevating the principle to the highest ranking among the sources of EU law, but mainly by virtue of its direct horizontal effect which, according to established case law of the Court of Justice, permits enforcement of the said principle in private litigations.[37]

Against such a background, the rationale for an expansion of anti-discrimination provisions beyond the domain of subordinate employment is seen favourably by legal scholars, although some have noted that EU legislation in this respect is still fragmented and ambivalent: therefore the process, to be completed, should be supported by way of interpretation.[38]

[32] Further analysis on this point will be developed in section IV.C.

[33] The applicability of the instruments of non-discrimination law to platform work is the exclusive topic of this sub-section. The feasibility of this branch of law to address the problems of digital work in general is addressed in ch 12 by Jeremias Adams-Prassl and ch 14 by Sylvaine Laulom in this volume.

[34] Council Directive 2000/78/EC of 27 November 2000 establishing a general framework for equal treatment in employment and occupation [2000] OJ L303/16.

[35] Article 21 CFREU covers a wider set of conditions including colour, ethnic and social origin, genetic features, language, membership of a national minority, property and birth, and its effects extend beyond employment relationships to every interpersonal and public–private relationship.

[36] E Muir, 'The Transformative Function of EU Equality Law' (2013) 5 *European Review of Private Law* 1231.

[37] M Bell, 'Article 21 CFREU. Non-discrimination' in E Ales, M Bell, O Deinert and S Robin-Olivier (eds), *International and European Labour Law: Article-by-Article Commentary* (Baden-Baden Hart-Beck-Nomos, 2018) 203.

[38] S Borelli and M Ranieri, 'La discriminazione nel lavoro autonomo. Riflessioni a partire dall'algoritmo Frank' (2021) 7 *Labour & Law Issues* 21; M Kullmann, 'Platform Work, Algorithmic Decision-Making, and EU Gender Equality Law' (2018) 34 *International Journal of Comparative Labour Law and Industrial Relations* 1. See also the contribution by Tamás Gyulavári, ch 7 in this volume.

An interesting application of the above considerations has been made by an Italian court in a case concerning a group of workers employed by a food delivery platform.[39] The judge found that the algorithm used by the platform to assign shifts and make other organisational decisions relating to the work performance had a discriminatory potential, insofar as it did not distinguish among the different personal situations of the 'riders'. In particular, the workers could be indirectly sanctioned for refusing a task regardless of the reasons for their refusal, and namely even in cases where it was due to the exercise of a constitutional right such as the participation in a strike or the fruition of a sick leave. In her line of reasoning, the judge bypassed the ascertainment of the classification of the contractual relationship at stake, simply noting that, pursuant to the domestic legislation enacted in application of the Equal Treatment Directive,[40] the prohibition of discrimination applied to employees and independent contractors alike.

A support to the effectiveness of non-discrimination law in the context of platform work could come from the Platform Proposal, which expressly states the purpose of protecting the right to non-discrimination.[41]

As a matter of fact, the prohibition of discrimination is not directly addressed in the body of the Proposal, which nonetheless introduces significant limitations and measures to discourage the actions that could lead to a potentially discriminatory decision and to sanction the effects of such actions. Such measures, which also cover the self-employed persons performing platform work,[42] include:

- The prohibition of processing data that are not intrinsically connected and strictly necessary for the work performance, like those concerning the emotional and psychological state of workers.[43]
- The obligation to ensure the regular monitoring of the impact of decisions taken or supported by automated systems.[44]
- The workers' right to obtain an explanation on any such decisions that significantly affect the working conditions and to request a review.
- The obligation on the platform to rectify decisions that are found to infringe workers' rights or offer adequate compensation in case a rectification is not possible.[45]

In this sense, the Platform Proposal should also be read in combination with the general protections laid down by Regulation (EU) 2016/679,[46] which the draft Directive by its

[39] Tribunale di Bologna, order 31 December 2020, *Filcams Cgil Bologna, Nidil Cgil Bologna, Filt Cgil Bologna v Deliveroo Italia srl* commented on by I Purificato, 'Behind the Scenes of Deliveroo's Algorithm: in the Blindness of "Frank" its Discriminatory Potential' (2021) 14 *Italian Labour Law e-Journal* 169.

[40] Namely Legislative Decree n 216/03.

[41] Recital 37.

[42] Article 10.

[43] Article 6.5.

[44] Article 7.1.

[45] Article 8.

[46] Regulation (EU) 2016/679 of the European Parliament and of the Council of 27 April 2016 on the protection of natural persons with regard to the processing of personal data and on the free movement of such data, and repealing Directive 95/46/EC [2016] OJ L119/1; on which see ch 15 by Frank Hendrickx in this volume.

express wording specifies and complements in order to adapt the rules to the peculiar features of platform work.

## C. The Right to Collective Bargaining and the Commission's Guidelines

Another interesting case concerns the entitlement of platform workers to the right to collective bargaining.

As is well known, EU law protects collective representation rights, and notably the right to collective bargaining, in a rather ambivalent way. On the one hand, it is qualified as a fundamental right and enshrined as such in the CFREU.[47] On the other hand, it is construed as an exemption from the general prohibition of cartels under EU competition law.[48]

The famous *Albany* doctrine of the CJEU admits only agreements pursuing the improvement of working and employment conditions that have been signed by representatives of employers and employees.[49] Following this line of reasoning, the Court of Justice excluded, in the equally famous *FNV Kunsten* case, that the same immunity could be enjoyed by agreements signed by associations of self-employed persons, unless the latter were found to be 'false self-employed', ie, 'service providers in a situation comparable to that of' subordinate workers.[50]

Once again, employment status functions here as the demarcation line of a binary system that separates workers covered by labour law protections and workers treated in the same way as undertakings, thus hampering the condition of those placed in a 'grey zone', including people employed by digital platforms.

Such a formalistic approach, which deprives increasing shares of the workforce of a crucial instrument for the improvement of their working conditions, has been counteracted by several proposals aimed at realigning the terms of the relationship between collective labour law and competition law to the social and economic reality.

One position relies on the qualification of collective bargaining as a fundamental right embedded into the human rights framework.[51] This argues that the meaning and

[47] Article 28, in connection with Article 12 (freedom of association).

[48] Article 101, Consolidated Version of the Treaty on the Functioning of the European Union [2016] OJ C202/1.

[49] Case C-67/96 *Albany International BV v Stichting Bedrijfspensioenfonds Textielindustrie* ECLI:EU:C:1999:430, ECR [1999] I-05751.

[50] Case C-413/13 *FNV Kunsten Informatie en Media v Staat der Nederlanden*, ECLI:EU:C:2014:2411 [2014] para 42.

[51] According to the famous 'Demir and Baykara' doctrine of the European Court of Human Rights: see ECtHR, Grand Chamber, Case *Demir and Baykara v Turkey*, 34503/97, 12 November 2008, ECLI:CE:ECHR:2008:1112JUD003450397. According to the Court, the right to collective bargaining is an essential element of the right to freedom of association enshrined in Article 11 of the European Convention on Human Rights (ECHR). The scheme also applies to the EU system, not only because the CFREU expressly recognises both rights (Articles 12 and 28), but by virtue of the provision at Article 52(3) CFREU which states that 'In so far as this Charter contains rights which correspond to rights guaranteed by the Convention for the Protection of Human Rights and Fundamental Freedoms, the meaning and scope of those rights shall be the same as those laid down by the said Convention'.

personal scope of the right should be interpreted broadly, as to also encompass the self-employed, or at least those self-employed who are in a position of contractual imbalance and vulnerability comparable to that of employees, in line with the ILO jurisprudence formed on Conventions 87 and 98.[52]

On a different line of reasoning, other commentators have proposed reconceptualising the rationale of the antitrust provisions enshrined in the Treaty and the very relationship between labour law and competition law. This position can be advocated from the perspectives of labour law and competition law alike. On the latter side, as Tihamér Tóth argues in this book, competition law tolerates the application of the antitrust immunity to both employees and self-employed if the economic characteristics of the actors are almost identical, particularly with regard to their bargaining power. From the labour law field, Nicola Countouris and Silvia Rainone maintained that the risks typically tackled by collective bargaining are no longer faced by employees alone, but in the factual reality they are extended to certain categories of independent contractors, such as platform workers. Therefore, these authors contend that the *Albany* immunity should also be extended to embrace all the contractual relationships characterised by dependency, as demonstrated by a set of alternative indicators such as: predominantly personal work (a situation that could easily apply to platform workers); provision of a service consisting in the same activity as the one run by the client; or provision of a service for a potential competitor in the market.[53]

Years of intense doctrinal debates have paved the way for an initiative launched by the European Commission, which in March 2021 started a consultation with the European Social Partners on possible measures to ensure that EU competition rules do not stand in the way of collective bargaining for certain solo self-employed people.[54] As a result, in December 2021 the Commission published the 'Guidelines on the application of EU competition law to collective agreements regarding the working conditions of solo self-employed persons'.[55]

The nature of the document is that of a self-commitment by the Commission on the way it will apply EU competition law. It does not aim to interfere with the legal definitions of worker and self-employed,[56] nor precludes the further interpretation of Article 101 of the Treaty on the Functioning of the European Union (TFEU) by the Court of Justice.[57] Interestingly, these statements of 'institutional fair-play' may also be

[52] N Contouris and V De Stefano, 'The Labour Law Framework: Self-Employed and Their Right to Bargain Collectively' (2021) *Bulletin of comparative labour relations*, available at SSRN: www.ssrn.com/abstract=3763214.

[53] S Rainone and N Countouris, 'Collective bargaining and self-employed workers. The need for a paradigm shift' (2021) 11 *ETUI Policy Brief* 5.

[54] The initiative is based on the assumption that 'Whilst it is not for competition policy to address the social challenges faced by self-employed people, the initiative could ensure that EU competition rules do not prevent self-employed in a weak position from engaging in collective negotiations or agreements to improve their working conditions': European Commission, 'Competition: Commission invites stakeholders to provide comments on the application of EU competition law to collective bargaining agreements for self-employed', Press Release, Brussels, 5 March 2021.

[55] European Commission, Communication Annex (n 26).

[56] Guideline 11.

[57] Guideline 12.

interpreted as a window that the Commission leaves open for a possible legal generalisation of its regulatory position. In the same sense, it is stressed that collective agreements concluded by self-employed persons that are not covered by the Guidelines should not be automatically considered as in breach of Article 101 TFEU.[58]

The Guidelines do not engage in a systematic discussion of the subjective scope of the right to collective bargaining under Article 28 CFREU. This comes as no surprise, considering that the initiative originates from the Directorate General on Competition. In fact, the focus of the document is on the concept of undertaking adopted by competition law, and on the conditions that determine the loss of the status of undertaking by a self-employed person.[59]

The personal scope of the Guidelines is determined by looking at the bargaining weakness of self-employed workers, which justifies the exemption from EU competition law. The main requirement is that the person shall be a 'solo self-employed', ie, an individual who is not in an employment relationship but nonetheless relies primarily on her personal labour for the provision of the services concerned.[60] In particular, the personal work must be the primary but not the exclusive means for the execution of the performance: hence the use of 'ancillary means' does not imply that the worker should be classified as un undertaking.

The additional criteria are articulated differently, depending on whether the solo self-employed is or is not in a situation comparable with that of a worker, regardless of whether she fulfils the criteria for being reclassified as a false self-employed.

To remain within the thematic boundaries of this chapter, it is remarkable to note that solo self-employed working through digital platforms are considered 'per se' in a situation comparable with workers,[61] in a sort of 'unrebuttable presumption' of economic dependency and contractual weakness that clearly stems from the accurate observation of the economic reality of platform work. However, it must be noted that the situation protected by the Guidelines as regards platform workers is not determined by market conditions alone (unlike the situation of economically dependent workers addressed by Guideline 24), but also by the functional integration of the worker in the business. In fact, the Guidelines adopt the same definition of a platform as laid down in the Platform Proposal, which requires that the service provided by the platform should involve as a necessary and essential component the organisation of work performed by individuals.[62]

It is probably unrealistic to expect that the acknowledgement of the right to collective bargaining for self-employed persons performing platform work will automatically enhance their collective power, considering that it does not imply any formal entitlement to force platforms into negotiations. However, it should be noted that the Guidelines extend the immunity to preparatory actions and other forms of pressure undertaken by associations or groups of solo self-employed persons to compel their counterparties to negotiate, such as the decision to refuse the provision of services to a

[58] Guideline 13.
[59] Guideline 9.
[60] Guideline 19.
[61] Guideline 28.
[62] A solution that resembles the Italian category of hetero-organised work under Article 2 of Legislative Decree n° 81/15.

client who is not willing to enter into an agreement, or the coordination and exchange of information between the parties of each bargaining side.[63]

The picture should then be completed with the prerogatives granted to the workers' representatives by the Platform Proposal. They include the possibility to use the digital infrastructure of the platform to communicate with workers,[64] the right to receive information from the platforms on the occupational status of their workers,[65] and the right to enforce workers' rights and obligations by engaging in judicial and administrative procedures.[66]

Read in this broader context, the likelihood of collective bargaining to represent an effective self-regulation tool, by which this category of platform workers can win better terms and conditions without relying only on statutory concessions, can be assessed more optimistically.[67]

## III. Working Conditions and Digital Employment Patterns: The Responsiveness of EU Law

Digital tools enable changes in the work organisation and work performance which impact on working conditions and workers' rights, questioning the capacity of the current regulatory instruments to maintain their protective function while safeguarding at the same time the efficiency of the production processes.

This section will examine the problem from the point of view of EU law, focusing on two examples: working time, and information and consultation (I&C). The first is a paradigm of how new employment patterns put under stress the established categories of labour law. The second is the typical instrument envisaged by the Union to provide workers with the power to influence collectively the managerial decisions on strategic and organisational issues that may affect their interests, like those implied in technological transformation.

### A. Working Time

The rules on working time typically play a twofold role. On the one hand, they are an instrument aimed at safeguarding occupational health and safety (OHS). This is the function specifically addressed by the Working Time Directive, in coordination with the 'right to limitation of maximum working hours, to daily and weekly rest periods and to an annual period of paid leave' affirmed by Article 31 CFREU.[68] On the other hand, they

[63] Guidelines 16 and 17.
[64] Article 15.
[65] Article 12.
[66] Article 14.
[67] On this point see also Ratti (n 30).
[68] V Leccese, 'Directive 2003/88/EC concerning certain aspects of the organization of working time' in E Ales, M Bell, O Deinert and S Robin-Olivier (eds), *International and European Labour Law: Article-by-Article Commentary* (Baden-Baden, Hart-Beck-Nomos, 2018) 1285.

are a parameter for the assessment of the fulfilment of the work obligation and for the remuneration of the work activity. Both these functions are deeply affected by digital technologies used in the work processes.

The binary structure of the Working Time Directive, based on the rigid separation of work and rest time, shows its limitations when faced with digitally enabled remote work arrangements. In particular, digital tools and fast-connectivity devices 'augment'[69] the managerial power to direct and control workers at any time,[70] while also facilitating the introduction of flexible time patterns characterised by the frequent succession of work and standby periods.[71]

While the issue is comprehensively addressed by Gábor Kártyás in this book, these notes will only consider some examples, useful to expose the structural deficiencies of the EU working time legislation in the face of the technological and organisational changes linked to digitalisation.

The first case concerns the employer's obligation to put into place a system for the measurement of working time, pursuant to the *CCOO v Daimler* judgment of the Court of Justice.[72] Digital devices may facilitate the compliance with the Court's requirements, since in most cases the software used for control and communication purposes could also be used to measure work hours remotely. However, while this may be true in situations in which the work activity is carried out according to regular time patterns, it could be more problematic in the case of the adoption of target-oriented organisational models that afford workers a certain degree of autonomy in the organisation of their working hours.[73] The Court itself has pointed out that the obligation to measure work hours does not apply in the cases covered by derogations under Article 17 Working Time Directive, including 'when, on account of the specific characteristics of the activity concerned, the duration of the working time is not measured and/or predetermined or can be determined by the workers themselves'.[74] On the other hand, Article 17 Working Time Directive requires that even when the derogations apply, the 'general principles on the protection of the safety and health of workers must be paid due regard': hence, even workers who self-determine their work hours must be granted specific OHS protections.[75]

This example helps to argue the case for an update to the regulatory toolkit. In particular, it seems clear that the rules should ensure that workers who self-organise their schedule are prevented from harming their health and wellbeing, not only when external interferences come from the employer, but also when they flow from their

[69] As maintained by Antonio Aloisi in ch 13 in this volume.

[70] LF Eisenstadt, 'Employer or Big Brother? Data Analytics and Incursion into Workers' Personal Lives' in T Addabbo et al (eds), *Performance Appraisal in Modern Employment Relations: An Interdisciplinary Approach* (Cham, Palgrave Macmillan, 2020) 165.

[71] R Krause, '"Always-on": The Collapse of the Work–Life Separation in Recent Developments, Deficits and Counter-Strategies' in E Ales et al (eds), *Working in Digital and Smart Organizations: Legal, Economic and Organizational Perspectives on the Digitalization of Labour Relations* (Cham, Palgrave Macmillan, 2020) 223.

[72] Case C-55/18 *Federación de Servicios de Comisiones Obreras (CCOO) v Deutsche Bank SAE* ECLI:EU:C:2019:402 [2019].

[73] A case that Gábor Kártyás, ch 8 in this volume, defines unlikely, but that still may theoretically occur or become more frequent with the further development of technologies and organisational models.

[74] Article 17(1), Working Time Directive (n 16).

[75] Leccese (n 68).

personal inclination to work long hours. The legislative elaboration on the right to disconnect, which will be addressed in section IV of this chapter, may bring about an improvement.[76]

A connected question may arise in the case in which the work obligation is fulfilled at home with the freedom to self-organise the working hours, but with a parallel obligation to remain available for calls in certain time slots.[77] The relevant question here is to distinguish the constraints on the enjoyment of free time during stand-by periods that depend on the worker's own choice from those owed to a contractual or organisational arrangement. Such blurred situations may be at odds with the straightforward scheme adopted by the CJEU, which considers decisive for a stand-by period to be classified as working time the fact that the constraints imposed on that worker during the given period are such as to affect her ability to manage freely the hours during which her professional services are not required, and to devote that time to her own interests.[78]

Finally, since the material scope of the Working Time Directive is limited to health and safety purposes, the definitions elaborated under its framework, and notably the binary divide between work and rest time, do not apply to other functions of working time, such as the assessment and the remuneration of the work performance. However, also from this different perspective the organisational patterns of digital work raise questions that involve the contents and the quality of EU law.

EU law neglects to qualify stand-by periods for purposes other than health and safety, although in some cases the Working Time Directive definitions have been used by national courts to decide on matters falling beyond their natural scope.[79] This leaves unaddressed the problems faced by the forms of digital work for which the fact of staying on-call in given time spans represents a distinctive and necessary element, as in the case of Uber drivers or food delivery riders.

The CJEU has consistently acknowledged that the remunerability of stand-by periods is excluded from the scope of the Working Time Directive and must be addressed by the law of the Member States.[80] This does not imply, however, that the issue could not be addressed by other pieces of EU legislation. The exclusion of a legislative competence of the EU on the matter of pay, pursuant to Article 153(5) TFEU, does not appear to be a sufficient ground to justify a total self-restraint. In fact, what is being discussed in this case is not how to fix the level of wages, but rather how to ensure fair

[76] E Ales, 'Adapting Labor Law to "Digital" Work: Between Scholarly Interpretation, Case Law and Legislative Intervention' in A Perulli and T Treu (eds), *The Future of Work: Labour Law and Labour Market Regulation in the Digital Era* (Alphen aan den Rijn, Kluwer Law International, 2020) 225.

[77] I Senatori and C Spinelli, '(Re-)Regulating Remote Work in the Post-pandemic Scenario: Lessons from the Italian Experience' (2021) 14 *Italian Labour Law e-Journal* 85.

[78] Leccese (n 68).

[79] Examples include the recent decision of the UK Supreme Court in *Uber v Aslam* [2021] UKSC 5, and the case examined by the referring court in the CJEU's decision *Radiotelevizija Slovenija* (n 80).

[80] Case C-344/19 *DJ v Radiotelevizija Slovenija* ECLI:ECLI:EU:C:2021:182 [2021], para 58: 'the way in which workers are remunerated for periods of stand-by time is not covered by Directive 2003/88 but by the relevant provisions of national law. Consequently, that directive does not preclude the application of a law of a Member State, a collective labour agreement, or an employer's decision that, for the purposes of the remuneration of stand-by time which makes a distinction between the treatment of periods in the course of which work is actually done and those during which no actual work is done'.

working conditions to a certain category of workers, in line with Article 153(1) TFEU.[81] The Directive on Transparent and Predictable Working Conditions in the European Union could have been the appropriate instrument to assert the principle that minimum pay should be provided for the stand-by periods in the situations protected by the Directive itself, at least in the cases of entirely or mostly unpredictable work patterns addressed in Article 10, ie, under the same conditions that preclude the worker from the right to refuse an assignment.[82] The choice made by EU lawmakers, that limits the compensation to the case in which the employer cancels a previous assignment after the expiry of a deadline, does not seem sufficiently aligned to the structure of the new forms of work, and as such it is not fit to wholly address the interests of the workers involved.

## B. Information and Consultation

I&C rights are the subject matter of a conspicuous body of secondary EU legislation that finds its 'constitutional' correspondence in Article 27 CFREU, stating that 'workers or their representatives must, at the appropriate levels, be guaranteed information and consultation in good time in the cases and under the conditions provided for by Community law and national laws and practices'.

The purpose of I&C rights is to promote the establishment of a method for the governance of the affairs of the company, in the form of a meaningful dialogue between workers and management on matters of common interest. By engaging directly with the decision-making authority of the undertaking ('at the appropriate levels'), in the course of the deliberative process and before it has come to an end ('in good time'), the workers, as individuals or (most likely) by means or their representatives, do not only enjoy the possibility to have their voice heard, but exert a power to influence the final managerial decision.

Considering that, as it has been recalled above, digital transformation is mostly about organisational decisions concerning the adoption and the use of new technologies in the production and work processes, I&C rights can represent a suitable instrument to govern the phenomenon in a manner consistent with the goal of improving of the quality of working conditions.[83]

[81] As recalled by E Ales, 'Article 153 TFEU' in E Ales, M Bell, O Deinert and S Robin-Olivier (eds), *International and European Labour Law: Article-by-Article Commentary* (Baden-Baden, Hart-Beck-Nomos, 2018) 155, 164, the CJEU holds that 'the "pay" exception cannot be extended to any question involving any sort of link with pay; otherwise, some of the areas referred to in Article 153(1) TFEU would be deprived of much of their substance'.

[82] Such conditions are that the work takes place within predetermined reference hours and days and that the worker is informed by his or her employer of a work assignment within a reasonable notice period established in accordance with national law, collective agreements or practice.

[83] The 'European Pillar of Social Rights Action Plan' supports this view where, as in was mentioned in the first section of this chapter, it commits itself to improve the implementation and enforcement of the *acquis communautaire* in the field of I&C: European Commission, 'The European Pillar of Social Rights Action Plan' (n 11).

First, the subject matters of I&C procedures resonate with the strategic and organisational situations that could occur in a context of digitalisation, as for instance:

- 'the situation, structure and probable development of employment within the undertaking or establishment and on any anticipatory measures envisaged, in particular where there is a threat to employment';[84]
- 'decisions likely to lead to substantial changes in work organization or in contractual relations';[85]

or

- 'substantial changes concerning organization, introduction of new working methods or production processes'.[86]

Second, I&C instruments cover both nation-scale and transnational business entities, a characteristic that makes them capable of intercepting, at least in principle, the new digital business models operating globally through platforms or supply chains.[87]

Third, while the I&C directives aim at ensuring the effectiveness of employee involvement (*effét utile*), they also take into account the economic interests of the company, by preventing decisional stalemates caused by excessively protracted consultations[88] and safeguarding the confidentiality on sensible issues.[89]

Lastly, I&C procedures can represent an empowerment tool for workers, facilitating their access to collective negotiations and to the conclusion of collective agreements and, more broadly, supporting the establishment of democratic methods to accompany the digital transformation of the workplace. EU law expressly provides for the possibility that information and consultation can lead to contractual relations.[90] The Court of Justice, in turn, has acknowledged that an agreement concluded in the course of a codetermination procedure is protected under Article 28 CFREU as an expression of the right to collective bargaining.[91]

[84] Directive 2002/14/EC of the European Parliament and of the Council of 11 March 2002 establishing a general framework for informing and consulting employees in the European Community/Framework Directive) [2002] OJ L80/29, Article 4(2)b.

[85] ibid, Article 4(2)c.

[86] Directive 2009/38/EC on the establishment of a European Works Council or a procedure in Community-scale undertakings and Community-scale groups of undertakings for the purposes of informing and consulting employees (Recast) [2009] L122/28 Annex I – Subsidiary requirements.

[87] EU law has created specific bodies and machineries to carry out employee involvement on a transnational scale, like the European Works Councils and the involvement procedures in the Societas Europaea and in the European Cooperative Company.

[88] Article 1(2) of the European Works Council (Recast) Directive (n 86) stipulates that 'The arrangements for informing and consulting employees shall be defined and implemented in such a way as to ensure their effectiveness and to enable the undertaking or group of undertakings to take decisions effectively'.

[89] Confidentiality provisions may function in two ways: they may limit, upon specific request from the company, the possibility of the employees' representatives entitled to I&C procedures to disclose the information to other employees, or may exempt the employer from discussing issues whose disclosure could harm or be prejudicial to the functioning of the undertaking, eg, Article 6 Directive 2002/14, see (n 84).

[90] Article 4(2) Directive 2002/14 (n 84) stipulates that consultation shall take place 'with a view to reaching an agreement'.

[91] Case C-699/17 *Allianz Vorsorgekasse AG* ECLI:EU:C:2019:290 [2019].

The high potential of I&C institutions may be further enhanced, in line with the purpose expressed by the European Commission to 'improve the implementation and enforcement of the *acquis communautaire* in the field'. This may happen by adapting the legal concepts and machineries to the new entrepreneurial structures and to the new dynamics of collective workers' representation, that are themselves a by-product of digital transformation. Among the challenges that require a specific response, the fragmentation and the 'de-materialisation' of the digital workplace[92] may suggest, for instance, a review of the concepts of undertaking and establishment, which demarcate the 'geographical' scope of the involvement procedures, as well as of the thresholds that activate the procedures. Also, the prerequisites of the confidentiality provisions, which may be highly controversial at the implementation stage, should be tested in order to ensure that the confidentiality exception is not abusively invoked by companies to hamper the effectiveness of employee involvement.

In the same direction, I&C has been relaunched by the Platform Proposal as a tool to strengthen the collective protections of platform workers. Article 9 of the Proposal stipulates that the representatives of platform workers, if existing,[93] must be informed and consulted on decisions 'likely to lead to the introduction of or substantial changes in the use of automated monitoring and decision-making systems'. The provision, which applies only to platform workers hired under a contract of employment, integrates the general rules enshrined in the I&C Framework Directive and addresses one of the topical issues of platform work.

## IV. Recent Policy Initiatives

As the two previous sections attempted to show, the current body of EU employment legislation is not totally ill-equipped to protect workers in the face of the changed working conditions prompted by digital transformation. In some cases a strategy of targeted adjustments of existing rules may suffice to improve the quality of the regulatory framework and realign it with the new patterns.

Nonetheless, in other cases the pervasiveness of the phenomenon and its capacity to disrupt the established categories and paradigms are such that a simple maintenance of the existing instruments may not be a satisfactory response. The European policymakers have undertaken several initiatives to dig deeper into these problems. Such initiatives follow different albeit interconnected trajectories, and it is not possible, within the limits of this chapter, to provide a systematic and comprehensive reconstruction of their contents, rationales and internal consistency. The analysis will therefore focus on three specific items that can be considered as representative of the general debate and present a connection with the arguments developed so far in this chapter: the right to disconnect, artificial intelligence and platform work.

[92] As addressed by Ales (n 76).

[93] The residual option of informing and consulting the individual workers concerned, in case no representative structure is in place (Article 9.1) goes in the direction of ensuring an effective involvement of workers, but it may represent a disincentive to the development of collective strategies for the advancement of workers' rights.

## A. The Right to Disconnect

The urgency for an effective regulation of the right to disconnect, which was referred to above in section III, is confirmed by the broad policy elaboration on the topic, which has engaged the European Commission, the Parliament and the European Social Partners alike.[94] The most advanced initiative so far is the one elaborated by the European Parliament with its Resolution of 21 January 2021,[95] that contains a legislative proposal for a Directive addressed to the European Commission (Disconnection Proposal).

Referring to the chapter by Gábor Kártyás for useful considerations on the coordination between the Parliament's initiative and the Working Time Directive, two elements are particularly worth mentioning here, as they pertain to the arguments developed in this chapter.

First, the scope of the Disconnection Proposal potentially extends beyond the realm of traditional employment relationships. By covering 'all workers, independent of their status and their working arrangements',[96] it refers to the notion of worker elaborated by the jurisprudence of the CJEU, aiming to encompass 'on-demand workers, part-time workers, intermittent workers, voucher based-workers, platform workers, trainees and apprentices'.[97] With its extensive approach, the Proposal qualifies itself as another tile in the mosaic of protections that EU law is building around platform work. More generally, it represents a significant acknowledgement of the 'horizontal' pervasiveness of the 'always-on' work patterns enabled by digitalisation, and a welcome attempt to address in a comprehensive way the problems it entails for different categories of workers.

Second, the Disconnection Proposal adopts a broad notion of the right to disconnect, defined as the right 'not to engage in work-related activities or communications by means of digital tools, directly or indirectly, outside working time'.[98] This formulation departs from the minimalist interpretations provided by the European Social Partners and some national jurisdictions,[99] which focus solely on safeguarding the worker from undue external interferences with her private time (like off-hour calls or emails). In fact, the words used by the Proposal encompass any kind of organisational or motivational coercion, even if implicit or self-produced, to exceed the work schedule.

This construction of the right has a strong potential, particularly for persons who work under flexible and self-managed work patterns. For such workers, it may provide the legal grounds to claim full sovereignty on the organisation of their work schedule. Interpreted in this sense, the right to disconnect may represent a first step towards a comprehensive reconceptualisation of working time, exceeding the sole function of protecting workers' health and safety.

[94] On the European Social Partners' position, enshrined in the Framework Agreement on Digitalisation, see ch 3 by Edoardo Ales in this volume.
[95] European Parliament, 'Resolution on the right to disconnect' (n 15).
[96] ibid, Article 1(1).
[97] ibid, Recital 15.
[98] ibid, Article 2(1).
[99] On the position of the European Social Partners' Framework Agreement on Digitalisation in this regard, see Senatori, 'The European Framework Agreement on Digitalisation' (n 18). On national legislations see ch 8 by Gábor Kártyás in this volume.

Besides these considerations, the European Parliament's initiative seems well integrated into the regulatory system. It complements existing instruments (mainly in the OHS domain) and aligns with the recent case law of the CJEU, where it commits Member States to 'ensure that employers set up an objective, reliable and accessible system enabling the duration of time worked each day by each worker to be measured'.[100] Furthermore, it rightly acknowledges that an effective work–life balance requires a change in the culture of work organisation, and mobilises to this end a mix of prescriptive and promotional measures. These circumstances qualify the Disconnection Proposal as a promising instrument for the improvement of the time-related working conditions in the digital context.

However, some clarifications could still be needed on specific issues. For instance, it is not clear how the obligation to ensure the measurement of working time will coordinate with the exemptions accorded by the CJEU in *CCOO*, in line with Article 17 Working Time Directive, and whether one may infer from the apparently unconditional provision of Article 3.2 of the Disconnection Proposal a removal of these exceptions. The solution to this problem may be provided by the European Social Partners. Collective agreements are, in fact, the instrument that the Disconnection Proposal puts in charge of establishing the practical arrangements for the exercise and the implementation of the right to disconnect at the level of each undertaking.[101]

## B. Artificial Intelligence

As Artificial Intelligence (AI) systems become more sophisticated and affordable for companies, their use in employment relationships increases, to the extent that AI will likely become the epitome of the digital transformation of work.

The workplace applications of AI (algorithmic decision-making, people analytics, data-driven management and the like) are punctually addressed in part III of this book.[102] What it is worth stressing here is their capacity to reshape power relations in employment by fragmenting, disguising and ultimately magnifying the managerial prerogatives. This pervasive process encompasses almost every aspect of the employment relationship, and challenges the effectiveness of the legal protections in place on issues like data processing, surveillance, transparency of managerial decisions, discrimination and health and safety.

The EU regulatory approach in the field, as stated in the Commission's 2020 'White Paper on Artificial Intelligence. A European approach to excellence and trust',[103] is

[100] European Parliament, 'Resolution on the right to disconnect' (n 15) Article 3(2).

[101] As provided for in Recital 21 of the Proposal: 'The practical arrangements for the exercise of the right to disconnect by the worker and the implementation of that right by the employer should be able to be agreed by the Social Partners by means of collective agreement or at the level of the employer undertaking'. For examples drawn from national experiences see ch 8 by Gábor Kártyás in this volume. See also Senatori and Spinelli (n 77).

[102] Particularly in ch 12 by Jeremias Adams-Prassl and ch 13 by Antonio Aloisi.

[103] European Commission, 'Artificial Intelligence – A European approach to excellence and trust' (White Paper) COM(2020) 65 final.

focused on the promotion of the development of market opportunities for AI. A goal only mitigated by commitment to the minimisation of the attached risks, including those affecting fundamental rights. In particular, the White Paper notes that:

> The use of AI can affect the values on which the EU is founded and lead to breaches of fundamental rights, including the rights to freedom of expression, freedom of assembly, human dignity, non-discrimination based on sex, racial or ethnic origin, religion or belief, disability, age or sexual orientation, as applicable in certain domains, protection of personal data and private life, or the right to an effective judicial remedy and a fair trial, as well as consumer protection.[104]

The Commission seems to acknowledge the 'horizontal' nature of AI, and consistently envisages a comprehensive regulation of its manifold implications. The follow-up initiative,[105] known as the 'Artificial Intelligence Act' (currently at the proposal stage; hereinafter the Act), proceeds along the same lines. However, its contents have raised a serious criticism as regards their capacity to live up to the commitment to guarantee an effective protection of fundamental rights, especially in the employment context.[106]

The rationale of the proposed Act is plainly clarified in the Explanatory Memorandum:

> The proposal presents a balanced and proportionate horizontal regulatory approach to AI that is limited to the minimum necessary requirements to address the risks and problems linked to AI, without unduly constraining or hindering technological development or otherwise disproportionately increasing the cost of placing AI solutions on the market.[107]

This idea of minimum harmonisation unveils the priority granted to market concerns over social considerations; an impression that is confirmed by the envisaged implementation strategy, inspired by the risk-based approach adopted in other sectors like product safety (again, a methodology quite far from those generally applied in labour law).[108]

AI systems used in employment relationships, workers' management and access to self-employment, for tasks such as recruitment, making decisions on promotion, termination and task allocation, monitoring or evaluation, are classified as high risk.[109] As such, they are not prohibited but are made subject to a risk-management procedure based on the principle of mitigation. This implies that the prior compliance with certain given requirements on data governance, drafting of technical documentation, record-keeping, transparency and information for users, human oversight on the functioning of the AI system is enough to render the use of the AI system permissible. In other words, the machinery accepts any residual risk stemming from the use of AI, provided

[104] ibid, 10.

[105] European Commission, Artificial Intelligence Communication (n 8).

[106] V De Stefano, 'The EU Proposed Regulation on AI: a threat to labour protection?' *Global Workplace Law & Policy* (16 April 2021), available at: www.regulatingforglobalization.com/2021/04/16/the-eu-proposed-regulation-on-ai-a-threat-to-labour-protection/.

[107] European Commission, Artificial Intelligence Communication (n 8) 3.

[108] M Veale and F Zuiderveen Borgesius, 'Demystifying the Draft EU Artificial Intelligence Act' (2021) 22 *Computer Law Review International*, Pre-print, July 2021, Version 1.1.

[109] Recital 35 of the Act.

that the software 'is used in accordance with its intended purpose or under conditions of reasonably foreseeable misuse'.[110]

It appears clearly that the regulatory scheme envisaged in the Act is at odds with a traditional labour law perspective. What emerges at first glance is that the Act makes no mention of imperative prohibitions in the interest of workers, and makes little if any effort to tackle the inherent power imbalance between workers and employers that AI is capable of sharpening.[111]

Of course the picture is not completely dark, and the Act includes some welcome innovations. One example is the attraction of AI providers in the area of liability.[112] This innovation can be explained by the high complexity of algorithms, that makes them hardly intelligible by users/employers but, on the other hand, facilitates the diffusion of responsibilities among the different actors involved in the design and use of technological systems, as noted by Jeremias Adams-Prassl in his contribution. However, there is an urgent need to clarify whether this prospective piece of legislation has the potential to overrule the existing (and more protective) instruments provided for by EU and domestic labour law, as may happen if the Act was to be interpreted as pre-empting any concurrent legislation for unduly hampering the free trade of AI products.[113]

Two provisions of the Act may be used to mitigate the concern for such paradoxical effects. First, Article 29(2), states that the user obligations to use systems in accordance with the instructions supplied by the provider 'are without prejudice to other user obligations under Union or national law'. Therefore, one may argue that the obligations that existing labour law provisions put on the employer/user are not affected by the Act, although the text should be improved to make such interpretation more straightforward. Second, Article 69 promotes the elaboration of provisions to

> encourage and facilitate the drawing up of codes of conduct intended to foster the voluntary application to AI systems of requirements related for example to environmental sustainability, accessibility for persons with a disability, stakeholders' participation in the design and development of AI systems.

A formulation that could pave the way for the creation of additional sources to regulate the use of AI in work contexts, possibly incremental in terms of worker protections, with the intervention of qualified stakeholders like trade unions and workers' representatives.

## C. The Platform Proposal and the Presumption of Employee Status

The Proposal for a Directive on improving working conditions in platform work, already mentioned in previous parts of this chapter (sections II and III.B), is part

[110] Article 9(4) of the Act.

[111] Leaving aside the specific dangers, like the possibility to fulfil the conformity obligations by simply meeting a set of harmonised standards and the lack of enforcement instruments in the hands of the individuals affected by AI systems: see Veale and Zuiderveen Borgesius (n 108).

[112] Article 16 of the Act.

[113] A similar concern is expressed by M Kullmann and A Cefaliello, 'The Interconnection between the AI Act and the EU's Occupational Safety and Health Legal Framework' *Global Workplace Law & Policy* (24 January 2022), available at: www.global-workplace-law-and-policy.kluwerlawonline.com/2022/01/24/the-interconnection-between-the-ai-act-and-the-eus-occupational-safety-and-health-legal-framework/.

of a package of two concurrent initiatives adopted by the European Commission to address the manifest under-protection of platform workers. The second element of the package is the Guidelines on collective bargaining for solo self-employed examined in section II.C. Although the scope of the Guidelines is actually broader than platform work, they provide for innovations that are of great relevance for the improvement of employment conditions in that area.

The proposed Directive aims at introducing a comprehensive regulation of the contractual relationships between workers and platforms. It integrates and adjusts existing concepts and instruments that, as such, either are not fully applicable to this category of workers or do not guarantee the protection of their specific needs and interests.

The measures envisaged by the Directive aim to fulfil three aims:[114]

- To ensure the correct classification of the employment status of platform workers.
- To promote transparency in algorithmic management.
- To improve transparency on the structure and activity of the platforms, with a particular concern for the number of people employed and the terms and conditions applied to the contractual relationships. Such concern for labour market transparency derives from the transnational nature of most platforms, which complicates the traceability of their conduct in the single Member State in which they operate.

While the contents of the Directive relating to algorithmic management have been addressed in other sections of this chapter, here the discussion will focus on the crucial topic of employee classification.

The policy assumption behind the initiative, as explained in the Memorandum that precedes its normative provisions, is that most of the people who provide services through platforms are genuinely independent, and yet they need a floor of basic rights. A quantitatively relevant minority is instead in the position of a false self-employed: this group needs further protections, although not in such a way as to hamper the sustainable growth of this business model.

This bipartition finds a correspondence in the definition of two categories of workers, who benefit from different sets of protections:

- 'Persons performing platform work'[115] are the broader group encompassing subordinate workers and self-employed, and are covered only by the provisions on algorithmic management.
- 'Platform workers'[116] are a sub-group that designates those employed under an employment contract, and are covered by all the provisions of the Directive.

In this sense, the Directive proposes a mix of the regulatory approaches recalled in section I of this chapter. The 'selective' side identifies a closed set of rights to be extended to a determined category of workers (persons performing platform work), whereas the 'universal' side provides for a general application of protections, based on the fact that the recipients meet the specific definition of platform workers.

[114] As declared in Article 1.1.
[115] Article 2.1(3).
[116] Article 2.1(4).

The classification criteria therefore become central in this architecture. The relevant elements in this regard are represented by organisation and control.

The organisation of work is the factor that qualifies the platform as relevant for the purposes of this legislation.[117] In other words, it represents the minimum necessary linkage between the worker and the client (or employer) to establish some degree of accountability in charge of the latter. This means that neither of the two categories of workers will be covered by the rights devised in the Directive if the service to the final user is not provided by means of an organisational mediation by the platform.

Control is, on the other hand, the meta-criterion that indicates the existence of an employment relationship between the worker and the platform. Control is hence one of the forms by which the platform exercises its (fundamental) organisational function.

The technique adopted by the Directive to ensure the correct classification of the platform workers, on the grounds of the meta-criterion of control, is the rebuttable presumption of employment status. As Martin Gruber-Risak maintains in his chapter, this procedural machinery is a crucial weapon in the hands of the workers, to counterbalance the information asymmetries that characterise the platform business model by shifting to the presumed employer the burden to prove the non-existence of an employment relationship between the parties.

To trigger the legal presumption of an employment relationship the worker must present evidence, by means of the 'appropriate procedures'[118] and 'framework of measures'[119] that Member States are required to put in place, that at least two out of five conditions recur in the case at stake. These conditions are set out at Article 4.2, and encompass situations of functional control by the platform on the execution of the performance[120] and situations that resemble more closely the contractual or economic dependency of the worker towards the platform.[121]

The limited space of this chapter allows for only a few brief comments on the classification criteria and, more broadly, on the regulatory strategy chosen by the Commission.

First, the presumptive criteria seem to be in continuity with the evolving jurisprudence of the CJEU on the concept of worker, which incorporates elements linked to the direction, functional integration and 'economic reality' of the contractual relationship.[122] The specific formulation of the Directive has certainly been influenced by the conspicuous case law elaborated in the past years by national courts, which has shed light on the factual circumstances that characterise the control exercised by most of the platforms.[123] Nonetheless, some commentators have critically stressed that the presumption criteria will rarely match the features of certain categories like crowdworkers.[124]

[117] Article 2.1(1).

[118] Article 3.1.

[119] Article 4.1.

[120] Subjection to binding rules on the appearance, conduct towards the recipient of the service, performance of work, supervision or control on the quality of the results of the work activity.

[121] Unilateral determination or limit-setting for the level of remuneration, effective restriction of the freedom to choose one's working hours or periods of absence, to accept or refuse tasks or to use subcontractors, effective restriction of the possibility to build an own client base or to perform work for any third party.

[122] See Menegatti (n 25).

[123] In particular, many indicators have been clearly inspired by the Uber business model, as analytically dissected in the famous ruling of the UK Supreme Court in *Uber v Aslam* (n 79).

[124] See Ratti (n 30).

Second, the text shows that the EU legislator is well aware of the enabling role that the digital devices play in shaping the mechanisms put in place by platforms to exercise the managerial prerogatives. In this regard, the Directive stipulates that the appreciation of the facts of the case must take into account the use of algorithms in the organisation of platform work.[125] Supervision and limitation of the worker's discretion may also (but not only) derive from sanctioning systems, reviews and ratings by the recipients.[126]

Third, it will be interesting to see whether the technique inaugurated by the Directive will prove convincing enough to influence the judicial approach to the classification of employment status also beyond the realm of platform work. In fact, the generalisation of the presumptive approach by means of interpretation may represent a step forward in the harmonisation of the concept of worker at EU level.

## V. Conclusions

The recent initiatives undertaken by the EU policymakers indicate the awareness of the urgency of a regulatory intervention aimed at filling the gaps and closing the loopholes that threaten the working conditions of people who work under business models and organisational arrangements enabled by digital technologies.

The 'social awakening' of the Von der Leyen Commission, in the shadow of the Social Pillar, has produced its more remarkable impact (although only a virtual one so far) in the field of platform work. This has probably more to do with the high attention of public opinion and the academic community on the matter than on the quantitative impact of the phenomenon. In any case, it represents a welcome attempt to combat the elusive and unfair market practices put in place by many operators in the sector.

On the other hand, the Commission's initiatives have been accompanied by relevant actions undertaken by the Parliament and the European Social Partners on issues like working time and the digitalisation of the workplace, that testify to the increasingly horizontal character of the challenges posed by the new technologies.

The mix between the targeted maintenance of existing statutory instruments that are still adaptable to the changing reality and more incisive innovations aimed at responding to totally new problems, promises to improve the quality of the regulation at EU level, in spite of the inevitable flaws. Regulating the digital transformation is certainly doomed to be an ongoing process, fast as is the speed of innovation. It is important, however, that regulators do not lose sight of the need to preserve the systemic coherence among the various instruments, and that they remember that the object of regulation must be work and not the technology, as several contributions in this book correctly maintain.

[125] Article 3.2.
[126] Recital 25.

# PART II

# Platform Work and Agile Work Arrangements

# 5

# Classification of Platform Workers: A Scholarly Perspective

MARTIN GRUBER-RISAK*

## I. Introduction

### A. What is Platform Work?

Developments in information and communication technology (ICT) have made it easier than ever before to match demand and supply of labour in real time, both locally and globally. This has led not only to fundamental changes in traditional employment relationships, but to the emergence of new forms of employment located in the grey and often uncharted territory between employment contracts and freelance work.[1] A particularly salient instance of this phenomenon is platform work, a relatively recent model also known as the crowdsourcing of labour, gig-work, on-demand work, or crowd employment. These models are ICT-based forms of organising the outsourcing of tasks to a large pool of workers. The work (ranging from transportation services and cleaning to digital transcription or programming tasks) is referred to in a variety of ways, including 'gigs', 'rides', or 'tasks', and is offered to a large number of people

* This contribution builds on my previous work on this topic, see J Prassl and M Risak, 'Uber, Taskrabbit, & Co: Platforms as Employers? Rethinking the Legal Analysis of Crowdwork' (2016) 27 *Comparative Labor Law & Policy Journal* 619; as well as J Prassl and M Risak, 'The Legal Protection of Crowdworkers – Four Avenues for Workers' Rights in the Virtual Realm' in P Meil and V Kirov (eds), *Policy Implications of Virtual Work* (Cham, Palgrave Macmillan, 2017) 273; and J Adams-Prassl and M Gruber-Risak, 'The legal protection of platform workers' in H Kurz, M Schutz, R Strohmaier and SS Zilian (eds), *The Routledge Handbook of Smart Technologies* (Abingdon, Routledge, 2022) 189.

[1] *cf* Eurofound, *New Forms of Employment* (Dublin, 2015) 107; A Aloisi, 'Commoditized Workers – The Rise of On-Demand Work, a Case Study Research on a Set of Online Platforms and Apps' (2016) 37 *Comparative Labor Law & Policy Journal* 653; V De Stefano, 'The Rise of the "Just-in-Time Workforce": On-Demand Work, Crowdwork, and Labor Protection in the "Gig Economy"' (2016) 37 *Comparative Labor Law & Policy Journal* 471; J Prassl, *Humans as a Service: The Promise and Perils of Work in the Gig Economy* (Oxford, Oxford University Press, 2018) ch 5.

(the 'crowd') by means of an internet-based 'crowdsourcing platform'.[2] This organisational model forms part of a larger set of processes known as 'crowdsourcing',[3] with customers (or indeed employers) referred to as 'crowdsourcers'. The resulting contractual relationships are manifold and complex: while the work is usually managed through an intermediary (the digital labour platform), some will insist on direct contractual relationships between crowdsourcer clients and platform workers, whereas others will opt for tripartite contractual structures, akin to traditional models of agency work and labour outsourcing.[4]

Eurofound, the European Foundation for the Improvement of Living and Working Conditions, a tripartite EU agency, has been shaping the European understanding of platform work significantly since its seminal report on the 'New Forms of Employment in Europe'.[5] It now defines platform work as follows for the purpose of its recent studies:

> Platform work is a form of employment that uses an online platform to enable organizations or individuals to access other organizations or individuals to solve problems or to provide services in exchange for payment. The main characteristics of platform work are as follows:
>
> - Paid work is organized through an online platform.
> - Three parties are involved: the online platform, the client and the worker.
> - The aim is to carry out specific tasks or solve specific problems.
> - The work is outsourced or contracted out.
> - Jobs are broken down into tasks.
> - Services are provided on demand.
>
> As the main traded good is labor, rather than materials or capital, sales platforms (such as eBay) or platforms providing access to accommodation (such as Airbnb) or financial services fall outside this definition. Furthermore, non-commercial transactions like volunteering, networking, social media (such as LinkedIn) or any other form of unpaid transaction (such as Couchsurfing, which matches people looking for accommodation with people offering it free of charge) are not considered platform work. Accordingly, the research focus is on online platforms matching the supply of and demand for paid labor.[6]

[2] Such as, notably, Amazon's Mechanical Turk (www.mturk.com). See S Strube, 'Vom Outsourcing zum Crowdsourcing' ['From outsourcing to crowdsourcing'] in Ch Benner (ed), *Crowdwork – Zurück in die Zukunft* (Frankfurt am Main, Bund Verlag, 2014) 75; for the German platform Clickworker, see D Lutz, 'Virtuelles Crowdwork: Clickworker' in D Lutz and M Risak (eds), *Arbeit in der Gig Economy* (Wien, ÖGB Verlag, 2017) 62.

[3] This term derives from a combination of the words 'outsourcing' and 'crowd', and was used by Jeff Howe for the first time, *cf* J Howe, 'The Rise of Crowdsourcing' *Wired Magazine* (June 2016), available at: www.wired.com/2006/06/crowds.

[4] *cf* A Kittur et al, 'The Future of Crowd Work', Paper presented at the 16th ACM Conference on Computer Supported Cooperative Work, available at: www.lri.fr/~mbl/ENS/CSCW/2012/papers/Kittur-CSCW13.pdf; JM Leimeister et al, 'Crowdwork – digitale Wertschöpfung in der Wolke' ['Crowdwork – digital value creation in the cloud'] in W Brenner and T Hess (eds), *Wirtschaftsinformatik in Wissenschaft und Praxis* (Berlin, Springer Verlag, 2014) 51.

[5] *cf* Eurofound, *New Forms of Employment* (n 1) 107.

[6] Eurofound, *Employment and Working Conditions of Selected Types of Platform Work* (Luxembourg, Publications Office of the European Union, 2018) 9. ibid, see Table 3 below for the different alternative terms for platform work used in selected Member States. The European Commission has also adopted this definition in its consultation document on possible action addressing the challenges related to working conditions in platform work, C(2021) 4230 final.

Unsurprisingly, the definition now used by the European Commission in its Proposal for a Directive on improving working conditions in platform work[7] moves along a similar vein (Article 2 (2)):

> [P]latform work means any work organised through a digital labour platform[8] by an individual on the basis of a contractual relationship between the digital labour platform and the individual, irrespective of whether a contractual relationship exists between the individual and the recipient of the service.

Work crowdsourced to an external crowd can be seen as clustered along a spectrum of services and arrangements.[9] At one end, we find physical services to be undertaken in the 'real' (offline) world, where the platform worker comes into direct contact with the customer. Examples include transportation delivered via apps such as Uber, domestic services (cleaning, repair work, etc) delivered via platforms such as Helpling,[10] and clerical work (eg, customer service or accounting) provided by platforms like UpWork.[11]

At the other end of the spectrum, there is digital work delivered in the virtual world, usually via an interface provided by the platform. The tasks involved here are often very simple, repetitive activities involving low pay and highly standardised or automated processes. These 'microtasks' include digital labelling and the creation of image descriptions, categorising data and products, and the translation or proofreading of short texts. They often originate from a larger task being broken down into smaller sub-tasks to be worked on independently. These micro-tasks are then posted on platforms, where platform workers can find and complete them. The leading platforms for this kind of 'cognitive piece work'[12] or 'Neo-Taylorism'[13] include Amazon's Mechanical Turk[14] and Clickworker.[15]

[7] COM(2021) 762 final, 33. This proposal was presented on 9 December 2021. *cf* European Commission, *Study to support the impact assessment of an EU initiative to improve the working conditions in platform work – Final Report* (European Commission, 2021) 32.

[8] A digital labour platform is defined in Article 2(2) as follows: '"digital labour platform" means any natural or legal person providing a commercial service which meets all of the following requirements:

(a) it is provided, at least in part, at a distance through electronic means, such as a website or a mobile application;
(b) it is provided at the request of a recipient of the service;
(c) it involves, as a necessary and essential component, the organisation of work performed by individuals, irrespective of whether that work is performed online or in a certain location'.

[9] cf for a typology of platform work Eurofound, *Platform work: Types and Implications for Work and Employment – Literature Review* (Dublin, Eurofound, 2018) 53; ILO, *The Role of Digital Labour Platforms Transforming the World of Work* (Geneva, ILO, 2021) 74 – the latter differentiates between online web-based and location-based platforms.

[10] www.helpling.com.

[11] www.upwork.com.

[12] FA Schmidt, 'The Good, the Bad and the Ugly' in C Benner (ed), *Crowdwork – Zurück in die Zukunft* (Frankfurt am Main, Bund Verlag, 2014) 378.

[13] J Leimeister et al, 'Crowdwork – Digitale Wertschöpfung in der Wolke' [Crowdwork – digital value creation in the cloud] in C Benner (ed), *Crowdwork – Zurück in die Zukunft* (Frankfurt am Main, Bund Verlag, 2014) 32.

[14] www.mturk.com/mturk/welcome.

[15] www.clickworker.com.

## B. The Mechanism behind Platform Work

Historically, the main advantage for employers of hierarchical employment relationships over contracts with independent contractors was understood to be the entrepreneur's degree of control, and the resulting decrease in transaction costs, whether in the search, selection and training of workers, or the employer's tight control over the production process.[16] An increasing desire for labour flexibility, on the other hand, was the driver behind the more recent creation of different forms of atypical work, including agency work, part-time work and fixed-term employment.[17]

Platform work is a rather novel combination of these factors, insofar as platforms attempt to increase flexibility for the employer or customer and reduce unproductive moments, while at the same time maintaining full control over the production process in order to keep transaction costs to a minimum. In order to meet these seemingly contradictory goals, some preconditions must be met: first, the crowd must be large enough to always have individuals available when needed, and to maintain enough competition between platform workers to keep prices low. This is usually achieved through platforms' large and active crowds, with different platforms specialising in different segments of the crowdsourcing market.

Second, instead of the command-and-control systems inherent in 'traditional' employment relationships, crowdsourcers and platforms rely on 'digital reputation' mechanisms to guide the selection of platform workers and to ensure efficient performance control. Individual models vary, but the fundamental approach is consistent: platform workers are awarded points, stars or other symbols of status by the crowdsourcer or customer after completing a task.[18] Quality control itself can thus be crowdsourced by the platform to its customers or other crowdsourcers, tapping the 'wisdom of the crowd' in order to determine the performance levels of each individual platform worker.[19]

## C. Advantages and Disadvantages of Platform Work

The potential upsides of this emerging model for firms and workers alike should not be underestimated.[20] Through the use of platforms, businesses ranging from restaurants to IT service providers can draw on a large crowd of flexible workers to reduce or even eliminate the cost of unproductive time at work, and rely on reputation mechanisms to maintain full control over the production process or service delivery. The resulting competition between platform workers will ensure that quality remains high while

[16] R Coase, 'The Nature of the Firm' (1937) 16 *Economica* 386.

[17] Eurofound, *Third European Survey on Working Conditions* (Dublin, Eurofound, 2000); European Parliament, *Atypical Work in the EU* (SOCI106EN, 1998).

[18] On some platforms, including Uber, customers are rated by crowdworkers in turn: *cf* S Langlois, 'Don't Tip Your Uber Driver? It Could Cost You a 5-Star Rating' *Market Watch* (12 August 2015), available at: www.marketwatch.com/story/dont-tip-your-uber-driver-it-could-cost-you-a-5-star-rating-2015-08-12.

[19] J Surowiecki, *The Wisdom of the Crowds* (New York, Doubleday, 2004).

[20] www.telegraph.co.uk/technology/uber/12086500/In-praise-of-the-gig-economy.html.

wages are low. As Lukas Biewald, founder of the platform Crowdflower, bluntly stated in 2010:

> Before the Internet, it would be really difficult to find someone, sit them down for ten minutes and get them to work for you, and then fire them after those ten minutes. But with technology, you can actually find them, pay them the tiny amount of money, and then get rid of them when you don't need them anymore.[21]

Platform work similarly offers significant potential upsides for (at least some of its) workers, first and foremost, in terms of flexibility: platform workers can decide when to work, where to work and what kinds of tasks to accept. Platform work might therefore be more compatible with other duties, such as childcare. The flexibility and potentially limited nature of individual engagements can also help the underemployed, providing additional income to their regular earnings,[22] and (at least through virtual platform work) allowing those excluded from regular labour markets due to disabilities or other factors to find opportunities for gainful employment.[23] Finally, there is an increasing number of genuinely successful small entrepreneurs, focused on particular niches or offering special skills, for whom platform work has become a very profitable source of new business.[24]

At the same time, however, it is important to note that working conditions for the vast majority of platform workers appear to be poor, irrespective of the work being delivered.[25] The lack of unions or organising powers, the oligopoly of but a few platforms offering certain kinds of tasks, and constant economic and legal insecurity result in a massive imbalance of bargaining power, noticeable primarily in low wage-rates and heavily slanted terms and conditions in platform use agreements. In the case of virtual platform work, global competition and dislocated physical workplaces further aggravate these problems, as a lack of regulation leads to what some have called 'digital slaves'[26] working away in their 'virtual sweatshops'.[27]

Two problems in particular are repeatedly highlighted: low wages, and workers' dependence on their ratings with a particular platform. As regards the former problem, for example, some reports suggest that the average wage on Amazon's *Mechanical Turk* is less than $2 per hour,[28] considerably below the US minimum wage.[29] Additionally

[21] As quoted in M Marvit, 'How Crowdworkers Became the Ghosts in the Digital Machine' *The Nation* (5 February 2014), available at: www.thenation.com/article/how-crowdworkers-became-ghosts-digital-machine/.

[22] www.dailyworth.com/posts/3410-flexible-side-gigs-to-bring-in-extra-income/4.

[23] *cf* K Zyskowski et al, 'Accessible Crowdwork? Understanding the Value in and Challenge of Microtask Employment for People with Disabilities', available at: www.research.microsoft.com/pubs/228714/crowdworkanddisability.pdf.

[24] ILO, *The Role of Digital Labour Platforms Transforming the World of Work* (n 9) 243.

[25] www.thenation.com/article/how-crowdworkers-became-ghosts-digital-machine/.

[26] M Rosenblum, 'The Digital Slave – That Would be You' *Huffingtonpost* (5 June 2013), available at: www.huffingtonpost.com/michael-rosenblum/the-digital-slave-that-wob3222785.html.

[27] See for 'so called gold farming' (professional online gaming to collect virtual money in games like World of Warcraft): J Dibbell, 'The Unreal Estate Boom' *Wired Magazine* (1 January 2003), available at: www.wired.com/2003/01/gaming-2; J Dibbell, 'The Life of the Chinese Gold Farmer' *NYT Magazine* (17 June 2006), available at: www.nytimes.com/2007/06/17/magazine/17lootfarmers-t.html?r=2&oref=slogin.

[28] *cf* J Ross et al, 'Who are the Crowdworkers? Shifting Demographics in Amazon Mechanical Turk', Paper prepared for Chi 2010, available at: www.dl.acm.org/citation.cfm?doid=1753846.1753873; A Felstiner, 'Working the Crowd: Employment and Labor Law in the Crowdsourcing Industry' (2011) 32 *Berkeley Journal of. Employment and Labor Law* 143.

[29] In the US, there are different minimum wages, depending on the State. *cf* www.dol.gov/whd/minwage/america.htm.

not all work relevant for the platform is paid, like waiting and search times or communication with clients.[30] A related aspect is insecurity regarding payment: in accordance with the general terms and conditions of some microtasking platforms, crowdsourcers have the right to reject the work without having to give a reason or provide payment, while still receiving the fruits of a worker's labour.[31]

Various systems of 'digital reputation', or rating mechanisms, which form one of the core elements of platform work, raise a second set of difficult questions: a customer input-based system of stars or points not only puts platform workers in a state of permanent probation, but infringes their mobility as it ties them to particular platforms. As the more attractive and better paid tasks are only offered and assigned to those who have the best reputation, and as a worker's digital reputation is not transferable between individual platforms, a change of platforms is difficult – a fact which also further impairs the bargaining position of platform workers. There is also the risk of discrimination that may be inherent to the platform design and the reputation system.[32]

## D. The Regulatory Challenges Resulting from Platform Work

One of the very purposes of employment and labour law is to draw a distinction between the genuinely self-employed and those requiring protection against many of the problems outlined above, bringing the latter group within its protective scope. Most jurisdictions have developed a more or less elaborate legal framework regulating the employment relationship based on the idea of the existence of an imbalance of bargaining power when negotiating pay and conditions of work.[33] This usually includes the right to organise, to bargain collectively and to take collective action. Self-employed persons, on the other hand, do not enjoy any of these rights, including minimum wages, sick pay, or protection against unfair dismissal. Indeed, they may even be forbidden from coming to mutual arrangements over basic terms on a collective level, such as minimum payments, as this might contravene competition or antitrust laws.[34]

It is therefore important to analyse where the line is drawn between the status of an employee and a self-employed person or independent contractor. As I have pointed out elsewhere,[35] this becomes very hard when more than two parties are involved, as the accepted analytical approach was developed in the context of bilateral employment relationships. Employment law thus struggles with the crowdsourcing of labour given the involvement of an intermediary or platform in addition to the platform

[30] V Pugliano et al, 'Does it Pay to Work?' (2021) *ETUI Policy Brief* 15.

[31] For an illustration in the context of *Mechanical Turk*, see Strube (n 2) 78, 83; D Martin et al, 'Being a Turker', Proceedings of the 17th ACM Conference on Computer-Supported Cooperative Work & Social Computing (2014), available at: www.dl.acm.org/citation.cfm?id=2531602.

[32] ILO, *The Role of Digital Labour Platforms Transforming the World of Work* (n 9) 245.

[33] M Freedland and P Davies, *Kahn-Freud's Labour and the Law*, 3rd edn (London, Stevens & Sons, 1983) 14, 69.

[34] *cf* Case C-413/13 *FNV Kunsten Informatie en Media v Staat der Nederlanden* ECLI:EU:C:2014:2411 [2014].

[35] J Prassl and M Risak, 'Uber, Taskrabbit, & Co: Platforms as Employers? Rethinking the Legal Analysis of Crowdwork' (2016) 27 *Comparative Labor Law & Policy Journal* 619.

workers and crowdsourcing customers. A traditional analysis would split the three-party arrangements underlying platform work scenarios into a series of bilateral contractual relationships, and attempt to classify each relationship separately. The economic situation of platform workers, however, is not accurately reflected in the sum of these fragments of contracts. Looking only at individual relationships one at a time, without also considering their interwoven nature because of the digital labour platform, is akin to determining the nature of a cloth by looking only at its differently coloured threads of wool, without taking into account the weaving pattern. The accepted analytical approach tends to ignore complex multi-party relationships, and analyses the resulting fragments without reference to the broader context and economic effects of platform work. This, then, is at the core of its shortcomings when faced with multiple parties: there is little analysis of contractual relationships as an interdependent net of contracts that only makes sense as a whole.

## II. Possible Solutions to the 'Platform Problem'

Based on the above, policymakers have now acknowledged the need to improve labour conditions for platform workers, but the solution is still open and very much under discussion, as there are different avenues available to achieve this aim.

- First there are interpretative approaches to the notion of employee that can be harnessed in an attempt to enlarge (or restore) the scope of employment law to include those working in the platform economy. The existing jurisprudence all over Europe shows that the following obstacles exist to include platform workers into the personal scope of labour law:
  - It seems that up to now, aspects of means of control in the virtual world are taken into account only to a limited extent when establishing whether the criteria for the concept of employee, especially the criterion of subordination, are fulfilled. Flexibility concerning working time, the physical place of work as well as the organisation of the course of work is sometimes wrongly overestimated and leads to the questionable conclusion that a platform worker is not classified an employee. But if one takes into account the means of control existing in the virtual realm and the distinct way directions are given in the platform economy, a different picture may emerge.
  - Another issue is the 'mutuality of obligations', ie, that an employment contract does not exist if there is no obligation to actually work or there is a right to reject offers to work. In this context, the question arises as to which situation is to be examined: the overall framework contract; the employee logging into the platform or opening the app to indicate they are available to work; or the employee accepting a task. Often, only the framework contract that in fact offers great flexibility to the platform worker is analysed; a legal examination of the other constellations might lead to different results.
  - Finally, there is the option available to the courts to redefine the concept of employee, emphasising economic arguments over organisational considerations.

- Another approach, also interpretative, is based on Jeremias Adams-Prassl's functional-typological concept of the employer, developed on the basis of a catalogue of five employer functions.[36] Where there is a potential multiplicity of employers, as in the case of platform work, such a concept can be helpful to identify the relevant persons in charge of complying with employer obligations.
- Another (much-disputed) approach to regulating platform work is based on the idea that an intermediate legal category, situated between the employee and the self-employed, might be the most suited for dealing with the legal issues arising from platform work. In many Member States of the EU such as Austria, Germany and Italy, such models exist but there is great variability in the protection available to this group of persons and the protection is rather limited. As it is easier to establish a worker's status in court, this avenue is sometimes chosen, as in the famous UK case of *Aslam, Farrar & Others*,[37] although the criteria for an employment relationship might also have been fulfilled.
- Again, another and maybe the most obvious way to deal with platform work is to enact special legislation dealing not only with the classification issue, but with the special problems connected to this form of organising work. There are a number of proposals available in the legal literature for what such legislation could look like.[38] Often they are rather general and reach from combating poor-quality work and non standard-work in general (including platform work),[39] to the extension of the Temporary Agency Work Directive to digital labour platforms[40] and the introduction of a new legal conceptual framework based on the idea of personal work relation.[41] At times they are more concrete and include a number of provisions tackling the problems unique to platform work like, among others, information obligations of the platforms, equal treatment with the workers employed directly by the requester, an adjusted definition of working time which includes stand-by time, and transparency obligations for the use of rating systems as well as the portability of ratings.[42]
- Solutions may also be found by opening arenas for collective bargaining at the sectoral and/or company level also for those platform workers who are considered self-employed. On the international level it seems to be clear that the relevant ILO instruments (in particular Conventions 87 and 98)[43] – as the responsible ILO

[36] J Prassl, *The Concept of the Employer* (Oxford, Oxford University Press, 2015).

[37] *London Central Employment Tribunal 28.10.2016, 2202551/2015 & Others, Aslam, Farrar & Others v Uber BV, Uber London Ltd & Uber Britannia Ltd*, available at: www.judiciary.gov.uk/judgments/mr-y-aslam-mr-j-farrar-and-others-v-uber/.

[38] *Cf* the recent overview in H Hauben, K Lenaerts and S Kraatz, 'Platform Economy and Precarious work: Mitigating Risks', Briefing for the EMPL Committee (European Parliament, 2020).

[39] S Garben, 'Tackling precarity in the platform economy – and beyond', *Social Europe* 2020, available at: www.socialeurope.eu/tackling-precarity-in-the-platform-economy-and-beyond.

[40] L Ratti, 'Online Platforms and Crowdwork in Europe: A Two-Step Approach to Expanding Agency Work Provisions' (2016) 38 *Comparative Labor Law & Policy Journal* 477.

[41] N Countouris and V De Stefano, *New Trade Union Strategies for New Forms of Employment* (Brussels, ETUC, 2019).

[42] M Risak, *Fair Working Conditions for Platform Workers: Possible Regulatory Approaches at the EU Level* (Berlin, FES, 2018).

[43] Freedom of Association and Protection of the Right to Organise Convention, 1948 (No 87); Right to Organise and Collective Bargaining Convention, 1949 (No 98).

> supervisory bodies regularly recall[44] – apply to all workers without distinction whatsoever. On the national level this is much disputed though and the self-employed often do not enjoy any of these rights. Indeed, they may even be precluded from coming to mutual arrangements over basic terms, such as minimum payments as this might contravene competition or antitrust laws.[45] In Australia therefore an exemption for some self-employed has been introduced[46] and also on the EU-level there is an ongoing initiative to make clear that competition law should not be an obstacle to collective bargaining agreement for the self-employed.[47] In other countries workers falling into the third or intermediary category explicitly enjoy the freedom of association and collective bargaining rights (*workers* in the UK,[48] *TRADE* in Spain,[49] *dependent contractors* in Ontario/Canada)[50] and competition law therefore does not seem to be an issue. In Italy, it is disputed if workers belonging to the third category (*lavoro etero-organizzato*) enjoy collective rights, as they are not mentioned in the relevant legislation.[51]

While the avenues to be chosen are thus potentially manifold, one thing is obvious: there is an urgent need for legislators and practitioners, especially judges, to address the prevalent vulnerable situation of persons working through platforms, offering maximum flexibility but getting very little security in return. This has to be changed, while keeping in mind that any proposed solution or mix of solutions must be able to respond flexibly to changing economic and organisational models, but at the same time must offer conceptual coherence in the face of factual complexity.

## III. Adapting the Concept of Employee to the Digital Age

Two of the core questions of labour law relate to the scope and justification of employment protection. Put differently: who is protected, and why? The scope of employment legislation should extend to those in need of protection because of their unique situation. This leads us to the second question, namely, what makes the employment relationship so special and the employee in need of special protection? One of the most frequently cited underlying rationales of labour law is the twofold economic dependence of the employee. This refers, first, to the fact that resources (eg, materials, machines or an

[44] See ILO, *Committee on Freedom of Association, Freedom of Association: Compilation of decisions of the Committee on Freedom of Association*, 6th edn) (2018) para 387.

[45] *cf* C-413/13 *FNV Kunsten* (n 34).

[46] Australian Competition and Consumer Commission, *Collective bargaining class exemption – Guidelines* (June 2020), available at: www.accc.gov.au/system/files/public-registers/documents/Collective%20bargaining%20class%20exemption%20-%20Guidelines%20June%202021.pdf.

[47] *cf* the Draft Guidelines of the European Commission on collective bargaining of self-employed, available at: www.ec.europa.eu/competition-policy/public-consultations/2021-collective-bargaining-2_en.

[48] In the UK though the UK Court of Appeal of 24 June 2021, in Case C1/2018/3104, decided that Deliveroo riders are not even workers and have no collective rights.

[49] Trabajadores autonónomos económicamente dependientes (TRADE) – economically dependent self-employed.

[50] Ontario Labour Relations Act 1995, s 1(1).

[51] Legislative Decree No 101/2019.

organisation) are typically needed to perform the work and that employees have, at least historically, depended on the employer to provide them. Second, it implies dependence of the employee on 'selling' his or her labour in exchange for remuneration from the employment relationship to sustain his or her living. Most legal orders, however, do not refer to these economic arguments, focusing instead on the way the work is actually performed.[52] The second aspect especially (dependence on salary to earn a living) is considered impractical, as employers often have no means of ascertaining whether their contractual partners actually have other sources of income or their reasons for working more generally.[53]

For decades, therefore, many jurisdictions have followed an organisational approach focusing on the notion of restricted self-determination when working, since it delivered both satisfactory results and was practical and relatively easy to apply. Its success was based on the fact that only those having enough resources were able to become self-employed and that they were able to negotiate for pay that satisfied their needs. On the other hand, those working under the close supervision of another person often did not have enough bargaining power when negotiating pay and conditions of work. Given those circumstances, it was rather unproblematic to equate organisational with economic dependency in the past.

Thus, at the core of the concept of employee in Europe stood and still stands the criterion of subordination, or, as it is called for instance in Germany and Austria, of 'personal dependency'. In all EU Member States, this represents the key criterion for determining whether a legal relationship between two parties qualifies as an 'employment relationship'.[54] This element is often further split up into the sub-criteria of subjection to the power of the employer, control (ie, the possibility to monitor the work of the employee) and integration (ie, forming part of the organisational structure of an undertaking).[55] In all countries, though, qualification of a relationship is far from clear-cut and requires an overall assessment of each individual case and application of the principle of 'primacy of facts'. Ultimately, a variety of indicators for the core-criterion of subordination are used, which in essence refer to the fact that the employees 'sell' their labour by subjecting themselves to the directives of another person who may 'use' them for his or her purposes. The main aspects of this limited personal freedom of the employee are the obligation to work at specified times and at a specified place, the right of the contractual partner to give orders, especially as regards time and place, as well as the employer's control over personal work-related behaviour and demands relating to integration in the partner's operational organisation.[56]

[52] For Austria *cf* M Risak, *Austria, International Encyclopaedia for Labour Law and Industrial Relations* (Alphen aan den rijn, Wolters Kluwer, 2010) 36; W Brodil, M Risak and C Wolf, *Arbeitsrecht in Grundzügen* [*Labour Law in General*], 10th edn (LexisNexis, 2019) 14; for Germany, M Weiss and M Schmidt, 'Germany (Fed Rep)' in *International Encyclopaedia for Labour Law and Industrial Relations* (Alphen aan den Rijn, Wolters Kluwer, 2008) 45.

[53] *cf* B Waas and G von Voss, 'Comparative Overview' in B Waas and G von Voss (eds), *Restatement of Labour Law in Europe, Vol I: The Concept of Employee* (Oxford, Hart Publishing, 2017) xlv.

[54] ibid, xxxix.

[55] ibid, xl.

[56] M Risak and R Rebhahn, 'Austria' in B Waas and G von Voss (eds), *Restatement of Labour Law in Europe, Vol I: The Concept of Employee* (Oxford, Hart Publishing, 2017) 4.

These criteria also apply when assessing if a platform worker is to be classified as an employee and therefore covered by protective labour legislation. In this context, it can be observed that courts tend to refrain from taking into consideration the virtual aspects of contemporary work, ie, the fact that employees not only work physically in the analogue world but often also at the same time in the virtual one, continuously creating data that can be used to monitor and control employee performance. Stated otherwise, the fact that the freedom and flexibility of platform workers concerning the physical aspects of work (especially the flexibility concerning the time and the location of work) are often neutralised by the intense control exercised virtually over their performance as well as by the extensive integration of the platform worker in the virtual structure of the platform, leaves them in need of legal protection.[57] This is often not recognised by the courts though.

As the following chapter by Emanuele Menegatti will show, in Europe and elsewhere, there exist a variety of different interpretations of the concept of employee in the platform economy. While some courts adapt their criteria to the changing ways work is organised and develop the received concept beyond a formal assessment, others remain rather formalistic and accept the contractual terms as plain facts. The situation is further complicated by different intermediate categories that exist in Europe. Often plaintiffs seek their rights via this category as this status is easier to prove in court and because it affords them at least some protection (eg, in the UK, an entitlement to the minimum wage and paid annual leave).[58] However, this intermediate status does not offer the full range of employee rights and it differs significantly from country to country.

The decisions of the national courts vary greatly depending on the importance they give to the individual elements of the concept of employee and on whether they adapt them to the new digital environment. This is particularly the case with the criteria of subordination and integration as well as mutuality of obligations. Another issue is the question of which contractual relationships are examined: if this is the framework contract, there is often enough autonomy of the platform worker to decide if and how much to work. This can vary, as in cases where the platform worker logs into the respective App, thereby communicating their availability, as a result of which the platform then expects the platform worker to react to job offers and also sanctions refusals. There may also be positive incentives for accepting tasks such as gaining access to more interesting and better jobs; in such arrangements, freedom to refuse offers by the platform is restricted. Finally, worker autonomy is often even more restricted when examining the fulfilment of single tasks.

## IV. Redefining the Notion of the Employee

As pointed out above, an organisational approach was used for decades for determining who is an employee and who is not, focusing on the restricted autonomy when

[57] *cf* M Gruber-Risak, 'Cyberwork' in A Reichel, W Pfeil and S Urnik, *Die Arbeit ist immer und überall* (Wien, Manz, 2020) 71.

[58] National Minimum Wage Act 1998, s 1; Working Time Regulations 1998, s 13.

working. The picture, however, has changed, due to a number of factors, and has led to the emergence of a growing number of self-employed workers: advances in digital technologies, the widespread availability of handheld devices, and ever-increasing high-speed connectivity have combined with the realities presented by several cycles of economic downturn, shifts in lifestyle and generational preferences.[59] These new 'solo-entrepreneurs' and freelancers are very different from those of the past, where white-collar professionals such as lawyers, architects and other high-skilled workers had the power to bargain for high remuneration and controlled their own working conditions.

Platform workers active in the virtual realms of the gig economy today resemble the workers of the nineteenth century who did not have any other alternative than to sell their labour in a highly competitive market. They compete with a large reserve army of virtual labour, unlike those self-employed in liberal professions. They are also similar to traditional employees as they do work in person and thereby sell their labour and not an end product. Finally, they are also vulnerable as they earn their livelihood by doing this vis-à-vis only one or a very limited number of immediate contractual partners (viz, the platforms). The only difference between them and traditional employees is the fact that they are formally free to work at what and when they choose – but this freedom may often be no more than formal, due to an economic situation which does not leave them a lot of alternatives to selling their labour in a certain way to certain contractual partners.[60]

Redefining the notion of the employee, or specifically including the self-employed within the scope of certain employment law norms, would widen the scope of the application of individual labour law, ie, the set of rules granting individual rights and entitlements, thereby protecting employees from unfair und unhealthy working conditions. This body of laws usually encompasses, among others, minimum wages, working time restrictions, right to paid sick leave and holidays, as well as protection against dismissals. If the economic situation of the employee is the reason that these rights and entitlements were developed in the first place, it is hard to argue against extending the scope of their application to persons in the same situation based only on the argument that they are not formally integrated enough into the business of their contractual partners.

In a study undertaken with Thomas Dullinger,[61] I have developed a non-exhaustive list of criteria for the group of persons in a comparable position to employees not working in a relationship of subordination (or of personal dependency), but who are economically dependent on their contractual partners, as they do not operate independently on the market:

- The services are provided in person; the right to use substitutes is limited or does not make sense economically.

[59] O Lobel, 'The Gig Economy & The Future of Employment and Labour Law' (2016) USD Legal Studies Research Paper Series Research Paper No 16-223, 2.

[60] M Risak and T Dullinger, 'The Concept of "Worker" in EU Law: Status Quo and Potential for Change' (2018) ETUI Research Paper – Report 140.

[61] ibid; for another approach see N Kountouris, 'The Concept of "Worker" in European Labour Law: Fragmentation, Autonomy and Scope' (2018) 47 *Industrial Law Journal* 192.

- The work is provided for only one or a very small number of contracting parties. The person concerned therefore does not operate independently of the market but depends on a limited number of contractual partners.
- Workers do not own operating resources and/or control other employees.
- Restrictions to work for other parties are in place.
- The worker is dependent on the earnings for his or her livelihood.

However, it is important to note that, in our view, these elements are to be considered as mere indicators and that they should be used in a flexible manner in response to the existing diversity of work arrangements; they should also take into account any new developments. Stated otherwise, the above-mentioned criteria do not necessarily have to be met in any given individual case, but rather it suffices to demonstrate that the criteria that define persons as being economically dependent on their contractual partners override those typical for an entrepreneur conducting his or her own business on the market.

In my view, this group of persons is in a vulnerable situation similar to that of traditional employees. This is mainly the result of the fact that they do not have the necessary bargaining power to secure fair contracts that reflect their interests in an appropriate way. The provisions of labour law should therefore also apply to them where necessary.

## V. Functional Concept of the Employer

In the case of multiparty employment relationships, prevalent in platform work, the functional concept of employer as developed by Adams-Prassl[62] can also be helpful. This concept is based on the finding that employment law identifies, at least indirectly, a series of five employer functions – from hiring workers to setting their rates of pay – and regulates them in one or several areas, from anti-discrimination law to minimum wage provisions.

For the purposes of this analysis, an 'employer function' is one of the various actions employers are entitled or obliged to perform as part of the bundle of rights and duties falling within the scope of an open-ended service employment contract. These functions are rarely set out explicitly: in most legal contexts, the definition of the employer is seen as an afterthought in determining the scope of worker-protective norms. Upon closer inspection, however, it quickly appears that the concept implicitly mirrors the definition of the employee or worker, allowing for a 'reverse-engineering' of employer functions based on factors defining the employee.[63]

Drawing from the established tests of employment status, such as control, economic dependence, or mutuality of obligation, the following set of functions was developed, with the presence or absence of individual factors becoming less relevant than the

[62] Prassl, *The Concept of the Employer* (n 36).
[63] ibid, 24–25.

specific role they play in any given context. Individual elements can vary from situation to situation, as long as they fulfil the same function when viewed as a whole.[64]

The five main employer functions and their functional underpinnings are:

1. *Inception and termination of the employment relationship*: this category includes all powers of the employer over the very existence of its relationship with the employee, from the 'power of selection' to the right to dismiss.
2. *Receiving labour and its fruits*: duties owed by the employee to the employer, specifically to provide his or her labour and the results thereof, as well as rights incidental to it.
3. *Providing work and pay*: the employer's obligations towards its employees, such as, for example, the payment of wages.
4. *Managing the enterprise-internal market*: coordination through control over all factors of production, up to and including the power to require both how and what is to be done.
5. *Managing the enterprise-external market*: undertaking economic activity in return for potential profit, while also being exposed to any losses that may result from the enterprise.[65]

Key to this multifunctional concept of the employer is the fact that not one function mentioned above is relevant in and of itself. Rather, it is the composite of the five functions that matters: each of them covers one of the facets necessary to create, maintain and commercially exploit employment relationships. Together, they make up the accepted legal concept of employing workers or acting as an employer, including the responsibility to uphold the appropriate range of employee-protective norms.

A functional conceptualisation of the employer, then, is one in which the contractual identification of the employer is replaced by an emphasis on the exercise of each function – whether by a single entity, as demonstrated immediately below, or in situations where different functions may be exercised from more than one *locus* of control.[66] Indeed, in the platform work context one particular challenge arises from the fact that functions may sometimes be jointly exercised by platforms, customers and potentially even the platform worker herself. A shared endeavour between two or more entities, or one where functions are parcelled out between different parties, arises when platform work arrangements lead to a fragmented exercise of employer functions. It is in these scenarios that the functional model of the employer is put to the test: there may be elements of genuine self-employment, platforms performing employer roles, and even customers potentially becoming subject to regulatory obligations.

[64] The 'equipollency principle' (*Äquivalenzprinzip*): L Nogler, 'Die Typologisch-Funktionale Methode am Beispiel des Arbeitnehmerbegriffs' ['The typological-functional method using the example of the term employee'] (2009) 10 *ZESAR* 459, 463.

[65] For earlier attempts at such lists see, eg, M Freedland, *The Personal Employment Contract* (Oxford, Oxford University Press, 2003) 40.

[66] The term '*locus* of control' is designed to avoid additional complexities arising from the fact, as noted inter alia by Freedland (n 65) 45–47, that even in traditional companies without external influence, management control is often exercised by more than one person among a group of relatively senior executives.

In order to disentangle these intertwined elements, and ensure a consistent application of employment law in the face of factual complexity, the conceptual notion of 'employer' needs to move from the current rigidly formalistic approach to a flexible, *functional* definition. In more concrete terms, the following working definition has been offered by Adams-Prassl:[67] the functional concept of the employer should come to mean 'the entity, or combination of entities, playing a decisive role in the exercise of relational employing functions, and regulated or controlled as such in each particular domain of employment law'.[68]

Jeremias Adams-Prassl and I have applied this functional approach to business models existing in the platform economy and reached the following conclusions:[69] an examination of the transportation service Uber's business model demonstrated that, where a platform exercises all employer functions, it can easily be identified as an employer, with drivers consequently viewed as workers, rather than independent contractors. Most platforms, however, lead to a fragmentation of employer functions as demonstrated in the case of TaskRabbit, which provides household services. We concluded that, just as different functions may be exercised by various parties, concomitant responsibility should be ascribed to whichever entity – or combination of entities – has exercised the relevant function. As a result, multiple entities may come to be seen as employers for different purposes; at the same time the model is able to recognise elements of (genuine) self-employment, as the examples have demonstrated.

## VI. Introduction or Extension of an Intermediate Category

Another option to protect persons working through platforms is the recognition of an intermediate category of worker between employee and independent contractor.[70] In this way, the argument runs, the level of protection may be graded, and the fact that the personal integration of some platform workers is less intense and that they enjoy a certain level of flexibility and freedom, can actually be used to their advantage.

The examples are numerous: in Canada, jurisprudence has developed the category of dependent contractor for cases in which a contractor has worked exclusively or largely exclusively for one client for an extended period. They are then deemed a dependent contractor for purposes of termination notification and representation.[71] In Italy, *para-subordinate* relationships enjoy some level of statutory protection,[72] and in Germany and Austria some employment regulations are to be applied also to employee-like (*arbeitnehmerähnliche*) persons.

[67] Prassl, *The Concept of the Employer* (n 36) 155.

[68] In a recent ruling the ECJ (*AFMB Ltd*, ECLI:EU:C:2020:565) has also used such a functional concept in the context of social security law when determining who is the employer of long-distance lorry drivers.

[69] Prassl, *The Concept of the Employer* (n 36) 636.

[70] Lobel (n 59) 10; SD Harris and AB Krueger, 'A Proposal for Modernizing Labor Laws for Twenty-First Century Work: The "Independent Worker"' Hamilton Project Discussion Paper 2015-10 (December).

[71] *cf* Superior Court of Justice, 14 August 2014, *Wyman v Kadlec* 2014 ONSC 4710 (CanLII), available at: www.canlii.ca/t/g8lnv (26 September 2016); Court of Appel for Ontario, 23 December 2009, *McKee v Reid's Heritage Homes Ltd* 2009 ONCA 916 (CanLII), available at: www.canlii.ca/t/27551.

[72] V De Stefano, *The Rise of the 'Just-in-Time Workforce': On-Demand Work, Crowdwork and Labour Protection in the 'Gig-Economy'* (Geneva, ILO, 2016) 20.

In Austria, these persons are defined as persons who perform work/services by order of and on account of another person without being in an employment relationship, but who may be considered employee-like due to their economic dependence. Only some provisions of labour law apply to those employee-like persons, for example those on the competence of the labour courts,[73] agency work,[74] employee liability[75] and anti-discrimination.[76] In Germany, the intermediate category is defined similarly, and is also covered by the Act on Collective Agreements (*Tarifvertragsgesetz*), and may therefore conclude collective agreements with normative effect.

In the United Kingdom, the extension of employee rights beyond the employment contract seems to be the furthest developed and was relevant in the decisions concerning Uber. In *Aslam v Uber BV* the Central London Employment Tribunal ruled, on 28 October 2016, that Uber drivers were workers for purposes of section 230(3)(b) of the Employment Rights Act 1996, rather than as independent contractors, as the company had long maintained. The Tribunal found that the Uber drivers were workers and as a result they will now be entitled to a small number of core rights attached to worker status, including, importantly, the National Minimum Wage Act 1998 and the Working Time Regulations 1998.[77] Such basic protection will overcome some of the worst problems faced by Uber drivers and other platform workers but in the longer run, however, they – even when classified as workers – will face many of the problems encountered by zero-hours workers across the United Kingdom:[78] from low income to struggling with unpredictable shifts due to a lack of guaranteed work. This, then, is the fundamental problem with the creation of a novel third status: not only would it fail to alleviate the uncertainty and classificatory problems identified above, it would provide persons working through platforms with a lower degree of protection even though, as previous discussion has shown, they might often be among the most vulnerable participants in the labour market.

Beyond the United Kingdom, the experience with this intermediate category is similarly varied. While its introduction does not, at first glance, appear to change anything to the disadvantage of traditional employees because of employers moving over to this now legitimate group, the Italian example seems to indicate otherwise. Valerio De Stefano points out that the workers who would qualify for full protection as employees under the traditional legal tests would likely become deprived of many rights if they were crammed into an 'intermediate bucket'.[79] He warns that regulating dependent self-employment as a distinct group is no panacea for addressing the changes in business and work organisation driven by the disintegration of vertical firms.

[73] Labour and Social Courts Act, s 51 (3)2.
[74] Act on Agency Work, s 3.
[75] Employees' Liability Act, s 1(2).
[76] Equal Treatment Act, ss 1(3) 2 and 16(3) 2.
[77] The Employment Tribunal's findings were upheld in the Employment Appeal Tribunal and by a majority (Underhill LJ dissenting) in the Court of Appeal. The UK Supreme Court heard Uber's final appeal and also decided in 2020 in favour of the plaintiffs.
[78] A Adams, M Freedland and J Prassl, 'The "Zero-Hours Contract": Regulating Casual Work, or Legitimating Precarity?' (2015) 147 *Giornale di Diritto del Lavoro e di Relazioni Industriali* 529.
[79] De Stefano, *The Rise of the 'Just-in-Time Workforce'* (n 72) 20.

Some argue, on the other hand, that as existing law no longer protects a growing number of persons who once would have enjoyed the status of employees and who are now slipping out of the protective scope of labour law due to their increased formal freedom and flexibility, there is nonetheless the need for such intervention. It is arguable, for example, that the lack of any intermediate status effectively provides greater incentives for employers to classify their workers as independent contractors and that an intermediary category may well provide them with those rights they actually need.[80]

## VII. Special Legislation for Platform Work

Another option is the creation of a special legislative act dealing with the issues involved with platform work, as has been done in many European countries with temporary agency work in the transposition of the Temporary Agency Work Directive 2008/104/EC. This is the most complicated solution as it must take into account that the platform economy is very diverse and that a one-size-fits-all approach will hardly work. As the chapter by Tamás Gyulavári will explore this option in depth, I will only highlight in very rough strokes what such an act might include concerning the issue of the classification of persons working through platforms.

The general aim of such legislation would be to ensure the protection of persons working through platforms and to improve the quality of platform work. It should also take into account that platform work may contribute to the creation of jobs and to the development of flexible forms of working by introducing creative and innovative business models, but also keep in mind that there is nothing innovative about precarious work. The primary goal thus would be the creation of a level playing field for those platforms that endorse an approach that is platform-worker friendly, rather than one based on low labour costs and value extraction.

The heart of such special legislation should be a rebuttable legal presumption that the underlying contractual relationship is an employment contract between the platform worker and the platform.[81] Attempts to classify the legal relationships underlying the platform economy have shown that it is very hard to get an insight into how the work is actually organised by the platform and the mechanisms behind it. This knowledge is of significant importance to prove before a court of law that an employment contract has been concluded – but, as the platform worker has no means of getting to the information necessary to do so, this often amounts to the impossibility of providing the court with the necessary evidence. Such a legal presumption would recalibrate the massive imbalance of information and thereby justify a departure from the otherwise existing contribution of the burden of proof.[82]

[80] Lobel (n 59) 12.

[81] This is now included in Article 4 of the Proposal for a Directive on improving working conditions in platform work C(2021) 762 final.

[82] Lutz and Risak (n 2) 356; Risak, *Fair Working Conditions for Platform Workers* (n 42) 14; see also, European Commission, 'Second-phase consultation of social partners under Article 154 TFEU on possible action addressing the challenges related to working conditions in platform work' C(2021) 4230 final. 621.

The very tricky question for legislation will be to draw the role and the responsibility of the digital labour platforms in a transparent way in order to give platform workers certainty of their legal position in this set-up, without, however, suffocating those crowdsourcing models that are based on genuine self-employment (and thus not necessarily in need of statutory protection). This final concern, however, should not be – in my view – a hindrance to, or excuse from, protecting those genuinely in need of protection. Finally, it should also be noted that any platform work-specific legislation ought not to fall into the trap of technological exceptionalism, and recognise that, fundamentally, platform work should be regulated as work first and foremost.

## VIII. Collective Bargaining

Another option to provide protection is the self-organisation of platform workers and collective bargaining in order to overcome the power inbalance existing on the individual level. The rights to freedom of association and collective bargaining are therefore a reconciliation of the market model and its failures when it comes to the labour market. The unequal bargaining power between employees and employers that would lead to unsatisfactory results is recalibrated by the employees' possibility to unionise and to bargain collectively. The resulting rights are even considered universal human rights and guaranteed on an international level as in Article 20 of the Universal Declaration of Human Rights, numerous ILO Conventions (especially 87 and 98), Article 11 of the European Convention on Human Rights, and Articles 12 and 28 of the Charter of Fundamental Rights of the European Union.

However, according to competition law theory such an association could also be seen as one that can create concentration of power within one party (the employees) against the other (the employers), which might have an impact on free competition. It can be argued that unionising results in price fixing, ie, a restrictive agreement between employees to maintain a minimum price at which their services are sold. It is settled case law of the Court of Justice of the European Union (CJEU) that, although certain restrictions of competition are inherent in collective agreements between organisations representing employers and employees, the social policy objectives pursued by such agreements would be seriously compromised if management and labour were subject to competition law when seeking jointly to adopt measures to improve conditions of work and employment. Thus, the CJEU has held that agreements entered into within the framework of collective bargaining between employers and employees and intended to improve employment and working conditions must, by virtue of their nature and purpose, be regarded as not falling within the scope of Article 101(1) of the Treaty on the Functioning of the European Union (TFEU) dealing with antitrust measures.[83] It is unclear though if and to what extent the self-employed may also profit from the right

[83] cf Case C-67/96 *Albany International BV v Stichting Bedrijfspensioenfonds Textielindustrie* ECLI:EU:C:1999:430 [1999] para 59; Case C-438/05 International Transport Workers' Federation and Finnish Seamen's Union ECLI:EU:C:2007:772 [2007] para 49; Case C-319/07 P *3F v Commission of the European Communities* ECLI:EU:C:2009:435 [2009] para 50; C-413/13 *FNV Kunsten* (n 34) para 22.

to association and to bargain collectively.[84] Due the importance of this discussion a chapter of this book by Tihamér Tóth is dedicated to this topic.

## IX. Conclusions

In this contribution a series of potential solutions to classification of persons working through platforms are explored. It is important to note that while the phenomenon of platform work is indeed a novel one, the legal implications – particularly as regards employment law – are much less so. Seen from a historical labour law perspective, platform work is but the most recent threat to emerge to the law's quest for underlying coherence in the scope of protective norms in the face of dramatic changes in the labour market: online platforms or 'apps' act as intermediaries in a spot-market for labour, providing clients with workers for a wide range of jobs that are, from a legal perspective, not all that different from traditional outsourcing and agency relationships, or the infamous zero-hours contracts in the United Kingdom.

At first glance, the advantages for business, customers and workers resulting from the platform business model are immense: platform work does away with many of the regulatory costs traditionally associated with employing individuals; customers can receive a nearly infinite number of services at cut-price rates; and workers can find flexible work to suit their schedules and income needs. Upon closer inspection, however, a series of problems arising from this fragmentation of traditional work arrangements quickly emerges – in particular for workers, who often find themselves outside the scope of employment protective norms as a result of digital platforms' business models, thus suffering low pay, no job security and challenging working conditions.[85]

Each of the possible solutions explored in this chapter has its peculiar advantages and drawbacks. In any case it is important to recognise that whichever regulatory solutions are adopted, one should be careful about reinventing the wheel: many of the problems encountered with platform work are not novel, so efforts should be made to fit it into existing regulatory structures, with only partial additions as and when required. It is equally important to point out that new regulatory measures, if adopted, should not lead to the dilution of workers' rights, as might be the case with some 'third-status' proposals, in particular. Finally, given the vast heterogeneity of platforms, users and working conditions, it is unlikely that an easy solution could be found: platform work can cater for the needs of successful entrepreneurs, but can also become a low-wage trap. Only a sophisticated and responsive approach will be able to address the vast range of problems identified.

[84] *cf* Countouris and De Stefano (n 41); I Lianos, N Countouris and V De Stefano, 'Re-thinking the Competition Law/Labour Law Interaction: Promoting a Fairer Labour Market' (2019) 10 *European Labour Law Journal* 291.

[85] See also European Commission, 'Second-phase consultation of social partners under Article 154 TFEU on possible action addressing the challenges related to working conditions in platform work' C(2021) 4230 final, 6; European Commission, 'Commission Staff Working Document' SWD(2021) 143 final, 66.

# 6

# The Classification of Platform Workers through the Lens of Judiciaries: A Comparative Analysis

EMANUELE MENEGATTI

## I. Introduction

According to a widespread definition, the so-called gig economy refers mainly to two forms of work: crowdwork performed by online labour platforms and work-on-demand via app through on-location labour.[1] They both involve the performance of labour-intensive services in a triangular relationship, in which workers – classified as independent contractors – and customers are matched by online platforms in a (relatively) new work paradigm. However, they differ regarding a very relevant element: whereas crowdwork encompasses the completion of electronically transmittable services through online platforms, work-on-demand is more connected to traditional jobs, requiring physical and localised delivery, often relating to easy tasks, such as driving, cleaning and personal services.

The following considerations will be mainly focused on work-on-demand via app and on-location labour platforms, which is far more interesting from a labour perspective than crowdwork for two reasons. First, it involves local labour markets, therefore platform activities and the problem arising from this business model can be dealt with through national labour laws and by national courts. The second reason of interest concerns the impact of work-on-demand via app on the labour market. Even if it is still just about a very small percentage of the total workforce, the number of workers

[1] For a comprehensive and up-to-date glossary, see European Commission, 'First-phase consultation of social partners under Article 154 TFEU on possible action addressing the challenges related to working conditions in platform work' C(2021) 1127 final. See also C Codagnone, F Abadie and F Biagi, *The Future of Work in the 'Sharing Economy'. Market Efficiency and Equitable Opportunities or Unfair Precarisation?* (Institute for Prospective Technological Studies, JRC Science for Policy Report, 2021), available at: www.ec.europa.eu/jrc/en/publication/eur-scien-tific-and-technical-research-reports/future-work-sharing-economy-market-efficiency-and-equitable-opportunities-or-unfair; V De Stefano, 'The Rise of the "Just-in-Time Workforce": On-Demand Work, Crowdwork, and Labor Protection in the "Gig-Economy"' (2016) 37 *Comparative Labor Law and Policy Journal* 471; MA Cherry, 'A Taxonomy of Virtual Work' (2011) 45 *Georgia Law Review* 951.

involved with on-location platform work has sharply increased over the last few years. To the point that, according to recent studies, in 2018 more than 10 per cent of the EU total workforce has performed gig-work to varying extents,[2] and the digital labour platform economy has increased overall five times from 2016 to 2020.[3]

Very intensive discussion has been taking place on the outcomes of gig-work, eventually convincing the European Commission to propose a legislative initiative aimed at improving the working conditions of people working through platforms. As shown by Martin Gruber-Risak, platform work involves some pros and cons for the various players involved. As for workers, the main issues stem from their classification: being normally considered by the platforms as independent contractors, they do not usually have any guaranteed amount of work or the rights and entitlements typically accorded to employees.

As this chapter is going to highlight, this classification is rather controversial and it has been challenged, with mixed fortune, in courts all over the world. The essential and hard question which judges from different jurisdictions have been trying to answer in the last few years is: are gig-workers really independent contractors or just misclassified employees?

The 'formal reality' emerging from customary contractual terms and conditions provided by platforms is normally the following:

(a) Platforms are not comparable to temporary work agencies or to employers; they just offer independent contractors, who are not employees, workers or agents, a technology platform as a referral tool for a service, and facilitate payments and other operational details.
(b) Workers are almost free from direction in the performance of their services. Platforms might just set certain quality standards. Platforms do not directly monitor workers. However, final-users rate and review the performance of workers at the end of any gig.
(c) Workers are not obliged to grant a minimum availability, and the platforms do not have to grant a minimum amount of work. Workers often have the opportunity to review jobs and select those that meet the preferred specifications regarding time frame, date, neighbourhood or geographic location.
(d) Platforms manage payments. They usually pay fees to their workers periodically while retaining their share. The workers must meet all expenses associated with running their business and carry the related risks.

Besides this approximate description, it should be considered that work-on-demand via app is a nuanced phenomenon, in which a rough distinction can be drawn between two main business models: that of platforms just matching workers to final users and managing payments and other operational details, which are mostly providing a business-to-business service; and that of 'vertically integrated' platforms, which tend to

[2] European Commission, 'Second-phase consultation of social partners under Article 154 TFEU on possible action addressing the challenges related to working conditions in platform work' C(2021) 4230 final, 5.

[3] WP de Groen, Z Kilhoffer, L Westhoff, P Doina and F Shamsfakhr, *Digital Labour Platforms in the EU: Mapping and Business Models*, Study prepared by CEPS for DG EMPL under service contact VC/2020/0360, 2021, available at: www.ec.europa.eu/social/main.jsp?catId=738&langId=en&pubId=8399&furtherPubs=yes.

maximise control over the 'affiliated' independent contractors in order to ensure coordination, speed, reliability and good quality of the service provided.[4] The latter platforms (eg, *Uber*, *Uber Eats*, *Fodoora* and *Deliveroo*) very often go as far as imposing working tools or equipment specifications, routes, strict timing for the gig and (almost) mandatory fees; the whole thing is enforced through a kind of disciplinary power which may involve the 'de-activation' of the worker.

No matter which model of business they are following, platforms are always really keen on excluding any employment relationship from the triangulation of platform–worker–final user. However, this is happening with less and less success for 'vertically integrated' platforms, as I am going to highlight.

In this chapter I will start my investigation by giving an account of the main employment tests applied in the various national jurisdictions, in conjunction with the relevant features of contractual arrangements involving platform workers (section II) I will then move, without claiming to be all-encompassing, to the examination of the courts' decisions in a number of jurisdictions (including the US, UK, France, Spain, Italy) delivered by mid-2021, trying to work out the common patterns behind their outcomes (section III). We will see how these decisions seem to be increasingly heading towards recognition of the employment status to platform workers. However, there are good reasons to believe that this solution is pretty unstable, mainly because of the failure of traditional employment tests to understand gig-work. This will take us to the exploration of some possible solutions to move past the current uncertainty (section IV), such as that of introducing a new legislative definition of the 'employee' category (section IV.A) or that of creating new intermediate categories of 'dependent contractors' (section IV4.B). I will, finally, consider a different approach, aimed at providing universal rights beyond the employment contract (section IV.C). This last approach looks that chosen by the European Court of Justice (ECJ) over the last decade. By endorsing a broad concept of 'worker', the ECJ has been able to work out a different distribution of employment protections between 'employee' and self-employed workers (section V). This might entitle gig-workers to the protections they really need, without a counterproductive and unnecessary change of the current understanding of the 'employee' category.

## II. The Toolbox Available to National Courts: Overview of the Customary Employment Tests

Before looking at the conclusion reached by national courts on the classification of the relationship between on-location platforms and workers, it would be appropriate to consider employment tests and indicia provided by judiciaries. This can allow us to understand the kind of toolbox available to national courts when making their decisions on disputes promoted by gig-workers.

In the matter of the classification of work relations, labour courts and tribunals have been in charge themselves in shaping the definition of subordinate employment all over

[4] Codagnone, Abadie and Biagi (n 1).

the world. This is because national legislations have not traditionally been really helpful in classifying work relations, rarely providing definitions of 'employee' or 'employment contract'.[5]

Legal subordination – that is to say, the employee's subjection to the employer's unilateral direction and supervision – used to be the main line of enquiry for most civil law countries.[6] Nonetheless, things have changed in the post-industrial era. The employer, especially for high-skilled or very low-skilled jobs, is often not interested in control over the manner of work, but she or he is more interested in the result of work.[7] Other indicators of subordination apart from direction and supervision, taking into consideration the changing prevailing models of employment, have then been put forward by judiciaries.

For example, French judicial authorities currently mainly use two tests to identify a legal relationship of subordination (*lien de subordination juridique*).[8] The first refers to the integration into an organised service (*service organisé*), meaning that the employer controls the execution of the work (ie, gives technical direction, establishes the place of work and the working time). The second considers the participation within one employer's business (ie, dependency on the employer's organisation), from a negative perspective: the worker does not employ anyone, he or she does not have his or her own clientele and he or she does not have to cover the business risk.

In German law, the distinction between subordinate employment and self-employment lies on the degree of personal dependence (*Persönliche Abhängigkeit*), identified by courts through a wide set of indicators, according to a classical typological method.[9] The most important refers to the integration into the employer's organisation (*Organisatorische Abhangigkeit*): workers offer their work within the frame of an organisation determined and directed by another;[10] aside from the fact that they do not have their own clientele, they do not employ anyone, they do not make investments, they are not free to determine the price of products or services, etc.

Dependency on an employer is also one of the main criteria for the recognition of an employment relationship in Spain. Significantly, employment tests are accompanied here by a rebuttable presumption of employment status provided by Article 8.1 of the Workers Statute, according to which the worker should just prove that the service is provided within the scope of the organisation and management by the client. This is a reversal of the burden of proof on employers.

In Italy, the employee's condition of technical subordination to the employer's control, functional for the organisation of the employer's business is still considered the

[5] G Casale, *The Employment Relationship: A Comparative Overview* (Oxford, Hart Publishing, 2011) 17–29.

[6] N Countouris, 'The Employment Relationship: A Comparative Analysis of National Judicial Approaches' in G Casale (ed), *The Employment Relationship. A Comparative Overview* (Oxford, Hart Publishing, 2011) 35, 57.

[7] A Supiot, 'Les nouveaux visages de la subordination' (2000) 2 *Droit Social* 131, 147.

[8] Supiot (n 7) 140; A Perulli, 'Subordinate, Autonomous and Economically Dependent Work: A Comparative Analysis of Selected European Countries' in G Casale (ed), *The Employment Relationship. A Comparative Overview* (Oxford, Hart Publishing, 2011) 137, 150; Countouris (n 6) 55.

[9] M Weiss and M Schmidt, 'Germany (Fed Rep)' in *International Encyclopaedia for Labour Law and Industrial Relations* (Alphen aan den Rijn, Wolters Kluwer, 2008) 45; L Nogler, *The Concept of 'Subordination' in European and Comparative Law* (Trento, Quaderni del Dipartimento di Scienze Giuridiche, 2009).

[10] W Däubler, 'Working people in Germany' (1999) 21 *Comparative Labor Law & Policy Journal* 77; Weiss and Schmidt (n 9); Perulli (n 8) 158.

principal characterisation of the employment status, also being expressly recognised in Article 2094 of the Civil Code. Integration (often referred as hetero-organisation) into the employer's organisation and continuity of the employee's obligation to cooperate are other common indicators of subordination.[11] The employee's duty to comply with a set working time, a fixed amount of remuneration, the absence of risk of loss, the 'label' attached by the parties to the contract are some of the subsidiary 'indicia', coming into relevance whenever the test based on the above-mentioned primary indicators are not conclusive.[12] Italian case law tends not to consider dependency on the employer's business, despite the emphasis placed on it by the Constitutional Court.[13]

The application of the above-mentioned indicators work, in all the civil law jurisdictions considered, on the primacy of facts principle: judges go beyond the description of the relationship given by the parties, looking at the way the relationship between them is carried out. Moreover, the indicators are assessed through a multifactor test/typological method, according to which the greater the number of employment indicia have been satisfied, the more likely it is that the individual will be an employee.

As far as the UK and other common law countries are concerned, the 'control test' was at the beginning the only test, according to which employment is a relationship of control, where the employer gives orders, plans out jobs in minute detail and monitors the employees' work. Other tests have then been developed by English courts: integration test, economic reality test and mutuality of obligation test. Integration corresponds exactly to the considered namesake indicator developed by civil law courts. Even the economic reality test, aimed at assessing whether the individual is not working for his own account, does not differ much from the negative tests used in civil law countries. Mutuality of obligation – looking for a promise by both parties to provide and accept future work – is known in other countries as continuity of obligation, and has had a strong and controversial impact.[14] Currently, UK courts tend to use the so-called 'multiple' test, taking into consideration the above-mentioned tests and all aspects of the relationship, no single feature being in itself decisive.[15] Eventually, courts still consider control and mutuality of obligation the 'irreducible minimum criteria' for the establishment of a contract of employment.[16]

The 'control' test is also at the core of the common law test in the US.[17] According to the Supreme Court, it applies to defining an 'employee' under statutes not providing their own definition. It does not concern the Fair Labor Standards Act (FLSA) – providing a wide range of employment rights, including the minimum wage – which has introduced a broader definition of employment in comparison to that based on the common law 'control' test. In that way, the FLSA definition of 'employ' includes

[11] Perulli (n 8) 144–49; Nogler (n 9) 88–89.
[12] L Spagnuolo Vigorita, 'Impresa, rapporto di lavoro, continuità (riflessioni sulla giurisprudenza)' (1969) I *Rivista di Diritto Civile* 570.
[13] Constitutional Court, sentence n 30 of 1996.
[14] Supiot (n 7) 141.
[15] Countouris (n 6) 51–52.
[16] S Deakin, 'Does the "Personal Employment Contract" Provide a Basis for the Reunification of Employment Law? (2007) 36 *Industrial Law Journal* 68, 79.
[17] K Dau-Schmidt et al, *Legal Protection for the Individual Employee*, 4th edn (St Paul, MN, West Academic Publishing, 2011) 31–45.

'suffer or permit to work' (section 203(g)), ie, the work that the employer directs or allows to take place. On the basis of the 'suffer or permit' concept, the Supreme Court and Circuit Courts of Appeal have developed the multifactorial 'economic realities' test: workers who are dependent on the business of the employer are considered to be employees. This shall be determined from several factors, none alone determinative, including that relating to an employer's control. In opposition to the multifactor test, State legislatures and administrative agencies (adopted by many legislations starting in Massachusetts in 2004, for employment insurance and protective statutes)[18] have increasingly made use of the so-called ABC test, based on a rebuttable presumption of employment. According to this, a worker is considered an employee, unless the hiring entity satisfies all three of the following conditions:

1. The worker is free from the control and direction of the hiring entity in connection with the performance of the work, both under the contract for the performance of the work and in fact (*control test*).
2. The worker performs work that is outside the usual course of the hiring entity's business.
3. The worker is customarily engaged in an independently established trade, occupation, or business of the same nature as that involved in the work performed.

Since it is not a multifactorial test, it is simpler, less vague and more predictable. It does not involve any balance between employment indicators, but leads to straightforward conclusions. This turned out to be very useful for the classification of gig-workers, and thus adopted by California legislation (as we will see later).

Despite the different labels, employment indicators and tests look remarkably similar across the above-mentioned countries. To sum up, judiciaries normally start their investigation from legal subordination, or in common law jurisdiction from the very similar control test. Whenever these have little relevance or no relevance at all in assessing the employment status, they tend to resort to a set of indicators/tests that, again, do not substantially differ from country to country: integration into the organisational framework created by the employer, dependency/economic reality test, legal continuity/mutuality of obligations.

## III. The Gig Economy Workers in National Courts

Bearing in mind the highlighted employment tests, the analyses of the judicial investigation should start from clearing the field of the ambiguous nature of the relationship between platforms and workers. In that regard, it should be remembered that the degree of control varies widely depending on the model of business on which the platform is based: some platforms just match workers and final users, others have strict control over the workers, as is typical of platforms providing ride-hailing and food delivery services.

[18] Session Law, Act, 2004, c 193, 'An Act Further Regulating Public Construction in the Commonwealth', amending chapter 149, § 148B of the Massachusetts General Laws, on 'Employee Status; Exceptions; Penalties'. It can be consulted here: www.malegislature.gov/Laws/SessionLaws/Acts/2004/Chapter193.

As far as the latter are concerned, it is interesting to quote the North California District Court in *O'Connor*, acknowledging that 'Uber does not simply sell software; it sells rides', by harnessing its drivers' performance. Similar conclusions have been reached by the ECJ in *Élite Taxi*[19] and *Uber France SAS*.[20] Asked to ascertain whether the services provided by Uber should be regarded as transport services, information society services or a combination of both, the ECJ concluded that: Uber provides 'more than an intermediation service', it 'simultaneously offers urban transport services'; 'Uber exercises decisive influence over the conditions under which that service is provided by drivers', determining 'at least the maximum fare' and exercising 'a certain control over the quality of the vehicles, the drivers and their conduct, which can, in some circumstances, result in their exclusion'.

It has therefore to be excluded that the relationship between the ride-hailing platform and the drivers – and, more generally, that involving a vertically integrated platform (including food delivery) – can be considered as a business-to-business relationship. On the contrary, workers should be seen as an integral part of the service provided by the platform. Thus, can platforms be considered as employers in the light of the employment tests shown above? The answer to that question has been at the core of the legal disputes raised all over the world by gig-workers. The outcome has been rather conflicting, even if apparent stabilisation looks on the way.[21]

Some decisions, especially the first to be delivered, when the phenomenon was probably still small and pretty unknown, have confirmed the 'independent contractor' status of the gig-workers. Among these decisions:

- District Court for the Northern District of California in *Lawson v Grubhub* (a British and US version of Foodora).[22]
- District Court for the Eastern District of Pennsylvania in *Razak v Uber Technologies*.[23]
- Torino Labour Court in *Pisano v Digital Services XXXVI Italy* (*Foodora*).[24]
- Conseil de prud'hommes de Paris (Labour Tribunal) in *Florian Menard v SAS Uber France and Societe Uber BV*.[25]
- Cour d'appel de Lyon (*Uber*).[26]
- Cour d'appel de Paris (*Deliveroo*).[27]

[19] Case C-434/15 *Asociación Profesional Elite Taxi v Uber Systems Spain*, SL ECLI:EU:C:2017:981 [2017].

[20] Case C-320/16 *Criminal proceedings against Uber France* ECLI:EU:C:2018:221 [2018].

[21] For a comprehensive review of the decisions delivered by courts and administrative tribunals in Europe, see C Hießl, 'Case Law on the Classification of Platform Workers: Cross-European Comparative Analysis and Tentative Conclusions' (2022) *Comparative Labor Law & Policy Journal*, available at SSRN: www.ssrn.com/abstract=3839603 or http://dx.doi.org/10.2139/ssrn.3839603.

[22] www.courthousenews.com/wp-content/uploads/2018/02/grubhub-ruling.pdf.

[23] www.isdc.ch/media/1591/14-razak-v-uber.pdf.

[24] www.globalworkplaceinsider.com/2018/05/italian-labour-court-hands-down-landmark-decision-on-foodora-case-with-potentially-far-reaching-implications-for-any-company-active-in-italys-growing-gig-economy.

[25] www.diritto-lavoro.com/wp-content/uploads/2018/02/sentenza-del-29-gennaio-2018.pdf.

[26] www.doctrine.fr/d/CA/Lyon/2021/C302A25A2F9007470EB8F.

[27] www.iuslaboris.com/insights/deliveroo-riders-are-independent-contractors-not-employees-in-france-confirmation-from-the-paris-court-of-appeal/.

- Firenze Labour Court (*Deliveroo*).[28]
- Australian Fair Work Commission in *Kaseris v Rasier Pacific*.[29]

Other decisions, which have become the majority over time, have qualified gig-workers as 'employees', including in the Supreme Courts sentences of three different countries:

- Cour d'appel Paris in *Florian Menard v SAS Uber France and Societe Uber BV*.[30]
- Cour de cassation on food delivery company *Take eat Easy*.[31]
- Cour de cassation, on 4 March 2020, n°19-13316 (*Uber*).[32]
- Corte di Cassazione on 24 January 2020, no 1663 (*Foodora*).[33]
- Valencia Tribunal in *Jose Enrique v Roofoods Spain SL* (*Deliveroo*).[34]
- Fair Work Commission in *Klooger v Foodora Australia*.[35]
- Tribunal Supremo Spanish Supreme Court (*Glovo*).[36]

A different outcome concerned Courts in countries where a third intermediate category, between employment and self-employment, is given by the legislature, variously referred to as dependent contractors, quasi-subordinate workers, economically dependent workers. These are:

- Central London Employment Tribunal in *Aslam, Farrar & Others v Uber*,[37] confirmed by the Employment Appeal Tribunal[38] and the Court of Appeal.[39]
- Madrid Labour Court in *Beatriz Victoria Prada Rodriguez v Glovo*.[40]
- Torino Court of Appeal in *Pisano v Digital Services XXXVI Italy* (*Foodora*).[41]

The varied solutions offered by courts seem not to depend on the diverging terms and conditions of platform work from country to country, which are on the contrary very similar. Sporadically, peculiar terms of the engagement emerged in one given country, such as the 'batching system' in the Australian Fair Work Commission decision in *Kloger v Foodora*.[42] Different outcomes do not correspond to different legislative definitions

[28] www.bollettinoadapt.it/ancora-sui-riders-cosa-dice-concretamente-il-tribunale-di-firenze.
[29] www.fwc.gov.au/documents/decisionssigned/html/2017fwc6610.html.
[30] www.legalis.net/jurisprudences/cour-dappel-de-paris-pole-6-ch-2-arret-du-10-janvier-2019.
[31] www.soulier-avocats.com/en/reclassification-of-the-contract-between-a-delivery-rider-and-a-digital-platform-a-strong-message-sent-by-the-cour-de-cassation/.
[32] www.courdecassation.fr/IMG/20200304_arret_uber_english.pdf.
[33] www.lexology.com/library/detail.aspx?g=fc305f7a-0c7b-4d7f-8cb2-1d2fd359616e.
[34] www.euronews.com/2018/06/04/judge-rules-against-deliveroo-in-landmark-decision-in-spain.
[35] www.fwc.gov.au/documents/decisionssigned/html/2018fwc6836.htm.
[36] www.eldiario.es/economia/tribunal-supremo-falla-primera-vez-caso-riders-concluye-falso-autonomo_1_6240803.html.
[37] www.judiciary.uk/judgments/mr-y-aslam-mr-j-farrar-and-others-v-uber/).
[38] www.assets.publishing.service.gov.uk/media/5a046b06e5274a0ee5a1f171/Uber_B.V._and_Others_v_Mr_Y_Aslam_and_Others_UKEAT_0056_17_DA.pdf.
[39] www.judiciary.uk/wp-content/uploads/2018/12/uber-bv-ors-v-aslam-ors-judgment-19.12.18.pdf.
[40] www.jurisprudencia.vlex.es/vid/740259545.
[41] wwww.ichinobrugnatelli.it/en/foodora-riders-comment-by-atty-marco-paoletti-on-the-judgment-of-the-court-of-appeal-of-turin/.
[42] As illustrated by the Fair Work Commission (n 35) it 'introduced a ranking of individual delivery riders/drivers as part of the process by which available shifts were offered and subsequently selected'.

and employment tests available in the considered jurisdictions either. As shown above, the employment tests elaborated by Labour Courts and Tribunals are remarkably similar, no matter whether civil law or common law systems are concerned, and they are applied on the basis of a primacy of facts principle and a multifactor test.

The combination of these employment tests can be summarised with regard to a selection of significant decisions shown in the following tables.

**Table 1** Spain

| Court and platform | Valencia Labour Court – food delivery[43] | | Madrid Labour Court – food delivery | | Supreme Court – food delivery | |
|---|---|---|---|---|---|---|
| Employment test | Control | YES | Control | NO | Control | YES |
| | Integration | YES | Integration | NO | Integration | YES |
| | Dependency | YES | Dependency | NO | Dependency | YES |
| | Mutuality of obligations | Not considered (NC) | Mutuality of obligations | NO | Mutuality of obligations | NC |
| Classification | EMPLOYEES | | INTERMEDIATE CATEGORY | | EMPLOYEES | |
| Main points of reasoning | 'The final decision on the work schedule was on Deliveroo … The company gave specific instructions about the way in which delivery had to be carried out, setting time and behaviours that they had to comply with … The worker lacked the freedom to refuse orders. The rejection of offers and repeated lack of availability led to the extinction of the relationship between the parties'. | | 'Plaintiffs decided how, where and when to provide services, they had full control of their activity and could even desist from a service previously accepted without suffering any penalty'. | | 'Riders who do not have their own and autonomous business organization, who provide their services within the employer's organization of work, subject to the management and organization of the platform, as evidenced by the fact that Glovo establishes all aspects related to the form and price of the collection and delivery service of said products'. 'The claimant did not have a true capacity to organise his work provision, lacking autonomy to do so. It was subject to the organizational guidelines set by the company'. | |

*(continued)*

[43] ibid.

**Table 1** ***(Continued)***

| Classification | EMPLOYEES | INTERMEDIATE CATEGORY | EMPLOYEES |
|---|---|---|---|
| | | | 'Glovo has the power to sanction its distributors for a plurality of different behaviours, which is a manifestation of the managerial power of the employer'.<br>'Through the digital platform, Glovo carries out a real-time control of the provision of the service, without the delivery person being able to carry out his task unrelated to said platform'. |

**Table 2** Italy

| Torino Labour Court – food delivery | | Torino Court of Appeal – food delivery | | Supreme Court – food delivery | |
|---|---|---|---|---|---|
| Control | NO | Control | NO | Control | NO |
| Integration | NO | Integration | YES | Integration | YES |
| Dependency | NO | Dependency | NO | Dependency | NO |
| Mutuality of obligations | NO | Mutuality of obligations | NO | Mutuality of obligations | NC |
| INDEPENDENT CONTRACTORS | | INTERMEDIATE CATEGORY | | EMPLOYEES | |
| 'Workers did not have to show up for work and the platform did not have to provide work … That is enough to exclude they were under legal subordination'. | | 'What looks relevant in order to exclude employment status is the circumstance that employees were free to give their availability for the shifts proposed by the company'.<br>However, according to Legislative Decree no 81 of 2015, the same regulation of the employment relationship shall also apply to hetero-organised relationships. Namely those relationships 'functionally integrated in the client productive organization, so that the work performance ends up being structurally linked to that (the organisation)'. | | Legislative Decree no 81/2015 extended 'the application of the legal discipline of the subordinate employment to forms of continuous and personal collaboration, carried out with the functional interference of the organization unilaterally prepared by the person commissioning the service'. | |

*(continued)*

**Table 2** ***(Continued)***

| INDEPENDENT CONTRACTORS | INTERMEDIATE CATEGORY | EMPLOYEES |
|---|---|---|
| | Those are the work relations involved in food delivery where 'the riders worked on the basis of a shift, in areas and on routes established by the client … as well as the delivery times (30 minutes from taking charge of the product)'. | The worker is not autonomous since the 'methods of work are substantially determined by a digital platform and a smartphone application'. |

**Table 3** France

| Paris Labour Tribunal – Uber | | Paris Court of Appeal and Supreme Court – Uber | | Supreme Court – food delivery | |
|---|---|---|---|---|---|
| Control | NO | Control | NO | Control | YES |
| Integration | NC | Integration | NC | Integration | NC |
| Dependency | NO | Dependency | NO | Dependency | NC |
| Mutuality of obligations | NO | Mutuality of obligations | NC | Mutuality of obligations | NC |
| INDEPENDENT CONTRACTORS | | EMPLOYEES | | EMPLOYEES | |
| 'Total liberty of organisation enjoyed by the driver sets up an obstacle to acknowledging an employment contract'. | | 'The freedom for the driver to connect to the application … is not likely to exclude the existence of a relationship of subordination, since it has been demonstrated that when the driver connects to the Uber platform, he integrates a service organised by the company, which gives him directives, monitors the execution of work and exercises a power of sanction'. | | 'The application was equipped with a system of geolocation allowing the real-time monitoring by the company of the position of the courier … and, secondly, that the company Take Eat Easy had the power to sanction the courier'. | |

| Supreme Court – ride hailing | | Paris Court of Appeal – food delivery | |
|---|---|---|---|
| Control | YES | Control | NO |
| Integration | YES | Integration | NC |
| Dependency | YES | Dependency | NC |
| Mutuality of obligations | NC | Mutuality of obligations | NO |

*(continued)*

**Table 3** ***(Continued)***

| EMPLOYEES | INDEPENDENT CONTRACTORS |
|---|---|
| 'The driver worked with the ride-hailing service created and entirely organised by the Uber platform which did not enable the driver to build up his own clientele, set his rates freely or establish the conditions under which he provides transport services. The fares were set by Uber by means of a predictive mechanism based on a route over which the driver has no control and the final destination of the journey is sometimes not known to the driver'. 'Uber had the ability to temporarily disconnect the driver from the application after he had refused three trips and the driver could lose access to his account if a defined order cancellation rate was exceeded or if he had been reported for "problematic behaviour"'. | A permanent legal subordination is excluded by: 'the freedom to choose whether or not to perform services according to their own convenience'; 'the possibility of collaborating with other platforms, which was the case in this instance for the delivery partner, who collaborated with several platforms directly competing with Deliveroo;' 'the ability to subcontract their delivery services'. Geolocation system was considered 'inherent to the service requested', therefore not conflicting with the independent contractors status. |

**Table 4** Australia

| Fair Work Commission – Uber | | Fair Work Commission – food delivery | |
|---|---|---|---|
| Control | NO | Control | YES |
| Integration | NO | Integration | YES |
| Dependency | NO | Dependency | YES |
| Mutuality of obligations | NO | Mutuality of obligations | NC |
| INDEPENDENT CONTRACTORS | | EMPLOYEES | |
| 'The Applicant was able to choose when to log in and log off the Partner App, he had control over the hours he wanted to work, he was able to accept or refuse trip requests (with some caveats) and he was free to choose how he operated and maintained his vehicle. All of these factors weigh in favour of an independent contractor relationship'. | | 'The level of control that might be exercised in employment situations was obtained by Foodora by virtue of the operation of, inter alia, the batching system. As a matter of practical reality, the applicant could not pick and choose when and where to work, or how fast or slow to make deliveries'. | |

**Table 5** United States

| District Court for the Eastern District of Pennsylvania – UBER | | Fair Work Commission – food delivery | |
|---|---|---|---|
| Control | NO | Control | NO |
| Integration | YES | Integration | NO |
| Dependency | NO | Dependency | NO |
| Mutuality of obligations | NO | Mutuality of obligations | NO |

*(continued)*

**Table 5** ***(Continued)***

| INDEPENDENT CONTRACTORS | INDEPENDENT CONTRACTORS |
|---|---|
| 'Because UberBlack drivers can work as little or as much as they want – the hallmark of a lack of "relationship permanence" with an alleged employer – this factor weighs heavily in favor of Plaintiffs' independent contractor status … Opportunity for profit or loss depending upon his managerial skill since they can concentrate their efforts around certain "high times" of the day, week, month, or year, in order to capitalise on "surge pricing"'. | 'Grubhub did not control the manner or means of Mr Lawson's work, including whether he worked at all or for how long or how often and neither Grubhub nor Mr Lawson contemplated the work to be long term or regular, but rather episodic at Mr Lawson's sole convenience'. |

What emerges from the analysis of the above-mentioned decisions is that, generally speaking, the application of the traditional employment tests has been fairly complicated. Quoting the District Court of California in a case concerning Lyft (Uber's main competitor in the US): it is like handling 'a square peg and asked to choose between two round holes', because the 'test the California courts have developed over the 20th Century for classifying workers isn't very helpful in addressing this 21st Century problem'.[44] The same conclusion can be true for all the jurisdictions considered here.

More precisely, while the personality of work is usually confirmed by gig-economy arrangements, which do not normally permit the worker to send along a replacement, the traditional control test, as many decisions seem to confirm, is more difficult to meet.[45] Even if a certain control was recognised, for example in the relationship between Uber and its drivers, they 'retain very little freedom to determine their working conditions since ride fees are not negotiable and they have to comply with a detailed performance protocol';[46] platforms do not seem to have the same control over workers' performances for a 'traditional' employer.[47] The fact that the workers retain the freedom to set up their own work schedule, deciding when, for how long and where they wish to work time after time, is for some courts also significant of a not complete integration of gig-workers into the organisation set up by platforms.[48] As far as the more comprehensive economic reality test is concerned, the degree of dependency of the worker on the platform again looks quite blurred. Let us consider for a moment again the example of Uber drivers. On the one hand, they seem to work for Uber, which decides the market strategies, deals with the clients, coordinates the result of workers' performances; on the other hand, the drivers do not get a fixed remuneration, they own the car – which is the relevant asset for the service at stake; all related expenses are for them, and if something goes wrong, they can even run a loss.

[44] United States District Court, Northern District of California, *Cotter et al v Lyft Inc*, Order Denying Cross-Motion for Summary Judgment, 11 March 2015, Document 94.

[45] Conseil de prud'hommes de Paris (Labour Tribunal), *Florian Menard v SAS UBER FRANCE and SOCIETE UBER BV*.

[46] United States District Court, Northern District of California Case No C-13-3826 EMC, *O'Connor v Uber Technologies, Inc et al*, available at: www.cand.uscourts.gov/home.

[47] O'Connor quote above and United States District Court, Northern District of California, Case No 13-cv-04065-VC, *Cotter et al v Lyft Inc*, available at: www.cand. uscourts.gov/home.

[48] This was, for example, the conclusion of Torino Labour Court *Pisano v Digital Services XXXVI Italy* and Australian Fair Work Commission, *Kaseris v Rasier Pacific*.

Though the employment tests so far considered can somehow be adapted to gig-economy workers, completely out of line is the legal continuity/mutuality of the obligations test. Platform workers do not have any obligation to show up for work if they do not want to and, in turn, platforms do not have any obligation to provide gigs to the workers. Thus, if the employment tests available have been very similar, the different classification of workers in the considered decisions should depend on the way they have been used. At the end of the day, it looks like that the decision to consider or ignore mutuality of obligations test/legal continuity has been the decisive factor. When judges have taken it into account, they attributed primary importance to it, and went on to say that other factors were also weighted in favour of an 'independent contractor' status. On the contrary, when they neglected it, they moved in the opposite direction.

It seems that in some jurisdictions (ie, France and Spain) there is a trend towards the adaptation of employment tests to the reality of gig-workers, giving little credit to the casual/on-call nature of the work relationship. For food delivery, especially, the reclassification of gig-workers has become very common. This is particularly true for Spain where dozens of sentences have been ruled in favour of workers in recent years.[49] However, this is in all probability the effect of the above-mentioned rebuttable presumption of employment status provided by the Spanish Workers Statute).[50]

Nonetheless, there is still a great deal of uncertainty and issues to be addressed about the classification of gig-workers for a variety of reasons.

By and large, judicial subjectivism – that is to say, a decision based on the judge's own value and conception of the good, rather than on objective application of the law – looks more widespread than usual here, mostly because of the poor guidance provided by traditional employment tests. This has created legal uncertainty, which is never good for the legal system and its legitimacy, and for the players here involved: platforms and workers.

And in fact, in some cases Supreme Court decisions have not been followed by subsequent lower courts decisions. That was, for example, the case in recent decisions by labour courts in Lyon[51] and Paris.[52]

In reaction to courts' decisions and legislative interventions, the organisation of platforms is constantly adapting in relation to the exclusion of the employment status.

Some platforms have applied the ruling only to the plaintiffs, without extending it to other employed workers. In some cases, arbitration clauses or choice of foreign courts are a way of preventing lawsuits.

## IV. How to Move Past Uncertainty?

The analyses of the relevant case law confirms that, despite the stabilising trend of decisions, there is still an urgent need to provide regulatory solutions aimed at granting

[49] A Todolí-Signes, 'Comentario a la Sentencia que consideraa los Riders empleados laborales' (2020) 6 *Labour & Law Issues* 2.

[50] Hießl (n 21).

[51] www.courthousenews.com/wp-content/uploads/2018/02/grubhub-ruling.pdf.

[52] www.isdc.ch/media/1591/14-razak-v-uber.pdf.

gig-workers access to employment and social protection when appropriate. The opinions of scholars on the possible regulatory approaches to the issue of classification of platform workers can be gathered around three main options explained in the following section.[53]

## A. New Legislative Definition of 'Employment'

One option could be that of elaborating a new broader legislative definition of 'employment' which is able to include gig-economy workers. This new definition should probably follow those court decisions which have given no relevance to mutuality of obligations. In this way, many forms of casual work would end up in the 'subordinate employment' category, receiving full employment rights.

One example is California Assembly Bill No 5 (AB5). It codifies the commonly known 'ABC test', following the ruling of the Supreme Court of California in *Dynamex Operations West Inc v Superior Court of Los Angeles*.[54] The ABC test makes easier the classification of a worker as 'employee'. And this is particularly true for gig-workers. Bringing back the above-mentioned requirements of the ABC test, while the ride-hailing and food delivery companies may be able to prove that workers are not under their control and direction, it seems almost impossible for 'vertically integrated' platforms to prove that the work performed is outside the usual course of the hiring entity's business. It is also very difficult, in most of the cases, to argue that the workers are engaged in an independently established trade, occupation, or business of the same nature as the work performed for the hiring entity. This could just, for example, be the case of a taxi driver working at the same time for Uber, but never that of food delivery rider.

Another example is the Spanish Riders Law (Real Decreto-ley 9/2021). It has introduced a rebuttable presumption of employment status for 'the activities of distribution of any type of product or merchandise, when the employer exercises its faculty of organisation, direction and control, directly, indirectly, or implicitly, through the algorithm management of the service or working conditions, via a digital platform'. Basically, the presumption already provided by Article 8.1 of the Spanish Workers Statute (see above, section II) has been extended to the case where work relations are managed by algorithm. The reversal of burden of proof is less broad than in AB5. In California legislation it can potentially apply every time a service is provided, while in Spanish law riders are requested to prove that the service is proved within the scope of the platform's organisation.

I believe that such a solution might create more problems than it would solve, especially in legislations that, unlike in the US, provide a broad range of employment rights to those who are employees. First, a detailed legislative identification of the precise boundary between 'employment' and 'self-employment' can create problems because judiciaries will lose room for adapting, as they have done so far, the 'employment status'

[53] On the possible ways for solving platform workers' issues, not only involving classification, see Tamás Gyulavári ch 7 and Martin Gruber-Risak ch 5 in this volume.

[54] *Dynamex Operations W v Superior Court and Charles Lee, Real Party in Interest* 4 Cal 5th 903 (Cal 2018), available at: law.justia.com/cases/california/supreme-court/2018/s222732.html.

to the social prevailing model of 'employee'. So, if the legislative definition turns out to be too broad or too strict at a precise moment in time, there will be little they can do to adapt it.

At the end of the day, we must then ask ourselves if it is really worth changing the current understanding of the employment relation because of a very small minority of workers. We must not forget that, thanks to the judicial adaptation of the concept, subordinate employment corresponds to the prevailing social model of it. This model is still based on the control granted by the employment contract to the employer over the employee, in order to allow the employer a smooth and efficient organisation of his or her business. Legal continuity is essential to this end as well, because the employer is (quite) sure that employees will regularly show up for work. Therefore, when a worker can decide whether and when to work, it is hard to say that he or she is nonetheless under an employer's control and so a subordinate worker.

In this regard, we should not confuse, as some judges have done, between:

a. 'subordination' (control) which means subjection to the employer's power to give instruction on how, when and where to do the work, also changing his or her mind at any time, even in an unpredictable way; and
b. a very detailed, but rather 'stable', work organisation set up by a client, which leaves to the worker the decision on if, when and for how long to join in. This does not correspond to the common understating of 'subordinate' work, but rather to 'coordinated' work, typically performed by genuine self-employed or, where existing, intermediate category workers.

Therefore, the argument that even if on-demand workers have no obligation to show up for work, they are nonetheless 'employees' because at a time when they are performing gigs they become an integral part of the platform's organisation, looks unacceptable. A certain degree of integration and coordination between client and contractor is quite normal even for 'genuine' independent contractors. The District Court for the Eastern District of Pennsylvania in *Razak v Uber* made a good example for this:

> [T]he homeowner may impose certain requirements while the carpenter/plumber is in the house, such as not permitting certain fumes, footwear, music, or other conditions – but all of these conditions apply only while the carpenter/plumber is in the home – and they certainly do not suffice to conclude that the carpenter/plumber is an employee.

Also, penalties for delays, shortcomings, low-quality performances are a rather customary characteristic of an independent contractor's relationship with his or her client.

Even the fact that the platform may push the worker to work more, by increasing the rate of pay or by giving him a preference in the selection of gigs, does not look like a decisive indicator of employment status. Again, even genuine self-employed persons are very likely to face similar situations: they should accept working proposals to make a living, and this does not make them employees. I believe that a relationship of subordination may be excluded as long as the worker does not have a formal legal obligation to accept the gigs. In short, we should not confuse 'legal obligations' with matter-of-fact reality. More particularly, we should not confuse legal continuity with factual continuity. If a worker on-demand performs for days, months, years for the same client-platform while he or she has no legal obligation to do so, this reflects a choice. It can certainly be imposed by necessity, but the same necessity concerns every worker, no matter whether he or she is an employee or an independent contractor.

These might sound like rather formal arguments, but they are not. They also bring very substantial implications, suggesting that a new definition of employment, just to include those workers, is not really something desirable.

First, many employment rights are customised on the traditional model of employment, and hence difficult to adapt to a model of work based on casual engagements. The adaptation customary employment rights would require if they were to be applied to gig-workers is the subject of the chapters by Gyulavári and Kártyás. Let us here just refer to the example of certain working time limitations: they assume the unilateral determination of the working hours by the employer, so they limit it in order to safeguard employees' health. But what if employees can determine their own working time? New interests come into play and the rule should be different.

But even assuming that the above-mentioned employment rights can somehow be adapted to gig-workers, there is another major, less theoretical, objection to consider: are we really sure that by considering gig-workers as 'employees' we would be doing them a favour? The employment status comes with employment rights but also duties. For instance, multiple jobs undertaken for competing platforms (ie, Foodora and Uber Eats), not unusual for gig-workers, will probably not be admitted.[55] Moreover, if platforms were forced to consider all workers as 'employees', they would probably change the contracts with the workers in order to reflect the mandatory employment status. Gig-workers would then become 'standard' employees and platforms would start behaving as 'standard' employers. Workers could lose flexibility – they perhaps could not decide any longer if and when to work – and decide to abandon gig-work. But, before that many platforms would probably quit the market, because their business model can only be competitive and profitable as long as it is based on independent contractors' cooperation.

All things considered, including gig-workers in the 'employment' category in an a-selective way could be counterproductive: for platforms, likely to be forced out of the market; for consumers, losing access to good quality cheap services; for workers, losing job opportunities.

## B. Creation of Intermediate Categories for Gig-Workers

A less radical solution is suggested by the British, Spanish and Italian experience. When an 'intermediate' category is given in legislation, it probably represents the most appropriate category for platforms workers; at least for those operating for 'vertically integrated' platforms.

Some authors have recently advocated for the creation of a new intermediate category, based on the concept of economic dependence,[56] which accurately describes the

[55] The topic is more deeply analysed by Tamás Gyulavári ch 7 and Tihamér Tóth ch 10 in this volume.

[56] S Harris and A Krueger, 'A Proposal for Modernizing Labor Laws for Twenty-first Century Work: The "Independent Worker"' (2015) Brookings Institute, Washington DC, available at: www.hamiltonproject.org/assets/files/modernizing_labor_laws_for_twenty_first_century_work_krueger_harris.pdf.

situation of on-demand via app workers providing a personal service mainly for one platform. According to these proposals, the main client of a dependent contractor should be considered responsible for some employment protections.

It is a very evocative possibility. Nevertheless, it reveals considerable problems in practice. First, as the attempts made by some legal systems testify, it is really difficult to find a suitable definition for this category, a definition able to identify the 'weak' contractors.[57,58] Thus, rather than providing a secure solution to the issues affecting gig-workers, a new category would probably lead to more uncertainty and litigation.[59] The empirical analysis of existing intermediate categories raises a second major counterargument. As a matter of fact, they have often created a good opportunity for a misclassification of workers hitherto considered 'employees' into a category of atypical and under-protected workers.[60] In most of the legislation where they exist, very few protections tend to be provided for these workers.

In sum, the creation of new intermediate categories appears to be a lose–lose solution, not able to solve the problems for workers of the gig economy and possibly creating new ones for 'regular' employees.

## C. Universal Rights for Personal Work Relations

A third option deals with the issue from a reverse perspective: rather than proposing a change in employment categories, it proposes a different distribution of rights between employment and self-employment.

The whole idea behind it is that 'gig' work is not 'paradigm shifting'[61] and does not bring anything really new, since some of its features can be traced back to the earliest days of capitalism[62] and they exist widely in other forms of non-standard work. It is rather a further confirmation that the all or nothing dichotomy attached to employment/self-employment is outmoded. More precisely, platform work does not seem to be putting into question the employment contract as the main gateway to employment protection. It challenges the idea, prevailing for a large part of the twentieth century, of providing protections only for those who, in order to make a living, had to accept subordinate employment and ignoring those who, for the same purpose, had invested in their self-organisation. But this idea has already become outdated, passing into obsolescence over the course of the 1980s. Over the last 30 years or so, self-employment has clearly become a survival strategy for those who are not able to get a 'regular' job through an employment contract, typically those belonging to the weakest segments of the labour

[57] De Stefano (n 1).

[58] MA Cherry and A Aloisi, '"Dependent Contractors" in the Gig Economy: A Comparative Approach' (2017) 66 *American University Law Review* 637.

[59] Perulli (n 8).

[60] N Countouris, *The Changing Law of the Employment Relationship: Comparative Analyses in the European Context* (Basingstoke, Ashgate Publishing, 2007).

[61] G Davidov, 'The Status of Uber Drivers: A Purposive Approach' (2017) 6 *Spanish Labour Law and Employment Relations Journal* 6.

[62] MW Finkin, 'Beclouded Work in Historical Perspective' (2016) 37 *Comparative Labor Law & Policy Journal* 603.

market (migrants, young workers, disabled, etc).[63] Gig-economy workers are just the latest example of low-income persons being particularly attracted by self-employment. It would now be appropriate and desirable to equip all workers performing personal work, whether employees or not, with some 'core rights'. This has already been proposed by highly authoritative scholars, like Marco Biagi with the 'Statuto dei lavori' ('Jobs Statute'),[64] and Mark Freedland with the 'personal employment contract' construction.[65]

In order to decide which employment protections could be extended beyond the employment contract, it is possible to make use of a purposive approach,[66] applying it to possible future legislation. If we consider, for example, the right to a minimum wage, it is necessary to understand whether, according to its justifications and purposes, the right can be provided with a scope broader than just 'employees'. Since the goals of the minimum wage are commonly intended to be a reduction of in-work poverty and respect for human dignity, there is merit in extending the right to the minimum wage to all personal work relations.[67] These goals are clearly appropriate for everyone who personally performs any work or service for another party, no matter whether he or she is an employee under the employer's control and integrated to his or her business or an independent contractor self-organising his or her work. Many independent contractors as well as employees obtain their livelihood by means of their personal work, selling their energies, often to just one client. Therefore, they might have dignity only if their work receives fair compensation. Otherwise, they might fall into in-work poverty and not be able to participate in society.

## V. EU Law is Moving Towards a Quasi-Universalisation of Core Employment and Social Security Rights

The Court of Justice of the European Union (CJEU) appears to be pushing EU labour law precisely in the direction of universalisation of employment and social protection beyond the employment contract. To this end, starting from the field of the free movement of workers, it has built a broad concept of worker, broader than that endorsed by national courts, according to the employment tests considered above. In particular, the concept of 'worker' has been further developed for the purpose of extending the scope of employment protection directives, and eventually for refining the boundaries of the so-called labour exception to antitrust law.[68] Following the development of the

[63] D Weil, *The Fissured Workplace: Why Work Became So Bad for So Many and What Can Be Done to Improve It* (Cambridge, MA, Harvard University Press, 2015).

[64] M Biagi, 'Le ragioni in favore di uno statuto dei nuovi lavoratori' [1998] *Stato e Mercato* 46.

[65] M Freedland, 'Application of Labour and Employment Law Beyond the Contract of Employment' (2007) 146 *International Labour Review* 3; M Freedland and N Kountouris, *The Legal Construction of Personal Work Relations* (Oxford, Oxford University Press, 2011).

[66] G Davidov, *A Purposive Approach to Labour Law* (Oxford, Oxford University Press, 2016).

[67] E Menegatti, 'A Fair Wage for Workers On-Demand via App' in E Ales et al (eds), *Working in Digital and Smart Organizations: Legal, Economic and Organizational Perspectives on the Digitalization of Labour Relations* (Cham, Palgrave Macmillan, 2018) 67.

[68] Case C-413/13 *FNV Kunsten Informatie en Media v Staat der Nederlanden* ECLI:EU:C:2014:2411 [2014]. For a comment about the implications of the case, see V De Stefano and A Aloisi, 'Fundamental Labour

ECJ jurisprudence the concept of worker can be summarised on the basis of three traditional employment tests.

1. Direction/control: the employer dictates the manner in which the work is to be carried out (this includes the time and place of work).
2. Integration into the employer's business organisation.
3. Economic reality: the worker does not bear any risk of loss, does not employ anyone, and does not act directly in the market concerned.

Even if this concept seems very similar to that of employee which many different national jurisdictions share, it differs from the latter in two very important respects: (i) *direction* has been significantly watered down by the Court of Justice so as to coincide with the idea of coordination; and (ii) the fact that little, if any, relevance attaches to the commitment to an ongoing engagement, either understood in light of the mutuality of obligation test developed by English courts or as the continuity of the employment relationship in other countries.

These differences make the EU notion of worker much broader than that of employee commonly used by national courts, to the point of including intermediate category workers – variously referred to in different jurisdictions as dependent contractors, economically dependent workers, 'para-subordinate' workers, or employee-like persons – and, more generally, all workers who (i) are engaged in 'effective and genuine activities'; (ii) are economically, functionally, and/or operationally dependent on a client/principal; and (iii) receive some kind of remuneration in exchange for such activities.

As discussed, there is a wide variety of atypical work arrangements – not properly falling within the purview of what in national law is deemed 'employment' – that in the case law of the CJEU have already been found to be encompassed within the single EU notion of worker, such as casual work, where work is irregular or intermittent, with no expectation of continuity, as in the case of lecturers paid by the hour (*Allonby*).[69] This list can be expanded, by analogy, so as to include various forms of casual work such as gig-work or zero-hour contracts, where workers perform their activity within the business cycle of a single main client.

The capacious 'container' that is the single EU concept of worker can be applied to workers 'without adjectives', excluding only genuinely self-employed workers and entrepreneurs, that is to say, workers with 'direct' access to the markets they work in, where they normally perform services for multiple clients, without any functional and operational subordination to any other business entity. In this way, the CJEU's jurisprudence has wound up entitling dependent contractors, including casually engaged ones, to a good share of the employment protections provided for in EU primary and secondary law.

Rights, Platform Work and Human-Rights Protection of Non-Standard Workers' in JR Bellace and B Ter Haar (eds), *Labour, Business and Human Rights Law* (Cheltenham, Edward Elgar Publishing, 2018); M Biasi, '"We will all laugh at gilded butterflies". The shadow of antitrust law on the collective negotiation of fair fees for self-employed workers' (2018) 9 *European Labour Law Journal* 354.

[69] Case C-256/01 *Debra Allonby v Accrington & Rossendale College, Education Lecturing Services, trading as Protocol Professional and Secretary of State for Education and Employment* ECLI:EU:C:2004:18 [2004].

These are protections the Court has so far expressly located in matters relating to pay equality between male and female workers (*Allonby*),[70] pregnant workers (*Danosa*),[71] the organisation of working time (*Fenoll*),[72] the regulation of collective dismissal (mass layoff) procedures (*Balkaya*),[73] temporary agency workers (*Betriebsrat der Ruhrlandklinik*),[74] and the right to collective bargaining, which may work in derogation of antitrust law (*FNV Kunsten*).[75] The process of extending employment protections beyond the employment contract has probably not run its full course yet: the CJEU's case law still seems to be moving towards extending the single EU concept of worker to other EU social welfare laws. A process supported by the Charter of Fundamental Rights of the European Union (CFREU) and ultimately reinforced by the Commission's initiative on a European Pillar of Social Rights. The legislative initiative stemming from the Pillar, such as the Directive on transparent and predictable working conditions[76] and the recent Proposal for a Directive on adequate wages in the EU[77] endorse the expansion of the scope of application of the rights by recalling the concept of 'worker' proposed by the ECJ jurisprudence.

Precisely focused on the challenges relating to working conditions in platform work is the recent consultation started by the European Commission under Article 154 of the Treaty on the Functioning of the European Union (TFEU), in view of enacting a common EU regulative framework. The initiative is aimed at granting gig-workers the correct employment status in the first place. To that end, the European Commission proposed the provision of a rebuttable presumption of an employment relationship, which can be countered in court.[78] However, unlike the very broad and perhaps too generous ABC test, its scope of application would be narrowed by a number of criteria to be met in order to trigger the presumption or by limiting it to relationships with a certain stability.

A 'lighter' solution may consist in the shift in the burden of proof: very basic facts from which it can be presumed that an employment relationship exists (ie, remuneration as well as specific rules unilaterally established by the platform), in which case it would be for the platform to prove that she or he is a self-employed. Both solutions, as considered by the Commission would require starting legal proceedings before courts. This would not be the case of an administrative procedure to be opened by the parties or worker's representative, aiming at providing a certification of the work contracts

[70] See www.jurisprudencia.vlex.es/vid/740259545.

[71] Case C-316/13 *Dita Danosa v LKB Līzings SIA* ECLI:EU:C:2010:674 [2010], para 41.

[72] Case C-316/13 *Gérard Fenoll v Centre d'aide par le travail 'La Jouvene' and Association de parents et d'amis de personnes handicapées mentales (APEI) d'Avignon* ECLI:EU:C:2015:200 [2015].

[73] Case C-229/14 Ender *Balkaya v Kiesel Abbruch- und Recycling Technik GmbH* ECLI:EU:C:2015:455 [2015].

[74] Case C-216/15 *Betriebsrat der Ruhrlandklinik GmbH v Ruhrlandklinik GmbH* ECLI:EU:C:2016:883 [2016].

[75] See above (n 68).

[76] Directive (EU) 2019/1152 of the European Parliament and of the Council of 20 June 2019 on transparent and predictable working conditions in the European Union [2019] OJ L186/105.

[77] 'Proposal for a Directive of the European Parliament and of the Council on adequate minimum wages in the European Union' COM(2020)682 final.

[78] European Commission, 'Second-phase consultation of social partners under Article 154 TFEU on possible action addressing the challenges related to working conditions in platform work' C(2021) 4230 final.

by labour authorities or independent bodies, as happens in the Italian work contracts certification. Either binding or purely indicative criteria or indicators valid only for platforms (and not with the general notion of 'employee') can be provided by legislation in order to support the tools above described.

## VI. Conclusion

The controversial classification of platform workers, also emerging from the conflicting labour courts and tribunal decisions from all over the world, is supporting the idea that legislative intervention is needed to protect workers and move past the judicial subjectivism which seems to be pervading courts' approach.

I considered three different options and shared the opinion that it is not worth changing our understanding of employment relations because an increasing but still small minority of workers (gig-workers) are difficult to include in current customary boundaries of the 'employee' category. The best way to protect workers involved in the gig economy is thinking bigger and thinking about the extension of some suitable employment rights and social protections beyond the employment contract, towards all those who personally perform any work or service for another party, from whose business they are functionally and operationally dependent. The European Court of Justice has been very active over the last decade in extending some core employment protections beyond the employment contract (ie, maternity leave, right to rest periods, right to annual paid leave, right to collective bargaining). To this end, the Court has endorsed a broad concept of workers for the purpose of determining the scope of several pieces of EU social legislation. It includes not only those who are normally considered as 'employees' under national employment tests, but workers commonly regarded as 'quasi-subordinate', whose work is precisely characterised by a functional and operational dependence on a principal's business.

This broad concept of worker should include all those employment rights and social protections which, looking at their justifications and purposes, appear appropriate to all those who work in the described condition of dependence.

# 7

# Floor of Rights for Platform Workers

TAMÁS GYULAVÁRI

## I. Introduction

Since the recent rapid expansion of platform work, remarkable attention has been paid to its disadvantages and particularly its legal classification. But far less has been written about the potential catalogue of platform workers' rights, in other words the necessary standards inevitable to improve their working conditions. Therefore, this chapter strives for identifying the floor of employment rights, and the regulatory methods to ensure the effective sources of enforcement of platform workers' rights.

The topic of potential employment protection and their effective regulation will be divided into three parts. Section II will outline the diversity of work relations and related rights in this sector, moreover, potential regulatory ways to cope with such heterogeneity. Section III will then turn to the list of potential employment rights. I will analyse the applicability of classic employment rights, but also standardise specific regulatory issues, which are presently not addressed by labour law. Transparency of work evaluation by algorithms, transferability of ratings, among others, are important concerns, which have a special relevance in platform work. Section III will wind up with a list of rights, which should be granted to platform workers.

Finally, section IV is dedicated to the regulatory methods that could ensure the rights examined in the chapters above. In this respect, I will consider national and international law, collective agreements, individual agreements and in particular unilateral statutes and codes. The underlying question is, how the essential employment protection could be most easily, rapidly and adequately guaranteed. While sections II and III concern the necessary rights, section IV moves to the issue of how to ensure them.

I will argue that the peculiarities of platform work necessitate the special regulation of certain employee rights, where the detailed rules are different from those of typical and even from atypical employees. Therefore, the automatic application of the labour laws of normal employees cannot be an adequate solution, which requires special labour law standards. As a whole, the focus will be on what employee rights and which specific standards shall be guaranteed, instead of the well-known paradigm of what contractual framework shall be applied.

# II. Heterogeneous Workers and Employment Rights

## A. Diverse Forms of Platform Work

Although platform work is a recent phenomenon,[1] several types of it have been developed, so it has become an umbrella notion.[2] Under varying names,[3] it is a complex labour market phenomenon with many innovative models. For instance, Eurofound identified 10 types of platform work in accordance with the type and place of work, respectively the required skills.[4] As a fundamental feature, we can state that there is a virtually unlimited variety of forms characterising platform work.[5]

The widespread clustering of the entire group of platforms workers classifies two main forms, such as 'crowdsourcing' and 'on-demand-work via apps'. On the one hand, 'crowdwork' is performed through online platforms that put in contact an indefinite number of businesses and individuals through the internet, potentially on a global basis. The nature of the tasks performed on crowdwork platforms may vary from low-skill (photo framing) to high-skill activities (car design). On the other hand, 'on-demand-work via apps' includes the performance of local services (such as transport, cleaning or clerical work), and it is offered to workers and clients via applications. The platforms running these apps typically set various minimum quality standards of service, selection and management of the workforce.[6]

So there are remarkable differences between the above-mentioned two main forms, based on the place of work (global or local), and the strength of the link between the platform and the worker. At the same time, there are several common features, such as the importance of the internet and the open call for an unlimited crowd. As regards potential and essential employment protection, crowdworkers and app workers are quite distinctive in many respects. Crowdworkers have a looser liaison with the platform, the client, but also in relation to the 'job', working time, and so on. Labour lawyers' position on app workers can be far easier, as the nature of their work relation is much closer to that of employees.

[1] It was labelled as 'crowdsourcing' only in 2006 (*cf* J Howe, 'The Rise of Crowdsourcing' *Wired Magazine* (June 2016), available at: www.wired.com/2006/06/crowds.

[2] It has been widely debated whether it is indeed a genuinely new form. The outstanding importance of the internet and IT devices is evidently novel in it, however, the legal structure is not without legal predecessors, as it has been pointed out by several scholars. See MW Finkin, 'Beclouded Work in Historical Perspective' (2016) 37 *Comparative Labor Law & Policy Journal* 603; M Risak and J Warter, 'Legal strategies towards fair conditions in the virtual sweatshop', Paper presented at the 4th Regulating for Decent Work Conference, ILO, Geneva, 8–10 July 2015, available at: www.rdw2015.org/uploads/submission/full_paper/373/crowdwork_law_RisakWarter.pdf, 9–14.

[3] Many other terms, beyond platform work, have been used for this part of the labour market, such as sharing economy, on-demand economy, on-demand work, collaborative economy, gig work and gig economy etc.

[4] Eurofound, *Employment and Working Conditions of Selected Types of Platform Work* (Luxembourg, Publications Office of the European Union, 2018) 5.

[5] M Risak, *Fair Working Conditions for Platform Workers: Possible Regulatory Approaches at the EU Level* (Berlin, FES, 2018) 5.

[6] V De Stefano and A Aloisi, 'Fundamental Labour Rights, Platform Work and Human-Rights Protection of Non-Standard Workers' (2018) Bocconi Legal Studies Research Paper 1, available at: www.researchgate.net/publication/323766255_Fundamental_Labour_Rights_Platform_Work_and_Human-Rights_Protection_of_Non-Standard_Workers, 6.

But why is this extreme heretogeneity in the gig economy? The answer is probably complex, as always in the field of precarious work. The platforms are manifold, from large companies like Uber, to small local food deliveries in Bangladesh. These colourful digital platforms come from a wide range of sectors, and certainly have divergent strategies, objectives, respectively economic and legal environment (often depending on the 'mother country'). Workers also have varied backgrounds regading their age, sex, country, social origin etc. Closing the triangular structure of platform work, clients also have various needs and expectations. One can say, that these features are rather similar in other forms of work, so there must be something special beyond these in the gig economy. One of the extra factors resulting in such a variety of forms is the unleashed flexibility provided by the internet, which enables platforms to find innovative and multicoloured ways of providing diverse services. If platforms or clients have unique ideas, there is the ultimate freedom of the internet to comply with these demands.

This unlimited web freedom is topped by the second factor, namely the lack of regulation, particularly that of taxation and labour law. Regulation always has a so-called' uniformisation effect', since the legal framework inevitably leads towards the elaboration of standardised models of work. If platform work was regulated, it would inevitably be squashed into regulatory boxes with limited legal options (status). On the contrary, the lack of norms in statutory law and collective agreements results in the total freedom of employers to determine working conditions. Presently, regulation means merely the unilateral power of the platform to dictate working conditions through accepting the terms of conditions on the platform's website by simply clicking on a button through the app. And this unilateral rule-making mirrors the wide range of expectations and interests of digital patforms and their clients.

## B. How to Handle Parti-Coloured Work Relations?

In my view, the detailed, strict rules of employment relationship(s) are inappropriate to manage all the variegations of platform work. The automatic application of the rules on employment relationships would be feasible in those forms of platform work (in particular on-demand-work via apps), which resemble the most to dependent employment. As an alternative, the various forms of platform work may be addressed by specific, varying standards, as 'regulators need to resist the idea of a homogenous form of work deserving of one-size-fits-all interventions'.[7]

The debate on platform work has been simplified to the issue of their legal status. Researchers have mostly focused on the extension of the employee status to platform workers, or, as a popular alternative, to create a specific (third) legal status for them.[8] Notably, platform workers even now, prior to any legal reform, do have a legal status in national law, for example as a private entrepreneur or company member. This legal status is used, however, only for the purposes of taxation and social security insurance, but employment rights are not attached. So the solution is not necessarily creating a

[7] A Aloisi, *Platform Work in the EU: Lessons learned, legal developments and challenges ahead* (Directorate General for Employment, Social Affairs and Inclusion, 20 November 2020) 2.

[8] Risak (n 5) 14–18.

new (third) status, or expanding an old one (employment relationship), but the extension of certain employee rights to platform workers.[9] The experience in relation to the third category of economically dependent workers (under various names in certain legal systems) may be used as a sample for the attachment of specific employment rights to a defined group of workers.[10] In international labour law the Transparent and Predictable Working Conditions Directive is the first step in this direction.[11] In national law, the French El Khomri Act of 2016[12] is not defining a special legal status, but contains a set of insurance and training rights for 'dependent' self-employed platform workers.[13] The big advantage of this right-by-right strategy is that the employment rights may be ensured and regulated separately, gradually, or at the same time, as is best in the national context.

If we stick to the clustering based on 'crowdsourcing' and 'on-demand-work via apps', the regulatory prospect is at least a bit more simple. Regulation of on-demand-work via apps is the easier task, since it is closer to dependent employment, so the classic employment standards may be adjusted to their special needs. Nevertheless, 'crowdsourcing' is the more flexible, globalised form, which takes place in the offline world and in the 'cloud' at the same time,[14] so it requires a looser regulatory approach. Accordingly, I will make remarks on these two forms regarding some regulatory topics below, where appropriate.

## C. Two Clusters of Employment Rights

In the next section, employment rights will be selected from 'classic' employee rights and 'specific' rights designed for platform workers. Classic employee rights are perceived as those entitlements of the workers, which have traditionally been guaranteed by statutory law, as reinforced by international labour standards, and supplemented by collective agreements. These rights are the usual, normally regulated topics of employment regulations. Labour law has elaborated a list of minimum standards for employees, which rights have similarly been guaranteed all around the world in the course of the twentieth century. In addition, these national employment standards have been generated and

[9] E Menegatti, 'On-demand Workers by Application: Autonomia o subordinazione?' in Z Grandi Gaetano and B Marco, *Commentario Breve allo Statuto del Lavoro Autonomo e del Lavoro Agile* (Padova, Wolters Kluwer, Italia, 2018) 109.

[10] See, for instance, CA García and CN González, 'The Regulation of Economically Dependent Self-Employed Work in Spain: A Critical Analysis and a Comparison with Italy' (2012) 1 *E-Journal of International and Comparative Labour Studies* 117; G Fontana, 'Dependent Workers and the Self-Employed in the Italian Experience' in B Caruso and M Fuchs (eds), *Labour Law and Flexibility in Europe: The Cases of Germany and Italy* (Baden-Baden, Nomos Verlagsgesellschaft, 2004); W Daubler, 'Protection of Working Relationships in Germany' in F Pennings and C Bosse (eds), *The Protection of Working Relations: A Comparative Study* (Alphen aan den Rijn, Kluwer Law International, 2011) 127.

[11] See Directive (EU) 2019/1152 of the European Parliament and of the Council of 20 June 2019 on transparent and predictable working conditions in the European Union [2019] OJ L186/105 (Transparent and Predictable Working Conditions Directive).

[12] Law 2016-1088 (8/8/2016) on labour, the modernisation of social dialogue and securing of professional careers. See new Art L 7341-1 and Art L 7342-1 of the French Labour Code.

[13] Aloisi (n 7) 2.

[14] Risak (n 5) 7.

also strengthened by international labour standards. So the regulation of platform work may dominantly rely on these fundaments.

However, in the new economic setting of the sharing economy, classic employee rights often need revised rules to fit the special nature of platform work. Automatic application of the rules of employment relationships (typical or sometimes atypical) may be a direct, easy solution for some rights. However, adjustment of technical and substantial provisions may be required in the case of other rights, just as in the case of some atypical employment relationships. Within the realm of labour law, the following rights have special relevance in the gig economy: establishment, amendment and termination of employment; working time and rest periods; minimum wage, including reimbursement of expenses; prohibition of forced, child labour and discrimination; and collective rights and collective bargaining.[15]

Certainly, several other employment rights may have a role in platform work, such as for instance liability for damages (eg, in case of an accident of a Foodora biker). However, I will focus on the above-mentioned core rights to create a catalogue of essential employment protections. In the following chapter, these employment rights will be scrutinised, whether they fully or partly fit the conditions and features of platform work. Social security insurance also has an outstanding importance in protection, but this chapter is restricted to topics of labour law. So, the following section will discuss, how the objectives of these traditional employee rights can be achieved in the new setting.

As is evident from literature, platform work raises certain issues which are not present in typical or even in atypical employment relationships, or are present in a very different way. The following regulatory questions will most probably require peculiar provisions focusing exclusively on platform workers: transparency and transferability of ratings; data protection and privacy; and exclusivity clauses. In the next section, I will also try to elucidate, how these specific rights could be regulated for the better employment protection of platform workers.

This multicoloured group of works presents a challenge for legislation, since it is extremely hard to provide uniform protection for non-uniform workers. Therefore, the feasible legislative strategy could approach this issue by attaching rights to the existing (tax, social security) legal status of platform workers instead of creating a new one, or force upon them a new status. The next section will make an attempt to make suggestions on a potential floor of rights for platform workers.

## III. Floor of Employment Rights for Platform Workers

In this section, I will outline the potential contents of protection right by right, starting with the classic, and finishing with the novel rights. At the end of the section, I will compile the set of minimum rights for platform workers.

[15] We may refer here to the ILO Declaration of Philadelphia 1944 (Declaration concerning the aims and purposes of the International Labour Organisation), available at: www.ilo.org/legacy/english/inwork/cb-policy-guide/declarationofPhiladelphia1944.pdf), which covers similar areas as fundamental rights.

## A. Conclusion, Amendment and Termination

Statutory standards on conclusion, amendment and termination of the contractual relationship are essential pillars of employee protection. Due to the similar nature of the work relationship elucidated by profuse labour law scholarship,[16] some of these standards should also be applied to the platforms concerning app workers and crowdworkers alike. The most important standards in the field call for universal application for all forms of personal work.

In terms of conclusion of the legal relationship, statutory law should set the minimum contents of the contract and the obligatory contents of written information provided for the worker at the time of conclusion and later amendments.[17] These legal obligations have long been embedded in European Union (EU) law, and the Transparent and Predictable Working Conditions Directive is a benchmark in this regard.[18] It is an analogue fundament of labour law, that amendment of the employment contract requires the mutual consent of the signing parties. Evidently, this principle should be also be incorporated into the regulation on platform workers.

The present practice of platforms mirrors their unleashed freedom of terminating the contractual relationship in the form of unreasoned inactivation by the algorithm, which practically coincides with the unreasoned, immediate termination of employment. However, such a termination raises the same problems for workers in most of the cases like termination of an employment relationship. It is evident that this situation must be changed by providing at least minimum protection against unfair dismissal and further rights connected to losing one's job. So protection against termination must be present in employment protection of non-standard, including platform workers. We have to keep in mind that termination is not just one matter of employment, but 'this tail wags the whole dog'.[19]

The need for existential protection in cases of loss of employment derives indirectly from the necessity to protect individual autonomy.[20] The underlying question is, what level of subordination and dependence should be protected in case of termination. Charles A Reich emphasises in his new property theory, that social resources of the individual depend on business organisations, and this leads to firm eceonomic dependence on these organisations, so economic dependence needs to be reasonably limited.[21]

[16] To mention just a few of these academic pieces: J Prassl and M Risak, 'Uber, Taskrabbit, & Co: Platforms as Employers? Rethinking the Legal Analysis of Crowdwork' (2016) 37 *Comparative Labor Law & Policy Journal* 619; J Prassl, *Humans as a Service: The Promise and Perils of Work in the Gig Economy* (Oxford, Oxford University Press, 2018); A Aloisi, 'Commoditized Workers – The Rise of On-Demand Work, a Case Study Research on a Set of Online Platforms and Apps' (2016) 37 *Comparative Labor Law & Policy Journal* 653; P Cappelli and JR Keller, 'Classifying work in the new economy' (2013) 38 *Academy of Management Review* 575.

[17] On modification of the employment relationship, see Article 6 of the Transparent and Predictable Working Conditions Directive Directive (n 11).

[18] On the minimum contents of written information, see Article 4 of the Transparent and Predictable Working Conditions Directive (n 11).

[19] H Collins, *Justice in Dismissal: The Law of Termination of Employment* (Oxford, Clarendon Press, 1992) 270.

[20] ACL Davies, *Perspectives on Labour Law* (Cambridge, Cambridge University Press, 2004) 162–63; Collins (n 19) 9–21.

[21] CA Reich, 'The liberty impact of the new property' (1989–90) 31 *William and Mary Law Review* 295.

Based on this dogmatic ground, two clusters of termination protections may be extended to platform workers. The first group may compile protection against unfair dismissal by requiring written valid reason of termination 'connected with the capacity or conduct of the worker or based on the operational requirements of the undertaking'.[22] Based on this requirement of presenting a valid reason, sanctions for unfair dismissal of employees should also be expanded, even if the worker is terminated by the algorithm.[23] The second group would include rights for workers in case of termination, such as severence pay, notice period, or collective dismissal rules. This would again be a decisive move towards universalisation of employment protection.

## B. Working Time and Rest Periods

Working time poses different regulatory questions regarding the more relaxed form of crowdwork in terms of time and place of work, and app work, which requires the physical presence of the worker at the time and place of performance. Thus, crowdworkers have more autonomy to organise their working time and rest periods. Statutory minimums would not be feasible here because of a lack of adequate enforcement. On the contrary, app workers' working time is precisely registered by the application, thus platforms can easily calculate working time and rest periods.

Since measuring and registering working time is certainly provided by the application, statutory minimums on employees shall also be applied to app workers on both working time and rest periods, such as daily minimum and maximum working time, monthly maximum working time including overtime, daily rest break, weekly rest days, paid leave. Working time banking is also feasible in platform work, however, its statutory employment provisions may need some level of adjustment. The statutory requirements on registration of working time could also be extended to applications and the underlying algorithm. The EU Working Time Directive may be an excellent basis to sort out unapplicable working time provisions. Protection of health and safety at work is the dogmatic basis of the above-listed working time provisions, and this is also extremely relevant for non-standard, including platform workers.[24] Consequently, app workers should enjoy, in my view, very similar working time rights to employees with necessary technical adjustments.

There are a few working time issues which entail explicit and peculiar provisions for platform workers. Such an important requirement should be that platform workers have an adequate period of time for performance of work. This condition is presently set unilaterally by the platforms in accordance with the algorithm, which often leads to work stress from irrational conditions and results in bad ratings. This is not an issue in normal employment, thus it calls for specific statutory limitations. Similarly, after a

[22] Article 4 of Termination of Employment Convention of the ILO, 1982 (No 158).

[23] J Prassl, 'What if your Boss was an Algorithm? Economic Incentives, Legal Challenges, and the Rise of Artificial Intelligence at Work' (2019) 41 *Comparative Labor Law & Policy Journal* 123, available at: papers.ssrn.com/sol3/papers.cfm?abstract_id=3661151, 14.

[24] International Labour Organization, *Non-Standard Employment Around the World: Understanding Challenges, Shaping Prospects* (Geneva, ILO, 2016), available at: www.ilo.org/wcmsp5/groups/public/---dgreports/---dcomm/---publ/documents/publication/wcms_534326.pdf, 18–19.

defined period of time spent actively in the legal relationship, the worker should have guaranteed minimum working hours on the basis of the average hours worked earlier.[25] The right to switch off could also be guaranteed through limits on working time and minimum rest periods.

The unambiguous definition of working time is also a necessity. In *Aslam v Uber* the UK Supreme Court stated that 'a driver was "working" under such a contract during any period when he (a) had the Uber app switched on, (b) was within the territory in which he was authorised to use the app, and (c) was ready and willing to accept trips'.[26] So Uber's argument, that the drivers were only working when they were actually driving passengers to their destinations, was refused by the Court. In this regard, statutory law should state that working time includes 'stand-by periods', when the worker is at the disposal of the platform to work, however, there is no provision of service due to the lack of potential assignment. This is again about the equitable allocation of financial risks between platform and worker.

## C. Minimum Wage and Compensation of Expenses

The low pay of platform workers is a fundamental problem, however, their income is not only inadequate, but incalculable and intermittent. Guaranteed minimum paid working time would be a solution for irregular, unpredictable income, which solution has already been introduced in some countries in on-call work (eg, Germany,[27] Turkey,[28] Ireland,[29] the Netherlands).[30] Low pay could be handled by the application of a statutory minimum wage in app work and crowdwork alike. There are several arguments for the application of a minimum wage. It ensures a just share of financial risks between platform and worker, and guarantees a minimum of employment protection in order to moderate exclusion and inequalities. A minimum wage creates fair competition between platforms of the sharing economy and traditional employers, so platforms cannot acquire a competitive advantage from depressed pay.[31] It protects workers, but also the market in a wider sense, as low pay often results in unemployment and economic depression as

[25] A Aloisi, V De Stefano and S Silberman, 'A Manifesto to Reform the Gig Economy' (Milan, 29 May 2017), available at: www.pagina99.it/2017/05/29/amanifesto-to-reform-the-gig-economy/.

[26] *London Central Employment Tribunal 28.10.2016, 2202551/2015 & Others, Aslam, Farrar & Others v Uber BV, Uber London Ltd & Uber Britannia Ltd*, available at: www.judiciary.gov.uk/judgments/mr-y-aslam-mr-j-farrar-and-others-v-uber/.

[27] B Waas, 'New Forms of Employment in Germany' in R Blainpain and F Hendrickx (eds), 'New Forms of Employment in Europe' (2016) 94 *Bulletin of Comparative Labour Relations* 223.

[28] K Bakirci, 'New Forms of Employment in Turkey' in R Blainpain and F Hendrickx, 'New Forms of Employment in Europe' (2016) 94 *Bulletin of Comparative Labour Relations* 361.

[29] Organisation of Working Time Act 1997, s 18, available at: www.irishstatutebook.ie/eli/1997/act/20/section/18/enacted/en/html#sec18.

[30] Eurofound, *New Forms of Employment* (Luxemboourg, Publications Office of the European Union, 2015), available at: www.eurofound.europa.eu/sites/default/files/ef_publication/field_ef_document/ef1461en.pdf, 55–56.

[31] E Menegatti, 'A Fair Wage for Workers On-Demand via App' in E Ales et al (eds), *Working in Digital and Smart Organizations: Legal, Economic and Organizational Perspectives on the Digitalization of Labour Relations* (London, Palgrave Macmillan, 2018) 68.

a consequence of low-key demand. Protection against such market failures is the main source of legitimation of labour law.[32]

So the solution for the above-mentioned problems is to guarantee a universal right to a minimum wage, irrespective of the contractual form, icluding on-demand-work via apps and also crowdwork.[33] National law has a high importance regarding, for instance, the amount of a minimum wage and the way it is defined, which certainly differs from country to country, even within the EU. The determination of the applicable national law is not always easy and evident, since Article 8 of the Rome I Regulation[34] arranges the choice of national law exclusively in relation to employment relationships.[35] Despite legal difficulties, expansion of the minimum wage to a wider range of work relations, including especially platform workers, would really improve the working conditions and living standard of these non-standard workers. A minimum wage would guarantee higher pay and it would also make their income more predictable.

It is a generally applied principle of labour law that necessary and reasonable expenses occurred in relation to work performance must always be covered or reimbursed by the employer, since economic activities are carried out for their interest and profit. There is no reasonable explanation for the present practice of platforms, whereby they push all the expenses deriving from using and operating work equipment onto the worker. It is highly reasonable that platforms should also compensate the platform worker for using her own computer, car, bike etc. Platforms should be obliged to provide adequate compensation for expenses and it shall be explicitly prohibited to include such compensation in pay. This legal obligation would contribute remarkably to the just allocation of risks and obligations deriving from work. The detailed regulation of compensation for expenses could be left for unilateral codes of conduct, or terms and conditions of platforms, in compliance with explicit statutory standards.

## D. Prohibition of Forced Labour, Child Labour and Discrimination

Crowdwork in particular involves the potential possibility of using forced labour and child labour, since work may be performed literally anywhere, even in a sweatshop, sweat factory.[36] So, there is an increased danger of forced labour, however, it cannot be investigated and banned with the usual methods and measures, due to the globalised nature of crowdwork. Similar risks arise regarding child labour taking into account the

[32] A Todolí-Signes, 'The End of the Subordinate Worker? Collaborative Economy, On-demand Economy, Gig Economy, and the Crowdworkers' Need for Protection' (2017) 33 *International Journal of Comparative Labour Law and Industrial Relations* 241, available at: ssrn.com/abstract=2899383, 21.

[33] See on this matter, M Freedland, *The Personal Employment Contract* (Oxford, Oxford University Press, 2003); M Freedland and N Kountouris, *The Legal Construction of Personal Work Relations* (Oxford, Oxford University Press, 2011); Menegatti, 'A Fair Wage for Workers On-Demand via App' (n 31) 78.

[34] Regulation (EC) No 593/2008 of the European Parliament and of the Council of 17 June 2008 on the law applicable to contractual obligations (Rome I).

[35] Risak and Warter (n 2) 5.

[36] J Zittrain, 'The Internet Creates a New Kind of Sweatshop' *Newsweek* (12 July 2009), available at: www.newsweek.com/internet-creates-new-kind-sweatshop-75751.

global setting of work, which entails the wide use of child labour in crowdwork in developing countries. Some platforms even generate the work of children by video game vouchers for good work performance. Platform workers are often young persons, who work in their free time for extra income.[37]

Despite the positive effects of platform work on discriminatory practices[38] deriving from the lack of face-to-face work performance in crowdwork,[39] many platform workers face discrimination (eg, women[40] and ethnic minorities).[41] The rating system is a crucial source of equal treatment violations (see below). Despite widespread discrimination, the legal weaponry is weakened by the fact that prohibition of discrimination has not been ensured as a universal human right. Self-employed workers (non-employees) are still in many countries excluded from the scope of anti-discrimination legislation.[42]

In the face of considerable legislative efforts in EU law, effective implementation of equal treatment for self-employed workers remains problematic.[43] Particularly, the personal scope of EU gender equality law is limited to a narrow concept of employees, while a large percentage of the labour market participants are excluded from this protection. Moreover, EU law contains clear rules only on gender equality regarding non-discriminatory access to labour market opportunities.

So equal treatment laws should be improved to cover all workers irrespective of the contractual form beyond the scope of employment, including explicitly self-employed workers. At the same time, the wide material scope of the equal treatment principle should cover engagement, terms and conditions of work (pay, rating etc) and termination. Finally, Erika Kovács rightly suggests that platforms should be liable for avoiding the discriminatory behaviour of clients against virtual workers through biased ratings.[44]

## E. Collective Rights, Collective Bargaining

Universal entitlement to collective rights is the approach under ILO Conventions;[45] at the same time, EU law is much more restrictive in terms of personal and material scope.[46] In this context, a less restricted provision of these rights would be particularly

[37] Todolí-Signes (n 32) 21.

[38] K Zyskowski et al, *Accessible Crowdwork? Understanding the Value in and Challenge of Microtask Employment for People with Disabilities*. Association for Computing Machinery, 2015, available at: www.research.microsoft.com/pubs/228714/crowdwork_and_disability.pdf.

[39] N Leong, *The sharing economy has a race problem* (*Salon*, 2 November 2014), available at: www.salon.com/2014/11/02/the_sharing_economy_has_a_race_problem/.

[40] RA Barzilay and A Ben-David, 'Platform Inequality: Gender in the Gig-Economy' (2017) 47 *Seton Hall Law Review*, available at: papers.ssrn.com/sol3/papers.cfm?abstract_id=2995906.

[41] Leong (n 39).

[42] De Stefano and Aloisi (n 6) 8.

[43] N Countouris and M Freedland, 'The Personal Scope of the EU Sex Equality Directives', European Network of Legal Experts in the Field of Gender Equality (European Commission, 2012) 17.

[44] E Kovács, 'Gender Equality in Virtual Work II: Regulatory Suggestions' (2018) 5 *Hungarian Labour Law E-Journal* 3.

[45] Universal rights could be ensured on the basis of Article 2 of the 1948 Convention on Freedom of Association and Protection of the Right to Organise No 87 (M Doherty and V Franca, 'Solving the "Gig-saw"? Collective Rights and Platform Work' (2020) 49 *Industrial Law Journal* 352.

[46] See Article 153 of the Treaty on the Functioning of the European Union (TFEU).

important for platform workers due to their vulnerable and individualised labour market position. However, their freedom of association as well as information and consultation rights are severely hampered in practice by several native features of platform work and also of the trade union movement.[47] Moreover, there are legal obstacles in force in several countries to the organisation of self-employed workers in trade unions.[48] As for the right to strike, a chief tool of private enforcement of labour rights, platform workers often suffer legal limitations in issues like strike ballots. Overall, many of the existing limitations and restrictions to freedom of association, the right to collective bargaining and the right to strike disproportionately affect non-standard workers.[49]

Thinking in terms of universalisation, collective rights should be ensured for all persons performing work personally, irrespective of its legal form. Based on the foregoing, the following collective rights should be guaranteed for platform workers, beyond the right to collective bargaining (which is discussed in the next section):

- The right to association shall ensure the right to join and form a trade union, or other special forms of interest representations.
- Rights to information and consultation.
- Right to participation, representation in works councils.[50]
- Right to strike and collective action.

There are promising developments in this regard for example in France, where the 2016 El Khomri Act extended the three collective rights (collective action, freedom of association and collective bargaining) to platform workers, which rights have traditionally been associated with employees.[51]

Collective organisation and collective bargaining is the 'smartest solution'[52] to improve the working conditions of platform workers. The right to collective bargaining is not the protection of the worker, but a tool to protect herself.[53] Regarding collective bargaining, the two main issues are whether the right of platform workers to collective agreements is desirable and possible. As for the question on relevance of collective

[47] See details M Doherty, 'Trade Unions and the "Gig Economy"' in F Hendrickx and V De Stefano (eds), *Game Changers in Labour Law: Shaping the Future of Work* (Alphen aan den Rijn, Wolters Kluwer, 2018) 108; De Stefano and Aloisi (n 6) 6; H Johnston and C Land-Kazlauskas, 'Organizing on-demand: Representation, voice, and collective bargaining in the gig economy' (2018) ILO Conditions of Work and Employment Series Working Paper No 94, available at: www.ilo.org/wcmsp5/groups/public/---ed_protect/---protrav/---travail/documents/publication/wcms_624286.pdf, 3; T Gyulavári, 'Collective rights of platform workers: The role of EU law' (2020) 27 *Maastricht Journal of European and Comparative Law* 413.

[48] S Engblom, 'Atypical Work in the Digital Age – Outline of a Trade Union Strategy for the Gig Economy' in M Rönnmar and J Julen (eds), *Festskrift till Ann Numhauser-Henning* (Lund, Juristförlaget i Lund, 2017) 225.

[49] V De Stefano, 'Non-Standard Work and Limits on Freedom of Association: A Human Rights-Based Approach' (2017) 46 *Industrial Law Journal* 186, 200.

[50] On limitations of the right to participation through works councils, see E Kovács, 'Regulatory Techniques for "Virtual Workers"' (2017) 4 *Hungarian Labour Law E-Journal* 17.

[51] I Daugareilh, D Degryse and P Pochet, 'The platform economy and social law: Key issues in comparative perspective' 2019 ETUI Working Paper 10 (Brussels, ETUI 2019), available at: www.etui.org/sites/default/files/WP-2019.10-EN-v3-WEB.pdf, 55.

[52] D Schiek and A Gideon, 'Outsmarting the gig-economy through collective bargaining – EU competition law as a barrier?' (2018) 32 *International Review of Law Computers & Technology* 1.

[53] Todolí-Signes (n 32) 27.

bargaining in the gig economy, we can conclude that regulation by collective agreements could have several advantages. The main outcomes would be compensation for the asymmetry of bargaining power between the parties, and the improvement of working and employment conditions, in particular the working conditions of vulnerable workers in order to balance structural inequalities.[54]

In particular, sector-level collective agreements could play a fundamental role, since they remove wages and employment conditions from competition between employers.[55] Since platform workers often accept lower wages than employees or other platform workers, extension of sector-level collective agreements (or parts of them) to platform workers could be the best way to increase and equalise wages in certain sectors, which may result in fair competition in the given market (eg, taxi services). In addition, collective agreements may also fill legislative gaps deriving from the lack of comprehensive legislation.[56] As a whole, collective bargaining is not merely desirable, but would be an essential regulatory method to ensure effective employment protection for platform workers.

Now we can turn to the second question, whether collective bargaining is legally acceptable in relation to platform work. As a starting point, we can state that collective bargaining is based on the employment relationship and the binary model of employment regulation (employees and self-employed). Therefore, the traditional collective labour law paradigm is that employees may conclude collective agreements, but self-employeed workers are naturally excluded from this employment right and its benefits. As a consequence of this admitted, traditional concept, platform workers are excluded from the right to collective bargaining, except if they are employees. This restrictive legal concept is clearly present in EU law in spite of some recent developments towards a wider interpretation of the notion of worker.[57]

The antitrust rules of competition law serve as a theoretical basis for this legislative policy excluding all non-employees from the right to collective bargaining (eg, Article 101 TFEU). Despite these legal constraints, there have been some remarkable attempts to conclude collective agreements covering platform workers;[58] however, the regulatory role of collective agreements is robustly restrained for the moment. In order to move forward, the right to collective bargaining should be allowed beyond employment. This may need remarkable changes in the legal framework, for instance in EU law.[59] Without conceptual changes in labour law and especially in competition law, collective agreements will not become an important pillar of employment protection in the sharing economy.

[54] Schiek and Gideon (n 52) 12–13.

[55] E Menegatti, 'The Impact of the European Union Economic Governance on the Hierarchy of National Labour Law Sources' in T Gyulavári and E Menegatti, *The Sources of Labour Law* (Alphen aan den Rijn, Kluwer Law International, 2020) 119.

[56] Gyulavári, 'Collective rights of platform workers' (n 47).

[57] Doherty and Franca (n 45); J Prassl, *Collective Voice in the Platform Economy: Challenges, Opportunities, Solutions* (ETUC, 2018); Doherty (n 47); Kovács (n 50); M Freedland and N Kountouris, 'Some Reflections on the "Personal Scope" of Collective Labour Law' (2017) 46 *Industrial Law Journal* 52.

[58] Eurofound, *'Platform economy initiatives'* (2021), available at: www.eurofound.europa.eu/data/platform-economy/initiatives#negotiation.

[59] I Lianos, N Countouris and V De Stefano, 'Re-thinking the competition law/labour law interaction: Promoting a fairer labour market' (2019) 10 *European Labour Law Journal* 291; Gyulavári, 'Collective rights of platform workers' (n 47).

## F. Transparency and Transferability of Ratings

Transparency and transferability of ratings is a highly relevant issue for platform workers, which is not a similarly important matter in the case of normal employees, thus its regulation is mostly missing from national labour laws. This topic includes some further problems, like transparency of work evaluation by algorithms, which will also be mentioned in the following in relation to data protection and privacy.

Platforms in essence outsource work evalution and monitoring to the clients through the internet.[60] Continuous and comprehensive online rating of workers, extending over every single detail of work performance, is a fundamental feature of platform work, in particular in on-demand-work via apps. Some platforms even generate problems by allowing dissatisfied clients to keep or refuse results of service without payment and an appropriate explanation, beyond rating. Platform workers lose their income in such a case without any explanation, remedy or compensation, hence, workers should have the (statutory) right to dispute false, dishonest or fraudelent consumer behaviour. For this reason, it is an indispensable requirement that the entire system and procedure of work evaluation (online rating) shall be clear, transparent and ascertainable, and this equally applies to employer measures applied as a response to evaluation results. This is an extremely serious matter in platform work, since online rating may result in inactivation of the worker, or deterioration of working conditions, such as pay.[61]

Hence, the most important requirements regarding national labour laws are to set precise and clear-cut rules, minimum standards in relation to ratings, pay and lawful consequences of refusal to work. There should be independent forums and efficient sanctions, especially regarding debates on quality of service.[62] Arbitration, for instance, could ensure an effective remedy, depending on the national legal context. For instance in *Cotter v Lyft*,[63] the parties finally agreed that drivers have the right to arbitration before termination of their legal relationship, so they cannot be inactivated by a simple message of the algorithm.[64]

Beyond transparency, transferability of ratings acquired by the worker should also be guaranteed by statutory law. According to the general practice of platforms, it requires a lot of effort to achieve a high rating, which results in better tasks, thus higher income. The right to transfer one's (good) rating from one platform to another, respectively portability of her personal data connected to the rating on work performance details and clients alike, would affirm income security of workers and would diminish vulnerability and dependence. In order to ensure tranferability of ratings, it should be declared that these data form the personal property of the worker.[65]

[60] Prassl and Risak (n 16) 625.

[61] V De Stefano, 'The Rise of the "Just-in-Time Workforce": On-Demand Work, Crowdwork and Labour Protection in the "Gig-Economy"' (2016) 37 *Comparative Labor Law and Policy Journal* 471, 500.

[62] Aloisi, De Stefano and Silberman (n 25).

[63] United States District Court, Northern District of California, *Cotter et al v Lyft Inc*, Order of 1[illegible] March 2015 Denying Cross-Motion for Summary Judgment (Case No 13-cv-04065-VC), available at: www.adapt.it/adapt-indice-a-z/wp-content/uploads/2015/06/Cotter_Lyft.pdf.

[64] M Cherry, 'Beyond misclassification: The digital transformation of work' (2016) 37 *Comparative Labor Law & Policy Journal* 597.

[65] Aloisi, De Stefano and Silberman (n 25); Prassl, *Humans as a Service* (n 16) 112.

## G. Data Protection and Privacy

Digital technology and online rating keep platform workers under the extremely close control of platforms competing with personal subordination and hierarchy of employment. Although workers can decide about their time of work, platforms may however closely follow, from minute to minute through GPS, when the worker sits down, drinks a coffee, or logs onto *Facebook*, instead of cooking for instance.[66] Technological progress opens up the possibilities of privacy-invading surveillance.[67] In crowdsourcing, there are also serious problems coming from informational assymetry between platform and worker, and also the lack of protection of privacy and personal data.[68] Statutory law should, therefore, expand the adjusted provisions on data protection and protection of privacy of employees, in accordance with international standards such as the General Data Protection Regulation.[69] Beyond statutory clauses, unilateral codes of conduct may also stipulate basic principles of data protection and privacy.[70]

## H. Exclusivity Clauses

In platform work, similar to on-call work, the legal issue of exclusivity of contractual relationship with one platform often arises in practice. Exclusivity in this regard means the contractual condition that platform wokers must not undertake any contractual relationship aimed at work with other platforms performing similar economicy activities during the period of contractual obligations with the given platform. As a relevant practical background, platform workers often use this work opportunity to earn suplementary income beside some other obligations, and they also often work with several similar platforms to ensure a solid and predictable income. Therefore, exclusivity clauses curtail such work strategies and apply excessive and disproportionate restraints.

In my view, the unilateral exclusivity (incompatibility) clauses of platforms should be banned, or at least restricted by statutory law. In the case of choosing restrictions, exclusivity clauses may be allowed if they protect a genuine legitimate interest of the platform, similar to restrictive covenants.[71] The main argument against exclusivity clauses is that they are extremely hard to implement in practice, as it has been argued regarding the ban on zero-hours contracts[72] in the United Kingdom.[73]

[66] See the example of Honor, available at: www.joinhonor.com/; www.sfchronicle.com/business/article/Honor-lands-20-million-for-senior-in-home-care-6173606.php.

[67] Prassl, 'What if your Boss was an Algorithm?' (n 23) 30.

[68] A Felstiner, 'Working the Crowd: Employment and Labor Law in the Crowdsourcing Industry' (2011) 32 *Berkeley Journal of Employment and Labor Law* 143, available at: www.wtf.tw/ref/felstiner.pdf, 157.

[69] Regulation (EU) 2016/679 of the European Parliament and of the Council of 27 April 2016 on the protection of natural persons with regard to the processing of personal data and on the free movement of such data, and repealing Directive 95/46/EC [2016] OJ L119/1 (General Data Protection Regulation).

[70] Aloisi, De Stefano and Silberman (n 25).

[71] B Kiss, 'Restrictive covenants from a comparative perspective' (2018) 5 *Hungarian Labour Law E-Journal* 88.

[72] Employment Rights Act 1996, s 27(2), inserted by Small Business, Enterprise and Employment Act 2015, s 153.

[73] Z Adams and S Deakin, 'Work Is Intermittent But Capital is Not: What To Do About Zero Hours Contracts' (*IER Blog*, 1 May 2014), available at: www.ier.org.uk/blog/work-intermittent-capital-not-what-do-about-zero-hours-contracts.

The prohibition of exclusivity clauses can be useful to restrict such practices of platforms, but their absolute ban or severe restriction can only be implemented in legal practice, on condition that the platform worker cannot be inactivated without any reason, written reasoning and effective remedies. This issue is, therefore, closely connected to the need for efficient protection against unfair dismissal (see above). It may be declared that workers cannot be terminated or retaliated against for also working for another platform.[74] The Transparent and Predictable Working Conditions Directive is a decisive step in this direction, as it allows parallel engagements with other employers: the worker must not be treated adversely, and incompatibility clauses must be limited to cases of 'objective grounds, such as health and safety, the protection of business confidentiality, the integrity of the public service or the avoidance of conflicts of interests'.[75]

## I. Floor of Employment Rights for Platform Workers

Based on the foregoing, the enlisted individual and collective rights should be at least guaranteed for platform workers to better their working conditions and labour market situation. Evidently, this is a list of minimum, however, dominantly tailor-made standards for platform workers:

- Statutory law should define minimum contents of the contract and information provided for the worker at the time of conclusion and later amendments.
- Any amendment of the contract should require mutual consent of the signing parties.
- Written valid reason of termination should be required, connected with the capacity or conduct of the worker or based on the operational requirements of the undertaking.
- Sanctions against unfair dismissal of employees should also be expanded to platform workers.
- Extra rights for workers should be provided in case of termination, such as severence pay, notice period and collective dismissal.
- Statutory definition of working time should include 'stand-by periods', when the worker is at disposal of the platform to work, but there is no provision of service due to the lack of potential assignment.
- An adequate period of time should be guaranteed by statutory law for the performance of work.
- The right to switch off should be guaranteed by statutory law in accordance with provisions on employees.

[74] See similar rules on non-call work in the UK: 2015 No 2021 Terms And Conditions Of Employment, The Exclusivity Terms in Zero Hours Contracts (Redress) Regulations 2015, available at: www.legislation.gov.uk/uksi/2015/2021/introduction/made; D Pyper, F McGuinness and A Powell, 'Zero-hour contracts' House of Commons Library, Briefing Paper 06553 (13 April 2017), available at: researchbriefings.parliament.uk/ResearchBriefing/Summary/SN06553#fullreport, 19-20.

[75] Article 9 of the Transparent and Predictable Working Conditions Directive; Aloisi (n 7) 8.

- The right to minimum wage should be granted, irrespective of the contractual form.
- Minimum paid working time should be guaranteed in statutory law.
- Platforms should be obliged by statutory law to provide adequate compensation for expenses in a separate amount from pay.
- App workers should enjoy similar working time rights like employees with necessary technical adjustments particularly on daily minimum and maximum working time, monthly maximum working time including overtime, daily rest break, exemptions from work, weekly rest days, paid leave.
- The right to transfer ratings from one platform to another, respectively portability of personal data connected to the rating on work performance details and clients; moreover these data should form the personal property of workers.
- The right to dispute false, dishonest or fraudelent consumer behaviour at independent forums, like court or arbitration.
- Statutory law should expand provisions on data protection and privacy of employees, in accordance with international standards.
- Unilateral exclusivity (imcompatibilty) clauses of platforms should be banned or restricted by statutory law.
- Prohibition of forced labour and child labour through elaborating statutory standards and incenting unilateral codes of conduct.
- Prohibition of discrimination through universal strandards and statutory provisions ensuring effective protection of all workers, including self-employed, with a wide material scope.
- Labour law liability of the employer for damages, accidents, sickness of the employee.
- Provisions on protection of health and safety at work of employees should be applied.
- The right to association shall ensure the right to join and form a trade union, or other special forms of interest representations.
- The right to information and consultation, similarly to employees and their trade unions.
- The right to participation, representation in works councils, similarly to employees.
- The right to strike and collective action without legal limitations.
- The right to collective bargaining for non-employee (self-employed) platform workers by finding lawful exception from antitrust rules.
- The right to coverage by sector level collective agreements, in particular through extended collective agreements, where applicable.
- Access to labour law disputes, remedies and alternative dispute resolution mechanisms, with reasonable, specific exemptions in material and procedural laws.

So the above-mentioned employment protections may be divided into three groups. The first group includes those rights of traditional employees, which may automatically be expanded to platform workers without the need for technical or substantial limitation or adjustment. The second group of rights may need such restrictions and amendments in order to comply with the needs of platform workers, with special regard to their various groups. Finally, the third cluster includes those rights from the above list (eg, ratings, exclusivity), which are not embedded in the employment protection of employees and thus require elaboration of new concepts and standards. In the following section the focus will be shifted from the charter of rights to the potentially effective sources of these employment rights.

## IV. Multilayered Regulation of Platform Work?

Modern labour law has elaborated a set of regulatory methods (law, collective agreements, by-laws) at various levels (international, national, regional, sector), which toolbox has proved to be rather stable in the last century, despite some recent trends in changes.[76] Evidently, the same regulatory methods and levels could potentially be used for the protection of platform workers as in the case of employees. The following regulatory methods may play a role in this framework:

- International standards, including EU law, particularly as a guarantee of universal protection.
- National laws, with emphasis on labour codes in several countries.
- Collective agreements at various levels (company, sector, region).
- Individual agreements of platform and worker.
- Unilateral by-laws, particularly terms and conditions, respectively codes of conduct of the platform or several platforms.

The effective regulatory methods may differ from employment relationships due to the distinguishing features of platform work. So the questions here are: which methods are best to guarantee minimum standards for platform workers; and how can a balanced interplay between law and unilateral regulation be created which diminishes misuses of potential legal standards by platforms?

### A. International and National Law

Starting logically with international standards which may play an important role in the long run; however, international standardisation has several inherent drawbacks. It usually takes a long time to find compromises in the form of new and extended (universalised) standards. Therefore, we cannot expect fast reaction to platform work from international organisations (eg, the ILO and EU), even if there has already been a 'small step forward'[77] in EU law.[78] Moreover, the inherent compromises of international negotiations may lead to steps towards universalisation of employment protection, but this process may also water down some labour standards.

[76] T Gyulavári and E Menegatti, 'Recent Trends in the Hierarchy of Labour Law Sources' in T Gyulavári and E Menegatti (eds), *The Sources of Labour Law* (Alphen aan den Rijn, Kluwer Law International, 2020).
[77] Aloisi (n 7) 7.
[78] See Transparent and Predictable Working Conditions Directive (n 11).

Soft and slow international laws may result in some developments, but they commonly leave a lot of room for manoeuvre for national legislations. In this situation, universalisation seems to be a viable concept in the case of certain employment rights, such as the right to association, collective bargaining, minimum wage, prohibition of forced child labour and discrimination. Since platform workers, like non-standard workers in general, are excluded from the protection of labour law, thus universalisation is not yet ensured concerning these fundamental rights, despite ILO efforts.[79]

As has been described, national legislations may be confined by international standards, however, this is not the case so far concerning platform work. Thus, national statutory law has an almost absolute freedom in regulating platform work, which opportunity has not been exploited yet. Regulation of platform work through statutory law has several advantages, such as fitting the national legal framework, aptitude for innovation and finding rapid solutions for emerging problems. Moreover, the role of statutory law has been increasing in labour law regulation in general all over the world in the last decade.[80] Therefore, national statutory law should play a primary role in setting minimum standards, and case law may also be a useful tool in this work in several common law countries.

## B. Collective Agreements at Various Levels

In addition to statutory law, collective agreements could also have a supplementary role in the regulation of platform work. Based on the principle of favour, collective agreements could provide better protection to platform workers than national labour law. As it has been argued in the part of this chapter on collective rights, regulation by collective agreements could have several advantages. In particular, sector-level collective agreements could play a fundamental role, which could be achieved, for instance, by extension mechanisms. However, platform workers are presently excluded from the right to collective bargaining, except if they are employees. Thus, collective agreements will most probably play a minor role in regulation in at least medium term, unless, for example, sector-level collective agreements, or at least some rights in it, are extended to certain groups of gig-workers. Remarkably, there are also several countries with digital platforms where the regulatory importance of collective agreements is inherently limited.[81]

## C. Unilateral Regulation by the Platform

Due to the lack of national, international regulations and collective agreements directed at platform work, the terms and conditions of work are now set unilaterally by the

[79] De Stefano and Aloisi (n 6) 6–8; De Stefano, 'The Rise of the "Just-in-Time Workforce"' (n 61) 501.

[80] Gyulavári and Menegatti (n 76) 6–8.

[81] J McCartin, *Repairing the crumbling system of collective bargaining? Trade Unions and Industrial Relations in USA* (Washington, Friedrich Ebert Stiftung, 2014); T Gyulavári, 'Chasing the Holy Grail? Stumbling Collective Bargaining in Eastern Europe and the Hungarian Experiment' in S Laulom, *Collective Bargaining Developments in Times of Crisis* (Alphen aan den Rijn, Kluwer Law International, 2017) 29.

platform by a click on the website. Unilateral law-making could also be used to improve statutory standards.

The predominance of unilateral regulation is presently almost exclusively unfavourable for workers due to the extreme inbalance of power between the platform and its workers, and the weak social commitment of platforms. Freedom of contract when accepting the terms is not genuine here, because the worker has two options: accepting the working conditions offered by the platform in the terms and conditions, or refusing it (and finding another job). In addition, these conditions may be changed by the platform at any time, without any legal constraint. In this context, the agreement (contract) between the worker and platform cannot really be understood in the usual sense, as the terms of such an 'agreement' are evidently dictated by the platform.

This unrestrained freedom of the platforms to set working conditions should be thoroughly confined by national (and indirectly international) legislation. Statutory law shall have the mission to define the obligatory topics and minimum contents of unilateral by-laws ('terms and conditions') of the platforms. The limitation of the freedom of contract, or rather restriction of unilateral 'working condition setting' by the platform, may be an efficient strategy. This legal technique is of course well known from the structure and principles of regulating employment relationships in the face of minimum statutory standards and *ius cogens*. However, more freedom should be left for digital platforms (than for normal employers) to define technical rules and those conditions not confined by statutory law. The above analysed employment rights and protections should be guaranteed by statutory law at some level. Clearly, statutory law cannot arrange all conditions and should also leave flexibility inherent in the sharing economy.

Unilateral law-making could also be used to improve statutory standards in another sense. Unilateral codes of conduct,[82] not restricted by national borders,[83] may set positive obligations for the platforms, such as basic principles, minimum wage, transparent ratings and data protection.[84] The 2019 French reform is a good example which encouraged the adoption of codes of practice defining mutual rights and obligations.[85]

Furthermore, the basic concept of favourable derogations should be applied between statutory law and unilateral statutes. Therefore, the platform could derogate from statutory standards merely for the benefit of workers. The same principle should arrange the relationship of collective agreements and unilateral statutes. I think it is important to state *expressis verbis* the rules of unilateral derogation in national statutory law to prevent abuse.

Regarding the sources, we may conclude that the regulation of platform workers' rights shall involve several regulatory layers of labour law. Employment right protection should be primarily based on the interplay between statutory minimum standards and unilateral terms and conditions, supplemented by codes of conduct potentially involving more platforms in a sector. National legislation shall demarcate the regulatory

[82] For instance: 'Crowdsourcing Code of Conduct' in Germany (www.crowdsourcing-code.com/); and 'Good Work Code' in the US (www.goodworkcode.org/).

[83] Kovács, 'Regulatory Techniques for "Virtual Workers"' (n 50) 3.

[84] Aloisi, De Stefano and Silberman (n 25).

[85] Aloisi (n 7) 2.

playing field of platforms in the form of minimum standards, which must be respected, and may unilaterally be improved. These two layers are supplemented by international standards with minimum standards, and more favourabe work conditions in collective agreements.

## V. Conclusions: A Limited Charter of Rights?

The chapter outlined a desirable charter of employment rights for platform workers. Therefore, my research concentrated on the potential floor of rights instead of the legal status of workers. Certainly, this employment right catalogue may easily be supplemented by further elements; however, I tried to compose a minimum floor of rights which are essential for employment protection. At the same time, the detailed regulation of each right shall depend on the national legal framework, so only the minimum contents of rights was outlined without the important substantial and technical details.

Beyond these minimum protections, I also addressed the issue of how these employment protections could best be achieved. In my view, it would be sensible to focus on which rights platform workers need and ensure that the platform provides them with an effective means of enforcement. This might even happen on a 'right-by-right basis', which strategy seems to be a minimalist approach compared with the classification of platform workers as employees. However, some expanded rights such as minimum wage for instance may reach a much wider range of platform workers than employee status. The main argument against such a solution is the weakening of the primary employment status (standard employment relationship) by introducing secondary ones with protection watered down. So this solution is recommended, where the primary status – standard employment relationship – is not a feasible option.

Finally, the sources of regulation and their legal relationship have a key role. International standards may take steps towards universalisation of key protections, such as minimum wage and collective bargaining. However, national statutory law will have the primary task to elaborate minimum standards which must be respected and may be suplemented by the unilateral statutes (terms and conditions, codes of conduct) of platforms. The right to collective bargaining is suffering from several legal flaws, but collective agreements may also have some say in regulation of platform work in the long run. Nevertheless, the interplay between statutory law and unilateral standards will be the decisive matter in regulation. If we put the proposed floor of rights in this context, the regulation of platform work seems to be a complex, and at the same time, challenging and promising adventure.

# 8

# Working Time Flexibility: Merits to Preserve and Potentials to Adjust to Change

GÁBOR KÁRTYÁS

## I. Introduction

Working time is a key working condition for both the economic interests of the employer and the economic and social interests of the employee. Nonetheless, it seems hard to adapt the traditional rules of working time to the modern work environment. New digital technologies enable many workers to perform work at any time and from anywhere. Innovative approaches to organise working time, where work is not limited by previously set schedules and not interrupted by compulsory rest periods, entice with enhanced productivity and competitiveness for employers and with flexible schedules to cope with non-work related duties and higher influence over their working hours for workers. The aim of this chapter is to explore the challenges that working time regulations face in the twenty-first century and to analyse whether traditional legal instruments such as the fixed measure of working time, overtime regulations or annual paid leave are still relevant.

The chapter highlights that the basic institutions of working time have their roots in the protection of the health and safety and private life of the worker and thus shall be respected regardless of how technology evolves. For that aim, the standards of European Union (EU) law will be examined in detail. The strict 'binary system' elaborated by the European Court of Justice (CJEU or Court) – dividing working time and rest periods with no third category in between – or taking the right to paid annual leave as a 'particularly important principle of EU social law' show that the protections in union law shall be interpreted to apply to the broadest range of cases (section II). With such solid fundaments, the introduction of the right to disconnect seems superfluous, at least regarding those covered by the Working Time Directive (section III). Even if digital workplaces are characterised with blurred boundaries between working time and rest periods, those employers building strongly on digital technologies shall not have technical difficulties in complying with their legal obligation to measure and record working time (section IV). The traditional instruments of working time can best be adjusted to the changing needs of the parties by collective agreements: the merits and drawbacks of this legislative technique will be explored in section V. It is argued that the promise of working time autonomy may have real substance for only a very limited group of workers and protective measures shall not be traded for vague concepts of flexibility (section VI), not even if it is initiated by the employee (section VII).

As a conclusion, the chapter argues that while labour law shall not keep employees and employers from making use of the benefits of modern technologies, the minimum guarantees of working time are necessary for all workers and shall certainly not be denied based on mere technical reasons.

# II. The Binary System of Working Time and Rest Periods in EU Law

## A. What Role for Working Time Regulations?

The regulation of working time is partly a social issue, which mainly concerns the protection of the health and safety of workers, and partly an economic problem affecting production.[1] Working time is the working condition – beyond wages – that has the most direct impact on the daily lives of workers. The extent of working hours and the way they are scheduled can have a significant impact on the quality of work and on private life outside the workplace, which has importance on the community level too. On the other hand, working time is a core issue for businesses, as it is a key factor in productivity, ensuring the profitability and sustainability of the business.[2] These economic aims are also important for society as a whole: limits on working hours help to reduce unemployment and effective organisation of working time is crucial in the undertakings' competitiveness in the (global) market.[3]

The two-track nature of working time is captured by Eurofound's approach to working time flexibility which differentiates between employee and employer-oriented flexibility. While the former embraces solutions to meet the workers' own personal or family needs, the latter aims to bring the human capital in line with the temporal requirements following from business.[4] Nonetheless, these two concepts do not necessarily exclude each other as there might be an overlap between the parties' interests.[5]

The dual objective of working time regulations is also reflected in EU law, but the emphasis is clearly on protecting workers' health. The Preamble of the Working Time

[1] International Labour Organization (ILO), 'Ensuring decent working time for the future. General Survey concerning working-time instruments' (Geneva, ILO, 2018) 2.

[2] ibid, 5.

[3] T Katsabian, 'It's the End of Working Time as We Know It – New Challenges to the Concept of Working Time in the Digital Reality' (2020) 17 *McGill Law Journal* 7–8.

[4] Eurofound, *Organisation of working time: Implications for productivity and working conditions. Overview Report* (2012) 53; Eurofound and the International Labour Office, *Working anytime, anywhere: The effects on the world of work* (Luxembourg and Geneva, Publications Office of the European Union and the International Labour Office, 2017) 24–25.

[5] I Campbell, 'Working-time flexibility. Diversification and the rise of fragmented time systems' in D Grimshaw et al (eds), *Making Work More Equal: A New Labour Market Segmentation Approach* (Manchester, Manchester University Press, 2017) 113.

Directive[6] states that the improvement of workers' safety, hygiene and health at work is an objective which should not be subordinated to purely economic considerations.[7] It appears desirable to provide for flexibility in the application of certain provisions of the Directive, while ensuring compliance with the principles of protecting the health and safety of workers.[8]

Court practice also builds remarkably on this objective. The CJEU has already ruled in its first decision concerning the Working Time Directive (WTD) that the aim of the Directive is to protect the health and safety of workers. The case was an annulment procedure brought by the United Kingdom, arguing that working time rules could not have been adopted on grounds of the protection of workers' safety and health. While rejecting this claim, the Court referred to the Constitution of the World Health Organization, which states that health is a state of complete physical, mental and social well-being that does not consist only in the absence of illness or infirmity.[9] Over two decades later, the Court still repeatedly highlights that the principle that the various requirements laid down in the WTD 'concerning maximum working time and minimum rest periods constitute rules of EU social law of particular importance from which every worker must benefit as a minimum requirement necessary to ensure protection of his safety and health'.[10]

The cornerstones of working time regulation today are protected as fundamental rights. In EU law, the right to limitation of maximum working hours, to daily and weekly rest periods and to an annual period of paid leave are also enshrined in the Charter of Fundamental Rights of the European Union, which has risen to the status of a primary law.[11] The relevant provisions of the WTD, that give specific form to these fundamental rights, must, therefore, be interpreted in the light of the Charter.[12] Court practice has given no less importance to the right to paid annual leave, which the Court considers to be regarded 'as a particularly important principle of Community social law from which there can be no derogations and whose implementation by the competent national authorities must be confined within the limits expressly laid down by' the Directive.[13] A similarly important measure is maternity leave[14] – regulated outside

[6] Directive 2003/88/EC of the European Parliament and of the Council of 4 November 2003 concerning certain aspects of the organisation of working time [2003] OJ L299/9 (Working Time Directive: WTD).

[7] WTD, Preamble (4).

[8] WTD, Preamble (15).

[9] Case C-84/94 *United Kingdom of Great Britain and Northern Ireland v Council of the European Union* ECLI:EU:C:1996:431 [1996], paras 15, 38.

[10] See, eg, Case C-266/14 *Federación de Servicios Privados del sindicato Comisiones obreras (CCOO) v Tyco Integrated Security SL and Tyco Integrated Fire & Security Corporation Servicios SA* ECLI:EU:C:2015:578 [2015], para 24; Case C-518/15 *Ville de Nivelles v Rudy Matzak* ECLI:EU:C:2018:82 [2018], para 45.

[11] Charter of Fundamental Rights of the European Union [2012] OJ C326/391 Article 31(2). Note that Article 2 of the European Social Charter sets out similar rights with a view to ensuring the effective exercise of the right to just conditions of work, which are softer than under EU law.

[12] Case C-55/18 *Federación de Servicios de Comisiones Obreras (CCOO) v Deutsche Bank SAE* ECLI:EU:C:2019:402 [2019], para 31; Case C-585/19 *Academia de Studii Economice din Bucureops ti v Organismul Intermediar pentru Programul Operațional Capital Uman – Ministerul Educației Naționale* ECLI:EU:C:2021:210 [2021], para 37.

[13] See, for instance, Case C-173/99 *Secretary of State for Trade and Industry v Broadcasting, Entertainment, Cinematographic and Theatre Union (BECTU)* ECLI:EU:C:2001:356 [2001], para 43; Case C-684/16 *Max-Planck-Gesellschaft zur Förderung der Wissenschaften eV v Tetsuji Shimizu* ECLI:EU:C:2018:874 [2018], paras 19–20.

[14] Council Directive 92/85/EEC of 19 October 1992 on the introduction of measures to encourage improvements in the safety and health at work of pregnant workers and workers who have recently given birth or are

the WTD – which again must be regarded as a particularly important mechanism of protection under employment law.[15]

However, the complexity of the regulation of working time is well indicated by the fact that, although the review of the WTD started after 2004 with the first judgments on on-call time, consensus has still not been reached. In May 2017, the Commission only issued a long non-binding interpretative communication on the WTD.[16] The document well incorporates the case law of the Court but naturally cannot in itself solve the questions raised in practice concerning the scope of the Directive, on-call work, scheduling annual leave etc.[17] Eventually, the WTD, as last amended in 2003, is still in force today.

## B. The Exclusivity of Working Time and Rest Period

Working time regulations gained importance not only at the level of rhetoric. The abovementioned principles are the basis of the Court's consistent case law, according to which working time and rest periods are mutually exclusive concepts in EU law and there is no intermediate category (some form of on-call time) in between. 'Working time' and 'rest period' may not be interpreted in accordance with the requirements of the various legislations of the Member States, but constitute concepts of EU law which must be defined in accordance with objective characteristics by reference to the scheme and purpose of that Directive.[18] Therefore, following this strict dichotomy for over two decades,[19] if it can be established for a given period that the employee was at the disposal of his or her employer or performed work during that period, it should be considered as working time. This practice had great importance in the categorisation of on-call and stand-by time, as well as travel time.

Thus, on-call time performed by an employee with a physical presence at the employer's establishment must be regarded as working time in its entirety, irrespective of the work actually performed during on-call time.[20] In the practice of

breastfeeding (tenth individual Directive within the meaning of Article 16(1) of Directive 89/391/EEC) [1992] OJ L348/1, Article 8.

[15] Maternity leave is intended, first, to protect a woman's biological condition during and after pregnancy and, second, to protect the special relationship between a woman and her child over the period which follows pregnancy and childbirth, by preventing that relationship from being disturbed by the multiple burdens which would result from the simultaneous pursuit of employment. Case C-116/06 *Sari Kiiski v Tampereen kaupunki* ECLI:EU:C:2007:536 [2007], para 49; Case C-463/19 *Syndicat CFTC du personnel de la Caisse primaire d'assurance maladie de la Moselle v Caisse primaire d'assurance maladie de Moselle* ECLI:EU:C:2020:932 [2020], paras 50, 52.

[16] Interpretative Communication on Directive 2003/88/EC of the European Parliament and of the Council concerning certain aspects of the organisation of working time, C/2017/2601, [2017] OJ C165/1.

[17] See, in detail, T Nowak, 'The turbulent life of the Working Time Directive' (2018) 25 *Maastricht Journal of European and Comparative Law* 118.

[18] Case C-151/02 *Landeshauptstadt Kiel v Norbert Jaeger* ECLI:EU:C:2003:437 [2003], para 58; Case C-14/04 *Abdelkader Dellas and Others v Premier ministre and Ministre des Affaires sociales, du Travail et de la Solidarité* ECLI:EU:C:2005:728 [2005], para 44.

[19] M Glowacka, 'A little less autonomy? The future of working time flexibility and its limits' (2020) 12 *European Labour Law Journal* 113.

[20] Case C-303/98 *Sindicato de Médicos de Asistencia Pública (Simap) v Conselleria de Sanidad y Consumo de la Generalidad Valenciana* ECLI:EU:C:2000:528 [2000], para 52; C-151/02 *Landeshauptstadt Kiel* (n 18)

the CJEU, time spent on daily travel between the place of residence and the first and last customer designated by the employer is also considered as working time if the employees do not have a permanent or usual place of work. During such journeys, the workers act on those instructions of the employer and are not able to use their time freely and pursue their own interests, so that, consequently, they are at their employer's disposal.[21]

It is also clear from the Court's practice, that even periods of stand-by time[22] shall be considered working time, on condition that during such stand-by time the constraints imposed on the worker are such as to affect, objectively and very significantly, the possibility for the latter freely to manage the time during which his or her professional services are not required and to pursue his or her own interests.[23] For example, if the worker is obliged to spend stand-by time at his home, to be available there to his employer and to be able to reach his place of work within eight minutes, this situation objectively limits the worker's opportunities to devote himself to his personal and social interests, and consequently it must be regarded as working time.[24] Nonetheless, an overall assessment of all the facts of the case is necessary to decide whether stand-by time shall be considered as working time, including the consequences of the time limit within which the worker shall return to work if called, and the average frequency of activity during that period. However, the limited nature of the opportunities to pursue leisure activities within the immediate vicinity of the place where the workers stays during stand-by time is irrelevant.[25]

## III. The Use of the Binary System in Digital Work: Is the Right to Disconnect Relevant?

The strict binary system of working time and rest periods is of high value in times of blurring boundaries between work and private life. In the era of working any time and from anywhere the CJEU's case law is the stable fundament to preserve the divide between the two areas. Under this regime, if the employee is at the disposal of or works for the employer, then that period shall be regarded as working time and the employee shall be remunerated for it, regardless of the place of work and the way the work was performed. Seen from this perspective, the legal debate over the so-called 'right to disconnect' seems superfluous, at least for employees falling under the scope of the WTD.

From a legal point of view, it is clear that employees browsing emails or answering phone calls outside their regular working hours are actually performing work

paras 71, 75, 103; Case C-397/01 *Bernhard Pfeiffer v Deutsches Rotes Kreuz, Kreisverband Waldshut eV* ECLI:EU:C:2004:584 [2004] para 93; C-14/04 *Abdelkader Dellas and Others* (n 18) para 46.

[21] C-266/14 *Federación de Servicios Privados del sindicato Comisiones obreras (CCOO* (n 10) paras 36, 39, 50.

[22] It means a period when the worker is required to be permanently accessible without being required to be present at the place of work.

[23] Case C-344/19 *DJ v Radiotelevizija Slovenija* ECLI:EU:C:2021:182 [2021], para 37.

[24] C-518/15 *Ville de Nivelles v Rudy Matzak* (n 10) paras 63, 65.

[25] C-344/19 *DJ v Radiotelevizija Slovenija* (n 23) para 66.

for their employer, thus such periods constitute working time. In other words – seen from the employees' perspective – they are not breaching their employment contracts if they are not available for work outside the scheduled working time (unless such performance is ordered as overtime as prescribed in the relevant national law). From this aspect, the right to disconnect means the non-existence of the work obligation.[26] Nonetheless, such theoretically clear-cut legal classification does not mean that it would be easy to implement it into daily practice. If working time with clear boundaries becomes the exception and continuous interference between working and personal time the rule, the enforcement of the binary concept turns out to be challenging. This could be especially true for workers who can schedule their own working time (flexible schedules). The emergence of a separate right to disconnect shows the struggle of how legal systems try to stop endless working time or employees' constant availability.

The right to disconnect has been addressed by a few legislative initiatives.[27] In 2016, France introduced a specific article in the Labour Code, which places an obligation on employers with at least 50 employees to start negotiations to ensure the respect for the rest and holiday periods of workers and their personal and family lives. In the lack of a negotiated agreement, the employer shall adopt measures unilaterally. In 2013, the German Ministry of Employment introduced a 'minimum intervention in leisure time' policy, whereby managers can contact employees outside their normal working hours only to deal with exceptional situations requiring action that cannot be postponed until the start of the next working period. Furthermore, employees cannot be put at a disadvantage for turning off their mobile phone or not picking up messages outside normal working hours. In Italian law, the right to disconnect is limited to work that is 'characterized by spatial and temporal flexibility of the work performance' and does not contain any concrete provisions on its exact meaning and does not provide any guidance for how it should be applied. Spanish law provides both private and public employees with the right to disconnect outside formal work time. However, the contents shall be agreed upon by the employer and the employees' representatives.[28] A common feature of all these initiations is that the law lacks real enforceable substance and its effect is conditional on the success of the social parties' negotiations. If no agreement is reached or it contains only formal declarations – like it reiterates only the vague wording of the law – it can hardly be expected that it will reach its target to change the spreading habit of unlimited (online) work.[29]

In a growing number of cases collective bargaining agreements include various technical solutions to combat constant online availability. For example, email inboxes may be set to holiday mode, while the sender is informed that the software automatically postpones the delivery of all incoming emails until the end of the leave period. A similar limitation may apply on sending emails in the evenings and at weekends: these messages will be forwarded to the recipient only at the beginning of the next working day. These can be supplemented by possible exceptions for cases requiring extraordinary urgency.

[26] Glowacka (n 19) 19.
[27] See, in detail, Eurofound and the International Labour Office, *Working anytime, anywhere* (n 4) 50–51.
[28] Katsabian (n 3) 12.
[29] ibid, 16.

Other agreements encourage employees to agree with their supervisors on fixed times of reachability – or the other way round: time periods during which the worker cannot be contacted – or to register time spent working outside the employer's premises as working time.[30]

At the beginning of 2021, the European Parliament adopted a resolution which requests the Commission to submit a proposal for an act on the right to disconnect.[31] The resolution also contains a detailed proposal for a future directive. At first glance, the proposal means no step forward compared with the mentioned initiatives as it does not intend to reform the definition of working time. The proposal aims to guarantee a right to workers not to engage in work-related activities or communications by means of digital tools, directly or indirectly, outside working time, where working time is to be understood as defined in the WTD. The proposal lists various measures to implement this right, from practical arrangements for switching off digital tools for work purposes, to – among others – an objective, reliable and accessible system for measuring working time and awareness-raising measures like in-work training The interesting novelty of the proposal, however, is its personal scope: the new directive would apply to all workers, independent of their status and their working arrangements. Thus, persons who work out of an employment relationship would also be guaranteed periods free from work-related obligations, even though the duration of such term is not defined.

An overview of the above-mentioned legislative steps and collective agreements reveals that the right to disconnect should not be regarded as a separate right, but rather a collection of various technical solutions to enforce the basic institutions of working time law. In its essence, the right to disconnect only calls employers to respect the long-standing statutory rules and contractual limits of working time.[32] Obviously it has a completely different importance outside the scope of labour law where workers are not protected by traditional working time regulations. In such a setting (as for gig-workers), the right to disconnect is crucial to guarantee minimum rest periods and to avoid excessively long hours of availability.

## IV. Immeasurability of Working Time? Accounting Working Time in the Digital Workplace

The diminishing boundaries between work and private life put the employer's obligations to properly account for working time to challenges. If workers have at least a partial autonomy to decide when to work and working hours might disperse through the whole day or week, it is obviously less convenient to track the exact amount of compulsory rest

[30] Eurofound and the International Labour Office, *Working anytime, anywhere* (n 4) 49–50.

[31] European Parliament 'Resolution of 21 January 2021 with recommendations to the Commission on the right to disconnect' 2019/2181(INL).

[32] G Rebelo, E Simões and I Salavisa, 'Working Time and Digital Transition: A Complex and Ambiguous Relationship' Paper presented at the Second European Conference on the Impact of Artificial Intelligence and Robotics, 2020) 134, available at: www.researchgate.net/publication/345726373_Working_Time_and_Digital_Transition_A_Complex_and_Ambiguous_Relationship.

periods and time worked.[33] Nonetheless, accurate accounting of working time should not be hampered by the fact that work is more difficult to measure if it is not performed during an uninterrupted period and/or in a particular place.

As the CJEU has pointed out in a recent judgment, in the absence of a system enabling the time worked each day by each worker to be measured there is nothing to ensure that actual compliance with the limitation on maximum working time and with minimum rest periods is fully guaranteed to workers, since that compliance is left to the discretion of the employer. Consequently, Member States must require employers to set up an objective, reliable and accessible system enabling the duration of time worked each day by each worker to be measured.[34] The Court acknowledged that a worker may rely on other sources of evidence, such as, inter alia, witness statements, the production of emails or the consultation of mobile telephones or computers, in order to provide indications of a breach of working time rights and thus bring about a reversal of the burden of proof. However, unlike a system that measures time worked each day, such sources of evidence do not enable the number of hours the worker worked each day and each week to be objectively and reliably established.[35] Nevertheless, it is for the Member States to determine the specific arrangements for implementing such a system, in particular the form that it must take, having regard, as necessary, to the particular characteristics of each sector of activity concerned, or the specific characteristics of certain undertakings concerning, inter alia, their size.[36]

While the Court made it clear that a reliable working time account is essential, it also added that its technical implementation can take various forms. Nevertheless, the technical difficulties of registering working time can be easily overcome with digital devices.[37] In the era of complex algorithms taking over a growing number of employers' functions,[38] it seems reasonable to expect that work time accounting is not a challenge of software developers. On the contrary, one may be concerned to see how close surveillance is possible by digital technologies. Any device used to keep account of working time shall not gather more data than necessary and shall by no means monitor the employees' activities too closely or intrude into private life.[39]

It is worth noting that the European Parliament's proposal on the right to disconnect would oblige employers to set up an objective, reliable and accessible system to measure daily working time, in accordance with workers' right to privacy and to the protection of their personal data. Workers shall have the possibility to request and obtain the record of their working times. Importantly this would apply not only to employees, but to all workers, independent of their status and their working arrangements.[40]

[33] See especially the case of independent contractors working for more than one employer simultaneously. SD Harris and AB Krueger, 'A Proposal for Modernizing Labor Laws for Twenty-First-Century Work: The "Independent Worker"' (2015) Hamilton Project Discussion Paper 10, 13.

[34] C-55/18 *Federación de Servicios de Comisiones Obreras (CCOO* (n 12) paras 58, 60.

[35] ibid, paras 53–55.

[36] ibid, para 63.

[37] ILO 'Ensuring decent working time for the future' (n 1) 298; E Shevchenko, A Efremova, N Oshovskaya, A Voloshin and A Finogentova, 'Improving Methods of Accounting for Working Time in the Context of Digitalization' (2021) SHS Web of Conferences 93, 03011, 3–4.

[38] See especially Martin Gruber-Risak, ch 5 in this volume.

[39] Glowacka (n 19) 9, 11; Katsabian (n 3) 32.

[40] European Parliament 'Resolution of 21 January 2021' (n 31) Articles 1(1) and 3(2).

# V. Adjusting Regulation to Changing Needs: Negotiated Flexibility

## A. The Possible Merits of Collective Bargaining

Even if the fundamental protections offered by the rules of working time cannot be put aside in digital work environments, this does not mean that all traditional legal institutions can apply without adjustment. The demarcation of working time and rest periods or the proper accounting of working hours – as seen above – are good examples. Nonetheless, adjustment shall not be understood as opt-out: merely technical reasons cannot justify the non-application of working time guarantees.

In my view the most convenient way to reconcile the needs of new types of work and working time regulations is collective bargaining. Bargaining on a collective level can introduce adequate protective measures against an overemphasis on employer-oriented flexibility and means a more transparent and formal standard-setting process than individual negotiations.[41] As opposed to legislation, the parties of collective bargaining have much better knowledge of the priorities of the affected workplace or sector and the process educes quick reactions to the rapidly changing market requirements.[42] However, an apparent practical drawback of this solution is that it is conditional on the sound operation of trade unions in the affected sectors. Thus, the effective regulation of working time by collective agreements can be easily hampered by low union representation levels in digital workplaces or the lack of collective labour rights of workers who are not classified as employees. While the importance of these barriers cannot be underestimated, in the following I attempt to demonstrate that EU law builds on the possibility of reaching flexible working time arrangements in collective agreements.

A traditional function of collective bargaining is to set the details not regulated by law or to fill in the legislative gaps and thus to adapt the general legal framework to the exact needs of the affected workers and their employers. Moreover, in most jurisdictions parties can even deviate from the law by their collective agreement but – in general – only in favour of the employee.[43] The same technique is also used at international level by the working time regulations of the International Labour Organization (ILO).[44] The relevant conventions set out the basic protective measures and collective bargaining is promoted to reach agreement on terms and conditions of employment that are

[41] Eurofound, *Organisation of working time* (n 4) 23–25.

[42] E Ales, 'The Regulatory Function of Collective Agreements in the Light of its Relationship with Statutory Instruments and Individual Rights: A Multilevel Approach' in T Gyulavári and E Menegatti (eds), *The Sources of Labour Law* (Kluwer Law International, 2020) 69.

[43] However, there are more and more exceptions in several countries (eg, Poland, Hungary), where *in peius* derogation is also allowed. T Gyulavári and E Menegatti (eds), *The Sources of Labour Law* (Alphen aan den Rijn, Kluwer Law International, 2020) 6–7.

[44] The ILO has placed great emphasis on the regulation of working time from the outset. The first ILO convention on the subject was adopted in 1919, followed over the years by further conventions and recommendations. The most important issues touched upon are the following: the measure of working time in Conventions 1, 30, 47 and Recommendation 116; weekly rest periods in Conventions 14, 10 and Recommendation 103; paid leave in Conventions 52, 101, 132 and Recommendation 98; night work in Conventions 4, 41, 89, 171 and Recommendations 13 and 178; part-time work in Convention 175.

more favourable than those already established by law.[45] Several instruments set out the requirement to consult the organisations of employers and workers concerned if it is intended to exclude some categories of workers from their scope. Others require consultation of workers' and employers' organisations for the introduction of permanent or temporary exceptions to the protective measures set in the relevant instrument.[46] However, it is not possible to set aside the standards prescribed in the conventions in a collective agreement.

Compared with the ILO's regime, EU law gives broader space for collective bargaining in setting working time standards. Article 18 of the WTD allows derogations from the Articles on daily rest, breaks, weekly rest period, length of night work and reference periods by means of collective agreements. Importantly, such derogations are open not only for agreements of universal application, but for 'agreements concluded between the two sides of industry at a lower level'.[47] Nonetheless, the Directive prescribes that such derogations shall be allowed on condition that equivalent compensating rest periods are granted to the workers concerned or, in exceptional cases where it is not possible for objective reasons to grant such periods, the workers concerned are afforded appropriate protection. The concept is clear: the European Social Partners may substitute the listed rules of the Directive by alternative solutions; however, they have to ensure 'equivalent compensating rest periods' or – exceptionally – appropriate protection by other means.

The WTD is not the only instrument using this technique. Member States may give the European Social Partners the option of concluding collective agreements that deviate from the equal treatment principle enshrined in the Agency Work Directive, 'while respecting the overall protection of temporary agency workers'.[48] Minimum requirement of working conditions enlisted in the Transparent and Predictable Working Conditions Directive may also be deviated from in collective agreements, 'while respecting the overall protection of workers'.[49] Member States may also entrust management and labour with defining freely and at any time through negotiated agreement the practical arrangements for informing and consulting employees. These agreements may be different from those referred to in the relevant directive, but shall still respect its objectives.[50]

## B. How to Interpret Derogations?

Although delegation of (de)regulatory functions to collective bargaining can be foreseen as an alternative to statutory instruments,[51] there is only a limited case law on how to interpret the mentioned clauses on possible derogations.

[45] ILO, 'Ensuring decent working time for the future' (n 1) 287–88.

[46] ibid, 276–77.

[47] Ales (n 42) 48.

[48] Directive 2008/104/EC of the European Parliament and of the Council of 19 November 2008 on temporary agency work [2008] OJ L/327/9, Article 5.

[49] Directive (EU) 2019/1152 of the European Parliament and of the Council of 20 June 2019 on transparent and predictable working conditions in the European Union [2019] OJ L186/105, Article 14.

[50] Directive 2002/14/EC of the European Parliament and of the Council of 11 March 2002 establishing a general framework for informing and consulting employees in the European Community [2002] OJ L80/29, Article 5.

[51] Ales (n 42) 65.

In *Accordo*, the CJEU emphasised that when Member States offer possibilities to derogations, such rules shall be consistent with general principles of EU law, which include the principle of legal certainty. 'To that end, provisions which permit optional derogations from the rules laid down by a directive must be implemented with the requisite precision and clarity necessary to satisfy the requirements flowing from that principle'.[52] In *Jager*, the Court stated that derogations 'must be interpreted in such a way that their scope is limited to what is strictly necessary in order to safeguard the interests which those derogations enable to be protected'.[53] As regards 'equivalent compensating rest periods', the Court – taking the Directive's aim as a starting point – set the requirement that such rest periods must follow on immediately from the working time which the workers are supposed to counteract in order to prevent the worker from experiencing a state of fatigue or overload owing to the accumulation of consecutive periods of work.[54] Moreover the Court confirmed that it is only in entirely exceptional circumstances that the Directive enables appropriate protection to be accorded to the worker where the grant of equivalent periods of compensatory rest is not possible on objective grounds.[55] The case law suggests that collective agreements making use of the derogation clauses will be subject to strict scrutiny if the question of their legal compliance with the Directive's requirements are questioned in a future case.

Nevertheless, empirical evidence shows that working time rules set by collective agreements in digital workplaces is not just an issue for theory. There are various examples in EU Member States of collective agreements applicable to gig-workers which also contain some basic protections of working time.[56]

# VI. Autonomy to Displace Protection?

## A. Not the Dying Days of Working Time

The most important claim to support the idea that labour law's traditional working time regulations are irrelevant in the modern workplace is that workers enjoy broad autonomy over the measure and schedule of their working time. Work time autonomy or sovereignty means that the working hours are not defined by the employer but workers can decide when and how much to work. While the traditional employment relationship is characterised by fixed working time defined by the mutual agreement of the parties and by the employer's prerogative to allocate the working hours by unilateral decisions,[57] in a growing number of cases there are either no fixed level of working time and/or the worker schedules his or her own working hours. As in these new settings the worker is no longer under the subordination of the employer as regards the temporal

[52] Case C-227/09 *Antonino Accardo et al v Comune di Torino* ECLI:EU:C:2010:624 [2010], para 55.

[53] C-151/02 *Landeshauptstadt Kiel* (n 18) para 89.

[54] ibid, para 94.

[55] ibid, para 98; see also, Case C-428/09 *Union syndicale Solidaires Isère v Premier ministre and Others* ECLI:EU:C:2010:612 [2010], para 55.

[56] See the regularly updated database of Eurofound on the platform economy at: www.eurofound.europa.eu/data/platform-economy.

[57] See, for instance, ILO Recommendation on the Employment Relationship 2006 (No 198) point 13.

aspects of employment: protective rules such as the maximum level of working time or minimum rest periods lose their original meaning.

The idea that autonomy displaces working time regulations shall be challenged by two basic reasons. First, some level of autonomy and flexibility is present in the typical employment relationship too. Standard working time is not a synonym of rigidity and not the opposite of flexibility.[58] The employer's right to order overtime, to schedule working time in shifts or to change the already scheduled hours within a certain deadline make possible the organisation of work also in special sectors requiring continuous production in manufacturing, or in emergency services, or maintenance work. For instance, EU law calls for a maximum level of 48 hours' weekly working time.[59] Consequently, Member States relying on the 40 hours of working a week can enable employers to order 416 hours of overtime (that is approximately two and a half months of working time) annually. Besides, labour law recognises employees as human beings with a life outside the workplace and offers a wide range of paid and unpaid leave to meet individual (or social) needs.[60] It is enough to refer to the 'force majeure' clause in the Parental Leave Directive, which entitles workers to time off from work on grounds of urgent family reasons in cases of sickness or accident making the immediate presence of the worker indispensable.[61] The clause may apply to a wide spectrum of work–private life interferences, irrespective of other provisions on paid annual leave, maternity and parental leave.

Second, full work time autonomy limits the employer's influence on the organisation of work at a level that would render the operation of most business impossible. For most workers such sovereignty is too good to be true, for the following reasons.

## B. Why Working Time Autonomy is Hard to Achieve?

Full work time autonomy – in a strict sense – would mean that whenever the worker decides to take up work, there is always paid work available. Be it any hour of the day, or during the night, the weekend or on feast days, the employer is always able to assign relevant tasks for the worker standing by for work. Only employers having a vast pool of clients or workload may claim that they are in fact able to offer work whenever the worker decides to accept tasks.[62] However, empirical evidence on both clusters of platform work (gig-workers and crowdworkers) suggests that this is rarely the case. Gig-workers often face waiting time because tasks are available only during

[58] Campbell (n 5) 112.

[59] WTD, Article 6.

[60] Campbell (n 5) 111.

[61] Council Directive 2010/18/EU of 8 March 2010 implementing the revised Framework Agreement on parental leave concluded by BUSINESSEUROPE, UEAPME, CEEP and ETUC and repealing Directive 96/34/EC [2010] OJ L68/13, Cl 7. See also the right to request flexible working arrangements for caring purposes in Article 9 in Directive (EU) 2019/1158 of the European Parliament and of the Council of 20 June 2019 on work–life balance for parents and carers and repealing Council Directive 2010/18/EU [2019] OJ L188/79.

[62] One basic expectation of online workers is that online platforms dramatically increase the pool of available jobs. In addition, they also increase the likelihood that workers will find suitable matches for their skills and preferences. A Agrawal, J Horton, N Lacetera and E Lyons, 'Digitization and the Contract Labor Market: A Research Agenda' (2013) NBER Working Paper 19525, available at: www.nber.org/papers/w19525.pdf.

certain periods.[63] The ILO Survey of Crowdworkers in 2015 reported that 90 per cent of respondents would like to do more crowdwork than they were actually doing.[64] Such a high level of underemployment reveals that crowdworkers rarely face adequate job opportunities when they decide to take up work, which excludes real work time autonomy. Workers with zero-hours contracts or on on-call work have no specific working hours set in their contract with the – at least theoretical – right to refuse the employer's call to work. However, in practice this contractual setting leads to a broad fluctuation of working hours, unreliable rests and little or no input for workers into their schedules.[65] Research from the EU, US and Japan shows that working from home arrangements often mean longer working hours than working from the office and time spent in a home office does not substitute but rather supplement regular working hours.[66] Such extension of working time clearly does not stem from the workers' autonomy but rather from the mere technical possibility that workers using information technologies can take up work from anywhere and at any time, even if it is not formally ordered by the employer. This is especially true in the case of sporadic teleworking, which is not based on the parties' mutual agreement.[67]

From another aspect, if workers have full autonomy over their schedules, such employers can only guarantee their clients that they will be actually serviced in a reasonable time if they also have a robust source of workforce. Otherwise, if employers waive their rights to order the worker to be available for a minimum amount of hours and/or during certain periods, such companies' clients must regularly wait until a worker appears (or logs into the online world) to answer their call. Nonetheless, the more workers the company employs to eliminate the risk to not have enough workforce standing ready for work, the higher the workers' competition for tasks will become and – at least at certain times – some workers will remain without a job to complete. This is especially apparent in crowdwork where workers around the globe can compete for online tasks, which also has an adverse effect on wages.[68] The competition for the job puts workers under a pressure to be available for excessively long or unsocial hours which exclude real work time autonomy. ILO research shows that many crowdworkers worked atypical hours: 36 per cent regularly worked seven days per week; 43 per cent reported working during the night; and 68 per cent reported working during the evening (6 pm to 10 pm), either in response to task availability (and differences in time zones) or because of other commitments.[69] These data show that, although workers are in principle free to decide on their working hours, in practice they are forced to work in schedules that are extremely hazardous to their health.

[63] V De Stefano, 'The Rise of the "Just-in-Time Workforce": On-Demand Work, Crowdwork, and Labour Protection in the "gig-economy" (2016) ILO Conditions of work and employment series 71, 5–6.

[64] J Berg, 'Income security in the on-demand economy: Findings and policy lessons from a survey of crowdworkers' (2016) ILO Conditions of Work and Employment Series 74, 13–14.

[65] ILO, 'Ensuring decent working time for the future' (n 1) 264–265.

[66] Eurofound and the International Labour Office, *Working anytime, anywhere* (n 4) 21–23.

[67] Katsabian (n 3) 12.

[68] De Stefano, 'The Rise of the "Just-in-Time Workforce"' (n 63) 5.

[69] ILO, *Digital labour platforms and the future of work. Towards decent work in the online world* (Geneva, ILO, 2018), available at: www.ilo.org/wcmsp5/groups/public/---dgreports/---dcomm/---publ/documents/publication/wcms_645337.pdf.

Such pressure may also appear in gig-work when the employer offers higher compensation for hours performed outside the standard working hours or by sanctioning workers not being available for work under an expected minimum level. For instance, UK workers in marginal part-time employment (on-call work or zero-hours contracts) often face the 'fear of being zeroed down', meaning that the employer might not offer any further job opportunities once the worker rejects a call to go to work.[70] As an ETUI study described the situation of gig delivery riders: 'The only liberty is to log in. But once one is online, any liberty becomes very restricted'.[71] Platforms can easily put pressure on workers who want to quit the application by simple tricks. For example, the algorithm comes up with an immediate message, encouraging the worker to stay and work more, by offering a better task, or simply by sending a convincing message. Lastly, it is also questionable whether formally time-sovereign workers are actually able to reach a decent wage without obeying the employer's direct or indirect pressure to be available during the most busy or underemployed times. This concern is all the more important as many workers employed in flexible time arrangements (platform workers, zero-hours contracts) are associated with income insecurity and low wages.[72] Aloisi points out that for platform workers 'flexibility is just a kind of solace: to earn a significant sum of money, workers might also have to work more hours every day than a "standard"' worker. Since they have to be available "around the clock", this kind of flexibility does not entail a greater freedom for the worker'.[73]

Considering all of these factors, there might be only a very limited number of employers who can offer full work time autonomy to their workers. Instead, in most cases workers have only a certain level of discretion over their working time but are still subject to the employers' (indirect) orders deciding when and how much to work.

## C. Legislative Gaps Caused by Fake-Autonomy

Nonetheless it is of crucial importance that no workers shall be left out of the protection of working time measures, who actually lack autonomy over their working time. The more they remain subordinated by the employer, the more the traditional guarantees of working time regulations shall stay in place. Otherwise some work time arrangements would simply allocate upon the worker a whole set of risks of insecurity of work and income.[74] Such 'protective gaps' can disconnect workers from the system of guarantees and lead to increased precariousness. For instance, protective measures including exemptions and exclusions, or being conditional on high thresholds or lengthy service

[70] JC Messenger and P Wallot, 'The Diversity of "Marginal" Part-Time Employment' (2015) ILO INWORK Policy Brief No 7, 8.

[71] I Daugareilh, C Degryse and P Poche (eds), 'The platform economy and social law: Key issues in comparative perspective' (2019) ETUI Working Paper 10 (Brussels, ETUI, 2019), available at: www.etui.org/sites/default/files/WP-2019.10-EN-v3-WEB.pdf, 48.

[72] ILO, 'Ensuring decent working time for the future' (n 1) 274; Messenger and Wallot (n 70) 8.

[73] A Aloisi, 'Commoditized Workers – The Rise of On-Demand Work, a Case Study Research on a Set of Online Platforms and Apps' (2016) 37 *Comparative Labor Law and Policy Journal* 653, 661–62.

[74] A Adams, M Freedland and J Prassl, 'The "Zero-Hours Contract": Regulating Casual Work, or Legitimating Precarity?' (2014) Working Paper, available at: www.labourlawresearch.net/papers/zero-hours-contract-regulating-casual-work-or-legitimating-precarity, 19.

requirements, may leave workers outside the scope of labour law's protection even if the affected workers do not really enjoy the advantages of self-organised working time.[75] Such one-sided, employer-oriented flexibility means no liberty for the worker but a simple risk allocation on him or her,[76] instead of a trade-off between the relaxation of working time protections and work time sovereignty. However, the principal function of labour law is to distribute risks equitably and manageably between the parties.[77] Moreover, the de-mutualisation of risks[78] may shift burdens away from the employer not only towards the employee, but even further towards his or her family or the state.[79] The lack of regular rest periods, paid annual leave or limits on daily or weekly working time can adversely affect workers' health or family responsibilities and put more burden on state childcare or elderly care institutions and public health systems.

To sum up, the more autonomy the worker enjoys over the organisation of working time, the fewer protective measures are necessary. Nonetheless, protection shall not be lifted in full in cases involving partial or formal autonomy. A strict assessment is necessary to establish what level of protective standards shall apply to a certain form of work. As Gruber-Risak argues, the means of control in the virtual world and the distinct way directions are given shall be considered when adjudging the flexibility concerning working time.[80]

## VII. Relaxing Protections to the Benefit of the Worker?

### A. Unwanted Protections?

The legal constraints on working time are often criticised by employees as well. There may be cases where it is the worker who wants to overstep the measures that were meant to protect him or herself and wishes to trade protections for flexibility.[81] For example, a worker living in a remote location would prefer to work 14 hours a day, in exchange for working only six days in a fortnight. Another worker raising more children would gladly perform overtime in addition to the annual statutory limit for the extra income. A highly trained young IT professional loves the challenges of his job and enthusiastically completes 50–60 hours a week when an interesting problem comes up. Daily or weekly limits of working time might appear as unwanted barriers for these workers, others might want to decide for themselves how much to rest.[82]

[75] Campbell (n 5) 115. A good example could be the situation of casual workers in EU law, as the part-time work and the written statement directives – adopted during the 1990s where the casualisation of work was not yet as widespread as today – do not apply to casual work. V De Stefano, 'Casual work beyond casual work in the EU: The underground casualisation of the European workforce – and what to do about it' (2016) 7 *European Labour Law Journal* 442.

[76] Glowacka (n 19) 9.

[77] Adams, Freedland and Prassl (n 74) 19.

[78] De Stefano, 'The Rise of the "Just-in-Time Workforce"' (n 63) 6.

[79] Campbell (n 5) 119.

[80] See ch 5, section III by Martin Gruber-Risak in this volume.

[81] Harris and Krueger (n 33) 13.

[82] M Jauch, 'The rat race and working time regulation' (2020) 19 *Politics, Philosophy & Economics* 293, 294.

Undoubtedly, rules of working time limits the employee's autonomy. Nonetheless, this intrusion to the worker's freedom to organise his or her own time is not without a reason. On the one hand, whatever we see as the purpose of working time regulations (such as the protection of health, safety or human dignity of worker or the reduction of unemployment), these shall obviously apply even if the request to exceed legal time limits is initiated by the worker. The regulation's interference with the workers' will seems justified even if taking the protection of private life as a basic aim of the regulation. The individual may have many obligations or interests outside the workplace which are important for society as a whole (like caring for children or elderly relatives or having adequate rest for him or herself), thus the legislation shall limit the time spent at work to enable the fulfilment of duties in other spheres of life.

Besides, it may well be the case that the employer itself opposes the employee's request to relax the constraints of working time regulations. In principle, the employer is responsible for the lawful operation of the workplace and in case of non-compliance authorities cannot accept the claim that the deviation from the rule was made at the request of the employee. In addition, if – as a result of fatigue – an employee becomes ill or suffers an accident, or causes damages to third persons during work, the responsibility lies with the employer. These considerations can motivate the employer to reject the employee's claim for the permissive interpretation of legal requirements of working time.

On the other hand, in my view labour law shall set limits of working time that are applicable to each employment (or other work-related) relationship separately. Thus, if the worker is unable to exhaust all of his or her energies, creativity and diligence within the framework of one employment contract, he or she may establish another legal relationship for further work. This obviously means less intrusion to autonomy. Moreover, restrictions on parallel work-related relationships would deprive many workers of the possibility to earn enough money.

There are a number of arguments to be put forward to justify why the law limits the amount of time that can be spent in work within a single legal relationship if the same standards shall not apply in the case of multiple parallel legal relationships. The idea that working time rules apply per contract and not per worker builds on the assumption that in the case of multiple legal relationships, the employee is less vulnerable. A multiple of parallel relationships in itself presupposes that the employee has undertaken further work upon his own consideration. In contrast, within one legal relationship, the extension of working time is in most cases ordered by the employer, or at least the 'consent' of the employee is questionable. In addition, if employees work 12 hours a day because they have taken a part-time job of four hours a day in addition to their full-time job, they can manage their working hours more flexibly than if they had to work 12 hours a day in the framework of one employment contract. The two legal relationships can be terminated separately if the worker feels that the workload is too demanding. Paid or unpaid leave can be taken independently and at different times in the two jobs, or in case of recovery from an illness or during times of childcare, the worker may perform in one job while staying on leave in the other. Having more work-related relationships may mean additional risks to the health and safety of the worker, but at the same time offers more possibilities to cope with such risks. The economic dependency is also reduced if the employee receives remuneration from two different employers.[83]

## B. Parallel Employment under EU Law

The WTD does not explicitly state whether its provisions set absolute limits in cases of concurrent contracts with one or more employer(s) or if they apply to each employment relationship separately. The Commission took the view that, in the light of the Directive's objective to improve the health and safety of workers, the limits on average weekly working time and daily and weekly rest should, as far as possible, apply per worker. Nonetheless, the Commission repeated that not all work-related relationships are covered by the Directive,[84] thus parallel employment as 'volunteers' or 'self-employed' and as employee does not interfere with the minimum requirements of EU law.

The CJEU tackled the issue of parallel employment for the first time in 2021. The Court confirmed that where an employee has concluded several contracts of employment with the same employer, the minimum daily rest period applies to those contracts taken as a whole and not to each of them taken separately. Although the case involved a situation where the worker had separate employment relationships with the same employer and only the application of the provision on daily rest periods was in question,[85] the Court's conclusions surely will have broader effect.

The Court underpinned its conclusion for the following reasons. First, as Article 3 of the WTD entitles 'every worker' to a minimum daily rest period of 11 consecutive hours per 24-hour period, this provision applies to workers regardless of whether or not they have concluded several contracts with the employer.[86] Second, following the strict division between working time and rest periods, the hours considered to constitute rest periods under one contract shall not be capable of constituting working time under another contract.[87] Third, the aim of the Directive – that is to guarantee better protection of the safety and health of workers – could be undermined by the combination of working time provided for separately by each of the contracts concluded with the employer which would make it impossible to guarantee the daily rest period of 11 consecutive hours for each 24-hour period.[88] Lastly, the Court took the view that the stricter interpretation is necessary to protect the worker, as the weaker party in the contract, from the possibility of pressure from his or her employer intended to split the working time into a number of contracts, which would be liable to render the provisions of daily rest periods redundant.[89]

Apparently, the Court's reasoning builds on the protective aim of the WTD and leaves little doubt that its findings shall be applied to cases involving separate contracts

[83] Nowak (n 17) 129.
[84] Interpretative Communication on Directive 2003/88/EC of the European Parliament and of the Council concerning certain aspects of the organisation of working time, C/2017/2601, [2017] OJ C165/1, 10.
[85] WTD, Article 3.
[86] C-585/19 *Academia de Studii Economice din Bucureops ti* (n 12) para 41.
[87] ibid, para 45.
[88] ibid, paras 47–50.
[89] ibid, paras 51–53.

with different employers and to the Directive's other protective measures too. However, this is not to say that EU law would limit the possibility of parallel employment. On the contrary, the Directive on Transparent and Predictable Working Conditions calls Member States to ensure that an employer neither prohibits a worker from taking up employment with other employers, outside the work schedule established with that employer, nor subjects a worker to adverse treatment for doing so, unless such restrictions are based on objective reasons, such as health and safety, the protection of business confidentiality, the integrity of public service or the avoidance of conflicts of interests.[90] The new directive read together with the CJEU's decision shows that the protective measures of the WTD cannot be put aside in cases of parallel employment relationships. However, other work-related relationships fall outside the coverage of the WTD, thus no constraints apply to self-employed or platform workers who perform for more employers.

## VIII. Summary

Basic working time regulations are needed regardless of the technical environment where the work is performed. To safeguard the health and safety of workers and to enable them to live an undisturbed private life are values that shall be respected in all non-standard forms of work. The fundamental institutions of working time – strengthened also by the European Charter of Fundamental Rights – shall not be set aside for the mere promise of autonomy. Research shows that it is only a minority of workers who in fact can enjoy a broad level of discretion over their working time, but for many employers flexible working arrangements mean only an excuse to escape protective measures.

From the employers' aspect, to exploit the benefits of the digital work environment, it is not necessary to systematically relax or revise working time standards. Even the traditional institutions of working time (like overtime or unequal schedules) grant a certain room for manoeuvre. Moreover, collective bargaining could be an important tool to overstep one-sided, employer-oriented flexibility and to adjust the legal framework to the needs of the parties by mutually beneficial agreements that respect the overall protection of workers. If we turn to the question how to handle the technological changes of the twenty-first century, the idea is to enable the parties to adjust the legal framework to the new circumstances but not to merely offer the employers an opt-out from it. Working time rules can be a serious constraint for employers, but they have an important function. The reservation of basic working time guarantees ensures that the risks are borne by the actors with whom they emerge and, after all, who are also entitled to the profits of the activity.

[90] Directive (EU) 2019/1152 (n 49) Article 9.

# 9

# Which Welfare Rights for Platform Workers?

MARIUS OLIVIER

## I. Introduction

Platform workers typically sell their time or labour through a digital platform to a user, with crowdwork and work-on-demand being the most prevalent forms. There is no single, agreed definition, although the general sentiment seems to suggest that platform work is narrower than gig-work – the latter is often understood to refer to work outside the traditional employer–employee relationship or, generally, non-standard work.[1] For the Organisation for Economic Co-operation and Development (OECD) platform workers are individuals who use an app or a website to match themselves with customers, in order to provide a service in return for money.[2] The recently adopted Indian Code on Social Security of 2020 defines a platform worker as a person engaged in or undertaking platform work, which in turn is defined to mean 'a work arrangement outside of a traditional employer–employee relationship in which organisations or individuals use an online platform to access other organisations or individuals to solve specific problems or to provide specific services or any such other activities which may be notified by the Central Government, in exchange for payment'.[3]

Worldwide, the social security position of platform workers is often influenced by their labour law position. In this regard, the position varies across different jurisdictions. In several countries, on the basis of (amending) legislative provisions or jurisprudence and depending on the categories of platform workers affected, these workers are seen as 'employees', attached to an employment relationship. To the extent that they are

[1] R Sreelakshmi, '#TIL: "Who is a platform worker?"', Ola Mobility Institute, 9 September 2020, available at: www.mobilityinstitute.medium.com/til-who-is-a-platform-worker-eed7cbf37d1e.

[2] OECD, *Measuring the Digital Transformation: A Roadmap for the Future* (2019) available at: www.oecd.org/publications/measuring-the-digital-transformation-9789264311992-en.htm.

[3] The Code on Social Security, 2020 (Act 36 of 2020), Article 2(60) and (61). See also A Broughton, R Gloster, Marvell R., Green M, J Langley and A Marti, *The experiences of individuals in the gig economy* (commissioned report prepared by the Institute for Employment Studies) (Her Majesty's Government, UK, 2018) 8.

regarded as employees, they would invariably enjoy the full spectrum of social security protection. The labour law systems of other countries have chosen a different route, and essentially view them, or at least certain groups of platform workers, as persons who provide an independent service. As such, self-employed gig (ie, platform) workers 'are engaged outside established systems of social security and the protections these afford, which means they may not have access to, among other things, pensions, statutory sick pay and holiday entitlement'.[4]

For several reasons, social security coverage and access for platform workers have been difficult to achieve – including the (mis-)classification of such workers, the concealment of the (true) nature of their relationship with the platform, limited working hours and low pay, and (lack of) contributory capacity. Also, given the peculiarity of many platform work relationships, coverage under labour law may not provide a sufficient social security coverage and access response – as these very relationships operate beyond the spectrum and boundaries of labour law. Yet, a range of comparative approaches to address these challenges have become evident – such as enhancing reliance placed on labour law-attached social security provisioning. Sometimes social security laws are adjusted to accommodate platform workers; alternatively unique social security solutions are forged. Fundamental rights protection embedded in national constitutions and supranational regulation (such as in the European Union (EU)) may also be relevant.

This raises the question of what the key principles and values are that should inform appropriate social security coverage extension and access. Fundamental in this regard should be the universal recognition of social security for all as a human right and the Sustainable Development Goal objective of leaving no one behind. Equally important is the social protection floor paradigm, which has attracted global endorsement. As noted by the ILO:

> [S]ocial protection floors are nationally defined sets of basic social security guarantees that should ensure, as a minimum that, over the life cycle, all in need have access to essential health care and to basic income security which together secure effective access to goods and services defined as necessary at the national level.[5]

It is suggested that countries could consider the variety of legal, policy, design and administrative techniques to achieve social security coverage extension to and access by platform workers practised elsewhere. These include – in addition to considerations indicated above – also the role played by collective agreements; accommodating private arrangements; lessons learnt from the worldwide extension modalities benefiting informal economy workers; reliance on contributory and non-contributory interventions; and the need for flexible approaches relating to financing and contribution modalities, appropriate entitlement conditions, and possibly dedicated benefit regimes. An appropriate representation model may also be required.

This chapter considers the issue of social security for platform workers from different perspectives. In the next section, the challenges impacting on social security for

[4] ibid, 13.

[5] ILO, *Social Protection Floor*, available at: www.ilo.org/secsoc/areas-of-work/policy-development-and-applied-research/social-protection-floor/lang--en/index.htm#:~:text=Social%20protection%20floors%20are%20nationally,defined%20as%20necessary%20at%20the.

platform workers are briefly discussed. The following section provides a comparative overview of current coverage and access modalities, as they are applied in various jurisdictions. The contribution then highlights the key principles and values that (should) inform the extension of social security coverage and access in relation to platform workers. In the penultimate section, the chapter critically reflects on legal, policy, design and administrative techniques for achieving social security coverage extension to and access by platform workers. Three dimensions are in particular investigated:

1. Decoupling employment status from coverage by and access to social security, and the need to adopt a differentiated approach in this regard.
2. Learning from other coverage extension modalities, with specific reference to social security coverage extended to vulnerable informal economy workers.
3. Collective bargaining, voice and representation.

The Conclusions bring together the key findings and messages of the chapter.

## II. Challenges Impacting on Social Security for Platform Workers

Several factors impact on platform workers' coverage by and access to social security. These include the (mis-)classification of such workers, even to the extent of the concealment of the (true) nature of their relationship with the platform. This may be done in an attempt to avoid contributions to and/or rely on social protection coverage relating to their main job in the traditional economy – resulting in the '"new economy" free riding the social security system with regard to the financing of social security at the expense of the "traditional economy", with implications for fair competition, as well as the equitable and sustainable financing of social protection systems'.[6]

In fact, the core of the problem seems to be that, traditionally, primarily workers involved in an employment relationship generally qualify for the more or less full spectrum of social security coverage arrangements, including contributory social security. This appears from the scope of coverage of both labour laws and even social security laws in several jurisdictions, despite recent attempts to expand the sphere of coverage to also include self-employed workers. This is true not only of many national legal systems, but also of supranational and even global instruments.

For example, the EU Directive on Transparent and Predictable Working Conditions in the European Union (2019) stipulates that platform and other non-standard workers who satisfy the criteria applied by the European Court of Justice for determining the status of a worker could fall within the scope of the Directive. This includes persons engaged in bogus self-employment, ie, where the person is declared to be self-employed while fulfilling the conditions characteristic of an employment relationship, in order to avoid certain legal or fiscal obligations. Such persons should fall within the scope of this Directive. However, genuinely self-employed persons should not fall within the scope of

[6] C Behrendt, Q Nguyen and U Rani, 'Social protection systems and the future of work: Ensuring social security for digital platform workers' (2019) 72 *International Social Security Review* 17, 24–25.

the Directive since they do not fulfil those criteria.[7] This distinction is also of relevance for purposes of social security dimensions covered by this Directive. Article 4(1) of the Directive, on the obligation to provide information, stipulates that Member States shall ensure that employers are required to inform workers of the essential aspects of the employment relationship. According to Article 4(2)(o), the information referred to shall include, among other, where it is the responsibility of the employer, the identity of the social security institutions receiving the social contributions attached to the employment relationship and any protection relating to social security provided by the employer.

It should be added, though, that the social security inclusion of the self-employed is specifically foreseen by another dedicated EU document, ie, the EU Council Recommendation on Access to Social Protection for Workers and Self-employed (2019).[8] Furthermore, Principle No 12 of the European Pillar of Social Rights of 2017 (on social protection) stipulates that regardless of the type and duration of their employment relationship, workers and, under comparable conditions, the self-employed, have the right to adequate social protection. Generally speaking, however, in the absence of dedicated legislative intervention, self-employed status (ie, as independent contractors) may imply exclusion from most publicly provided contributory social security arrangements. Also, self-employed persons rarely have access to non-contributory social security arrangements (eg, in the form of social assistance), as these arrangements are seldom extended to able-bodied workers.

The peculiarity but also heterogeneity of work relationships through which platform workers are engaged pose similar problems at the level of global normative instruments. The ILO Employment Relationship Recommendation (1998) recognises the difficulties in establishing whether or not an employment relationship exists, given the lack of clarity of the respective rights and obligations of the parties, or where there has been an attempt to disguise the employment relationship. It also acknowledges the need for special protection for vulnerable workers and that national policy should include measures to combat disguised employment relationships and contractual arrangements hiding the true legal status of workers. Nevertheless, it also makes it clear that 'National policy for protection of workers in an employment relationship should not interfere with true civil and commercial relationships, while at the same time ensuring that individuals in an employment relationship have the protection they are due'.[9]

A related challenge concerns the cross-border and global nature of platform activity. Many platforms operate as multinational entities, which procure and/or utilise the services of platform workers through a web of complex work and control arrangements. National legal systems seldom have extraterritorial application, especially in the absence of a legislative mandate to that effect. For example, the platform worker may contractually render services for a holding, or other entity registered in another country, and not

[7] Directive (EU) 2019/1152 of the European Parliament and of the Council of 20 June 2019 on transparent and predictable working conditions in the European Union [2019] OJ L186/105, para 8. For a detailed discussion of the Directive, see Iacopo Senatori, ch 4 in this volume.

[8] EU Council Recommendation of 8 November 2019 on access to social protection for workers and the self-employed [2019] OJ C387/01.

[9] ILO, Employment Relationship Recommendation 2006 (R198) clause 8.

for a locally registered entity. Consequently, a court may not be able to adjudicate the dispute for want of jurisdiction.[10]

Furthermore, according to the Global Commission on the Future of Work, the greater exposure of workers to social risks increases the demand for comprehensive and adequate social protection that guarantees income security and access to healthcare throughout people's lives, and facilitates life and work transitions.[11] Also, Behrendt et al describe the novel context of challenges experienced by platform workers as follows:

> While some of the challenges are not new, the surge of the platform economy presents new challenges for the social protection of workers. The trend whereby businesses can outsource tasks – that in former days would have been delegated to a single employee – to a large pool of virtual workers in different countries mediated through digital platforms renders it even more difficult to identify the party responsible for contributing to social insurance. Despite the fact that their work may be closely supervised and characterized by a dependency relationship vis-à-vis their client(s), and that their relationship with the platform can resemble an employment relationship in practice, workers are usually classified as independent contractors, leaving workers solely responsible for the payment of social insurance contributions, if any.[12]

Finally, the fluidity of the work engagement with a particular platform and the fact that the platform worker may also hold another, in many cases, primary job, may imply loss of benefits when the worker moves to a new work environment, as coordinated social security coverage approaches, including portability of social security benefits, have not been adopted.

## III. Comparative Conspectus of Current Coverage and Access Modalities

Various approaches have been adopted in a range of jurisdictions to inform social security coverage and access for platform workers. One of these concerns the attempt to accord employee status to the worker concerned and to deem the platform as the employer – which would imply the accrual of rights and obligations in labour law and social security. Yet, it is evident that consistency in approach has not been achieved across jurisdictions, with some assuming employee status and others upholding self-employed or a different status – for example, in relation to transportation network company drivers.[13] Davidov argues for a nuanced approach, which he terms a purposive

[10] eg, see the South African Labour Court case of *Uber SA Technology Services (Pty) Ltd v National Union of Public Service & Allied Workers* 2018 39 *ILJ* (LC). For different views on the judgment, see S Van Eck and N Nemusimbori, 'Uber drivers: Sad to say, but not employees of Uber SA' (2018) 81 *THRHR (Journal of Contemporary Roman-Dutch Law)* 473–83; K Mokoena, 'Are Uber drivers employees or independent contractors?' A comparative analysis' (2018) 39 *Industrial Law Journal* 1453; and A Govindjee, 'Extending social protection in the digital age: The case of transportation network company drivers in South Africa' (2020) 83 *THRHR* 48.

[11] Behrendt, Nguyen and Rani (n 6).

[12] ibid (authorities included in original text omitted).

[13] See Behrendt, Nguyen and Rani (n 6) 30; G Davidov, 'The Status of Uber Drivers: A Purposive Approach' (2017) 6 *Spanish Labour Law and Employment Relations Journal* 6; S Fredman and D Du Toit, 'One Small Step Towards Decent Work: *Uber v Aslam* in the Court of Appeal' (2019) 48 *Industrial Law Journal* 260 (277); and Mokoena (n 10).

approach, suggesting that it is fallacious to consider one category of employees and then to apply the entire gamut of 'labour law' to this group. Conceptually, according to him, a worker can be conceptualised as an 'employee' for one purpose and an 'independent contractor' for another. The main advantage of a purposive approach seems to be that it avoids overly legalistic applications of tests that could be outdated, instead seeking the ultimate objectives behind the law in order to determine who should be protected. As such, according to Davidov, the approach is well suited to dealing with new forms of work arrangements.[14] Other researchers have suggested a range of alternative approaches for determining worker status, including,

> a 'for-hire drive' classification; a 'hybrid' approach that would provide workers with a basic level of protection while still maintaining flexibility; a 'platform contractor classification', 'taxonomy' or 'continuum' approaches.[15] There are also the 'independent employee' approach and a 'dependent contractor' classification recognised in Canada, Germany, New Zealand and the UK for workers who do 80% or more of their work for a single company.[16]

In addition to an approach focusing on redefining the employee (and for that matter, the employer) concept for social security purposes, a range of adaptive social protection approaches have sought to expand coverage to an increasing number of vulnerable and excluded workers. Expanding the scope of contributory social security schemes to include all workers could imply significant coverage extension and support for labour mobility, in addition to ensuring a significantly enlarged risk pool.[17] The same is true of universal schemes, for example universal pension schemes (eg, Argentina, Cabo Verde and China); universal health schemes (eg, Philippines, Thailand and Viet Nam, having established all-encompassing national health insurance schemes); and universal maternity schemes (eg, Ukraine and Uruguay), ensuring coverage of all. Non-contributory tax-financed schemes, in particular universal or categorical schemes, imply coverage beyond employment-based social security mechanisms. In fact, the modern tendency is to provide social security needs through an aligned and calibrated combination of contributory and non-contributory arrangements.[18]

Furthermore, modalities to streamline contributions and find innovative funding solutions are evident. One example is the welfare funds established in India. They are financed through levies collected from selected employers and manufacturers,[19] and provide a range of benefits, including social security-related benefits such as medical care and maternity assistance. Also at a state level, a tax (*cess*) is imposed by state governments on the aggregate output of selected industries (eg, the Beedi Welfare

[14] Davidov (n 13).
[15] A Andoyan, 'Independent Contractor or Employee: I'm Uber Confused! Why California Should Create an Exception for Uber Drivers and the "On-Demand Economy"' (2017) 47 *Golden Gate University Law Review* 153, 155; RL Redfearn, 'Sharing Economy Misclassification: Employees and Independent Contractors in Transportation Network Companies' (2016) 31 *Berkeley Technology Law Journal* 1023.
[16] Govindjee (n 10).
[17] Typically, in European countries, self-employed workers are mostly covered under compulsory, full, contributory social insurance systems. However, this is not usually the case in most other countries. Also, other vulnerable categories of persons/workers may be excluded from coverage, especially if they do not qualify to be indicated as self-employed persons – eg, informal economy workers, as discussed below.
[18] Behrendt, Nguyen and Rani (n 6) 27–28.
[19] F Lund, 'Work-related social protection for informal workers' (2012) 65 *International Social Security Review* 9, 23–24.

Fund is financed by a tax on beedis).[20] Similarly, 'the German artists' social insurance (*Künstlersozialversicherung*) covers performing artists and publicists through a (non-individualised) global contribution on total contract value by the contracting "employer", complemented by workers' contributions if earnings exceed a certain level, as well as a government subsidy'.[21] Another example concerns several Latin American countries, that have introduced a Monotax system: tax payments and social security contributions are paid as a single package, instead of separate payments. Referred to as the Montributo scheme in Uruguay, but also applied in Argentina, Brazil and Ecuador, this has been an effective tool for the extension of social security coverage to small businesses and independent workers, especially women.[22]

The Monotax systems simultaneously provide good examples as to how the potential of digital technology can be utilised to achieve enhanced coverage of platform workers.[23] In fact, as noted, coverage for workers on digital platforms calls for simplifying or streamlining administrative and financing requirements and procedures, harnessing the potential of digital innovation to develop adapted administration and financing mechanisms. Behrendt et al remark:

> This can include introducing more flexible contribution collection schedules or using flat contribution or broad contribution categories (as in Brazil, Cabo Verde, Costa Rica and Thailand); introducing simplified tax and contribution payment mechanisms (as found in Argentina, Brazil, France and Uruguay); as well as facilitating electronic and mobile access to registration, consultation and contribution payment mechanisms and using coordinated data systems, smart cards and other emerging technologies, such as artificial intelligence and big data. Some countries, such as Uruguay and Indonesia, have introduced adapted mechanisms whereby the digital applications automatically add a social insurance contribution to the price of each ride to ensure that platform workers are covered. In Malaysia, self-employed taxi drivers and drivers of digital platforms can register and undertake their contribution payments for the employment injury scheme online.[24]

The authors further indicate the importance of effective information-sharing to support social security payment modalities in relation to platform workers:

> In Estonia, Lithuania and Sweden, Uber drivers can voluntarily authorize Uber to share income data and other information directly with tax authorities on their behalf, facilitating tax payment for individual drivers and tax collection for tax authorities. In Estonia, the automatic data transmission is facilitated through an electronic tool, which shares standardized income information with the tax authorities and automatically enters the worker's data into his or her prefilled tax return. Since the launch of the new regime, the number of workers declaring their income through Uber and similar transport platforms has increased fourfold. Such simplified declaration and payment mechanisms could also be envisaged for social

[20] M Olivier, *Informality, Employment Contracts and Extension of Social Insurance Coverage* (Report prepared for the International Social Security Association (ISSA) 2009) 15.

[21] Behrendt, Nguyen and Rani (n 6) 32.

[22] See F Durán-Valverde, *Monotax: Promoting formalization and protection of independent workers* (ILO, Social Protection in Action: Building Social Protection Floors, No 02/2014, 2014); F Durán-Valverde, J Aguilar, J Vindas, D Corea, A Vieira and L Tessier, *Innovations in extending social insurance coverage to independent workers: Experiences from Brazil, Cape Verde, Colombia, Costa Rica, Ecuador, Philippines, France and Uruguay* (ILO, ESS – Document No 42, 2013).

[23] Behrendt, Nguyen and Rani (n 6) 31.

[24] ibid. Authorities included in original text omitted.

> insurance, thereby ensuring workers' social security coverage. Belgium created a favourable tax regime for companies in the platform economy in which participating platforms transmit information about the workers' incomes directly to tax authorities who then forward the information to the social insurance institution.[25]

In the EU, the reality is that clarity, streamlining and consistency regarding the treatment of platform workers across the EU Member States have been apparent, accompanied by a clear understanding of the vulnerable social protection status of affected platform workers, among others – as is evident from the provisions of a number of key EU instruments and documents.[26] Pursuant to a study on working conditions of platform workers, in 2020 the Commission President published in a Letter of Intent the Initiative to improve the working conditions of people working in the platform economy. Following consultations, publication of the European Commission's Proposal for an EU Directive on Digital Platform Workers occurred on 9 December 2021.[27] The scope and intent of the proposed Directive have been summarised as follows:

> The proposed Directive seeks to ensure that people working through digital labour platforms are granted the legal employment status that corresponds to their actual work arrangements. It provides a list of control criteria to determine whether the platform is an 'employer'. If the platform meets at least two of those criteria, it is legally presumed to be an employer. The people working through them would therefore enjoy the labour and social rights that come with the status of 'worker'. For those being reclassified as workers, this means the right to a minimum wage (where it exists), collective bargaining, working time and health protection, the right to paid leave or improved access to protection against work accidents, unemployment and sickness benefits, as well as contributory old-age pensions. Platforms will have the right to contest or 'rebut' this classification, with the burden of proving that there is no employment relationship resting on them. The clear criteria the Commission proposes will bring the platforms increased legal certainty, reduced litigation costs and it will facilitate business planning.[28]

Recently, the European Parliament's draft report on fair working conditions, rights and social protection for platform workers explicitly argued for:

- Addressing the occupational health and safety needs of platform workers.
- Considering the need to ensure that platform workers should receive compensation in case of work accidents and occupational diseases, and be offered sickness and invalidity insurance coverage.
- Formal and effective coverage, adequacy and transparency of social protection systems should apply to all workers including the self-employed.[29]

[25] ibid, 31–32. Authorities included in original text omitted.

[26] In particular, the European Agenda for the Collaborative Economy (2016), the EU Directive on transparent and predictable working conditions in the European Union (2019), building on the *European Pillar of Social Rights* (2017), and the EU Council Recommendation on access to social protection for workers and the self-employed (2019).

[27] European Commission, 'Proposal for a Directive of the European Parliament and of the Council on improving working conditions in platform work' COM(2021) 762 final 2021/0414 (COD). See also: www.europarl.europa.eu/legislative-train/theme-a-europe-fit-for-the-digital-age/file-improving-working-conditions-of-platform-workers.

[28] ec.europa.eu/commission/presscorner/detail/en/ip_21_6605.

[29] European Parliament, Committee on Employment and Social Affairs, Draft report on fair working conditions, rights and social protection for platform workers – new forms of employment linked to digital

## IV. Key Principles and Values Informing the Extension of Social Security Coverage and Access in Relation to Platform Workers

International instruments provide the fundamental basis for the protection of the social security rights of platform workers, despite the generalised nature of the provisions of these instruments. These instruments are given further meaning through clarifying documents and reports concerning their implementation emanating from the international organisations concerned.

The foundational UN instrument confirming the right of every person to social security is the 1948 UN Declaration of Human Rights. Article 22 stipulates that:

> Everyone, as a member of society, has the right to social security and is entitled to realization, through national effort and international co-operation and in accordance with the organization and resources of each State, of the economic, social and cultural rights indispensable for his dignity and the free development of his personality.

Article 25(1) in turn emphasises that 'Everyone has the right to a standard of living adequate for the health and well-being of himself and of his family, including … the right to security in the event of unemployment, sickness, disability, widowhood, old age or other lack of livelihood in circumstances beyond his control'. The UN Sustainable Development Goals, building on the premise of ending poverty in all its forms everywhere, and that no one should be left behind, stipulates that countries should 'implement nationally appropriate social protection systems and measures for all, including floors, and by 2030 achieve substantial coverage of the poor and the vulnerable'.[30]

Furthermore, the widely ratified UN International Covenant on Economic, Social and Cultural Rights (ICESCR) (1966) in Article 9, stipulates that 'The States Parties to the present Covenant recognise the right of everyone to social security, including social insurance'. The UN's General Comment No 19 of 2008 (on Article 9 ICESCR) does not mention platform workers specifically, presumably as they were not as such appreciated as an identifiable worker category at that stage. However, the General Comment does impose concrete obligations on ratifying countries in respect of 'workers inadequately protected by social security', referring particularly to part-time, casual, self-employed and homeworkers, by stipulating that (in paragraph 33):

> Steps must be taken by States parties to the maximum of their available resources to ensure that the social security systems cover workers inadequately protected by social security, including part-time workers, casual workers, the self-employed and homeworkers. Where social security schemes for such workers are based on occupational activity, they should be adapted so that they enjoy conditions equivalent to those of comparable full-time workers. Except in the case of employment injury, these conditions could be determined in proportion to hours of work, contributions or earnings, or through other appropriate methods. Where such occupation-based schemes do not provide adequate coverage to these workers, a State party will need to adopt complementary measures.

development (2019/2186(INI)) (Rapporteur: Sylvie Brunet) paras 7–10, available at: www.europarl.europa.eu/doceo/document/EMPL-PR-657498_EN.pdf.

[30] UN, Transforming our World: The 2030 Agenda for Sustainable Development, Target 1.3 (2015).

From the perspective of ILO instruments, the Social Protection Floors Recommendation[31] is particularly important, providing guidance to Member States in respect of the establishment and maintenance of social protection floors as a fundamental element of the national social security system, to be implemented in a progressive manner so that higher levels of social security may be made available to as many people as possible.[32] The national social protection floors referred to are essentially basic social security guarantees designed to ensure that people are able to live in dignity, and that they have access to essential healthcare and to basic income security in the event of sickness, unemployment, maternity and disability.[33] The guarantees so indicated should apply to all residents, evidently capturing platform workers and all other worker categories as well. The Recommendation stipulates that a variety of scheme design and funding techniques could be considered to ensure a social protection floor for all.

In the ILO General Survey concerning Recommendation 202, the ILO's Committee of Experts on the Application of Conventions and Recommendations emphasised that

> while relief and anti-poverty measures provide some form of protection and constitute an essential component of social protection floors in many countries, securing a life in health and decency for all people requires the establishment of other types of social security measures, such as tax-funded social assistance and adapted social insurance mechanisms enshrined in law which are sustainable, rights-based and provide adequate levels of protection.[34]

In addition, social protection, with reference also to coverage extension considerations, is an essential part of the ILO's Decent Work Agenda, as it makes up one of the four constituent parts of the Agenda.[35]

Also, the recent ILO Centenary Declaration for the Future of Work (2019) calls upon all ILO Member States to further develop its human-centred approach to the future of work by 'Strengthening the institutions of work to ensure adequate protection of all workers'.[36] The Declaration recognises the urgent need to enhance social protection systems to ensure universal access to adequate, comprehensive and sustainable social protection adapted to the world of work. Of particular relevance is the need for normative direction at the global level: it calls on the ILO to develop an international governance system for digital labour platforms that ensures minimum rights and protections for workers on these platforms, including social protection.

An earlier document, the ILO Declaration on Social Justice for a Fair Globalization,[37] recognises that full and productive employment and decent work should be at the centre

[31] ILO, National Floors of Social Protection Recommendation, 2012 (No 202).

[32] Social Protection Floors Recommendation 2012 (No 202) para 1.

[33] ibid, paras 5 and 8.

[34] ILO, *Universal social protection for human dignity, social justice and sustainable development* (General Survey concerning the Social Protection Floors Recommendation, 2012 (202), Report of the Committee of Experts on the Application of Conventions and Recommendations, 2019) 89.

[35] www.ilo.org/global/topics/decent-work/lang--en/index.htm.

[36] ILO, *Centenary Declaration for the Future of Work* par III (emphasis added). See ILO, Global Commission on the Future of Work, *Work for a brighter future* (ILO, 2019).

[37] ILO, Declaration on Social Justice for a Fair Globalization), 2008 (adopted by the International Labour Conference at its Ninety-seventh Session, Geneva, 10 June 2008).

of economic and social policy, and should be based on developing and enhancing sustainable measures of social protection adapted to national circumstances, including the extension of social security to all. Various ILO social security standards, including the Social Security (Minimum Standards) Convention,[38] the Income Security Recommendation,[39] and the Medical Care Recommendation[40] remain relevant.

As indicated elsewhere in this contribution, also of importance are supranational approaches, such as the application of current and in particular recent EU-level instruments and initiatives (eg, the Initiative to Improve the Working Conditions of People Working in the Platform Economy).[41] National-level constitutionally entrenched fundamental rights further support the protection of platform workers as regards their coverage by and access to social security.

In view of the challenges outlined earlier in this contribution, and the direction given by international instruments and guiding documents, it is suggested that the following principles and values should be heeded when considering extending social security coverage and access to platform workers:

- Continued coverage and portability/transferability: social protection arrangements relevant to platform workers should be adapted in a way that ensures continued protection for workers who move between different employment arrangements, jobs, sectors of the economy or countries, and ensures that rights and benefits are accessible and portable, including for platform workers (see also the Global Commission for the Future of Work, 2019). It should be ensured that social protection systems positively support labour market mobility, and take into account the structural transformation of the labour market and economy.
- Universality of protection, coverage and effective access: effective access for platform workers regardless of work status, whether as employees or otherwise, adapted to their situation and needs.
- Adequacy: social protection arrangements relevant to platform workers do not only effectively prevent poverty, but provide appropriate income replacement, in an equitable and sustainable way.
- Transparency: all platform actors should be made fully aware of their rights and responsibilities; legal frameworks should provide for clear and predictable entitlements; and administrative procedures should be as simple and clear as possible, fully harnessing the potential of digital technology while protecting personal data and respecting privacy.
- Risk-sharing: an appropriate level of risk-sharing in the social protection system is required, including with regard to solidarity in financing through collective financing mechanisms, that avoids that individual workers have to bear an undue level of financial and economic risk.

[38] ILO, Social Security (Minimum Standards) Convention, 1952 (No 102).
[39] ILO, Income Security Recommendation, 1944 (No 67).
[40] ILO, Medical Care Recommendation, 1944 (No 69).
[41] See ch 4 in this volume by Iacopo Senatori on developments at EU law in the labour law arena, and his reference to experimentation with a parallel pathway, relating to the extension of universal protections beyond the domain of the employment relationship.

- Gender equality: social protection systems/arrangements should be sensitive to the realities that women and men engaged in platform work face in the labour market, in employment and society, and should promote gender equality.
- Good governance: social protection systems/arrangements should be financed in a sustainable and equitable way, as well as have efficient management and administration.
- Social dialogue: engagement and collaboration with and formally consulting social partners are critical to the devising of social security arrangements relevant to platform workers. However, as indicated below, where a credible and representative trade union engagement is not possible, representative institutions of platform workers should be formally engaged.[42]

# V. Legal, Policy, Design and Administrative Techniques for Achieving Social Security Coverage Extension to and Access by Platform Workers

## A. Decoupling Employment Status from Coverage by and Access to Social Security: The Need for a Differentiated Approach

It is suggested that an approach which seeks to classify platform workers as either employees or self-employed persons is not necessarily particularly helpful. A hybrid classification may be apposite, which would require that platform workers who are not in an employment relationship are nevertheless ensured of protection, including social protection.[43] Harris and Kroeger argue that the traditional distinction between employees and independent contractors may not be suitable, and that legislation establishing a new worker classification may be needed. According to them, none of the traditional notions of 'employee', 'independent contractor' or even 'worker' adequately describe the position of transportation network company drivers; they argue for the legislative introduction of the concept of 'independent workers'.[44] Fredman and Du Toit conclude that 'it is time to consider ways of transcending this binary divide and ensuring decent work in the labour market irrespective of employment status'.[45]

From a conceptual perspective, lessons may be learnt from the ongoing debate concerning the expansion of labour law to non-standard workers, but also the boundaries of labour law. It has become commonplace in several jurisdictions, including in a range of developing countries, for labour laws (which often have social security consequences as well), to achieve extended protection through a deliberate widening of the

[42] Adjusted from and essentially relying on Behrendt, Nguyen and Rani (n 6) 26–27.
[43] Andoyan (n 15).
[44] S Harris and H Krueger, 'A Proposal for Modernizing Labor Laws for Twenty-First-Century Work: The "Independent Worker"' (2015) Hamilton Project, Discussion Paper (Washington, DC, Brookings, 2015). See also Mokoena (n 10).
[45] Fredman and Du Toit (n 13) 274.

employee (and at times also the employer) concept. This technique may have value in the case of employee-like workers, but would rarely suit the context of independent workers, the self-employed and several other categories of non-standard workers. It may also not be apposite for platform workers.

Other regulatory experiences include the adoption of special regulatory frameworks introduced for specific categories of workers – for example, teleworkers in the EU – as well as the impact of anti-discrimination law in the EU, which has had the effect of extension of protection to part-time and fixed-term employees, but not to multi-employer intermediated arrangements. Note should be taken of the influential report to the EC by Alain Supiot,[46] suggesting the extension of different rights to other groups: for example, independent contractors should be entitled to healthcare schemes; occupational health and safety; a right to equal treatment at work; and protection against sexual harassment. Embedded in this approach is the view of various concentric circles of labour and social protection and that the largest circle encompasses universal and constitutional social rights for all kinds of workers, including the rights to dignity, equality and non-discrimination, together with individual rights to work.[47] It further suggests, as per the Supiot report, the 'redesigning the notion of security' to prevent the working world being split in two: employment status should be redefined to guarantee the continuity of employment status in order to protect workers during transitions between jobs.[48] In fact, as the Supiot report suggests, it is necessary to move beyond employment; all forms of work are worthy of protection, not only subordinate work. Such an approach also sits well with the Decent Work Agenda of the ILO and recently found expression in the European Parliament's recent report, arguing for the guarantee of a minimum set of rights for platform workers, regardless of their employment status.[49]

Social security laws have been slow to follow the labour law lead. Nevertheless, modern occupational health and safety legislation[50] has deliberately extended its personal sphere of application to cover all persons affected by health and safety risks, including workers beyond the employment relationship framework, and through an expanded understanding of 'workplace', which is not restricted to premises of the employer. Furthermore, note can be taken of the example of other regulatory techniques to support coverage extension, in relation to supply chain scenarios.[51] Especially in contexts where collective bargaining outcomes are absent or weak, through supply chain regulatory techniques, coverage extension could be achieved through the statutory application/extension/adjustment of a statutory floor of minimum conditions of employment.

The Australian example regarding expanded coverage in supply chain contexts and relating to labour law dimensions may provide some useful guidance for extended

[46] A Supiot and P Meadows, *Beyond Employment: Changes in Work and the Future of Labour Law in Europe* (Oxford, Oxford University Press, 2001).

[47] ibid. J Landa Zapirain, 'Regulation of dependent self-employed workers in Spain: A regulatory framework for informal work?' in J Fudge, S McCrystal and K Sankaran (eds), *Challenging the Legal Boundaries of Work Regulation* (Oxford, Hart Publishing, 2012) 158.

[48] Supiot and Meadows (n 46) 221.

[49] European Parliament, Draft report on fair working conditions (n 29) para 4.

[50] See, eg, the Australian model occupational health and safety law, introduced in 2010.

[51] Lund (n 19) 23–24; M Rawling, 'A generic model of regulating supply chain outsourcing' in C Arup et al (eds), *Labour Law and Labour Market Regulation* (Sydney, Federation Press, 2006) 520.

application also in social security contexts. Here supply chain regulation has been introduced to deal with (supply chain) outsourcing via an interconnected series of commercial arrangements, in the textile, clothing and footwear industry (and also the truck drivers and cash-in-transit industries), in some of the States. The key dimensions of this approach have been described by Rawling in the following terms:[52]

> The statutory model consists of deeming provisions designed to clarify the employment status of outworkers,[53] rights of recovery allowing outworkers to make a claim for their lawful entitlements against parties throughout the contracting chain and provisions for the making of mandatory codes applicable to the retailer sector.

In terms of this approach, these employer deeming provisions provide for an outworker to make a claim against any party in the contracting chain (aside from the retailer), including principal contractors and a person directly engaging the outworker, 'despite there being no direct employment relationship or common law employment contract between the outworker and the person giving out the work'.[54]

## B. Learning from Other Coverage Extension Modalities: Vulnerable Informal Economy Workers

Coverage extension has been a central theme in the protection of vulnerable workers. Informed by a normative framework to this effect,[55] in recent years social security has seen significant developments towards the extension of coverage for a particularly vulnerable group of workers, ie, informal economy workers.[56] These developments can be summarised as follows:

- Innovative and at times extensive conceptualisation has been introduced to widen the application of social security, so as to also include those in the informal economy, through extensive (re)-definition(s) of the range of workers/persons and/or the

[52] M Rawling, 'Supply Chain Regulation: Work and regulation beyond the employment relationship' (PhD thesis, University of Sydney, 2010) 11.

[53] 'Outworkers are contractors or employees who perform their work at home or at a place that wouldn't normally be thought of as a business premises. Outworkers are common in the textile, clothing or footwear industry'. See: www.fairwork.gov.au/starting-employment/types-of-employees/outworkers.

[54] Rawling, 'Supply Chain Regulation' (n 52) 138–39.

[55] Key standards and principles have been flowing from instruments such as ILO Recommendation on National Floors of Social Protection, 2012 (Recommendation 202) and ILO Recommendation on the Transition from the Informal to the Formal Economy, 2015 (Recommendation 204) and include: (i) International (UN; ILO) and regional standards confirm the right of all persons and all workers, including informal economy workers, to social security protection; (ii) The adoption of an appropriate policy and legal foundation to inform, support and mandate the extension of (contributory) social security to informal (economy) workers is advised; (iii) Coverage extension should occur progressively via any one or combination of a non-exclusive list of modalities, including contributory and non-contributory arrangements; and (iv) Recent ILO instruments emphasise that contributory arrangements should be sensitive to the context and contributory capacity of these workers.

[56] For a summary of these principles, applied particularly in the developing world context, see M Olivier, 'Social security protection for informal economy workers: Developing world perspectives' in M Westerfeld and M Olivier (eds), *Social Security Outside the Realm of the Employment Contract: Informal Work and Employee-like Workers* (Cheltenham, Edward Elgar Publishing, 2019) 2; and (for an African emphasis) UNDP, *Informality and Social Protection in African Countries: A Forward-looking Assessment* (2021).

occupations/industries[57] and sectors covered by the enabling legislation (eg, India,[58] Tanzania)[59] – via revisions to social security and labour laws.

- Non-contributory schemes have been adapted to ensure inclusion of these workers – for example, through the introduction of universal pension arrangements (eg, Namibia,[60] Nepal).[61]
- Contributory schemes have been extended to achieve inclusion, at times even on a compulsory basis (eg, domestic workers in South Africa),[62] and are increasingly supported through government incentives, including government subsidies; the introduction of national health insurance schemes also serves this purpose (eg, Thailand,[63] Viet Nam).[64]
- Some governments have introduced comprehensive arrangements to extend social security coverage to the whole of the informal economy. Examples include China,[65] India,[66] Indonesia,[67] Ghana[68] and Rwanda.[69]

[57] For an example of the definitional extension occurring on an industry basis, see the Indian Beedi and Cigar Workers (Conditions of Employment) Act (Act 32 of 1996), which covers a person employed in the beedi industry (hand-rolled cigarettes) directly or through any agency and who is given raw materials by an employer or a contractor: in this way, outworkers and homeworkers are included.

[58] See the Code on Social Security Act (Act 36 of 2020) (India), which incorporates a vast number of worker categories within the framework of the law, including among other 'platform workers' – defined as a person engaged in or undertaking platform work. 'Platform work' is in turn defined to mean 'a work arrangement outside of a traditional employer employee relationship in which organisations or individuals use an online platform to access other organisations or individuals to solve specific problems or to provide specific services or any such other activities which may be notified by the Central Government, in exchange for payment' – see Article 2(60) and (61).

[59] s 3 of the Social Security (Regulatory Authority) Act (Act 8 of 2008), defines the 'informal sector' as the sector that includes workers who work informally and who do not work in terms of an employment contract or another contract contemplated in the definition of employee.

[60] s 3 of the National Pensions Act 1992 (Act 10 of 1992) extends various social assistance grants to all Namibian citizens resident in Namibia.

[61] In 1995, Nepal introduced the Senior Citizens Allowance (colloquially called Old Age Allowance, OAA), a universal non-contributory social pension (HelpAge International *The universal social pension in Nepal* (2009)). At that stage, this non-contributory social pension scheme was hailed as a scheme unique to Asia. See now s 3 of the Social Security Act 2075 (2018), which extends social security allowances to several categories of vulnerable Nepali citizens. The universal scheme must be understood against the background of Nepal's new Constitution (2015), which guarantees social protection for the poor and vulnerable.

[62] Coverage of South African social security legislation has incrementally been extended to domestic workers: see Lund (n 19) 26; M Olivier, *Informality, employment contracts and extension of social insurance coverage* (ISSA Project on 'Examining the existing knowledge of social security coverage', Working Paper, no 9, Geneva, International Social Security Association ISSA, 2009) 23–37. Recently, their exclusion from the scope of coverage of South Africa's main employment injury system was found to be unconstitutional – see *Mahlangu v Minister of Labour (Commission for Gender Equality & another as amicus curiae)* (2021) 42 *ILJ* 269 (CC).

[63] K Damrongplasit and G Melnick, 'Early results from Thailand's 30-baht health reform: Something to smile about' (2009) 28(3) *Health Affairs* 457, 457.

[64] Law on Health Insurance (2008) (Law No 25/2008/QH12) 2008; Law amending the Law on Health Insurance (Law No 46/2014/QH13) 2014; Q Nguyen and N Cunha, *Extension of social security to workers in informal employment in the ASEAN region* (Geneva, ILO, 2019) 58–59; M Olivier, *Viet Nam social security law reform: An integrated framework* (Geneva, ILO, 2022) 55–59.

[65] The voluntary rural and urban pension schemes were introduced in 2009 and 2011 respectively, and are (co)-funded by government via matching contributions. By the end of the first quarter of 2012, 376 million people were already participating in the two schemes, despite weak incentives to contribute above the minimum (see M Dorfman, M Wang, P O'Keefe and J Cheng, 'China's pension schemes for rural and urban residents' in R Hinz, R Holzman D Tuesta and N Takayaka (eds), *Matching Contributions for Pensions* (Washington, DC, The World Bank) 217; M Olivier, 'Social protection innovation and challenges in China and Africa: Selected comparative perspectives' (2017) 12 *Frontiers of Law in China* 429.

- Some countries have included informal economy workers sector by sector, usually on the basis of separate or dedicated schemes. Examples include Ecuador,[70] Tunisia[71] and the Indian welfare funds modality.[72]
- Tailor-made design modalities have been introduced, including:[73]
  - Specialised contribution modalities (eg, flexible contribution options allowing workers to contribute according to their ability and at a frequency that reflects the reality of their income-generation, such as in the case of seasonal workers (Ghana,[74] Philippines,[75] Viet Nam);[76] the setting of realistic income baselines as a basis upon which contributions are calculated (Tunisia); and, importantly, the increasing tendency of government subsidies to support or even replace the contributions of poor informal economy workers (India (proposed),[77] Rwanda, Viet Nam);

[66] See the Code on Social Security Act (Act 36 of 2020) (India); and Olivier, 'Social security protection for informal economy workers' (n 56) 19–23.

[67] See the National Social Security Law of Indonesia, Act 40 of 2004.

[68] Through the Informal Sector Fund and other (private) arrangements: see M Guven, 'Extending Pension Coverage to the Informal Sector in Africa' (2019) Social Protection & Jobs Discussion Paper No 1933, World Bank, 31, available at: https://documents1.worldbank.org/curated/en/153021563855893271/pdf/Extending-Pension-Coverage-to-the-Informal-Sector-in-Africa.pdf; K Douglas, *Ghana's first pension fund targeting the informal sector*, 6 December 2016, available at: www.howwemadeitinafrica.com/ghanas-first-pension-fund-targeting-informal-sector/56924/.

[69] In December 2018 Rwanda launched a long-term savings scheme named Ejo Heza ('Brighter Future') which offers opportunity and incentives for all Rwandans to save a voluntary share of regular or irregular earnings to mitigate against the risk of old-age poverty. The scheme has been described as 'the first national-level universal pension program in the world being launched by leveraging existing digital financial inclusion infrastructure in the true spirit of Public–Private Partnership'. See E Rwigamba, 'An inclusive and integrated pension model for informal sector workers in Rwanda' in P Khana, W Price and G Bhardwaj (eds), *Saving the Next Billion from Old Age Poverty: Global Lessons for Local Action* (Singapore, Pinbox Solutions, 2018) 157.

[70] See PA Ortiz, 'Informal and self-employed workers in Latin America: from an excluded category to an example of innovate inclusive measures' in M Westerfeld and M Olivier (eds), *Social Security Outside the Realm of the Employment Contract: Informal Work and Employee-like Workers* (Cheltenham, Edward Elgar Publishing Ltd, 2019) 141, 156–57.

[71] Economic and Social Commission for Western Asia (ESCWA) (2016), *Social Protection Country Profile: Tunisia* (UN; Beirut) 6; M Chaabane, 'Towards the universalization of social security: The experience of Tunisia' (2002) Extension of Social Security, ESS Paper No 4 (Geneva, ILO) 11–12.

[72] Indian welfare funds are financed through levies collected from selected employers and manufacturers, and provide a range of benefits, including social security-related benefits such as medical care and maternity assistance. Also at a state level, a tax (cess) is imposed by state governments on the aggregate output of selected industries (eg, the Beedi Welfare Fund is financed by a tax on beedis): Lund (n 19) 23; Olivier, *Informality, employment contracts and extension of social insurance coverage* (ISSA Project) (n 62) 15.

[73] See above for the references in relation to the different country experiences.

[74] Provided for within the framework of the Ghana Informal Sector Fund, referred to above.

[75] In addition to compulsory arrangements, the Philippines Social Security System has adopted several flexible approaches to meet the requirements of informal sector workers who do not have access to formal banking arrangements and who are only able to contribute irregularly, by introducing specific social security programmes and (in the process) partnering with organised informal sector groups (ISGs) and Local Government Units (LGUs) (see J Mines, *Moving towards inclusive growth: The Philippine Social Security System* (Philippine Social Security System, 2015), available at: www.sss.gov.ph/sss/DownloadContent?fileName=2015_Updated_ISSA_Report_on_ISCoverage_FINAL.pdf.

[76] Government subsidies are available in particular for more vulnerable categories of persons within the framework of both the social health insurance and the voluntary insurance schemes: see Olivier, *Viet Nam social security law reform* (n 64) 58.

[77] According to the Code on Social Security Act (Act 36 of 2020), India, public social security schemes can be partly funded by the union and/or state governments.

- Relaxed entitlement criteria (accessing benefits without complying with lengthy contribution periods or other onerous conditions).
- Dedicated, context-sensitive benefit arrangements addressing the key short-term and long-term needs of informal workers (Ghana[78] and Rwanda).[79]

In addition to the above, it is clear that extending coverage to and enhancing social security-related protection of the informally employed cannot be achieved in isolation. The following supporting arrangements are of particular importance:[80]

- Stakeholder consultation: firstly, there is need to ensure that appropriate stakeholder consultation takes place, to determine concrete options – and consider challenges and solutions – in relation to extending coverage to the informally employed and developing suitable protection modalities for them. World-wide experience has shown that successful coverage extension and suitable forms of protection in social security terms for those who work informally have been preceded by thorough consultation with stakeholder groups and institutions. In fact, this appears to be called for also by prevailing international standards.[81]
- Communication: secondly, as supported by evidence emanating from other countries where the self- and informally employed have been included in social security schemes, there has to be thorough communication of envisaged new arrangements. In particular, those who are affected by the new arrangements, including informally employed workers and, where relevant, their providers of work, have to be properly informed. Given the national relevance of such arrangements, awareness-raising interventions targeting the general public also have to be introduced.
- Enabling framework: thirdly, extending coverage and enhancing protection would require that a proper enabling framework has been established and is operational. Among others, steps that would enhance the ability in the informal economy to contribute to and access (contributory) social security, have to be considered and

[78] Under the Informal Sector Fund, informal economy workers contribute to two accounts: (a) a Retirement Account (a pension account, from which a member is permitted to withdraw only in the event of retirement, death or disability occurring); and (b) an Occupational Scheme Account, which serves as a form of a personal savings account, from which the contributor can withdraw after five months of initial contributions, provided the account has a credit balance (with rules for withdrawals before retirement, eg, for education and business enhancement).

[79] It has been noted, with reference to the new long-term savings scheme, Ejo Heza, that: 'Members of the scheme shall be expected to keep savings in their assigned account for a minimum pre-defined number of years. Upon completion of the minimum period, a member may be authorized to withdraw part of his/her benefits as a pre-retirement package. The pre-retirement package may be invested in housing and education or/and any other investment (for those with sufficient savings under the RSSB mandatory scheme). However, it should be noted that the amount of the authorized pre-retirement package will be capped to a maximum percentage of the total individual savings to ensure that the beneficiary retains sufficient funds under the scheme to cater for his/her retirement days': Rwigamba (n 69) 157–58.

[80] Largely taken from Olivier, 'Social security protection for informal economy workers' (n 56) 15–17.

[81] ILO Recommendation 204 (2015) (*The transition from the informal to the formal economy*) requires, in relation to the need to consult appropriately with institutions representing the interests of informal economy workers: 'Consultation with the most representative employers' and *workers' organizations, which should include in their rank, according to national practice, representatives of membership-based representative organizations of workers and economic units in the informal economy*' (emphasis added) (see in particular paras 6, 34, 38 and 39 of the Recommendation).

introduced. Fixing the minimum wage at a level that would enable them to contribute would be one such matter to be considered. Providing incentives in the form of government subsidies or contributions would be another.

## C. Collective Bargaining, Voice and Representation

It is important to consider adjusting and expanding the use of labour law techniques and responses to achieve appropriate improved social security coverage. Collective agreements may provide such an avenue. The role of trade unions in the public and policy debate and the regulatory role of collective agreements are particularly relevant, as the recent experience in Europe has shown. For example, for the first time, in April 2018, in Denmark, a collective agreement was signed between a trade union (3F) and platform operator (Hilfr.dk). In terms of the agreement, once the freelance workers of the platform have completed at least 100 hours of work, they are reclassified as 'employees', which provides them with higher wages and social protection. Also, in Germany, through the involvement of the trade union IG Metall all self-employed workers have been included in the statutory pension scheme and the minimum contributions of self-employed workers to statutory health insurance.[82]

And yet, particular challenges remain. In many countries, trade unions yet have to show a commitment to engage on behalf of this non-traditional constituency. Also, in several jurisdictions, in particular in a range of African countries, trade unions' legal representative mandate is restricted to employees involved in an employment relationship – thereby impacting on the ability and (legal) authority of unions to represent non-employee platform workers in relation to social protection issues covered in, for example, collective agreements.

In the absence of trade union engagement, other alternatives have to be considered. Some lessons can possibly be learnt from the informal economy experience, bearing in mind the representative capacity of stakeholder institutions to exert appropriate influence on social security policy development to the advantage of informal economy workers. There is some indication of innovative attempts to ensure that other cooperatives and other (often community-based) institutions represent the interests of informal economy workers.[83] However, the efficiency of these interventions remains limited due to (at times) lack of scale, and the absence of recognition in the regulatory and policy realm of the status, role and capacity of these institutions – both in domestic and international systems. There may be a need to revisit the traditional approach to representation of workers when it comes to platform workers: it may be necessary to adjust the historical tripartite model for this purpose.

[82] Behrendt, Nguyen and Rani (n 6) 33; Eurofound (European Foundation for the Improvement of Living and Working Conditions) *Platform work* (29 June 2018), available at: www.eurofound.europa.eu/sr/node/94271.

[83] A Routh, 'Forms of solidarity for informal workers in India: Lessons for future?' Paper presented at the Labour Law Research Network: Inaugural Conference (Barcelona, 13–15 June 2013) 21–22; J Fudge, 'Blurring Legal Boundaries: Regulating for Decent Work' in J Fudge, S McCrystal and K Sankaran (eds), *Challenging the Legal Boundaries of Work Regulation* (Oxford, Hart Publishing, 2012) 1, 8–9, 21–22.

A recent report of the European Parliament summarises the prevailing position by recognising that freedom of association and the right to collective bargaining are fundamental rights for all workers, and believing that a directive on platform workers should ensure that these rights are effective and enforced. The report notes the potential for imbalanced relationships between digital labour platforms and workers, who may lack the individual bargaining power to negotiate their terms and conditions; and notes further that there are also practical issues such as a lack of common means of communication and opportunities to meet online or in person, which can prevent collective representation in practice.[84] The report further notes the legal difficulties in collective representation faced by platform workers, and that the solo self-employed are considered 'undertakings', and as such are subject to the prohibition on agreements that restrict competition; it welcomes in this regard the inception impact assessment published by the Commission, and the planned initiative to address this obstacle.[85]

It should also be noted that in accordance with the provisions of the recently published proposed European Commission Proposal for a Directive on improving conditions in platform work, those who, as a result of correct determination of their *employment* status (as opposed to genuine self-employed people working through platforms), are recognised as workers[86] will enjoy improved working conditions – including health and safety, employment protection, statutory or collectively bargained minimum wages and access to training opportunities – and gain access to social protection according to national rules. Furthermore, at the end of 2021 the European Commission published draft Guidelines on collective bargaining of self-employed, for public comment.[87]

## VI. Conclusions

It is apparent that a no one-size-fits-all approach may be called for when it comes to social security coverage and access in favour of platform workers. Comparatively, countries have adopted a wide array of means and techniques informed by different legal regimes and varied abilities to implement coverage and access modalities. The traditional labour law-infused focus on an employment relationship as a trigger for social

[84] European Parliament, Draft report on fair working conditions (n 29) para 11.

[85] ibid, para 12.

[86] European Commission Proposal for a Directive of the European Parliament and of the Council on improving working conditions in platform work (n 27) 15: 'As a general rule, the Directive covers persons who have, or who based on an assessment of facts may be deemed to have, an employment contract or employment relationship as defined by the law, collective agreements or practice in force in the Member States, with consideration to the case-law of the CJEU', available at: ec.europa.eu/competition-policy/public-consultations/2021-collective-bargaining-2_en#consultation-document---questionnaire.

[87] European Commission Communication from the Commission: Approval of the content of a draft for a Communication from the Commission – Guidelines on the application of EU competition law to collective agreements regarding the working conditions of solo self-employed persons C(2021) 8838 final (Brussels, 9.12.2021). As noted by the Commission: 'The draft Guidelines aim to ensure that competition law does not stand in the way of collective agreements to improve the working conditions of certain self-employed persons, who may have little influence over their working conditions, while guaranteeing that consumers and SMEs continue to benefit from competitive prices and innovative business models, including in the digital economy. The draft Guidelines seek to achieve this objective by clarifying the applicability of EU competition law to collective bargaining by solo self-employed'.

security coverage evidently does not produce satisfactory outcomes. Many platform workers and the platform through which they are engaged do not fit the mould of an employment relationship, given the variation and heterogeneity of work relationships through which platform workers are engaged. The complexity of their position in social security terms is exacerbated by the fluidity of their work engagement and by issues of jurisdiction, given the cross-border and international nature of platform activity.

It would appear necessary to decouple employment status as a prerequisite for platform workers' coverage by and access to social security. Much can be gleaned from the experience globally with innovative regulatory, conceptual and institutional techniques aimed at extending social security coverage and access to platform workers outside the confines of the employment relationship. The experience in particular with the extension of social security to workers in the informal economy provides a useful point of departure. Policymakers and legislatures should also take their cue from the developing normative framework, including key overall principles and values informing coverage and access extension, with a particular focus on following a rights-based approach to ensure that no one – and no platform worker – is left behind when it comes to coverage by and access to social security.

# 10

# Competition Law Implications of Platform Work

TIHAMÉR TÓTH

## I. Introduction

The unprecedented space of technological development and digitalisation is reshaping many industries and is creating new markets. Platform work creates new opportunities for individuals and businesses, but also presents regulatory challenges. Some of them emerge as gatekeepers of the digital economy. Questions are asked whether antitrust is suitable for the task of dealing with the complexity and pace of these changes.

I will explore the question whether the traditional antitrust concept of an undertaking can provide a meaningful basis to understand and evaluate the developments in digital platform markets. The clear lines we used to draw between hierarchical labour relations versus actions among business actors supplying goods to serve consumer demand have been blurred. Traditional labour relations are evolving, and the pace of change is accelerated by the mandatory restrictions and voluntary adaptations following the global Covid-19 pandemic. Existing roles have been recalibrated, new tasks have been defined. Traditional distinctions between working as an employee and working as an individual entrepreneur are not evident any more. All this may impact the well-established labour exemption under competition rules. In addition, the realm of platform work is fairly heterogeneous: some types of platform work may be subject to competition rules while others may not.

The chapter discusses the interactions of labour law and competition law in the 'gig' economy with special regard to the characterisation of digital platform workers as potential subjects of competition law. Section II starts with a discussion of the personal scope of competition rules. I summarise how European and United States (US) competition laws deal with actions involving natural persons. I will discuss traditional examples like professional services, taxi drivers and professional sportsmen which may be used as analogy when we discuss the gig economy. In section III, I will present the labour specific exemption both (European Union) EU and US case law has developed.

In section IV, I will discuss some of the features of platform services like Uber which may impact the classification of workers as employees or undertakings. Next, assuming that individuals in some platform markets are subject to competition rules, I will explore how their cooperation can be evaluated under rules prohibiting anticompetitive agreements. I will conclude that broadening the scope of competition rules to cover gig-economy relations would not necessarily obstruct the operation of these new businesses.

# II. The Personal Scope of Competition Rules

## A. Differences in Personal Scope

Although the substantial competition rules in the EU and US are similar, they differ in one thing: the way personal scope is defined in the statutes. In the US, the Sherman Act (1890) prohibits anticompetitive agreements and unilateral conduct that monopolises or attempts to monopolise the relevant market. Section 1 of the Act is structured in a way to focus on the subject matter of the unlawful conduct rather than the person: 'Every contract, combination in the form of trust or otherwise, or conspiracy, in restraint of trade or commerce among the several States, or with foreign nations, is declared to be illegal'.[1] In contrast, section 2 uses the fairly general term of 'person': 'Every person who shall monopolise, or attempt to monopolise, or combine or conspire with any other person or persons, to monopolise any part of the trade or commerce among the several States, or with foreign nations, shall be deemed guilty of a felony'.[2] This is the widest personal scope that can be imagined, covering not only business entities, but natural persons and even government and other public bodies. In fact, case law had to carve out state governments' actions and related private conduct, rationalising the reach of antitrust.[3]

As a contrast, EU competition law applied a narrower term to draw the boundaries of competition rules. Article 65 ECSC Treaty and Article 81 EEC Treaty both used the terms 'undertaking' and 'associations of undertakings' defining the persons who can engage in anticompetitive conduct. The text has not changed over time, today's Articles 101 and 102 of the Treaty on the Functioning of the European Union (TFEU) still regulate the conduct of undertakings. Through a number of cases in the 1990s, the concept of undertaking has acquired a unique EU law meaning, distinct from similar definitions existing under national competition, company or tax laws.

The EU concept of an undertaking has a fairly vague positive and more precise negative dimension. As early as 1962, the European Court of Justice (ECJ) held, interpreting the ECSC, that an undertaking is constituted by a single organisation of personal, tangible and intangible elements, attached to an autonomous legal entity and pursuing a

[1] 15 USC § 1. The second sentence, providing for sanctions, uses the term 'person': 'Every person who shall make any contract or engage in any combination or conspiracy hereby declared to be illegal shall be deemed guilty of a felony, and, on conviction thereof, shall be punished by fine not exceeding $100,000,000 if a corporation, or, if any other person, $1,000,000, or by imprisonment not exceeding 10 years, or by both said punishments, in the discretion of the court'.

[2] 15 USC § 2.

[3] *Parker v Brown*, 317 US 341 (1943). The Supreme Court held at 351 that '(t)here is no suggestion of a purpose to restrain state action in the Act's legislative history'. The sponsor of the bill which was ultimately enacted as the Sherman Act declared that it prevented only 'business combinations'.

given long-term economic aim.[4] The first definition of an undertaking under the EEC was delivered in 1984.[5] Accordingly, the term must be understood as 'designating an economic unit for the purposes of the subject-matter of the agreement in question, even if in law that economic unit consists of several persons, natural or legal'. An undertaking subject to the rules of competition law can be any person or entity that carries out an economic activity.[6] Economic activity is loosely defined as the production of goods, provision of services in a market.[7] Purchasing can also become an economic activity if the product is used for another economic activity.[8]

The negative dimension of the definition involves identifying categories of conduct which shall not be covered, and certain features which should be inconclusive. Activities linked to the exercise of public authority (law-making, law enforcement, protection of public order and the environment, etc)[9] and services regulated by the solidarity principle (especially in healthcare and social security) are thus excluded from the concept.[10] It is also irrelevant whether the entity is for-profit or non-profit, the way it is financed, whether it is publicly or privately owned, or whether it was created by law or through a private contract. What is decisive is the economic nature: the function of the activity. The definition of undertaking is thus functional, and its boundaries can thus be flexible, depending on how we define the economic character of a conduct.

As an example, we should recall the *Höfner* judgment. German labour law in the 1980s entrusted the federal labour office with the task of providing employment procurement services. This legal monopoly was challenged in a private litigation between a company and two managers. The Court held that 'the concept of an undertaking encompasses every entity engaged in an economic activity, regardless of the legal status of the entity and the way in which it is financed and, secondly, that employment procurement is an economic activity'.[11] Employment procurement, especially executive recruitment, has not always been, and is not necessarily, carried out by public entities.[12] This case is a good example of the *functional definition*: the federal labour office exercised mainly public authority functions, and thus was not an undertaking in those respects; however, when it came to the provision of headhunting services, it qualified as an undertaking.

We can conclude that the wording of the US antitrust law gives room for the inclusion of workers as employees within the scope of competition rules, whereas the EU law response will depend on how broadly the term 'undertaking' can be interpreted. It is

[4] Joined cases 17/61 and 20/61 *Klöckner-Werke AG and Hoesch AG v High Authority of the European Coal and Steel Community* ECLI:EU:C:1962:30 [1962], para 341.

[5] Case 170/83 *Hydrotherm Gerätebau GmbH v Compact del Dott Ing Mario Andreoli & C Sas* ECLI:EU:C:1984:271 [1984], para 11.

[6] Case C-41/90 *Klaus Höfner and Fritz Elser v Macrotron GmbH* ECLI:EU:C:1991:161 [1991], para 21.

[7] Case C-35/96 *Commission of the European Communities v Italian Republic* ECLI:EU:C:1998:303 [1998], para 36.

[8] Case C-205/03 *Federación Española de Empresas de Tecnología Sanitaria (FENIN) v Commission of the European Communities* ECLI:EU:C:2006:453 [2006].

[9] Case C-343/95 *Diego Calì & Figli Srl v Servizi ecologici porto di Genova SpA (SEPG)* ECLI:EU:C:1997:160 [1997], paras 22–23 (exercising environmental control in a sea port).

[10] Case C-160/91 *Christian Poucet v Assurances Générales de France and Caisse Mutuelle Régionale du Languedoc-Roussillon* ECLI:EU:C:1993:63 [1993] (compulsory social security system scheme based on principle of solidarity).

[11] ibid, para 21.

[12] ibid, para 22.

not the exact identity of the person which is important, rather the nature of the activity. As we will see, working under the control of another entity, lacking genuine business autonomy means that the conduct is not economic.

## B. The Boundaries of an Undertaking: Group of Companies

In some cases, the EU concept of undertaking covers a *group* of legal persons. As a rule, parent and subsidiary companies are considered to form one single undertaking if the subsidiary is directed by the parent company. This concept, I believe, is also similar to how the employer is held responsible for the actions of its employee. Under EU competition law, there are two conditions that have to be met: the ability and the actual exercise of influence over the conduct of the subsidiary. The Court of Justice of the European Union (CJEU) established a rebuttable presumption that both of the criteria are fulfilled where the parent company owns 100 per cent of the subsidiary.[13] There is no need to prove that the subsidiary actually received instructions from the parent company as to its unlawful behaviour on the market. However, a 100 per cent ownership is not necessarily required; the case law seems to follow the path of merger control rules at large.[14] Consequently, a parent company may be held liable for infringements of its subsidiaries even though it was neither involved in the anticompetitive conduct, nor was aware of it.

The economic unit doctrine also works on the other side of the Atlantic. The US Supreme Court made it clear that a parent and its wholly owned subsidiary were incapable of conspiring with each other, even if the parent does not actually exercise day-to-day business control.[15]

Before analysing the intra-undertaking relations in more detail, we can state that the conduct of an employee in relation to his or her employer is not a subject that competition rules should regulate. Intra-entity issues are 'family problems' which should not be judged by third parties. Once a person makes the decision to tie herself or himself to a company, her or his independence will be lost and will form an integral part thereof, just like subsidiaries constitute one single undertaking with their parent company.

## C. The Boundaries of an Undertaking: The Agency Exemption

There is another aspect of the concept of undertaking which may be relevant for the discussion of the status of normal and platform workers. Genuine agents and genuine

[13] Case C-97/08 P *Akzo Nobel NV and Others v Commission of the European Communities* ECLI:EU:C:2009:536 [2009], para 61.

[14] In the Banana information cartel case an 80% limited partnership interest was enough to prove the ability to exercise decisive influence. See Case C-293/13 P *Fresh Del Monte Produce Inc. v European Commission and European Commission v Fresh Del Monte Produce Inc* ECLI:EU:C:2015:416 [2015], para 29.

[15] *Copperweld Corporation v Independence Tube Corporation*, 467 US 752, 769, 767–72 (1984). 'With or without a formal "agreement" the subsidiary acts for the benefit of the parent, its sole shareholder … They share a common purpose whether or not the parent keeps a tight rein over the subsidiary; the parent may assert full control at any moment if the subsidiary fails to act in the parent's best interests'.

employees are considered in the same way in competition law. Agents, acting as distributors of another undertaking may be regarded as an integral part thereof, just like an employee would be. Principal and agent, just like employer and employee form one single entity: neither agents, nor employees are regarded as separate undertakings, hence their contracts with the principal or the employer are not subject to competition rules.[16] The CJEU ruled in the *Suiker Unie* case, that

> if … an agent works for the benefit of his principal he may in principle be treated as an auxiliary organ forming an integral part of the latter's undertaking, who must carry out his principal's instructions and thus, like a commercial employee, forms an economic unit with this undertaking.[17]

The European Commission's Vertical Guidelines elaborate on agency agreements. Unlike genuine contract-specific risks, such as financing of stocks, the risk of the agent's income being dependent upon its success or general investments in for instance premises or personnel, are not material to this assessment.[18] The Guidelines list additional factors, such as the agent shall not undertake product liability, nor take responsibility for the customer's non-performance. A genuine agent shall not be obliged to contribute to the advertising budget, nor make market-specific investments. These activities are fairly similar to those which would also not be expected to be performed by an employee. Consequently, the analogy between the classification of a person as an employee and an agent may come in handy.

An important feature of the agency exemption, which is also relevant for the evaluation of work relations, is that it applies only for the period when the agency agreement ties the two persons. Before, and after, the agent company may be regarded as an undertaking, offering its distribution services on the market on which it offers its services to potential principals.[19]

To conclude, the agent forms an integral part of the principal's undertaking if it does not bear any, or only negligible financial and commercial costs and risks linked to sales of goods to third parties on behalf of the principal. Interestingly, the fact that the agent acts for more than one principal in parallel does not make the agent an independent undertaking.[20] The same approach may be helpful when deciding whether platform workers are separate undertakings or are integrated into another one.

## D. Applying Competition Rules to Individuals

One of the questions discussed in this chapter is to what extent workers, by definition natural persons, may qualify as an undertaking for the purposes of competition law.

[16] Case C-266/93 *Bundeskartellamt v Volkswagen AG and VAG Leasing GmbH* ECLI:EU:C:1995:345 [1995], paras 18–19.

[17] Joined cases 40/73 to 48/73, 50/73, 54/73 to 56/73, 111/73, 113/73 and 114/73 *Coöperatieve Vereniging 'Suiker Unie' UA and others v Commission of the European Communities* ECLI:EU:C:1975:174 [1975], para 480.

[18] Guidelines on Vertical Restraints, Brussels, SEC(2010) 411 final, point 15.

[19] Case C-279/06 *CEPSA Estaciones de Servicio SA v LV Tobar and Hijos SL* ECLI:EU:C:2008:485 [2008], para 41.

[20] ibid, para 36.

Bearing this in mind, I explore the more general question: under what conditions do individuals have to comply with competition rules?

Natural persons may be held liable for competition law infringements in two ways. First, a person may be sanctioned for the infringement committed by a company. Sanctions like this do not exist at EU level, but most Member States introduced some kind of personal liability against managers and employees who were involved in the unlawful action personally or did not exercise their supervisory functions properly.[21] The liability of individuals is secondary as it depends upon the liability of their company in the first instance. The second way is when the individual is the undertaking, a person directly addressed by the norm. The term 'undertaking' can cover anyone who carries out an economic activity. The person does not even have to take the legal form of an individual entrepreneur. The individual may act in a personal capacity, without being able to issue invoices and be a separate subject of tax law. The same applies under US antitrust, where the 'open' prohibition of the Sherman Act reaches anyone who may be in the position to conclude anticompetitive agreements or take part in conspiracies.

An important part of competition law cases connected to individuals in the EU relates to (regulated) professions. In *Commission v Italy*, the CJEU took into account that customs agents assume the financial risks involved in their activity and bear the deficit themselves.[22] The conclusion was that the intellectual nature of the activity and that it required authorisation, did not exclude it from the scope of the competition rules of the Treaty. Similarly, in *Wouters*, the CJEU held that members of the Dutch bar who offered legal services for a fee and bore the financial risks carried on economic activities and so constituted undertakings.[23]

Another set of cases involving individuals relates to professional sports activities. The CJEU in 1974 had already pointed out in its *Walrave and Koch* judgment that sport is subject to EU law as long as it constitutes an economic activity.[24] European case law evolved mainly through the application of the free movement rules prohibiting discrimination.[25] The first seminal competition law judgment was delivered in 2006. The CJEU confirmed in *Meca-Medina* that sporting regulations with economic effects also fall under the aegis of competition rules.[26] More recently, in its *International Skating Union* (ISU) decision of 2017, the EU competition authority condemned the speed skate eligibility rules of the ISU that could even result in a lifetime ban at ISU competitions in a case of skating at an event not approved by ISU. The General Court approved the

[21] Among others, Spain, Belgium and Germany.

[22] C-35/96 *Commission of the European Communities v Italian Republic* (n 7) para 38.

[23] Case C-309/99 *JCJ Wouters, JW Savelbergh and Price Waterhouse Belastingadviseurs BV v Algemene Raad van de Nederlandse Orde van Advocaten, intervener: Raad van de Balies van de Europese Gemeenschap* ECLI:EU:C:2002:98 [2002], paras 46–49 and 64.

[24] Case 36/74 *BNO Walrave, LJN Koch v Association Union cycliste internationale, Koninklijke Nederlandsche Wielren Unie e Federación Española Ciclismo* ECLI:EU:C:1974:140 [1974]. The Court also explained that the Treaty does not affect the composition of sports teams, the formation of which is a question of purely sporting interest and is outside the boundaries of economic activities.

[25] I believe that since both competition and free movement rules have the common goal of protecting the single market, classifying an activity as economic should follow the same path.

[26] Case C-519/04 P *David Meca-Medina and Igor Majcen v Commission of the European Communities* ECLI:EU:C:2006:492 [2006].

Commission decision's most important points in 2020.[27] Interestingly, the personal scope of competition rules was not even raised by the applicants. No one doubted that professional skaters are undertakings, hence the association of national associations is an association of undertakings for the purposes of competition rules.

## III. The Provision of Work as a Service: The Labour Exemption

### A. EU Competition Law Jurisprudence on Workers

The scope of competition law in relation to workers depends on two questions:

1. To what extent can definitions of another legal field (labour law) have an impact on the interpretation of competition rules?
2. Should more weight be given to formal considerations (ie, contract title) than to economic realities?

Both competition law and labour law struggle with the proper characterisation of workers: some employees may in fact carry out economic services, while there are independent contractors who work under circumstances similar to those of an employee.

EU competition law had to deal with situations where the application of competition law to labour relations was at the heart of the case. These cases related to a legal rule unique to EU competition law. Article 106(1) TFEU prohibits Member States from creating exclusive, or special, rights, or putting public undertakings into a situation where another Treaty provision, especially competition rules, would be infringed. Before condemning a restrictive state measure, it is essential to clarify whether the related activity comes under the personal and material scope of the competition rules, ie, whether the conduct is of an economic nature. In *Becu*, the CJEU ruled that employees, in that case dock workers who worked for and under the direction of their employers, did not constitute separate undertakings, rather, they were incorporated into the undertaking of their employer.[28]

To what extent the provision of work is distinct from the provision of goods and services in a market is a complex question. This issue was discussed by AG Jacobs in *Albany* relating to a supplementary pension scheme, just one year after *Becu*.[29] AG Jacobs

[27] Case T-93/18 *International Skating Union v European Commission* ECLI:EU:T:2020:610. The decision was partially annulled as far as it related to arbitration clauses. The judgment is now pending at ECJ, Case C-124/21 P.

[28] Case C-22/98 *Criminal proceedings against Jean Claude Becu, Annie Verweire, Smeg NV and Adia Interim NV* ECLI:EU:C:1999:419 [1999], para 26. There was another competition law case involving dock work. In Case C-179/90 *Merci Convenzionali Porto di Genova SpA v Siderurgica Gabrielli SpA* ECLI:EU:C:1991:464 [1991] the CJEU held that Article 106(1) of the Treaty, in conjunction with free movement and competition rules, precludes national rules which require an undertaking established in that State to have recourse, for the performance of dock work, to a dock-work company formed exclusively of national workers.

[29] Case C-67/96 *Albany International BV v Stichting Bedrijfspensioenfonds Textielindustrie* ECLI:EU:C:1999:430 [1999]. See also, eg, CNSD [1993] OJ L203/27; Joined cases C-180/98 to C-184/98 *Pavel Pavlov and Others v Stichting Pensioenfonds Medische Specialisten* ECLI:EU:C:2000:428.

acknowledged that the provision of labour could be characterised as the provision of any other service from an economic point of view. However, the legal interpretation of this term, in the context of the Treaty, would lead to a different result:

> Dependent labour is by its very nature the opposite of the independent exercise of an economic or commercial activity. Employees normally do not bear the direct commercial risk of a given transaction. They are subject to the orders of their employer. They do not offer services to different clients, but work for a single employer. For those reasons there is a significant functional difference between an employee and an undertaking providing services.[30]

The Court followed the path of its Advocate General and created a 'qualified labour exemption'[31] for collective agreements concluded by workers and employers. The judges were aware that certain restrictions of competition are inherent in collective agreements between organisations representing employers and workers. However, the social policy objectives pursued by such agreements would be seriously undermined if management and labour were subject to competition rules when seeking jointly to adopt measures to improve conditions of work and employment.[32]

In 2014, the CJEU was invited to give a preliminary ruling interpreting competition rule as regards collective agreements. The outcome of the *FNV Kunsten* judgment, another reference originating from the Netherlands, was different from *Albany*.[33] FNV concluded a collective labour agreement with the Netherlands Musicians' Union and the Association of Foundations for Substitutes in Dutch Orchestras. The collective labour agreement laid down minimum fees not only for substitutes hired under an employment contract, but for self-employed substitutes. The CJEU ruled that such mixed agreements involving both workers and self-employed persons are subject to the competition rules of the Treaty. The CJEU acknowledged that although they perform the same activities as employees, service providers are undertakings within the meaning of Article 101(1) TFEU, since they offer their services for remuneration on a given market and perform their activities as independent economic operators in relation to their principal.[34] The judges followed the Opinion of AG Wahl who argued that an organisation representing self-employed persons does not act as a trade union, but as an association of undertakings.[35]

The CJEU's position in *FNV Kunsten* was certainly in line with previous jurisprudence, however, it seems to give more weight to formalities than to economic reality. A more thorough investigation into the economic circumstances of how contracted musicians perform their work could have shown similarities with those of employed orchestra members. Why is a fixed rate among contracted musicians more harmful to society than the same agreement among employees? Treating entities with similar attributes differently due to the title of their contract does not bring about a level playing

[30] ibid, Opinion of Advocate General Jacobs, delivered on 28 January 1999, point 215.

[31] N Countouris, V De Stefano and I Lianos, 'The EU, Competition Law and Workers Rights' in S McCrystal, E McGaughey and S Paul (eds), *The Cambridge Handbook of Labor in Competition Law* (Cambridge, Cambridge University Press, 2021) 4.

[32] See (n 29) para 59.

[33] Case C-413/13 *FNV Kunsten Informatie en Media contro Staat der Nederlanden* ECLI:EU:C:2014:2411 [2014].

[34] ibid, para 27.

[35] ibid, para 28.

field. A radical, yet logical solution would be to either allow the collective price negotiation for both employed and self-employed workers, or prohibit it for both groups.

## B. US Case Law on Workers

On the other side of the Atlantic, neither workers, nor labour unions were originally excluded from the rather general scope of the Sherman Act. Interestingly, the Ohio senator giving his name to the Bill, believed that the act would not cover labour relations. Sanjukta M Paul cites Senator Sherman responding to a question during the debate of the bill: 'combinations of workingmen to promote their interests, promote their welfare, and increase their pay are not affected in the slightest degree, nor can they be included in the words or intent of the bill'.[36] Paul notes, reviewing the adoption process of the antitrust bill and the early jurisdiction of courts, that

> the Sherman Act, originally the child of a republicanism that opposed huge conglomerations of capital and sought to protect the small enterprise and artisan of traditional American economic life, soon enough became a weapon against the working people who labored for those new conglomerations.[37]

In 1914, the adoption of the Clayton Act created the statutory labour exemption, making it clear that 'the labor of a human being is not a commodity or article of commerce'.[38] This was interpreted to apply only to relations between an employer and its existing employees. This resulted in the adoption of the Norris–LaGuardia Act 1932, which broadened the scope of the labour exemption, expressly favouring arrangements of labour organisation, representation and negotiation of terms and conditions of employment.[39] The labour exemption granted by later statutes brought labour union specific arrangements into the sphere of legality, regardless of their potential anticompetitive effects This reflects the victory of social policy favouring fundamental labour rights over the value of free competition.

The exemption was built on the existence of an employment relationship. A union of independent contractor truckers could thus not have benefited from the benefits of the labour exemption.[40] The dominant view was driven by the Supreme Court's *Columbia River Packers Association v Hinton* decision and provides that independent

[36] SM Paul, 'The enduring ambiguities of antitrust liability for worker collective action' (2016) 47 *Loyola University Chicago Law Journal* 969, 999.

[37] ibid, 1000.

[38] 38 Stat 738 (1914), codified at 29 USC s 52. Section 20 of the Clayton Act reads: 'No restraining order or injunction shall be granted by any court … in any case between an employer and employees … involving, or growing out of, a dispute concerning terms or conditions of employment … And no such restraining order or injunction shall prohibit any person or persons, whether singly or in concert, from terminating any relation of employment, or from ceasing to perform any work or labor … nor shall any of the acts specified in this paragraph be considered or held to be violations of any law of the United States'.

[39] 47 Stat 70 (1932), codified at 29 USC ss 101–15. Section 2 provides that: 'Whereas under prevailing economic conditions … the individual unorganized worker is commonly helpless to exercise actual liberty of contract and to protect his freedom of labor, and thereby to obtain acceptable terms and conditions of employment … it is necessary that he have full freedom of association, self-organization, and designation of representatives of his own choosing, to negotiate the terms and conditions of his employment'.

[40] *Conley Motor Express, Inc v Russell*, 500 F.2d 124, 126 (3rd Cir, 1974).

contractors are not exempt from the restrictions posed by antitrust rules.[41] The Court held that

> a dispute among businessmen over the terms of a contract for the sale of fish is something different from a 'controversy concerning terms or conditions of employment, or concerning the association of persons seeking to arrange terms or conditions of employment'.[42]

The existence of a labour exemption highlights the importance of how labour laws define workers. Competition rules may allow other laws, like labour law, to restrict its field of application. The qualification of a person as an employee under labour law should take into account similar factors than competition law would rely on to establish that someone is not an undertaking. Consequently, the legal status of individuals under national labour laws has an influence on the lawfulness of cooperation taking place on and in relation to the platform. This topic will be explored in the next section.

## IV. Competition Law Analysis of Platform Relations

### A. Competition Law Rules Weighing the Positive and Negative Effects of Restrictive Practices

Agreements restricting competition (ie, regulating prices, sharing markets, restricting output) relating to platform work can be justified in various ways. Using EU terminology, it can be argued that: (i) the restriction falls outside the scope of competition rules (non-economic activities); (ii) the restriction is necessary for the proper functioning of a market (a sort of ancillary doctrine and public policy rule of reason); (iii) the restriction of competition is of minor importance (*de minimis* exemption); (iv) the restriction is block-exempted by a regulation; or (v) the restriction can be justified through an individual exemption.

EU and harmonised national competition laws prohibit agreements, concerted practices between undertakings, as well as decisions by associations of undertakings which either have the aim or effect of harming competition. Such anticompetitive practices may be exempted from the prohibition, either by a specific block exemption regulation (ie, distribution contracts), or through a detailed analysis of the individual effects of the agreement. Mainstream competition policy exempts anticompetitive practices which enhance economic efficiency to the benefit of consumers. Restrictions bringing about other economic and social benefits are difficult to justify. According to well-established dogma, price fixing and market allocation schemes are anticompetitive in their aim, could not benefit from an exemption and are clearly prohibited regardless of their market effects.

As we have seen in previous chapters, a restrictive practice may fall outside the scope of EU competition rules if the actors are not undertakings, ie, the conduct is not economic in nature. In addition, EU case law developed an exemption for minor restrictions of competition. According to the practice of the EU Commission, the prohibition

[41] *Columbia River Packers Association v Hinton* 315 US 143 (1942).
[42] 315 US 146.

of Article 101(1) TFEU shall not apply if the combined market share of the competing undertakings is below 10 per cent.

Furthermore, according to the jurisprudence of the CJEU testing the limits of the textual interpretation of Article 101(1) TFEU, not every agreement between undertakings falls under the prohibition of Article 101 TFEU. This approach could be labelled as a public policy rule of reason exception. In *Wouters*, the professional regulation prohibiting multidisciplinary practices with accountants, despite its inherent negative effects on competition, was necessary for the proper practice of the profession, as organised in the Netherlands. The Commission also emphasised that restrictions objectively necessary to guarantee the proper practice of the profession fall outside the scope of the prohibition.[43]

US antitrust walks a different path, yet the outcome is the same. Since there is no exemption in the Sherman Act, judicial interpretation of the concept 'in restraint of trade' filtered out unharmful contracts including some kind of restriction on the parties' behaviour. As a result, only practices that unreasonably restrict trade are prohibited. Courts would apply one of the following three standards nowadays. First, overlapping with the European 'by object' concept, the per se rule is followed in cases where the restriction at stake is so inherently anticompetitive that there is no need to analyse its effects or objective competitive justification.[44] The catalogue of per se restrictions includes horizontal price fixing (vertical price fixing no longer applies), horizontal market allocation, bid-rigging, group boycotts, some types of tying agreements. Price fixing and market allocation may only be accepted if they are ancillary to an otherwise lawful cooperation, like the creation of a joint venture with positive economic effects.[45]

In the US, for restraints not fitting into the per se category, the analysis of the market effects, in various depths, is required. In its full-blown form, the rule of reason approach involves for the plaintiff: (i) the definition of the relevant market; (ii) identifying the market power of the defendant; and (iii) the existence of anticompetitive effects. In turn, the defendant can prove that positive effects outweigh negative effects, and can justify the restricion.[46] The third option is a sub-section of the rule of reason analysis. The so-called 'quick look' does not require the plaintiff to go through all the steps of the full-blown rule of reason; it is sufficient to prove that the conduct appears likely to have anticompetitive effects. That is the case when an observer with even a rudimentary understanding of economics could conclude that the arrangement in question would have negative effect on consumers.[47]

As far as labour matters are concerned, EU case law excluded agreements between employees and employers as falling outside the personal scope of competition rules. US law provides immunity for some agreements through specific legislation. Yet, since the exact scope of the labour exemption is far from clear, there may be restrictions which require a case-by-case competition law analysis.

[43] AG Jacobs in his Opinion in Case C-67/96 *Albany International BV v Stichting Bedrijfspensioenfonds Textielindustrie* ECLI:EU:C:1999:28 [1999].

[44] See, eg, *US v Socony-Vacuum Oil Co*, 310 US 150 (1940).

[45] Federal Trade Commission and Department of Justice, 'Antitrust Guidelines for Collaborations Among Competitors, April 2000', available at: www.ftc.gov/sites/default/files/documents/public_events/joint-venture-hearings-antitrust-guidelines-collaboration-among-competitors/ftcdojguidelines-2.pdf.

[46] See, eg, *Continental TV, Inc v GTE Sylvania Inc*, 433 US 36, 49 (1977).

[47] *California Dental Ass'n v FTC*, 526 US 756 (1999).

## B. Models of Coordination in Platform Markets

The most important features of platform markets is discussed by Gruber-Risak in this book. I would just add, that these services often bring about regulatory disruptions, especially in their growing phase. Platform companies compete with existing services, but by using sophisticated new structures they avoid existing regulations, face fewer costs, thereby gaining market share quickly. It takes some time for regulators to decide what is best for society: whether deregulating traditional services or extending the regulation to the platform company. Many European countries imposed strict regulations on Uber and Airbnb which had a chilling effect on these companies and their partners.[48]

Digital platforms are manifold, from large companies like Uber, to small food deliveries in Bangladesh. Platforms are organised in different ways, so the status and working conditions of their workers may vary. Consequently, regulators, including those shaping labour and competition laws, should resist the idea of a homogenous form of work deserving of one-size-fits-all interventions.[49] Anderson and Huffman distinguish between various platforms as regards the degree of integration and risk sharing between the platform operator company and the individual workers. We borrow their figure to illustrate this theory.[50]

**Figure 1** Types of platforms according to the degree of risk sharing and integration

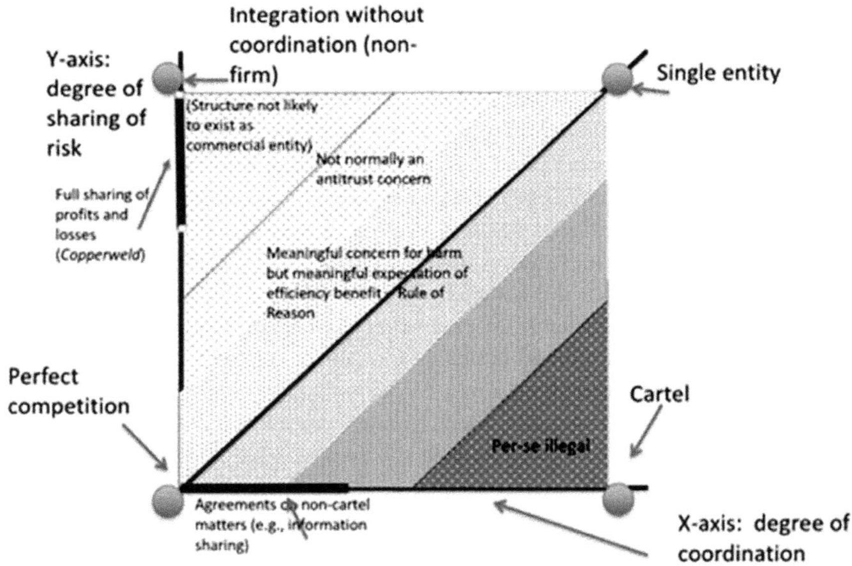


[48] In Hungary, for example, following demonstrations by taxi drivers, Uber was practically banned through transport regulation in 2016. AirBnb services can also be regulated by municipalities, limiting the period when entire apartments can function as hotels.

[49] A Aloisi, *Platform Work in the EU: Lessons learned, legal developments and challenges ahead* (Directorate General for Employment, Social Affairs and Inclusion, 20 November 2020) 2.

[50] M Anderson and M Huffman, 'The Sharing Economy Meets the Sherman Act: Is Uber a Firm, a Cartel, or Something in Between?' (2017) 3 *Columbia Business Law Review* 919. See: www.ssrn.com/abstract=2954632. The figure is published under a CC-BY 4.0 licence, available at: creativecommons.org/licenses/by/4.0/.

On the X-axis, representing the degree of coordination, the left-hand corner represents minimum coordination, while the further right we move, the more competition-sensitive forms of coordination arise (with a hard-core, per se unlawful cartel as an extreme). On the Y-axis, at the junction with the X-axis, we can find the ideal form of perfect competition where there is no risk sharing among the companies. At the end where Y approaches infinity, we can see full risk sharing: this represents a firm, or an economic unit. Anderson and Huffman conclude that antitrust law should allow for increased levels of coordination when a sharing economy enterprise involves increased levels of risk sharing.

# V. Selected Competition Law Issues in Platform Markets[51]

## A. Horizontal Restrictions: Collective Bargaining

One of the most important horizontal issues, where competition law may seriously limit the abilities of platform workers, is their right to bargain collectively for better working conditions, particularly wages. On the one hand, the right to collective bargaining is a fundamental right protected by international, EU and national legal instruments.[52] On the other, competition lawyers condemn most of these collective agreements, if concluded by undertakings, as evil cartels. It makes a huge difference whether one is characterised as an employee, or an individual entrepreneur.[53] Creating associations, councils and other forms of gatherings is not unlawful per se. However, meeting with competitors under the aegis of such associations and discussing prices and other sensitive business information does not provide protection against competition law investigations. Competing undertakings should be careful not to exchange sensitive, especially price-related information concerning their businesses, since this may be condemned as an information sharing cartel. Furthermore, organising a strike translates into a collective boycott in the realm of competition law.

A crucial question is to what extent competition law should consider the goals of other public policies. EU competition rules clearly state that they apply, 'unless otherwise provided' either by the TFEU or Acts of Parliament. The concurrent rule has to be very specific and clear to change the universal reach of competition rules. This means, for example, that the right to bargain collectively would not be challenged under competition rules, however, when this negotiation covers prices/wages, it would be regarded as an anticompetitive agreement, provided that employees could be characterised as undertakings. For example, France extended the rights of collective action, freedom

[51] In this section I will focus on bi- or multilateral actions, ie, cartels and vertical restrictions. As shown by the *Sidecar* litigation in California, monopolisation, abuse of dominance may also be a legal base challenging unilateral conduct of powerful platform companies.

[52] ILO Conventions 87 and 98, as well as Article 28 of the Charter of Fundamental Rights of the EU.

[53] There are legal obstacles in force in several countries to the organisation of self-employed workers in trade unions, see, eg, S Engblom, 'Atypical Work in the Digital Age – Outline of a Trade Union Strategy for the Gig Economy' in M Rönnmar and J Julén Votinius, *Festskrift till Ann Numhauser-Henning* (Lund, Juristförlaget, 2017) 225.

of association and collective bargaining to platform workers.[54] Would this limit the application of competition law prohibitions? Most probably yes, if we take into account French competition law. National legal regimes often provide for an antitrust exemption if a certain activity is expressly regulated by another statute. However, national rules would not pre-empt the application of supranational EU competition rules. Even if France were to decide that platform workers should be categorised as traditional employees and, thus, be exempted from French competition rules, the EU Commission, the EU courts and most probably also the French Competition Authority, enforcing Article 101 TFEU, could disagree if the conditions for defining the platform worker as an undertaking as interpreted by EU case law are fulfilled.

This tension between national and EU competition rules on the one hand, and international labour law on the other has arisen in Ireland recently. In 2016, the Irish Congress of Trade Unions (ICTU) lodged a collective complaint against Ireland with the European Committee on Social Rights (Council of Europe) regarding an alleged breach of Article 6.2 of the European Social Charter. This was prompted by a decision of the Irish Competition Authority in the Actors' Equity case.[55] The Competition Authority found an infringement of competition rules through a fee-setting arrangement between the trade union representing actors (Actors' Equity) and the Institute of Advertising Practitioners in 2004. These actors provided services to advertisers as, for example, voice-over actors in radio advertisements. The actors were found to be self-employed persons, and were thus classified as undertakings. The Committee found that the ban on collective bargaining was not necessary in a democratic society, and thus the situation before the entry into force of the 2017 Act amending Irish competition law was in breach of the Charter.

In the aftermath of the public debate prompted by the national Competition Authority's decision, an amendment of the Competition Act was adopted in 2017. This provides for a specific exemption for three named categories of self-employed workers: voice-over actors, session musicians and freelance journalists.[56] Such exceptions apply only to national competition rules and do not restrict the applicability of EU competition rules. Yet, the CJEU may take into account these national developments when interpreting EU law in a preliminary ruling procedure. In Ireland, these individuals now have the right to bargain collectively with employers in relation to working conditions, including pay rates. Under strictly defined conditions, other groups of self-employed workers could also be allowed to bargain collectively. In the course of the preparation of this amendment, the government refused to include general practitioners (family doctors contracted by the state) and other self-employed professionals (eg, barristers, dentists, pharmacists) from providing services to the state under similar contracts to collectively negotiate.[57]

[54] I Daugareilh, D Degryse and P Pochet (eds), The platform economy and social law: Key issues in comparative perspective' (2019) ETUI Working Paper 10 (Brussels, ETUI, 2019), available at: www.etui.org/sites/default/files/WP-2019.10-EN-v3-WEB.pdf, 55.

[55] Case E/04/002. Decision available at: www.ccpc.ie/business/wp-content/uploads/sites/3/2017/04/E_04_002-Actors-Fees-Enforcement-Decision.pdf.

[56] I should note that such exceptions apply only to national competition rules and do not restrict the applicability of EU competition rules.

[57] See Irish note to the OECD, 5 June 2019, available at: one.oecd.org/document/DAF/COMP/WD(2019)39/en/pdf, section 2.2.2.

As the Irish case proves, competition lawyers believe that individuals who do not qualify as genuine employees should not be exempt from the competition law prohibition. However, Nicola Countouris and his co-authors believe that the personal scope of this collective bargaining right should be interpreted broadly, to also cover self-employed people like agricultural workers and members of liberal professions.[58] They cite the report of the ILO Committee on Freedom of Association that requested the South Korean government to ensure that this fundamental trade union right should also extend to self-employed workers.[59] This issue was also discussed recently within the framework of the EU–Korean free trade regime, where in 2021 a panel of experts decided that the South Korean legislation excluding self-employed truck drivers from the category of 'workers' was in breach of ILO standards.[60]

From a competition law perspective, if the *Wouters*-like creative exception is not applied, collective agreements would most likely fall under the by-object restrictions, since they regulate price/wage terms. One important implication is that the *de minimis* rule relating to by-effect analysis would not apply as even collaborations between just a few workers would be caught by Article 101(1) TFEU. This does not mean, however, that collective bargaining would in the end be prohibited. Even by-object restrictions may be exempted under Article 101(3), as noted for example by the CJEU in *Irish Beef*, involving an output limitation cartel arrangement.[61] For an individual exemption, four cumulative conditions have to be fulfilled: the anti-competitive agreement (i) creates efficiencies or contributes to economic development; (ii) some part of these benefits are passed on to consumers; while (iii) the restriction of competition is necessary to achieve those positive goals; and (iv) does not eliminate all competition. The general problem with price related restrictions is that consumers would not benefit; to the contrary, they would ultimately pay the bill for collective agreements guaranteeing better working conditions. Although competition takes many forms beyond pricing, experience is that higher prices cannot be justified by other, often long-term benefits to consumers.

Some authors argue that despite the inherent upward price effects, such collective deals should be analysed as by-effect restrictions of competition, as they are significantly different from traditional naked collusions, and due to their social character, they do not seek to attain goals incompatible with core EU values.[62] Unlike a price cartel, which is by its nature secretive, collective bargaining is often reported even in the media. Such an approach would indeed fit in well with the broader framework of the EU Treaties, allowing the harmonisation of various EU goals better than trying to interpret the individual exemption rules so widely that the outcome may be disconnected from its actual wording. Such an interpretation would certainly require a ruling from the CJEU.

Following the *FNV Kunsten* judgment, the Dutch competition authority (ACM) issued its guidelines on how to deal with collaborative price arrangements between

[58] ibid, 12.

[59] ILO, Committee on Freedom of Association (2012) Report no 363, Case no 2602, para 461.

[60] The report is available at: trade.ec.europa.eu/doclib/docs/2021/january/tradoc_159358.pdf.

[61] Case C-209/07 *Competition Authority v Beef Industry Development Society Ltd and Barry Brothers (Carrigmore) Meats Ltd* ECLI:EU:C:2008:643.

[62] MJ Schmidt-Kessen, C Bergqvist, C Jacqueson, Y Lind, and M Huffman, '"I'll call my Union", said the driver – Collective bargaining of Gig Workers under EU Competition Rules' (2020) Copenhagen Business School, CBS LAW Research Paper no 20-43, available at SSRN: www.ssrn.com/abstract=3744177, 14.

self-employed workers who use their own equipment (eg, car, bike or computer) to provide their services.[63] The ACM will likely not find competition rules applicable if the individual works side-by-side in an identical manner with other employees.[64] If the platform worker constitutes an undertaking, there are still several ways their cooperation can be cleared under competition rules. The ACM also noted that they are not going to intervene if the collective agreement's goal is to secure a normal income. The difficulty with this approach is how to set a just income level. In countries, where there are statutory rules or collective agreements on minimum wage, this may serve as such a reference point.

Since labour law is predominantly regulated at national level, national competition regimes may also feel tempted to introduce labour specific exemptions at that level (see the Dutch and Irish examples).[65] Most competition regimes do not seem much harm in collective buying arrangements by small businesses. If the combined market share of these entities is not more than 10 per cent, then they are saved by the *de minimis* exception. If they are bigger, but still not reaching a level of dominance, individual exemption under Article 101(3) TFEU can be substantiated. This favourable treatment is available even if these agreements set an identical purchase price, thus excluding a form of price competition between competing small business entities.

As far as US antitrust is concerned, collective price agreements would be subject to automatic prohibition as a *per se* violation of section 1 of the Sherman Act. Even if such agreements were analysed under the more permissive rule of reason test, analysing the positive and negative market effects of the agreement, the narrow definition of what constitutes economic efficiencies would make the legalisation of such agreements rather difficult. Anderson and Huffman develop an argument however, so that organisation by workers can overcome market inefficiencies created by buyers of labour with monopsony power by exerting countervailing power, moving the price for labour up and closer to the equilibrium price.[66] This would lead to more labour output and increases the level of production for the benefit of consumers. Ultimately, the effect of labour organisation is to lower prices for the consumer.

A similar approach, considering factors going beyond price competition, is represented by the Australian Competition and Consumer Act that permits business entities to engage in collective negotiations with their suppliers if they result in overall public benefit. They have also recently introduced a class exemption for collective bargaining for small businesses, agribusinesses and franchisees.[67] A rule like this acknowledges that such small business entities, in some cases individuals, may be able to negotiate more

[63] Available at: www.acm.nl/sites/default/files/documents/2020-07/guidelines-on-price-arrangements-between-self-employed-workers.pdf.

[64] ibid, point 29.

[65] A former exemption that existed under Hungarian law as regards countervailing supplier power between 1991 and 1997 could also be reinvented. The law at that time provided for a special exemption for anticompetitive agreements concluded by small market players with a view to creating a level playing field with a dominant supplier or buyer.

[66] M Anderson and M Huffman, 'Labor Organization in Ride Sharing – Unionization or Cartelization?' (2021) 23 *Vanderbilt Journal of Entertainment and Technology Law* 715.

[67] See ACCC Guidelines on collective bargaining class exemption, June 2021, available at: www.accc.gov.au/system/files/public-registers/documents/Collective%20bargaining%20class%20exemption%20-%20Guidelines%20June%202021.pdf.

efficiently with larger businesses, and achieve better terms and conditions, than they can on their own. The class exemption covers three kinds of cooperation: (i) a business entity or independent contractor with an aggregated turnover of less than $10 million[68] which forms a collective bargaining group to negotiate with suppliers; (ii) franchisees which collectively bargain with their franchisor regardless of their size; and (iii) fuel retailers which collectively bargain with their fuel wholesaler regardless of their size. The favourable competition law treatment also has its limits in Australia: the collaboration shall not extend to a collective boycott.

In Europe, the European Commission announced an initiative, connected to the public consultation of the Digital Services Act, to ensure that EU competition law should not prohibit collective bargaining by self-employed individuals, including those working through platforms.[69] The Commission will consider how to balance the right to conclude collective agreements promoting the wellbeing of platform workers, with the right of consumers and SMEs to benefit from competitive prices and innovative business models in the digital economy. Margrethe Vestager, in charge of competition policy, emphasised in June 2020 that:

> The Commission has committed to improving the working conditions of platform workers during this mandate … As already stressed on previous occasions the competition rules are not there to stop workers forming a union but in today's labour market the concept 'worker' and 'self-employed' have become blurred. As a result, many individuals have no other choice than to accept a contract as self-employed. We therefore need to provide clarity to those who need to negotiate collectively in order to improve their working conditions.[70]

As a next step, the Commission published a set of initiatives in December 2021 to improve the working conditions in platform work.[71] Among these, draft Guidelines aim to clarify the application of EU competition law to collective agreements of solo self-employed people. The draft Guidelines aim to bring legal certainty and make sure that EU competition law does not stand in the way of certain solo self-employed people's efforts to improve collectively their working conditions, including remuneration, in cases where they are in a relatively weak position, for example where they face a significant imbalance in bargaining power. A key concept to distinguish these self-employed, including platform workers, is economic dependence. This will be assumed whenever the worker earns 50 per cent or more of her or his annual income from the same counterparty.[72] As the Guidelines cannot change EU law, the Commission, by explaining its priorities, declares that it will not actively enforce the law against these collective agreements.

[68] This amount is consistent with the threshold used by the Australian Tax Office to determine if a business is a 'small business entity' for tax concession purposes. See ibid, 4.

[69] Inception impact assessment on 'Collective bargaining agreements for self-employed – scope of application of EU competition rules' launched in January 2021.

[70] EU Commission Press release of 20 June 20 2020, IP/20/1237, available at: www.ec.europa.eu/commission/presscorner/detail/pt/IP_20_1237.

[71] See Commission Press release of 9 December 2021, available at: www.ec.europa.eu/commission/presscorner/detail/en/ip_21_6605. These draft guidelines were published following the submission of this chapter, so a detailed analysis thereof is not included here.

[72] ibid, point 25 of the draft Guidelines.

There is a similar attitude on the other side of the Atlantic. Federal Trade Commission member Slaughter noted that the misclassification issues as regards self-employed and employees should be solved by legislation; until then she had urged that the Federal Trade Commission should not use its limited resources to bring enforcement actions against such collective action by platform workers.[73]

## B. Vertical Restrictions on Competition

Vertical restrictions, which are concluded between a manufacturer and its distributors, or a supplier and its business partners are also the subject matter of competition policy. They often include restrictions that have an effect on third parties, creating artificial entry barriers, limiting consumer choice and other benefits in the long run. However, due to their inherent efficiencies most vertical restrictions can be justified from a competition policy perspective, as long as none of the parties has significant market power.[74] On the other hand, restrictions fixing the price consumers have to pay, or eliminating intra-brand trade between EU Member States, qualify as by-object anti-competitive restrictions, often subject to heavy fines. In the US, after the late 1970s, the welfare-oriented jurisprudence on vertical restraints became much less worried about the inequalities of bargaining power and the anticompetitive effects that could be effectuated through them, and more concerned about efficiencies.[75]

Competition rules on vertical restrictions may be analogous to most labour relations. Economic power and subordination are relevant for rules protecting the weaker party in both realms.[76] Manufacturers often tend to exercise control over the activities of their distributors, just like employers over their employees. For this reason, I introduce a view relevant to competition law topics which may be used to discuss work relations.

### *i. Franchise Agreements*

Many platform markets show similarities with the franchise way of distribution. The franchisor, just like the owner of a platform, owns a set of intellectual properties and know-how, and licences these to independent companies under strict conditions. Franchising thereby enables the franchisor to establish, with limited investments, a uniform network for the distribution of his products. The *Pronuptia* case in 1986 was the first franchising judgment by the CJEU.[77] The Court ruled that restrictions of a

[73] 'New Decade, New Resolve to Protect and Promote Competitive Markets for Workers', remarks of Commissioner Rebecca Kelly Slaughter, FTC Workshop on Non-Compete Clauses in the Workplace Washington, DC 9 January 2020. See: www.ftc.gov/system/files/documents/public_statements/1561475/slaughter_-_noncompete_clauses_workshop_remarks_1-9-20.pdf, 7.

[74] In the EU Vertical Block Exemption Regulation (n 79), this is reflected in the 30% market share threshold which is a condition to the applicability of the exemption.

[75] 'Monopsony and the Business Model of Gig Economy Platforms' – note by Marshall Steinbaum, point 11, available at www.one.oecd.org/document/DAF/COMP/WD(2019)66/en/pdf.

[76] This can be witnessed especially under EU rules applicable to the distribution of new vehicles.

[77] In the US, there is no distinction between franchising and other types of distribution systems, which require essentially a rule of reason analysis.

franchise agreement which are essential to the working of the franchise system do not harm competition.[78] The Court's reasoning as to why franchise restrictions themselves are not anticompetitive could also be applied to the organisation of many platforms. Companies relying on sharing of resources owned by their contractors enhance through their technology and brand image the conclusion of transactions between individuals who othwerwise would not have traded with each other. Such an approach would imply that most restrictions relating to the functioning of a platform would be held ancillary, hence not restricting competition in the market.

### *ii. Non-Compete Clauses*

Non-compete contracts between companies, but also those between the employer and their employees, can raise competition law issues. Although such agreements may be less common in the gig economy during the existence of a given platform-based activity, they may arise after the termination of this relationship. EU competition rules, for example, tolerate such post-non-compete restrictions in trade, if they do not last longer than one year.[79]

### *iii. Vertical Price Fixing*

In the EU setting the consumer price, or a minimum price level by the manufacturer is a hardcore restriction of competition. This is a 'dogmatic' prohibition in as much as even very small companies without any market power are barred from interfering with consumer prices. This does not apply if the distributor is not an independent undertaking, ie is a subsidiary of the seller, or acts as a genuine agent.

The US policy is more lenient, vertical price restraints after *Leegin* come under a rule of reason interpretation where the pros and cons of such a restraint are balanced. In *Leegin*, the US Supreme Court held that minimum resale price maintenance agreements are not per se unlawful under federal antitrust law, but should be evaluated under a rule of reason analysis like most other vertical restraints.[80] The *Leegin* court overruled century-old precedent[81] holding that such agreements were per se unlawful. This ruling does not make resale price restrictions lawful, but at least allows the manufacturer, or in the case of the gig economy the platform operator, to justify the restriction.

Vertical retail price restrictions can have similar effects to horizontal price cartels. Hub-and-spoke agreements, not uncommon in the retail trade business, have both vertical and horizontal features. According to a definition provided by the OECD, hub-and-spoke arrangements are 'cartels that are not co-ordinated through direct exchanges between the horizontal competitors, but through indirect exchanges via a vertically

[78] Case 161/84 *Pronuptia de Paris GmbH v Pronuptia de Paris Irmgard Schillgallis* ECLI:EU:C:1986:41 [1986], para 24.

[79] Commission Regulation (EU) No 330/2010 of 20 April 2010 on the application of Article 101(3) of the Treaty on the Functioning of the European Union to categories of vertical agreements and concerted practices, [2010] OJ L102/1–7, Article 5 (3)(d) (Vertical Block Exemption Regulation).

[80] *Leegin Creative Leather Prods v PSKS, Inc* 551 US 877 (2007).

[81] *Dr Miles Medical Co v John D Park & Sons Co* 220 US 373 (1911).

related supplier or retailer'. Price coordination through a platform can be considered as a hub-and-spoke cartel.

This topic is important since some gig economy platforms fix the prices that their independent service providers have to charge consumers. If the contractor is regarded as an independent undertaking, agreements like this are prohibited under competition rules. Platform operators resorting to this strategy would find it difficult to justify their policy. As Anderson and Huffman rightly observe, it would be rather difficult for Uber to prove the logical nexus between the procompetitive effects of entry and the agreement on price. An argument that price competition needs to be eliminated faces a high hurdle.[82]

In a recent class action litigation against Uber, alleging a horizontal price conspiracy between Uber and the Uber drivers, Judge Rakoff rejected the defendant's argument that the agreement with drivers created a bundle of vertical agreements subject to less strict antitrust scrutiny. The judge denied the motion to dismiss the price fixing conspiracy claim with a reference to hub-and-spoke agreements.[83]

### *iv. Exclusivity*

The possibility of multi-homing is an important feature of many digital markets, including platform works. This means essentially that users may use different platforms, in some cases on different tools, in parallel. Multi-homing is important for competition, since it may help counter the economic power that large platforms benefit from.[84]

Restricting multi-homing may take the form of prohibitions, or the withdrawal of advantages, binding the service provider to the dominant platform. There are also 'natural' reasons for single homing by a service provider. In the ride-hailing industry, for example, drivers may find it difficult to use more than one app while driving. Platforms often offer incentives for both their service providers and their customers. For example, they may pay bonuses to drivers who complete a certain number of trips or have the best customer ratings.

Such practices have effects similar to exclusive dealings which can be allowed under some conditions, depending upon the market structure and the length of such a commitment. For example, EU rules exempt exclusivity clauses up to five years if both parties have market shares of less than 30 per cent of the relevant market.[85]

## VI. Conclusions

Selling one's labour to another entity on a lasting basis and for remuneration is a sort of economic activity which, like any other economic activity, could fall, at least in theory,

[82] Anderson and Huffman, 'Labor Organization in Ride Sharing' (n 66) 913 and 916. Uber requires its drivers to charge the price determined by the Uber pricing algorithm.

[83] 'US judge denies claims Uber won price-fixing suit because arbitrator was scared' *CNBC* (2 August 2020), available at: www.cnbc.com/2020/08/04/us-judge-denies-claims-uber-won-price-fixing-suit-because-arbitrator-was-scared.html.

[84] PPMI, 'Study on "Support to the Observatory for the Online Platform Economy"' (2021) Analytical paper #7, Multi-homing: obstacles, opportunities, facilitating factors), available at: www.platformobservatory.eu/app/uploads/2021/01/AP-7-Multihoming-Jan-2021-EC-final-for-pbl.pdf.

[85] Vertical Block Exemption Regulation (n 79).

under the scrutiny of competition rules. The same applies to platform-related work in the digital economy. Yet, once a person becomes an employee agreements with other employees or their organisations on the one hand, and agreements between employer and employee, on the other are, as a rule, immune from competition rules. The same would not apply to platform workers who would be considered as undertakings. This could make various coordination connected to a platform anticompetitive and even unlawful. The reaction of the CJEU on how to treat non-traditional workers was to extend the scope of the definition of an employee and thereby limit the reach of competition law (the *Albany* labour exemption). The *FNV Kunsten* judgment held that some self-employed individuals should be characterised as 'false self-employed' and thus their cooperation should be excluded from competition law.

The Commission's draft Guidelines, even if they do not expressly legitimise collective agreements among platform workers as such, are a welcome development to clarify when the EU competition authority will abstain from investigating such agreements.

The Commission's proposal is a step in the right direction. I am not advocating that agreements either between employees or self-employed gig-workers seeking to secure a fair income should be condemned at the outset. My point is that we should have the same regulatory approach, regardless whether labour law (miss)classifies these individuals as employees or non-employees. From this point of view, the CJEU's ruling on the Dutch musicians sets a good precedent: self-employed musicians should be regulated in the same way as employed musicians if the characteristics of their work are almost identical. The same regulation, the level playing field, can either be an exemption from competition rules or a subordination to those rules. Both outcomes are acceptable from a fairness point of view. The unfavourable result would be treating these two categories differently just because of the different title of their contracts.

In reality, the distinction between employees and independent contractors/undertakings is oversimplified by law. Considering the extent to which a person is independent from his or her employers/business partner, we could place her or him somewhere in a spectrum, rather than make a binary choice. This is true both for traditional and digital platform markets. At the one extreme, we have employees spending their mandatory working hours in a factory, using the tools provided and following the orders of their employer. On the other end of the spectrum, there is a medical service provider or a lawyer who could not be instructed and would bear fully the risks of her or his actions. Labour law (and most probably also tax and social security laws) would draw a line between these two categories, making the unavoidable mistake of granting the employed status to either too many or too few people.

I believe that both labour law's worker and competition law's undertaking concept are flexible enough so that they could complement each other, avoiding overlapping areas causing concern for legal certainty.

# 11

# Decent Teleworking: Lessons from the Pandemic

CARLA SPINELLI

## I. Introduction

In the face of the unfolding Covid-19 crisis, many actions have been taken to minimise its impact on businesses, workers and citizens all over the world. A really important form of labour market adjustment has been the mass shift to working from home, which has not only prevented further job losses, but has supported public health efforts by reducing social contacts.[1] However, such a sudden and huge shift to telework has been implemented nearly everywhere without appropriate organisational arrangements and within an emergency legislation framework. Inadequate equipment, lack of organisational support, unrealistic expectations with regard to performance and productivity, blurred boundaries between work and private life, and higher gender inequalities have been common concerns for workers during the lockdowns.[2]

Nevertheless, as a consequence of such a widespread use of it, teleworking has gained higher appeal in business reorganisations, with longer-term demands for remote work likely to grow in the post-pandemic scenario. Moreover, the mass uptake of telework during the Covid-19 pandemic has reduced some stigmas associated with this type of working arrangement. Working outside the employer's premises is presented as a potentially win–win work organisation pattern, which can match the employers' interests in improving flexibility and productivity and workers' interests in work–life balance. Telework is also endorsed as a means to safeguard the environment, reducing commuting time and carbon emissions, and redirecting housing from big cities to provinces and small towns, with lower costs and a better standard of living.

[1] S Soares, F Bonnet J Berg and R Labouriau, 'From potential to practice: Preliminary findings on the numbers of workers working from home during the COVID-19 pandemic' (2021) *ILO Policy Brief*, March 2021.

[2] Eurofound, *Living, working and Covid-19*, survey April 2020 (Luxembourg, Publications Office of the European Union, 2020); Eurofound, *Living, working and Covid-19*, survey update July 2020.

From this perspective, remote work could give a new impetus to the much needed human-centred agenda for the future of work,[3] provided that regulators, companies, workers and their unions become aware of the pitfalls of contractual distancing. Therefore, to have a truly liberating effect and positive economic and social impacts, future telework schemes must swiftly depart from the 'lockdown work' paradigms.[4]

The chapter aims at identifying some of the major challenges of telework regulation consistent with decent work policy, moving from the current experience of teleworking across Europe, as influenced by the pandemic. To address this purpose, the chapter is structured as follows. Section II analyses recent trends in teleworking. Section III presents some strategic assets to implement telework in work organisations. Section IV deals with legal frameworks and collective agreements regulating telework at EU and national level. Section V explores the major weaknesses arising from the regulations in force, and section VI identifies some policy implications relating to the potential spread of telework in the near future.

## II. Telework as a Multifaceted and Evolving Phenomenon

Since the end of the 1970s, due to the development and spread of information and communication technologies, telework has established itself as a way of performing work outside the company's premises and often from home, through an ICT connection with the company. The benefits of teleworking were identified from the beginning: on the one hand, in the achievement of greater flexibility and efficiency by the company and, on the other, in meeting the workers' needs of reconciling work and family life. However, telework has had a limited application and has been only marginally integrated into the labour market.[5]

Before the pandemic, working from home was a comparatively marginal experience.[6] During lockdown periods in 2020, only 13 per cent of European workers were willing to work from home each day if there were no Covid-19 restrictions.[7] On the contrary, as shown by the results of the Eurofound online survey conducted in July 2020, over three-quarters of EU employees declared they want to continue working from home at least some of the time in the post Covid-19 future, while a few (13 per cent) wish to work remotely all the time.[8] In early 2021, the findings of the Eurofound survey show that while the incidence of working from home was declining in that phase of the pandemic, the preference to do so has further increased, the most popular choice being to work from home several times a week.[9] Therefore, the use of teleworking is

[3] ILO, Global Commission on the Future of Work, *Work for a brighter future* (Geneva, ILO, 2019).

[4] N Countouris and V De Stefano, 'The "long Covid" of work relations and the future of remote work' (2021) *socialeurope.eu* (14 April 2021).

[5] Eurofound, *Telework in the European Union* (Luxembourg, Publications Office of the European Union, 2010).

[6] M Sostero, S Milasi, J Hurley, E Fernández-Macías and M Bisello, *Teleworkability and the COVID-19 crisis: a new digital divide?* (Seville, Joint Research Centre European Commission, 2020).

[7] *Living, working and Covid-19*, survey April 2020 (n 2).

[8] *Living, working and Covid-19*, survey update July 2020 (n 2).

[9] *Living, working and Covid-19*, survey April 2020 (n 2).

expected to remain a permanent feature after the coronavirus crisis abates, although not on a full-time basis. Hybrid forms are more likely to prevail, combining remote and office working (alternating telework).

As is well known, with the recent emergence of digital technologies and the high levels of automation of production processes, the need to be present at the workplace has been further reduced and limited to some phases of those processes. The work of digital manufacturing, in fact, is designed to be performed both inside and outside the company's premises. Since the beginning of the pandemic, the pace of the digitalisation process has quickened as well as the adoption of digital technologies by enterprises. Those two factors have encouraged workers to carry on working outside the employer's premises.

In this new scenario, remote work is carried out through ICT and digital media, out of a predefined place for the execution of the work. ICT-based mobile work is a form of remote work with a high rate of mobility.[10] Companies are often motivated to make use of it for reasons relating to the strengthening of the company appeal, since this form of remote work is considered consistent with the goal of finding more flexible and innovative ways of organising work and attracting highly qualified personnel, while reducing costs and improving productivity.[11] ICT-based mobile work is considered as third-generation telework,[12] made possible thanks to wireless technologies and mobile devices. ICT-based mobile work differs from the more traditional form of teleworking as it is not bound to a specific place. The work activity, in fact, can be carried out without a fixed location, anywhere and at any time, given that the intensive use of digital technology and online data is perfectly combined with the high mobility of workers, which takes place between real and virtual environments.[13]

Working anywhere and at any time using digital devices are the main features of advanced teleworking also shared by smart/agile working, but they do not exhaust the peculiarities of the latter. In particular, smart/agile working is performed in a dynamic

[10] It is defined as a new form of employment 'where workers do not use their employer's premises (or their own premises if they are self-employed) as their main place of work, and spend most of their time working with information and communication technologies (computers, the Internet, e-mail and social networks). Their work differs from familiar forms of mobile work such as visiting clients or patients working on construction sites, making deliveries or driving vehicles, and can be characterised as remote work without a fixed location'. Cfr. Eurofound, *New Forms of Employment*, (Luxembourg, 2015) 72 ff.

[11] G Valenduc and P Vendramin, 'Work in the digital economy: sorting the old from the new' (2016) ETUI *Working Paper* 3, 31 ff.

[12] According to Jon Messenger, Team Leader for the ILO Working Conditions Group, first-generation telework was *home office*, second generation telework was *mobile-office*, third generation telework is *virtual office*. See E Dagnino, '*What does telework mean in the 21st century? Face to face with Jon Messenger*' (2016) *Bollettino Adapt* (27 July 2016), available at www.englishbulletin.adapt.it/wp-content/uploads/2016/07/Messenger_Bulletin_Final.pdf. According to G Valenduc and P Vendramin: 'The virtual work carried out by ICT-based mobile workers is undoubtedly an offshoot of remote work, but it is now a feature of increasingly intangible and globalized environments which are not rooted in time or space and where the boundaries between work and home, between employment and self-employment and between producers and consumers of digitised information are blurred', See Valenduc and Vendramin (n 11) 46.

[13] The *e-workers* and *e-nomads*, according to EU Commission, *The Increasing Use of Portable Computing and Communication Devices and its Impact on the Health of EU Workers* (Luxembourg, 2010), available at: www.osha.europa.eu/en/legislation/guidelines/the-increasing-use-of-portable-computing-and-communication-devices-and-its-impact-on-the-health-of-eu-workers.

work environment, in which spaces, hours and work tools are reshaped providing greater freedom and empowerment to workers. Smart/agile work is a system of organisational flexibility that combines remote working and results orientation, so as to operate a balance between business goals and individual needs.[14]

To sum up, in the post-pandemic digital age working outside the employer's premises has a much greater chance to develop than in the past. Moreover, it can be performed through more flexible arrangements, no longer limited to working from home. New forms of remote work, such as ICT-based mobile work and smart/agile work, are gaining ground as potential game-changers in the world of work. They combine various degrees of highly performing digital technology and a performance-oriented organisational approach with alternative worksites beyond the default place of work.

## III. The Organisational Dimension of Telework: Some Critical Issues

All three forms or sub-categories of remote working (home-based, mobile and smart/agile work) are favoured by those who value their potential and push for change, and viewed with suspicion by those who highlight the risks and resist them. Digitalisation as an evolving process that takes place at the organisational level and across all sectors, attracting companies' investments, can be supportive for working from remote locations, but also a source of increasing possible side-effects on workers' dignity and privacy.

Teleworking, even in its evolutionary form, is not a one-size-fits-all solution but requires many factors to be aligned in terms of a supportive culture, appropriate systems and a trust-based work environment.[15] The sudden and therefore unstructured use of telework, necessitated by the pandemic, has highlighted several problems with respect to the organisational setting.[16] Some empirical studies have highlighted that the benefit of organisational flexibility in the interests of the worker is fully realised only if he or she decides with real autonomy where, when and how to perform work. On the contrary, very often the discretionary choices of the worker of the place, time and methods of work can only be made within constraints imposed by management.[17]

To be effective, teleworking needs to maintain a high standard of team performance. The best method to manage remote workers is through a process called 'Management by Results', whereby both manager and employee agree on a common productivity

[14] D Sarti and T Torre, 'Is Smart Working a Win-Win Solution? First Evidence from the Field' in T Addabbo et al (eds), *Well-being at and Through Work* (Torino, Giappichelli, 2017) 231 ff.

[15] P Bérastégui, 'Teleworking in the aftermath of the Covid-19 pandemic' (2021) 2 *ETUI Policy Brief* 6.

[16] M Fana, S Milasi, J Napierala, E Fernandez Macias, I Gonzalez Vazquez, 'Telework, work organisation and job quality during the COVID-19 crisis: a qualitative study' (2020) 11 JRC Working Papers on Labour, Education and Technology.

[17] R Albano, S Bertolini, Y Curzi, T Fabbri and T Parisi, 'DigitAgile: The Office in a Mobile Device. Threats and Opportunities for Workers and Companies' in E Ales et al (eds), *Working in Digital and Smart Organizations: Legal, Economic and Organizational Perspectives on the Digitalization of Labour Relations* (London, Palgrave Macmillan, 2018) 193 ff.

measurement mechanism. For this to be effective, it is necessary to identify objectives, tasks and milestones and then monitor and discuss progress, allowing personnel to have the flexibility and autonomy to organise their work.

To safeguard employees' wellbeing and maintain the agreed work performance standards, both workers and managers are required to reassess working habits and learn new skills. Adequate training is therefore required to keep workers motivated, adopt different working methods and maintain good team collaboration. In this respect, it also has to be highlighted that the lack of face-to-face interaction with colleagues represents another main concern for teleworkers, not only during the pandemic. Teams that work remotely face more significant communication challenges than face-to-face teams. The more time team members spend working apart, the more the degrees of separation between them and the sense of professional isolation increases. As a consequence, teamwork can be eroded: workers tend to share less information with their colleagues and in some cases have difficulty interpreting and understanding the information they receive. Therefore, full-time teleworking implies a real risk of social and professional isolation which could become potentially massive. For this reason, organisations should introduce and increase informal opportunities for workers to connect (eg, intranet, coaching programmes, virtual meetings) and favour hybrid forms of telework, which allow workers not to lose contact with their colleagues.

Existing social and economic gender inequalities and challenges for women were aggravated by the pandemic, not only for those women working on the front line in healthcare, but for those working from home while also dealing with childcare and the household. In this regard, organisations should become more gender-responsive in their actions and should improve HR policies regarding flexible working from a gender-oriented perspective.

Above all, working on a redefinition of a work–life balance culture is necessary. It should be more sensitive to the negative implications of the conflict between life and work experienced by men and women in a e-workplace, which certainly impacts on performance and wellbeing. Family friendly HR actions should encompass policies based on time management as well as organisational options designed to give economic benefits (fringe benefits, economic facilities) and provide direct services to employees (eg, wellbeing services inside the company).

Policies aiming at promoting a cultural change, such as diversity training programmes, oriented to change stereotypes and to manage diversity, are also needed, provided that a monitoring of the needs of the specific population chosen as a target is conducted before the implementation of such programmes.

## IV. Telework Regulation at EU and National Level

### A. Regulating Telework at EU Level

According to the European Social Partners Framework Agreement of 2002 (European Telework Agreement), telework is defined as 'a form of organising and/or performing work, using information technology, in the context of an employment contract/

relationship, where work, which could also be performed on the employers' premises, is carried out off those premises on a regular basis'. A critical point in this definition concerns the expression 'on a regular basis' referring to the work carried out outside the company's premises. It seems to leave out, beyond the intention of the Social Partners to adopt a broad notion of telework,[18] those types of telework in which this regularity could be lacking, as in the case of occasional, mobile or alternating telework.

In the Report on Implementation of the European Telework Agreement,[19] as a result of the analysis of the national regulations considered, the European Commission suggested a modification of the definition of telework adopted by the Social Partners, consistent with what had been its original proposal in this regard, ie, to provide for a quantitative threshold for qualifying remote work.[20]

There is no doubt that the expression 'on a regular basis' could have more than one meaning. On the one hand, it can be considered as inherent to the temporal continuity of telework, which cannot be occasionally performed to be qualified as such. On the other hand, it could entail that work shall be performed permanently outside the workplace.

Adopting a narrower interpretation of the definition of telework would mean that ICT-based mobile work and smart/agile work could not be covered by the European Telework Agreement concerning teleworkers' working conditions. From this perspective, to address the challenges of these new kinds of working arrangements strong EU legislation on working conditions can be applied anyway, for example the European Framework Directive on Safety and Health at Work,[21] the Working Time Directive,[22] the Work–life Balance Directive,[23] the Transparent and Predictable Working Conditions

[18] *cf* ETUC, *Framework Agreement on Telework – Interpretation Guide*, available at: www.resourcecentre.etuc.org/linked_files/documents/Telework%20-20ETUC%20interpretation%20guide%20EN.pdf (European Telework Agreement).

[19] EU Commission, *Report on the implementation of the European social partners' Framework Agreement on Telework*, SEC(2008) 2178, Bruxelles, available at: www.ec.europa.eu/social/BlobServlet?docId=463&langId=en.

[20] 'The Commission therefore proposed the following definition of telework: 'Telework is a method of organising and/or performing work which accounts for at least a considerable proportion of working time and which is done by a natural person in the framework of an employment relationship, in the following cumulative conditions:

- the work is done at a distance (away from the firm's premises or away from the place where the work is expected),
- the work is performed using information technology and technology for data transmission, in particular the internet'. Definitions based on these factors could cover the three types of telework identified: teleworking from home, mobile teleworking (via portable communication systems) and work in telework centres (outstations, neighbourhood offices, telecottages). They could also cover both permanent and alternating telework, ie, arrangements whereby the worker spends part of his/her working time at the employer's premises and the rest elsewhere' (para 3.1).

[21] Directive 89/391/EEC of 12 June 1989 on the introduction of measures to encourage improvements in the safety and health of workers at work [1989] OJ L183/1.

[22] Directive 2003/88/EC of the European Parliament and of the Council of 4 November 2003 concerning certain aspects of the organization of working time [2003] OJ L299/9 which is relevant insofar as it limits weekly working hours and regulates minimum daily rest periods.

[23] Directive (EU) 2019/1158 of the European Parliament and of the Council of 20 June 2019 on work–life balance for parents and carers and repealing Council Directive 2010/18/EU [2019] OJ L188/79 which extends the existing right to request flexible working arrangements (including remote work arrangements and flexible work schedules) to all working parents and carers.

Directive,[24] provided that the possibility to adjust employment conditions to the particular characteristics of this form of work is duly considered.

In the same vein, the European Social Partners Framework Agreement on Digitalisation of 2020, adopted within the framework of the European Social Dialogue, also covers remote work-related issues in a broad sense.[25] More precisely, the crucial questions afforded in the Agreement concern digital skills, modalities of connecting and disconnecting, as well as intrusive monitoring through remote surveillance. All these topics will be analysed in detail in the next section, since they constitute the major weaknesses of working conditions relating to home-based telework, ICT-based mobile work and smart/agile work, that the pandemic has brought to light.

## B. Regulating Telework in EU Member States

It is mainly on the basis of the definition and regulation of telework foreseen by the European Telework Agreement that the national legal frameworks of EU Member States were enacted before the pandemic, while in some countries only more recently and as a result of that. The rapidly growing adoption of teleworking during the Covid-19 pandemic has shown the weaknesses of the existing legal framework across EU Member States. Some of them had rules which were too restrictive and did not meet the specific needs relating to responding to the pandemic.[26]

The approach of reducing existing regulations was adopted by national governments in their emergency legislation, to make it easier to implement a high level of home-based telework to face the pandemic through social distancing. As a consequence of the widespread experiment in telework forced by the pandemic, a debate has spread in these countries about the necessity to adapt or integrate the existing regulations to address the challenges and opportunities of teleworking, also in a post-pandemic scenario. Hungary[27] and Poland,[28] for example, are still in the middle of a legislative process, quite controversial, which aims at amending the existing provisions of their respective Labour Codes in order to introduce less strict regulation of telework.

In other countries, where there were no regulations on telework at all, the debate arose on the opportunity and/or necessity to introduce ad hoc legislation. One notable example is Spain, which adopted Royal Decree-Law No 28 in September 2020,

[24] Directive (EU) 2019/1152 of the European Parliament and of the Council of 20 June 2019 on transparent and predictable working conditions in the European Union [2019] OJ L186/105 which contains provisions relating to place of work and work patterns.

[25] I Senatori, 'The European Framework Agreement on Digitalisation: A Whiter Shade of Pale?' (2020) 13 *Italian Labour Law e-Journal* 159.

[26] *cf* (2020) 13(1S) *Italian Labour Law e-Journal*: Special Issue: 'Covid-19 and Labour Law. A Global Review'.

[27] A Kun, I Rácz and I Szilárd Szabó, *ICT-enhanced remote and mobile work. National Report on Hungary*, iRel-Smarter Industrial Relations to Address New Technological Challenges in the World of Work (2021), available at: www.irel.fmb.unimore.it/archive/research-output/national-reports.

[28] I Florczak and M Otto, *ICT-enhanced remote and mobile work. National Report on Poland*, iRel-Smarter Industrial Relations to Address New Technological Challenges in the World of Work, available at: www.irel.fmb.unimore.it/archive/research-output/national-reports.

introducing comprehensive legislation covering remote working.[29] This Spanish telework law introduces a distinction between

- remote working, that occurs away from company premises regularly; and
- teleworking, a sub-category of remote working that occurs exclusively or predominantly online.

However, despite extensive regulation there are still some remaining areas where the decree does not provide the level of detail and clarity that employers might reasonably expect in order to help them implement these working arrangements in practice.

The Scandinavian countries have confirmed the regulation of telework among the competences of collective bargaining, according to their voluntary industrial relations tradition. In Finland, for example, teleworking levels were already relatively high compared with the EU average in pre-pandemic times due to several factors, such as the larger proportion of workers in knowledge and ICT-intensive service sectors, the institutional setting, the level of digitalisation and the prevailing culture of trust. Presently, the definition of telework is not foreseen by the Finnish legislation, but is rooted in workplace practices and collective agreements.

Indeed, in most EU countries collective agreements are the main instruments in large companies currently shaping the use of telework, ICT-based mobile work and smart/agile work. This is the case in Germany,[30] for example, where, according to the traditional industrial relations system, it is left to the Social Partners to regulate these aspects of work organisation.

In Italy, the European Telework Agreement has been implemented by the National Cross-sectoral Agreement of 2004, signed by the leading trade unions and employers' organisations of the private sector. Indeed, specific clauses on telework are present in industry-wide collective agreements of prominent sectors, such as trade, banking, telecommunications, clothing and cleaning, embracing roughly 70 per cent of employees in the private sector. Even the concept of smart/agile work was originally elaborated by a number of pioneering company agreements, which inspired the later enactment of Law No 81 of 2017 on 'agile work'. Notwithstanding the legislative choice to support individual autonomy, leaving the parties to the employment contract to determine a wide range of working conditions through the so-called 'agile work pact', the Social Partners did not give up their negotiating prerogatives, neither before, nor during the pandemic.[31] In December 2021, a Protocol for the private sector was signed by the government and the Social Partners to define the guidelines for the further developments of agile work.[32] The Ministry for Public Administration has adopted

[29] MB Fernández Collados, 'El teletrabajo en España antes, durante y después del confinamiento domiciliario' (2021) 9 *Revista Internacional y Comparada de Relaciones Laborales Y Derecho Del Empleo* 1.

[30] R Krause, and JW Kühn, *ICT-enhanced remote and mobile work. National Report on Germany*, iRel-Smarter Industrial Relations to Address New Technological Challenges in the World of Work, available at: www.irel.fmb.unimore.it/archive/research-output/national-reports.

[31] I Senatori and C Spinelli, '(Re-)Regulating Remote Work in the Post-pandemic Scenario: Lessons from the Italian Experience' (2021) 14 *Italian Labour Law e-Journal* 85.

[32] *Protocollo nazionale sul lavoro in modalità agile*, available at: www.lavoro.gov.it/notizie/Documents/PROTOCOLLO-NAZIONALE-LAVORO-AGILE-07122021-RV.pdf.

guidelines on the same topic.[33] In both documents collective agreements have been given a fundamental regulatory role with respect to the main critical issues concerning agile work as emerged during the pandemic.

As comes out of the analysis developed above, there is a plurality of sources of law, at EU and national level, that have to be taken into account when looking for regulatory solutions for critical issues relating to telework, ICT-based mobile work and smart/agile work. Therefore, extensive room is left to interpretation, which explains the heterogeneity of the approaches and the uncertainty of the results, as we will see in the next section dealing with how employment protections can be granted to those flexible workers.

## V. Employment Protection for Teleworkers

The employment contract remains the background regulation to look at for the European Telework Agreement and most of the national legislations on telework. However, ICT-based mobile work and smart/agile work can be performed as employees or self-employed. In the latter case, the workers cannot benefit from the protective regulation provided for employees, therefore they remain much more exposed to the deterioration of their working conditions. In this respect, the forthcoming EU guidelines, which exempt collective agreements on working conditions for individual self-employed service providers from the scope of application of EU competition law,[34] could remove an obstacle and be of assistance. As a matter of fact, self-employed ICT-based mobile workers and smart/agile workers could gain protections by collective agreements.

Teleworkers are mainly subordinate workers and, if they are not hired to perform that work as such, the switch to telework does not affect their employment status, because it only modifies the way in which work is performed. Therefore, as far as working conditions are concerned, teleworkers shall benefit from the same rights, guaranteed by applicable legislation and collective agreements, as comparable workers at the employer's premises.[35] Telework shall be a voluntary choice for both the employer and employee, which means that the latter does not have a right to telework but he or she cannot be dismissed because of a refusal of telework. The decision to switch to telework shall be reversible by individual and/or collective agreement, which shall provide for specific modalities in this respect. The reversibility could imply returning to work at the employer's premises, at the worker's or at the employer's request.[36]

Whatever the form of flexible work in terms of space and time they adopt, employers will need to confront the new challenges posed by such a relevant change in working

[33] *Linee guida in materia di lavoro agile nelle amministrazioni pubbliche*, available at: www.funzionepubblica.gov.it/sites/funzionepubblica.gov.it/files/lineeguidalavoroagile_0.pdf.

[34] European Commission Press release of 9 December 2021, 'Guidelines on the application of EU competition law to collective agreements on working conditions for individual self-employed workers' para (21). See N Countouris, *Regulating digital work: from laisser-faire to fairness* (2021), available at: www.*socialeurope.eu* (8 December 2021).

[35] Article 4 of the European Telework Agreement (n 18).

[36] ibid, Article 3.

arrangements. The main critical issues to deal with when telework, ICT-based mobile work and smart/agile work are included in the work organisation concern mainly two features of working conditions: health and safety protection and performance-based work arrangements. More precisely, a specific regulation is needed with respect to employees' work-related health and safety outside the office, working time schedules, the establishment of a right to disconnect, monitoring performance and working time, and effectively coordinating the workforce remotely.

In the following sub-sections all these aspects will be analysed from the perspective of avoiding the infringement of workers' rights when telework, ICT-based mobile work and smart/agile work are performed. In particular, the lens of the health and safety protection (V.A) is also adopted to highlight criticalities in working time patterns and monitoring (V.B), while the implementation of the right to disconnect is taken into account as a mean to respect work–life balance and the right to privacy (V.C). The latter constitutes the strictest boundary of remote surveillance and work performance monitoring (V.D). In this regard, enforcing collective rights of teleworkers, ICT-based mobile workers and smart/agile workers plays a fundamental supporting role (V.E).

## A. Health and Safety

Telework can bring advantages to both employers and workers by improving productivity and work–life balance; however, it has some potential disadvantages, such as the possible negative implications on a worker's health. Performing telework can affect both physical and psychosocial health. The main hazards for the health of teleworkers are: the unavailability of ergonomic work equipment and a dedicated working area, the risk of overwork, and psychosocial implications of working from home.[37] The physical and environmental characteristics of the home office and the related work habits can be critical with respect to the workers' capability to perform remotely and effectively.

According to most national laws and collective agreements regarding health and safety, the employer is responsible for the protection of the workers' occupational health and safety. Such a responsibility applies to teleworking as well. The employers' responsibilities include identifying and managing the occupational risks of home-based teleworkers.

The European Telework Agreement attempts to clarify this aspect, noting that teleworkers are covered by all the general protection offered to workers and that the employer, workers' representatives and/or relevant authorities should have access to the place of teleworking to check that health and safety provisions are correctly applied in the home context, albeit within the limits of national legislation and collective agreements. Furthermore, the teleworker has the right to request inspection visits from health and safety inspection bodies.[38]

[37] G Buomprisco, S Ricci, R Perri and S De Sio, 'Health and Telework: New Challenges after COVID-19 Pandemic' (2021) 5 *European Journal of Environment and Public Health* 2.

[38] Article 8 of the European Telework Agreement (n 18).

Recent research conducted by the European Agency for Safety and Health at Work looked at trends in relation to musculoskeletal diseases, finding that much still remains to be done in the area of risk assessments. Overall, it found that larger organisations were more likely to carry out risk assessments, although there remains some room for improvement, while small and medium-sized enterprises are less likely to have written risk assessments. Furthermore, it found that risk assessments are often carried out as an afterthought, ie, when something goes wrong, rather than at the design stage of the work process. It also found that risk assessments generally tend to give little consideration to diversity (eg, gender or age).[39]

In the case of ICT-based mobile work and smart/agile work the main problem concerns how the employer can be considered responsible for the employee's work-related health and safety outside the office, when he cannot have access to the place in which the work is performed, since he does not know where that place is as it is freely chosen by the employee. Working anywhere, as a consequence of the worker gaining a major degree of autonomy in choosing the workplace, risks putting on his shoulders the responsibility for health and safety protection. In this respect, defining by collective agreements or individual negotiation a range of workplaces where the work can be performed at the worker's choice could be supportive. This being the case, the employer would be aware of the possible remote workplaces where the work will be performed. Therefore, he would be able to provide risk-assessment systems.

Digital technologies and, above all, the hyper-connectivity that can result from their use represent a potential threat to the workers' physical and mental health. As a matter of fact, the workers are exposed to peculiar pathologies such as techno-stress, technological addiction or burn-out. Other potential risks of psychosocial harm are associated with remote-only jobs, like the increased risk of social isolation in the professional sphere and the increased risk of blurring of boundaries between work and personal life. In this respect, national legal frameworks should cover the means to evaluate the legitimacy of these arrangements and specify additional measures employers should take to prevent psychosocial risks.

However, under the umbrella of Council Directive 89/391/EEC ('duty of care' principle) and the European Telework Agreement, management strategies should clearly reflect the prioritisation of occupational health and safety, not only with respect to ergonomic risks but also psychosocial risks. Therefore, developing and implementing psychosocial risk-assessment and management at company level is also an essential part of identifying and mitigating possible health risks for remote workers. In this respect, it is of paramount importance to involve health and safety representatives in the process, with the obligation of consultation, information and training.[40]

[39] EU-OSHA, *Work-related musculoskeletal disorders: From research to practice. What can be learnt?* (Luxembourg, Publications Office of the European Union, 2020).

[40] EU-OSHA, *Teleworking during the COVID-19 pandemic: risks and prevention strategies* (Luxembourg, Publications Office of the European Union, 2021).

## B. Working Time

Flexible working time arrangements, which are quite commonly combined with working outside the employer's premises, can be settled to accomplish the workers' interests or the employers' interests,[41] which makes a difference in terms of their suitability for workers' wellbeing.[42]

According to several surveys, employees working from home tend to work longer hours than when they are working on the employer's premises. This tends to happen partly because the time to commute to the workplace is replaced by work itself, partly due to the changes in work routines and to the blurring of the boundaries between paid work and personal life.[43] During the pandemic, many organisations in which previous teleworking experience had been very limited fell into a critical work system, due to lack of clarity around the priorities to be given and the tasks to accomplish. One in four workers (27 per cent) who worked from home in 2020 stated that they were working in their free time to meet the demands of their work.[44]

ICT-based mobile work and smart/agile work offer workers a higher degree of autonomy in organising time and space of their work performance, which is an asset. Autonomy, however, can also lead to an intensification of work when combined with heavy workloads and work cultures dominated by competition, self-management or mechanisms to enforce performance. These kinds of remote work pose some risks for the mental and physical wellbeing of workers. Not only are they more likely to report stress and other psychosocial and physical problems, they are also more likely to engage in a new phenomenon enabled by digitalisation: virtual *presenteeism* – ie, working from home when one is sick but not so sick as to preclude working.[45]

To face the negative consequences of working time flexibility in telework, ICT-based mobile work and smart/agile work, it is useful to make reference to the Working Time Directive provisions, and especially to its derogations to verify if they apply to these remote workers.

Workers may be excluded from the scope of some provisions concerning maximum weekly working time and minimum rest periods 'when, on account of the specific characteristics of the activity concerned, the duration of the working time is not measured and/or predetermined or can be determined by the workers themselves'.[46]

In order to identify the scope of the derogations set out in Article 17(1) of the Working Time Directive there are some relevant rulings from the Court of Justice of the European Union (CJEU) to consider. First, as exceptions to the European Union

[41] C Spinelli, *Sustainable Work, Work–Life Balance and Flexible Working Time* in T Addabbo et al (eds), *Well-being at and Through Work* (Turin, Giappichelli, 2017) 221.

[42] See especially ch 8 by Gábor Kártyás in this volume.

[43] Eurofound and the International Labour Office, *Working anytime, anywhere: The effects on the world of work* (Luxembourg and Geneva, Publications Office of the European Union and the International Labour Office, 2017); J Messenger, *Telework in the 21st century: An evolutionary perspective* (Cheltenham, Edwar Elgar Publishing, 2017).

[44] *Living, working and Covid-19*, survey April 2020 (n 2).

[45] Eurofound, *Telework and ICT-based mobile work: Flexible working in the digital age* (Luxembourg, Publications Office of the European Union, 2020).

[46] Article 17(1), Directive 2003/88/EC (n 22).

system for the organisation of working time put in place by Directive No 2003/88, those derogations must be interpreted in such a way that their scope is limited to what is strictly necessary in order to safeguard the interests which those derogations enable to be protected.[47] Moreover, derogation applies to workers whose working time, *as a whole*, is not measured or predetermined, or can be determined by the workers themselves on account of the specific characteristics of the activity carried out, which is for the national court to ascertain.[48] Therefore, the derogation set out in Article 17(1) of the Working Time Directive can be applied to teleworkers, ICT-based mobile workers and smart/agile workers provided that they can determine by themselves not only when to work (working time slot), but also how much time they work (working time duration), which is not often what they are really allowed to do.

The same criterion shall be applied to determine if and how working time has to be measured in telework, ICT-based mobile work and smart/agile work, considering that working time maximum limits and minimum rest periods are measures aiming to protect the workers' health and safety. In this respect, the CJEU has stated that, out of the cases in which workers' working time, as a whole, is not measured or predetermined, or can be determined by the workers themselves, a law of a Member State that does not require employers to set up a system enabling the duration of time worked each day by each worker to be measured is precluded by the Working Time Directive.[49]

To summarise, teleworkers, ICT-based mobile workers and smart/agile workers are entitled to benefit from maximum daily and weekly working time limits and minimum rest periods, as health and safety measures, like all other workers who perform their work entirely at the employer's premises, unless they can determine themselves the duration of working time as a whole.

## C. The Right to Disconnect in a Work–Life Balance Perspective

As already stressed in the previous two sub-sections, digital devices allow workers to be always-on and therefore constantly at the employer's disposal, blurring the boundaries between professional and personal life, in contradiction to the very purpose towards which remote work is assumed to be oriented, ie, work–life balance. In this regard, the concept of time porosity[50] has been coined, to indicate the mutual interference and overlap between working time and private life, which can trigger personal and family conflicts.

The blurring of boundaries between work and personal life has been a continuing issue of teleworking and one of the biggest problems occurred during the pandemic, due to the unique circumstances in which it took place. Indeed, many home-based

[47] Case C-428/09 *Union syndicale Solidaires Isère v Premier ministre and Others* ECLI:EU:C:2010:612 [2010], para 40.

[48] Case C-484/04 *Commission of the European Communities v United Kingdom of Great Britain and Northern Ireland* ECLI:EU:C:2006:526 [2006], para 20.

[49] Case C-55/18 *Federación de Servicios de Comisiones Obreras (CCOO) v Deutsche Bank SAE* ECLI:EU:C:2019:402 [2019].

[50] E Genin, 'Proposal for a Theoretical Framework for the Analysis of Time Porosity' (2016) 32 *International Journal of Comparative Labour Law and Industrial Relations* 280.

teleworkers had to carry out additional education and caring duties, because home schooling was the norm, and faced challenging household conditions. In the end, the Covid-19 crisis shattered the notion that paid work and personal life are two entirely separate domains, as well as dispelled the myth that workers can and should always be available to perform their work-related functions.

## *i. National Regulations*

As a consequence, the debate on the efficacy of the right to disconnect as a means to counteract workers' hyper-connectivity has intensified. Some Member States have already taken into account the right to disconnect before the Covid-19 outbreak, while other States are still discussing the necessity for regulation.[51] It is important to underline that not only is the necessity to regulate the employees' disconnection related to the massive use of telework, but in general to the constantly growing digitalisation of the workplace. In fact, some Member States which had regulated on disconnection before the pandemic, applied the legislation to every kind of work, not only remote work.

As is well known, France was the first Member State which regulated the right to disconnect in 2016. The El-Khomri Law introduced the duty for the employer to assure the employees' disconnection.[52] It obliges the employer with more than 50 employees to reach an agreement at company level or issue a code of conduct to regulate how to disconnect from work and when. Although it has been a great achievement for trade union struggles in terms of human rights protection, many criticisms have been raised against this law. Many scholars have contested on the one hand, the lack of sanctions against the employer who will not apply the rule and, on the other, the decision to limit the scope of application of this new rule to the biggest industries only.[53] This limitation leaves aside businesses such as, for example, start-up, in which most of the time there are fewer employees, but they are involved in intensive use of technologies and very difficult to disconnect, since, in many cases, they belong to Gen-Z, which means that they are used to staying connected at all times even in their own private life.

In Italy, the regulation of the right to disconnect offers a good example of the ambiguities of the legal framework: 'technical and organizational measures necessary to ensure that the worker can disconnect from digital devices' shall be defined through the individual negotiation between the employer and the employee.[54] The right to disconnect applies only to agile workers, who share their working time between home/remote site and the employers' workplace. Moreover, the legal regulation does not foresee any condition or limitation to guarantee that the individual agreement on agile working actually pursues the goal of work–life balance and facilitates its accomplishment. It is

[51] Eurofound, *Right to disconnect in the 27 EU Member States* (Luxembourg, Publications Office of the European Union, 2020).

[52] Law No 1088/2016.

[53] C Mathieu, 'Le droit à la déconnexion: une chimère? Pas de droit à la déconnexion (du salarié) sans devoir de déconnexion (de l'employeur)' [2016] *Revue du droit du travail* 592; JE Ray, 'Grande accélération et droit à la déconnexion' [2016] *Droit social* 912.

[54] Article 19, para 1, Law No 81/2017.

assumed, instead, that better possibilities of reconciliation are the natural and virtuous result of this way of working.[55]

In Spain, the right to disconnect is dealt with in Ley Orgánica No 3/2018.[56] Although it was initially intended to merely implement the General Data Protection Regulation (GDPR), its scope was suddenly expanded to include what have been defined as 'digital rights'. Ley Orgánica No 3/2018 grants for the first time a right to digital disconnection for employees, also known as a 'digital detox'.[57] Employees have the right not to be connected or be at the disposal of the employer during rest time and holidays in order to ensure they have a proper work–life balance. This means that employers in Spain will have to promote a work organisation culture and design a disconnection policy that guarantees the employees' right to digital disconnection in accordance with their job position. The disconnection policy should be especially enhanced in remote working for the above-mentioned goals.

In other countries the right to disconnect is a matter for codes of conduct and/or collective bargaining, mainly at company level. The first company that really applied the disconnection is German. Since 2015 Volkswagen employees have been granted the right to disconnect: once working time is accomplished every device is switched off until the next morning, so that it is impossible to contact workers. In the last decade, prominent corporations, such as BMW, Audi and Telekom, have all implemented codes of conduct to regulate that employees should not, apart from exceptional circumstances, be contacted outside regular working hours. In the Nordic countries the issue is not very prominent and tends to be part of collective bargaining on work–life balance.

### *ii. EU Regulations*

The relevance of the right to disconnect in the digital economy has also been recognised at EU level. The European Social Partners have dealt with the necessity to guarantee a right to disconnection in the European Framework Agreement on Digitalisation of 2020. In the same vein, at the beginning of 2021, the European Parliament issued a resolution concerning the right to disconnect to push Member States – especially those still reluctant, such as Eastern European countries – to take action against what it considers one of the biggest health issues in the world of work.

In June 2020, the European Social Partners adopted the Framework Agreement on Digitalisation to engage in a share commitment 'to optimise the benefits and deal with the challenges of digitalisation in the world of work'. One of the four topics addressed by this Agreement is 'modalities of connecting and disconnecting'. This includes a commitment to collective bargaining in order to clarify the 'legitimate expectations' of workers when using digital work devices. Matters that should be addressed during such

[55] E Dagnino, 'Working Anytime, Anywhere and Working Time Provisions. Insights from the Italian Regulation of Smart Working and the Right to Disconnect' (2020) 9 *E-Journal of International and Comparative Labour Studies* 3, available at: www.englishbulletin.adapt.it/wp-content/uploads/2021/06/DAGNINO_FINAL.pdf.

[56] Protección de Datos Personales y Garantía de los Derechos Digitales.

[57] Article 88.

bargaining include: ensuring compliance with working time rules; creating a culture that avoids out-of-hours contact and where workers are not obliged to be contactable; and developing guidance on the risks to health and safety of being overly connected coupled with 'alert and support' procedures.

Although the power to propose legislation on the right to disconnect lies with the Commission, the European Parliament adopted a draft text of such a Directive in 2021. It is described as an instrument that 'particularises and complements' the existing Directives on related topics such as health and safety, working time, transparent and predictable working conditions and work–life balance. The Proposal provides for a definition: 'disconnect means not to engage in work-related activities or communications by means of digital tools, directly or indirectly, outside working time'. Consistent with the Working Time Directive, employers must have an 'objective, reliable and accessible system' for measuring working time; such data must also be available to workers. The most interesting element of the proposed Directive is a duty to ensure that detailed arrangements are made to enable workers to exercise the right to disconnect. These should address: practical arrangements for switching off digital tools; systems for measuring working time; health and safety assessments, including psychosocial risk-assessments; criteria for derogations and any related compensation for work outside normal working hours; and awareness-raising measures and in-work training to be taken by employers.

The proposed Directive includes measures designed to enhance its effectiveness in practice. First, each worker would be provided by his or her employer with written information on the right to disconnect. Moreover, workers would be entitled to a right of redress in case of a breach of the rights provided by the Directive, including a right for trade unions to engage in proceedings on behalf of or in support of workers. In order to ensure the right to disconnect be properly respected and is not treated as a simple recommendation without real effects, such as in several Member States' legislation in force, the Parliament Resolution requires Member States to adopt a sanction system, whose penalties should be effective, proportionate and dissuasive.

During the discussion on the proposed Directive, a significant issue was its relationship with the Framework Agreement on Digitalisation. It has been suggested that the enactment of the Directive is postponed to after the three-year period for the implementation of the Framework Agreement, in order not to disregard the role of the European Social Partners laid down in the Treaty on the Functioning of the European Union, notwithstanding the European Trades Union Confederation calling on the Commission to bring forward a legislative proposal. Therefore, the way forward for the definition of a common legal framework at EU level on the right to disconnect still seems an uphill one.[58]

### *iii. Qualification of the Right to Disconnect*

The different regulatory approaches examined above confirm that, either at national level or at EU level, the qualification of the right to disconnect is still controversial,

[58] See also, ch 4 by Iacopo Senatori in this volume.

concerning whether it should be considered as a new kind of workers' digital right, linked to 'hyper-connectivity', or merely a specification of the worker's right to rest time.

In this regard, it is certainly useful to include the right to disconnect in the measures to protect the workers' health and safety, as a technological version of the right to rest, which is recognised at EU level and by national laws, as a right-duty of the worker which implies a corresponding obligation for the employer. According to this interpretative approach, the regulation of the right to disconnect is linked to rest time and the obligation of the employee to be at disposal of the employer. Therefore, the minimum level of disconnection can be considered equivalent to the 11 hours of daily rest. However, referring to this provision seems to be not enough to solve the problem of limiting the obligation of the teleworker, ICT-based mobile worker and smart worker to be available to be reached by the employer beyond the limits of working time. This purpose could be better satisfied through the on-call and/or standby service regime, including the related economic treatment. Beyond this hypothesis, the worker will have the right to disconnect from the technological tools and interrupt contacts with the employer (not responding to emails, turning off the mobile phone, etc), without thereby incurring the non-fulfilment of work performance and suffering disciplinary sanctions as a consequence.

According to a different interpretative thesis, which highlights the potential prejudice that unlimited availability causes to the personal sphere of the worker, the right to disconnect should be placed among a new generation of human rights, the so-called digital rights, as an expression of the right to privacy.[59] This has been the approach adopted by the Spanish jurisdiction, as mentioned above, which appears preferable in terms of strengthening the employee's protection. In this perspective, the right to disconnect should be defined as the worker's right to prevent the employer intruding on his or her personal life. This right would thus be connected to the value of dignity and the need of its protection and could consequently benefit, in terms of effectiveness, from the supervisory action of the national Privacy Authority.

## D. Remote Surveillance

Mass teleworking, coupled with digitalisation, offers many opportunities but carries several risks as well. Digital technology, data processing and artificial intelligence surveillance systems allow improving enterprise efficiency while also securing the working environment and ensuring healthy and safe working conditions. At the same time, however, the risk of compromising the dignity of the human being increases, especially when personal monitoring is carried out.[60] Therefore, companies need to weigh the risks against the possibilities before they invest and roll out any new piece of technology to their workforce.

The pervasiveness of technologies exposes the workers – all workers, but especially those fully or partially working outside the employer's premises – to new forms of

[59] Ray (n 53) 939 ff.
[60] See ch 16 by David Mangan in this volume.

control by the employer. This could lead to the deterioration of working conditions and of the wellbeing of workers. Therefore, it is necessary to identify new ways of balancing the protection of the legitimate interests of the latter to the correct fulfilment of the work performance, as well as the defence of company assets, with the protection of the worker's freedom, dignity and privacy.

During the pandemic the volume, variety and velocity of data collection have increased rapidly, not only or necessarily for sanitary reasons but also for productivity tracking. The door has been opened to a new generation of employee monitoring widgets beyond the traditional and currently regulated system. Due to the adoption of emergency legislation, fundamental principles such as meaningful consent, collective involvement and prior administrative authorisations, commonly adopted by Member States in this respect, have been eroded if not cancelled altogether.[61] Several tools were – and are still being – developed to track and monitor the activity of employees working from remote locations (ie, home, telework centre, or elsewhere), turned into performance management devices to measure whether workers are meeting their expected key performance indicators. As a consequence, increasing possible side-effects on their dignity and privacy emerged.

The GDPR offers the strictest boundary of remote surveillance and work performance monitoring, being the leading source of privacy and personal data protection in Europe, which also provides for rules in relation to the processing of personal data of workers in the employment context.[62] While the importance of these rules is not to be underestimated, it has been argued that the effectiveness of the GDPR is undermined by a long list of specific derogations.[63] As a consequence, a rather manifold legal framework has developed in Europe, depending on the Member States' regulations and the national data protection authorities' rulings.[64]

The European Social Partners Agreement on Digitalisation of 2020 stresses the risk of deterioration of working conditions and wellbeing of workers and calls for 'data minimisation and transparency along with clear rules on the processing of personal data limits the risk of intrusive monitoring and misuse of personal data'. According to Article 88 of the GDPR, the European Social Partners leave to the collective agreements the duty to enable specific rules to ensure the protection of the rights to privacy, consent and use of data linked with the surveillance.[65]

A critical approach to personal data sharing is required. Therefore, it is of fundamental relevance that the Social Partners launch a new round of bargaining on monitoring instruments, also at a decentralised level, with the aim of setting transparent and clear

[61] Eurofound, *Employee monitoring and surveillance: The challenges of digitalisation* (Luxembourg, Publications Office of the European Union, 2020).

[62] See especially, ch 15 by Frank Hendrickx in this volume.

[63] They can be found respectively in Article 6 and Article 9 GDPR for the lawful processing of this special category of personal data. Moreover, Article 89(2) GDPR allows the domestic lawmaker to restrict (some) of the data subject's rights as set out in Chapter 3 of the Regulation. See A Aloisi and V De Stefano, 'Essential Jobs, Remote Work and Digital Surveillance: Addressing the COVID-19 Pandemic Panopticon' (2021) *International Labour Review*, available at www.onlinelibrary.wiley.com/doi/10.1111/ilr.12219.

[64] Relevant national legislation addressing employee monitoring and surveillance are listed and analysed in Eurofound, *Employee monitoring and surveillance* (n 61).

[65] Sostero et al (n 6).

rules in relation to the processing of personal data of workers, so to profit from the good opportunities offered by technology. Moreover, the European Framework Agreement on Digitalisation advocates for worker representatives' involvement to address issues relating to consent, privacy protection and surveillance. As a matter of fact, works councils or other forms of employee representation have an important role to play in setting boundaries to the use of intrusive technologies for employee monitoring. In this respect, the Social Partners call for providing workers representatives with facilities and (digital) tools to fulfil their duties in a digital era.

## E. Collective Rights

As highlighted in section III, improvements in work organisation and change management patterns are necessary to introduce flexible working arrangements. In this regard, involving workers in the design and implementation of teleworking, and/or ICT-based mobile working, as well as smart/agile working is of paramount importance since workplace-level initiatives could facilitate this process and be helpful in tackling the associated risks.[66] In addition to being a legal obligation as far as health and safety is concerned,[67] discussing and achieving consensus on organisational and regulatory solutions 'will set the tone and foster confidence before a structural teleworking programme begins'.[68]

Social dialogue at company level would be equally important to ensure that teleworkers enjoy all the same rights as other workers, including the right to contact and join a union and the benefits of collective agreements. Although most of these requirements are already included in the European Telework Agreement, their regulation would demand a more effective implementation and enforcement. More precisely,

> teleworkers have the same collective rights as workers at the employers' premises. No obstacles are put to communicating with workers' representatives. The same conditions for participating in and standing for elections to bodies representing workers or providing worker representation apply to them. Teleworkers are included in calculations for determining thresholds for bodies with worker representation in accordance with European and national law, collective agreements or practices. The establishment to which the teleworker will be attached for the purpose of exercising his/her collective rights is specified from the outset. Worker representatives are informed and consulted on the introduction of telework in accordance with European and national legislations, collective agreements and practices.[69]

Indeed, enforcing these rights seems to be even more challenging in workplaces becoming increasingly virtual. There is clear evidence of the necessity to modernise the exercise of collective rights, so that they allow the trade union and workers' representatives to

[66] On the fundamental role of workers' representatives in the digital era, see ch 3 by Edoardo Ales in this volume.
[67] Article 11, Directive 89/391/EEC (n 21).
[68] Bérastégui (n 15).
[69] Article 11 of the European Telework Agreement (n 18).

intercept and regulate the epochal changes that the world of work is facing with the evolution of digital technologies.[70]

At international level, trade unions show a great awareness about their strategic role in order to ensure that teleworking arrangements improve access to decent work rather than deteriorate it. In 2020, the International Trade Union Confederation (ITUC) issued a legal guide on telework to ask for proper regulations, promoting social dialogue and denouncing the existing gaps in national and international law.[71] UNI Global Union, the global union federation with affiliates in 150 countries, has developed key principles to support those affiliated trade unions around the world, who are negotiating working conditions to advance remote workers' rights, in relation to the developing trend of teleworking, in all its available forms. The Union denounces the large-scale restructuring of corporations via 'digital off-shoring' as a growing cost-saving strategy and claims for remote workers the need to negotiate collectively through their trade unions to ensure that they also benefit from these savings. In this respect, full awareness is shown of the greater hurdles for trade unions to organise and negotiate collective agreements in an increasingly virtual and digital format. Therefore, the first concern is to prevent telework being used to diminish or obstruct workers' rights to form or join a trade union, weaken social dialogue and collective bargaining or impinge trade union rights, activities and organising. To ensure that remote workers can fully exercise their rights to freedom of association, the UNI Global Union has called for a written statement of these rights, access to electronic communication, fair representation, inclusion of remote workers in the determination of bargaining thresholds and in elections, and voting regarding collective action.[72]

## VI. Concluding Remarks: Which Future Scenarios?

The chapter has moved from the peculiar experience of teleworking during the pandemic and looked into the existing and expected regulations at EU and national level, trying to highlight the major weaknesses and possible solutions, so as to find paths for its development consistent with a decent work approach.

In the light of the foregoing analysis, the European Union and Member States need to take further steps to allow a well-established and decent development of telework, overcoming the unstructured kind we became used to seeing during the pandemic. To take the right direction, it is necessary to understand the amount of telework that could be expected in the future and the kinds of workers who will be the main characters in what could represent one of the greatest changes in the labour market.

It should be noted that work is 'teleworkable' only in some sectors and occupations, and therefore not all workers will benefit from teleworking arrangements. This raises

[70] A Forsyth, *The Future of Unions and Worker Representation: The Digital Picket Line* (Oxford, Hart Publishing, 2022).

[71] ITUC, *Legal Guide – Telework*, 2020, available at: www.ituc-csi.org/ituc-legal-guide-telework?lang=en.

[72] UNI Global Union, *Key Trade Union Principles for Ensuring Workers' Rights when Working Remotely*, 2021, availableat:www.opencorporation-blog.s3.amazonaws.com/uploads/2021/03/UNI-Remote-Work-Guidelines-Report_compressed.pdf.

the possibility of a new divide between those who can telework and those who cannot. In the EU, the service sector has historically been dominant in terms of teleworking, and particularly in occupations linked to information and communications, finance and insurance, professional, scientific and technical activities, and public administration.[73] The *teleworkability divide* may result in segments of workers experiencing heightened job insecurity and financial uncertainties. This increased vulnerability comes in addition to existing labour market inequalities, as most low-skilled and low-income occupations are not teleworkable. Workers who do not have the opportunity to telework are at increased risk of temporary layoff or even permanent termination of their contracts of employment on economic grounds.[74] Workers in jobs that are not teleworkable should be provided with additional social safety nets. Lifelong learning is becoming the main source of job security in the digital era for guarding against age discrimination in the workforce.

Another possible adverse impact of the widening of telework concerns mainly home-based teleworkers, since they are often perceived by colleagues and managers as having less commitment. This negative evaluation, combined with lack of visibility, could jeopardise their career development opportunities.

Last but not least, if high levels of telework are here to stay, it is likely to lead to an increase in cross-border teleworking,[75] something that so far has not been addressed in new national legislation nor at EU level, but which could have implications for working conditions and social security rights.

Therefore, policymakers should now take the opportunity to reflect on what the current experience of teleworking means in terms of the nature of work and its future. Otherwise, the risk is that switching to remote-only work will be used by companies only as a strategy to reduce the costs of managing the workplace under the guise of innovation and at the expense of workers' protection.

[73] Sostero et al (n 6).

[74] A Aloisi and V De Stefano, *People and work in times of the Covid 19 emergency*, 2020, available at: www.rivistailmulino.it/news/newsitem/index/Item/News:NEWS_ITEM:5121.

[75] P Pochet, *Globalisation, telemigrants and working conditions* (2021), available at: www.socialeurope.eu (19 November 2021).

# PART III

# Regulating the Algorithm

# 12

# The Challenges of Management by Algorithm: Exploring Individual and Collective Aspects

JEREMIAS ADAMS-PRASSL*

## I. Introduction

Discussion of algorithms at work has traditionally focused on the implications of automation for the *existence* of jobs. This is not necessarily a novel concern: in the 1930s, John Maynard Keynes famously expressed his concerns about the rise of 'technological unemployment. This means unemployment due to our discovery of means of economising the use of labour outrunning the pace at which we can find new uses for labour'.[1] His predictions, of course, did not instantiate. But the advent of ever-faster processing power and increased storage capacity supporting rapid improvements in machine learning technology has led to a resurgence of fears. Economists on both sides of the Atlantic have once more sounded alarm bells, identifying large swaths of the labour market as at a 'high risk' of being automated,[2] and warning of the ensuing stark polarisation in the labour market flowing on from technological progress.[3] Legal scholars

* This contribution draws on work first developed in J Adams-Prassl, 'What if your Boss was an Algorithm? Economic Incentives, Legal Challenges, and the Rise of Artificial Intelligence at Work' (2020) 41 *Comparative Labor Law & Policy Journal* 123. I acknowledge funding from the European Research Council under the European Union's Horizon 2020 research and innovation programme (grant agreement No 947806).

[1] JM Keynes, 'Economic Possibilities for Our Grandchildren' in *Essays in Persuasion* (London, Palgrave Macmillan, 2010) 321, 325. Similar fears have been voiced throughout the past century. President Kennedy, for example, regarded maintaining full employment 'as the major domestic challenge, really, of the '60s … when automation, of course, is replacing men': News Conference 24 (14 February 1962), available at: www.jfklibrary.org/Research/Research-Aids/Ready-Reference/Press-Conferences/News-Conference-24.aspx archived at www.perma.cc/LDS6-Y8X7.

[2] C Frey and M Osborne, *The Future of Employment: How Susceptible are Jobs to Computerisation?* (Oxford, Martin School, 2013) 38, 42.

[3] E Brynjolfsson and A McAfee, *The Second Machine Age: Work, Progress, and Prosperity in a Time of Brilliant Technologies* (New York, WW Norton & Company, 2014) ch 1.

have voiced similar concerns: 'Automation is an entirely lawful – indeed, almost unassailable – way to avoid the costs of employing people'.[4]

Not everyone agrees, however;[5] and the ensuing discussion is explored in a number of fascinating contributions to this edited collection. The focus of the present contribution, on the other hand, is not on automation's impact on the quantity of jobs, but rather their quality. More specifically, it looks at the rapid rise of algorithmic management – defined for present purposes as the augmentation or full automation of traditional employer functions, from hiring to firing workers – and explores some of the individual and collective challenges which ensue for labour law.

To this end, discussion is structured as follows: section II provides a short primer on management by algorithm, from its roots in the gig economy platform's tight algorithmic surveillance and control to today's widespread deployment across the socio-economic spectrum, not least as a result of the Covid-19 pandemic. Section III then takes a step back to look at the potential advantages of management by algorithm – such as the potential for fairer and more consistent decisions, or its uses in protecting safety and health at work – before considering different ways in which the automated exercise of employer function can pose serious harms to decent working conditions, from persistent discrimination and bias to intensive surveillance and unpredictable and potentially inexplicable decision-making. Section IV then maps these dangers onto existing regulatory regimes in employment law, from anti-discrimination norms and unfair dismissal to collective bargaining to identify a number of challenges which arise for existing labour market rules. A brief conclusion returns to a crucial question hovering in the background: in regulating the deployment of algorithmic management systems, how can we ensure that the peculiarities of the employment relationship are sufficiently taken into account?

Before embarking on this discussion, one important point should be noted: the broad definition of employment law adopted for present purposes, as relevant regulatory domains not just limited to traditional facets such as working time regulation or collective bargaining rights. To understand the legal challenges raised by management by algorithm, we also need to consider closely related fields such as data protection and anti-discrimination law.

## II. Management by Algorithm: A Primer

Any absence of widespread mass unemployment should not be taken as evidence that technological advances are not in the process of fundamentally reshaping employment relationships: 'technology can change both the search and hiring process and also facilitate new monitoring and performance management schemes once an employment relation is initiated'.[6]

[4] C Estlund, 'What Should We Do After Work? Automation and Employment Law' (2017) 578 New York University Public Law and Legal Theory Working Papers 21, 23. See now also C Estlund, 'What Should We Do After Work? Automation and Employment Law' (2018) 128 *Yale Law Journal* 254.

[5] D Autor, 'Polyani's Paradox and the Shape of Employment Growth' (2014) NBER Working Paper No 20485 129, 136.

[6] A Adams, 'Technology and the Labour Market: The Assessment' (2018) 3 *Oxford Review of Economic Policy* 349, 355.

## A. Rewiring the Firm

It is this monitoring which is the key enabler of management by algorithm: economists have long been concerned with the cost of monitoring employees;[7] such costs are one of the key reasons behind the failure of earlier attempts to 'automate' managerial functions, including those (in-)famously described in Taylor's theory of 'scientific management'.[8] The advent of algorithmic management fundamentally changes this equation: in principle, at least, the marginal cost of monitoring workers is rapidly tending towards zero.[9]

In a remarkably prescient note, David Autor in 2001 explored the consequences of 'wiring the labour market'.[10] As I have argued elsewhere, however, rather than bringing about mass unemployment, it appears that the immediate consequence of automation has been a '(re-)wiring of the firm':[11] as the cost of data collection and processing continues to fall, employers are increasingly able to deploy technology to monitor – and control – the workplace to a hitherto unimaginable degree.

Not unlike the early days of the gig (or the 'sharing economy', as it then was), there is yet to be a settled label for this phenomenon. One of the earliest terms deployed was 'people analytics', viz,

> how sensing technology and big data about organizations in general, can have massive effects on the way companies are organized. From changing the org chart to changing coffee areas, no aspect of organizations will be untouched by the widespread application of this data.[12]

The impact of data-driven Human Resource Management, its proponents argue, will by no means be limited to large corporations:

> The people analytics system would essentially be 'management in a box' for small business … with only a few sensors and some basic programs, [they] could get automated help setting up their management structure and generating effective collaboration patterns. They could even receive feedback on their progress [… as well as] automated suggestions on org structure, compensation systems, and so on.[13]

## B. Artificial Intelligence at Work

What does this mean in practice? As Alexandra Mateescu and Aiha Nguyen explain:

> Algorithmic management can describe systems of varying degrees of complexity, but they typically include:
>
> - Prolific data collection and surveillance of workers through technology;
> - Real-time responsiveness to data that informs management decisions;

[7] P Davies, 'Efficiency Arguments for the Collective Representation of Workers: A Sketch' in A Bogg et al (eds), *The Autonomy of Labour Law* (Oxford, Hart Publishing, 2017) 367.

[8] FW Taylor, *The Principles of Scientific Management* (New York, Harper & Brothers, 1919).

[9] I say in principle because such accounts exclude important externalities, including notably the environmental impact of energy- and resource-intensive computational techniques.

[10] DH Autor, 'Wiring the Labor Market' (2001) 15 *Journal of Economic Perspectives* 25.

[11] J Adams-Prassl, 'What if your Boss was an Algorithm? Economic Incentives, Legal Challenges, and the Rise of Artificial Intelligence at Work' (2020) 41 *Comparative Labor Law & Policy Journal* 123.

[12] B Waber, *People Analytics* (New York, FT Press, Pearson, 2013) 178.

[13] ibid 191.

- Automated or semi-automated decision-making;
- Transfer of performance evaluations to rating systems or other metrics; and
- The use of 'nudges' and penalties to indirectly incentivize worker behavio[u]rs.[14]

The first, and perhaps starkest, illustration of algorithmic management could be seen in the gig economy, with platforms relying on sophisticated rating mechanisms to manage their workforce. Designed, at first glance, to provide consumers and workers with accurate feedback about other platform providers, it quickly became apparent that, as Tom Slee has argued, reputation algorithms were designed to exercise control over platforms' workforces, operating as

> a substitute for a company management structure, and a bad one at that. A reputation system is the boss from hell: an erratic, bad-tempered and unaccountable manager that may fire you at any time, on a whim, with no appeal.[15]

What began with customer-driven rating mechanisms in the gig economy a decade ago, then, is today no longer limited to non-standard forms of work.[16] Start-ups and established software providers compete in offering software that promises to support, and potentially automate management decision-making across all dimensions of work, as well as the entire life cycle of the employment relationship: whether it is in factories or offices, universities or professional services firms, the exercise of employer functions from hiring and managing workers through to the termination of the employment relationship can already be automated.[17]

When it comes to the *inception of the employment relationship*, for example, AI-driven software now allows prospective employers to conduct extensive screening of an applicant's online presence,[18] but is by no means limited thus: the entire process, from analysing CVs through to ranking candidates, making offers and determining salary levels can be automated – and increasingly is, with sometimes deeply problematic consequences. In early 2019, media reports suggested that Amazon had been forced to abandon its automated recruitment tool after the machine learning algorithm had begun systematically to reject female applicants for engineering roles within the firm.[19]

Once employees are hired, they might find themselves under the watchful eye of the algorithmic boss: the day-to-day *management of the enterprise-internal market* (another core employer function) can similarly be automated to a surprising degree.

[14] A Mateescu and A Nguyen, *Explainer: Algorithmic Management in the Workplace* (*Data&Society*, 2019) 3, available at: www.datasociety.net/library/explainer-workplace-monitoring-surveillance/.

[15] T Slee, *What's Yours is Mine: Against the Sharing Economy* (New York, O/R Books, 2015) 101.

[16] Which have always been merely on a spectrum with digitally intermediated work: International Labour Office, *Non-Standard Employment Around the World: Understanding Challenges, Shaping Prospects* (Geneva, ILO publications, 2016) 2.

[17] In previous work, I have defined a 'function' of being an employer as one of the various actions employers are entitled or obliged to take as part of the bundle of rights and duties falling within the scope of the open-ended contract of service: J Prassl, *The Concept of the Employer* (Oxford, Oxford University Press, 2015) 24–25. For a context-specific application, see also J Prassl and M Risak, 'Uber, TaskRabbit, & Co: Platforms as Employers? Rethinking the Legal Analysis of Crowdwork' (2016) 37 *Comparative Labor Law & Policy Journal* 619.

[18] www.fama.io/about.

[19] www.independent.co.uk/life-style/gadgets-and-tech/amazon-ai-sexist-recruitment-tool-algorithm-a8579161.html.

From the deployment of regular screen-shotting software[20] to the assignment of individual productivity scores,[21] there are few elements of the employment relationship which have not been transformed by the advent of 'data-driven management'[22] and 'talent analytics'.[23]

Workforce analytics software, finally, can even be relied upon in exercising the employer's power of *terminating the employment relationship*. When faced with allegations of retaliatory dismissals in response to concerted trade union activity in one of its warehouses, Amazon revealed the extensive use of algorithmic management: the claimant's employment had been terminated for a lack of productivity, as determined by a neutral algorithm. Local warehouse management, the company's defence asserted, had had no input, control, or understanding of the details of the system deployed.[24]

### C. The Impact of the Covid-19 Pandemic

In concluding this overview, the role of the Covid-19 pandemic should briefly be highlighted. Whilst management by algorithm has been a growing market – and concern – for several years, the advent of a global pandemic and the ensuing changes to workforce organisation have been a significant booster to the deployment of monitoring, surveillance and management software.[25] With a significant proportion of the labour market confined to their homes, nearly all interactions between workers are now recorded, whether through webcams and video cameras, screenshot- and key-logging, or metadata harvesting from common software applications. In thinking about the ensuing challenges for employment law, it is therefore particularly important not to take the status quo at the time of writing as the baseline for future regulatory efforts: the exceptional measures required by an unprecedented public health crisis should not justify the long-term entrenchment of potentially harmful technologies.

## III. Mapping Advantages – And Harms

As the previous section has shown, the rise of management by algorithm opens up the possibility of the full range of employer functions. The picture emerging from a quickly

[20] www.bbc.co.uk/news/business-54289152.

[21] www.technologyreview.com/2020/06/04/1002671/startup-ai-workers-productivity-score-bias-machine-learning-business-covid/.

[22] MK Lee, D Kusbit, E Metsky and L Dabbish, 'Working with Machines: The Impact of Algorithmic and Data-Driven Management on Human Workers', Proceedings of the 33rd Annual ACM Conference on Human Factors in Computing Systems (CHI 2015, Crossings, Seoul).

[23] M Nocker and V Sena, 'Big Data and Human Resources Management: The Rise of Talent Analytics' (2019) 8 *Social Sciences* 273.

[24] www.theverge.com/2019/4/25/18516004/amazon-warehouse-fulfillment-centers-productivity-firing-terminations.

[25] www.cipd.co.uk/news-views/changing-work-views/future-work/thought-pieces/coronavirus-workforce-surveillance.

growing literature on point is clear:[26] management automation enables the exercise of hitherto impossibly granular control over every aspect of the working day.

What does it mean for the quality of jobs when managerial prerogatives are no longer exercised by a human, but rather a low-cost automated system? As Adams explains, from a labour economics perspective, there are both upsides and downsides to this lowering of monitoring cost:

> The increased ease with which firms can monitor their employees should help to raise productivity by limiting moral hazard in the workplace. [Software provider] Evolv claims that its monitoring can help to improve productivity by at least 5 per cent in two-thirds of jobs, although this claim has not been independently verified. Insights from wearables can also allow firms to restructure jobs in a way that benefits its workers. Bank of America, for example, found that workers were more productive when they were allowed to take breaks together. Upon rolling out this policy universally, performance improved by 23 per cent and the 'amount of stress in workers' voices fell 19 per cent'.
>
> However, there are reasons to be cautious about developments in this area. If not all aspects of a job can be monitored and performance managed to the same degree, employers will need to be careful not to distort their employees' efforts across tasks that are more or less captured by the technology. Further, some studies have found that wearables and monitoring increase workplace stress with potentially detrimental effects on productivity and retention.[27]

Both facets of this observation are borne out in practice. Several facets of management by algorithm have significant positive potential – whereas others pose a direct threat to decent working conditions.[28]

## A. Key Technical Features

A number of technical features of algorithmic management distinguish it from traditional management practices, including the kinds of information gathered and analysed, the probabilistic patterns relied upon in machine learning, and new forms of direction and supervision.

When it comes to fine-grained information about individual employees, first, there are a host of sources of data in the modern workplace, from digital information to sensors and even employee self-tracking. As regards digital information, for example, a large number of providers offer software solutions that allow employers to capture employees' digital activities, from key stroke logs through to screenshots taken at regular (yet random) intervals.[29] Information about phone calls, emails and other communication channels can similarly be recorded. Even where the actual substance of such communications is not disclosed or analysed, so-called 'meta-data' (eg, the duration and

[26] See, eg, E Ales et al (eds), *Working in Digital and Smart Organizations: Legal, Economic and Organizational Perspectives on the Digitalization of Labour Relations* (London, Palgrave McMillan, 2018).

[27] Adams (n 6) 357.

[28] Present space limitations dictate a focus on the threats to decent working conditions as the basis for the ensuing legal challenges, which explains the somewhat skewed length of the two sub-sections.

[29] www.support.upwork.com/hc/en-us/articles/211068518-Use-Your-Work-Diary.

frequency of calls between specific individuals, or the size and timing of email attachments sent to external recipients) can easily be captured. In addition to these digital crumbs, increasingly sophisticated sensors allow the capture of physical information: Uber famously pioneered the use of its drivers' iPhones to measure how quickly individuals accelerate and/or break, thus capturing smooth and abrupt driving patterns.[30]

Recording and organising large amounts of data in and of itself is not enough, however: key to the rise of management by algorithm is the availability of increasingly powerful tools to process and analyse what has been captured. The advent of large data sets and precipitous drops in the cost of processing power have fuelled the rise of machine learning – probabilistic analyses of large data sets, relying on sophisticated statistical modelling to spot patterns or correlations in the data.[31] This is a crucial step away from our traditional understanding of algorithms: machine learning is designed to rely on a constant evolution and redefinition of parameters – algorithmic control is no longer just confined to experiences taught through training data sets and pre-programmed analytical routines.[32] The results are ever-changing decision structures: as increasing amounts of data are collected about individual employees and every aspect of their working lives scrutinised on an ongoing basis, the factors considered relevant for key metrics such as productivity or innovation will continue to change.[33]

Initially, machine learning algorithms would scour big data sets for important insights into the workplace, from the arrangement of physical spaces to productive and unproductive team behaviours, and then provide the automation to management in order to inform their choices. At least from a technical perspective, however, there is nothing inherent in the capabilities of such software to limit itself to informing traditional managers: in principle, at least, their actual decisions can be fully automated.[34]

## B. Positive Potential – Or a Threat to Decent Work?

The promise of management by algorithm should not be underestimated. Existing management structures can pose threats to decent working conditions, from unconscious biases and favouritism to downright illegal managerial behaviour. Indeed, there is an emerging body of evidence that the thoughtful deployment of algorithmic management structures will be welcomed by a workforce which perceives the automated system to be fairer and more rational than previous structures. A 2020 study on the effects of using participatory working time scheduling software in Finnish hospitals, for example,

[30] www.eng.uber.com/telematics/.

[31] N Polson and J Scott, *AIQ: How Artificial Intelligence Works and How We Can Harness its Power for a Better World* (London, Bantam Press, 2018).

[32] D Heaven (ed), *Machines That Think* (London, New Scientist, 2017).

[33] I Goodfellow, Y Bengio and A Courville, *Deep Learning* (Cambridge, MA, MIT Press, 2016).

[34] In jurisdictions covered by the European Union's General Data Protection Regulation, such an approach would not be legal, given a right to have a 'human in the loop', ie, not to be subject to fully automated decisions: see Regulation (EU) 2016/679 of the European Parliament and of the Council of 27 April 2016 on the protection of natural persons with regard to the processing of personal data and on the free movement of such data, and repealing Directive 95/46/EC (General Data Protection Regulation) [2016] OJ L119/1, Article 22 (GDPR).

found that improvements in working time allocation led to significantly lower sickness absence when compared to more traditional shift allocation systems.[35] Algorithmic management tools can also play an important role in ensuring safety and health at work, for example in monitoring for signs of fatigue which could lead to dangerous working conditions, or when deployed to monitor workers' physical distance in warehouses during the Covid-19 pandemic: image recognition technology can constantly monitor and calculate workers' positioning, and provide real-time feedback about potentially dangerous proximity and/or exposure.[36]

At the same time, however, management by algorithm can also pose a number of serious threats to decent working conditions. On the basis of an in-depth study of algorithmic management practices, Gina Neff and colleagues at the Oxford Internet Institute conclude that

> there are broadly three major ways that AI fails workers and workplaces. 1) Integration challenges happen when settings are not yet primed for AI use, or when these technologies operate at a disjoint between workers and their employers. 2) Reliance challenges stem from over and under reliance on AI in workplace systems. 3) Transparency challenges … arise when the work required by these systems – and where that work is done – is not transparent to users.[37]

If not managed properly, these challenges can quickly translate into specific harms. Take privacy as a first example: given the sheer quantity of information that is captured by algorithmic management systems, the traditional boundary between the workplace and individuals' private lives is rapidly breaking down. Information about an individuals' weekend activities can easily be combined with measures of Monday morning productivity, revealing patterns far beyond traditional employer concerns. Furthermore, even where information is collected and stored in anonymised form, as information is increasingly organised in machine-readable formats, data sets from different sources can – at least in principle and subject to data processing consent and privacy laws in jurisdictions such as the European Union – easily be combined to build large employee databases, and – again, at least in principle – identify individuals within a firm with relative ease.

A second and closely related concern is the tight control which can be exercised over workers – whilst also potentially dissimulating its origins as employer orders and making it difficult, if not impossible, to obtain and/or understand the reasons for particular decisions. The use of algorithmic management software can quickly go far beyond mere monitoring, up to and including automated terminations. Crucially, however, employer orders need no longer be explicitly framed as directives aimed at the workforce: algorithmic control is exercised in myriad ways, often eschewing direct orders or explicit instructions.[38] As a result of the advent of management by algorithm, the use

[35] J Turunen et al, 'The effects of using participatory working time scheduling software on sickness absence: A difference-in-differences study' (2020) 112 *International Journal of Nursing Studies* 103716.

[36] www.theverge.com/2020/6/16/21292669/social-distancing-amazon-ai-assistant-warehouses-covid-19

[37] G Neff, M McGrath and N Prakash, *AI @ Work: Artificial Intelligence in the Workplace* (Perth, Minderoo Foundation, 2020) 3.

[38] The operation of algorithmic control mechanisms tallies closely with 'the most effective and insidious use of power' identified by Steven Lukes. He argues that control over a situation can be exercised in myriad ways, 'whether through the operation of social forces and institutional practices or through individuals' decisions': to put the matter sharply, 'A may exercise power over B by getting him to do what he does not want to do, but

of automated rating mechanisms,[39] gamification[40] and incentive-based 'nudge' mechanisms,[41] become increasingly effective in controlling large, heterogeneous workforces whilst scrupulously avoiding the appearance of traditional employer control.[42]

Alex Rosenblat and Luke Stark were amongst the first to conduct an extensive study of such control mechanisms. They demonstrate how working conditions can easily be 'shaped by the company's deployment of a variety of design decisions and information asymmetries via the application to effect a "soft control" over workers' routines'.[43] Even though instructions are 'carefully designed to be indirect, presumably to avoid the appearance of a company policy',[44] they can achieve essentially the same outcome as direct orders:

> Individualized metrics … foster a 'highly individualized sense of responsibility for one's own job stability', even though [workers] have limited control over how passengers interact with the rating system or how [the company] assesses it. By design, systematic accountability for the whole interactive process is downloaded onto individual [workers].[45]

When a Uber driver is ready to quit at the end of her shift, for example, algorithmic control can be quick to step in. Rosenblat and Stark demonstrate how the app prompts drivers with an enticing pop-up message accompanied by the surge-price icon: 'Are you sure you want to go offline? Demand is very high in your area. Make more money, don't stop now!'[46] Similar mechanisms can be deployed in the context of white-collar jobs, for example through the use of regular 'feedback' emails to workers such as Microsoft's Cortana, which promises to act as a 'personal productivity assistant', which 'helps you achieve more with less effort while allowing you to focus on what matters'.[47]

In summary, then, whilst there is some clear promise in the deployment of algorithmic management systems, many of the technical features involved have the potential to pose inherent threats to decent working conditions.

## IV. Illustrating Specific Challenges

It is this realisation which sits at the heart of the labour law challenges to which the deployment of management by algorithm systems gives rise: core elements of the novel

he also exercises power over him by influencing, shaping or determining his very wants. Indeed, is it not the supreme exercise of power to get … others to have the desires you want them to have – that is, to secure their compliance by controlling their thoughts and desires?' (S Lukes, *Power: A Radical View* (London, Palgrave 2005), 27.)

[39] Slee (n 15) 101.

[40] M Bodie, M Cherry, ML McCormick and J Tang, 'The Law and Policy of People Analytics' (2016) 88 *University of Colorado Law Review* 961, 962.

[41] A Rosenblat and L Stark, 'Algorithmic Labor and Information asymmetries: A Case study of Uber's Drivers' (2016) 10 *International Journal of Communication* 3758.

[42] P Moore, M Upchurch and X *Whittaker* (eds), *Humans and Machines at Work: Monitoring, Surveillance and Automation in Contemporary Capitalism* (London, Palgrave Macmillan, 2017).

[43] Rosenblat and Stark (n 41) 3775.

[44] ibid.

[45] ibid, 3772.

[46] ibid, 3768.

[47] www.microsoft.com/en-us/cortana/.

approach to exercising the managerial prerogative differ fundamentally from the traditional management structures around which employment law has been designed.

## A. Individual Employment Law

Perhaps most significantly, it can be difficult if not impossible to understand in practice how a system has arrived at a particular decision or recommendation – yet the giving of reasons is key in many domains of employment law, such as unfair dismissal protection. As we have seen, the iterative approach inherent in modern machine learning techniques can make algorithmic management highly unpredictable – and inexplicable, as evolving decision parameters can be near impossible to reconstruct, or document exhaustively.[48] In concrete terms, this means that the reason why a worker was fired at any given moment may no longer be relevant – or even discernible – a few days after the event.

Another domain in which algorithmic management raises serious concerns is discrimination law. A large body of empirical work has clearly demonstrated that automated decision-making can replicate – or even bolster – patterns of discriminations prevalent in the labour market. And yet it is not entirely clear how the law should respond. Can discrimination law's long-standing emphasis on causation be reconciled with machine learning's reliance on correlation?[49] As predictive algorithms improve their accuracy with ever-larger data sets, what sanctions should be in place for a pre-emptive dismissal on grounds of an unprotected characteristic (such as a preference for sugary drinks) which is highly correlated with a protected ground (eg, developing a disability in old age)?[50] Existing legal categories, including notably direct discrimination, may well be insufficient to hold employers accountable for algorithmic control resulting in such discriminatory outcomes: as long as we proceed on the assumption that algorithms operate as neutral criteria (thus only triggering the prohibition on indirect discrimination), a large space is opened up for potential justification of their ongoing deployment.

Perhaps most important, however, are questions relating to data protection, specifically the extent to which the European Union's General Data Protection Regulation may provide some level of protection for employees across the Union's Member States.[51] Key aspects of this question have been explored in the Article 29 Data Protection Working Party's extensive documentation, including in particular Opinion 2/2017 on data processing at work.[52]

[48] M Temme, 'Algorithms and Transparency in View of the New General Data Protection Regulation' (2017) 3 *European Data Protection Law Review* 473.

[49] AG King and M Mrkonich, '"Big Data" and the Risk of Employment Discrimination' (2016) 68 *Oklahoma Law Review* 555.

[50] S Hoffman, 'Big data and the Americans with Disabilities Act' (2017) 68 *Hastings Law Journal* 777.

[51] GDPR (n 34).

[52] www.ec.europa.eu/newsroom/article29/item-detail.cfm?item_id=610169. Today, the Article 29 Working Party ('WP29') has been replaced by the European Data Protection Board, an independent body responsible for the consistent implementation of the GDPR. The Board has endorsed some, though not all, Opinions and Guidelines of WP29 (Endorsement 1/2018): see www.edpb.europa.eu/news/news/2018/endorsement-gdpr-wp29-guidelines-edpb_en.

The 'collection, recording, organisation, structuring, [and] storage' of Data (perhaps somewhat confusingly included in the broader definition of 'processing'[53] will only be lawful, for example, where the employer can show a legal ground for doing so.[54] As the recitals make clear, however, consent, the primary lawful reason in many areas, 'should not provide a valid legal ground for the processing of personal data in a specific case where there is a clear imbalance between the data subject and the controller'.[55] Recognising the specific features of the employment relationship, the Opinion therefore concludes that

> [u]nless in exceptional situations, employers will have to rely on another legal ground than consent – such as the necessity to process the data for their legitimate interest. However, a legitimate interest in itself is not sufficient to override the rights and freedoms of employees.[56]

Another potentially promising aspect of the GDPR is its Article 22, which prohibits (or at least severally constrains) 'automated processing, including profiling, which produces legal effects concerning him or her or similarly significantly affects him or her'.[57] Recently launched litigation in the Amsterdam District Court against gig economy platforms such as Uber shows the potential of this provision in avoiding some of the worst excesses of management by algorithm, such as the automation of worker sanctioning and termination.[58]

## B. Collective Labour Law

The challenges are by no means limited to the domain of individual employment law: ensuring the effective representation of collective worker voice is just as challenging a task. Regulatory regimes should be designed to ensure that the deployment and ongoing operation of algorithmic management systems can only take place in close consultation with trade unions and/or other forms of worker organisation.

One potential angle for such worker involvement at the European level is the need, under the GDPR, for the employer to conduct a Data Protection Impact Assessment (DPIA) '[w]here a type of processing in particular using new technologies, and taking into account the nature, scope, context and purposes of the processing, is likely to result in a high risk to the rights and freedoms of natural persons';[59] and particular safeguards surrounding sensitive personal data, including 'racial or ethnic origin, political opinions, religious or philosophical beliefs, or trade union membership'.[60] An explicit stipulation that worker representatives be involved in the DPIA process would go a long way towards alleviating many of the concerns identified in the previous sections. Whilst

[53] Article 4(2), GDPR.
[54] Article 6(1), GDPR.
[55] Recital 43, GDPR.
[56] WP29, Opinion, 4.
[57] Article 22(1), GDPR.
[58] www.ekker.legal/2020/10/26/uber-drivers-challenge-dismissal-by-algorithm/.
[59] Article 35(1), GDPR.
[60] Article 9(1), GDPR.

wholesale reform of the GDPR itself is unlikely in the near future, Member States are free to lay down such specifications in domestic law or implementing measures.[61]

## V. Conclusion

A rich and fascinating literature on algorithmic accountability has emerged at the intersection of computer science, the law, humanities and the social sciences in the years since Frank Pasquale's work on the 'black box society' was published.[62] Despite that fact, however, management by algorithm has been relatively under-explored, with general discussion only relatively rarely straying into the specific context of employment.[63] This is not necessarily surprising, given the number of specific features which heighten many of the underlying tensions, including most importantly the fundamental inequality of bargaining power between an employer and her employees,[64] as well as vast differences in industrial relations structures and labour market organisation in different jurisdictions.[65]

As a result, even the most promising regulatory strategies developed in contexts such as financial regulation or data protection will rarely fit into the workplace without further adjustment: whereas increased transparency can be a powerful tool in scrutinising financial markets,[66] imposing similar obligations on employers might quickly run up against employees' privacy expectations.[67] Advocates of unconditional counterfactual explanations as a promising strategy to explain algorithmic decision-making whilst avoiding complex technical arguments, have similarly explicitly highlighted that 'counterfactuals do not provide the statistical evidence needed to assess algorithms for fairness or racial bias'.[68]

What these observations show is that the rise of management by algorithm poses a novel and complex paradox for labour market regulation. From a legal perspective, the dramatic increase in managerial control which results from the 'rewiring of the firm' might at first be thought to be welcome: most employment law systems place significant emphasis on control and/or subordination as a key factor in determining when a relationship should come within the scope of protective norms. At the same time as dramatically concentrating employer control, however, key elements of algorithmic management can also be relied upon to diffuse responsibility: questions as to

[61] Article 88, GDPR.

[62] F Pasquale, *The Black Box Society: The Secret Algorithms that Control Money and Information* (Cambridge, MA, Harvard University Press, 2015).

[63] With the notable exception of discrimination in the automated hiring context. See, eg, A Kelly-Lyth, 'Challenging Biased Hiring Algorithms' (2021) 41 *Oxford Journal of Legal Studies* 899.

[64] K Wedderburn, *The Worker and the Law*, 3rd edn (London, Penguin 1986).

[65] O Kahn-Freund, 'On Uses and Misuses of Comparative Law' (1974) 37 *Modern Law Review* 120.

[66] Pasquale (n 62).

[67] J Atkinson, 'Workplace Monitoring and the Right to Private Life at Work' (2018) 81 *Modern Law Review* 688.

[68] S Wachter et al, 'Counterfactual explanations without opening the black box: automated decisions and the GDPR' (2018) 31 *Harvard Journal of Law & Technology* 842, 883.

who should be liable – the employing enterprise? The designers of the software? The providers of contaminated training data? – can no longer necessarily be tackled with the traditional tools of employment law alone. Any regulatory effort designed to restore the coherent application of individual and collective standards will only succeed if it fully takes both the specific harms (and advantages) as well as the core technical features of management by algorithms into account.

# 13

# Automation, Augmentation, Autonomy: Labour Regulation and the Digital Transformation of Managerial Prerogatives

ANTONIO ALOISI*

## I. Introduction

Technologies together represent a constitutive component of modern societies, which is why their multifarious impacts have long been at the centre of scholarly and popular discourses. Understandably, their emergence has prompted both rosy expectations and justified anxieties. In addition to permeating almost all aspects of human life, digital advances are significantly altering workplace interactions and reshaping industrial processes.

The world of work is arguably one of many areas in which the influence of new technology is increasingly tangible. Over the last few years, workers in all sectors have witnessed the frantic acceleration of the digital transformation, which has been further exacerbated (if not validated) by the Covid-19 pandemic necessitating the reorganisation of production methods while contributing to the widespread adoption of digital solutions intended to enable business continuity, facilitate remote working arrangements and keep people safe.[1] Both during the most severe phases of the Covid-19 lockdowns and after the related restrictions were relaxed, the penetration of digital applications continued to reach astonishing peaks, corroborating their role as 'privatised utilities' for workers, employers and public institutions alike.[2] Yet, the relevance

* This chapter is written within the framework of the 'Boss Ex Machina' project, which has received funding from the European Union's Horizon 2020 research and innovation programme under the Marie Skłodowska-Curie grant agreement No 893888. I am extremely grateful to Valerio De Stefano, Nastazja Potocka-Sionek, Silvia Rainone, the editors of this volume and my colleagues at IE University Law School for participating in an enriching discussion and providing invaluable feedback.

[1] A Gilbert, A Thomas, S Atwell and J Simons, *The Impact of Automation on Labour Markets: Interactions with Covid-19* (London, Institute for the Future of Work, 2020). See also A Aloisi and V De Stefano, 'Essential Jobs, Remote Work and Digital Surveillance: Addressing the COVID-19 Pandemic Panopticon' (2022) 161 *International Labour Review*, available at www.onlinelibrary.wiley.com/doi/10.1111/ilr.12219.

[2] JY Chen and JL Qiu, 'Digital Utility: Datafication, Regulation, Labor, and DiDi's Platformization of Urban Transport in China' (2019) 12 *Chinese Journal of Communication* 274.

of digital automation was prominent well before the pandemic struck. This exogenous event could, therefore, serve as a litmus test of the soundness of theories concerning human substitution, expanded managerial powers, skill displacement and efficiency enhancement.

All too often, the seismic shifts brought about by digital infrastructure are considered through the distorting prism of utopian or dystopian ideologies, which in some cases privileges beliefs over facts due to the adoption of a rather polarised approach. During several epochs, the consequences of this attitude have materialised in the form of short-sighted policy measures, dysfunctional company rulebooks and misguided regulatory interventions, which all fail to offer concrete responses to radical changes. Although firmly anchored in employment law, this chapter contributes to the literature by disentangling the main trajectories of the digital transformation at the workplace level from a cross-disciplinary perspective. More specifically, the analysis concentrates on the three main vectors of the digital transformation, namely smart machines, algorithms and online platforms. These transformative forces affect the full array of options available to entrepreneurs: the potential dislocation of tasks and jobs, opportunities for outsourcing, digitisation of decision-making processes, augmentation of command-and-control roles and impact on job quality and task discretion.[3] By distinguishing between hype and reality, the goal of this chapter is to reassess the influence of technological means on the basis of a three-pronged scenario comprising the following complementary possibilities: (i) automation, (ii) augmentation and (iii) autonomy.

## A. Game-Changing Technologies and the World of Work

A comprehensive definition of 'game-changing technologies' that includes material gadgets and immaterial infrastructure will be embraced in this chapter.[4] There is no denying that such tools are highly heterogeneous in terms of their usages and purposes, as are the reasons behind their introduction. Despite this, they enable the reconfiguration of organisational procedures, workplace practices, skills acquisition, retention and enhancement. Consequently, rather than dissecting each distinct means, an examination of technological artefacts should necessarily include a deep dive into the benign or harmful alterations they can make to the (already unbalanced and asymmetric) power relationship between bosses and workers.

Before proceeding any further, a note of caution must be sounded. It is debatable whether the current period really deserves such tantalising labels as the 'Second Machine Age' or 'Fourth Industrial Revolution'.[5] Labour historians have almost unanimously linked the previous industrial revolutions to enabling engines associated with

[3] In this chapter, the term 'augmentation' is used to describe the expansion of employer powers. In other fields, it is considered to be a value-added alternative to automation. S Raisch and S Krakowski, 'Artificial Intelligence and Management: The Automation–Augmentation Paradox' (2021) 46 *Academy of Management Review* 192.

[4] Eurofound, *Game-Changing Technologies: Transforming Production and Employment in Europe* (Luxembourg, Publications Office of the European Union, 2020).

[5] E Brynjolfsson and A McAfee, *The Second Machine Age: Work, Progress, and Prosperity in a Time of Brilliant Technologies* (New York, WW Norton & Company, 2014).

profound change, including in relation to the social fabric.[6] Without dwelling on the matter too much, changes are periodised according to the main disrupting force that determined the redesign of production, distribution and consumer attitudes.[7] Thanks to steam engines and railways, a transition occurred from manual to mechanised production methods, which boosted coal-powered manufacturing (from the end of the eighteenth to the beginning of the nineteenth century, a period known as the 'First Industrial Revolution'). Then, at the end of the nineteenth century, steel, electricity and heavy engineering facilitated the shift to mass production based on a stricter division of labour, which defines the second stage of this progression. Finally, the 'Third Industrial Revolution' commonly refers to the first wave of the automation and computerisation of production cycles thanks to newly invented tools such as microprocessors in the information and communication technology (ICT) arena during the 1970s.[8]

Scholars have expressed strongly diverging views, but to paint as accurate a picture of the current landscape as possible, it is important to consider what machines, algorithms and platforms have in common with the forces redesigning human history, which have previously been used to classify industrial shifts.[9] The most critical underlying asset related to these new technologies is data, particularly personal data,[10] without which new technologies could not operate in such efficient and effective ways. Indeed, 'big' or 'smart' data capture, storage and processing now constitute the backbone of digital operators' strategies, ensuring sustained exponential advances in reprogramming business models and redeploying complex activities due to the high availability of data-collecting devices and enhanced computational power.[11] As will be discussed later in this chapter, the 'datafication' of employment relationships is also a precondition for the magnification of managerial prerogatives.[12] The other significant characteristic considered to indicate that an inflexion point of unprecedented progress has occurred, at least in the Global North, could be the peculiar capacity of the current wave of digitalisation to be re-combinatory, self-reinforcing and interconnected.[13]

[6] D Acemoglu and JA Robinson, *Why Nations Fail: The Origins of Power, Prosperity, and Poverty* (New York, Crown Publishing Group, 2012).

[7] N von Tunzelmann, 'Historical Coevolution of Governance and Technology in the Industrial Revolutions' (2003) 14 *Structural Change and Economic Dynamics* 365.

[8] M Castells, *The Information Age: Economy, Society, and Culture* (London, Blackwell Publishers, 1996).

[9] EG Popkova, YV Ragulina and AV Bogoviz, 'Fundamental Differences of Transition to Industry 4.0 from Previous Industrial Revolutions' in EG Popkova, YV Ragulina and AV Bogoviz (eds), *Industry 4.0: Industrial Revolution of the 21st Century* (Cham, Springer, 2019) 21. See also E Macias, D Klenert and JI Anton, 'Not So Disruptive Yet? Characteristics, Distribution and Determinants of Robots in Europe' (2021) 58 *Structural Change and Economic Dynamics* 76.

[10] Regulation (EU) 2016/679 of the European Parliament and of the Council of 27 April 2016 on the protection of natural persons with regard to the processing of personal data and on the free movement of such data, and repealing Directive 95/46/EC (General Data Protection Regulation) [2016] OJ L119/1, Article 4(1).

[11] D Angrave, A Charlwood, I Kirkpatrick, M Lawrence and M Stuart, 'HR and Analytics: Why HR Is Set to Fail the Big Data Challenge' (2016) 26 *Human Resource Management Journal* 1.

[12] PV Moore and J Woodcock (eds), *Augmented Exploitation: Artificial Intelligence, Automation, and Work* (London, Pluto Press, 2021). See also S Adler-Bell and M Miller, *The Datafication of Employment: How Surveillance and Capitalism Are Shaping Workers' Futures Without Their Knowledge* (New York, The Century Foundation, 2018).

[13] E Brynjolfsson and A McAfee, *Race Against the Machine* (Lexington, Digital Frontier Press, 2012). See also SG Leonhard, *Technology vs Humanity: The Coming Clash Between Man and Machine* (London, Fast Future Publishing, 2016).

Parallel to previous industrial revolutions, new modes of production have complemented or supplanted some activities while purportedly increasing efficiency, minimising transaction costs and catering to evolving customer appetites. There is more. Similar to the preceding cases, game-changing technologies give rise to stark tension between the changing social organisation of production and the underlying institutional framework,[14] thereby causing social unease and, possibly, political unrest. This divergence places social institutions and the resultant coordination mechanisms under severe strain, resulting in a situation that has commanded the attention of regulators, social partners and the general public. In short, workplace disruption can be associated with substantial social costs for those directly affected if they are not appropriately compensated. It is undeniable that this alteration in the power equilibria leads to both winners and losers.[15] Consequently, innovations often face resistance and lead to upheaval.[16]

## B. Research Hypothesis and Structure of the Chapter

The potential of modern tools is barely comparable to that of ancient practices that were bound by the limitations of the scope, latitude and precision of direct human power.[17] Their magnitude constitutes a challenge for traditional institutions, which often struggle to adapt to new organisational and production patterns. This spectacular turnaround demands that we look at things differently and raises the captivating question of whether employer authority today is the same as it was in the past. There is abundant evidence that advanced technologies are not making humans redundant; rather, they are making workers submissive and managers superfluous.[18] Therein lies the puzzle that has motivated the examination of what I term the 'genetic mutation' of the employer's functions (ie, an exorbitant augmentation of their breadth and reach). This expansion in both the spatial and the temporal scope of hierarchical powers raises issues regarding the adequacy of the existing statutory and collectively agreed upon legal frameworks.[19]

The trajectory of the ongoing work transformation is certainly not a linear one. However, it would be wrong not to recognise the role of labour regulation in addressing these manifold challenges: technology's evolution is shaped by the legal environment through mutually reinforcing interactions with individual and collective labour regulations.[20] While innovations cannot be uninvented, effectively shaping the ways in which their benefits are shared and their risks mutualised represents a crucial task for all involved supranational and domestic actors.

[14] B Jovanovic and PL Rousseau, 'General Purpose Technologies' in P Aghion and S Durlauf (eds), *Handbook of Economic Growth*, vol 1 (Amsterdam, Elsevier BV, 2005) 1181.

[15] K Crawford, *The Atlas of AI* (New Haven, CT, Yale University Press, 2021).

[16] D Spencer, M Cole, S Joyce, X Whittaker and M Stuart, *Digital Automation and the Future of Work* (Brussels, European Union, 2021).

[17] R Bodei, *Dominio e sottomissione, Schiavi, animali, macchine, Intelligenza artificiale* (Bologna, Il Mulino, 2019).

[18] A Aloisi and V De Stefano, '*Introducing the Algorithmic Boss*' (Madrid, IE Insights, 20 April 2021), available at: www.ie.edu/insights/articles/introducing-the-algorithmic-boss/.

[19] S Zuboff, *In the Age of the Smart Machine: The Future of Work and Power* (New York, Basic Books, 1988).

[20] S Deakin and C Markou, 'The Law–Technology Cycle and the Future of Work' (2018) Cambridge, Centre for Business Research, University of Cambridge, Working Paper No 504.

The remainder of this chapter, which applies an analytical-descriptive approach, is structured into three main sections. The second section debunks the rhetoric of a 'world without work', explaining how a more accurate portrayal of the ongoing transformation would reveal complementarity rather than substitution effects and, more worryingly, the significant potential for quality erosion in relation to several middle-income professional contexts. After providing a thorough overview of the legal and economic functions of both employers and managers, the third section examines the transformation of related prerogatives, as spurred on by the widespread adoption of so-called automated decision-making systems (ADMS), which have the potential to render authority more intense, distributed and deceitful. Prior studies in the organisation, surveillance and human resources management (HRM) fields inform the multidisciplinary examination of the genetic variation of employer prerogatives, a trend that results in the reduction of workers' agency (here defined as freedom of choice with regard to time and place of work as well as the methods used to achieve the objectives set), which may negatively affect productivity, competitiveness and propensity to innovate. By openly opposing the prevailing deterministic approach, the final section engages with the importance of fostering a professional ecosystem in which self-determination is promoted in order to empower workers, attract talent and achieve lasting organisational success.

## II. Challenging the 'Workless Future' Narrative

There is arguably only one topic that has been researched as extensively as the 'future of work' and that is the alleged soon-to-be end of work. When conceived as a vector replacing human labour inputs, automation ends up being treated as a job-destroying force. Over the last century, philosophers, sociologists and economists have speculated about the much-vaunted demise of work due to unstoppable technological breakthroughs rendering humans unnecessary. In this field of study, wishful thinking and illusions have often been conflated with reality.

As a source of apprehension and even discontent, this conventional wisdom regarding the threat posed by technologies and their winner-takes-all nature has ample historical precedent. However, claims that human work will shortly disappear require evidence that has not been provided. In the meantime, there is much confusion concerning how to frame the issue from a legal standpoint. Although this ongoing dispute is unlikely to be settled within legal circles, it may severely affect policy responses as well as the way in which regulators design the accompanying measures. For instance, skill obsolescence and enhanced mechanisation could trigger large restructuring operations, the social implications of which ought to be mitigated.[21] Similarly, anticipating the development of new demands could inform reskilling processes. Alternatively, fewer jobs may usher in downward competition in terms of the wages and other conditions associated with the jobs that survive the turbulence. Thus, as suggested by Estlund,[22] employment law

[21] V De Stefano, '"Negotiating the Algorithm": Automation, Artificial Intelligence, and Labor Protection' (2019) 41 *Comparative Labor Law & Policy Journal* 15.

[22] C Estlund, 'What Should We Do After Work? Automation and Employment' (2018) 128 *Yale Law Journal* 254.

scholars cannot afford to ignore the discussion that is currently raging among labour economists and business leaders.

## A. Is the Job Destruction Anxiety Exaggerated?

When it comes to tracing the evolution of the unfulfilled prophecy of the jobless society, it is striking that the futurists of work disappearance tended to perceive the available rudimentary technology as a positive force that was expected to free humans from non-meaningful, tedious and menial duties. In short, the coming abundance of machines, gadgets and widgets appeared to promise the liberation of human energies that could be devoted to more rewarding tasks. The seminal voice in this political and economic theorising was that of Keynes, who memorably projected the tremendous convenience of a 15-hour working week by 2030 thanks to inventions purported to suffer on behalf of humans.[23] Technological advances were awaited with a mixture of hope and relief. More recently, in an astonishing and utterly cynical reversal of perspective, ICT progress has been accused of paving the way for a reduction in employment and task immiseration. Over time, this dismal understanding of the ongoing digital transformation has escalated, becoming a widespread mythology.[24] However, massive dislocation has yet to materialise, despite ongoing digital progress. Workers are transferring from declining to fast-growing sectors or concentrating on less routine and skill-intense occupations, while new occupations are absorbing the available labour supply. Undeniably, interim adjustments may prove traumatic. What is worse, the highly perceptible abundance of automation technology is not triggering a corresponding growth in productivity rates.[25] The same applies to wages.

Several commentators rushed to forecast an upsurge in automation during the early phases of the recent pandemic for a panoply of reasons.[26] First, unlike human labour, technology is not affected by dreadful viruses ('robots cannot get sick' was the catchy headline). Second, machines offer the prospect of potentially significant cost-saving for firms. Indeed, it is no mere accident that the same storyline gained traction during previous recessions.[27] Throughout similar exogenous shocks, automation occurred in bursts and was concentrated during times of economic downturn. However, recent data have demonstrated that the current levels of job destruction anxiety are exaggerated.[28] In fact, there is little evidence of growing interest in automation, and even the pandemic has had only a fairly modest impact. It has not intensified the adoption of robots, although aggregate unemployment has risen, while the feasibility of in-person labour

[23] JM Keynes, 'Economic Possibilities for Our Grandchildren' in *Essays in Persuasion* (London, Palgrave Macmillan, 2010) 321.

[24] CB Frey, *The Technology Trap: Capital, Labor, and Power in the Age of Automation* (Princeton, NJ, Princeton University Press, 2019).

[25] RM Solow, 'We'd Better Watch Out' (1987) *New York Times Book Review* 36.

[26] C Coombs, 'Will COVID-19 Be the Tipping Point for the Intelligent Automation of Work? A Review of the Debate and Implications for Research' (2020) 55 *International Journal of Information Management* 102182.

[27] 'Robots Threaten Jobs Less Than Fearmongers Claim' *The Economist* (10 April 2021), available at: www.econ.st/3wECso3.

[28] A Georgieff and A Milanez, 'What Happened to Jobs at High Risk of Automation?' (2021) Paris, OECD Social, Employment and Migration Working Papers No 255, available at: www.bit.ly/32YMLKe.

has been severely compromised.[29] Despite positively altering public attitudes towards the adoption of new technology, mainly in terms of customer mindsets, the pandemic has also made evident the previously overlooked human network that upholds the operation of the digital world.[30] Nevertheless, such preoccupations are not new, and it may be useful to look backwards in order to see forwards.

Catastrophic forecasts regarding the number of jobs that will be lost in the future occupy the pages of myriad bestsellers. This posturing has seemingly prevailed thanks to numerous evocative titles and false alarmist proclamations.[31] Even worse, fuelled by the rhetoric of relentless technological obsolescence, the idea of a 'post-work utopia' has gained widespread recognition,[32] suggesting that breakthroughs in robotics and artificial intelligence (AI) will make it possible to abolish various jobs in the name of cost-effectiveness.[33] Over the last two centuries, there have been periodic warnings that automation and new technologies will wipe out or downgrade large numbers of middle-class jobs while leaving workers at a permanent disadvantage, at least since the Luddites attempted to smash mechanised looms during the nineteenth century after marching on a textile mill in Huddersfield, England.[34] Optimists have highlighted past examples of how technology has improved the human condition, often stressing factories and warehouses as a positive externality. By contrast, scaremongers have fretted about the devastating impacts of new inventions on the intrinsic value of human labour. In the current climate, it appears that technology has turned out to be less favourable to labour than expected,[35] thereby failing to deliver on its promise of making our lives easier. Such a culture of uncertainty may also have played a role in curbing contestation and collective claims. Indeed, anxiety over the magnitude of technological displacement has frequently been weaponised to force workers 'to accept *any* jobs as a means of survival'.[36]

## B. A Brief History of Unfulfilled Prophecies

Decades ago, Rifkin claimed that automation and technological progress in the field of agriculture would inevitably lead to work destruction, which would cause soaring unemployment.[37] At the same time, the noted labour economist predicted polarisation

[29] Gilbert et al (n 1).

[30] HR Ekbia and BA Nardi, *Heteromation, and Other Stories of Computing and Capitalism* (Cambridge, MA, MIT Press, 2017).

[31] RD Atkinson and J Wu, *False Alarmism: Technological Disruption and the US Labor Market, 1850–2015* (Washington DC, Information Technology and Innovation Foundation, 2017), available at: www.bit.ly/3oNO4nR. See also E McGaughey, 'Will Robots Automate Your Job Away? Full Employment, Basic Income, and Economic Democracy' (2018) Cambridge, Centre for Business Research, University of Cambridge, Working Paper No 496.

[32] D Thompson, 'A World Without Work' *The Atlantic* (July/August 2015), available at: www.theatln.tc/2qsVCM3.

[33] J Wiecki, 'Robopocalypse Not' *Wired Magazine* (September 2017), available at: www.wired.com/2017/08/robots-will-not-take-your-job/.

[34] S Deakin, 'Luddism in the Age of Uber' *Social Europe* (3 November 2015), available at: www.socialeurope.eu/luddism-in-the-age-of-uber.

[35] D Acemoglu, 'AI's Future Doesn't Have to Be Dystopian' *Boston Review* (20 May 2021) www.bostonreview.net/forum/science-nature/daron-acemoglu-redesigning-ai.

[36] A Aloisi and V De Stefano, 'Regulation and the Future of Work: The Employment Relationship as an Innovation Facilitator' (2020) 159 *International Labour Review* 52.

[37] J Rifkin, *The End of Work: The Decline of the Global Labor Force and the Dawn of the Post-Market Era*, 1st edn (New York, Tarcher, 1994).

between a select group of high-skilled workers and a growing number of permanently displaced workers, with the latter facing limited professional, economic and territorial opportunities in an increasingly globalised and digitised world. The debate in this regard has been freshly stimulated by the publication of a much cited and highly contested working paper quantifying prospective human redundancy due to susceptibility to computerisation. As Frey and Osborne put it, 47 per cent of the total employment in the United States is vulnerable to automation 'relatively soon, perhaps over the next decade or two'.[38] More than 700 occupations were studied by assessing the likelihood that a given occupation will be affected and eventually replaced by advanced machinery such as AI-driven applications, with jobs in logistics, production and administrative support being found to be particularly exposed. This exercise has been repeated with many adjustments and country- or sector-specific adaptations, and several authors have shared similarly sinister messages.[39]

From the vantage point of the present, such pessimistic predictions have not corresponded to actual developments. Perhaps unwillingly, the authors overestimated how quickly and profoundly machines would take over. In fact, they predicted that AI would be increasingly capable of executing even non-routine cognitive activities such as financial compliance checks, medical diagnostics and legal writing. Over the years, the methodology applied by Frey and Osborne has been strongly criticised: occupations considered to be at high risk often remain responsible for a substantial share of tasks that are almost impossible (or too costly and difficult) to automate. Moreover, the likelihood of substitution does not always result in the most obvious consequence. This linear extrapolation appears to overlook the principle of comparative advantage as well as the social organisation of the production process. Being concerned merely with the actual or potential speed at which technology performance improves, a purely numerical approach says very little or nothing about the qualitative aspects of a change whose contours are extremely complex to forecast.

Considering the variety of workers' tasks within even a single occupation, instead of the average task content of all jobs within each occupation, several authors have re-evaluated the original estimate and claimed that, on average across the 21 Organisation for Economic Co-operation and Development (OECD) countries, only approximately 9 per cent of jobs face the automability risk.[40] More importantly, 44 per cent of employed people will soon experience a radical change in their work-related tasks. Indeed, the effect of the widespread recourse to digital technology 'will be felt more in the content of work, rather than in its volume'.[41]

When assessing the risk of automation, recent studies have focused on a single task rather than an entire occupation, which is in line with the universally acclaimed 'task-based approach'.[42] Other studies have applied the approach adopted by Autor and his

[38] CB Frey and MA Osborne, 'The Future of Employment: How Susceptible Are Jobs to Computerisation?' (2017) 114 *Technological Forecasting and Social Change* 254.

[39] M Ford, *Rise of the Robots: Technology and the Threat of a Jobless Future* (New York, Basic Books, 2015).

[40] M Arntz, T Gregory and U Zierahn, *The Risk of Automation for Jobs in OECD Countries: A Comparative Analysis* (2016) Paris, OECD Social, Employment and Migration Working Papers No 189. See also J Manyika et al, *A Future That Works: Automation, Employment, and Productivity* (McKinsey Global Institute, 2017).

[41] Spencer et al (n 16).

[42] DH Autor, 'The "Task Approach" to Labor Markets: An Overview' (2013) Cambridge, Centre for Business Research, NBER Working Paper No 18711.

co-authors, showing that occupations are far more multifaceted than previously assumed. In fact, occupations involve the performance of a bundle of tasks,[43] not all of which may be at risk of substitutability by machines. The task-based approach dramatically reduces the (over)estimated impact of automation. An ample amount of work remains difficult to mechanise. It involves tasks that require a mixture of skills, including abstraction, imaginative capacity, critical thinking, charismatic acumen, analytical judgement, common sense, physical dexterity and craftsmanship.[44] Humans can perform many valuable activities that are beyond the reach of technology or specialise in non-automatable niches within their profession. While the direct impact of automation intended to foster the productivity-enhancing process might be job-destroying, innovations leading to the partial automation of a given task or lower prices and new products have the 'spillover' potential to trigger new economic activities and create several jobs to replace those that are lost (with a net positive effect at the aggregate level).[45]

Conversely, the catastrophist belief discussed above has been dubbed the 'Lump of labour fallacy', a misguided interpretation given that there is no static lump of labour, as the amount of available work can, at least in theory, increase without quantitative limits or, rather, workers can be soaked up by different industries and specialise in new and complementary tasks.[46] This view has gained support in mainstream economics, although it is taking a long time to establish itself as a significant fact among lawmakers.

In summary, there are a number of overwhelming limits to automation. The first is connected to the difficulty of unpacking and programming activities that may seem trivial yet involve a considerable deal of tacit expertise. The substitutability of human tasks is, therefore, challenging since intellectual and manual activities are relatively hard to teach to computers and robots. Second, robots and cobots are still far from becoming mainstream in many jobs in which human labour continues to be preferred, mainly due to the comparatively low cost and significant practical challenges involved in their automation. The third limit to automation is particularly worrying, as it depends on the large availability of poorly paid jobs. A gradual yet seemingly inexorable process whereby workers are rendered interchangeable, expendable or fungible constitutes a valid alternative to full automation. This limit also brings into sharp focus a pressing issue, namely that of potential realisation. Indeed, the key question is not simply 'whether a job can be mechanised but if it is economically worthwhile given the cheap labour available'.[47] It is surely no coincidence that, in the era of disruptive technologies, we are witnessing the proliferation of bad jobs rather than seeing them disappear due to automation.[48]

[43] DH Autor, F Levy and RJ Murnane, 'The Skill Content of Recent Technological Change: An Empirical Exploration' (2003) 118 *Quarterly Journal of Economics* 1279.

[44] They draw upon 'tacit' knowledge that cannot be codified. See M Polanyi, *The Tacit Dimension* (Chicago, IL, University of Chicago Press, 2009).

[45] J Mokyr, C Vickers and NL Ziebarth, 'The History of Technological Anxiety and the Future of Economic Growth: Is This Time Different?' (2015) 29 *Journal of Economic Perspectives* 31. See also D Acemoglu and P Restrepo, 'Robots and Jobs: Evidence from US Labor Markets' (2017) Cambridge, Centre for Business Research, NBER Working Paper No 23285.

[46] DH Autor, 'Why Are There Still So Many Jobs? The History and Future of Workplace Automation' (2015) 29 *The Journal of Economic Perspectives* 3.

[47] P Fleming, 'Robots and Organization Studies: Why Robots Might Not Want to Steal Your Job' (2019) 40 *Organization Studies* 23, 28.

[48] Raisch and Krakowski (n 3).

Worse still, the large availability of cheap and under-protected labour may lead to a reduction in employment by reducing the incentive for businesses to innovate.

To date, much less emphasis has been placed on the quality and content of the jobs that will outlive digital automation.[49] Ultimately, the automation debate fails to grasp the current practices within AI-modulated workplaces, particularly for those in low-wage occupations and sectors. Today, workers face a routine-biased transformation that is wiping out the more repetitive mid-level tasks in clerical occupations and on factory floors. At the same time, labour markets worldwide are experiencing simultaneous growth at the bottom and top of the skill distribution accompanied by the substantial contraction of middle-skill jobs, which is leading to growing polarisation. Game-changing technologies 'hollow out' the distribution of jobs into either high-paying skilled positions or low-paying routine positions through the destruction of jobs in the middle. Indeed, the main threat to labour is the slow and persistent downward pressure placed on the value and availability of work.[50] As 'automation is thus part of a larger menu of options by which those who own or manage capital seek to maximise their returns … seeking more profitable ways to produce other goods and services',[51] it is essential to focus on the cases in which automation is not economically viable or technically possible. Such businesses will most likely be able to organise, monitor and discipline workers in relation to their task performance in an unprecedented and stricter manner than before, which will prove detrimental.[52]

This theme represents the central focus of the following section, which considers the most popular target of automation: decision-making tasks.

## III. From Automation to Augmentation: Redefining Power Dynamics at Work

While it is largely agreed that technology is not rendering human labour redundant, its effects on the content and quality of jobs remain poorly understood. Unsurprisingly, power augmentation efforts are 'less attention grabbing than full job automation',[53] as they cause iterative and uneven shifts to management processes and jobs. In today's work contexts, people are often still working alongside machines or, more recently, with AI-enabled tools and algorithms.[54] This section examines the role played by digital automation at the level of workplace interactions, where it takes the form of complementarity

[49] De Stefano, '"Negotiating the Algorithm"' (n 21).

[50] A specific division of labour has been and remains the condition associated with the possibility of digital automation. See Eurofound, *Automation, Digitisation and Platforms: Implications for Work and Employment* (Luxembourg, Publications Office of the European Union, 2018).

[51] Estlund, 'What Should We Do After Work?' (n 22).

[52] M Ivanova, J Bronowicka, E Kocher and A Degner, 'The App as a Boss? Control and Autonomy in Application-Based Management' (2018) 2 *Arbeit, Grenze, Fluss, Work in Progress interdisziplinärer Arbeitsforschung*.

[53] B Rogers, 'The Law and Political Economy of Workplace Technological Change' (2020) 55 *Harvard CR–CLL Review* 532, 563.

[54] A Taylor, 'The Automation Charade' *Logic* (1 August 2018), available at: logicmag.io/failure/the-automation-charade/.

with or substitution for directional roles traditionally played by employers. To date, this scenario has only been considered from a limited perspective whereby human actions are 'supported with augmenting technologies that are related to perceiving, affecting, or cognitively processing the world and information around the user'.[55] By contrast, the following paragraphs examine the potential delegation of managerial powers to technological tools.[56] The hypothesis here is that machines, algorithms and platforms have the potential to reinforce (rather than replace) human workers, particularly in relation to executive tasks and strategic decisions. Paradoxically, modern technologies deployed for the hiring, scheduling, promoting and firing of workers are both potentiating the role of decision-makers and distancing them from decisions, thereby diluting liabilities and confounding responsibilities.

A growing body of evidence shows that downward pressure is leading to workforce homogenisation and deskilling, which can both be considered enabling factors in terms of the introduction of automated decision-making systems.[57] This triggers a process of simultaneous regimentation, parcellisation and uniformisation of work, which is compounded by the risk of harm, thereby partially disproving popular theories according to which automation should abolish highly demanding and psychosocially dangerous jobs.[58] While skill specialisation has often been cited as the foundation of modern economic growth,[59] workers are increasingly forced to comply with standardised rules in constrained environments, reproducing the most basic precepts of Taylorism.[60] In this perverse cycle, once work is stripped of its abstract and creative components, it rapidly becomes outsourceable either to individuals without extensive training or to dysfunctional machines fed by 'invisible workers'.[61] In the latter case, human intervention is often confined to tasks such as supervising algorithms, fixing errors, handling exceptions or even personifying machines.[62] Such task impoverishment represents a distortionary incentive for broader substitution. Platform work is yet another illustrative example of what the fragmentation of activities into simple tasks, when coupled with relentless feedback systems, ferocious self-regulation and 'organised irresponsibility' on the part of the employing entity, can entail.[63] The lessons learned through comprehensive evaluations of work organisation in this area facilitate a more comprehensive and systematic understanding of the practices of managerial augmentation.

[55] R Raisamo et al, 'Human Augmentation: Past, Present and Future' (2019) 131 *International Journal of Human-Computer Studies* 131. The 'augmentation' phrase was originally adopted in the technology design field and then imported to 'describe mediated communication processes which incorporate both the affordances of digital tech and the established feature of face-to-face interaction'.

[56] A Aneesh, 'Global Labor: Algocratic Modes of Organization' (2009) 27 *Sociological Theory* 347.

[57] JG Harris and TH Davenport, 'Automated Decision Making Comes of Age' (2005) 46 *MIT Sloan Management Review* 2.

[58] A Gilbert and A Thomas, *The Amazonian Era: How Algorithmic Systems are Eroding Good Work* (London, Institute for the Future of Work, 2021).

[59] A Smith, *The Wealth of Nations* (London, W Strahan and T Cadell, 1776).

[60] M Crowley, D Tope, LJ Chamberlain and R Hodson, 'Neo-Taylorism at Work: Occupational Change in the Post-Fordist Era' (2010) 57 *Social Problems* 421.

[61] A Casilli, *En attendant les robots-Enquête sur le travail du clic* (Paris, Média Diffusion, 2019).

[62] J Smids, S Nyholm and H Berkers, 'Robots in the Workplace: A Threat to – or Opportunity for – Meaningful Work?' (2020) 33 *Philosophy & Technology* 503.

[63] H Collins, 'A Review of The Concept of The Employer by Dr Jeremias Prassl' (*Labour Law Blog*, University of Oxford, Faculty of Law, 10 November 2015), available at: bit.ly/2Lp6PcG.

## A. Disentangling the Premises and Promises of Hierarchical Powers

An overview of the distinctive features of the employment relationship could offer an important means of verifying the assumption of the current technological augmentation of managerial prerogatives.[64] Scholars have long sought to untangle the foundations of the 'rights or authority to organize and direct men, machinery, materials, and money in order to achieve the objectives of the enterprise'.[65] However, the fact is often overlooked that a private party is legitimately entitled to exercise its unilateral authority over the other contracting party in an employment relationship. This theme has regained traction due to the increasing potential of modern technologies. More recently, this peculiar yet underestimated trait of the employment contract has become topical alongside escalating litigation concerning the professional status of workers engaged in the so-called 'gig economy'.[66] Technical subordination is the effect of the exercise of fully-fledged command-and-control power. This factual condition is universally considered to be a meta-indicator, part of a comprehensive multifactorial test that may aid in proving the existence of an employment relationship. The dyadic relationship between domination and subordination has prompted renewed interest in the legal determinants of employment in the context of the concurrent thinning of canonical parameters and stiffening of new elements of supremacy.

Yet, this examination has understandably been conducted on a case-by-case basis and from the workers' perspective in an effort to solve the legal conundrum of their appropriate status classification.[67] Adams-Prassl bemoaned the fact that the concept of the employer has been neglected in both judicial and academic discussions or, occasionally, considered in a residual fashion from a purely contractual perspective.[68] Despite the emergence of multilateral arrangements and complex corporate settings placing pressure on the unitary notion of the employer and impairing the ascription of employment-related responsibilities,[69] managerial coordination has stimulated a less

[64] This section draws and expands on Aloisi and De Stefano, 'Regulation and the Future of Work' (n 36).

[65] S Young, 'The Question of Managerial Prerogatives' (1963) 16 *ILR Review* 240, 241.

[66] For a comprehensive overview, see E Kocher, *Digital Work Platforms at the Interface of Labour Law. Regulating Market Organisers* (Oxford, Hart Publishing, 2022) and chapters in part II of this volume.

[67] The Court of Justice of the European Union has repeatedly held that 'the essential feature of an employment relationship is that, for a certain period of time, a person performs services for and *under the direction* of another person, in return for which he receives remuneration' (emphasis added). Case 216/15 *Betriebsrat der Ruhrlandklinik v Ruhrlandklinik* ECLI:EU:C:2016:883 [2016]. See also N Kountouris, 'The Concept of "Worker" in European Labour Law: Fragmentation, Autonomy and Scope' (2018) 47 *Industrial Law Journal* 192; E Menegatti, 'Taking EU Labour Law Beyond the Employment Contract: The Role Played by the European Court of Justice' (2020) 11 *European Labour Law Journal* 26; S Deakin, 'The Comparative Evolution of the Employment Relationship' in G Davidov and B Langille (eds), *Boundaries and Frontiers of Labour Law* (Oxford, Hart Publishing, 2006).

[68] J Prassl, *The Concept of the Employer* (Oxford, Oxford University Press, 2015). There are notable exceptions, however. See also L Corazza and O Razzolini, 'Who is an Employer?' (2014) Centre for the Study of European Labour Law, Working Paper "Massimo D'Antona" INT–110/2014; S Deakin, 'The Complexities of the Employing Enterprise' in G Davidov and B Langille (eds), *Boundaries and Frontiers of Labour Law* (Oxford, Hart Publishing, 2006).

[69] S Vallas and JB Schor, 'What Do Platforms Do? Understanding the Gig Economy' (2020) 46 *Annual Review of Sociology* 16.

intense debate than the thorny issue of the scope of employment.[70] This section emphasises that, while strictly intertwined, the notion of employment and the concept (or, even better, the functions) of the employer should be addressed separately. Indeed, their symbiotic interconnection could hamper the sound interpretation and proper mapping of the evolution of the latter entity. Thus, it would be beneficial to insulate managerial prerogatives from the current 'misclassification' quandary. The heavy theoretical baggage might overshadow current variations in such powers and, while courts are often guided by remedial logic in the case of law avoidance, this focus fails to successfully grasp the intensification and diffusion of employer prerogatives. This recalibration may help to establish a more encompassing understanding of the power relationships at work.

It is interesting to consider this dynamic tension from the employing entity's perspective. Drawing on multidisciplinary insights, it must be acknowledged that the legal authority to direct an enterprise has always been considered functional in relation to attaining genuine organisational objectives. Edwards explained how workplaces are ruled from the top down because hierarchies are far more profitable than one-off decentralised arrangements.[71] Managerial prerogatives can be conventionally unboxed into three complementary powers: direction, evaluation and discipline. Direction is defined as setting 'what needs to be done' in what order and time frame, evaluation consists of supervising and assessing workers' performance, while discipline illustrates the apparatus for administering sanctions and rewards, eliciting collaboration and enforcing compliance.[72] Whatever the means used to wield them, such powers are strictly intertwined and should be seen as a functional continuum. Due to being 'overlapping and complementary',[73] they operate jointly and in pursuit of the efficient coordination of economic factors and productive activities.[74] Practically speaking, employee monitoring is conducted to verify whether workers are abiding by instructions and to ensure the virtuous correspondence between specific tasks and larger projects.[75] In a similar vein, disciplinary power is exercised to discourage defiance and punish misdemeanours while influencing behaviours 'by example'.[76]

As an employment contract is by default expected to be lasting, reaching endless agreements on all aspects of it would prove a titanic task, not to mention the need to amend the agreed upon terms to adjust production to meet constantly changing internal needs and external fluctuations. The various theories of relational contracts have clarified that superior–subordinate arrangements are necessarily incomplete, as it would be impossible to specify all contingencies in advance.[77] Such incompleteness may not

[70] S Deakin, 'The Changing Concept of the "Employer" in Labour Law' (2001) 30 *Industrial Law Journal* 72. See also H Collins, 'Ascription of Legal Responsibility to Groups in Complex Patterns of Economic Integration' (1990) 53 *Modern Law Review* 731.

[71] R Edwards, *Contested Terrain: The Transformation of the Workplace in the Twentieth Century* (New York, Basic Books, 1982).

[72] ibid.

[73] Deakin, 'The Changing Concept of the "Employer" in Labour Law' (n 70).

[74] L Tebano, *Lavoro, potere direttivo e trasformazioni organizzative* (Naples, Editoriale Scientifica, 2020). See also M Persiani, *Contratto di lavoro e organizzazione* (Milan, Giuffrè, 1966).

[75] A Topo and Razzolini, 'The Boundaries of the Employer's Power to Control Employees in the ICTs Age' (2018) 39 *Comparative Labor Law & Policy Journal* 389.

[76] K Ball, 'Workplace Surveillance: An Overview' (2010) 51 *Labor History* 87.

[77] CJ Goetz and RE Scott, 'Principles of Relational Contracts' (1981) 67 *Virginia Law Review* 1089. See also U Muehlberger, 'Hierarchies, Relational Contracts and New Forms of Outsourcing' (Torino, ICER Working

be cost-effective. Coase observed that, within a firm, 'market transactions are eliminated' and replaced with 'the entrepreneur-coordinator, who directs the production'.[78] As argued elsewhere,[79] transaction costs, namely the costs incurred when it comes to obtaining information, bargaining regarding contractual terms, securing consent and enforcing agreements, are reduced within the firm because formal, hegemonic powers replace time-consuming negotiation and price-mechanism governance. Authority is unmistakably vested in the person of the employer, who commonly (and implicitly) transfers their prerogatives to a group of managers and supervisors who are subject to the upstream power despite their ample room to manoeuvre. This private governance structure, which is seen as 'a miniature legal system' with neat separation between task definers and task executors,[80] has traditionally been used to elucidate the vital socio-economic functions of the employment relationship.

The contract of employment reserves for the employer 'a space for discretion in decision-making, beyond any express agreement for the performance of the contract'.[81] The source of this authority is the legal framework, which acknowledges a pre-existing situation of power. Indeed, legislation aims to streamline production by legitimising the prerogative to change the terms without the consent of the contractual debtor (ie, the worker).[82] The French Labour Code states that 'working time is the time during which the employee is at the employer's disposal and complies with her directives'.[83] In Italy, Article 2086 of the Civil Code provides that 'the entrepreneur is the head of the business and her collaborators hierarchically depend on her'.[84] Simultaneously, according to Article 2104, 'the employee must also observe the instructions for the work execution given by the entrepreneur and by her collaborators (managers and supervisors)'. According to the gravity of the infringement, failure to fulfil the duty of loyalty and obedience may give rise to the application of disciplinary sanctions. In Spain, the personal ambit of the application of the Workers' Statute is defined as follows: 'workers who voluntarily provide their paid services on behalf of others and within the scope of organisation and management of another natural or legal person, called employer

Paper No 22, 2005); OE Williamson, *The Economic Institutions of Capitalism: Firms, Markets, Relational Contracting* (New York, Free Press, 1985).

[78] RH Coase, 'The Nature of the Firm' (1937) 16 *Economica* 386, 388.

[79] A Aloisi, 'Hierarchies Without Firms? Vertical Disintegration, Outsourcing and the Nature of the Platform' (2020) 8 *Quaderni del Premio Giorgio Rota* 11.

[80] H Collins, 'Market Power, Bureaucratic Power, and the Contract of Employment' (1986) 15 *Industrial Law Journal* 1.

[81] S Deakin, *The Many Futures of the Contract of Employment* (Cambridge, ESRC Centre for Business Research, University of Cambridge, 2000).

[82] D Landes, *The Unbound Prometheus: Technological Change and Industrial Development in Western Europe from 1750 to the Present* (Cambridge, Cambridge University Press, 1969). Landes argues that the colocation of workers in factories started occurring before the advent of mechanical infrastructure in an effort to exercise organisational power in a more efficient way than in the case of fragmented and less controllable home-based work.

[83] Article L3121-1, modifié par Loi n° 2016-1088 du 8 août 2016 – art 8 (V). In the absence of a statutory definition of employment, the French Supreme Court stated that 'the relationship of subordination is characterised by the performance of work under the authority of an employer who has the power to give orders and directives, to control their execution and to sanction the breaches of her subordinate'. Cour de Cassation, Chambre sociale, du 13 novembre 1996, 94-13.187. See also G Auzero, D Baugard and E Dockès, *Droit du travail* (Paris, Dalloz, 2021).

[84] A Perulli, 'Il potere direttivo dell'imprenditore. Funzioni e limiti' (2002) 16 *Lavoro e diritto* 397. See also S Sciarra, 'Diritti e poteri nei luoghi di lavoro. Una lettura dello Statuto dei lavoratori nel tempo della pandemia' (2021) 293 *Moneta e Credito* 11.

or entrepreneur'.[85] Relatedly, Article 5(c) states that '[workers must] comply with the orders and instructions issued by the employer in the regular exercise of his managerial powers'.[86]

Employers and their delegates can observe, redeploy and evaluate work on a minute-by-minute basis and in terms of its microscopic components down to the last observable movement. In short, employers rule the workforce and the workplace. Despite differing domestic specificities, a relatively standard model can be found across jurisdictions in both civil and common law systems.[87] Due to a single scheme that encapsulates a set of developmental rules and conditions, the employee consents to the employer's authority and agrees to follow the orders promulgated by managers in a 'zone of acceptance'.[88] Within this area of constructive ambiguity, workers can be transferred to different locations, assigned to new and distinct tasks, assessed, reprimanded and even dismissed as long as procedural and substantive rules are followed. Unilateral managerial variations should be exercised reasonably and rationally, pursuing the interests of the enterprise without biases or irrelevant considerations. By providing firms with broad, albeit not completely unfettered or arbitrary, discretionary power, this arrangement nurtures functional flexibility, which spurs on adaptability and versatility,[89] thereby guaranteeing responsiveness to the ever-changing nature of socio-economic contexts.

Several studies, not necessarily in the employment law field, have focused on the power dynamics engendered by this legal template.[90] For instance, Anderson compared the employment relationship to the vertical rapport between public institutions and citizens. From a philosophical perspective, according to this model, those 'governed are kept out of decision-making',[91] not infrequently in a despotic way, resulting in a 'democratic deficit'.[92] The pervasiveness of this open-ended authority is echoed in Collins' studies, which describe the authoritarian structure 'that appears to be at odds with the commitment in liberal societies to values such as liberty, equal respect, respect for privacy'.[93] While it is true that the most irritating aspects of domination, including the right to change the normative situation of the employee and the requirement that

[85] Real Decreto Legislativo 2/2015, de 23 de octubre, por el que se aprueba el texto refundido de la Ley del Estatuto de los Trabajadores.

[86] Article 20 ('1. The worker must carry out the agreed work under the direction of the employer or her delegates. 2. Fulfilling the obligation to work assumed in the contract, the worker owes the employer the diligence and collaboration in the work established by the legal provisions, the collective agreements and the orders or instructions adopted in the regular exercise of [the employer's] powers and, failing that, by the uses and customs … 3. The employer may adopt the most appropriate measures of surveillance and control to verify compliance by the worker of her obligations and duties').

[87] G Racabi, 'Abolish the Employer Prerogative, Unleash Work Law' (2022) 43 *Berkeley Journal of Employment and Labor Law* 79. See also R Nielsen, *Employers' Prerogatives: In a European and Nordic Perspective* (Copenhagen, Handelshøjskolens Forlag, 1996).

[88] HA Simon, 'Organizations and Markets' (1991) 5 *Journal of Economic Perspectives* 25.

[89] M Rönnmar, 'The Managerial Prerogative and the Employee's Obligation to Work: Comparative Perspectives on Functional Flexibility' (2006) 35 *Industrial Law Journal* 56.

[90] Collins, 'Market Power, Bureaucratic Power, and the Contract of Employment' (n 80).

[91] E Anderson, *Private Government* (Princeton, NJ, Princeton University Press, 2017) 45.

[92] G Davidov, 'The Three Axes of Employment Relationships: A Characterization of Workers in Need of Protection' (2017) 52 *University of Toronto Law Journal* 357. See also A Gorz, 'The Tyranny of the Factory: Today and Tomorrow (1973) 16 *Telos* 61.

[93] H Collins, 'Is the Contract of Employment Illiberal?' in H Collins, G Lester and V Mantouvalou (eds), *Philosophical Foundations of Labour Law* (Oxford, Oxford University Press, 2018) 48.

workers obey all instructions to the letter, have been mitigated in modern societies, ongoing tectonic shifts call into question the capability, role and significance of employment-related constraints on managerial prerogatives and the conditioned authority of non-human bosses.

Given the unbalanced bargaining power and information asymmetries, employment protection legislation limits the employer's legal powers of command. The task of labour regulation is actually twofold, as it both allows for and constrains autonomous norm creation.[94] In short, the law and worker representatives are expected to regulate, support and restrain the power of management. Upon closer inspection, this model aims to prevent abuses of managerial power by rationalising the managerial prerogative to safeguard human dignity and autonomy.[95] To offer a cursory overview, in most European Union (EU) jurisdictions, case law has identified professionalism as an intrinsic limit to the power to change duties, several provisions prevent the infringement of workers' privacy when it comes to monitoring, and mandatory rules against unfair dismissal apply.[96] A vast array of rules are mobilised to temper and tone down the level of capricious decision-making.[97] While labour law is designed to eradicate the imperfections typical of human bosses, technologies profoundly displace and disrupt this set of counterweights. For instance, algorithmic management represents a stark illustration of the difficulties associated with limiting employers' exuberance.[98] Moreover, there has been non-negligible movement from centralised decision-making towards scattered, outsourced centres of power, often involving co-workers and even customers.[99] In a nutshell, power is now shedding its skin.

## B. Addressing the *Boss Ex Machina*, the Marvel and the Menace of Power Expansion

Most cases concerning the existence of 'direction' have dealt with this defining element from the perspective of the 'on/off' toggle of employee status, thereby addressing the dilemma using a binary approach. Platform workers have been found to be employed by the relevant company when the claimants have succeeded in demonstrating the exercise

[94] D Dukes, 'Constitutionalizing Employment Relations: Sinzheimer, Kahn-Freund, and the Role of Labour Law' (2008) 35 *Journal of Law and Society* 341.

[95] S Deakin and F Wilkinson, *The Law of the Labour Market: Industrialization, Employment, and Legal Evolution* (Oxford, Oxford University Press, 2005). See also H Collins, 'Market Power, Bureaucratic Power, and the Contract of Employment' (1986) 15 *Industrial Law Journal* 1.

[96] C158 – Termination of Employment Convention, 1982 (No 158); Article 24 European Social Charter (Revised); Article 30 Charter of Fundamental Rights of the European Union (2000/C 364/01). See also P Collins, 'Automated Dismissal Decisions, Data Protection and The Law of Unfair Dismissal' (*UK Labour Law Blog*, 19 October 2021), available at: www.bit.ly/3oaNfnu.

[97] D Cabrelli and R Zahn, 'Theories of Domination and Labour Law: An Alternative Conception for Intervention?' (2017) 33 *International Journal of Comparative Labour Law and Industrial Relations* 339.

[98] A Rosenblat and L Stark, 'Algorithmic Labor and Information Asymmetries: A Case Study of Uber's Drivers' (2016) 10 *International Journal of Communication* 3758.

[99] K Levy and S Barocas, 'Refractive Surveillance: Monitoring Customers to Manage Workers' (2018) 12 *International Journal of Communication* 23.

of organisational prerogatives by management, either directly or indirectly, including through technological devices. In the well-known Uber case, Advocate General Szpunar argued that

> indirect control [not exercised in the context of a traditional employer–employee relationship] based on financial incentives and decentralised passenger-led ratings, with a scale effect, makes it possible to manage in a way that is just as, if not more, effective than management based on formal orders given by an employer to his employees and direct control over the carrying out of such orders.[100]

Very little is currently known about the extent, form and scope of this power or about the 'potential flaws and drawbacks associated with machine decision-making, and systematic and effective institutional mechanisms to guard against them'.[101] The present section aims to fill this gap in the literature. From a practical perspective, the findings could offer meaningful resources for judges and litigators. More importantly, developing a faithful representation of managerial authority throughout the entire lifecycle of working relationships represents a valuable starting point in the process of enforcing and reinforcing limits in both innovative and conventional sectors of the labour market.

Today, workers in manufacturing and office-based occupations can receive orders from an automated system, be constantly monitored by Global Positioning System (GPS) trackers or digital log-stamps, and be dismissed for not achieving the goals set by computational tools measuring average targets and clients' level of satisfaction, with little if any possibility of objection and rectification. Many workers operate within a system based on incentives and penalties, which are defined on the basis of granular data collected from myriad sources through digital tools or feedback from final clients and colleagues.[102] Constant evaluation renders this problem even more acute. Additionally, the pandemic has prompted the adoption of employee-monitoring software in relation to both front line and remote workers in an effort to fine-tune work processes, implement distancing requirements and uphold productivity. Moreover, this invasion has strengthened the myth that decisions made by means of mathematical processing could reduce the weight of human subjectivity, thereby resulting in fairer and more accountable outcomes. Precisely because employer prerogatives are mutually reinforcing, this section contends that the expansion of surveillance impacts the nature and scope of the organisation and its disciplinary prerogatives. This leads to a 'genetic variation' in terms of the administration of workplace interactions, representing 'as much a technical challenge as it is a legal one'.[103]

[100] Opinion of Advocate General Szpunar delivered on 11 May 2017, Case C-434/15 *Asociación Profesional Élite Taxi v Uber Systems Spain* ECLI:EU:C:2017:364 [2017], para 52.

[101] K Yeung, 'Why Worry about Decision-Making by Machine?' in K Yeung and M Lodge (eds), *Algorithmic Regulation* (Oxford, Oxford University Press, 2019) 21, 23.

[102] MT Bodie, MA Cherry, ML McCormick and J Tang, 'The Law and Policy of People Analytics' (2016) 88 *University of Colorado Law Review* 961. See also C Safak and J Farrar, 'Managed by Bots: Data-Driven Exploitation in the Gig Economy' (London, Worker Info Exchanges, 2021), available at: www.workerinfoexchange.org/wie-report-managed-by-bots.

[103] J Adams-Prassl, 'When Your Boss Comes Home: Three Fault Lines for the Future of Work in the Age of Automation, AI, and COVID-19' (2020) *Ethics of AI in Context* 1. See also Jeremias Adams-Prassl, ch 12 in this volume.

This variation can be considered from various perspectives. First, while the literature in the field of omnipresent AI-enabled employee monitoring has recently blossomed,[104] it would be misleading to consider these practices as representing a mere threat to privacy rights. Indeed, something more structural is taking place. What is generally omitted from the story is that surveillance, which is now deeply ingrained in all workplaces,[105] is only one of many complex jigsaw pieces and, further, is not exercised per se.[106] Conversely, it is instrumental in allocating decision-making prerogatives to separate agents, either human or mechanic – an activity that also entails the dispossession of workers' autonomy. At the same time, monitoring informs the imposition of sanctions. In addition, the boss–worker pyramid traditionally embedded within a centralised organisation is now spreading across the labour market, without the corresponding entitlements compensating for the lack of agency enshrined in the employment relationship. Such aggrandisement of power distorts the already weakened boundaries between categories. The hallmarks of the employment relationship, ie, the possibility of dictating terms, appraising compliance and sanctioning noncompliance, are now shared features in several professional contexts. This results in legal uncertainty triggered by the diffusion of managerial prerogatives across the full spectrum of contractual arrangements.

Thus, it is through the prism of workplace governance that the introduction of new technologies ought to be viewed. While platforms operating in the last-mile logistics sector or exchanging back-office tasks have been accused of abandoning employer obligations and avoiding the associated costs (thanks to a panoply of strategies, the most common of which is the adoption of debatable self-employment formats), their legacy lies in the intensification of the power to instruct workers, assess their performance and downgrade their profile due wholly or partly to automated decision-making systems. Interestingly, Estlund has reasoned that autocratic control has now been abandoned in favour of alternative arrangements, in a way challenging traditional assumptions that employees are preferred over external suppliers due to the wide managerial latitude afforded by this legal template.[107] While it is true that 'employers are increasingly choosing to forego their dictatorial power over workers in favour of more indirect but cost-effective means',[108] managerial prerogatives are now spilling over beyond the realm of the contract of employment, with businesses also exercising intense direction, monitoring and disciplinary powers in relation to self-employed workers and external providers.

Managerial prerogatives are being radically magnified in their extent and extended in their scope beyond the often blurred (legal, temporal and spatial) confines of employment.[109] While the apparent goal of this aggrandisement of power is not necessarily to

[104] Ball (n 76); I Ajunwa, K Crawford and J Schultz, 'Limitless Worker Surveillance' (2017) 105 *California Law Review* 735. See also O Solon, 'Big Brother Isn't Just Watching: Workplace Surveillance Can Track Your Every Move' *Guardian* (6 November 2017), available at: bit.ly/3iVFos6.

[105] A Nguyen, *The Constant Boss: Work Under Digital Surveillance* (New York, Data & Society Research Institute, 2021), available at: www.apo.org.au/node/312352.

[106] M Martinez and MP Iacono, 'Dealing with Critical IS Research: Artifacts, Drifts, Electronic Panopticon and Illusions of Empowerment' in R Baskerville, M De Marco and P Spagnoletti (eds), *Designing Organizational Systems* (New York, Springer, 2013) 83.

[107] C Estlund, 'Rethinking Autocracy at Work' (2017) 131 *Harvard Law Review* 795.

[108] ibid.

[109] V De Stefano. '"Masters and Servers": Collective Labour Rights and Private Government in the Contemporary World of Work' (2020) 36 *International Journal of Comparative Labour Law and Industrial Relations* 425.

dodge legal obligations,[110] the hybridisation makes it possible for companies to resort to effective means of exercising control 'in a guise that courts, armed with conventional metrics for employment vs independent contracting, may not recognize'.[111] When centrifugal forces are matched by an intensification of power and an extensification of its impact,[112] the condition of workers' perennial subordination may suffer the looming consequences of this profound shift. Nowadays, people analytics and algorithmic governance, methods aimed at running a business in a hyper-efficient and data-driven way, are salient instantiations of new evidence-based HRM practices, which I boil down into the *boss ex machina* formula.[113] Various groups of workers are on the verge of experiencing not replacement by machines but treatment as robots. Sectoral investigations and anecdotal reports abound, although we lack a comprehensive and systematic account that could help to explain whether the transformation of managerial prerogatives is quantitative (determined by the increase in agents embodying authority) or qualitative (affecting the very nature of power).[114]

In the past, different forms of digital surveillance were used to make classifications and identify workflow bottlenecks or deviant conduct. Essentially, the use of data was eminently *descriptive*, being nothing more than a sometimes chaotic, concise and imprecise digital representation of numbers and statistics used to portray reality. Now, a deeper reliance on inferential analytics, which is favoured by machine learning, helps managers to detect patterns and generate predictions concerning team dynamics, future behaviours and career prospects thanks to probabilistic evaluations of data sets.[115] This role can be defined as *predictive*, as forecasts are performed in accordance with a set of programmed objectives that rely on advanced statistical modelling to identify patterns or correlations within data in order to make informed HRM decisions regarding quotidian issues.[116] At the same time, the predominant system of tacit penalty and reward is used to enforce compliance, thereby subtly reconfiguring interactions with near-perfect information, which represents the most advanced yet still under-researched facet of algorithmic governance. Potent data-driven policies aim to subtly change human conduct. Workers' choice is severely constrained by *prescriptive* or *pre-emptive* algorithmic tools that 'shap[e] an environment in which there are no alternatives to performing

[110] Adams-Prassl, 'When Your Boss Comes Home' (n 103).

[111] Estlund, 'Rethinking Autocracy at Work' (n 107) 821.

[112] D Weil, *The Fissured Workplace: Why Work Became So Bad for So Many and What Can Be Done to Improve It* (Cambridge, MA, Harvard University Press, 2014).

[113] A calque from the Latin expression 'god from the machine'. According to the *Encyclopaedia Britannica*, 'a person or thing that appears or is introduced into a situation suddenly and unexpectedly and provides an artificial or contrived solution to an apparently insoluble difficulty. The term was first used in ancient Greek and Roman drama, where it meant the timely appearance of a god to unravel and resolve the plot. The *deus ex machina* was named for the convention of the god's appearance in the sky, an effect achieved by means of a crane (Greek: *mēchanē*)'. A Aloisi and V De Stefano, *Your Boss is an Algorithm: Artificial Intelligence, Platform Work and Labour* (Oxford, Hart Publishing, 2022).

[114] I Manokha, 'New Means of Workplace Surveillance' *Monthly Review* (1 February 2019), available at: www.bit.ly/3uaShCj.

[115] KC Kellogg, MA Valentine and A Christin, 'Algorithms at Work: The New Contested Terrain of Control' (2020) 14 *Academy of Management Annals* 366.

[116] Gilbert and Thomas (n 58). See also J Meijerink, M Boons, A Keegan and J Marler, 'Algorithmic Human Resource Management: Synthesizing Developments and Cross-Disciplinary Insights on Digital HRM' (2021) *International Journal of Human Resource Management* 1.

the work as prescribed'.[117] In some cases, this model leaves employees with the impression that they own their actions in reality.[118] By applying the same logic with relentless consistency, even bosses that operate through technologies stop being self-reflecting agents.

Both during and after the hiring process, an almost unthinkable number of data points, including contact lists on social media, emails sent, websites visited, cookies and documents in shared repositories, may serve as indicators for personnel management decisions, leading to new forms of anticipatory conformity.[119] Both oppressive and tenuous command-and-control positions are transitioning to the next level in a situation in which digitised systems impose not only rhythms and locations, but remuneration, rewards and penalties.[120] This transformation of managerial prerogatives displaces existing social institutions because most limitations on managerial domination were designed for a pre-digital context, where power was exercised directly or using tools whose reach was far less developed than today. The inadequacy of the systems designed to temper bosses' authority risks frustrating 'the range of normative values and goals pursued by employment law'.[121] This results in the exacerbation of vulnerability, in addition to the complexity of ascribing responsibility when power sources are fragmented and distributed across multiple actors. While technologically encoded to increase standardisation and reduce the risk of human error,[122] it can perpetuate and deepen prior discrimination patterns and generate related harms, such as short-term thinking, loss of human expertise and lock-in effects.[123]

Although human flexibility has been criticised as a source of arbitrariness, it is also expected to promote the 'virtues of human discretion, judgment and agency, which have long been recognised in socio-legal scholarship as vital in overcoming the inevitable imperfection associated with legal rules'.[124] Material workplaces and human bosses are far from perfect; however, the delegation of executive prerogatives to ADMS ends up displacing the wide variety of procedural and substantive norms stemming from legislative intervention and collective negotiation. Although modern legal systems have a wealth of practices for confronting flaws in human decision-making,[125] the rise of 'algorithmic bosses' fundamentally unsettles existing mechanisms. The ongoing and wide-ranging transformations make gaps in protection systems and loopholes in regulations even more palpable.

Under the veneer of innovation, code-based governance systems are too rigid to depart from predetermined solutions as well as being less adaptable than human authority. Their

[117] Aneesh (n 56).

[118] MK Lee, D Kusbit, E Metsky and L Dabbish, 'Working with Machines: The Impact of Algorithmic and Data-Driven Management on Human Workers' Proceedings of the 33rd Annual ACM Conference on Human Factors in Computing Systems (2015) 1603; Fleming (n 47).

[119] Ball (n 76).

[120] A Delfanti, 'Machinic Dispossession and Augmented Despotism: Digital Work in an Amazon Warehouse' (2019) 1 *New Media & Society* 23.

[121] P Collins and J Atkinson, 'Labour Rights, Labour Values and Technology at Work' (Paper presented at the LLRN5 Conference, June 2021).

[122] S Wiblen and JH Marler, 'Digitalised Talent Management and Automated Talent Decisions: The Implications for HR Professionals' (2021) *International Journal of Human Resource Management* 1.

[123] Raisch and Krakowski (n 3).

[124] Yeung, 'Why Worry about Decision-Making by Machine?' (n 101) 29.

[125] ibid.

'accuracy', 'precision' and 'impartiality' guarantee the infinite replication of hidden flaws, biases and disparities without the possibility of halting feedback loops.[126] Hence, not only is assuming the objective or neutral nature of data-driven governance largely disingenuous, it also downplays the importance of existing legal remedies by shifting decisions to a level of presumed non-explicability that impedes objections and contestations. What are the legal strategies for countering autonomous decision-making processes in the workplace and rendering them reasonable, legible and assessable? How can prior authorisation requirements be met when workers freely consent to gamification tools collecting data and then surreptitiously assessing them? What is the role of dismissal regulation when self-employed or non-standard workers can be simply 'discontinued' following negative feedback from disappointed customers? These questions are all worth addressing while technology continues to be adopted and improved.

The routinisation of all management functions evoking an air of infallibility also represents a challenge for firms, especially large-scale companies wherein the chains of command are complex, as it can thwart productivity. Indulging data-centric obsessions pushes workers to satisfy formal requirements that are tracked and assessed through metrics, leaving quality objectives unmet.[127] Continuous performance reviews, unpredictable alterations in terms of task and slot allocation, and real-time nudges foster an environment in which the importance of praising the *boss ex machina* by far exceeds the relevance of delivering meaningful results. At the same time, while making instructions more persuasive, the constant threat of disciplinary action discourages unorthodox initiatives and unanticipated actions, which impairs creativity and promotes subservient behaviours in monolithic workplaces. Such attitudes may lead to burn-out and increased turnover, thereby wasting accrued know-how and the skills developed or improved over time. Disjointed information often leads to illogical HRM solutions. Moreover, from a legal perspective the unpredictability and limited explicability of executive choices made by 'black boxes' cannot insulate employers from responsibilities.[128] Paradoxically, the intricacy of reverse-engineering or documenting decision-making processes amplifies the vulnerability of bosses' legal position, as systems based on presumptions may be in force in courts.

Bosses' authority is not only targeting new subjects, it is also becoming less palpable and more effective, departing from traditional at-a-glance management, including when professional activities are decoupled from the physical workplace premises.[129] This more sophisticated form of power benefits from delayered and flattened bureaucratic hierarchies, with workers being encouraged to indicate their availability, track themselves, rate colleagues and utilise variable scheduling models in gamified environments.[130] Workers

[126] RE Kidwell and R Sprague, 'Electronic Surveillance in the Global Workplace: Laws, Ethics, Research and Practice' (2009) 24 *New Technology, Work and Employment* 194.

[127] T Prasanna, P Cappelli and V Yakubovich, 'Artificial intelligence in human resources management: Challenges and a path forward' (2019) 61 *California Management Review* 15.

[128] F Pasquale, *The Black Box Society: The Secret Algorithms that Control Money and Information* (Cambridge, MA, Harvard University Press, 2015).

[129] G Sewell and L Taskin, 'Out of Sight, Out of Mind in a New World of Work? Autonomy, Control, and Spatiotemporal Scaling in Telework' (2015) 36 *Organization Studies* 1507.

[130] AJ Wood, *Despotism on Demand: How Power Operates in the Flexible Workplace* (Ithaca, NY, Cornell University Press, 2020).

personally contribute to the generation of insights into workplace dynamics, from booking spaces in the case of hot-desk models to identifying less productive moments during the working day. In recent decades, something similar has occurred in the service sector due to the involvement of final clients, customers and shoppers in activities once viewed as part of the core business.[131] Managerial prerogatives have 'mostly moved away from an authoritarian regime, wherein workers were subjected to discreet and predictable surveillance at the hands of employers'.[132] Notably, these practices have now been redesigned to leverage an 'ostensibly participatory character, wherein workers are expected to aid employer[s]' and supervisors in their own administration.[133] The use of these less coercive means of control risks placing workers on an electronic leash,[134] while bosses could then assume decisions to be informed by the wealth of gathered information.

Warehouses, fulfilment centres, logistic hubs, fast food and dark kitchen chains, and cleaning and maintenance services – places where working conditions are physically demanding, and bad-paying jobs coexist with oppressive managerial regimes – have all served as large sites of experimentation. In these industries, despotism predated the arrival of game-changing technologies, although it is now coupled with manipulation strategies that claim workers enjoy greater autonomy. What is perceived as freedom is simply a form of deception based on nudging techniques constantly refining individuals' choice ecosystems. As shown by Yeung, decisional choice contexts are 'intentionally designed in ways that systematically influence human decision-making in particular directions'.[135] In fact, behaviour change is considered most effective when it leaves the person being managed feeling that they own their choices.[136] A highly detailed standard-setting model leads to outcomes considered desirable by those who have the authority to set targets.[137] In this case, technology allows for the realisation of continuous and dynamic adjustments, constantly reconfiguring an individual option architecture, which alters behaviours in a very opaque manner by tailoring inescapable cages. Due to unwritten rules and design features, a gentler version of power facilitates 'nimble, unobtrusive and highly potent' persuasion camouflaged as autonomy, thereby realising the subtlest version of coercion.[138]

The diagnosis of the augmentation of upstream authority reveals the parallel erosion of self-government. As hierarchical pressure mounts, workers end up experiencing a loss of agency and a sense of alienation from their work,[139] which impairs their abstract

[131] U Huws, *Labor in the Global Digital Economy: The Cybertariat Comes of Age* (Hatfield, JSTOR, 2014).

[132] Ajunwa, Crawford and Schultz (n 104).

[133] ibid.

[134] Aneesh (n 56). See also D Lyon, 'The Search for Surveillance Theories' in D Lyon (ed), *Theorizing Surveillance: The Panopticon and Beyond* (Portland, OR, Willan Publishing, 2006) 3.

[135] K Yeung, '"Hypernudge": Big Data as a Mode of Regulation by Design' (2017) 20 *Information, Communication & Society* 118.

[136] Gilbert and Thomas (n 58).

[137] M Stelmaszak Rosa and A Aaltonen, 'As firms collect their data, employees learn to game the system' (*LSE Blog*, 16 January 2020), available at: www.bit.ly/3CSvr6l.

[138] Gilbert and Thomas (n 58). See also B Callaci, *Puppet Entrepreneurship: Technology and Control in Franchised Industries* (New York, Data & Society Research Institute, 2021).

[139] Despite the nuances in terms of their meaning, in this section 'autonomy' and 'agency' are used interchangeably and are intended to refer to the possibility of setting goals and choosing the methods through which they can be achieved.

thinking and inventive contribution while promoting diligent homogeneity. The consequence of this is that they 'can be deprived of the right to conceive [of] themselves as the directors of their own actions'.[140] As a result, workers adopt subservient behaviour that they assume will be viewed positively by bosses. The ultimate consequence of this could be a gradual stifling of business competitiveness. More often than not, technologies unduly compromise the space available for autonomy.[141] To address and forestall this problem, labour regulation and modern management theories should uphold more benign uses of new tools and practices in an effort to open up emancipating opportunities for workers.[142]

## IV. Concluding Remarks: Building Emancipating Work Environments

This final section appraises the role of individual and collective self-determination in promoting prosperous working environments in which innovation is harnessed sustainably.[143] It will be argued that 'freedom as non-domination' not only entails that individuals are 'not subject to the arbitrary or uncontrolled will of another', but that they are vested with meaningful discretion to shape their own actions.[144]

While the current research on work quality is scattered across several disciplines, including the organisational psychology, economics and sociology fields,[145] this concept is almost unanimously defined as a multidimensional construct. One of several determinants contributing to its definition is the degree of decisional latitude, ie, personal agency in terms of defining the actions by which the indicated goals must be achieved. A higher level of agency at the task level is associated with a higher level of work quality.[146] According to Szekér and colleagues,[147] this is reflected in the organisation of the work to be performed when it comes to the order, method and tempo of the tasks. In the near-endless litigation concerning legal status, the amount of flexibility that a worker enjoys in relation to executing a task for a company has been pivotal in denying the existence of a relationship of subordination.[148] This narrow understanding of flexibility,

[140] Lee, Kusbit, Metsky and Dabbish (n 118).

[141] In this chapter, I use 'agency' and 'autonomy' interchangeably.

[142] A Licht, 'Entrepreneurial Spirit and What the Law Can Do About It' (2006) 28 *Comparative Labor Law & Policy Journal* 817.

[143] T Kato and M Morishima 'The Productivity Effects of Participatory Employment Practices: Evidence from New Japanese Panel Data' (2002) 41 *Industrial Relations: A Journal of Economy and Society* 487

[144] Collins and Atkinson (n 121).

[145] GS Lowe, *The Quality of Work: A People-Centred Agenda* (Oxford, Oxford University Press, 2000).

[146] M Bisello, E Peruffo, E Fernandez-Macias and R Rinaldi, *How Computerisation is Transforming Jobs: Evidence From the Eurofound's European Working Conditions Survey* (European Commission, Joint Research Centre, No 2019/02, 2019).

[147] L Szekér, I Smits and G Van Gyes, 'It Takes More Than One Measure. Capturing the Multidimensionality of Job Quality with Job Types and Multiple Job Quality Outcomes' (2017) InGRID Working Paper.

[148] The concept of nominal autonomy in terms of work organisation has been used to defeat the subordination test in court, especially in recent litigation concerning the legal status of platform workers. Case C-692/19 *B v Yodel Delivery Network Ltd* ECLI:EU:C:2020:288 [2020].

which is currently weaponised in the most advanced labour market areas,[149] should not be confused with agency.

Ultimately, agency encompasses direct control over the design, implementation and maintenance of all aspects of organisation, performance and execution. Indeed, as demonstrated by the job demands – job control model, the amount of discretion moderates the effects of the job demands on psychological pressure.[150] As a result, the psychosocial wellbeing of employees can be enhanced by offering a higher level of self-determination.[151] Together with investment in human capital, direct or mediated (via worker representatives) participation in job crafting through the selection and allocation of tasks provides a unique opportunity to foster workers' moral power, self-worth and meaningfulness. Contrary to the widespread misconception that humans are not trustworthy or responsible (a myth partially disproved by the fact that productivity has not declined following the adoption of remote working schemes during the Covid-19 pandemic),[152] individual and collective self-government represents one of the best ways to achieve long-lasting organisational success.

For instance, theories of self-determination in the workplace have been employed to explain how workers' participation in the definition of performance measurement systems can 'improve [the] validity of the operational performance metrics and increase their sensitivity, precisions and verifiability'.[153] When coupled with transparent and constant feedback delivered in a supportive environment, job autonomy is a crucial determinant of both self-motivation and worker morale.[154] In turn, intrinsic motivation is key to engagement and efficiency, and it facilitates the learning of new skills. Admittedly, this does not mean that organisations should be run in an entirely bottom-up fashion. Proponents of self-determination theory acknowledge that there can be autonomy even in relation to tasks that are mandated or in circumstances that are controlled if the motivation behind the actions demanded is made clear and recognised. In contrast to freedom and independence, agency should be understood as the volition to pursue a goal, even in a context in which the specific means of attaining it are obligatory or dictated by bosses. It has also been considered an attractiveness factor for companies striving to entice and retain talent. Workers are not inspired by rigid organisational templates in highly vertical structures, which prevents them from pursuing project-based arrangements and time and space sovereignty. In this

[149] Platform giants have long sought to claim that, by classifying platform workers as employees, they would lose a great deal of flexibility, which is defined as 'the ability to choose if and when to work'. A Adams-Prassl, J Adams-Prassl and D Coyle, 'Uber and Beyond: Policy Implications for the UK' (2021) The Productivity Institute, Productivity Insights Paper No 001.

[150] RA Karasek Jr, 'Job Demands, Job Decision Latitude, and Mental Strain: Implications for Job Redesign' (1979) 24 *Administrative Science Quarterly* 285; A Wrzesniewski and JE Dutton, 'Crafting a Job: Revisioning Employees as Active Crafters of their Work' (2001) 26 *Academy of Management Review* 179.

[151] CEPS, EFTHEIA and HIVA-KU Leuven, *Study to Gather Evidence on the Working Conditions of Platform Workers* (Social Europe, Final Report VT/2018/032, 2020).

[152] R Bregman, *Humankind: A Hopeful History* (London, Bloomsbury Publishing 2020).

[153] BA Groen, MJ Wouters and CP Wilderom, 'Employee Participation, Performance Metrics, and Job Performance: A Survey Study Based on Self-Determination Theory' (2017) 51 *Management Accounting Research* 5.

[154] S Viete and D Erdsiek, 'Mobile Information Technologies and Firm Performance: The Role of Employee Autonomy' (2020) 51 *Information Economics and Policy* 100863.

regard, technology should be used in an emancipating fashion in order to better adapt workloads and methods to individual needs and preferences.[155]

Co-determining both tasks and objectives may prove particularly beneficial for businesses, as workers are in the best position to define internal rules due to their vast knowledge of operational practices. The parallel involvement of the manager ensures that the developed metrics align with the broader organisational strategy. In short, the active participation of workers offers two types of advantages. First, given the correspondence between the designer of the assessment model and the evaluation subjects, noisy metrics that imperfectly signal effective conduct can be excluded. Second, due to the peer knowledge of the framework, workers are less inclined to game it as their colleagues would likely respond reciprocally. When autonomy, mutual trust and competence are all safeguarded, workers feel empowered 'to improve the measurement properties rather than risk the imposition of metrics that poorly reflect the operational characteristics of their work'.[156] Harnessing their full potential might require employees to be provided with appropriate decision-making rights concerning when and where work is completed. From a theoretical perspective, technology-enabled flexibility might increase employees' efforts and enhance their performance through job enrichment, thereby boosting work capacity and forging a positive social identity.[157]

In several contexts, technological devices fully embody a means of consistently exercising power according to a logic of productivity enhancement, whose goals and benchmarks are only co-determined between labour and management to a very limited extent. When new practices or digital tools intended to replace bosses in the all-encompassing spectrum of employer functions are introduced with the sole purpose of cost reduction, their reception by employers turns out to be negative, while it adversely affects workers' overall commitment to the organisation. By contrast, when technologies are adopted in order to improve the overall work experience and enhance employees' wellbeing, such methods have been received positively and had a positive effect on workplaces. In an 'autonomy-supportive context',[158] allowing more self-determination in terms of selecting meaningful outcomes and the means of achieving them positively correlates with successful performance.[159] When it comes to mitigating the dominance of companies, building worker power is essential to attaining a future characterised by shared prosperity. Circularly, empowering workers represents a concrete way of promoting tasks that face a lower risk of substitution.

After minimising the catastrophic narrative of mass joblessness thanks to more persuasive analyses, the overarching objective of this chapter has been to demonstrate that digital automation is unexpectedly leading to the augmentation of organisational, control and disciplinary prerogatives in both conventional and innovative sectors.

[155] V Cirillo, M Rinaldini, J Staccioli and ME Virgillito, 'Technology vs Workers: The Case of Italy's Industry 4.0 Factories' (2021) 56 *Structural Change and Economic Dynamics* 166.

[156] Groen, Wouters and Wilderom (n 153) 10.

[157] Viete and Erdsiek (n 154).

[158] SC Rigby and RM Ryan, 'Self-Determination Theory in Human Resource Development: New Directions and Practical Considerations' (2018) 20 *Advances in Developing Human Resources* 133.

[159] L Manganelli, A Thibault-Landry, J Forest and J Carpentier, 'Self-Determination Theory Can Help You Generate Performance and Well-Being in the Workplace: A Review of the Literature' (2018) 20 *Advances in Developing Human Resources* 227.

At the same time, it has assessed the potential of technologies when it comes to developing an emancipating new work environment in which agency is encouraged. Advanced technologies should arguably be designed and implemented in such a way as to support workers, not to 'conspire' against them. Hopefully, the future of work will be built around task autonomy rather than around job automation or, even worse, employer power augmentation. Indeed, the direction of the technological transformation of the labour market is not predetermined: the goal should be to foster a human-centred workplace in which game-changing technologies support rule crafting rather than rule adherence, thereby enabling authentic spatial, temporal and decision-making agency.

# 14

# Discrimination by Algorithms at Work

SYLVAINE LAULOM

## I. Introduction

From a very naive point of view, algorithms cannot be discriminatory. Can we not trust science to eliminate all the subjectivity of human decisions and, more precisely here, of management decisions? At first glance, algorithms sort, categorise and organise information by eliminating any prejudice and bias specific to human beings. Discriminatory practices are based on prejudices. Thus, algorithms should be able to ensure equal treatment by applying the same criteria and weighting regardless of the requester's origin or sexual orientation for example. However, this trust in science has not lasted long and practice has very quickly shown not only that algorithms can be discriminatory, but they can exacerbate discrimination.

An important literature is already documenting this risk.[1] Indeed, within few years almost all international and European institutions had set up groups of experts and issued communications, recommendations, reports and declarations highlighting the ethical problems raised by the development of artificial intelligence (AI).[2] Among them, the risk of discrimination is clearly identified. The same enthusiasm can be witnessed at national level.[3] Far from slowing down this process, Covid-19 has amplified the

[1] J Gerards and R Xenidis, *Algorithmic discrimination in Europe, Challenges and opportunities for gender equality and non-discrimination law* (European network of legal experts in gender equality and non-discrimination EELN, 2020) (EELN Report); S Barocas and AD Selbst, 'Big Data's Disparate Impact' (2016) 104 *California Law Review* 62; J Kleinberg, J Ludwig, S Aullainathan and CR Sunstein, 'Discrimination in the age of algorithms' (2019) NBER Working Paper Series; F Zuiderveen Borgesius, *Discrimination, Artificial Intelligence and algorithmic decision-making* (Council of Europe Report, 2018); R Xenidis and L Senden, 'EU non-discrimination law in the era of artificial intelligence: Mapping the challenges of algorithmic discrimination' in U Bernitz et al (eds), *General Principles of EU law and the EU Digital Order* (Alphen aan den Rijn, Kluwer Law International, 2020); P Adam, M Le Friant and Y Tarasewicz (eds), *Intelligence artificielle, gestion algorithmique du personnel et droit du travail, les travaux de l'AFDT* (Paris, Dalloz, 2010); J Porta, 'Algorithme et risque discriminatoire' in M Mercats-Bruns (ed), *Nouveaux modes de détection et de prévention de la discrimination et accès au droit* (Paris, Société de Législation comparée, 2020) 61.

[2] See the website of the Council of Europe dedicated to addressing human rights issues raised by AI. A page of the website lists all policies, recommendations, declarations, guidelines and other legal instruments issued by Council of Europe bodies or committees on AI: www.coe.int/en/web/artificial-intelligence.

[3] See the data visualisation of AI initiatives elaborated by the Council of Europe: www.coe.int/en/web/artificial-intelligence/national-initiatives.

digitalisation of our societies and strengthened the need to understand what is at stake in these processes, and particularly their consequences for human rights. The actual and possible impact of AI is such that the European Union (EU), the Council of Europe and the International Labour Organization (ILO), each in their scope of competences, are now considering the adoption of some regulation on these issues.[4]

Should we fear the development of algorithms at work? Is their use likely to reinforce existing discriminations and generate new ones? Do they pose a danger to decent work, and under what conditions can they be used to ensure decent work? To answer these questions, it is necessary to define precisely in this chapter what we are talking about. Therefore, section II will discuss the meaning and types of algorithms that are actually used at work. In this context, section III investigates the potential discriminatory impact of algorithmic management of work. Once the risk of algorithmic discrimination at work is identified, section IV analyses how algorithms may be regulated. At EU level, two sets of regulations are intertwining: data protection and non-discrimination legislation. The use of algorithms in the context of work makes it possible to assess the capacity of EU law to catch this type of discrimination.

## II. The Use of Algorithms at Work

### A. Different Types of Algorithms

The terms 'AI' and 'algorithm' have become part of our everyday language without a common definition of these concepts, or a clear understanding of the reality behind these terms. Indeed, the various international organisations that have worked on AI have produced some definition and/or glossary of the various terms used,[5] but until now no common definition has emerged. It is, therefore, necessary to give an overview of how algorithms can be used at work to be able to understand which discrimination they can generate.

Recourse to algorithms as a basis for public or private decision-making is not such a recent phenomenon. The use of algorithms to calculate, for example, insurance or premiums is nothing new. Strictly speaking, an algorithm is 'the description of a finite and unambiguous sequence of steps (or instructions) for producing results (output) from initial data (input)'.[6] Therefore any list of instructions aimed at a certain result is technically an algorithm. A recipe could be defined as an algorithm since a dish can be made from its ingredients.[7]

[4] At the European level, see European Commission, 'Proposal for a Regulation of the European Parliament and of the Council Laying Down Harmonised Rules on Artificial Intelligence (Artificial Intelligence Act) and Amending Certain Union Legislative Acts' COM (2021) 206 final. Also see the first feasibility study on a legal framework on AI design, development and application based on Council of Europe standards: www.rm.coe.int/cahai-2020-23-final-eng-feasibility-study-/1680a0c6da.

[5] See the Glossary of the Council of Europe: www.coe.int/en/web/artificial-intelligence/glossary.

[6] See CNIL, '*How can humans keep the upper hand? The ethical matters raised by algorithms and artificial intelligence*' (2017) Report on the public debate led by the French Data Protection Authority (CNIL) as part of the ethical discussion assignment set by the digital Republic Bill, available at: www.cnil.fr/sites/default/files/atoms/files/cnil_rapport_ai_gb_web.pdfb.

[7] ibid.

The glossary published by the European Council defines algorithms as a 'finite suite of formal rules (logical operations, instructions) allowing to obtain a result from input elements. This suite can be the object of an automated execution process and rely on models designed through machine learning'.[8] The place of algorithms in computer science is also clarified:

> For a computer to be able to run an algorithm, it must be written in a computer language and coded into a program (a sort of text comprising written instructions, also known as 'source code'). This program can then be run in a software or compiled in the form of an application. Software generally makes use of a number of algorithms: for inputting data, computing and displaying the results or communicating with other software programs, etc.[9]

If the use of algorithms as decision support tools is not new, the computational capacity of today's and tomorrow's computers and the volume, speed and flexibility of data processing are fundamentally changing the place and the role of algorithms in all aspects of any process of decision-making.

The growing complexity of algorithms has generated new classifications: (a) 'classical' algorithms which are deterministic, since their operating criteria are clearly defined by the people wishing to run them; and (b) machine learning algorithms, called 'probabilistic' algorithms.[10] Probabilistic algorithms represent a much more powerful technology than classical ones, as their output is always changing depending on the learning basis they were given, which itself changes in step with their use. Machine learning algorithms do not only apply predefined rules, they identify similarities to reproduce some thinking skills.

The place of algorithms in decision-making is very different depending on the category of algorithm used – ie, a classical algorithm or a machine learning one. If in both cases the end goal of applications making use of these classes of algorithm consists of automating tasks that would otherwise be performed by humans, in the case of machine learning, the decision itself could be delegated to the machine.

## B. Algorithms at Work

If we look now at the role algorithms actually play at work, it is possible to distinguish three very different types of impact. First, AI technologies imply a change in the structure of the labour market itself. Second, some new organisations of work have emerged with platform work which create some specific risks of algorithmic discrimination. Third, the use of algorithms could also change the management of work. Human resources (HR) departments are now assisted, or even replaced for some of their functions, by various AI instruments. The risk of algorithmic discrimination at work generally refers to this specific use. To appreciate the risk of discrimination, it is therefore necessary to have a more precise idea of how algorithms are currently used in HR and which discriminations they could generate. In this section, I will have a closer look at these three impacts.

[8] www.coe.int/en/web/artificial-intelligence/glossary

[9] See CNIL (n 6).

[10] ibid.

### *i. Changes in Labour Market Structure*

One of the first impacts of AI at work is on jobs themselves. At a global level, the debate is concentrating on what will be the 'future of work' and the 'jobs of the future'. How many jobs will be lost as a consequence of technological innovation, and how deeply will the nature of jobs change? It is acknowledged that the development of AI technology might imply some specific public policies especially training policies in order to qualify workers for these new jobs and to mitigate the possible social consequences for workers.

These changes could also have important consequences for inequality as they could reinforce the structural inequalities existing in the labour market or lead to new ones. According to an ILO research paper:

> For the opportunities to exceed the risks, however, policies need to be adjusted at both the national and the international levels. This paper argues that skills policies in and of themselves, albeit necessary, will not be sufficient in this regard. Policy-makers and social partners need to ensure that individual companies cannot gain market dominance, thereby excluding users from their algorithm or maintaining and replicating existing biases.[11]

Gender inequalities could also be reinforced. For example, the number of women in high technology jobs is still low, which means that they will not have the best jobs in these fields. According to the World Economic Forum Global Gender Gap Report 2020,[12] female workers make up an estimated 26 per cent of workers in data and AI roles globally. Only 17 er cent of ICT specialists in the EU are women even though women-led entrepreneurial start-ups are more likely to be successful. Globally, women make up 12 per cent of all AI researchers. They hold 20 per cent of technical positions within major machine-learning companies. The subset of the population that currently shapes and designs AI systems is thus very narrow, and with a clear underrepresentation of women.

AI technology does not only imply changes in the structure of the labour market, in displacing workers, introducing new jobs and destroying others, it could also imply some new forms of work organisation.

### *ii. A New Form of Work Organisation: Platform Work*

The diffusion of platform work is also deeply influenced by algorithms, as online platforms rely heavily on them. As investigated by the chapters included in part II of this book, such algorithms determine how supply and demand are matched, what the pay is and what the consequences are when a platform worker receives positive and/or negative ratings. The algorithmic management of work raises specific issues because of the disappearance of the employer behind the algorithm. The algorithms assign work, fix prices and evaluate work.

[11] E Ernst, R Merola and D Samaan, 'The economics of artificial intelligence: implications for the future of work' (2018) ILO Future of Work Research Paper Series. V De Stefano, '"Negotiating the Algorithm": Automation, Artificial Intelligence and Labour Protection' (2018) Employment Working Paper 246.

[12] World Economic Forum, Global Gender Gap Report 2020, available at: www3.weforum.org/docs/WEF_GGGR_2020.pdf.

The promoters of platform work usually present the potential of these new types of work to include new workers in the labour market. Platforms would provide important income and employment opportunities for a growing number of workers. They would enable workers, who could normally be excluded from the labour market on account of their age, disability, illness, origins, gender, care responsibilities, to participate. Another potential positive effect of platform work is that some forms of it could avoid 'real' personal contacts using the anonymity on the net, which can contribute to reducing risks of discrimination. Following this presentation, platform work could even be a useful tool to improve equality in the labour market by improving its 'scope': ie, participation in the labour market.

As highlighted by Eurofound:

> Both workers and clients benefit from the efficiency and neutrality of this feature: tasks are listed, users customise their selection criteria according to their needs, and the algorithm performs a match. There are some grounds for assuming that automated matching is more objective than a human and hence prevents discrimination against workers based on factors such as ethnicity or disability status. This can be particularly advantageous in platform work types such as online click-work, which is dominated by groups who are generally disadvantaged in the labour market.[13]

However, here again there is a significant gap between discourse and reality. The quality of platform work has been questioned. Despite the potential of platforms to provide employment opportunities, there are a number of concerns relating to workers' unclear employment status, unfair treatment, low earnings, non-payment, lack of social protection and lack of voice. It is therefore obvious that far from contributing to the reduction of discrimination and inequalities, platform work can increase them. In this regard the role of algorithms is significant. According to Eurofound, 'if the algorithm is programmed in an unfavourable way, it can increase discrimination … This is not necessarily intentional but a consequence of the still insufficient development of algorithms'.[14]

Another crucial issue regarding algorithms in platform work is the importance of rating, where the explicit and implicit preferences of customers may play an important role in evaluating workers. Since customers' reviews may be essential in preserving the possibility of acceding to the app and to future jobs, biased reviews could entail major detrimental effects on workers' employment opportunities.

Finally, the use of algorithms could also change the management of work in companies.

### *iii. An Algorithmic Management of Work?*

The risk of algorithmic discrimination at work usually refers to the risks generated by the various AI instruments conceived to assist HR departments. Software and hardware are spreading in modern workplaces and are developing solutions that allow management to recruit workers, to give them instructions on the work they do, to control their

[13] Eurofound, *Platform work: Maximising the potential while safeguarding standards* (Luxembourg, Publications Office of the European Union, 2019).

[14] ibid.

performances through digital tools, to manage their careers, predict their departures, etc. For example, these tools can define career guidelines in line with individual profiles, detect any employees who are likely to resign in the coming months, match a list of applicants to a job vacancy, understand social phenomena in the workplace, etc.

The major driving forces for algorithmic decision-making are certainly minimising risks, costs and time. They could also be seen as diminishing human biases (prejudice and personal beliefs) thereby increasing the objectivity, consistency and fairness of managerial decisions.[15]

Recruitment is now a primary playing field for AI. Various stakeholders are developing solutions for assisting recruitment (by matching supply with demand in particular):

> Firms increasingly rely on social media platforms and digital services, such as Facebook, Instagram, LinkedIn, Xing, Monster, and CareerBuilder, to advertise job vacancies and to find well-fitting candidates. These digital services are called recommender systems and search engines and use algorithmic decision-making tools to recommend suitable candidates to recruiters and suitable employers to candidates … Hiring platforms, such as Xing and LinkedIn, already implement predictive analytics. Their algorithms go through thousands of job profiles to find the most eligible candidate for a specific job and recommend this candidate to the recruiter. Firms also examine data about job seekers, analyze them based on past hiring decisions, and then recommend only the applications that are a potential match. Consequently, firms can more precisely target potential candidates.[16]

Recruitment is not the only area of HR management where the recourse of algorithms is developing. Another increasingly popular area of AI integration is 'people analytics', defined broadly as the use of big data and digital tools to manage workforce, ie, to 'measure, report and understand employee performance, aspects of workforce planning, talent management and operational management'.[17] Also referred to as 'human analytics', 'talent analytics' and 'human resource analytics', in an era of 'strategic HR', this application of AI-enabled tools is defined broadly as the use of individualised data about people to help management and HR professionals make decisions about recruitment, ie, who to hire, for performance appraisals and promotion considerations, to identify when people are likely to leave their jobs, and to select future leaders. People analytics are also used to look for patterns across workers' data, which can help to spot trends in attendance, staff morale and health issues at the organisational level.[18]

However, there is a gap between discourse and communication around the use of algorithms in HR departments and their actual use, especially with regard to the most developed forms of algorithms, the machine-learning algorithms. As observed by Capelli et al:

> While the deployment of general-purpose AI is still a long shot in any domain of human activity, the speed of progress towards specialized AI systems in health care, automobile

[15] A Köchling and MC Wehner, 'Discriminated by an algorithm: a systematic review of discrimination and fairness by algorithmic decision-making in the context of HR recruitment and HR development' (2020) 13 *Business Research* 795.

[16] ibid.

[17] De Stefano (n 11).

[18] European Agency for Safety and Health at Work, 'OSH and the future of work: benefit and risks of artificial intelligence tools in workplaces' (2019) Discussion Paper.

> industry, social media, advertising and marketing has been considerable. Far less progress has been made in issues around the management of employees on the first step of the AI path, which is decisions guided by algorithms.[19]

Software developers could present their solutions to assist HR departments as being much more advanced than they really are and companies prefer to communicate on how good they are in using the most advanced models of AI.[20] Today, it would be a good idea to communicate on its AI policy. Admitting to not have one would be in a way admitting an unforgivable delay in development. According to some authors, the incorporation of AI into the HR management must necessarily be understood in relation to its historical development, as a progressive quantification function (which is not the only possible perspective) and the central importance given to data, both in terms of quantity and quality. The proposals are extremely ambitious and one can legitimately wonder what has really been achieved so far given the current limits of attempts in this direction.[21]

Indeed, the figures that can be found show a contrasted and limited use of AI applications. About 40 per cent of HR functions in international companies are now using them – but this does not give any indication on the level of their development. These companies are mostly based in the United States, even if some European and Asian organisations have started to use AI applications.[22] An Equinet Report[23] observes that in recruitment, complex AI is being used in Finland to assess candidates for roles including automated video analysis and assessment of social media presence. Companies are also deploying technology in the recruitment field in France, the Netherlands, Sweden and the UK. It must be admitted that we are still a long way from managing human resources through algorithms and that deep learning using neural networks do not seem to be so widespread.

Outside the recruitment process, the development of AI seems much more limited than it is generally presented. Four reasons for that have been identified: the difficulty to identify the outcome (a 'good employee'); constraints imposed by small data sets; accountability questions associated with fairness and other ethical and legal constraints; and possible adverse employee reactions to management decisions via data-based algorithms.[24]

In the end, with the exception of platform work where algorithms play a central role, HR management is far from being placed in the hands of AI. It is true that they can intervene in the recruitment process, but more rarely in other areas of human resources (I exclude here the tools that can intervene in other fields in companies such as, for example, the use of algorithms in matters of health and safety at work to try, for

[19] P Tambe, P Cappelli and V Yakubovich, 'Artificial intelligence in human resources management: Challenges and a path forward' (2019) 61 *California Management Review* 15.

[20] S Fischman and B Gomes, 'Intelligences artificielles et droit du travail: contribution à l'étude du fonctionnement des plateformes numériques' in P Adam, M Le Friant and Y Tarasewicz (eds), *Intelligence artificielle, gestion algorithmique du personnel et droit du travail* (Paris, Dalloz, 2020) 37.

[21] L Benraïss-Noailles and O Herrbach, 'Enjeux organisationnels et managériaux de l'IA pour la gestion du personnel. Ver un DRH augmenté'? [2021] *Droit social* 110.

[22] European Agency for Safety and Health at Work (n 18).

[23] R Allen and D Masters, *Regulating for an equal AI: a new role for equality bodies* (Brussels, Equinet, 2020).

[24] Cappelli, Tambe and Yakubovich (n 19).

example, to limit the number of accidents at work). The decision itself also seems to be very rarely entirely delegated to machine and the algorithm will instead intervene as a tool for decision. These elements must be kept in mind when analysing the risk of algorithmic discrimination in the following section.

## III. Potential Discriminatory Impact of Algorithmic Management of Work

> There is no technological magic or mathematical neutrality: algorithms are designed by humans using data that mirror human practices. As such, bias can be introduced into every stage of the development and deployment of systems: as from the intention that initially governs the algorithm's development, during the creation of the computer code, the executable code, during execution, in the context of execution and maintenance.[25]

Various kinds of discrimination can arise at different stages of the process and bias, that can be discriminatory or lead to discrimination, can be introduced into every stage of the development and deployment of systems.[26] To work, algorithms need data. The output will therefore necessarily depend on the quality of data, which in turn depends on their number, diversity, accuracy and relevance. For example, a completely intentional bias could result from the inclusion of prohibited grounds for discrimination in an algorithm itself. If the code excludes the recruitment of pregnant women, it is obvious that no pregnant women will be offered a job. The use of algorithms does not change anything: the active source encoder discriminates against women which is prohibited by law. Indeed, as the inclusion of prohibited grounds for discrimination in an algorithm is prohibited by law, and as it will be possible to discover this discrimination in examining the set of variables and the source code to identify the prohibited criteria, the use of algorithms in direct sources could prevent discrimination. So the algorithm can avoid direct discrimination, as it will be prohibited for the coder to use prohibited criteria.

Of course, the discriminatory effects of algorithms will usually be much less apparent because they could be based on mechanisms much less visible than the inclusion of easily identifiable prohibited grounds for discrimination in the algorithm. It is now well known that one of the most frequent biases is based on a lack of representativeness in the data used. When the algorithms learn by example, 'the character of the training data can have meaningful consequences for the lessons that data mining happens to learn'.[27]

> As computer science scholars explain, biased training data leads to discriminatory models. This can mean two rather different things though: (1) if data mining treats cases in which prejudice has played some role as valid examples to learn from, that rule may simply reproduce the prejudice involved in these earlier cases; or (2) if data mining draws inferences from a biased sample of the population, any decision that rests on these inferences may systematically disadvantage those who are under- or overrepresented in the dataset. Both can affect the training data in ways that lead to discrimination.[28]

[25] Défenseur des Droits, 'Algorithms: preventing automated discrimination' (2020).
[26] See, eg, the classification proposed by Barocas and Selbst (n 1) and Kleinberg et al (n 1).
[27] Barocas and Selbst (n 1)
[28] ibid, 681.

In work relations, the Amazon system of selecting candidates is a well-known example of the problems generated by a lack of representativeness in the data used. Amazon stopped using an AI system for screening job applicants because the system was biased against women. The company realised its system was not rating candidates for software developer jobs and other technical posts in a gender-neutral way. Based on historical training data, Amazon's system taught itself that male candidates were preferable.[29] Here the system, by learning from a previously segregated labour market, exacerbates the segregation in excluding women. In this case, the algorithm designers should teach the algorithm not to use this prohibited criterion to select candidates.

In work relations, as we have seen above, one of the actual limits for developing algorithms in companies is the constraint imposed by small data sets. Furthermore, the use of external data may be limited by the General Data Protection Regulation (GDPR), which provides that the collection of information is for a defined purpose and limits the reuse of data for another purpose (see below).

Another discrimination could arise in defining the model or the result that the algorithm should reach. For example, in defining the qualities of a good employee one can choose to value the presence in the company and give fewer points to those with a high absenteeism rate. The risk of discriminating on the ground of sex (women are more likely to stay home to take care of their ill children), or health or trade union activity is high. In choosing the criteria to define a 'good employee', the algorithm will have a performative effect, and if the criteria is biased, it will here again reinforce discrimination.

Finally, a specific risk of discrimination is linked to the 'proxy' mechanism. Machine-learning algorithms identify correlations between various data points, which they use to detect patterns and make predictions. However, correlations are different from causalities.

> Some proxies might yield a high level of predictive accuracy but at the same time discriminatory … In the absence of perfect information or more granular data and in front of the cost of obtaining such data, stereotypes and generalisations regarding certain groups of population might be relied on as a way to approximate reality.[30]

The landmark *Test-Achats* decision of the Court of Justice of the European Union (CJEU) shows very clearly how a proxy can work.[31] A common practice of insurance companies, based on statistical data, was to differentiate premiums according to sex regarding car and life insurance. After an intense lobby of insurance companies, Directive 2004/113, which prohibits discrimination based on sex in the access to and supply of goods and services, allowed Member States to permit differences relating to sex in respect of insurance premiums and benefits, if sex was a determining risk factor and that it could be substantiated by relevant and accurate actuarial and statistical data.[32] A consumer organisation challenged this provision and the Court was asked whether that provision of the Directive was compatible with the European general principle of sex equality.

[29] Zuiderveen Borgesius (n 1).

[30] Xenidis and Senden (n 1).

[31] Case C-236/09*Association Belge des Consommateurs Test-Achats ASBL and Others v Conseil des ministres* ECLI:EU:C:2011:100 [2011].

[32] Article 5.2 of Council Directive 2004/113/EC of 13 December 2004 implementing the principle of equal treatment between men and women in the access to and supply of goods and services [2004] OJ L373/37.

As stated by the Advocate General:

> Admittedly, it is especially easy to implement distinctions on the basis of sex in respect of insurance products. The correct recording and evaluation of economic and social conditions and of the habits of insured persons is much more complicated and is also more difficult to verify, particularly since those factors may be subject to changes over time. Practical difficulties alone do not however justify the use, to an extent for reasons of convenience, of the insured person's sex as a distinguishing criterion. The use of a person's sex as a kind of substitute criterion for other distinguishing features is incompatible with the principle of equal treatment for men and women. It is not possible in that way to ensure that different insurance premiums and benefits for male and female insured persons are based exclusively on objective criteria which have nothing to do with discrimination on grounds of sex.[33]

The Court followed this reasoning and ruled that the derogation was contrary to the prohibition of discrimination based on sex.

As this example shows, if unquestioned and uncorrected, the emphasis on finding correlations may lead to unfoundedly discriminatory algorithmic outputs. In addition, even when protected characteristics (such as gender) are removed from the pool of available inputs, algorithms might select apparently unrelated but de facto correlated data points ('proxies') for prediction purposes. Indirectly, this might still lead to discriminatory outcomes.[34]

## IV. Regulation of the Risk of Algorithmic Discrimination

'The Achilles' heel of all algorithms is the humans who build them and the choices they make'. A critical element of regulating algorithms is therefore 'regulating humans'.[35] Specifically, the field of labour relations is regulated with two sets of rules, with a clear interaction between these two regulatory bodies: data protection and non-discrimination legislation. From this point of view, EU law is a particularly relevant field of analysis insofar as it offers fairly comprehensive regulations in these two areas. The existence of these regulations, applicable in 27 Member States, and which could be completed in the near future, makes the European Union a laboratory for the role that the law can play in containing the risk of algorithmic discrimination. As the operation of an algorithm is based on data, I will first analyse the protections offered by the European regulation on data protection, before seeing how European non-discrimination law deals with the risk of algorithmic discrimination.

### A. The Data Protection Regulation

'The algorithm without data is blind. Data without algorithms is dumb'.[36]

[33] Case C-236/09, Opinion of advocate general Kokott, delivered on 30 September 2010, § 66.
[34] See the EELN Report (n 1)
[35] ibid, 107.
[36] Défenseur des Droits (n 25).

Because of the unbalanced relationship in work relations, protection of workers' data is essential. One way to avoid algorithmic discrimination is not to feed the algorithm with personal data. For example, if you do not want to have any decision based on trade union membership, one can prevent this data from being published.

Article 8(1) of the Charter of Fundamental Rights of the European Union and Article 16(1) of the Treaty on the Functioning of the European Union (TFEU) provide that everyone has the right to the protection of personal data concerning him or her. Implementing this fundamental right, the General Data Protection Regulation (GDPR) is the first piece of European legislation that recognises the phenomenon of algorithmic discrimination.[37]

The GDPR sets out several principles for the lawful processing of personal data and some of them are of particular relevance to tackle the risk of algorithmic discrimination at work. The first regards the treatment of personal data and data minimisation laid down in Article 5 of the GDPR: the personal data shall be 'adequate, relevant and limited to what is necessary in relation to the purposes for which they are processed'. Moreover, the GDPR provides a specific protection for sensitive data. Certain categories of data are particularly sensitive because they can easily lead to discrimination. The GDPR 'sanitises' these data to 'prevent the inclusion of variables related to protected categories'.[38] According to Article 9,

> processing of personal data revealing racial or ethnic origin, political opinions, religious or philosophical beliefs, or trade union membership, and the processing of genetic data, biometric data for the purpose of uniquely identifying a natural person, data concerning health or data concerning a natural person's sex life or sexual orientation shall be prohibited.

The GDPR recognises the principle of removal of sensitive data used by algorithms and it imposes a duty of care on designers: they must provide for settings that guarantee the protection of data subjects' rights.[39]

Regarding the issue of sensitive data, two failings of the GDPR have been identified. This first is a lack of cohesion between the European data protection regulation and that on non-discrimination. It is stressed that

> the list of categories of data the processing of which could give risk to discrimination does not neatly fit with the list of protected grounds under EU gender equality and non-discrimination law. Importantly, the issue of gender equality or sex discrimination is altogether absent from the GDPR and neither gender nor sex are mentioned as sensitive categories of personal data.[40]

Although the list of sensitive data is much larger than the list of prohibited grounds of discrimination, age, sex and disability are not mentioned in the GDPR. If disability is

[37] Regulation (EU) 2016/679 of the European Parliament and of the Council of 27 April 2016 on the protection of natural persons with regard to the processing of personal data and on the free movement of such data, and repealing Directive 95/46/EC [2016] OJ L119/1. Xenidis and Senden (n 1); BW Goodman, 'A step towards accountable algorithms? Algorithmic discrimination and the European Union general data protection' Paper presented at the 29th Conference on Neural Information Processing Systems (2016). Even though the term 'algorithm' is not used in the Regulation, the risk of discrimination by the processing of personal data is clearly identified in the Preamble of the Regulation.

[38] Regulation (EU) 2016/679, ibid.

[39] See Article 25, GDPR.

[40] EELN Report (n 1).

understood to be included in the terms 'health status' or 'data concerning health', age and sex are absent from the regulation. However, it is questionable whether age and gender are really sensitive data. Moreover, the absence of age and sex as sensitive data obviously does not exclude the prohibition of discrimination based on these criteria.

Another consequence of the ban on the collection of sensitive data is denounced: how will it be possible to detect algorithmic discrimination, if the algorithm cannot use these sensitive data? Identifying and reducing discrimination in algorithms can only be possible if data on those belonging to special groups are available, but Article 9(1) of the GDPR prohibits the categorisation of individuals based on sensitive data.[41] Taking into account this problem, Article 10(5) of the European Commission proposal on AI addresses the criticism that the prohibition on processing sensitive data is an obstacle to proving discriminatory bias in algorithms.[42]

In addition to data minimisation, the GDPR provides for algorithmic transparency.[43] In the context of work relations, it means that employees must be informed about the data processed and their sources, as well as about the purpose of the algorithm and the way it is implemented.

Several provisions of the GDPR are devoted to transparency: a right to be notified of solely automated decision-making; a right of both notification and access to meaningful information about the logic involved; a right to be informed of the significance of and envisaged effects of solely automated decision-making; and a right not to be subject to solely automated decision-making, with safeguards and restraints for the limited cases in which automated decision-making is permitted. Those safeguards include, but are not limited to, a right to contest a decision, to express one's point of view, and to human intervention.[44]

The gaps and weaknesses of the GDPR have been debated. For example, what constitutes a meaningful information in practice, 'has been the subject of hot debate, including whether it is a system-wide (model-wide) explanation or specific to individual decisions, and what depth of explanation is required'.[45] In the employment context, what is essential is that workers have a right to clear information and explanation about the algorithm. The information must be provided 'in a concise, transparent, intelligible and easily accessible form, using clear and plain language'.[46]

A whole series of rights are therefore recognised for individuals. The question of effectiveness of these rights was of course raised. The issue is crucial, particularly in the context of labour law, where the ability of workers to effectively claim the rights recognised to them is a problem as old as labour law itself. In companies, the role of trade unions and workers' representatives is therefore very important. The GDPR recognises this specificity of labour law in providing that EU Member states may introduce, 'by law or by collective agreements', 'specific rules to ensure the protection of the rights and freedoms in respect of the processing of employees' personal data in the employment

[41] Goodman (n 37).
[42] Commission, Com(2021) 206 final (n 4).
[43] Articles 13–15, GDPR on rights of information and access to personal data.
[44] Articles 13, 14, 15 and 22 GDPR.
[45] ME Kaminski and G Malgieri, 'Algorithmic Impact Assessments under the GDPR: Producing Multi-layered Explanations' (2021) 11 *International Data Privacy Law* 125, 127.
[46] See Recital 42, GDPR.

context'. These rules shall 'include suitable and specific measures to safeguard the data subject's human dignity, legitimate interests and fundamental rights' with particular regard to 'monitoring systems at the work place', 'transparency of processing and transfer of personal data'.[47]

Moreover, individual rights are complemented by what is called governance rules. Indeed, the GDPR

> combines a series of individual rights (Articles 12–23) with a systemic governance regime overseen by regulators, targeted at more comprehensive oversight over the algorithm and the people around it (Articles 24–43 and throughout). These two systems interact and overlap. An individual right is often also a company's duty. But even if individuals (data subjects) fail to invoke their rights, companies (data controllers) have significant obligations – both procedural and substantive – under the GDPR.[48]

These specific enforcement mechanisms include third-party auditing, the appointment of Data Protection Officers and Data Protection Impact Assessments, codes of conducts and certification.[49] Among the various governance instruments, impact assessment is certainly one of the most promising ways for avoiding the risk of discrimination.

The actual proposal on an AI Act goes further.[50] High-risk AI systems will have to comply with a series of mandatory horizontal requirements,[51] and follow conformity assessment procedures before they can be placed on the EU market. This means that ex ante 'accountability' obligations, prior to deployment, will have to be met by the AI systems supplier. The regulation explicitly classifies AI systems dealing with employment in high risks systems.

Another initiative should also be taken into account.

In June 2020, the European Social Partners signed a framework agreement on digitalisation. The agreement establishes the principle that an AI system 'should be lawful, fair, transparent, safe and secure, complying with all applicable laws and regulations as well as fundamental rights and non-discrimination rules'. It also states that

> social partners at the level of the enterprise and at other appropriate levels should pro-actively explore the potential of digital technology and AI to increase the productivity of the enterprise and the well-being of the workforce, including a better allocation of tasks, augmented competence development and work capacities, the reduction to exposure to harmful working conditions. The potential tensions between respect for human autonomy, prevention of harm, fairness and explicability of decision making should be acknowledged and addressed.[52]

The agreement also recognises a still soft but interesting right for workers representatives to be provided with facilities and (digital) tools, for example digital notice boards to fulfil their duties in a digital era.

[47] Article 88, GDPR on 'Processing in the context of employment'.
[48] Kaminski and Malgieri (n 45) 126.
[49] Articles 24, 40 and 42, GDPR.
[50] COM(2021) 206 final (n 4).
[51] Chapter 2 of Title III (46) of the Proposal.
[52] *European Social Partners Framework Agreement on Digitalisation*, June 2020, available at: www.etuc.org/system/files/document/file2020-06/Final%2022%2006%2020_Agreement%20on%20Digitalisation%202020.pdf.

The GDPR has only been applicable in the Member States since 25 May 2018. It is a complex regulation that will take time to be mobilised by the different actors. Like any legal text, its understanding gives rise to debate and avenues of interpretation, which are already open. It should also be completed soon if the regulation proposed by the European Commission is adopted.[53] Nevertheless, it will be an essential tool in the understanding of the risk of algorithmic discrimination.

Unfortunately, the EELN report found that

> there seems to be limited awareness in European countries' public space of specific issues such as those relating to the interaction between data protection law and gender equality and non-discrimination law. While issues of data protection and privacy are often flagged as central self-standing issues in national debates, a majority of national experts report that the interaction between the two bodies of norms – data protection law and equality law – have not been explored in the public domain. In countries where discussions have tackled the interaction between data protection and discrimination, there is a clear consensus on the relevance of the General Data Protection Regulation (GDPR) and in particular its Articles 5 (on the treatment of personal data), 13–15 (on rights of information and access to personal data) and 22 (the right not to be subject to an individual decision based solely on automated processing, including profiling).[54]

Nevertheless, the transposition and application of the GDPR as well as the growth in European initiatives, both on the part of the European institutions and the European Social Partners, should help to consolidate the articulation between the GDPR and the non-discrimination legislation.

## B. Non-Discrimination Law

It can be assumed that the existence of an important body of European legislation on non-discrimination, as well as the place occupied by the principle of non-discrimination and equality in the European Union, have also meant that the issue of the risk of algorithmic discrimination has very quickly attracted attention. Very swiftly, the question arose as to whether and how the current gender equality and non-discrimination legislative framework can adequately capture and redress algorithmic discrimination.[55]

Basically, the European legal framework of non-discrimination[56] is based on key concepts of discrimination, which include particularly the prohibition of direct and indirect discrimination and a specific system of proof of the discrimination.

[53] COM(2021) 206 final (n 4).

[54] EELN Report (n 1) 95–96.

[55] This is precisely the purpose of the comprehensive report prepared by the European Network of legal experts in gender equality and non-discrimination law. See EELN Report (n 1).

[56] I refer here to the provisions of the Treaties and the various directives adopted prohibiting discrimination based on the criteria protected by Article 19 TFEU, ie, sex, race or ethnic origin, disability, sexual orientation, religion or belief and age (Directive 2006/54/EC of the European Parliament and of the Council of 5 July 2006 on the implementation of the principle of equal opportunities and equal treatment of men and women in matters of employment and occupation (recast) [2006] OJ L204/23; Council Directive 2000/43/EC of 29 June 2000 implementing the principle of equal treatment between persons irrespective of racial or ethnic origin [2000] OJ L180/22; Council Directive 2000/78/EC of 27 November 2000 establishing a general framework for equal treatment in employment and occupation [2000] OJ L303/16).

EU law defines direct discrimination as a situation in which 'one person is treated less favourably than another is, has been or would be treated in a comparable situation on the basis of one of the protected grounds defined in the relevant directives'.[57] According to this definition, it will therefore be prohibited for an algorithm, ie, for the developers, to choose not to recruit women. This is obvious and it is not really a problem. Indeed, 'it has been pointed out in the literature on algorithmic discrimination that direct discrimination is unlikely to arise because it is improbable that designers of algorithmic systems directly input protected grounds as negative variables in supervised algorithmic models'.[58] The prohibition of discrimination is further reinforced by the application of the GDPR rule not to collect sensitive data.

Furthermore, the use of an algorithm could allow the avoidance of certain direct, and unfortunately still persisting, discrimination. If the recruiter decides, in the black box of his or her mind, not to hire a woman or a man because he or she belongs to an alleged race or ethnic group, it could be very difficult to prove actual discrimination. These direct discriminations should disappear, on the condition that the components of the algorithms are accessible. And, as considered above, the GDPR recognises this right. We can here draw a parallel with a French experiment in which companies were asked to only examine anonymous CVs to select job applicants for interview. In practice it meant omitting information, such as name, ethnic origin, age, gender and address.[59] In the same way, in selecting job applicants, algorithms will not take into account these criteria. The assistance of an algorithm to select job applicants for a specific role, compels the developers of the algorithm to formalise which criteria and which data should be used and which weight should be given to each data and this process could lead to a more objective selection.

Two other strengths of the European definition of direct discrimination have been characterised in the context of the risk of algorithmic discrimination.[60] The element of intentionality is irrelevant for direct discrimination. Hence, proving a case of direct discrimination requires showing neither that the perpetrator was conscious of the discrimination, nor showing that he or she intended to discriminate. The irrelevance of intentionality means that the concept of direct discrimination potentially covers situations where the developers of an algorithm did not intend to build a discriminatory model, but designed it in a way that allows the algorithm to treat individuals and groups belonging to certain protected categories in a less favourable way than others. A second strength of the concept of direct discrimination is that it extends to situations where a person is treated unfavourably because he or she is associated with a protected group, without sharing the protected characteristic himself or herself.[61]

A second key concept of the EU non-discrimination legal framework is that of indirect discrimination, which could be a very valuable way to limit the risk of algorithmic discrimination. Indirect discrimination is defined as situations

> where an apparently neutral provision, criterion or practice would put [members of a protected category] at a particular disadvantage compared with other persons, unless that

[57] Article 2(2)(a) Directive 2000/43/EC; Article 2(2)(a) Directive 2000/78/EC; Article 2(1)(a) Directive 2006/54/EC.

[58] EELN Report (n 1) 78.

[59] The law was adopted in 2006 but was never enforced before it was finally repealed.

[60] See EELN Report (n 1) 67.

[61] Case C-303/06 *S Coleman v Attridge Law and Steve Law* ECLI:EU:C:2008:415.

> provision, criterion or practice is objectively justified by a legitimate aim and the means of achieving that aim are appropriate and necessary.[62]

Hence, indirect discrimination is just taking into account the effect of a decision, or if we want to use a more algorithmic vocabulary, to the output produced by the algorithm. If the output reveals a particular disadvantage for a protected category, it must be scrutinised.

The indirect discrimination mechanism is perfectly suited to tackle the situations of proxy discrimination where decisions are made on the basis of characteristics relating to, but different from, protected grounds. For example, the criteria of residency could be a proxy for ethnicity as migrants are more likely to live in certain areas of a city than others. The 'apparently neutral provision' of the European definition of indirect discrimination works exactly as a proxy, which could produce a discriminatory effect. The indirect discrimination concept could therefore capture what is known as covert direct discrimination.[63]

Not only would the notion of indirect discrimination make it possible to capture discrimination when it results from the operation of an algorithm, but it would even be better suited to this type of discrimination:

> As the algorithm is based on the mining of large datasets, it could also make visible a discriminatory effect faster and more clearly … If used by algorithms as training material, the patterns of inequality engrained in this data will be further reproduced, reified and performed by algorithms in their output. The operation of algorithms, because of their reliance on de facto biased social data, thus increases the likeliness of occurrences of indirect discrimination.[64]

However, some important limits on the concept of indirect discrimination are highlighted in the context of algorithmic discrimination.[65] Two practical difficulties are generally pointed out: the issue of justification and proof. When direct discrimination is established, only a few exceptions, interpreted restrictively, are admitted. On the contrary, establishing a disproportionate impact of a measure is only the first step before recognising indirect discrimination. The directives provide that no indirect discrimination is to be found, where the implicated 'provision, criterion or practice is objectively justified by a legitimate aim, and the means of achieving that aim are appropriate and necessary'. A wide pool of possible justifications is therefore opened and the courts have to use a proportionality test.

Legally, it will be easy for the defendant to demonstrate that the algorithm at stake is serving a legitimate aim. 'This is an easy step for defendants as the use of algorithm models in itself will serve legitimate business purposes (eg, ranking or scoring algorithms to find out which employees are most performant, estimating a default risk, etc)'.[66] Similarly, even when prima facie evidence can be gathered, it might be a challenge for judges to operate the necessary proportionality and objective justification test

[62] Article 2(2)(b) Directive 2000/43/EC; Article 2(2)(b) Directive 2000/78/EC; Article 2(b) Directive 2004/113/EC; Article 2(1)(b) Directive 2006/54/EC.
[63] EELN Report (n 1) 70.
[64] ibid, 72.
[65] Porta (n 1) 61.
[66] Xenidis and Senden (n 1).

in cases of indirect discrimination. It might also be difficult to assess whether a software company responsible for the discriminatory output of an algorithm could have opted for a less impactful solution in light of the highly technical explanations the company is likely to present in relation to the trade-offs that it must make. For some authors the conclusion is that the control of the decision implied by the control of justifications, would not be adapted to the logic of algorithms.[67] A psychological factor may come into play. It would be very difficult to go against the supposed neutrality of the algorithm, adorned with all the assets of science.[68]

Legally, it will be also very difficult to open the famous 'black box' of the algorithm. The question then is not so much the limits of the concept of indirect discrimination but the question of proof. How to prove the discriminatory effect of an algorithm? 'How to overcome the lack of transparency in the nature and effects to algorithms?'[69]

Most of these criticisms are well founded, but most of them relate more to the difficulty for the law in grasping discrimination in general than to specific difficulties linked to algorithms. Even without the use of algorithms, identifying discrimination in companies has proven to be particularly difficult because discrimination is based on stereotypes and prejudices and rooted in the way organisations go about their day-to-day business. It is reasonable to ask whether, on the contrary, the use of algorithms, provided that their use is regulated, might not become an instrument for combating discrimination. In the field of work, the legal tools exist so that discrimination generated by algorithms can be better identified. The articulation of the concept of indirect discrimination, with the specific system of proof of the discrimination and the right to information and explanation recognised by the GDPR, could prove to be quite effective instruments in the fight against discrimination.

As we have seen, the concept of indirect discrimination thus makes it possible to capture discrimination when it results from the operation of an algorithm. Concerning the control of justification and proportionality, I believe it can take place.[70] On the one hand, there is no reason why the proportionality test should be lighter in an algorithmic context. The Court of Justice, in the *Achbita* case has shown that it does not accept general justification and that the proportionality test is strict.[71] The *Test-Achats* case also demonstrates that a correlation established by an algorithm does not prove any causality.[72]

It is also important to consider the rules of the burden of proof. According to the EU directives, if persons who consider themselves discriminated against bring facts from which it may be presumed that there has been direct or indirect discrimination, it shall be for the respondent to prove that there has been no breach of the principle of equal treatment. It means that once a prima facie case of indirect discrimination has been established, the burden of proof shifts onto the defendant. If he or she cannot open the

[67] See Porta (n 1) 61.

[68] Concerning this argument, it seems to me that the intense debates around AI reveal fears rather than blind trust in the functioning of algorithms.

[69] ibid.

[70] Xenidis and Senden (n 1).

[71] Case C-157/15 *Samira Achbita and Centrum voor gelijkheid van kansen en voor racismebestrijding v G4S Secure Solutions NV* ECLI:EU:C:2017:203; and Case C-188/15 *Asma Bougnaoui e Association de défense des droits de l'homme (ADDH) v Micropole SA* ECLI:EU:C:2017:204.

[72] C-236/09 *Association Belge des Consommateurs Test-Achats ASBL and Others* (n 31).

black box of the algorithm to explain the functioning of the algorithm and how the algorithm arrives at a certain result, the discrimination will be established. Here again, the GDPR gives the right to obtain information and explanation on the algorithms but if no explanation is given or if the information is insufficient, the discrimination may nevertheless be established. Of course, a preliminary question will be whether there is sufficient evidence to establish this presumption of discrimination.

A final limitation concerns the general approach to discrimination in the EU directives. First, algorithmic profiling based on a granular analysis of personal and behavioural data entails heightened risks of intersectional discrimination, a type of discrimination that until now the directives and the Court of Justice have failed to recognise.[73]

Second, the right not to be discriminated against has been initially defined as an individual right and the traditional European approach has been to rely on an individual complaints model. In this perspective, the EU legal system guarantees the right to effective judicial protection with due regard to the principles of effectiveness and equivalence. Indeed, the right to effective judicial protection, which is now a general principle of EU law recognised in the European Charter of Fundamental Rights (Article 47), was first recognised in cases dealing with discrimination issues. The limits of this model have quickly emerged. Here again, this limitation is inherent in discrimination law in particular, and in labour law in general.

Different rights have been recognised to support individual claims and to mitigate the difficulties faced by the claimant, like the recognition of trade unions or associations to help the claimant, or the obligation on Member States to set up a body or bodies whose tasks include providing independent assistance to victims of discrimination on the ground of sex and of racial or ethnic origin. They shall also ensure that associations, organisations or other legal entities, which have a legitimate interest in ensuring that the provisions of the directives are complied with, may engage, on certain conditions, judicial procedures and/or administrative procedures provided for the enforcement of obligations under the directives. These rights are essential as it is otherwise very difficult for workers alone to fight against a discriminatory algorithm. Employees' rights to non-discrimination and data protection will be effective if they can rely on actors like trade unions, workers' representatives, equality bodies, labour inspectorates. Collective agreements can also play a role. For this reason, the situation of platform workers could be much more problematic. Without entering into the debate on the legal qualification of their contract (self-employed, employees or belonging to a third category), the issue will not be so much the recognition for these workers of their right not to be subjected to a discriminatory algorithm, but the effectiveness of their right.

## V. Conclusion

In conclusion, it seems to me that the risk of algorithmic discrimination at work today remains limited for a series of reasons. First, the use of algorithms in human resources management is still rather limited and the existence of anti-discrimination legislation

[73] Case C-443/15 *David L Parris v Trinity College Dublin and Others* ECLI:EU:C:2016:897.

may be a brake on the spread of these practices. Second, the articulation of non-discrimination with the data protection regulations seems promising. Third, dealing with discrimination in our societies is particularly complex because discrimination is the result of historical, social and economic processes.

The use of algorithms can indeed reveal certain discriminatory processes. For example, cross-referencing salary data in a company can provide a better understanding of the reasons for persistent inequality. Algorithmic human resource tools, because they must identify an issue to be addressed and define criteria to achieve a result, allow for objectification of decision making. From this perspective, they open the black box of human decision-making and allow for better control. However, it is important not be overly optimistic. At the European level, the European regulation on AI should be further developed, but the central issue in companies and in platform work will be the possibility for workers to claim the rights granted to them.

I will end with an example demonstrating the ability of non-discrimination law to deal with algorithmic operation. This is a decision of the Bologna Labour Court of 27 December 2020.[74] The case was referred to the Court by a trade union organisation. The dispute concerned the digital platform *Deliveroo Italia*. The algorithm used by the platform favoured the allocation of deliveries to the 'best' deliverers, with this quality depending on two indices: the reliability index, which measures the number of times the deliverer has not connected to the platform; and the participation index, which measures the willingness of the deliverer to work during peak hours.

From the analysis of the functioning of these two indices, the Court concludeed that delivery personnel who do not participate in the booked work without informing the platform in advance (late cancellation) are given a lower score than other delivery personnel. The judge deduced from this system the existence of indirect discrimination against striking workers contrary to the freedom of association. While the system is apparently neutral, it disadvantages workers who would like to participate in a surprise strike, which is legal in Italy. In other words, riders whose availability does not allow them to accept all the rides proposed by the algorithm are disadvantaged in subsequent allocations of work and are at risk of being completely excluded from work opportunities. This is therefore indirect discrimination, for which the platform has not provided any justification in terms of the legitimacy of the aim pursued and the appropriate and necessary nature of the means implemented to achieve it.

Here the tribunal did not look at the details of the algorithm. The judge accepted as factual elements suggesting the existence of discrimination in the documents surrounding the use of the algorithm: the contract between the platform and the delivery drivers which mentions the rules concerning the reservation or the FAQ available on the platform's website. It is these documents explaining to users how the algorithm works (the reliability and participation indices taken into account in the score of the delivery drivers) that constitute in this case the factual elements suggesting the existence of discrimination within the algorithm.

[74] The decision is available at: www.bollettinoadapt.it/wp-content/uploads/2021/01/Ordinanza-Bologna.pdf in italian, L Ratti, 'La neutralité algorithmique à l'épreuve de ses effets discriminatoires' [2021] *Revue de droit du travail*; L Ratti and M Peyronnet, 'Controverse: Algorithmes et risque de discrimination: quel contrôle du juge?' [2021] *Revue de Droit du Travail* 81.

This is, of course, a single decision, but it is indicative of the risk of algorithmic discrimination at work and of the ability of non-discrimination law to deal with it. On the other hand, it is essential that the use of algorithms in the employment relationship be regulated, and that workers' rights be effective so that this use contributes to making work decent.

# PART IV

# Data Protection and Privacy at Work

# 15

# Regulating Worker Privacy and Data Protection: Exploring the Global Source System

FRANK HENDRICKX

## I. Introduction

The workplace is a main place of concern for privacy and data protection. Originating as a traditional 'civil' right, the right to privacy has increasingly provided important milestones in the employment context. In 1890, Warren and Brandeis defined the right to privacy as 'the right to be let alone'.[1] Since then, privacy protection has strongly evolved over time. In light of this, data protection has become a growing issue. Employment and labour relations provide legitimate grounds for data collection and processing, not only in the recruitment process, but during and even after the whole employment. In the employment context, personal data flows come as an almost natural logic.

A key development from which privacy and data protection has been able to prosper has technological origins and comes from the growing digitalisation of work. Information needs and the exchange of data are growing, while technological developments make data collection and processing increasingly complex, as well as easier and faster. Internet, email, location tracking or GPS systems, recording systems, electronic badges, computer software, smart cameras and intelligent systems including algorithms, big data, the internet of things and profiling, are becoming increasingly intervening and influential factors in our world of work.

During the last decades, coming out of the twentieth century and into the new millennium, technological evolutions have brought the relevance of data protection to the fore. Various (international) regulators started to address the right to personal data protection. Also during this time frame, the International Labour Organization (ILO) adopted a Code of Practice (1996) concerning the protection of workers' personal data.[2]

[1] SD Warren and LD Brandeis, 'The right to privacy' (1980) 4 *Harvard Law Review* 193.
[2] International Labour Organization, *Protection of workers' personal data, An ILO code of practice* (1997) 47.

The European Union's General Data Protection Regulation (GDPR)[3] is a more recent addition to this proper and relevant perspective, following earlier twentieth-century legislative work. In this broader context, the privacy notion has also shown itself to be flexible, responsive and adaptive to new circumstances. Case law in the field was multiplied. In the later developments, the right to privacy appears to have strong potential in supporting and developing a human-in-command agenda of labour law, and thus to secure future proof regulation in a context of artificial intelligence (AI) and robotisation.[4]

The right to privacy and data protection would thus seem to have the potential to be everywhere in the world of work, while it is perhaps not yet an actual reality. At the same time, developments do not stop and progress is still being made in the field. Furthermore, this is a global phenomenon. While the right to privacy and data protection is universally accepted as a human right, its understanding has a social, cultural, even politico-historical bind.[5] It implies that international and global principles may receive further shape, but need to take into account differences in jurisdictional approaches, though with a common baseline.[6] This legal-contextual environment of privacy protection is not only pointed out from a 'Western' perspective, but far beyond this, as for example in African literature.[7] It is this potential for a global approach that meets the interest of the present contribution.

In earlier work, I have focused on the European approach of workplace privacy[8] as well as the evolving pathways of the privacy notion and approach in light of the workplace context.[9] It has been argued that the dynamic privacy concept has adapted itself over time to the pace of new technological challenges, and the idea of 'privacy 4.0'[10] has been seen as a response to 'Industry 4.0' and other disruptive models that attempt to explain the complex future of the world of work.[11] It not only marks the right to privacy as a 'layered' concept, but confirms its technological responsiveness in a broader perspective.

The present contribution looks into international legal frameworks. It aims to deliver an overview and analysis of international and regional instruments in the field

[3] Regulation (EU) 2016/679 of the European Parliament and of the Council of 27 April 2016 on the protection of natural persons with regard to the processing of personal data and on the free movement of such data, and repealing Directive 95/46/EC (General Data Protection Regulation) [2016] OJ L119/1.

[4] F Hendrickx, 'From digits to robots: The privacy–autonomy nexus in new labour law machinery' (2019) 40 *Comparative Labor Law & Policy Journal* 365.

[5] JQ Whitman, 'The Two Western Cultures of Privacy: Dignity versus Liberty' (2004) 113 *Yale Law Journal* 1151.

[6] RJ Krotoszynski, *Privacy Revisited: A Global Perspective on the Right to be Left Alone* (Oxford, Oxford University Press, 2016) 9.

[7] AB Makulilo (ed), 'African Data Privacy Laws' in *Law, Governance and Technology Series*, Vol 33 (Berlin, Springer, 2016) 4.

[8] See F Hendrickx, 'Article 7 – Protection of Private and Family Life' in F Dorssemont, K Lörcher, S Clauwaert and M Schmitt (eds), *The Charter of Fundamental Rights of the European Union and the Employment Relation* (Oxford, Hart Publishing, 2019) 229; F Hendrickx, 'Article 8 – Protection of Personal Data' in F Dorssemont, K Lörcher, S Clauwaert and M Schmitt (eds), *The Charter of Fundamental Rights of the European Union and the Employment Relation* (Oxford, Hart Publishing, 2019) 249.

[9] F Hendrickx, 'Privacy 4.0. at work: regulating employment, technology, and automation' (2019) *Comparative Labor Law & Policy Journal* 147.

[10] ibid.

[11] K Schwab, *The fourth industrial revolution: what it means and how to respond* (14 January 2016) *World Economic Forum*; K Schwab, *The Fourth Industrial Revolution*, 1st edn (Redfern, NY, Currency Books, 2017).

of workplace privacy. Hereby, the aim is to discover the dominant effects of privacy and worker personal data protection. As will be explained below, with the adoption of the GDPR in the European Union (EU), the influence of European standard-setting seems to be quite strong, if not authoritative, on the global scene. At the same time, many different international and regional initiatives have been undertaken, with instruments and principles which – taken together – may emerge as a global approach.

In light of this, the aim of this contribution is to give an overview of the status of global law – or global regulatory frameworks – on the subject and to give critical insights into trends and principles. It implies that both international and regional perspectives and sources will be taken into account. With the global dynamics in the development of international, regional and national instruments with regard to the right to privacy and data protection, an exploration can be undertaken in view of a growing international consensus-building relevant in this domain. This chapter uses a multiple set of legal research methods and sources, including library searches and official websites (specific attention is given to government departments for justice, labour and data protection), applying key terms relying on main literature references in law and the world of work.

In view of the aims of this contribution, the following structure is applied. First, in section II a 'global source development' is presented in order to create both a global and coherent overview of human rights and data protection instruments, at international and regional level. It will be demonstrated that the global picture may be seen as a combination of both globalism and regionalism. Second, against this background, in section III some global privacy and data protection principles are identified. They will be approached as belonging to global consensus building. However, some differences in language will be pointed out and when related to the employment context, the abstract principles will be shown to be adapted to the specific contexts of the instruments at stake. Finally, taking into account recent developments connected with privacy and data protection frameworks, reference is made in section IV to the issue of AI in the workplace. For this issue, the step from data protection to AI regulation will be illustrated, but also tested in light of the future prospects for privacy and data protection principles.

## II. Global Source Development

### A. Global Trends

A global approach to privacy and data protection law deserves attention for its dynamics and evolutions in global consensus building. This falls back on the assumption that privacy approaches are partly universally, but also partly culturally driven. Whereas privacy and data protection, as notions, have arisen in Western legal systems where they strongly developed in the twentieth century, they have clearly evolved throughout the globe. While the legal notion of privacy appeared first in the US legal system, it has subsequently been conceptually imported, elaborated and adapted in Europe, where approaches on human dignity and personality rights pre-existed.[12]

[12] Whitman (n 5).

Driven by the case law of the European Court of Human Rights, primarily under the European Convention on Human Rights (1950), the privacy right steadily expanded through a number of issues in Europe. Following this, regulation of data protection gained momentum, with a lot happening in Europe. The Council of Europe adopted Convention 108 with regard to personal data protection on 28 January 1981.[13] It followed an initiative from the Organisation for Economic Co-operation and Development (OECD) in 1980. The EU adopted legislation in 1995,[14] which was later replaced by the GDPR in 2016.

In the meantime, the development of the right to privacy and data protection slightly evolved in other regions of the world. Privacy and data protection laws became a phenomenon in different parts of the world, such as in Asian and African countries, or within the broad Latin America and Pacific region. While countries like Australia had already had data protection legislation since the 1980s, most central, southeast and East Asian countries, followed more recently with regulatory interventions.[15] Also many African countries have drafted data protection legislation, or are in the process of creating it.[16] The initiatives in these parts of the world also brought new driving forces in transnational cooperation on standard setting in the field. Many of these initiatives either resonate or reflect the model of the OECD or European data protection standards. Against the background of these dynamics and global legal developments, EU legislation, and mainly the GDPR, influenced data protection legislation around the world. It served as an example or benchmark for various worldwide initiatives.[17]

From a global perspective, the human rights dimension of the issue of privacy and data protection cannot be overlooked. Within the United Nations, the right to privacy is referred to in its International Bill of Rights. It is guaranteed by Article 12 of the Universal Declaration of Human Rights and by Article 17 of the International Covenant on Civil and Political Rights.

Most regions in the world would now also recognise the right to privacy and/or data protection as a fundamental right. The most important European instruments are the European Convention on Human Rights (Article 8 ECHR) and the Charter on Fundamental Rights of the European Union (Articles 7 and 8 CFREU). It goes along with a vast area of case law of the European Court on Human Rights (ECtHR). The human rights dimension also comes through in other regions. Privacy protection can be found in Article 11 of the American Convention on Human Rights (1969).[18] A number of US constitutions have explicit reference relating to this right. The federal

[13] Convention for the Protection of Individuals with Regard to Automatic Processing of Personal Data (Strasbourg, 28 January 1981, ETS no 108).

[14] Directive 95/46/EC of the European Parliament and of the Council of 24 October 1995 on the protection of individuals with regard to the processing of personal data and on the free movement of such data [1995] OJ L281/31.

[15] R Walters, L Trakman and B Zeller (eds), *Data Protection Law A Comparative Analysis of Asia-Pacific and European Approaches* (Berlin, Springer, 2019) VII.

[16] *cf*: www.deloitte.com/content/dam/Deloitte/za/Documents/risk/za_Privacy_is_Paramount-Personal_Data_Protection_in_Africa.pdf.

[17] White Paper of the Committee of Experts on a data protection framework for India (2017), available at: www.innovate.mygov.in/wp-content/uploads/2017/11/Final_Draft_White_Paper_on_Data_Protection_in_India.pdf, 10.

[18] www.oas.org/dil/access_to_information_American_Convention_on_Human_Rights.pdf.

afforded privacy protections mirror the Fourth Amendment of the US Constitution.[19] Within ASEAN, the Association of South-East Asian countries, also protects the right to privacy, including the right to data protection, through section 21 of the ASEAN Human Rights Declaration.

While the African Charter on Human and Peoples' Rights (African Charter) does not expressly recognise the right to privacy, this right is nevertheless inferred from other fundamental rights that are guaranteed in the Charter, such as the right to life and human dignity.[20] Furthermore, the African Commission on Human and Peoples' Rights adopted in 2019 the 'Declaration of Principles of Freedom of Expression and Access to Information in Africa' (African Declaration), providing that 'everyone has the right to privacy'.[21]

## B. Regional Data Protection Instruments

Beyond the general human rights framework, different regional initiatives have come into play in the field of data protection. The global outlook thus rather relies on regionalism, as the United Nations does not have a specific standard with regard to data protection, although it follows the subject closely and has adopted a few resolutions.[22]

The OECD has been one of the first organisations to respond to the increase in automated data processing. In 1980, the OECD adopted a Recommendation concerning guidelines governing the protection of privacy and transborder flows of personal data,[23] and updated it in 2013.[24] The guidelines have been very influential and prominent in international consensus building. They have exercised a direct influence on the making of national data protection laws around the world.[25]

The European legal order provides another important and 'leading' source of privacy and personal data protection, certainly with the GDPR. As already indicated, it is often used as a mirror for other regional or national regulatory initiatives. The origins of EU data protection legislation can be found in the Data Protection Directive 95/46/EC (1995),[26] with which the EU created a major legal instrument on the subject. However, new technological developments and the need for effective data protection rights[27]

[19] For an overview, see: www.ncsl.org/research/telecommunications-and-information-technology/privacy-protections-in-state-constitutions.aspx.

[20] www.unctad.org/page/data-protection-and-privacy-legislation-worldwide.

[21] Principle 40 of the Declaration.

[22] Resolution adopted by the General Assembly on 18 December 2014 [on the report of the Third Committee (A/69/488/Add.2 and Corr.1)] 69/166. The right to privacy in the digital age; www.daganun.org/bitstream/handle/11176/158167/A_RES_69_166-EN.pdf?sequence=3&isAllowed=y; Resolution adopted by the Human Rights Council 28/16. The right to privacy in the digital age; www.repository.un.org/bitstream/handle/11176/311688/A_HRC_RES_28_16-EN.pdf?sequence=3&isAllowed=y.

[23] See for the full text: www.oecd.org/sti/ieconomy/oecdguidelinesontheprotectionofprivacyandtransborderflowsofpersonaldata.htm.

[24] See for the full text: www.oecd.org/internet/ieconomy/privacy-guidelines.htm.

[25] www.oecd.org/sti/ieconomy/oecd_privacy_framework.pdf.

[26] See above (n 14).

[27] Communication from the Commission to the European Parliament, the Council, the European Economic and Social Committee and the Committee of the Regions Safeguarding Privacy in a Connected World A European Data Protection Framework for the 21st Century COM/2012/09 final.

led to the adoption of the 'General Data Protection Regulation', known as the GDPR, on 27 April 2016. The Regulation is applicable as from 25 May 2018 and replaces the 1995 Directive. The GDPR is, furthermore, complemented with a new Directive.[28]

The Council of Europe (CoE) adopted a specific Convention with regard to personal data protection on 28 January 1981,[29] which was modernised in 2018[30] and referred to as 'Convention 108+'. While the concern was to bring more unity and greater protection in national legal systems throughout Europe,[31] the new Convention aims to be a 'global' convention, promoting accession by countries outside Europe. In addition to the 47 European participating states, eight countries outside Europe have become parties.[32]

Further, outside the European or Western region, many different initiatives in the field of privacy and data protection have been taken. In the Asia-Pacific region, a new ASEAN 'Framework on Personal Data Protection' was adopted in 2016, containing a set of principles to guide the implementation of data protection measures at national and regional level.[33] Also APEC, the Asia-Pacific Economic Cooperation, developed data protection norms. This was done through the APEC Privacy Framework, first adopted in 2005 and updated in 2015. This Framework is modelled upon, and consistent with, the OECD Data Protection Guidelines, rather than the GDPR.[34] Furthermore, APEC adopted the 'Cross Border Privacy Rules system', which was endorsed by APEC leaders in 2011.[35] Attempts are being made to bridge the initiatives from ASEAN and APEC in order to reach a single and more coherent framework for the whole region.[36]

The legal notions of privacy and data protection also appeared in the African region. While the concept of privacy may be rather new to the cultural and legal traditions of African countries, the value of a regulatory approach has increased over the years. Different African countries have taken initiatives for regulating data protection

[28] Directive (EU) 2016/680 of the European Parliament and of the Council of 27 April 2016 on the protection of natural persons with regard to the processing of personal data by competent authorities for the purposes of the prevention, investigation, detection or prosecution of criminal offences or the execution of criminal penalties, and on the free movement of such data, and repealing Council Framework Decision 2008/977/JHA [2016] OJ L119/89.

[29] Convention for the Protection of Individuals with Regard to Automatic Processing of Personal Data (Strasbourg, 28 January 1981, ETS no 108).

[30] Explanatory Memorandum, to the Protocol amending the Convention for the Protection of Individuals with regard to Automatic Processing of Personal Data, Council of Europe Series n 223.

[31] It has been, moreover, ratified by countries outside the Council of Europe. See: www.coe.int/en/web/conventions/full-list/-/conventions/treaty/108/signatures?p_auth=mScbc290.

[32] Including, Uruguay, Mauritius, Senegal, Tunisia, Cape Verde, Mexico, Argentina and Morocco, with further outreach to Burkina Faso: www.coe.int/en/web/conventions/full-list/-/conventions/treaty/108/signatures; G Greenleaf and B Cottier, 'Comparing African Data Privacy Laws: International, African and Regional Commitments' (2020) University of New South Wales Law Research Series, available at: SSRN: www.ssrn.com/abstract=3582478.

[33] www.asean.org/storage/2012/05/10-ASEAN-Framework-on-PDP.pdf.

[34] For a comparison between the APEC Privacy Framework and the GDPR, see: www.iapp.org/news/a/gdpr-matchup-the-apec-privacy-framework-and-cross-border-privacy-rules/

[35] APEC Privacy Framework (2015), section 12: www.apec.org/publications/2005/12/apec-privacy-framework.

[36] www.gsma.com/publicpolicy/wp-content/uploads/2018/09/GSMA-Regional-Privacy-Frameworks-and-Cross-Border-Data-Flows_Full-Report_Sept-2018.pdf.

and various African constitutions have adopted a right to privacy.[37] These legislative initiatives have been promoted, supported and underpinned by African regional initiatives, partly in response to a need for benchmarking and harmonisation. An important initiative came from ECOWAS, the intergovernmental organisation of Western Africa countries. The 'ECOWAS Data Protection Act', adopted in 2010,[38] can be seen as the first real sub-regional initiative to develop a framework of personal data protection law in Africa. In 2013, a Model Law on Data Protection was drafted as an initiative from sub-Saharan Africa.[39]

In 2014, the African Union adopted a 'Convention on Cyber Security and Personal Data Protection',[40] however, only five (of the needed 15) ratifications have been realised so far.[41] The 2014 Convention has been completed with personal data protection guidelines in 2018 in order to facilitate the further promotion of the instrument.[42] Another relevant African regional document is the revised Declaration of Principles of Freedom of Expression and Access to Information in Africa, adopted by the African Commission on Human Rights in 2019, giving guidance on surveillance, privacy and data protection.[43]

Latin American countries are gradually arriving at a regional common standard development on privacy and data protection. The region has seen many data protection law reforms, some of which have been inspired by, or modelled on, the European GDPR.[44] Latin American countries have tried to establish their own initiatives, resonating a combination of the GDPR, OECD and APEC regulatory models.[45] Within the Ibero-American Data Protection Network,[46] the Data Protection Standards of the Ibero-American States was adopted in 2017.[47] Reflecting the EU's GDPR model, it has served as a blueprint for data protection law reforms and initiatives in this region.[48]

[37] A Rogers, 'Africa's Multilateral Legal Framework on Personal Data Security: What Prospects for the Digital Environment?' in R Zitouni, M Agueh, P Houngue and H Soude (eds), *E-Infrastructure and e-Services for Developing Countries 11th EAI International Conference*, AFRICOMM 2019 (Porto-Novo, Benin, 3–4 December 2019) Proceedings (Berlin Springer, 2020) 46; For an overview of enacted data privacy laws in Africa, see: Greenleaf and Cottier (n 32).

[38] Supplementary Act A/SA.1/01/10 Personal Data Protection within ECOWAS: www.tit.comm.ecowas.int/wp-content/uploads/2015/11/SIGNED-Data-Protection-Act.pdf.

[39] www.itu.int/en/ITU-D/Projects/ITU-EC-ACP/HIPSSA/Documents/FINAL%20DOCUMENTS/FINAL%20DOCS%20ENGLISH/sadc_model_law_data_protection.pdf.

[40] www.au.int/sites/default/files/treaties/29560-treaty-0048_-_african_union_convention_on_cyber_security_and_personal_data_protection_e.pdf

[41] Ghana, Guinea, Mauritius, Namibia, Senegal: ccdcoe.org/organisations/au/.

[42] Personal Data Protection Guidelines for Africa: A joint initiative of the Internet Society and the Commission of the African Union 9 May 2018, available at: www.internetsociety.org/wp-content/uploads/2018/05/AUCPrivacyGuidelines_2018508_EN-1.pdf.

[43] www.achpr.org/legalinstruments/detail?id=69.

[44] www.lexology.com/library/detail.aspx?g=b62b37fd-54dc-4fd4-9c81-36b32767a101.

[45] www.repositorio.cepal.org/bitstream/handle/11362/44629/1/S1900395_en.pdf; HJ Lehuedé, 'Corporate governance and data protection in Latin America and the Caribbean' (2019) 223 *ECLAC Production Development Serie* 58.

[46] www.phaedra-project.eu/wp-content/uploads/PHAEDRA-D1-30-Dec-2014.pdf (*cf* 128).

[47] For the text see: www.iapp.org/media/pdf/resource_center/Ibero-Am_standards.pdf.

[48] *cf*ec.europa.eu/fpi/sites/fpi/files/ann8_international_digital_cooperation_personal_data_protection_and_flow.pdf.

## C. Guidance for the Work Environment

One of the issues in the field of worker privacy and data protection is not just the establishment of general principles, but to develop more specific guidance. While major data protection instruments are in principle applicable in the employment context, efforts have been made to create more specific rules for the work environment. The concern has arisen prominently within the ILO, which took the lead in 1996 with the adoption of a Code of Practice.[49] This Code has not been adopted as an ILO Convention or a Recommendation, but rather as a reference for the development of legislation, regulations, collective bargaining agreements, work regulations, policies and other practical measures.

The creation of specific employment-related principles has also inspired the EU institutions. The EU has had the idea of legislating specifically in the area of employment data protection. After having conducted some comparative studies,[50] the European Commission initiated a consultation process on this subject with the European Social Partners under the Treaty's social policy title. The initiative, however, ultimately did not succeed.[51]

Under the (former) 1995 European Data Protection Directive, the European Data Protection Working Party adopted some guidance on data protection in the employment context. The Working Party[52] adopted Opinion 8/2001 on the processing of personal data in the employment context.[53] Another instrument is the EU Working Document on workplace communications (2002).[54] The Working Party also issued Opinion 2/2017 on data processing at work, which made a new assessment of issues 'by outlining the risks posed by new technologies and undertaking a proportionality assessment of a number of scenarios in which they could be deployed'.[55] Under the GDPR and its new governance model, the Working Party was replaced by the European Data Protection Board. However, many of the Working Party's Opinions are still authoritative and some even included projected references to the GDPR framework.

The desirability of adapting general data protection principles to the particular requirements of the employment sector also raised concerns in the Council of Europe. It led to the adoption of Recommendation No R(89)2 on the Protection of Personal Data Used for Employment Purposes. In 2015, the Committee of Ministers adopted a

[49] International Labour Organization, *Protection of workers' personal data, An ILO code of practice* (Geneva, 1997) 47.

[50] See the study of M Freedland and the studies of F Hendrickx: www.ec.europa.eu/social/main.jsp?catId=708.

[51] See: www.ec.europa.eu/social/main.jsp?catId=708.

[52] The Working Party is an advisory group composed of representatives of the data protection authorities of the Member States, which acts independently and has the task, inter alia, of examining any question covering the application of the national measures adopted under the Data Protection Directive in order to contribute to the uniform application of such measures.

[53] Opinion 8/2001 of 13 September 2001 on the processing of personal data in the employment context, 5062/01/EN/Final, WP 48, 28, available at: www.ec.europa.eu/justice/article-29/documentation/opinion-recommendation/files/2001/wp48_en.pdf.

[54] Data Protection Working Party, *Working Document on the Surveillance of Electronic Communications in the Workplace*, 29 May 2002, 5401/01/EN/final, 35.

[55] See: www.ec.europa.eu/newsroom/just/item-detail.cfm?item_id=50083.

new Recommendation on the processing of personal data in the employment context,[56] 'notably due to the increased use of information and communication technologies (ICTs) and the globalisation of employment and services'.[57]

In short, in addition to a major ILO initiative, only European regional initiatives seem to have put worker data protection to the fore.

# III. Global Principles on Privacy and Data Protection

As the worldwide growth of data protection regulation is unstoppable and a logical follow-up from technological evolutions and societal needs, it is clear that, mainly, regional data protection instruments attempt to give their respective responses. However, with the creation of different regional instruments, mutual inspiration and benchmarking has been used. An important influence has been exercised by the standard setting of the OECD, the Council of Europe and the EU (GDPR). While the different instruments have their own language and choices, it is important to recognise and appreciate the underlying global dimension and an emerging 'global consensus' of data protection standards.

## A. Global Consensus

Only a few studies have been conducted that compare and synthesise the major data protection standards on a global scale. A leading study came in 2020 from the Global Privacy Assembly, an organisation that groups data protection authorities worldwide.[58] The study produced a comparative inventory of the main and globally shared principles of data protection departing from 10 regional and global standards.[59] From the comparison of these instruments, the following global key principles emerged:

1. Fairness: personal data should be processed fairly.
2. Legitimacy (or lawfulness): personal data should be processed for legitimate purposes, or should be processed lawfully.
3. Purpose specification: personal data should be processed only for specified, defined, explicit and legitimate purposes.
4. Proportionality: personal data should be processed taking into account general requirements of proportionality, data minimisation requirements, requirements of non-excessive processing, or requirements of relevance to purpose.
5. Data quality: personal data should be accurate, complete and up to date.
6. Openness/transparency: the inclusion of some degree of openness or transparency can be found in all frameworks. Degrees range from general requirements to have

[56] CM/Rec(2015)5, available at: www.search.coe.int/cm/Pages/result_details.aspx?ObjectID=09000016805c3f7a.

[57] See the Preamble of Recommendation CM/Rec(2015)5.

[58] Formerly known as the International Conference of Data Protection and Privacy Commissioners – ICDPPC: www.globalprivacyassembly.org.

[59] Another interesting comparison departing from the African instruments: Greenleaf and Cottier (n 32).

transparent policies, and to ensure that information about personal data processing is made available, to specific lists of information that must be provided directly to data subjects.

7. Security: there should be appropriate (or sufficient) measures to secure personal data (processing).
8. Data retention: personal data should not be retained longer than is necessary for the purposes of processing.
9. Accountability: a slightly less generally shared principle, with six out of ten frameworks, requiring that data controllers (and where applicable, processors) are accountable for the personal data they process.
10. Access: data subjects have the right of access to their personal data and have these data rectified and/or deleted or erased, with (for some instruments) additional guarantees of objecting or contesting the data processing.[60]

Some of these principles will be further discussed below, in order to illustrate their common ground and mutual relationship in the global legal source system, but also to point out at nuances.

## B. Globalism versus Regionalism

While a global consensus on data protection principles takes shape, the translation of those general principles to the work environment may still be open for further development. It is also likely that specificities relating to regional approaches will come through. Looking at concrete issues there is clearly overlap, but also room for differences. This can be demonstrated with some of the key principles relating to three typical applications in the employment context.

### *i. Legitimacy*

A first example is that relating to the legitimacy principle. One of the main principles of data protection is that personal data must be processed on a legitimate basis. In other words, personal data processing has to be justified on the basis of a legitimate ground, reason or purpose. A legitimate basis requires, above all, that it is lawful.

In light of this, the ILO Code of Practice provides that 'personal data should be processed lawfully and fairly, and only for reasons directly relevant to the employment of the worker'.[61] This principle of lawfulness or legitimacy stands central in data protection law and has been further specified in different data protection instruments around the globe. Some will refer to this as a data collection limitation principle, as is made clear in section 7 of the OECD Guidelines on data protection (2013). There is a similar reference in the APEC Privacy Framework. The principle of lawfulness is also explicitly provided in the GDPR, and in the ECOWAS data protection act.

[60] Global Privacy Assembly, Policy Strategy Working Group 1: Global frameworks and standards, October 2020, available at: www.globalprivacyassembly.org/wp-content/uploads/2020/10/Day-1-1_2a-Day-3-3_2b-v1_0-Policy-Strategy-Working-Group-WS1-Global-frameworks-and-standards-Report-Final.pdf.

[61] s 5.1, ILO Code of Practice.

The evaluation of this legitimacy principle will be much dependent on the context and circumstances of data processing. However, it must be clear that the employment relationship is recognised as a legitimate basis for personal data processing under data protection law. Obviously, the link with the employment relationship should be established in an appropriate way. The language is, however, not always the same.

The ILO Code of Practice, referred to above, aims for a justification of data processing 'directly relevant to the employment of the worker'. This formula looks like a rather narrow approach, not including every legitimate business interest. Other instruments, such as the GDPR show that employers who want to process the personal data of workers may based the legitimacy of the processing on a wider variety of grounds. Under GDPR Article 6, processing is considered to be lawful when necessary:

- For the performance of a contract to which the data subject is party or in order to take steps at the request of the data subject prior to entering into a contract.
- For compliance with a legal obligation to which the controller is subject.
- In order to protect the vital interests of the data subject or of another natural person.
- For the performance of a task carried out in the public interest or in the exercise of official authority vested in the controller.
- For the purposes of the legitimate interests pursued by the controller or by a third party.

This European standard thus shows that personal data processing is not only legitimate when employers are required or obliged to process these data, but in cases where employers have a contractual or other 'legitimate interest'.

It may be assumed that together with the other instruments, employers may justify data processing in areas such as: recruitment and selection; the exercise of rights, such as the right to exercise authority and control, or to direct the enterprise and plan the work, under the employment contract; payroll, administration and human resources services; health and safety obligations and actions; diversity policies, and so on.

In the APEC Framework, this aspect is instead found in the principle on 'use of information', where reference is made to the condition that personal data should be collected only when necessary to provide a service or product requested by the individual, or by the authority of law and other legal instruments, proclamations and pronouncements of legal effect. This seems to be somewhat stricter than the GDPR, or the ECOWAS instrument. In the commentary to the APEC Framework provision, it is explained that justifications may be made for 'a centralized database to manage personnel in an effective and efficient manner' or for 'the processing of employee payrolls by a third party'.[62]

In this context, for the more obvious data processing activities like personnel administration, there will most likely be room for justification under all instruments. The difference in language might nevertheless play a more decisive role in dealing with 'hard' cases, for example in cases of electronic monitoring (see below), or in cases where employers would invoke public interest reasons, involving external circumstances to the business, such as, for example, during a pandemic.

[62] *cf* Commentary to Article 25 APEC Privacy Framework.

### *ii. Proportionality*

Another interesting principle is proportionality. It is one of the most general and overarching principles in data protection law, and most legal systems would apply and follow it. There are, however, different ways to label and define it. Some instruments refer to conditions of relevancy, adequacy, necessity, besides proportionality of data processing.

Proportionality also requires specification or interpretation. The principle of proportionality allows a legal assessment to work with the term 'necessary' and to distinguish it from 'legitimacy'. This may be complicated, since the legitimacy principle is also referring to a requirement of necessity, such as in 'necessary for the performance of a contract', as shown in Article 6.1(b) of the GDPR. An explanation may be that 'necessity' should be evaluated in light of the aims of processing,[63] so that the processing has to remain proportionate to the legitimate purposes.[64] As the OECD's Explanation to the Guidelines phrases it: 'The requirements in this respect are linked to the purposes of data, ie they are not intended to be more far-reaching than is necessary for the purposes for which the data are used'.[65] It requires a rather careful, judicious and prudent use of data in light of the intended purposes.

This proportionality principle is also mentioned as a principle in CoE Convention (108+), and in the Ibero-American Standards for Personal Data Protection (18th principle). In some instruments, proportionality is seen to be included in the principle of 'data quality', such as in the OECD Guidelines (2013). But all instruments use one or more of the principles of relevance, adequacy, non-excessiveness, and so on. The CoE Recommendation (2015), relating to employment, provides that 'personal data collected by employers for employment purposes should be relevant and not excessive, bearing in mind the type of the employment as well as the changing information needs of the employer'.[66]

The use of different language may have an influence on the ultimate legal assessment. The principle of proportionality is, under the GDPR, strongly interwoven with the concept of 'data minimisation'. This concept seems to be increasingly relevant in the context of AI, or in electronic monitoring, and even more generally in a human resources context. The data minimisation principle, mentioned in Article 5.1(C) of the GDPR, looks stronger – and perhaps more severe – than proportionality. The Ibero-American Standards for Personal Data Protection's 18th principle, referring to proportionality, perhaps comes closest to data minimisation as it demands that personal data should be 'appropriate, pertinent and limited to the minimum necessary for the purpose'. Also CoE Recommendation (2015) provides that 'employers should minimise the processing of personal data to only the data necessary to the aim pursued in the individual cases concerned'.[67]

[63] s 4.1, CoE Recommendation 2015.
[64] WP Opinion 2/2017 (n 55) 7.
[65] Explanation 53. See: www.oecd.org/sti/ieconomy/oecdguidelinesontheprotectionofprivacyandtransborderflowsofpersonaldata.htm#memorandum.
[66] s 5.2, CoE Recommendation 2015.
[67] s 4.1, CoE Recommendation 2015.

### iii. *Monitoring and Surveillance*

A third example, where more specificity for the employment context is relevant, is monitoring and surveillance in the workplace.

In Europe, a landmark case was delivered by the ECtHR with *Bărbulescu*.[68] The ECtHR gave a number of principles for email monitoring, such as: (i) prior notification; (ii) the extent of the monitoring and the degree of intrusion; (iii) the need for legitimate reasons; (iv) the presence of less intrusive methods or measures; (v) the consequences of monitoring; (vi) the presence of adequate safeguards.[69] These principles show some overlap with what is provided in the ILO Code of Practice, where it is also required that workers are informed in advance;[70] that employers must minimise the intrusion;[71] or that technical or organisational measures have to be put in place.[72] It seems nevertheless that the *Bărbulescu* case has embarked on elaborating the proportionality principle, mentioned above, and made the balancing between purposes and means more specific in the monitoring case.

The ILO Code of Practice nevertheless goes further with specific concerns in an employment context, such as the point that personal data collected by electronic monitoring should not be the only factor in evaluating worker performance, which seems to go beyond *Bărbulescu*.[73] Overlaps between *Bărbulescu* and the ILO Code of Practice are not fully surprising given the approach of the ECtHR in cross-referring to international sources in organising its legal assessment. In other words, in important cases the ECtHR is also trying to look into an emerging global consensus.

# IV. Artificial Intelligence and Industry 4.0

## A. Challenges

With the rise of 'Industry 4.0' and new technologies based on AI and robotics, new challenges are brought to the workplace, as well as to the field of privacy and data protection law.[74] The future outlook for technology increases the relevance of further thinking along the lines of the key principles of personal data protection, but also to look for strategies and concepts to address new phenomena. The world – and the workplace – has become a place of increased and almost unlimited possibilities for data processing, the centralisation and interconnection of data, making fast and complex flows of data possible. It also goes further as new technologies include the rise of AI, algorithmic decision-making and robotics. This 'intelligent technology' is on the rise and the forecast is that algorithms, big data, smart technology and profiling systems

[68] *Bărbulescu v Romania* App No 61496/08 (ECtHR 5 September 2017).
[69] ibid, para 121.
[70] s 6.14, ILO Code of Practice.
[71] ibid.
[72] s 5.4, ILO Code of Practice.
[73] s 5.6, ILO Code of Practice.
[74] Hendrickx, 'From digits to robots' (n 4).

are becoming increasingly influential factors in our world of work. New 'intelligent' techniques do not only accelerate the levels of personal data collecting and processing, but can also be turned into relevant workplace decision-making and monitoring tools. It may require a new understanding of data protection problems taking into account additional or novel approaches, taking account of (information) power and (de)humanisation.[75]

This is also confirmed in the work of the Global Commission on the Future of Work, stating that

> new technologies generate large amounts of data on workers. This poses risks for workers' privacy. There may be other consequences, depending on how the data are used. Algorithms used for job matching may reproduce historical biases and prejudices, for example. Regulation needs to be developed to govern data use and algorithmic accountability in the world of work.[76]

In light of the thirtieth anniversary of the OECD Guidelines on data protection (see above), an accompanying report not only describes the new technological evolutions, but its implications for privacy protection.[77] As a result of this, 'privacy relations are certainly changing in the employment relationship'.[78] These trends and findings were confirmed in a digital economy paper for the Global Privacy Assembly.[79]

Current data protection standards are crucial in addressing AI and 'Industry 4.0'. For example, as the gig economy shows, data protection standards are not always equipped to deal with a diversity of parties in a larger accountability concept, in online 'ecosystems' that go beyond a single data controller.[80] Another example is 'data quality', an often underestimated problem in the use of AI systems and the application of algorithms. Issues like bias, discriminatory effects, inaccurate or coincidental correlations between data, simplified conclusions, lack of context of data, irrelevant data, are various additional problems.[81]

Some data protection instruments address profiling and/or automated decision-making. The provisions are relevant to respond to algorithmic processes. Examples in the employment context may be: recruitment assessment; performance evaluation; selection for dismissal; analysis of workers' preferences; and analysis of workers'

[75] *cf* DJ Solove, 'Privacy and Power: Computer Databases and Metaphors for Information Privacy' (2001) 53 *Stanford Law Review* 1393.

[76] ILO, Global Commission on the Future of Work, *Work for a brighter future* (Geneva, ILO, 2019) 44, available at: www.ilo.org/global/publications/books/WCMS_662410/lang--en/index.htm.

[77] Thirty years after the OECD Privacy Guidelines, OECD (2011), 30, available at: www.oecd.org/digital/ieconomy/49710223.pdf.

[78] P Moore, 'Data subjects, digital surveillance, AI and the future of work' (2020) *STUDY Panel for the Future of Science and Technology, EPRS – European Parliamentary Research Service Scientific Foresight Unit (STOA)* PE 656.305, 32, available at: www.europarl.europa.eu/RegData/etudes/STUD/2020/656305/EPRS_STU(2020)656305_EN.pdf.

[79] Global Privacy Assembly Report, Policy Strategy Working Group 2, Digital Economy, October 2020, available at: www.globalprivacyassembly.org/wp-content/uploads/2020/10/GPA-PSWG2_Digital_Economy_Working_Group_Report_public.pdf,15.

[80] P Keller, 'The reconstruction of privacy through law: A strategy of diminishing expectations' (2019) 9 *International Data Privacy Law* 151.

[81] Future of Privacy Forum, *The Privacy Expert's Guide to Artificial Intelligence and Machine Learning* (2018), available at: www.fpf.org/wp-content/uploads/2018/10/FPF_Artificial-Intelligence_Digital.pdf, 8.

whereabouts. Under the GDPR, fully automated decision-making is also regulated. It concerns the ability to make decisions by technological means without human involvement. The ILO Code of Practice contains a reference to this: 'decisions concerning a worker should not be based solely on the automated processing of that worker's personal data' (section 5.5). Furthermore, the GDPR provides (in Article 22.1), that a data subject has the right not to be subject to a decision based solely on automated data processing (including profiling), which produces legal effects concerning him or her, or similarly significantly affects him or her.

The approach of these instruments is that they regulate, but do not exclude, nor can they avoid, artificially intelligent techniques and management in the employment context. New and additional principles would in such context seem to become relevant. For example, under the GDPR[82] the data subject (worker) has at least the right to obtain human intervention on the part of the controller (the employer) relating to fully automated decision-making. According to the European Working Party, human intervention is a key element in the GDPR's data protection, and any review of AI decisions must be carried out by someone who has the appropriate authority and capability to change the decision.[83] According to the Global Commission on the Future of Work, 'it also means adopting a "human-in-command" approach to artificial intelligence that ensures that the final decisions affecting work are taken by human beings'.[84]

## B. Towards AI Regulation

With the increasing development of AI systems and the close relationship of these phenomena with data protection standards, various new initiatives have been taken, amongst which is a resolution from the Global Privacy Assembly, grouping national data protection authorities globally, which adopted a 'Declaration on Ethics and Data Protection in Artificial Intelligence' in 2018.[85] It promotes principles such as fairness, governance, transparency and intelligibility, ethics by design, empowerment, avoiding bias and discrimination. These principles are related to and partly overlapping with data protection, but also go beyond the current known standards. They, thus, mark a possible new future outlook of AI-based data processing.

Different intergovernmental initiatives have come into existence in order to seek a regulatory framework for AI. The United Nations is obviously an important actor in the field of AI. The International Telecommunication Union (ITU) publishes an annual directory of all relevant AI initiatives throughout the UN system, including the work of its specialised agencies.[86] Within the UN system, UNESCO took the initiative to create an instrument in the form of a recommendation with principles on AI.

[82] Article 22.3.

[83] Data Protection Working Party, *Guidelines on Automated Individual Decision-making and Profiling for the Purposes of Regulation 2016/679*, adopted on 3 October 2017, last Revised and Adopted on 6 February 2018, 17/EN WP251rev.01, 27.

[84] Global Commission on the Future of Work, *Work for a brighter future* (n 76) 13.

[85] www.globalprivacyassembly.org/wp-content/uploads/2018/10/20180922_ICDPPC-40th_AI-Declaration_ADOPTED.pdf.

[86] See: www.itu.int/dms_pub/itu-s/opb/gen/S-GEN-UNACT-2019-1-PDF-E.pdf.

In September 2020, the ad hoc expert group of UNESCO proposed a first draft of this 'Recommendation on the Ethics of Artificial Intelligence'.[87] The ambition is to reach an officially adopted document by the end of 2021. The recommendation includes four values that should be respected with regard to AI,[88] including respect, protection and promotion of human dignity, human rights and fundamental freedoms. The OECD is another important international actor in the field of regulating AI. By 2018, the OECD had adopted a Recommendation on Artificial Intelligence.[89] The 'principles on AI' in this recommendation are the first international standards agreed by governments.[90] The principles include human-centred values and fairness, as well as transparency.[91]

At regional level, the EU has been an important actor. The European Commission first launched a 'White Paper on Artificial Intelligence in 2020.[92] The EU aims to establish a regulatory framework,[93] drafted in accordance with the guidelines of the High-Level Expert Group, which published guidelines on trustworthy AI in April 2019.[94] Again, also here human agency and oversight remains very important.

In its next step, the EU institutions launched a proposal for an EU Regulation on a European Approach to Artificial Intelligence.[95] The 36th recital of the proposal holds that:

> AI systems used in employment, workers management and access to self-employment, notably for the recruitment and selection of persons, for making decisions on promotion and termination and for task allocation, monitoring or evaluation of persons in work-related contractual relationships, should also be classified as high-risk, since those systems may appreciably impact future career prospects and livelihoods of these persons.[96]

AI systems that constitute a high risk for the safety or fundamental rights of citizens will have to comply with specific requirements and obligations. However, the last word has not yet been said about the issue and critical reflection will remain necessary.[97]

The work of international and regional organisations will inevitably continue over the next years. All the signs are there to bring the question of AI to a broader than just pure data protection approach. However, at the same time privacy and data protection standards and approaches provide important answers to the technological, ethical and legal challenges posed by AI.

[87] www.unesdoc.unesco.org/ark:/48223/pf0000373434/PDF/373434eng.pdf.multi; with follow up: www.events.unesco.org/event?id=1736064082&lang=1033.

[88] www.unesdoc.unesco.org/ark:/48223/pf0000373434/PDF/373434eng.pdf.multi.

[89] www.legalinstruments.oecd.org/en/instruments/OECD-LEGAL-0449.

[90] www.oecd.org/going-digital/ai/.

[91] www.legalinstruments.oecd.org/en/instruments/OECD-LEGAL-0449#mainText.

[92] www.ec.europa.eu/info/sites/info/files/commission-white-paper-artificial-intelligence-feb2020_en.pdf.

[93] www.ec.europa.eu/digital-single-market/en/news/communication-artificial-intelligence-europe.

[94] www.ec.europa.eu/futurium/en/ai-alliance-consultation/guidelines#Top.

[95] European Commission, 'Proposal for a Regulation of the European Parliament and of the Council laying down harmonised rules on artificial intelligence (Artificial Intelligence Act) and amending certain union legislative acts' COM(2021) 206 final.

[96] *cf* Recital 36.

[97] *cf* V De Stefano and S Taes, 'Algorithmic management and collective bargaining' (2021) *Foresight Brief* 10, available at: ETUI: www.etui.org/sites/default/files/2021-05/Algorithmic%20management%20and%20collective%20bargaining-web-2021.pdf.

## V. Conclusions

The chapter looked into the international and regional legal frameworks relating to privacy and data protection, in light of their relevance for the employment context. Examining the different initiatives and pathways followed to develop privacy and data protection rules and principles, not only does a global 'source system' start to emerge, but a growing global consensus towards principles of privacy and personal data protection.

Technology and data protection issues seemed to have accelerated this global body of rules and principles. The enlargement from privacy to personal data protection brought a need to determine guiding principles. In this context, there is a visible interdependence between the different international and regional initiatives. The OECD Guidelines on data protection and the EU GDPR are clearly major influencing instruments. They have served as models for other initiatives, at least implicitly.

At the same time, while the right to privacy and data protection is universally recognised as a human right, the work towards more specific principles and data protection standards is also a question of regional specificities and adaptation. So globalism is confronted with regionalism. It confirms that privacy and data protection need an understanding, which remains embedded in a historical, social, cultural, even political context. It means that, even with different international and regional initiatives leading to a global approach, diversity would still be prevalent. That may be more apparent in the sphere of employment relationships, where local context remains very relevant.

The field of technology and the world of work covers extremely global phenomena. This makes the case for interdependence and interpenetration of legal developments and norms more obvious. Mutual influencing of international and European legal instruments is, therefore, neither uncommon, nor unrealistic.

In this light, the role of regulating AI seems to require a global approach. When looking at the various initiatives already undertaken, simultaneous strategies come into view. Also here, there seems to be a growing consensus and a form of convergence of instruments on the international scene. A human-centred approach, human oversight, accountability and transparency constitute important factors in regulating AI and related systems. This development is still fully under way. It not only makes the findings of this contribution almost per definition explorative. But looking into the future, the uncovering reveals that the role of privacy and data protection within the context of employment will not be diminishing. On the contrary, the essence of privacy – respect for human dignity and human relations – will increasingly and strongly overlap with the essence of labour law. This reflects a reasonable and global aspiration.

# 16

# From Monitoring of the Workplace to Surveillance of the Workforce

DAVID MANGAN

## I. Introduction

Workplace monitoring has existed in some form for a lengthy period. In the early twenty-first century, there has been a change. Surveillance[1] has moved from being of the workplace, to being of the workforce. The distinction is between the orthodox fixed location of work and the broad capture area of twenty-first century surveillance technologies. Digitalisation of work has not only extended the scope of the managerial gaze, but has expanded the type of information collected. The spectrum includes workers' conduct at the place of business as well as their off-duty activities, existing simultaneously in the physical and online spaces. Monitoring of online activities offers a range of data about individuals that may not be easily gleaned from common workplace interactions. Restrictions on the data aspects of employers' surveillance have not been as significantly addressed in case law at this point.[2] Instead, adjudication of employers' monitoring activities has largely focused on video surveillance, as well as an increasing number of decisions relating to social media postings, and some on email and internet use. In many decisions, the monitoring itself has not been challenged because employers' authority (pursuant to contract or management rights) to monitor workers has been accepted, or the impugned activity has been voluntarily posted online by workers and drawn to employers' attention. Surveillance, then, has become a more complicated and layered topic as a result of advances in information technology.

Innovations in information technology have deepened the subordination within the employment relationship. Contract has filled in where the law has been left somewhat languishing. Contract provisions relating to matters of surveillance (if explicitly

[1] 'Surveillance' and 'monitoring' will be used interchangeably. The difference between these terms is discussed in K Ball, 'Workplace Surveillance: An Overview' (2010) 51 *Labor History* 87, 88.

[2] This is not to suggest the matter has not been raised. See, eg, Article 29 Data Protection Working Party, *Opinion 2/2017 on data processing at work 17/EN WP 249* (adopted 8 June 2017) 12. See also, Eurofound, *Employee monitoring and surveillance: The challenges of digitalisation* (Luxembourg, Publications Office of the European Union, 2020) Part 2, where data analytics are being used to monitor employee performance.

spelled out and not relegated to a more general management rights clause) are not likely at the forefront of workers' thoughts when signing the employment contract. Concerns with boilerplate or standard form contracts were ably and aptly raised some time ago in common law jurisdictions.[3] Surveillance draws attention to the contractual authority employers grant themselves. Although management rights are not unfettered, limitation of workplace surveillance necessitates some form of interjection by a legislature or court.

The range of surveillance tools enlarge the imbalance of bargaining power,[4] particularly with regard to information asymmetry between the parties. Workers may be unaware of surveillance activities undertaken by their employers. If they do know, they may be unacquainted with the extent of the surveillance. They may be unfamiliar with the related technologies, thereby bringing into question workers' understanding of any notification or consent given. Information asymmetry intensifies the imbalance of bargaining power within the employment relationship by adding another layer by which employers are in a superior position; ie, understanding the scope and range of monitoring, as well as the extent and implications of processing of data thereby collected.

In endeavouring to balance the competing interests (workers' right to privacy and employers' right to manage their businesses), some jurisdictions have instituted notice and consent requirements. This obligation is of equivocal utility if workers do not understand to what they are being given notice. This procedural focus should be viewed with some scepticism because it only leads to a 'right' to notice, and does not lay out a substantive right to privacy. Furthermore, procedural entitlements alone reinforce subordination. In considering the content of a substantive right to privacy at work, we are confronted with questions (such as on what bases can employers' surveillance extend beyond the workplace?) that demand further deliberation.

The chapter commences with an elaboration, in the next section, of the reasons for employers deploying surveillance. Largely, it is based upon security and safety concerns; though these premises offer a broad scope with a wide capture area. The chapter then considers approaches to surveillance in the UK, Europe[5] and Canada. In the space of this chapter, overviews from each of these jurisdictions indicate differing treatments of the topic: a light-touch, contract-focused approach in the UK; followed by the European analysis which is premised on the European Convention on Human Rights (ECHR) as well as the Charter of Fundamental Rights of the EU (CFREU); and, finally Canada, where there has been some recognition of a right to employee privacy, particularly in the labour arbitration case law. These examples illustrate that the case law of the jurisdictions under study remains somewhat tentative when it comes to an engagement with a worker's right to privacy in relation to an employer's surveillance activities. The situation remains of concern, particularly bearing in mind significant challenges, such

[3] KN Llewellyn, *The Common Law Tradition: Deciding Appeals* (Boston, MA, Little, Brown & Co, 1960); MJ Radin, 'Reconsidering Boilerplate: Confronting Normative and Democratic Degradation' (2012) 40 *Capital University Law Review* 617. See also, Article 29 Data Protection Working Party (n 2) 4.

[4] P Davies and M Freedland, *Kahn-Freund's Labour and the Law*, 3rd edn (London, Stevens & Sons, 1983) 18.

[5] Since decisions of the European Court of Human Rights will be discussed, the reference to Europe recognises that the ECtHR is not an EU body. The European Union (EU) is used as a shorthand, but with this proviso.

as employer surveillance of remote work undertaken during the Covid-19 pandemic, as well as the complications posed by algorithmic surveillance.

## II. Why Employers Use Surveillance

'Supervision is part of employment'.[6] This crude statement could be accurately applied to most any period of labour study. The traditional form of monitoring, prior to the largely remote, digital means currently available, had been through human physical oversight, whether of the workforce in action or their production. This form of surveillance was limited to the supervising individual's time and attention. Factory architecture from the first industrial revolution to the office cubicle layout provided management with opportune vantage points for monitoring the workforce.[7] In the later twentieth century, technology offered employers other means by which to oversee the workforce with phone call monitoring and video surveillance. In 1987, the US Congress released its report *The Electronic Supervisor*.[8] That same year, an estimated 75 per cent of large companies electronically monitored workers.[9] Employers benefited from the 'constant, pervasive, and unblinking'[10] character of this form of surveillance. Twenty-first century technological innovations have scaled up workforce surveillance making continuous oversight not only possible, but widely available to a range of employers.

The decision to monitor insinuates some level of management distrust of the workforce (even if unintended), where this distrust can lead to or include micro-managing of staff. In the context of a private law right to privacy in 1968, Fried used 'constant surveillance' as an example of the absence of trust: '[a person] cannot know that [s/he] is trusted unless [s/he] has a right to act without constant surveillance'.[11]

Four categories of purposes may be discerned from a management perspective of surveillance: '(a) performance appraisal, loss prevention, and profit; (b) development, growth, and training; (c) administrative and safety; and (d) surveillance and authoritarian control'.[12] A means of identifying efficiencies or improvements and legal obligations may also be added to this list.[13] Security and safety in the workplace has been the most often relied upon basis for surveillance.[14] A study by the UK Trades

[6] *Janes Family Foods (Surveillance Grievance)* (2006), 156 LAC (4th) 304, [40]. At the close of the 20th century, Michael Ford QC wrote of surveillance being almost as old as work: M Ford, *Surveillance at Work* (Liverpool, Institute of Employment Rights, 1998).

[7] On the architecture and layout of the office, see the discussion in N Saval, *Cubed: A Secret History of the Workplace* (New York, Anchor Books, 2015).

[8] US Congress, Office of Technology Assessment, *The Electronic Supervisor: New Technology, New Tensions*, OTA-CIT-333 (Washington, DC, US Government Printing Office, 1987).

[9] G Stoney Alder, 'Employee reactions to electronic performance monitoring: A consequence of organizational culture' (2001) 12 *Journal of High Technology Management Research* 323.

[10] ibid, 324.

[11] C Fried, 'Privacy' (1968) 77 *Yale Law Journal* 475, 478.

[12] DM Ravid, DL Tomczak, JC White and TS Behrend, 'EPM 20/20: A Review, Framework, and Research Agenda for Electronic Performance Monitoring' (2020) 46 *Journal of Management* 100, 103.

[13] For a thorough discussion see, C Degryse, *Digitalisation of the economy and its impact on labour markets* (Brussels, European Trade Union Institute, 2016).

[14] Trades Union Congress (TUC), 'I'll be watching you: A report on workplace monitoring' (London, 2018) 19.

Union Congress (TUC) found there is greater acceptance for common forms of surveillance.[15] Respondents in the same study determined that monitoring of employees' social media outside working hours as well as workers' browser histories when using their own devices connected to the employer's WIFI were deemed unacceptable.[16] The TUC study indicates an urgent need for action regarding the establishment of parameters for workforce surveillance.[17]

The range of information that may be collected and processed by contemporary forms of surveillance suggests more than only distrust because the scope of surveillance extends beyond the work day and the workplace. Employers may, based upon the content of this surveillance, enforce perceived performance and behavioural norms insofar as they may be said to be in relation to the workforce. Recognising that a workforce generates data and that employers collect and process this information on a daily basis has been accepted slowly. Society's growing awareness of data has arisen in concert with an enlargement of the ways in which data can be generated as well as how it may be collected and processed. Surveillance is both a technological and a conceptual challenge. Although data had been observable (and to some extent collected) long before computer technologies, there are three further capabilities in the early twenty-first century: (1) massive amounts of data can be easily collected about people; (2) it can be readily disseminated; and (3) this information can be quickly analysed to meet a variety of information retrieval goals.

In the twenty-first century, email and internet usage monitoring, global positioning system (GPS) tracking, electronic time clocks and wearable technologies (including fitness devices)[18] add to an increasingly vast array of tools for workforce surveillance. Digitalised monitoring permits persistent widespread surveillance that provides a broader range of information, as well as data of greater depth. All workers within the range of monitoring platforms may be observed at once and the type of information collected may include work performance, and workers' feelings or sentiments.

## III. Approaches to Legal Constraint of Employers' Surveillance

Contracts, internal rules, policies and handbooks have provided employers with the authority to oversee their workforces. Employers have scope within which they can exert this control. The innovations of information technologies have created an opening into which this management power has extended.

[15] ibid, 23.

[16] ibid, 22–23.

[17] 79% of workers surveyed by the TUC study believe employers should be legally required to consult the workforce and come to an agreement on the matter prior to implementing (let alone enforcing) any new form of surveillance; with 81% contending that employers should additionally be obligated to set out a 'clear and understandable justification' for these new forms of monitoring: TUC (n 14) 25–26.

[18] See C Farr, 'Fitbit Has a New Health Tracker, But You Can Only Get It Through Your Employer or Insurer' *CNBC* (8 February 2019), available at: www.cnbc.com/2019/02/08/fitbit-releases-insprire-foremployers.html.

Case law on worker rights of three jurisdictions are considered in the following sub-sections. These jurisdictions offer a range of approaches to the matter. The UK continues with a light-touch approach to the managerial prerogative, with cases largely enforcing the powers employers grant themselves in employment contracts to monitor the workforce. The European courts endeavour to balance workers' right to privacy and employers' right to administer their businesses. With this effort, there has been some development in workers' rights. However, it will be argued that the EU courts rely upon a largely procedural approach whereby employers are obligated to notify or obtain consent of workers prior to monitoring them. Finally, Canada mixes the approaches of the preceding two jurisdictions under study. Unionised workers have benefited from labour arbitration where there has been recognition of some right to privacy. However, non-unionised workers largely rely upon rights obtained through employment contracts, with the potential for a common law claim in privacy.

## A. The United Kingdom's Monitored Workforce

A TUC survey found that a strong majority of the workforce believed it likely that they were being monitored in their workplace.[19] Although the TUC's publication captures a widespread suspicion that monitoring takes place at work, it is hard to argue that some form of surveillance has not been historically part of most workplaces. The contemporary wariness centres on technological advances, such as computer monitoring (emails, files and internet browsing histories), closed circuit television, phone logs.[20] The TUC survey did not mention surveillance through handheld devices, or algorithms. Technology deepens the distrust[21] which seems endemic to labour relations. No legislation in the UK (including the Data Protection Act 2018)[22] precludes workplace surveillance, as is the case for many jurisdictions. Described by the Information Commissioner's Office (ICO) as setting out to 'collect information about workers by keeping them under some form of observation, normally with a view to checking their performance or conduct',[23] workforce monitoring must be consistent with the Act.[24] The ICO's Code is only guidance for employers, which uses examples to illustrate degrees of intrusiveness and what steps should be undertaken in particular situations, including a good practice recommendation listing.

Compared with the EU and Canada, there are not many cases where employees have challenged employer surveillance in the UK. Employers have the authority to direct

[19] 56% believed it likely they were being monitored; while 72% believed it to be fairly likely that at least one form of monitoring was being undertaken in their workplace: TUC (n 14) 5.

[20] ibid, 5–6.

[21] ibid, 5.

[22] On 28 June 2021, the EU Commission recognised the UK's data protection regime as providing 'an essentially equivalent level of protection to that guaranteed under EU law': European Commission, 'Data Protection: Commission Adopts Two Adequacy Decisions for the UK' (28 June 2021), available at: www.ec.europa.eu/commission/presscorner/detail/en/ip_21_3183.

[23] Information Commissioner's Office (ICO), *The Employment Practices Code* (November 2011) 59. Part 3 of the Code focuses on monitoring at work. This Code has not been updated to include references to the 2018 Act.

[24] ibid, 58.

the workforce.[25] When an employer suspected an employee of not working his proper hours, in *McGowan v Scottish Water*, video surveillance was set up outside his home which recorded him and his family members. The Employment Appeal Tribunal upheld the dismissal, observing there was no breach of Article 8 ECHR because Scottish Water was 'bound to carry out' the surveillance 'to protect assets of the company'.[26]

Employers may take disciplinary action where employees' private life activities may potentially harm employers' business interests (though, actual harm does not need to be proven). Anticipating the European Court of Human Rights (ECtHR) case law below, in *Pay v UK*,[27] the employer became aware that Pay engaged in sado-masochistic hobbies because he had modelled some attire on a freely accessible website. He was dismissed when he refused to cease the activity. The ECtHR found his conduct to be incompatible with his position as a prisons officer dealing with sexual misconduct.[28]

Employers also benefit from workers' voluntary posts to their publicly available social media accounts. These postings are then viewed by employers independently,[29] or are drawn to their attention by members of the public (such as patrons or business affiliates).[30] And so, surveillance is not raised as a contested matter. More often, as András Koltay outlines in his chapter,[31] workers' arguments centre on free speech. The brief decision of the employment tribunal in *Greenwood v William Hill Organisations Ltd*[32] provides one example. William Hill (a prominent betting agency) dismissed Greenwood who had been employed for over a decade. He was last a betting shop manager. Greenwood posted comments to a *Facebook* group set up for those working in the betting industry (allegedly named 'I no longer fear hell'). His *Facebook* comments (stemming from the uncertainty created by company restructuring) resulted in his termination for gross misconduct.[33] The case was not clear on how Greenwood's posts came to the employer's attention. William Hill's social media policy warned that serious breaches of the policy could result in dismissal for gross misconduct (summary dismissal): 'We will not tolerate wilful misuse of social media and will continue to take a tough stance on this. We must guard against the risk of reputational damage or malicious behaviour driven by misuse of social media channels'.[34] He unsuccessfully

[25] 'It is a feature of an employment contract that an employee is subject to the reasonable direction of his employer. An employer is thus entitled to know where someone is and what they are doing in the employer's time. An employee can have no reasonable expectation that he can keep those matters private and secret from his employer at such a time. To do so would be to run contrary to the contract he had entered with his employer': *City and County of Swansea v Gayle* [2013] IRLR 758 (Employment Appeal Tribunal), [15].

[26] *McGowan v Scottish Water* [2005] IRLR 167 (Employment Appeal Tribunal), [13].

[27] *Pay v UK* [2009] IRLR 139 (ECtHR).

[28] ibid, [41].

[29] In *British Waterways Board (t/a Scottish Canals) v Smith* UKEATS/0004/15/SM, the dismissed employee posted *Facebook* entries about drinking while on standby, as well as his offensive views of colleagues.

[30] In *Preece v JD Wetherspoon plc* ET/2104806/10 the daughter of two customers saw Preece's derogatory remarks about her parents on *Facebook* and made a complaint to the employer.

[31] See ch 17 by András Koltay in this volume.

[32] *Greenwood v William Hill Organisations Ltd*, [2017] UKET 2404408/2016 (28 March 2017)

[33] 'Ok – I have been walking a tightrope here – media policy – we have had the odd mention of strikes joining unions etc – I suggest smash an FOBT (Fixed Odds Betting Terminal) – most of us have four, why not smash two of them all – a large size hammer should do the trick – touch screen is probably the best to damage – Luddites unite!!!': ibid [6].

[34] ibid, [10].

contended that the punishment was too severe for someone with an otherwise unblemished work record.[35]

Data protection arises as a potentially useful tool here.[36] The TUC has commented that the General Data Protection Regulation (GDPR)[37] 'has the potential to provide increased protection for workers'.[38] UK-based Uber drivers, who successfully challenged their employment status at the UK Supreme Court,[39] have also launched a claim grounded in the Data Protection Act 2018 (and GDPR) against Uber to obtain data such as working time in order to calculate minimum wage. The case is currently making its way through the Dutch courts (as Uber's European operations headquarters are in Amsterdam).[40]

## B. Europe: What is the Essence of the Right Protected?

In this section, the case law of the two European level courts (Human Rights and Court of Justice) garners attention. There remain questions regarding the intersection of these two courts' case law that are beyond the present chapter. The emphasis here is on discerning a clear statement by these courts with regard to the workforce and surveillance. The ECtHR directly engages with this issue, applying only the ECHR. The Court of Justice of the European Union (CJEU) has produced some decisions pertaining to privacy and data protection where Articles 7 and 8 of the CFREU are challenged. In these cases, the Court has been concerned with the 'essence' of the Charter rights. It remains to be seen if a holistic European approach may be determined.[41]

### *i. The Procedural Focus of the European Court of Human Rights*

Consideration of surveillance falls under the Court's case law on Article 8 ECHR. The ECtHR has understandably determined that it will adapt existing concepts to the

[35] ibid, [38].

[36] This is the subject matter of ch 15 by Frank Hendrickx in this volume.

[37] Regulation (EU) 2016/679 of the European Parliament and of the Council of 27 April 2016 on the protection of natural persons with regard to the processing of personal data and on the free movement of such data, and repealing Directive 95/46/EC [2016] OJ L119/1. On 28 June 2021, the European Commission adopted two adequacy decisions regarding the UK, one of which was under the GDPR, available at: www.ec.europa.eu/commission/presscorner/detail/en/ip_21_3183.

[38] TUC (n 14) 29.

[39] *Uber v Aslam* [2021] UKSC 5. Of interest on the employment status issue, on 16 February 2021, the Amsterdam Court of Appeal found Deliveroo riders to be employees: ECLI:NL:GHAMS:2021:392, Gerechtshof Amsterdam, 200.261.051/01.

[40] After requesting and receiving data from Uber, the drivers sought further information: ECLI:NL:RBAMS:2021:1020, Amsterdam District Court (X/Uber BV). Largely the Court dismissed these requests, ordering only that Uber provide access to (anonymised) personal data regarding individual ratings See the Court's comments on transparency and automated decision-making.

[41] One problem is that the European Union has employed an expansive definition of personal data as 'any information relating to an identified or identifiable individual' (Council of Europe, *Convention for the Protection of Individuals with regard to Automatic Processing of Personal Data* 28 Jan 1981: www.rm.coe.int/1680078b37). The breadth of the definition of personal data (Article 4 GDPR) means there is a wide regulatory capture area that, interestingly, threatens to shrink the legal force of these laws: N Purtova, 'The law of everything. Broad concept of personal data and of future EU data protection law' (2018) 10 *Law, Innovation and Technology* 40. Some form of threshold for actionability may be needed to avert a potential for such withering.

technological challenges posed.[42] The Court has made some bold statements about private life and the workplace in the context of surveillance. It remains unclear, though, how these broad statements may be implemented.

There are layers to the Court's case law. The Court has put forward a broad understanding of a right to private life in relation to work. This right protects individuals' access to work as a locale for developing relationships with the 'outside world'. To determine whether the Article 8 right has been interfered with, the Court considers the scope of the right's protection, and the workers' reasonable expectation of privacy, leading to assessing whether the interference with the right is justifiable. Pursuant to Article 8 ECHR, states have a negative undertaking to abstain from interfering with the right. They also have a positive obligation to secure respect for private life in relations amongst individuals.[43]

In its 1992 *Niemietz* decision, the Court set out its broad interpretation of the protection provided to workers by Article 8.[44] The case speaks to a wider perspective of a working individual who participates in the workplace, but also has a private life. Intersection, however, does not negate a right to privacy because there is 'a zone of interaction of a person with others, even in a public context, which may fall within the scope of "private life"'.[45] The workplace facilitates human development through these relationships, as demonstrated by *Sidabras and Dziautas v Lithuania*.[46] And yet, it is also the location of an employer's business and that entity's interests require consideration. Consequently, the employment relationship remains one of subordination where the worker's privacy right is qualified by this very connection.[47]

Two decisions coming from the UK provide some direction regarding a worker's reasonable expectation of privacy. In *Halford v UK*,[48] the Assistant Chief Constable applicant had a reasonable expectation of privacy, failing some notification to the contrary, when her employer (Merseyside Police Authority) monitored her work phone.[49] Ms Halford had launched a gender discrimination case and the Authority set in motion a campaign of monitoring and press leaks to discredit her. The information gathered from the monitoring (data, length of calls, the telephone numbers dialled) constituted an 'integral element' of the telephone communications, thereby falling within

[42] 'The Court is aware of the rapid developments in this area. Nevertheless, it considers that proportionality and procedural guarantees against arbitrariness are essential': *Bărbulescu v Romania* App no 61496/08 (ECtHR, Judgment 5 September 2017), [121].

[43] On these obligations see, eg, *López Ribalda and Others v Spain* App nos 1874/13 and 8567/13) (ECtHR, Judgment, 17 October 2019), [110].

[44] *Niemietz v Germany* App no 13710/88 (ECtHR, Judgment 16 December 1992), [29].

[45] *PG and JH v UK* (44787/98) [2001] ECHR 546 (25 September 2001), [56]. The same phrase is repeated in *Antović and Mirković v Montenegro* App no 70838/13 (28 November 2017), [42].

[46] *Sidabras and Dziautas v Lithuania* App nos 55480/00 and 59330/00, Judgment of 27 July 2004, (2006) 42 EHRR 6, [48]: 'The ban has … affected the applicants' ability to develop relationships with the outside world to a very significant degree, and has created serious difficulties for them as regards the possibility to earn their living, with obvious repercussions on their enjoyment of their private life'.

[47] F Hendrickx and A Van Bever, 'Article 8 ECHR: Judicial Patterns of Employment Privacy Protection' in F Dorssemont, K Lörcher and I Schömann (eds), *The European Convention on Human Rights and the Employment Relation* (Oxford, Hart Publishing, 2013) 185.

[48] *Halford v UK* [1997] ECHR 32, [45].

[49] The Court found no violation of Article 8 in respect of her home phone because it found there was no evidence of such action.

the protection of Article 8.[50] Based upon the Court's ruling in *Copland v UK*,[51] the reasonable expectation of privacy in *Halford* was not limited to the applicant who had sole use of her office and two telephone lines with one dedicated for personal use.[52] Ms Copland, a personal assistant in a state school, had not been warned that calls on her work telephone, email and internet usage would be monitored (personal information was also collected and stored). Consequently, she had a reasonable expectation of privacy. The Court relied upon its decision in *Halford* as setting out protection of telephone conversations by a worker while using a workplace phone; that email and internet usage also attracted protection 'follow[ed] logically'.[53] Once again, the data collected fell within Article 8's protection and interference with that right could not be justified.

These decisions suggest that a reasonable expectation of privacy may be held at work, even when using work equipment such as telephones, computers and internet connections. They also set out a modest legal constraint on employers that is largely expressed as a procedural matter, obliging employers to warn workers when they are monitored.

An obligation to inform workers regarding monitoring was confirmed in *Bărbulescu v Romania*.[54] The private-sector employer in that case contractually prohibited any 'disturbance of order and discipline' at the workplace, and named, amongst other points, the 'personal use of computers, photocopiers, telephones or telex or fax machines'.[55] Bărbulescu's use of his *Yahoo*! *Messenger* accounts for personal reasons during work hours while on the premises formed the basis of the employer's decision to terminate his employment.[56] Although the applicant knew of these regulations (having signed a confirming document), it seemed as though he had not been notified the employer was monitoring him, nor to the potential that the contents of these communications may be accessed. The Court's reasoning affirmed the importance of notification prior to surveillance being undertaken. Additionally, the Grand Chamber declared that an employer could not reduce 'private social life in the workplace to zero'.[57] The Court then turned to consider whether the state met its positive obligation to secure compliance with Article 8. Bearing in mind a margin of appreciation accorded to states, the Court laid down several factors in ensuring the state's steps are proportional and that there are procedural guarantees against arbitrariness.[58] Applying the aforementioned factors as part of this assessment, the Court found the domestic courts failed to assess: the extent of monitoring; the justification for such surveillance by the employer; to consider whether less intrusive methods (avoiding accessing of the messages' contents)

[50] The ECtHR applied its earlier decision in *Malone v UK*, Series A, No 82 (1984) 7 EHRR 14, [84].

[51] *Copland v UK* [2007] ECHR 253, [42].

[52] The Article 29 Working Party suggested a professional and personal line of communication for workers to protect their privacy: Article 29 Data Protection Working Party, 'Working document on the surveillance of electronic communications in the workplace' 5401/01/EN/Final WP 55 (29 May 2002) 5.

[53] *Copland* (n 51) [41].

[54] *Bărbulescu v Romania* (n 42).

[55] ibid, [12].

[56] Bărbulescu had one *Yahoo!* account at the request of his employer.

[57] *Bărbulescu v Romania* (n 42) [80].

[58] ibid, [121]–[122].

were available; the seriousness of the consequences of this monitoring (including the subsequent disciplinary steps) which was 'the most severe disciplinary sanction';[59] at what point in the disciplinary process the surveillance commenced; the question of prior notice of monitoring; the reasons for undertaking such activity against Bărbulescu.

The procedural approach to determining a violation of Article 8 in *Bărbulescu* complements employers' authority to manage its workforce. In *Köpke v Germany*,[60] covert surveillance was permissible because it had been limited to two weeks in duration and targeted two employees who had been suspected prior to monitoring being put in place. While no legislation was directly applicable, the employer had followed the domestic employee monitoring case law. *Köpke* guides as to the extent and degree of surveillance. The rights of workers set out above in *Halford*, *Copland*, and *Bărbulescu*, are not unfettered and workers cannot violate workplace policies, expecting cover under Article 8 ECHR.[61]

Employers utilising constant video surveillance that captures all activity within its scope must comply with certain parameters, particularly the developmental aspects of interaction at work identified in *Niemietz*. Video surveillance in a university lecture hall, that captured all activities, violated the claimants' section 8 rights (as well as domestic law) in *Antović and Mirković v Montenegro*.[62] The Second Section wrote: 'university amphitheatres are the workplaces of teachers. It is where they not only teach students, but also interact with them, thus developing mutual relations and constructing their social identity'.[63]

While the recording of human interactions leading to the development of mutual relations was curbed in *Antović and Mirković*, the Grand Chamber's decision in *López Ribalda and Others v Spain* recognised that surveillance for a legitimate purpose (theft of the employer's goods in this case) can be justified.[64] To cut down on (if not eliminate) losses due to theft, a supermarket installed both visible and hidden cameras. The visible cameras were aimed at the entrance/exit areas, targeting customers. Employees were told of the visible but not the hidden cameras. Both sets of cameras continuously recorded all individuals that passed within their view. The cameras were functional for a 10-day period. Concealed surveillance recorded the dismissed applicants and others stealing (helping co-workers and customers to do so, as well as committing this act themselves) and were terminated. In this case, the Court identified the failure to inform employees about covert surveillance as problematic. However, the employer's conduct was found to be proportionate in the circumstances considering the degree of intrusion into employees' privacy factored together with the 'legitimate reasons'[65] justifying deployment of surreptitious surveillance technology. The Grand Chamber was also satisfied that the employer's decision to install the surveillance equipment was premised upon

[59] ibid, [137].

[60] *Köpke v Germany* App no 420/07 (ECtHR, Judgment 5 October 2010).

[61] Another illustration, though not a surveillance case, is *Libert v France* App no 588/13 (ECtHR, Judgment 22 February 2018).

[62] *Antović and Mirković v Montenegro* App no 70838/13 (ECtHR, Judgment 28 November 2017), [44].

[63] ibid, [44].

[64] *López Ribalda and Others v Spain* (n 43).

[65] ibid, [134].

a 'reasonable suspicion that serious misconduct has been committed and the extent of the losses identified in the present case may appear to constitute weighty justification'.[66] Difficulties in discerning a coherent path through these decisions is partly attributable to the trouble in finding a balance between management authority to conduct its business and the privacy interests of workers. The continuing evolution of technology also contributes to the challenge of clarity in adjudication.

The primary criticism here is that the prohibition on reducing workplace privacy to zero (where work is a space for self-development) is incongruent with the simple threshold of notice and consent to monitoring.[67] The concept of a right to workplace privacy stated in *Niemietz* and elaborated upon in later cases remains difficult to reconcile with notice and consent.[68] While these rights do not absolutely end at the office,[69] the workplace filters out more than may be initially recognised. Simply being informed must be viewed as a low bar and therefore incompatible with the court's statement that employees' privacy at work cannot be reduced to zero.

### *ii. The Court of Justice of the European Union and the Essence of a Right*

Article 52(3) CFREU requires that 'the meaning and scope' of Article 7 CFREU 'shall be the same' as that set out in Article 8 ECHR.[70] It may be that the decisions of these courts could be treated as aligned.[71] Though this approach is not adopted here,[72] these CJEU cases are viewed as instructive for present purposes in that they identify broad points for consideration. In the area of surveillance of the workplace, the CJEU does not provide direct discussions. Instead, the following cases offer some judicial commentary regarding the right to privacy and monitoring technologies, focusing on data collection and processing.[73] There is scope for the conduct of parties in relation to Articles 7 (protection of private life) and 8 (data protection) CFREU.[74] A further factor must be borne in mind. The Court has found that Article 16 CFREU provides employers with 'the freedom to conduct a business' which is 'in principle, legitimate'.[75]

[66] ibid. See also the factors in assessing the proportionality of video surveillance at *López Ribalda*, [116].

[67] See further D Mangan, 'Beyond Procedural Protection: Information Technology, Privacy and the Workplace' (2019) 44 *European Law Review* 559.

[68] Contrast *Bărbulescu* with M Otto, *The Right to Privacy in Employment: A Comparative Analysis* (Oxford, Hart Publishing, 2016) 76.

[69] Article 29 Data Protection Working Party, 'Working document on the surveillance of electronic communications in the workplace' (n 52) 4.

[70] The *Explanations* to the CFREU draw attention to a change in wording between the two instruments; where the ECHR referenced correspondence, the CFREU uses communications to 'take account of developments in technology': *Explanations relating to the Charter of Fundamental Rights* (2007/C 303/02).

[71] See the discussion in F Hendrickx, 'Article 7 – Protection of Private and Family Life' in F Dorssemont, K Lörcher, S Clauwaert and M Schmitt (eds), *The Charter of Fundamental Rights of the European Union and the Employment Relation* (Oxford, Hart Publishing, 2019) 229.

[72] There is scope for nuanced differences between the two courts, where alignment would suggest a level of shared interpretation that has yet to materialise. On the latter point see T Lock, 'Rights and Principles in the EU Charter of Fundamental Rights' (2019) 56 *Common Market Law Review* 1201.

[73] There is some overlap here with Frank Hendrickx' chapter in this volume.

[74] The protection of personal data in Article 8 is 'closely connected' to the right of privacy in Article 7 CFREU: Joined Cases C-92/09 and C-93/09 *Volker und Markus Schecke GbR and Hartmut Eifert v Land Hessen* ECLI:EU:C:2010:662 [2010], [47].

[75] Case C-157/15 *Samira Achbita and Centrum voor gelijkheid van kansen en voor racismebestrijding v G4S Secure Solutions NV* ECLI:EU:C:2017:203 [2017], [38].

The CJEU's two decisions relating to Max Schrems[76] provide some general commentary on privacy and data protection that may be applied to surveillance and the workplace. Both decisions deal with mass data collection and processing in the context of international data transfers from the EU to the US, where the impugned schemes failed because of their interference with the rights in Articles 7 and 8.

In its October 2015 decision of *Schrems*, the CJEU found (what is more commonly known as) the Safe Harbour agreement[77] to be invalid.[78] Safe Harbour was an agreement between the EU and the US regarding third-country data transfers (from the EU to the US) whereby the EU Commission had determined there was an adequate level of protection for individuals whose data was being transferred. *Schrems* continued the scrutiny of US practice with data that was initiated in *Digital Rights Ireland*.[79] The CJEU invalidated Safe Harbour on the basis that it interfered with the essence of the fundamental right to respect for private life[80] because the US had in place 'legislation permitting the public authorities to have access on a generalised basis to the content of electronic communications'. Safe Harbour did not allow 'any possibility for an individual to pursue legal remedies … as enshrined in Article 47 of the Charter'.[81] This was sufficient to invalidate the agreement without moving on to a proportionality analysis.[82] Safe Harbour 'emptie[d] those rights of their content [and] call[ed] their very existence into question';[83] 'there was simply no privacy as [US] authorities could have unlimited access to the content of all the personal data transferred from the EU to the US'.[84] In *Digital Rights Ireland*, the CJEU touched upon a distinction that was not picked up in this case. In *Digital Rights Ireland*, the Court appeared to distinguish between accessing the content of communications (which would interfere with the essence of Article 7) and meta-data.[85] Meta-data and interference with the essence of a right would be a valuable point for further evaluation.

[76] The *Schrems* cases also contribute to themes such as a clash between the US and EU titans (as noted by A Charlesworth, 'Clash of the Data Titans? US and EU Data Privacy Regulation' (2000) 6 *European Public Law* 253) or the 'Brussels effect', with its effect digital matters elaborated upon in A Bradford, *The Brussels Effect: How the European Union Rules the World* (Oxford, Oxford University Press, 2020) ch 5.

[77] Commission Decision 2000/520/EC of 26 July 2000 pursuant to Directive 95/46/EC of the European Parliament and of the Council on the adequacy of the protection provided by the safe harbour privacy principles and related frequently asked questions issued by the US Department of Commerce [2000] OJ L/215/7.

[78] Case C-362/14 *Maximillian Schrems v Data Protection Commissioner* ECLI:EU:C:2015:650 [2015].

[79] Case C-293/12 *Digital Rights Ireland v Minister for Communications, Marine and Natural Resources* ECLI:EU:C:2014:238 [2014]. This point was made by the referring court: Case C-362/14 *Maximillian Schrems v Data Protection Commissioner* ECLI:EU:C:2015:650 [2015], [13].

[80] *Maximillian Schrems v Data Protection Commissioner* (n 79) [94]. *Schrems* contrasts with *Digital Rights Ireland* when there was no interference with the essence of Article 7 regarding widespread data retention even though it affected the entire European population.

[81] *Maximillian Schrems v Data Protection Commissioner* (n 79) [95].

[82] ibid, [98].

[83] K Lenaerts, 'Limits on Limitations: The Essence of Fundamental Rights in the EU' (2019) 20 *German Law Journal* 779, 784.

[84] ibid.

[85] For treatment of metadata, see E Guild and S Carrera, 'The political and judicial life of metadata: Digital Rights Ireland and the trail of the Data Retention Directive' (2014) 65 CEPS Paper in Liberty and Security in Europe 1.

In July 2020, the CJEU found the successor to Safe Harbour (Privacy Shield)[86] to also be invalid based upon the CFREU.[87] The CJEU applied the GDPR.[88] *Schrems* (2020) assessed whether the bulk data transfer from the EU to the US pursuant to the Privacy Shield agreement was valid. Concerns about Privacy Shield centred around the US failing to provide an adequate level of protection with regard to the bulk transfers of data to US public authorities. The reasons for the Court rendering Privacy Shield invalid[89] focused on the inadequacy of safeguards, including:[90] the absence of limitations on the power to implement surveillance or guarantees for persons targeted by these programmes;[91] the lack of actionable rights in courts before US authorities for data subjects;[92] the failure to 'delimit in a sufficiently clear and precise manner the scope of such bulk collection of personal data';[93] as well as the lack of independence of the ombudsperson (an addition in Privacy Shield from Safe Harbour).[94] These reasons tied together Articles 7, 8 and 47 CFREU.[95]

Overall, the CJEU marks out rather broad points. The Court found a need for clear and precise rules governing the scope and application of the measure in question and imposing minimum safeguards, so that the persons whose data had been transferred could have sufficient guarantees to effectively protect their personal data against the risk of abuse. These measures must indicate in what circumstances, and under which conditions a measure providing for the processing of such data may be adopted, thereby ensuring that the interference is limited to what is strictly necessary. These considerations are heightened with automated processing of personal data. The essence of the right to private life was interfered with when public authorities had generalised access to the content of electronic communications, without data subjects' recourse to legal challenge. It is wondered what is meant, ultimately, by protecting the essence of a right.

[86] Commission Implementing Decision (EU) 2016/1250 of 12 July 2016 pursuant to Directive 95/46 on the adequacy of the protection provided by the EU-US Privacy Shield [2016] OJ L/2071.

[87] Case C-311/18 *Data Protection Commissioner v Facebook Ireland and Maximillian Schrems* ECLI:EU:C:2020:559 [2020] (*Schrems* 2020).

[88] The Data Protection Commissioner had not yet rendered a decision (having only put forward a draft decision) and the Data Protection Directive had been repealed in favour of the GDPR by the time the case came to the CJEU.

[89] *Schrems* 2020 (n 87) [199]–[201].

[90] More precisely, the ECJ wrote that the 'Privacy Shield Decision [could] not ensure a level of protection essentially equivalent to that arising from the Charter': ibid, [181].

[91] ibid, [180].

[92] '[N]ot providing for any possibility for an individual to pursue legal remedies in order to have access to personal data relating to him or her, or to obtain the rectification or erasure of such data, does not respect the essence of the fundamental right to effective judicial protection, as enshrined in Article 47 of the Charter': ibid, [187].

[93] ibid, [183].

[94] ibid, [195]–[197].

[95] The Standard Contract Clauses should be noted because of the number of qualifications in the decision: see *Schrems* 2020 (n 87) [131]–[135]. The EDPB also identified the potential need to supplement guarantees: European Data Protection Board, 'Frequently Asked Questions on the Judgment of the Court of Justice of the European Union in Case C-311/18 – *Data Protection Commissioner v Facebook Ireland Ltd and Maximillian Schrems*' (23 July 2020), available at: www.edpb.europa.eu/sites/edpb/files/files/file1/20200724_edpb_faqoncjeuc31118_en.pdf. See also, Commission Implementing Decision (EU) 2021/915 of 4 June 2021, [175].

## C. Canada: The Unionised and the Non-Unionised

The Canadian approach approximates that of the EU case law.[96] Canada makes a number of distinctions with regard to the workforce and the law. Non-unionised workers do not benefit from protections that are found in the unionised setting (both employees and dependent contractors),[97] largely through labour arbitration decisions.[98] This discussion commences with the unionised sector where labour arbitration cases have set out several distinctions regarding employers' surveillance efforts. The non-unionised workforce remains an area that has a number of questions regarding surveillance.

Security and safety of the workplace tend to be the most common bases for surveillance.[99] This concern would certainly apply to the majority of businesses.[100] The security and safety premise has permitted employers to not only be reactive, but to take preventative measures.[101]

### *i. Unionised Workplaces*

There is no consensus amongst Canadian labour arbitrators as to whether employees have privacy rights.[102] If privacy rights are recognised, the extent of the right stands out as a further point of contention. Where it exists, provincial legislation providing for a right to privacy has been relied upon (in conjunction with the 'value system imposed by the *Charter*')[103] to find that employees have a right to privacy.[104] There has been movement towards recognising some form of a right to privacy generally in Canada, but it has been slow in developing. Having noted the debate, this section adopts Robert Sharpe's perspective that some form of privacy protection exists in private law,[105] and the following paragraphs consider the texture of such a right in the Canadian labour setting.

Overt surveillance of the workforce is assessed by a standard of reasonableness in all the circumstances.[106] This is a lower standard than is used for covert surveillance.[107]

[96] Otto suggests the Canadian approach is 'more sensitive to the myriad privacy issues' than the European: Otto (n 68) 171.

[97] See *Canadian Union of Postal Workers, Applicant v Foodora Inc dba Foodora*, OLRB Case No 1346-19-R (25 February 2020).

[98] Canada has a strong private labour arbitration system in which companies and trade unions divert (through collective agreements) disputes to binding private labour arbitration where the parties pay for the arbitrator's involvement in adjudicating the dispute. These arbitrators are largely former labour lawyers from both management and union sides.

[99] *Kadant Carmanah Design* (2015), 266 LAC (4th) 119; *Woodstock (City)* 2015 CanLII 20641, [49]

[100] *Carte International Inc* (2018), 291 LAC (4th) 190, [45].

[101] *New Flyer Industries Ltd. (Cameras Grievance)*, [2011] MGAD No 27, [63]; *Kadant* (n 99) [102].

[102] RM Snyder (ed), *Palmer & Snyder: Collective Agreement Arbitration in Canada*, 6th edn (Markham, Lexis Nexis, 2017) 9.

[103] Reference is made in this quotation to Canada's Constitution, specifically the Charter of Rights and Freedoms, enacted as Schedule B to the Canada Act 1982, c 11 (UK).

[104] *Doman Forest Products Ltd* (1991), 13 LAC (4th) 275, [27], interpreting Privacy Act, RSBC 1979, c 336, s 1, which is now Privacy Act, RSBC 1996 c 373, s 1. *Re Pope & Talbot Ltd* (2004), 123 LAC (4th) 115, 125 reiterated the influence of the Charter on arbitral jurisprudence.

[105] RJ Sharpe, *Good Judgment: Making Judicial Decisions* (Toronto, University of Toronto Press, 2018) ch 9. See also his reasoning in *Jones v Tsige* [2012] ONCA 32.

[106] *New Flyer Industries* (n 101) [38].

[107] *Unisource Canada Inc* [2003] BCCAAA No 309; *Leon's Mfg Co Ltd*, [2006] SLAA No 12, [56]–[65].

The absence of complaint would be taken as at least 'circumstantial evidence of the subjective acceptance of the cameras as reasonable'.[108] And yet, this does not excuse an unreasonable invasion of workers' privacy.[109] Labour arbitrators have generally found surreptitious surveillance for the purposes of recording workers' productivity to be unreasonable[110] and contrary to human dignity.[111] Cameras could be placed in other areas such as loading docks, the parking lot and storage areas.[112]

The reasonableness standard aims to balance employer and employee interests.[113] The employer must: show that its concerns are 'real and meaningful';[114] that surveillance meets its objective;[115] and that a less intrusive means is not possible.[116] Employers may also need to demonstrate the loss of privacy was proportional to the benefit gained.[117] Employers, however, are not required to exhaust all alternatives as a prerequisite to deploying visible surveillance cameras.[118] Instead, a failure to use alternatives would be a factor in the reasonableness consideration.[119]

A worker cannot contend that she did not expect to be observed by her employer while at work. However, while supervision may be part of employment,

> there is no expectation of having one's image recorded and kept for as long as an employer chooses to keep it. The appropriating of that personal information is a significant intrusion on privacy interests which is being made more and more possible by the availability of increasingly sophisticated digital equipment.[120]

This statement contemplates an orthodox workplace where an employer requires the worker to perform her duties at a fixed location, maintained by the employer, with tools also provided by the employer.[121] A distinction can be made between observing a worker, for a short period and for a specific reason or reasons, and continuous recording of a worker, with that material being kept indefinitely.[122]

With surreptitious or covert surveillance, arbitrators have noted that some further attention is needed in these cases: 'It is particularly this kind of surveillance that arbitrators will be astute to require strict justification by the employer and the purpose of the surveillance will be examined carefully'.[123] Analysis of surreptitious surveillance recalls some of the points noted above with overt surveillance. The points common to both analyses include: an evident problem; and a strong possibility that surveillance will be

[108] *Cascade Aerospace, Inc (Surveillance Group/Policy Grievance)*, [2009] CLAD No 95, [91].
[109] *Carte* (n 100) [50].
[110] *Woodstock* (n 99) [47]–[50], [69], [79]; *Tri-Krete Ltd* (2005), 142 LAC (4th) 289, [47].
[111] *Puretex Knitting Co Ltd* (1979), 23 LAC (2d) 14, [29]; cited in *Eastmond v Canadian Pacific Railway* [2004] FC 852, [139].
[112] ibid.
[113] *Janes Family Foods (Surveillance Grievance)* (n 6) 304, [38], [45]; *Woodstock* (n 99) [49]–[50].
[114] *Woodstock* (n 99) [49].
[115] ibid, [50].
[116] *Janes Family Foods* (n 6) [45]; *Unisource* (n 107) [48]–[49]; *New Flyer Industries* (n 101).
[117] This point was included with the aforementioned three in Snyder (n 102) [9.97].
[118] *New Flyer Industries* (n 101) [60]–[61].
[119] *Leon's* (n 107) [67]; *New Flyer Industries* (n 101) [61]; *Carte* (n 100) [46].
[120] *Janes Family Foods* (n 6) [40].
[121] See further the decisions in *Cargill Foods* [2008] OLAA No 393, [96]; *Leon's* (n 107); *Cascade* (n 108).
[122] In *Pope & Talbot Ltd* (2004), 123 LAC (4th) 115, the arbitrator found 24-hour surveillance of a production area to be an unreasonable exercise of management rights that could not be justified.
[123] *St Mary's Hospital* (1997), 64 LAC (4th) 382, [51].

effective. Surreptitious or covert surveillance of employees by employers also requires some basis, such as safeguarding legitimate business interests, which would outweigh employees' interests.[124] This does not condone 'resort to random videotape surveillance in the form of an electronic web, cast like a net, to see what it might catch'.[125] In addition, employers will need to establish the reasonableness of the way in which they have conducted surveillance.[126] Surreptitious surveillance of specified employees in public spaces can take place where the employer has reasonable grounds to conduct an investigation.[127]

### *ii. Non-Unionised Workplaces*

Workers not part of a unionised workplace must rely upon whatever protections are provided by employment statutes, contract clauses or private law actions. Generally, employers may only disclose an employee's personal information once the employee has provided consent.[128]

Rights with regard to surveillance largely depend upon the existence of a private law action in the jurisdiction.[129] Private sector workplaces governed by federal legislation would be subject to the Personal Information Protection and Electronic Documents Act (PIPEDA).[130] Of interest, workers may still elect to bring a private law tort action instead of making a complaint through PIPEDA, which would be to the Privacy Commissioner of Canada and would not carry the possibility of an award in damages.[131] The Federal Government signalled its intention in November 2020 that it will be amending this legislation, with the possibility of repealing PIPEDA.[132] Each of British Columbia[133] Manitoba,[134] Newfoundland & Labrador,[135] and Saskatchewan[136] have legislation explicitly providing for a tort based upon violation of another person's privacy.[137] The identified provincial statutes are similar in content insofar as they each

[124] *Janes Family Foods* (n 6) [46].

[125] *Canadian Pacific Ltd* (1996), 59 LAC (4th) 111, [34].

[126] *Fairmont Royal York Hotel (Policy Grievance Re Video Surveillance)* (2011), 215 LAC (4th) 62, where surveillance was reasonable aside from that of the staff changing area. See also ABeatty, DM Beatty and DJM Brown, *Canadian Labour Arbitration*, 5th edn (Toronto, Carswell, 2019) [7:3625].

[127] *McKesson Canada* (2004), 136 LAC (4th) 102, [45]–[49], [56]–[57].

[128] *Mountain Province Diamonds Inc v DeBeers Canada Inc*, 2014 ONSC 2026.

[129] See *New Flyer Industries* (n 101) [58].

[130] SC 2000, c 5. The Federal Court of Canada confirmed PIPEDA has quasi-constitutional status in *Eastmond v Canadian Pacific Railway* [2004] FC 852, [100].

[131] *Jones v Tsige*, 2012 ONCA 32.

[132] Innovation, Science and Economic Development Canada, 'Bill Summary: Digital Charter Implementation Act, 2020' (23 November 2020), available at: www.ic.gc.ca/eic/site/062.nsf/eng/00120.html.

[133] Privacy Act, RSBC 1996, c 373, s 1(1). The Supreme Court of Canada discussed this legislation (particularly s 4) in the context of a forum selection clause (contained in an online consumer contract of adhesion) in *Douez v Facebook Inc*, 2017 SCC 33.

[134] Privacy Act, CCSM, c P125, s 2. Under this Act, it was determined that only an individual's personal information was protected and not that of a corporation: *Dowd v Skip the Dishes Restaurant Services Inc*, 2019 MBQB 63, [72].

[135] Privacy Act, RSNL1990, c P-22, s 3.

[136] Privacy Act, RSS 1978, c P-24, s 2.

[137] These acts are broadly similar: B von Tigerstrom, *Information & Privacy Law in Canada* (Toronto, Irwin Law, 2020) 71ff.

provide for a limited right of action where the defendant acted wilfully (except for Manitoba) and without claim of right.[138]

Illustrating the more difficult path for non-unionised workers, *Eastmond v Canadian Pacific Railway (CP)*[139] remains a leading decision applying PIPEDA to a workplace setting. CP had installed six digital video surveillance cameras in one of the employer's railyards. Recordings were made, but only viewed if an issue arose. The recordings were erased after 96 hours. Eastmond complained to the Privacy Commissioner of Canada, who upheld the complaint as well founded.[140] Eastmond then applied to the Federal Court for an order requiring CP to comply with the Privacy Commissioner's report.[141] The Federal Court dismissed the application. PIPEDA (section 7(1)) permitted employers to collect personal information without an employee's knowledge and consent.[142] The Court also accepted the employer's argument that collection of personal information only takes place when the employer's official view the recording to investigate an incident.[143] *Eastmond* 'is the precedent that is currently being followed'.[144]

At common law, *Jones v Tsige*[145] confirmed the existence of a right of action for intrusion upon seclusion,[146] with the court adopting the American Law Institute's definition.[147] The key features of this tort are: 'the defendant's conduct must be intentional [including being reckless]'; the defendant 'invaded, without lawful justification, the plaintiff's private affairs or concerns'; 'a reasonable person would regard the invasion as highly offensive causing distress, humiliation or anguish'.[148] The plaintiff is not required to demonstrate 'proof of harm to a recognised economic interest'. Damages would be 'measured by a modest conventional sum' because of the 'intangible nature of the interest protected'.[149] Claims for intrusion upon seclusion are limited to situations of 'deliberate and significant invasions of personal privacy'.[150] This action offers redress for significant invasions: 'such as one's financial or health records … employment … that, viewed objectively on the reasonable person standard, can be described as highly offensive'.[151]

[138] See, eg, Privacy Act, RSNL 1990, c P-22, s 3(2).
[139] [2004] FC 852.
[140] *PIPEDA* Case Summary #114 (2003) (Privacy Commissioner).
[141] The matter related to personal information and the collective agreement did not deal with this matter. Therefore, it was not a matter that could have been heard by a labour arbitrator: *Eastmond* (n 130) [114]–[115]. This application was not a judicial review of the Privacy Commissioner and was a fresh proceeding: *Eastmond* [118]-[120].
[142] *Eastmond* (n 130) [187].
[143] ibid, [189].
[144] Snyder (n 102) [9.32]. See, eg, *Englander v Telus Communications Inc*, 2004 FCA 387.
[145] *Jones* (n 131). For a more extensive discussion of the decision, see D Mangan, '*Jones v Tsige* (2012)' in P Wragg and P Coe (eds), *Landmark Cases in Privacy Law* (Oxford, Hart Publishing, 2022).
[146] *Jones* (n 131) [65].
[147] ibid, [19].
[148] ibid, [71].
[149] ibid, [71].
[150] ibid, [72].
[151] ibid, [72].

## IV. Refocusing the Legal Constraint on Surveillance

Based upon preceding analyses, three points should be further considered. First, there must be more pointed scrutiny of the bases for surveillance, with particular attention to the extent of monitoring (duration and scope of activities captured).[152] It should not be sufficient to rely upon a broad interpretation of common bases for surveillance (legal obligations, safety, security, identifying efficiencies) with no defined purpose. It may be that continuous, broad-based monitoring is more cost-effective, if we presume that greater specificity requires further tailoring and therefore more preparatory work to devise the monitoring platform. Nevertheless, the capacity of information technology for greater precision in monitoring should be harnessed. There should be greater precision in what safety and security interests, for example, are being met with specific monitoring activities. Collection of information for a defined purpose can yield positive results.[153]

Second, employers should have an ongoing obligation to inform workers about the full extent of monitoring activities that are undertaken. The argument that the assessment of any data produced through monitoring is only undertaken by a select number of individuals, seen in the Canadian arbitration cases, should be scrutinised further. Limiting the number of people who view the product of surveillance does not sufficiently engage in the fact of monitoring.

Finally, there must be greater attention to and examination of the data collection and processing that is part of surveillance (whether incidental, collateral, or the primary objective). There should be recognition that surveillance activities collect a remarkable amount of data, whether it is video surveillance, network or computer-based monitoring of work activities, or postings on social media unrelated to work. At present, this subject is being guided by technology, instead of being purpose-driven.

There is an urgency underlying the need to ameliorate constraints on employers' monitoring activities. Two reasons are put forward here: the Covid-19 pandemic, and algorithms. Common to both is that the current state of the legal constraint on surveillance does not provide an adequate foundation upon which to build in order to adapt the law to the challenges posed by each reason.

The Covid-19 pandemic may be a demarcation point for employment. The means by which employers can monitor workers even while they worked from home (a result of widespread stay-at-home orders by the state) has drawn much media attention.[154] At this time, it is likely that we are at an early stage of being aware of monitoring efforts. It is difficult to determine to what extent surveillance of workers who have been working from home during the pandemic has been conducted.

[152] As one illustration, see the argument against permitting employers to have access to and process fitness data on the basis of the GDPR in P Collins and S Marassi, 'Is That Lawful? Data Privacy and Fitness Trackers in the Workplace' (2021) 37 *International Journal of Comparative Labour Law and Industrial Relations* 65.

[153] Ravid et al (n 12) 107.

[154] See, eg, D Harwell, 'Managers turn to surveillance software, always-on webcams to ensure employees are (really) working from home' *Washington Post* (30 April 2020), available at: www.washingtonpost.com/technology/2020/04/30/work-from-home-surveillance/; A Hern, 'Shirking from home? Staff feel the heat as bosses ramp up remote surveillance' *Guardian* (27 September 2020), available at: www.theguardian.com/world/2020/sep/27/shirking-from-home-staff-feel-the-heat-as-bosses-ramp-up-remote-surveillance.

Surveillance using algorithms[155] ostensibly offers an expedient way to scan through vast amounts of data. When applied to the workplace, though, a number of issues arise, including: inaccuracy, unfairness, incompleteness and the opaqueness of how the data is processed. The latter point relates to the gulf in understanding between a worker and an employer. Article 22 of the GDPR has been the subject of queries in respect of what protection it in fact affords.[156]

## V. Conclusion

The case law to date, focused on common technologies for surveillance, provides employers, in the jurisdictions under study, with a good spectrum within which to manage their workforces. It does not portend well for the more nuanced and technologically sophisticated means of surveillance (such as algorithms) which are increasing in use. This is a particular problem to be addressed. It should be noted that regulatory frameworks such as the GDPR fall short of being adequate responses to this difficulty because they do not clearly address the nuances of workforce monitoring. As noted in the introduction, surveillance has moved from being of the workplace, to being of the workforce. Consequently, more dynamic approaches need to be developed that deal with the inadequacy of the current state of the law.

[155] A topic discussed more further in the chapters by Antonio Aloisi (ch 13) and Jeremias Adams-Prassl (ch 12) in part III of this volume. For a definition of algorithmic regulation, see K Yeung, 'Algorithmic Regulation: A Critical Interrogation' (2017) 2 *Regulation & Governance* 429, 507.

[156] A Seifert, 'Employee Data Protection in the Transnational Company' in F Hendrickx and V De Stefano (eds), *Game Changers in Labour Law: Shaping the Future of Work* (Alphen aan den Rijn, Wolters Kluwer, 2018) ch 12.

# 17

# Social Media and Freedom of Speech in Employment: Limitations on Employees' Right to Self-Expression

ANDRÁS KOLTAY

## I. Introduction

Freedom of speech is one of the most precious rights protected by European states and legal systems in many parts of the world. Centuries of struggle have led to a situation where today most people can express their opinions on public and private matters without any fear. In certain situations, however, constitutional protection may be put aside. An agreement between parties, or the legal relationship between private parties, may be such that the constitutional right to freedom of speech, which is primarily binding on the state and state bodies, is not enforced in full. Among the most important such areas are employment and freedom of speech at the workplace. If employers and employees are allowed to set aside the matter of protecting freedom of speech with no external limitations, this may lead to this constitutional right being emptied of content in practice. Certainly, the state and the legal system must approach the area of private autonomy cautiously, and can only influence it within limits; but the issue of ensuring freedom of speech may be of sufficient importance to justify such an intervention.

In what follows, I will review the basic issues of freedom of speech in the workplace, focusing on the use of social media by employees, and its possible limitations. Section II will examine the general issues relating to employees' freedom of speech, a right which is relevant irrespective of the nature of the means they use, be it their vocal cords or a medium of some kind. Section III reviews specific social media-related issues, while section IV briefly deals with the conditions for electronic monitoring of employees. Finally, in the last part, section V, I will attempt to draw certain general conclusions.

## II. Freedom of Speech in the Workplace

The right to freedom of speech applies to all individuals, not only at political rallies, other public events or in the media, but at each and every moment of their lives. People usually spend more time at their workplace (at work), than at home, or indulging in their hobbies, and most certainly more time than they devote to public appearances. So it follows that expression at work is more common, important and frequent to the individuals, than speaking in fora which are dedicated to being open for expression (media, public gatherings etc).

In principle, the limits on freedom of speech apply to the same degree at the workplace as they do outside the world of work. So, if a staff member belittles other persons or spreads untruths about them, the general rules on the conflict between the protection of personality and freedom of speech apply. The protection of freedom of speech in the workplace is underpinned by the same arguments as apply in general: freedom to debate public affairs; the search for truth; or interest in the autonomy and fulfilment of the individual. From the democratic perspective, the primary objective and purpose of the right to free speech is citizens' participation in the debate of, and decisions about, public affairs.[1] In contrast, according to the individualist theory, humans deserve free speech, because the existence of freedom in itself contributes to the creation of a 'good life'. In Ronald Dworkin's interpretation, everyone is entitled to this right, because in a just political system, the state treats every adult citizen as a 'responsible moral being'.[2] Both these approaches also underline the importance of the protection of freedom of expression in the workplace context.[3] In addition to the general rules on freedom of speech, other rules apply in the workplace, while working and in the relationship between the employee and the employer in general, which typically restrict the employee's ability to speak. The interests of the employer may require that employees shall not be able to exercise their freedom of speech to the full extent, that they would be allowed through the protection of that fundamental right.

These considerations may be legitimate and protected by law such as the protection of the employer's economic interests and its social image, ensuring its operation, and allowing it to operate efficiently, which may provide a basis for restricting the employee's freedom of speech. Ecomonic interests can be damaged even by fair and honest critique or truthful communication, but the law needs to focus on the restriction of unfair or untrue public speech. However, it is very difficult to separate interests that need to be protected in a legitimate way from an employer's arbitrariness. Employees are typically in a weaker, more vulnerable position in this relationship, so labour law seeks to protect them through a number of measures, but those can only be used to protect their freedom of speech in a fragmentary way. Legislation cannot anticipate all the situations in which the protection of employers' interests may give rise to a restriction of rights, so it is up to the courts to strike the right balance between conflicting interests.

[1] See A Meiklejohn, *Free Speech and its Relation to Self-Government* (New York, Harper, 1948), later published under a new title and with extended content: A Meiklejohn, *Political Freedom: The Constitutional Powers of the People* (Oxford, Oxford University Press, 1960).

[2] R Dworkin, *Freedom's Law: The Moral Reading of the American Constitution* (Oxford, Oxford University Press, 1996) 199–202; and R Dworkin, *Taking Rights Seriously* (Cambridge, MA, Harvard University Press, 1977) 266–78, 364–68.

[3] On the justifications of freedom of speech, see: RL Weaver, 'The Philosophical Foundations of Free Expression' in RL Weaver, A Koltay, MD Cole and SI Friedland (eds), *Free Speech and Media Law in the 21st Century* (Durham, NC, Carolina Academic Press, 2019) 183; A Koltay, *Freedom of Speech: The Unreachable Mirage* (Budapest, CompLex, 2013) 3–20.

It is arguable, whether, if an employee forms an opinion that her employer rejects so imposes a sanction on them, any infringement of freedom of speech has occurred at all. After all, by concluding an employment contract, the employee typically also agrees to the restriction of his or her freedom of speech.[4] According to Justice Oliver Wendell Holmes, deciding the fairness of a dismissal under US law, the dismissed worker is not in fact referring to the right to speak, but to the right to maintain an employment relationship, although this latter does not exist as a constitutional right.[5] Contrary to Holmes's approach, US courts these days take employees' right to speak into account, but not necessarily to the appropriate extent.

A fundamental question is whether it is necessary to distinguish between speech on public affairs and speech in general, and whether the extent to which the employer is allowed to intervene is affected by the circumstances to which the employee's speech relates. The constitutional protection of freedom of speech is stronger when participating in debates on public affairs and, starting from here, restricting the employee's freedom of expression in matters of a private nature (including internal workplace disputes) would not be inconceivable. A more pertinent question is that of what acceptable interests the employer has in sanctioning expression rather than what the employee was talking about. Is an employer entitled to restrict their employee's freedom of speech if the latter's speech has nothing to do with their employment or workplace?[6]

Paul Wragg argues that English case law does not take employees' freedom of speech seriously enough.[7] Controversial situations usually do not arise after an individual expresses an opinion on important public affairs but after chats between employees, and the protection of opinions that are of paramount importance for democracy does not extend to these unrefined, sometimes offensive, trivial statements. However, speaking on 'petty' issues is also important to the speaker, and is far from certain that extensive restrictions on such expressions does not violate the fundamental principles of freedom of speech, especially the protection of the interest in individual self-expression and self-fulfilment.[8]

Courts often take it for granted that general labour law provisions (principles) for the protection of the employer's interests and, possibly, relevant clauses in the employment contract jointly provide a basis for the employer to take action in cases where an employee expresses an opinion with which the employer disagrees.[9] Labour law rules may give excessive authority to an employer, even when on the surface they seem to aim to protect the employee. For instance, according to the Hungarian Labour Code, 'the employee may not exercise his right to free speech in any way that is materially detrimental or endangering to the reputation or legitimate economic and organisational

[4] E Barendt, *Freedom of Speech*, 2nd edn (Oxford, Oxford University Press, 2005) 488.

[5] *McAuliffe v Mayor of New Bedford*, 25 NE 517 (1892).

[6] Barendt (n 4) 490.

[7] PM Wragg, 'Free Speech Rights at Work: Resolving the Differences Between Practice and Liberal Principle' (2015) 44 *Industrial Law Journal* 1.

[8] ibid, 27.

[9] Nonetheless, employment contracts usually cannot deviate from statutory law in many jurisdictions, particularly not on such gerenal issues as free speech.

interests of the employer'.[10] It is clear that this provision gives the employer a nearly unrestricted tool for taking action against expression by employees.

In the English legal system, on the other hand, while not specifically mentioning freedom of speech for employees, its protection can be derived indirectly from the legislation. Section 94 of the Employment Relations Act 1999 stipulates that an employee has the right not to be unfairly dismissed by the employer, whereas section 3 of the Human Rights Act 1998 states that each and every piece of UK legislation must be read and given effect in a way which is compatible with the rights as established in the European Convention on Human Rights, including the right to free expression enshrined in Article 10.[11] In essence, it does not matter whether a separate labour law rule mentions an employee's freedom of speech or not; the level of protection does not depend primarily on that, as free speech is protected on the constitutional level.

In addition to statutory labour law and employment contracts, other legislation enshrining equal treatment (non-discrimination), constitutes a relevant set of additional rules. Although the European Union has adopted several directives aimed at combating discrimination against workers, they however do not protect political or other opinion as a discrimination ground.[12] At the same time, in several national equality laws political or other opinion is often a protected discrimination ground, on which basis it is not permitted to treat any person communicating such an opinion less favourably than any another person or group in a comparable situation.[13]

An employment relationship is a legal relationship which belongs to the sphere of private autonomy, based on the parties' free disposition and mutual agreement, the prima facie content of which may be influenced to a lesser extent by constitutionally protected rights. However, the fundamental rights of the parties must also be taken into account in such private law legal relationships. According to the concept of *Drittwirkung*, originating in German constitutional law, the parties must pay regard to each other's constitutional rights in their relations with each other.[14] Consequently, the employer must respect its employee's freedom of speech and it may restrict that freedom only on appropriate grounds, subject to imposing a proportionate penalty. This principle could possibly be taken into account by the national courts in Europe, even in the absence of a special statutory rule. It would be appropriate to set the range of relevant grounds to be sufficiently narrow and it would not suffice for any harm to an employer's interests or a minor risk of it to justify restricting the employee's freedom of speech.

[10] Act I of 2012 on the Labour Code, Paragraph (3) of Section 8.

[11] D Seah, 'Social Media and Freedom of Expression in the Workplace: Is the Law and Practice in the UK Fit for Purpose?' (2016) 11 *Bristol Law Review* 21.

[12] See, for instance: Council Directive 2000/43/EC of 29 June 2000 implementing the principle of equal treatment between persons irrespective of racial or ethnic origin [2000] OJ L180/22; Council Directive 2000/78/EC of 27 November 2000 establishing a general framework for equal treatment in employment and occupation [2000] OJ L303/16; Directive 2006/54/EC of the European Parliament and of the Council of 5 July 2006 on the implementation of the principle of equal opportunities and equal treatment of men and women in matters of employment and occupation (recast) [2006] OJ L204/23.

[13] See, for instance, Hungarian Act 125 of 2003 on Equal Treatment and Promotion of Equal Opportunities, s 8.

[14] On issues of the horizontal scope of fundamental rights in the labour law context, see G Kiss, *Alapjogok kollíziója a munkajogban* (Pécs, Justis, 2010) 125–84.

The protection of the employer's economic and business interests may be the strongest argument for restricting rights. This presupposes demonstrating that the employee's speech has caused harm to the employer or created a risk of harm occurring. Decision 14/2017 (VI. 30) of the Hungarian Constitutional Court was adopted following a lawsuit in which the employer (a bank) claimed in a dismissal case that its employee had caused financial disadvantage to it. The employee, who worked as a human resources expert, operated an internet portal jointly with others, on which he discussed human resource management matters. According to the employer's reasoning for termination, both the topic of the internet portal and the articles published there were closely related to the employee's responsibilities at work. The financial disadvantage claimed was essentially that the employee thus shared the knowledge, experience and information he had acquired in the course of his work for his employer with the public. The Constitutional Court rejected the complaint on the grounds that the writings published by the complainant were of a professional nature and not related to public debates, so the published writings could not benefit from the protection of freedom of speech.[15] The complainant appealed against this decision to the European Court of Human Rights (ECtHR), which ruled in its decision delivered in *Herbai v Hungary*[16] that freedom of speech is not limited to public issues in the strict sense.[17] Furthermore, in the Hungarian court proceedings it was not proved that the applicant's conduct had in fact adversely affected the employer's economic interest.[18] So the ECtHR established a violation of Article 10 of the Convention.

However, the interests to be protected may not be purely economic. According to the decision of the Hungarian Supreme Court,[19] it is a violation of the duty to cooperate if an employee, exercising his freedom of speech, acts in disregard of his employer's important interests and the requirement of modesty – in this case, a journalist employee published strong criticism of his employer. Besides these cases (which are at least easier to judge at the level of principles), employers may also find it easy to dismiss employees when they publish their views outside the context of their employment relationship. It is difficult to strike a balance between protecting employees' opinions and the employer's image and social standing. In the past, this problem did not occur en masse, because no platform for employee opinion was available that was as public as social media is today, which at the same time unequivocally prove that publication took place. These days, anyone can express an opinion free of charge, immediately and as frequently as they desire on online platforms which previously they could only share with their office neighbours or during lunch or cigarette breaks, under much more confidential circumstances. The other circumstance is the employers' vigorous effort, acting in the name of social justice, that rigorously enforce current moral standards with a view to protecting their business interests against their employees who do not behave *comme il faut*.[20]

[15] Constitutional Court decision no 14/2017 (VI. 30) Statement of Reasons, para 40.

[16] *Herbai v Hungary* App no 11608/15 (ECHR 5 February 2020).

[17] ibid, para 43.

[18] ibid, para 48.

[19] EBH2004, 1050.

[20] H Engler, '"Cancel Culture" in the Workplace: New Challenges and Risks for Compliance, HR & Boards' *Thomson Reuters* (15 September 2020), available at: www.thomsonreuters.com/en-us/posts/news-and-media/cancel-culture-in-the-workplace.

The commitment to maintaining a favourable image and being seen to support social justice not only drives some employers to take action against unlawful opinions, but also on the ground of minor slips, and envisages the strongest possible retaliation (dismissal, in the case of employees).[21] This is particularly worrying when it takes place following the expression of an opinion on an important public issue, as in the following example of a case that to date has not yet been followed by court proceedings. Zsolt Petry, the goalkeeping coach of the Hertha BSC football club in Berlin, lost his job in the spring of 2021 after expressing opinions in an interview. In the article[22] the coach stated that Europe was morally 'deeply sunk' and Western European immigration policy was a 'manifestation of moral degradation' that is 'sweeping across the continent'. Petry was dismissed for sharing his opinion, because it was incompatible with the values, openness, tolerance and diversity that Hertha represented.[23] The culture of German society today is largely based on these values, and the coach undoubtedly infringed them. In the wake of this case, it may seem that freedom of speech is no longer a fundamental pillar of a common set of European values and cultures, as it was in Western Europe after the Second World War and then, after the fall of the Iron Curtain, across the entire Continent. It is understandable and acceptable if the protection of diversity and tolerance is important for the football club, but if this aspect overrides everything and speech incompatible with the Berlin club's social values provokes the strongest possible response, the employer is treating both the supporters of diversity and its sceptics as minors. It does not consider the former to be able to defend their position or the latter to be worthy of expressing their views.

Of course, it can sometimes be difficult to say whether an opinion relates purely to a public matter, or whether it has a connection with and an impact on the work of the person communicating the opinion. The Berlin football club's commitment to an open society may be such an important part of its identity that incompatible opinions issuing from the mouths of an employee would have a devastating effect on that public identity. However, the connection between this and the work of a goalkeeping coach is still very distant and contingent. Furthermore, a private association or company in Europe, such as a football club, may also observe the protection of freedom of speech and tolerance of dissenting views as a building block of its identity. A case where an employee makes a manifestation that violates the rights of specific, identifiable persons may qualify, however, and this would be compatible with the constitutional principles regarding the restriction of freedom of speech. On the other hand, the remarks made by Zsolt Petry as

[21] 'A Letter on Justice and Open Debate' *Harper's Magazine* (7 July 2020), available at: harpers.org/a-letter-on-justice-and-open-debate ('it is now all too common to hear calls for swift and severe retribution in response to perceived transgressions of speech and thought. More troubling still, institutional leaders, in a spirit of panicked damage control, are delivering hasty and disproportionate punishments instead of considered reforms. Editors are fired for running controversial pieces; books are withdrawn for alleged inauthenticity; journalists are barred from writing on certain topics; professors are investigated for quoting works of literature in class; a researcher is fired for circulating a peer-reviewed academic study; and the heads of organizations are ousted for what are sometimes just clumsy mistakes').

[22] The debated interview in Hungarian: 'Dárdai magyar segítője nem ért mindenben egyet Gulácsi véleményével' *Magyar Nemze* (5 April 2021), available at: www.magyarnemzet.hu/sport/2021/04/dardai-magyar-segitoje-nem-ert-mindenben-egyet-gulacsi-velemenyevel.

[23] See the statement of the club: 'Hertha BSC part ways with Zsolt Petry', available at: www.herthabsc.com/en/news/2021/04/statement-regarding-zsolt-petry.

a club employee in the public eye, seemed not to respect other important values openly embraced by the club. A delicate balance is difficult to set in similar cases, not that the club made an effort and tried to reached that.

Protecting the identity of employers is a sensitive issue in other contexts as well. State institutions are obliged to neutrality in religious, world-view and political terms. In *Vogt v Germany*,[24] which came before the ECtHR, this was not raised in relation to the applicant, a teacher, who was a member of the Communist Party in West Germany in the 1970s (when the Communist Party had engaged in activities incompatible with the German Constitution) and tried to influence the children entrusted to her, or that she would have created a security risk to them. Her dismissal due to her party membership and the decisions of the German courts were found to have violated her right to free speech.[25]

The situation may be different in the case of a (private) institution which is committed to a world-view or religion, for example in the decision delivered in *Rommelfanger v Germany*.[26] The applicant, a doctor, was dismissed by a hospital run by the Catholic Church after he published a letter in one of the weekly papers in which he advocated abortion. This is incompatible with the teachings of the Church. Both German courts and the ECtHR held that the loyalty required by ecclesiastical institutions to the values of the Church may constitute a restriction on an individual's freedom of speech, but that must not be disproportionate. In this case, however, not speaking of abortion unless he shared the position of the Church was not an unreasonable and excessive burden on the employee. Conversely, actions taken by religiously neutral institutions against employees who express religious opinions, typically by wearing a religious symbol or a certain garment as a sign of their religious commitment, also affect the employees' freedom of expression.[27]

The scope of private and public sector employers' rights to take action against their employees does not differ just because of the requirement of neutrality for the latter. Beyond this, guaranteeing constitutionally protected rights is directly binding on the public sector (state and state-affiliated, as well as local government institutions). Moreover, for armed bodies the requirement of neutrality is more important than for other public employers.[28] The US Supreme Court has deeply investigated the issue of freedom of speech for civil servants in its practice.[29] In *Pickering v Board of Education*,[30]

[24] *Vogt v Germany* App no 17851/91 (ECHR, 26 September 1995).

[25] ibid, paras 60–61.

[26] *Rommelfanger v Germany* App no 12242/86 (ECHR, 6 September 1989) Admissibility Decision.

[27] Dismissal due to a small cross worn on a necklace violates freedom of speech and religion for an airport worker, but does not violate it for a nurse [*Eweida and Others v the United Kingdom* App nos 48420/10, 59842/10, 51671/10 and 36516/10 (ECHR, 27 May 2013); the ban on wearing headscarves is not discriminatory unless it is specifically against Muslim women (judgment on a reference for a preliminary ruling of 14 March 2017 in Case C-157/15 *Samira Achbita and Centrum voor gelijkheid van kansen en voor racismebestrijding v G4S Secure Solutions NV* [GC] ECLI:EU:C:2017:203 [2017]; judgment on a reference for a preliminary ruling of 14 March 2017 in Case C- 188/15 *Asma Bougnaoui and Association de défense des droits de l'homme (ADDH) v Micropole SA* [GC] ECLI:EU:C:2017:204 [2017]. See more on the Burqa cases around Europe: *Hungarian Labour Law E-journal* 2019/1, www.hllj.hu.

[28] See *Rekvényi v Hungary* App no 25390/94 (ECHR, 20 May 1999).

[29] FE Langan, 'Likes and Retweets Can't Save Your Job: Public Employee Privacy, Free Speech, and Social Media' (2018) 15 *University of St Thomas Law Journal* 228, 228–41.

[30] *Pickering v Board of Education*, 391 US 563 (1968).

the Court ruled that an opinion expressed on public affairs by a civil servant (who wrote a reader's letter criticising his employer in the local newspaper) could not qualify as grounds for dismissal. In *Connick v Myers*,[31] the Court clarified that this protection does not, however, apply to opinions on any matter other than public affairs. In *Rankin v McPherson*,[32] the Court established that any public opinion, not intended for the public, but which may be considered extreme (in this instance expressing the hope, following a failed attempt to assassinate President Reagan, that the next attempt would be successful) also falls under the protection of freedom of speech. *Garcetti v Ceballos*[33] revealed that if an employee's job is to form an opinion on certain public matters, the fulfilment of his obligations arising from his employment relationship cannot qualify as the exercise of their freedom of speech. This level of detail and sophistication in the case law or constitutional case law is not present in Europe, although the shift of employee expression to social media has also largely put US practice in parentheses. What Ardith McPherson said about President Reagan would hardly be considered protected speech if it were published on social media.

Whistleblowers should not be retaliated against because they have exposed abuses, the exposure of which serves the public interest. Such informants, if they are determined to act, may, as the case may be, contact either the public authority competent in the matter or the press. The protection of whistleblowers is not a separate right of the press, as the press can ensure their anonymity through the right to the protection of sources, but the press is also the beneficiary of the rules protecting them, as it has a better chance of accessing important and worthwhile content. A particularly piquant problem arises when journalists themselves become 'whistleblowers' of abuses in the press. The German *Walraff/Bild* case was triggered by an article by a covert journalist: the deception of his identity, through which he infiltrated another editorial office, was necessary to obtain the information and thus qualifies as an activity protected by the freedom of the press.[34] The ECtHR has also ruled in cases where journalists have drawn public attention to abuses by their own employers; the ECtHR decisions protected journalists from sanctions by their employer.[35] EU Directive 2019/1937 on whistleblowers needs to be mentioned here also, as it covers employees (civil servants among them), and expressly prohibits retaliation by dismissal in its Articles 4 and 19.

## III. Freedom of Speech, Workplace and Use of Social Media

Expressing opinions through social media is an opportunity for all users to make their views known to the public, but it also carries previously unknown dangers for them. Opinions can be communicated quickly or even instantaneously, which may increase the likelihood of offensive, thoughtless, hasty speech that usually appears without

[31] *Connick v Myers*, 461 US 138 (1983).
[32] *Rankin v McPherson*, 483 US 378 (1987).
[33] *Garcetti v Ceballos*, 547 US 410 (2006).
[34] BVerfGE 66, 116; 1 BvR 272/81 (*Wallraff/Bild* decision); Barendt (n 4) 441–44.
[35] *Fuentes Bobo v Spain* App no 39293/98 (ECHR, 29 February 2000); *Matúz v Hungary* App no 73571/10 (ECHR, 21 October 2014); *Wojtas-Kaleta v Poland* App no 20436/02 (ECHR, 16 July 2009).

filtering. Opinions that used to be delivered orally and thus restricted to a few people may be made public, and their spread is beyond the control of the speaker. Even unarguably legitimate opinions may be followed by a sanction on the part of the speaker's employer. In addition to statutory rules, employment contracts can further restrict employee expression, and many employers have special policies for social media use that can cover not only employment-related manifestations, but the employee's general social media presence.[36] Imposing a social media policy is a particularly sensitive issue for public sector employers, where guaranteeing the employees' right to freedom of speech is a constitutional obligation on the part of the employer.[37] However, employers may take strong action against social media views if they see them as 'potentially disruptive' to workplace communities.[38]

Internal regulation of the use of social media cannot be objected to in cases where the employer has a legitimate interest in regulating the activities of employees, in particular if their posts or tweets on the platforms may seem to be the views of the employer. This is why the *New York Times* introduced guidelines for the use of social media by its journalists. It may seem ironic that the social media presence of journalists working for a traditional medium is subject to such internal regulation, but the reasons for this regulation can easily be appreciated. As it has also been admitted by the journalists themselves, whatever they publish, even as a private individual, might be construed as the position of the paper they work for.[39]

On social media, not only text, images or video posted by users but other expressive acts may be considered 'speech', such as sharing or responding to content, which may be performed by a single click. In terms of the use of the *Facebook* 'like' function, it had to be clarified whether its use constituted an expression of opinion at all. In *Bland v Roberts*,[40] a US federal district court ruled that 'liking' a given piece of content does not qualify as protected speech, since it lacks any substance or material content that would be eligible for constitutional protection. In other words, the actual content of an opinion is still missing, as pressing the 'like' button does not reflect any affiliation to or endorsement of the content concerned. The facts of this case occurred during the campaign to elect the sheriff of the town of Hampton (since the sheriff is a directly elected official), when a new candidate was running against the eventually re-elected former sheriff. Certain staff members working in the sheriff's office expressed their support for the challenger by using the 'like' button on the *Facebook* campaign page. When the eventually re-elected sheriff did not reappoint those workers to their former position, they filed a lawsuit due to the violation of their freedom of association and speech. The district court ruled against the plaintiff and refused to apply the doctrine of symbolic speech, thereby exposing itself to harsh criticism from communities of professionals

[36] K McGarvey Hidy, 'Social Media Policies, Corporate Censorship and the Right to be Forgiven: A Proposed Framework for Free Expression in an Era of Employer Social Media Monitoring' (2020) 22 *University of Pennsylvania Journal of Business Law* 346.

[37] Langan (n 29) 241–43.

[38] DS Smith and CR Bates, 'The Evolution of Public Employee Speech Protection in an Age of Social Media' (2020) 22 *Atlantic Law Journal* 1.

[39] 'The Times Issues Social Media Guidelines for the Newsroom' *New York Times* (13 October 2017), available at: www.nytimes.com/2017/10/13/reader-center/social-media-guidelines.html.

[40] *Bland v Roberts*, 857 FSupp 2d 599 (ED Va, 2012).

dealing with social media platforms.[41] On appeal against the district court's judgment, the Fourth Circuit court established the violation of the freedom of speech.[42] The Court accepted the pressing of a 'like' button as symbolic speech that expresses an opinion that can be perceived without any words, similar to displaying a sign in support of a candidate on one's front lawn during an election campaign (as is customary in the United States). The interest of employees in expressing their opinion prevails over the sheriff's interest in serving the community without any disturbance. What an employee does on social media may be considered speech almost without exception, and as such freedom of speech may be raised in connection with it; however, as speech may harm the interests of the employer, it may therefore constitute a basis for action against the speaker.[43]

Social media has become the primary domain for publishing rushed and often foolhardy opinions en masse and without any filter or editorial control.[44] As a result, any employee who expresses an opinion in a hurry can find themselves in an extremely awkward position in the blink of an eye. The question is whether the courts – and employers – should deviate from the standards applied so far to public communication in this world of opinions issued quickly and without recourse to any external filter. In 2012, Welsh football player Daniel Thomas published a homophobic message on *Twitter* concerning the British Olympic diving team. The Director of Public Prosecutions (DPP) believed that the message was offensive, but not grossly offensive, in particular because it was meant to be humorous by its author, sent to followers (mostly family and friends) and swiftly removed after it became public, the author showed remorse and was punished by his team, and the targeted divers were not among the addressees, but learned about the message after it became public.[45] This shows that the context of speech on social media ought to be considered broadly and should be taken into account before an act is considered a criminal offence. In other cases, in contrast, the authors of statements meant to be humorous were eventually sent to prison. For example, the actions of a user who made racist and offensive remarks when he got into a heated debate for joking about a footballer who suffered a cardiac arrest should be considered a criminal offence.[46]

In *Chambers v DPP* (UK), the proceeding court needed to consider another quality mentioned in section 127(1)(a) of the Communications Act 2003 – the 'menacing' nature of the message.[47] Paul Chambers was charged and sentenced because he 'threatened' to blow up the Robin Hood Airport in Doncaster when he realised that his flight

[41] IP Robbins, 'What Is the Meaning of Like: The First Amendment Implications of Social-Media Expression' (2013) 7 *Federal Courts Law Review* 127; LE Gray, 'Thumb War: The Facebook "Like" Button and Free Speech in the Era of Social Networking' (2013) 7 *Charleston Law Review* 447.

[42] *Bland v Roberts* No 12-1671 (4th Cir, 2013).

[43] Langan (n 29) 245.

[44] P Coe, 'The Social Media Paradox: An Intersection with Freedom of Expression and the Criminal Law' (2015) 24 *Information & Communications Technology Law* 16, 32–33.

[45] DPP Statement on Tom Daley Case and Social Media Prosecutions (*Crown Prosecution Service Blog*, 20 September 2012), available at: www.blog.cps.gov.uk/2012/09/dpp-statement-on-tom-daley-case-and-social-media-prosecutions.html.

[46] S Morris, 'Student Jailed for Racist Fabrice Muamba Tweets' *Guardian* (27 March 2012), available at: www.theguardian.com/uk/2012/mar/27/student-jailed-fabrice-muamba-tweets.

[47] *Chambers v DPP* [2012] EWHC 2157.

had been cancelled due to bad weather conditions. The case became known in England as the 'Twitter joke trial', because Chambers did not have any actual intention of acting on his foolhardy threats.[48] Nonetheless, he was found guilty by the lower courts, based on the consideration that the message was menacing in and of itself, and was capable of causing unease in average citizens.[49] Eventually, Chambers was found not guilty by the proceeding Divisional Court due to the absence of any real threat, considering that the message was not capable of creating fear or apprehension in those to whom it was communicated, or who may reasonably be expected to see it.[50]

Another issue is that employers may act not only in the case of unlawful content, but according to the standards applied by them, the application of which may result in termination of employment. In essence, it is left to employers to decide what they allow their employees to do and what they do not. In this regard, social media speech is not a 'mitigating circumstance' which, by its very nature, encourages the tolerance of ill-considered, offensive speech, but, on the contrary, one which makes it more difficult for an employee trying to rely on freedom of speech as a voice amplifier of employee speech. The public 'visibility' of offensive speech entails a more serious problem than if the speech had been published orally, away from the cyberworld. To cite Frank LoMonte's apt example, a school teacher drinking a glass of beer at home cannot be a problem, but posting a picture of himself on *Facebook* while drinking alcohol can get him in trouble with his employer. Social media speech, which is often symbolic, figurative or light-hearted, may be punished more severely than the behaviour actually presented.[51]

With a view to assessing communication through social media platforms appropriately, Jake Rowbottom recommends using the category of low-level speech as an element of the doctrine of free speech.[52] The differentiation between high and low-value speech already exists: for example, the former might include discussions concerning public affairs, while the latter might include pornography or commercial speech.[53] According to the doctrine proposed by Rowbottom, the more an utterance is related to a public discourse, the more valuable it is and the greater the level of protection it should be afforded. The new category would take the context of publishing an utterance into account, meaning that disputes, quarrels, threats and hatred expressed on a platform would be considered low-level speech, and as such they would be protected more than utterances with the same content published in traditional media or expressed among persons who are physically present; both may be considered more threatening or dangerous.[54]

Social media lies somewhere between fully public and private fora, and closer to full publicity. In terms of its purpose, however, it cannot be considered to have the same

[48] M Beckford, 'Twitter Joke Trial Conviction Quashed in High Court' *Telegraph* (27 July 2012), available at: www.telegraph.co.uk/technology/twitter/9431677/Twitter-joke-trial-conviction-quashed-in-High-Court.html.

[49] *Chambers v DPP* (n 47) para 17.

[50] ibid, para 30.

[51] FD LoMonte, 'The "Social Media Discount" and First Amendment Exceptionalism' (2019) 50 *University of Memphis Law Review* 387, 405–06.

[52] J Rowbottom, 'To Rant, Vent and Converse: Protecting Low Level Digital Speech' (2012) 71 *Cambridge Law Journal* 355, 370–76.

[53] JM Shaman, 'The Theory of Low-Value Speech' (1995) 48 *SMU Law Review* 297.

[54] Rowbottom (n 52).

purpose as a traditional medium that always tries to reach as many people as possible. Social media speech on the part of employees is usually aimed at their friends and not at other users unknown to them, yet they cannot be regarded as purely private communications because their circle of friends and acquaintances on the platform can be very wide, even up to thousands of people, and they are also aware that their manifestations may be spread by sharing, even against their will, or may even be transmitted by traditional media. Users may not know who their speech will reach out of their friends and acquaintances on the platform. This intermediate status between the private sphere and full publicity might warrant special consideration from employers and courts. While an offensive, hurtful, incompatible comment on an employee's social media profile is not identical to writing an article in the *New York Times*, it is not like a speech at the family table. It would be necessary to take this into account when acting against an employee.[55]

Employee expressions posted via social media may lead to difficulties in their relationship with their employer in a number of different situations. They may even get into trouble before gaining employment.[56] Employers often check the social media accounts of employees wishing to join them. If their profiles are public, it cannot threaten their privacy, but the risk of discrimination in the recruitment decision may be present even in such cases.[57] Another problem is the use of social media during working hours, which can obviously be prohibited without any concern. Such a content-neutral restriction, independent of the employee's opinion to be expressed and which serves a good reason (protection of the employer's interests for organised, efficient work) does not, in principle, raise any constitutional concern. At the same time, social media has become part of everyday life to such an extent, and employees often log in to their own account several times daily by default, that such disproportionate punishment for social media use that does not significantly impair work performance may be unjustified. Surveillance of whether employees use social media may also constitute a privacy-invasive practice.[58] The question of what IT device the employees use to access their social media pages may be subject to a similar assessment. The use of employer-owned devices for private purposes, including communication via social media, may be prohibited for data and IT security purposes.

A particularly thorny question concerns instances when an employee's opinion posted on social media is judged by the employer. A distinction must be made between cases where employees post about their job, workplace and colleagues, and where they publish content completely independent of these.[59] The employer's room to manoeuvre is, in principle, wider in the former case, since the damage to its interests is easier to perceive if the employee criticises their workplace or publishes an offensive opinion about their colleagues. However, employers also often act in cases where their employee publishes an opinion that takes a position on a public issue whose content is incompatible

[55] DÁ Alonso, 'Social Media in the Employment Relationship Context: A Typology of Emerging Conflicts, and Notes for the Debate' (2018) 39 *Comparative Labor Law & Policy Journal* 287, 304–06.

[56] E Kajtár and B Mestre, 'Social networks and employees' right to privacy in the pre-employment stage: Some comparative remarks and interrogations' (2016) 1 *Hungarian Labour Law E-journal.*

[57] Alonso (n 55) 291–92.

[58] ibid, 293–96.

[59] D Mangan, 'Online Speech and the Workplace: Public Right, Private Regulation' (2018) 39 *Comparative Labor Law & Policy Journal* 357, 361.

with the employer's social image or which the employer considers detrimental to its interests for some other reason. Even an old pre-employment social media post can provide a basis for terminating an individual's employment. In these cases, employers and courts should pay regard to the value of freedom of speech; the more distant the relationship between the content of the opinion and the activity of the employer, the less vigorous action against the employee can be justified. Cara Magatelli has argued that employees are free to pursue any kind of activity outside work as long as such activities are not illegal and do not violate the legitimate business interests of their employer.[60]

Mary-Rose Papandrea raised the interesting issue of whether an employee may communicate with others through social media concerning a work-related matter (as if doing so were part of her job). This issue could be particularly sensitive in the context of exchanges between teachers and students. If an employer prohibits teachers from communicating with students (eg, to prevent inappropriate communication and relationships), the prohibition might limit the teachers' freedom of speech, even in situations where they wish to discuss a non-educational matter with a student.[61] The English and Canadian judicial decisions presented by David Mangan show that employers often act in cases where their employees express views on a public affairs topic, for example on gender and racial equality, LGBTQ rights or other political issues.[62] According to Mangan,

> speech of workers on social media platforms garners noticeably less protection in the United Kingdom. The matter is made stark by the disconnect between these decisions and recent legislative and common law movement regarding UK defamation law. The potential for an employer to dismiss (coupled with case law vindicating the decision) has a deterrent effect on speech in general as it contrasts unfavorably with protection of a wide spectrum for speech that guides libel adjudication. While workers' speech on social media is the subject of legitimate concerns over business interests, this matter alone should not displace the prima facie right to free expression.[63]

The situation is somewhat similar in the United States, and 'business organizations may choose to engage in censorship of this speech by adopting and implementing social media policies that regulate and control employees' expressive activity online'.[64] This has a detrimental effect on the employees' freedom of speech, and empties its constitutional protection while sidestepping meticulously developed doctrines.

## IV. Workers' Right to Privacy on the Internet

For it to judge the content published on social media sites presupposes that the employer checks, or, in the event of a signal to that effect, accesses the profile of its

[60] C Magatelli, 'Facebook is Not Your Friend: Protecting a Private Employee's Expectation of Privacy in Social Networking Content in the Twenty-First Century Workplace' (2012) 6 *Journal of Business, Entrepreneurship & the Law* 103.

[61] M-R Papandrea, 'Social Media, Public School Teachers, and the First Amendment' (2012) Boston College Law School Legal Studies Research Paper Series No 267.

[62] Mangan (n 59).

[63] ibid, 387.

[64] McGarvey Hidy (n 36) 384.

employee. This control, especially if it is continuous monitoring, may in itself be detrimental to the employee. An employee's activity on social media is part of their private life. However, public posts or posts of a particular employee shared by others become part of the public domain and may hardly be interpreted as confidential information. Such posts are accessible continuously and even for a long time, therefore, even pre-employment posts can be accessed, on which basis decisions detrimental to the employee may be made.[65]

Approached from the perspective of data protection, the title of websites visited, the date and time of downloading the website and other data are deemed to be personal data, because they may be linked to a specific identified natural person.[66] Usage of the internet may be monitored, conditional upon the consent of the employee, which may be allowed by their employment contract. If, according to rules established by the empoyer, it is forbidden to use the internet for private purposes, and the employee had been explicitly informed of the possibility of checks and they agreed to that, then the employee, by visiting a website, gives her consent to data processing (the criteria for the consent are set in the General Data Protection Regulation. Nevertheless, monitoring internet use is not allowed if the employer permits using the internet for private purposes.

The Grand Chamber of the ECtHR established the basic principles on the monitoring of online activities of employees in *Bărbulescu v Romania*.[67] The Court found that monitoring the employee's email account violated the right to privacy and correspondence enshrined in Article 8 of the European Convention on Human Rights. Although this case was not related to social media use, the decision has important implications in general for employees' rights to online privacy in the workplace. According to the Court, the applicant had not been informed of the scope and nature of the employer's monitoring activities, or that it might gain access to the content of communication. The ECtHR pointed out that the national courts did not pay enough attention to the scope and depth of the monitoring, or to whether there was any legal basis for it. They did not specify the specific purpose of this strict monitoring and failed to examine the severity of the consequences for the applicant, or determine what other, less intrusive means could have been applied.

Nevertheless, it becomes clear from the decision delivered in *Libert v France*,[68] that employers are allowed to monitor employees' online activities, subject to appropriate guarantees put in place for the protection of personal data. In this case, the ECtHR rejected the application of an employee who kept pornographic files on his work computer and was dismissed on this ground, because the French authorities had paid regard to the protection of private data. In general, if the employer has a legitimate interest in knowing about the employee's online activities, and it has informed the

[65] Mangan (n 59) 385–86.

[66] C Morgan, 'Employer Monitoring of Employee Electronic Mail and Internet Use' (1999) 44 *McGill Law Journal* 849.

[67] *Bărbulescu v Romania* App no 61496/08 (ECHR, 5 September 2017).

[68] *Libert v France* 588/13 (ECHR, 22 February 2018).

employee about the opportunity for and conditions of such monitoring, then it may be permissible as long as the set of conditions is clear, transparent and compliant with the law, and if the monitoring is not conducted secretly, hidden from the employee.[69] However, all this applies to the monitoring of activity on devices at the workplace but not on private ones. The employee's social media profile is part of her private sphere, and only the publicly available content published by her may be accessed by the employer. Of course, this does not exclude the possibility that the employer may have recourse to other sources to find out about its employee's activities, for example through a non-public post forwarded to it.[70]

## V. Conclusions

Freedom of speech, in the context of the workplace, involves restrictions departing from constitutional limitations on the expression of opinions. It is a matter of concern that employers may not only impose restrictions on the employee in the workplace, or in the context of their employment relationship, but retaliate for opinions expressed on public affairs, if these are harmful to their interests. Moreover, 'harm to interests' is also broadly construed, and a possible deterioration in the employer's social perception or image, or a weakening of the cohesion of the workplace community may also be sufficient for it to take action. This tendency is supported by social media platforms in many regards. For employees, social media is an opportunity to express their opinions and to participate in the public sphere, and at the same time is an unprecedented potential source of danger to them. In this regard, social media may be used as a tool that helps justifying the restriction of the freedom of employees.

It would seem necessary to provide stronger protection for employees, even at the cost of risking damage to the external image of employers. If freedom of speech is seen as a democratic core value (and we cannot regard it as anything else), then emptying it of its strict constitutional protection where employers are concerned is an undesirable development. If an employee faces the threat that they will be put at a disadvantage in their workplace on the grounds of their opinion, which is otherwise not illegal, their freedom will be impaired and, ultimately, public discourse will be harmed. There is no need for legislation to increase employees' freedom of speech, since the constitutional rights of the employee, including freedom of speech, may be taken into account in the fundamentally private law relationship between the parties, and the courts may be able to enforce this. However, addressing this problem is not possible through legal means alone: a social culture that attributes more value to freedom of speech will also be needed.

[69] Alonso (n 55) 306–09.
[70] See more in ch 16 by David Mangan in this volume.

# INDEX

www.ingramcontent.com/pod-product-compliance
Ingram Content Group UK Ltd.
Pitfield, Milton Keynes, MK11 3LW, UK
UKHW020233290926
15470UKWH00002B/508

9 781509 958238